HANDBOOK OF NEUROPSYCHOLOGY

HANDBOOK OF NEUROPSYCHOLOGY

Series Editors

FRANÇOIS BOLLER
Unit 324 INSERM, Centre Paul Broca, Paris, France

JORDAN GRAFMAN
Medical Neurology Branch, NINCDS, Bethesda, MD, U.S.A.

Editorial Board:

G. BERLUCCHI (Verona), G. W. BRUYN (Leiden), S. CORKIN (Cambridge, MA),
A. DAMASIO (Iowa City), E. DE RENZI (Modena), G. GAINOTTI (Rome),
H. GARDNER (Boston), H. GOODGLASS (Boston), R. KATZMAN (La Jolla),
R. D. NEBES (Pittsburgh), I. RAPIN (New York), G. RIZZOLATTI (Parma),
S. SEGALOWITZ (St. Catharines, Ont.), H. SPINNLER (Milan),
L. R. SQUIRE (La Jolla)

ELSEVIER

Amsterdam – London – New York – Tokyo

HANDBOOK OF NEUROPSYCHOLOGY

Section Editors

S. CORKIN

J. GRAFMAN
F. BOLLER

VOLUME 5

1993

ELSEVIER

Amsterdam – London – New York – Tokyo

© 1993, ELSEVIER SCIENCE PUBLISHERS B.V. All rights reserved

No part of this publication may be reproduced, stored in a retrieval system or transmitted in any form or by any means, electronic, mechanical, photocopying, recording or otherwise without the prior written permission of the publisher, Elsevier Science Publishers B.V. Copyright & Permissions Department, P.O. Box 1527, 1000 BM Amsterdam, The Netherlands.

No responsibility is assumed by the Publisher for any injury and/or damage to persons or property as a matter of products liability, negligence or otherwise, or from any use or operation of any methods, products, instructions or ideas contained in the material herein. Because of the rapid advances in the medical sciences, the publisher recommends that independent verification of diagnoses and drug dosages should be made.

Special regulations for readers in the USA: This publication has been registered with the Copyright Clearance Center Inc. (CCC), Salem, Massachusetts.

Information can be obtained from the CCC about conditions under which the photocopying of parts of this publication may be made in the USA. All other copyright questions, including photocopying outside of the USA, should be referred to the publisher.

ISBN Series: 0-444-90492-1

First published (hardbound edition) by Elsevier Science Publishers B.V. (Biomedical Division), 1991.
ISBN: 0-444-81233-4.

This edition (paperback) published by Elsevier Science Publishers B.V., 1993.
ISBN: 0-444-81501-5.

This book is printed on acid-free paper

Published by:
ELSEVIER SCIENCE PUBLISHERS B.V.
P.O. BOX 211
1000 AE AMSTERDAM
THE NETHERLANDS

Library of Congress Cataloging-in-Publication Data
(Revised for vol. 5)

Handbook of neuropsychology.

Editors vary for each vol.
Includes bibliographies and indexes.
1. Clinical neuropsychology. [DNLM:
1. Neuropsychology. WL 103 H236] I. Boller,
Francois.
RC343.H225 1988   612.8   88-21312
ISBN 0-444-90492-1 (set : alk. paper)

RC 343 H225 1988 v.5

Handbook of
neuropsychology

Preface

In the preface to Volume 1 of the Handbook of Neuropsychology, we stated that in recent years, there has been an enormous increase in interest into disorders of higher cortical functions and into brain-behavior relationships. This interest is exemplified by the success met so far by the first four Volumes. We believe that the Handbook has become an essential reference source for clinicians such as neurologists, psychiatrists and psychologists, as well as for all scientists engaged in research in the neurosciences.

The Handbook has been planned as a reference source in order to provide for the first time comprehensive and current coverage of experimental and clinical aspects of neuropsychology. To this end, the chapter authors have produced in-depth reviews that go beyond a summary of their own results and points of view. Each chapter is up-to-date, covering the latest developments in methodology and theory. Discussion of bedside evaluations, laboratory techniques, as well as theoretical models are all to be found in the Handbook.

The first two Volumes comprise an introductory section (edited by Boller and Grafman), and sections on attention (Rizzolatti), language, aphasia and related disorders (Goodglass) and visual behavior (Damasio). Volume 3 contains Section 5 dedicated to memory and its disorders (Squire) and Section 6 dedicated to emotional behavior and its disorders (Gainotti). Volume 4 starts with the section (Section 7, Nebes) dealing with the commissurotomized brain. The rest of Volume 4 includes the first part of the Section dealing with aging, age-related disorders and dementia (Section 8, Corkin).

Volume 5 which we now present also includes two sections. The first one includes the second part of Section 8 covering aging, age-related disorders and dementia. The Topic Editor is Professor Suzanne Corkin. The section includes chapters on epidemiology, the problem of possible subgroups in Alzheimer's disease, pathological and chemical correlates of dementia, disorders of attention and motor functions, as well as additional chapters on memory. It concludes with reviews of specific disorders (Parkinson's disease, Huntington's disease and HIV infection) and a chapter on treatment strategies for cognitive impairments.

The second part of Volume 5 includes Section 9 (edited by Grafman and Boller) dealing with cognitive models, neurolinguistic approaches to aphasia, and with methodological and practical issues in neuropsychology.

Two volumes (Volumes 6 and 7) dealing with developmental neuropsychology are in an advanced stage of preparation under the leadership of Professors Isabelle Rapin and

AUGUSTANA UNIVERSITY COLLEGE
LIBRARY

Sidney Segalowitz as Topic Editors. The Volumes will include chapters on the immature brain, structural, functional and behavioral assessment, mental deficiency, disorders of sensorimotor functions, language, memory, attention, mood and noncognitive aspects of behavior. Additional chapters will deal with academic disorders (dyslexia and dyscalculia), and with epilepsy, autism and childhood psychosis.

Recent developments in the field of Neuropsychology have prompted us to add further material to the Series. Volume 8 will be prepared in collaboration with Professor Hans Spinnler, a new and welcome addition to our Editorial Board. It will include a section on the frontal lobes, and additional sections on selected aspects of memory (with emphasis on current work on implicit memory), dementia and other current topics in neuropsychology research. The Topic Editors for this Volume are Spinnler and Boller.

Many people have contributed to the successful preparation of the Handbook. We again wish to emphasize our appreciation for the commitment of the Topic Editors who have spent long hours in the planning stage and in the actual compiling of the various sections. Marie-Cécile Masure has painstakingly prepared the index of this volume as well as that of the four preceding volumes; we are most grateful to her for her efforts. The editorial staff of Elsevier in Amsterdam continues to provide invaluable technical assistance.

François BOLLER
Jordan GRAFMAN

List of contributors

Y. Agid   INSERM U 289, Hôpital de la Salpêtrière, 47 Boulevard de l'Hôpital, 75651 Paris Cedex 13, France

L. Amaducci   Department of Neurology, University of Florence, Viale Morgagni 85, 50134 Florence, Italy
S.M.I.D. Centre (Italian Multicentre Study on Dementia), Via il Prato 58–62, 50123 Florence, Italy

F. Boller   INSERM U 324, Centre Paul Broca, 2ter rue d'Alésia, 75014 Paris, France

J. Brandt   Department of Psychiatry and Behavioral Sciences, Meyer 218, The Johns Hopkins Hospital, 600 North Wolfe Street, Baltimore, MD 21205, U.S.A.

D. Caplan   Neuropsychology Laboratory, Neurology Department, Vincent Burnham 827, Massachusetts General Hospital, Fruit Street, Boston, MA 02114, U.S.A.

A. Caramazza   Cognitive Science Center, The Johns Hopkins University, Baltimore, MD 21218, U.S.A.

T.N. Chase   Experimental Therapeutics Branch, National Institute of Neurological Disorders and Stroke, Bethesda, MD 20892, U.S.A.

H.C. Chui   Department of Neurology, University of Southern California, School of Medicine, 2025 Zonal Avenue, Los Angeles, CA 90033, U.S.A.

G. Denes   Clinica Neurologica dell'Università Policlinico, Via Giastiniani 5, 35128 – Padova, Italy

List of contributors

B. Dubois

INSERM U 289, Hôpital de la Salpêtrière, 47 Boulevard de l'Hôpital, 75651 Paris Cedex 13, France

M.M. Forbes

Pittsburgh Alzheimer Disease Research Center, Iroquois Building, Suite 400, 3600 Forbes Avenue, Pittsburgh, PA 15213, U.S.A.

J.D.E. Gabrieli

Department of Brain and Cognitive Sciences and Clinic Research Center, Massachusetts Institute of Technology, Cambridge, MA 02139, U.S.A.
Present address Department of Psychology, Northwestern University, 102 Swift Hall, Evanston, IL 60208, U.S.A.

F.A. Huppert

Department of Psychiatry, University of Cambridge, Level 4, Addenbrooke's Hospital, Hills Road, Cambridge CB2 2QQ, U.K.

D. Lanska

Neurobehavior Section, Department of Neurology, Case Western Reserve University and Alzheimer Center, University Hospitals of Cleveland, Cleveland, OH 44106, U.S.A.

A. Lippi

S.M.I.D. Centre (Italian Multicentre Study on Dementia), Via il Prato 58 – 62, 50123 Florence, Italy
Department of Neurology, University of Florence, Viale Morgagni 85, 50134 Florence, Italy

R.K. Mahurin

Department of Neurology, Baylor College of Medicine, One Baylor Place, Houston, TX 77030, U.S.A.

K. Marder

Neurological Institute, 710 West 168th Street, New York, NY 10032, U.S.A.

E. Mohr

Royal Ottawa Hospital, 1155 Carling Avenue, Ottawa, Ontario, K1Z 7K4, Canada

A. Olson

Cognitive Science Center, The Johns Hopkins University, Baltimore, MD 21218, U.S.A.

J.W. Pettegrew

Western Psychiatric Institute & Clinic, Room A741, Graduate School of Public Health, Pittsburgh, PA 15213, U.S.A.

B. Pillon

INSERM U 289, Hôpital de la Salpêtrière, 47 Boulevard de l'Hôpital, 75651 Paris Cedex 13, France

F.J. Pirozzolo   Department of Neurology, Baylor College of Medicine, One Baylor Place, Houston, TX 77030, U.S.A

H. Spinnler   First Neurological Department, University of Milan, Ospedale San Paolo alla Barona, Via di Rudini 8, 20142 Milan, Italy

Y. Stern   Neurological Institute, 710 West 168th Street, New York, NY 10032, U.S.A.

A.A. Swihart   Center for Neuropsychological Rehabilitation, 8925 North Meridian Street, Suite 100, Idianapolis, IN 46260, U.S.A.

M. Tabaton   Departments of Pathology and Neurology, Case Western Reserve University and University Hospitals of Cleveland, Cleveland, OH 44106, U.S.A.

G. Vallar   Istituto di Clinica Neurologica, Università di Milano, Via F Sforza 35, 20122 Milano, Italy

P.J. Whitehouse   Department of Neurology, Case Western Reserve University School of Medicine and Alzheimer Center, University Hospitals of Cleveland, Cleveland, OH 44106, U.S.A.

Acknowledgements

The editors and publisher gratefully acknowledge Sandoz Ltd, Basle, Switzerland, CIBA-Geigy, Summit, NJ, U.S.A., Fondation IPSEN, Paris, France, and Farmitalia Carlo Erba, Milan, Italy, for partially supporting the publication of this volume.

Contents

Section 8: Aging and Dementia (continued) (S. Corkin)

Contents

Section 9: Cognitive, Methodological and Practical Approaches
(J. Grafman and F. Boller)

Section 8

(Part 2)

Aging and Dementia

editor

S. Corkin

© 1991 Elsevier Science Publishers B.V.
Handbook of Neuropsychology, Vol. 5
F. Boller and J. Grafman (Eds)

CHAPTER 1

The epidemiology of dementia, Alzheimer's disease and Parkinson's disease

Luigi Amaducci[1] and Andrea Lippi[2]

[1]Department of Neurology and Psychiatry, University of Florence, Viale Morgagni 85, 50134 Florence, Italy, and [2] S.M.I.D.
Centre (Italian Multicentre Study on Dementia), Via il Prato 58, 50123 Florence, Italy

Introduction

The world population aged 60 years and over amounted to approximately 371 million in 1980, and reached 415 million by 1985. Moreover, it is expected to reach 1.1 billion by 2025 (United Nations, 1986). In the United States, it is anticipated that the populaton group aged 65 years or more will increase about 8-fold by the end of this century; the same population group will increase 4-fold in Italy (Rocca et al., 1984).

The increase in the elderly segment of the world's population due to reductions in fertility, infant mortality and deaths from infectious diseases is becoming of great importance in developing as well as in developed countries. In 1980, 6% of the world's total population aged 60 years and over lived in developing countries. In 1985 this percentage reached 6.3. By 2025, persons aged 60 and over living in the developing regions will represent 11.9% of the world total population (United Nations, 1986). It follows therefore that the growth in the number of elderly people increases the number of individuals at risk for age-associated disorders of the nervous system, including dementia and Parkinson's disease.

Epidemiology of dementia

Dementia is one of the most common mental health problems in the aged population. Clinically,

it is characterized by memory loss associated with impairment in abstract thinking and judgement, disturbances in higher cortical functions, and personality change (DSM III-R, American Psychiatric Association, 1987).

The magnitude of dementia in the population can be expressed by epidemiological indices, such as prevalence and incidence. Such indices are expressed as rates: with rates the frequency of dementia (numerator) is related to the population at risk of having disease (denominator). The prevalence measures the frequency of all current cases of dementia within a specific population and is calculated for a given time and given place. The prevalence rate for dementia is the number of persons suffering from dementia at a specified time per 100,000 (per 100 in this chapter) persons capable of having dementia at the same time.

The prevalence rate of severe dementia for people aged 65 and older has been estimated as between 1.3% (Akesson, 1969) and 6.7% (Sulkava et al., 1985b); moreover, the prevalence of mild to severe dementia was estimated to vary from 4.5% (Hasegawa, 1979) to 18.5% (Nielsen, 1963).

As estimated by Jorm (1987), prevalence rates for dementia increase with age, ranging from 0.72% in the age group 60 – 64 years to 38.63% in the age group 90 – 95 years.

The incidence measures the rapidity with which the dementia occurs or the frequency of addition of new cases of dementia within a specific population. It is calculated for a given time interval and given place. The incidence rate for dementia is the number of new cases of dementia during a specified period (usually 1 year) per 100,000 (or per 100) persons at risk of having dementia for the first time per year.

The incidence of dementia is difficult to assess, because disease onset is insidious and may escape detection until the disease becomes quite advanced. Relatively few population-based studies have assessed incidence rates. Based upon a five-year longitudinal study carried out on a random sample of people living in Newcastle upon Tyne in England, Roth (1978) estimated the annual incidence of dementia among people 65 years old and over to be 1.4%. Based upon a ten-year follow up study of the population of Lundby in Sweden, Hagnell (1966) estimated the annual incidence of 'senile psychosis' among people over 60 to be 2.3%. Like prevalence, the incidence rate increases steeply with age. Molsa et al. (1982), in a population-based survey carried out in the city of Turku in Finland, found the incidence rate of dementia to be 0.027% in the age group 55 – 64 years, 0.121% and 0.671% in those 65 – 74 and 75 – 84 respectively, and 1.928% over the age of 85 years. Moreover, the incidence rates were consistently higher in women. Similar data have been shown by Schoenberg et al. (1987) in Rochester, MN. In this study the incidence rate in the age group 60 – 69 years was 0.13%, 0.74% in the age-class 70 – 79 and 2.175% after the age of 80. Rates of similar magnitude (2.7%) were reported by Jarvik et al. (1980) in a cohort of people with an average age of 83 years. Katzman et al. (1989) studied a volunteer cohort with a mean age of 80 years and found a 3.53% incidence rate for all dementias.

The syndrome of dementia may have several causes. Dementing disorders can be classified as primary or secondary according to the etiology (Wells, 1979). Recently, the National Institutes of Health (U.S.A.) (1988), in the report of the Consensus Conference on the Differential Diagnosis of Dementing Diseases, proposed the distinction bet-ween diseases that appear to be primary in the brain and those which are outside the brain and affect it secondarily. A fruitful distinction for clinical purposes has also been made between progressive or fixed dementing pathological states, and arrestable or reversible causes of dementia. Arrestable or reversible causes of dementia include intoxications, infections, metabolic disorders, nutritional disorders, vascular diseases, space-occupying lesions, normal pressure hydrocephalus and affective disorders. These arrestable or reversible dementias represent 10 – 15% of all cases of dementia and every effort must be made to recognize them, because they are potentially reversible if an appropriate therapy is applied (Mardsen and Harrison, 1972).

However, the most frequent causes of dementia, as documented by clinical studies of dementia (Wells, 1979), post-mortem examinations (Tomlinson et al., 1970) and population-based surveys (Schoenberg et al., 1987; Rocca et al., 1990; Evans et al., 1989) are Alzheimer's disease (AD) and vascular dementia, followed by secondary dementias. Jorm (1987) observed that the relative prevalence of AD and vascular dementia changes across the countries: vascular dementia was more common in Japanese and Russian studies, AD in western European countries, while no significant differences were found in Finnish and American studies. The relative importance of AD and vascular dementia in different studies may be explained, in part, by the way mixed cases were handled (Jorm, 1987). On the other hand, real geographical differences may exsist: high rates of stroke have been reported in Japan, consistent with the higher rates for vascular dementia. In Italy, AD seems only slightly more frequent than vascular dementia. However, the most common type of dementia varies across age groups. In fact, vascular dementia prevalence is low in the age group 60 – 69, increases rapidly thereafter, and becomes slightly more common than AD in the age class 70 – 79 (Rocca et al., 1990). Jorm (1987) reviewed thirteen studies reporting overall prevalence rates for AD and vascular dementia and concluded that the rates for AD tend to be higher among females than males, whereas the rates for vascular dementia tend to be higher among males.

Descriptive epidemiology of Alzheimer's disease

Some important problems in the descriptive epidemiology of Alzheimer's disease (AD) are the choice of the population study and the type of sample, the methodology for case ascertainment, and the accuracy of clinical diagnosis.

The study population may be obtained from the general population by randomization or by complete enumeration of the subjects. An alternative method in some community surveys is to collect only data coming from hospitals, nursing homes and health authorities. The latter approach was principally used in north-European surveys (Akesson, 1969; Molsa et al. 1982). Since many demented subjects may not be referred to medical attention, the true incidence may be underestimated in a clinic-based population survey. On the other hand, severe dementia cases may be overrepresented in an institutionalized population. Therefore, study designs based on existing medical documentation are likely to generate biased rates, and recent studies tend to use more and more the door-to-door approach.

For the ascertainment of cases in population studies, two general strategies have been proposed: the one- and the two-phase approach. The first is less expensive, but the second leads to more accuracy in the diagnosis. In the two-phase approach a brief cognitive test with high sensitivity (the screening test) is administered to all people under investigation. Subjects scoring below the cut-off level at the screening test are then extensively studied from a clinical point of view in order to confirm the presence of mental impairment, to diagnose dementia, and to classify the type of dementia. However, the definite diagnosis of dementing disorders, especially AD, requires pathological examination of the brain.

Several sets of clinical diagnostic criteria for AD have been proposed. Although originally used to refer to patients with presenile degenerative dementia, the term AD is now generally applied to both presenile (before the age of 65 years) and senile dementia (after the age of 65 years) of the Alzheimer type, since there are few clinical, neuropathological, or biochemical distinctions between these two forms of the disorder (Katzman, 1978; see, however, Chapter 2 of this volume). Recent population-based surveys have used the NINCDS-ADRDA criteria (McKhann et al., 1984). The CAMDEX by Roth et al. (1986) provided a useful set of diagnostic criteria for differential diagnosis of mental disturbances in the elderly, and has been used successfully in some recent British surveys (Brayne and Calloway, 1989).

Prevalence of Alzheimer's disease

Available prevalence rates (cases per 100 population aged 65 and over) of AD range between 0.6 in the study by Shen et al. (1987) in China, and 10.3 in the study by Evans and colleagues (1989) in East Boston, MA, U.S.A. This variability in the prevalence rates can be influenced by different definitions of the disease under study and different case ascertainment procedures. Some investigations (Akesson, 1969; Molsa et al., 1982; Sulkava et al., 1985b; Schoenberg et al., 1985) considered only severe dementia, while in other studies mild dementia was included too (Kay et al., 1964; Broe et al., 1976; Evans et al., 1989). Akesson (1969), who found very low prevalence rates, adopted very restrictive diagnostic criteria: constant disorientation to time and place was required to make the diagnosis of dementia. Case ascertainment procedures also differ in various studies. Shen and colleagues (1987) in Beijing, in a small population, found a low prevalence rate, while a more recent Chinese prevalence survey carried out in a more representative population sample yielded a prevalence rate of 2.03 in a population aged 55 years and over (Zhang et al., 1990). Molsa and colleagues (1982) in Finland and Akesson (1969) in

Sweden collected data only from health and social services and reported low prevalence rates of dementia. Sulkava and colleagues (1985) used the door-to-door approach in a random sample representative of the whole Finnish population and found higher prevalence rates than previous community-based surveys.

All the studies conducted to date consistently showed an exponential increase in the prevalence rates of dementia with age. In the study by Molsa and colleagues (1982) in Finland, the prevalence rate increased from 0.025 in the age class 45 – 54 to 6.295 in the age class 85 years and over. In an Italian survey, the prevalence rate was 2.6 for subjects aged 60 and over and rose to 3.3 in those aged 65 and over (Rocca et al., 1990). In East Boston, MA, U.S.A., Evans and colleagues (1989) found prevalence rates of AD rapidly increasing with age. In fact, of those 65 – 74 years old, 3.0% had AD, compared with 18.7% of those 75 – 84 years old and 47.2% of those over 85 years.

In many studies the age-specific prevalence ratios were consistently higher in women than in men, especially in the older age groups (Broe et al., 1976; Molsa et al., 1982; Sulkava et al., 1985b; Rocca et al., 1990). Molsa and colleagues (1982) found the age-specific prevalence rates to be higher for men in the age group 45 – 54 years and higher for females in the other age groups. Kaneko in Japan (1975) reported prevalence rates consistently higher for males, while a more recent Japanese survey showed a pattern which is consistent with those reported in European and American studies (Karasawa et al., 1982). Finally, Schoenberg and colleagues (1985) in a population-based survey carried out in Copiah County, MS, found consistently higher prevalence rates of AD for females and Blacks.

Incidence of Alzheimer's disease

Consistent with the prevalence pattern, the incidence rate for AD rises exponentially with age. As summarized by Mas et al. (1987), the incidence rate can be estimated as about 0.01 per 1000 in the age group 40 – 60 years. It rises to 1 per 1000 in the age group 65 – 74 years and reaches 10 per 1000 in subjects aged 75 years and over. Akesson (1969) in Sweden, in a community-based survey, found that incidence rates rapidly increased with age from 0.29 per 1000 in the age group 60 – 69 years to 4.58 per 1000 in the ages over 80. The rates were consistently higher in females in all age groups. Molsa and colleagues (1982) in Finland, in a community-based survey, found that the age-specific annual incidence rates for AD were 0.06 cases per 1000 in the age class 45 – 54 years old and rose to 11.44 per 1000 in the age group 85 years and over. The incidence rates were higher in females, except for the 45 – 54 age group. Nilsson (1984) in Sweden in a sample of 70 – 79-year-old people showed a rapid increase in the incidence rates with age, from 3.6 per 1000 in subjects aged 70 – 74 years to 13.3 in those aged 75 – 79 years; rates were higher in men than women. Treves et al. (1986) in Israel, using the Israeli National Neurological Register as the source of cases, found lower incidence rates than Nilsson, but confirmed the age effect: from 0.01 cases per 1000 in the age class 45 – 49, to 0.87 per 1000 in subjects aged 60 years and over. Females showed higher incidence rates after the age of 59 years old. Moreover, in this study the age-specific incidence rates were higher in the European-American-born citizens, than in those who were Afro-Asian-born.

Sluss et al. (1981) followed up a cohort of 519 white males and observed that the age-specific incidence rate declined between ages 60 and 70 and then rose steeply after age 70. This finding is probably due to the small number of subjects on whom the estimates are based. The incidence rate of AD and other dementing illnesses over age 29 was estimated in a study based upon the medical record-linkage system in Rochester, MN (Schoenberg et al., 1987). In this study, 178 patients in an average annual at-risk population of 18,991 persons over age 29 developed dementia during 1960 – 1964, yielding an average annual incidence rate of 187.5 new cases/100,000/year. The corresponding rate for clinically and/or pathologically diagnosed AD was 123.3 new cases/100,000/year, based upon 117 cases. Consistent with the European studies, the incidence rates for all dementias and for AD rose rapidly with age. Contrary to previous studies, there were no significant sex differences in the age-specific rates.

No significant variations seem to have occurred in AD incidence rates across the years. Kokmen et al. (1988) in Rochester, MN determined the age- and sex-specific annual incidence rates for dementing disorders and AD between 1960 and 1974. They found that the incidence of dementia overall, and dementia specifically due to AD, had not significantly changed in this 15-year period. In the period 1960 – 1964, Schoenberg and colleagues (1987) found an annual incidence rate of 123.2 per 100,000 in the population over 30 years of age. Kokmen in the period 1970 – 1974, by using the same methodology, found an incidence rate of 147.2 per 100,000 in the same age group. Both the studies showed higher incidence rates in women than in men.

Analytic epidemiology of Alzheimer's disease

Analytic epidemiology is concerned with the etiology of disease. It is aimed at identifying factors associated with a high risk of disease. There are two general approaches to this type of study: retrospective and prospective.

Our knowledge of risk factors for AD is principally based upon findings coming from retrospective case-control studies. In these studies, one group of subjects with the disease (cases) is compared with one or more groups of subjects without the disease (controls) with respect to exposure to one or more hypothesized risk factors. Because demented people suffer from memory impairment, information is usually obtained from a surrogate respondent and the same procedure must be used with control subjects for comparability reasons. Rocca et al. (1986) assessed the reliability of surrogate respondents in providing data for the specific items of an Italian case-control study on AD (Amaducci et al., 1986). Agreement ranged

between 80 and 100% for the majority of questions. Lower agreements were observed for alcohol consumption and the number of cigarettes smoked per day; agreement was very poor for information about antacid drug use.

In case-control studies, once having identified a group of cases and controls, it is possible to measure the presence or absence of the risk factors, and estimate what is referred to as relative risk. The relative risk is a ratio of two incidence rates, or absolute risks; using the case-control approach it is not possible to calculate an absolute risk or incidence rate. It is possible to determine an absolute risk by employing a prospective study design. However, the case-control approach allows us to estimate the relative risk. Table 1 shows the design of a case-control study.

In cases and in controls we determine the presence or absence of a hypothesized risk factor. Cases and controls with the factor present are categorized in groups A and B respectively, and those without the factor in groups C and D. The estimation of the relative risk derives from the ratio of the cross-products AD/BC. This ratio is also referred to as an odds ratio. As underlined by Schoenberg (1978), for this estimate to be valid, three assumptions must be made: the disease under investigation is relatively uncommon; cases included in the study are representative of all cases of the disease; controls are representative of the population without the disease. When the frequency of the factor is the same in cases and controls the odds ratio will be equal to 1.0, and no increased risk is linked to the factor under investigation, while an odds ratio greater than 1.0 indicates an increased risk of disease. Of course, for odds ratios

TABLE 1

Design of a case-control study

Factor	Cases	Controls
Present	A	B
Absent	C	D

greater than 1.0 we have to carry out an appropriate statistical test to determine whether the observed deviation from 1.0 is statistically significant.

Based upon case-control studies, risk factors for AD include a positive family history of dementia and a previous head trauma in the history of the subject. In the case-control study by Amaducci and colleagues (1986), the presence of dementia in any first-degree relative yielded an odds ratio equal to 5.0 in the comparison with hospital controls and over 2.0 in the comparison with population controls, while the presence of dementia in any siblings yielded odds ratios equal to 11.0 in the comparison with hospital controls and over 5.0 in the comparison with population controls. Similar findings were found in other case-control (Heyman et al., 1984; Graves et al., 1987; Shalat et al., 1987) and comparative studies (Heston et al., 1981; Whalley et al., 1982; Breitner and Folstein, 1984). Mortimer (1990), using the Mantel-Haenszel statistical method (Schlesselman, 1982), carried out a meta-analysis of case control studies of AD. He found a summary odds ratio (95% C.I.) for the risk factor 'family history of dementia' equal to 3.96 (2.84, 5.52). Indications of the role of genetic factors in the etiology of AD come also from pedigree studies, twin studies and genetic studies. Rocca and Amaducci (1988) reviewed from an epidemiological point of view all the contributions to the problem of familial aggregation of AD. The authors suggested that at least three types should be considered regarding occurrence: autosomal dominant, familial and sporadic. The autosomal dominant type is linked to a genetic defect located on chromosome 21 in some families (St. George-Hyslop et al., 1987), while in other families its location is unknown (Schellenberg et al., 1988), suggesting the existence of a genetic heterogeneity. The familial type is defined as patients having at least one first-degree relative affected, without clear inheritance. Some of these cases are probably of the autosomal dominant type and they are misclassified because information on family members is insufficient. On the other hand

sporadic cases may also be misclassified as familial, because AD is a common condition in advanced age and two or more sporadic cases may be present in the same family simply by coincidence. Finally, the familial cases could be inherited not as single-gene but as polygenic disorders.

Despite the limitations of this classification of AD by type of occurrence, the authors feel it might be very useful in future etiological investigations.

Among hypothesized environmental risk factors for AD head trauma has to be seen as a probable even if unconfirmed risk factor. In fact a history of previous head trauma was significantly associated with the disease in more than one case-control study (Heyman et al., 1984; French et al., 1985; Mortimer et al., 1985; Graves et al., 1987). In some other studies (Amaducci et al., 1986; Chandra et al., 1987a,b; Shalat et al., 1987), head trauma was more frequent in cases than in controls, but the difference did not reach statistical significance. On the other hand, several studies were not able to find any association between head trauma and AD (Soininen and Heinonen, 1982; Bharucha et al., 1983; Sulkava et al., 1985a; Chandra et al., 1989). However, Mortimer (1990) observed that the association with head trauma is highly significant ($p < 0.001$) when considered across studies, despite the fact that the majority of studies failed to find significant associations for this risk factor.

Other factors found associated with AD in case-control studies include smoking and exposure to aluminum.

Shalat et al. (1986) found an increased risk of AD among smokers, and a significant increase in risk with increased cigarette consumption. This suggestive finding is not confirmed by other studies (French et al., 1985; Amaducci et al., 1986; Chandra et al., 1987b).

Accumulation of aluminum in paired helical filaments and in senile plaques in AD is now well established, but the role of this metal as risk factor is unclear. Chronic ingestion of aluminum-containing antacids was found not to be associated with an increased risk of AD (Heyman et al., 1984; Amaducci et al., 1986), while Graves et al. (1987)

found an increased risk of AD in users of anti-transpirants containing aluminum. Among the exposures proposed as risk factors for AD (Henderson, 1990), aluminum is one of the most interesting and further studies are expected. Possible sources of aluminum in the environment include cooking pots (Levick, 1980), tap water and acid rain (Pearce, 1985). A crucial issue to be clarified in this respect is the bioavailability of the metal, little aluminum being adsorbed from the gut (Mayor et al., 1987).

Parkinson's disease

Parkinsonism is a clinical syndrome characterized by hypokinesia, rigidity and tremor. This syndrome may result from primary parkinsonism (idiopathic Parkinson's disease) or from many types of secondary parkinsonism or parkinsonism associated with neurological system degeneration. Because the differential diagnosis of parkinsonism is difficult, and diagnostic methods often vary in different countries, epidemiological profiles for primary Parkinson's disease obtained in different surveys are not strictly comparable.

This section will deal principally with idiopathic PD (also called Lewy body disease). The epidemiology of the cognitive changes (including dementia) found in PD is discussed in the chapter by Dubois et al. (this volume, Ch. 10).

Prevalence of Parkinson's disease

Several studies have reported data on the prevalence (cases per 100 population) of Parkinson's disease (PD) in geographically defined populations. The prevalence ratio for PD ranges from 0.044 in China (Li et al., 1985) to 0.187 in Rochester, MN, U.S.A. (Kurland, 1958). In Italy two published surveys conducted in Sardinia (Rosati et al., 1980) and in the independent Republic of San Marino (D'Alessandro et al., 1987) report prevalence ratios of 0.065 and 0.185 respectively. Because of the variability in diagnostic criteria and case ascertainment of the

surveys, no clear geographic pattern emerges.

Two surveys based on medical records, one from Baltimore, U.S.A. (Kessler, 1972a), and one from South Africa (Reef, 1977), reported a considerably lower prevalence ratio among the black population than among the whites resident in the same geographical area. In contrast, a population-based survey conducted in Copiah County, MS, U.S.A., showed very similar prevalence ratios in whites and blacks in the population over 40 years old (Schoenberg et al., 1985). There seem to be lower prevalence ratios in Chinese and Japanese populations than among Caucasian (Marttila, 1987), but the relative influence of genetic and environmental effects cannot be established.

The prevalence ratio for PD increases sharply with age. Based upon the Rochester, MN, survey (Kurland, 1958), parkinsonism was rare before age 40, whereas 1% of the population over the age of 60 years were affected and the rate exceeded 2% in the oldest age group.

As the proportion of the population over 65 years old increases, and survival among patients with PD improves because of pharmacological therapy, there will be a further increase in this prevalence ratio and in the total number of affected subjects.

The prevalence ratio for PD has been found to be higher in males than in females in some studies (Kurland, 1958; Chalmanov, 1986; Mutch et al., 1986), but the reverse was true in several other studies (Jenkins, 1966; Marttila and Rinne, 1976a; Harada et al., 1983; Schoenberg et al., 1985). The reason for sex differences in prevalence remains unclear.

Incidence of Parkinson's disease

The mean annual incidence rate for PD in several surveys ranges from 4.9 cases per 100,000 population in Sardinia, Italy (Rosati et al., 1980), to 23.8 cases per 100,000 population in Rochester, MN, U.S.A. (Kurland, 1958). In Europe, the incidence of PD in mediterranean areas seems to be lower than in northern countries (Rosati et al., 1980).

However, this hypothesis is not supported by the results of some northern European studies (Garland, 1952; Broman, 1963) and variations in incidence rates cannot be explained only by a different risk of PD in different populations, because of the methodological variability in different surveys.

The onset of PD is rare before the age of 30 years, but incidence rates sharply increase with advancing age. The peak incidence rates occur during the ages 70 – 79 years, when 1 or 2 annually out of 1000 persons develop PD. After the age of 80 years, the incidence of PD declines, possibly due to incomplete ascertainment of cases in older subjects (Kurland et al., 1979; Gudmundsson, 1967).

Sex-specific incidence rates are higher in males than females for all ages (Kurland, 1958; Rajput et al., 1984), in contrast with some of the available prevalence data.

Risk factors

A major issue in the etiology of PD is whether the disease is inherited or caused by environmental factors. The proportion of patients with PD in their relatives varies from 2 to 62% (Marttila and Rinne, 1981). Inaccuracy in diagnosis of secondary cases, identified on the basis of anamnestic information, can explain these differences and preclude the drawing of firm conclusions about the relative importance of genetic and environmental factors.

Twins studies have shown low concordance rates for PD in twins; the rates were no higher in other relatives and approximated rates in the general population (Eldrige and Ince, 1984). These findings suggest that environmental factors are more important than genetic factors in determining the disease.

We do not know definite environmental risk factors for idiopathic PD. Several studies have indicated that smoking is negatively associated with PD (Baumann et al., 1980; Godwin-Austen et al., 1982; Bharucha et al., 1986), but this observation remains to be explained.

Several personality traits have been identified as

significantly different in the monozygotic twin affected with PD as compared with the unaffected twin (Ward et al., 1984). A typical personality in PD has been described as rigid, introverted and susceptible to depressive illness (Marttila, 1985).

One study (Kessler, 1972b) reported an association between PD and several pre-existing illnesses such as cerebrovascular disease encephalitis, head injury and psychiatric disorders, but another study did not confirm these findings (Marttila and Rinne, 1976b). A negative association with arterial hypertension has repeatedly been observed (Kondo, 1984; Marttila and Rinne, 1976b; Rajput, 1983). A possible explanation is the autonomic dysfunction of PD, which tends to lower blood pressure and thus prevent the development of hypertension (Marttila, 1985). A number of other possible environmental risk factors such as alcohol consumption, coffee consumption, vaccinations, mild tranquilizers, anesthetic agents, radiation, animal contacts, neurotoxins and birth order have been investigated, but none was found to be significantly associated with PD (Rajput, 1983; Marttila, 1985).

The discovery of MPTP-induced parkinsonism has renewed the interest in toxic substances as a cause of PD (Langston et al., 1983). A relationship between areas of agricultural pesticide use and high prevalence of PD in Canada was suggested by Barbeau et al. (1987). The hypothesis of a toxic substance present in the agricultural environment is also supported by a study comparing possible risk factors in cases of PD with early onset versus cases with late onset (Tanner, 1986). However, the hypothesis is not supported by a study of a rural population in the U.S.A. (Yesalis et al., 1985). Further investigations are needed.

References

Akesson HO: A population study of senile and arteriosclerotic psychoses. *Hum. Hered.: 19*, 546 – 566, 1969.
Amaducci LA, Fratiglioni L, Rocca WA, Fieschi C, Livrea P, Pedone D, Bracco L, Lippi A, Gandolfo C, Bino G, Prencipe M, Bonatti ML, Girottti F, Carella F, Tavolato B, Ferla S, Lenzi GL, Carolei A, Gambi A, Grigoletto F, Schoenberg

BS: Risk factors for clinically diagnosed Alzheimer's disease: a case-control study of an Italian population. *Neurology: 36*, 922 – 931, 1986.

American Psychiatric Association: *Diagnostic and Statistical Manual of Mental Disorders*, Third edn., Revised. Washington: American Psychiatric Association, p. 103, 1987.

Barbeau A, Roy M, Bernier G, Campanella G, Paris S: Ecogenetics of Parkinson's disease: prevalence and environmental aspects in rural areas. *Can. J. Neurol. Sci.: 14*, 36 – 41, 1987.

Baumann RJ, Jameson HD, McKean HE, Haack DG, Weisberg CM: Cigarette smoking and Parkinson's disease. I. A comparison of cases with matched neighbors. *Neurology: 30*, 839 – 843, 1980.

Bharucha NE, Schoenberg BS, Kokmen E: Dementia of Alzheimer's type (DAT): a case-control study of association with medical conditions and surgical procedures. *Neurology: 33* (Suppl 2), 85, 1983.

Bharucha NE, Stokes L, Schoenberg BS, Ward C, Ince S, Nutt JD, Eldridge R, Calne DB, Mantel N, Duvoisin RC: A case-control study of twin pairs discordant for Parkinson's disease: a search for environmental risk factors. *Neurology: 36*, 284 – 288, 1986.

Brayne C, Calloway P: An epidemiological study of dementia in a rural population of elderly women. *Br. J. Psychiatry: 155*, 214 – 220, 1989.

Breitner JCS, Folstein MF: Familial Alzheimer dementia: a prevalent disorder with specific clinical features. *Psychol Med.: 14*, 63 – 80, 1984.

Broe GA, Akhtar AJ, Andrews GR, Caird FI, Gilmore AJJ, McLennan WJ: Neurological disorders in the elderly at home. *J. Neurol. Neurosurg. Psychiatry: 39*, 362 – 366, 1976.

Broman T: Parkinson's syndrome, prevalence and incidence in Goteborg. *Acta Neurol. Scand.: 39* (Suppl 4), 95 – 101. 1963.

Chalmanov VN: Epidemiological studies of parkinsonism in Sofia. *Neuroepidemiology: 5*, 171 – 177, 1986.

Chandra V, Kokmen E, Schoenberg BS: Head trauma with loss of consciousness as a risk factor for Alzheimer's disease using prospectively collected data. *Neurology: 37* (Suppl 1), 152, 1987a.

Chandra V, Philipose V, Bell PA, Lazaroff A, Schoenberg BS: Case-control study of late onset 'probable Alzheimer's disease'. *Neurology: 37*, 1295 – 1300, 1987b.

Chandra V, Kokmen E, Schoenberg BS, Beard M: Head trauma with loss of consciousness as a risk factor for Alzheimer's disease. *Neurology: 39*, 1576 – 1578, 1989.

D'Alessandro R, Gamberini G, Granieri E, Benassi G, Naccarato S, Manzaroli D: Prevalence of Parkinson's disease in the Republic of San Marino. *Neurology: 37*, 1679 – 1682, 1987.

Eldridge R, Ince SE: The low concordance rate for Parkinson's disease in twins: a possible explanation. *Neurology: 34*, 1354 – 1356, 1984.

Evans DA, Funkenstein HH, Albert MS, Scherr PA, Cook NR, Chown MJ, Hebert LE, Hennekens CH, Taylor JO: Prevalence of Alzheimer's disease in a community population of older persons. *JAMA: 262*, 2551 – 2556, 1989.

French LR, Schuman LM, Mortimer JA, Hutton JT, Boatman RA, Christians B: A case-control study of dementia of the Alzheimer type. *Am. J. Epidemiol: 121*, 414 – 421, 1985.

Garland HG: Parkinsonism. *Br. Med. J.: 1*, 153 – 155, 1952.

Godwin-Austen RB, Lee PN, Marmot MG, Stern GM: Smoking and Parkinson's disease. *J. Neurol. Neurosurg. Psychiatry; 45*, 577 – 581, 1982.

Graves AB, White E, Koepsell T, Reifler B: A case-control study of Alzheimer's disease. *Am. J. Epidemiol: 126*, 754, 1987.

Gudmundsson KR: A clinical survey of parkinsonism in Iceland. *Acta Neurol. Scand.: 43* (Suppl 33), 9 – 61, 1967.

Hagnell O: *A Prospective Study of the Incidence of Mental Disorder*. Stockholm: Svenska Bokforlaget, 1966.

Harada H, Nishikawa S, Takahashi K: Epidemiology of Parkinson's disease in a Japanese city. *Arch. Neurol.: 40*, 151 – 156, 1983.

Hasegawa K: Aspects of community health care of the elderly. *Int. J. Ment. Health: 8*, 36 – 49, 1979.

Henderson AS: Epidemiology of dementia disorders. In Wurtman RJ, Corkin S, Growdon JH, Ritter-Walker E (Editors), *Advances in Neurology, Vol. 51: Alzheimer's Disease*. New York: Raven Press, 1990.

Heyman A, Wilkinson WE, Stafford JA, Helms MJ, Sigmon AH, Weinberg T: Alzheimer's disease: a study of epidemiological aspects. *Ann. Neurol.: 15*, 335 – 341, 1984.

Heston LL, Mastri AR, Anderson VE, White J: Dementia of the Alzheimer type: clinical genetics, natural history, and associated conditions. *Arch. Gen. Psychiatry: 38*, 1085 – 1090, 1981.

Jarvik CF, Ruth V, Matsuyama SS: Organic brain syndrome and aging. A six-year follow-up of surviving twins. *Arch. Gen. Psychiatry: 37*, 280 – 286, 1980.

Jenkins AC: Epidemiology of parkinsonism in Victoria. *Med. J. Aust.: 2*, 496 – 502, 1966.

Jorm AF, Korten AE, Henderson AS: The prevalence of dementia: a quantitative integration of the literature. *Acta Psychiatr. Scand.: 76*, 465 – 479, 1987.

Kaneko Z: Care in Japan. In Howells JG (Editor), *Modern Perspectives in the Psychiatry of Old Age*. New York: Brunner/Mazel, pp. 519 – 530, 1975.

Karasawa A, Kawashima K, Kasahara H: Epidemiological study of the senile in Tokio metropolitan area. In Ohashi (Editor), *Proceedings of the World Psychiatric Association Regional Symposium, Tokio 1982*. The Japanese Society of Psychiatry and Neurology, pp. 285 – 289, 1982.

Kay DWK, Beamish P, Roth M: Old age mental disorders in Newcastle upon tyne. Part I: a study of prevalence. *Br. J. Psychiatry: 110*, 146 – 158. 1964.

Katzman R, Terry RD, Bick KL: Recommendations of the nosology, epidemiology, and etiology and pathophysiology commissions of the workshop-conference on Alzheimer's Disease: senile dementia and related disorders. In Katzman, R, Terry RD, Bick KL (Editors), *Alzheimer's Disease: Senile Dementia and Related Disorders*. New York: Raven Press, pp. 579 – 585, 1978.

Katzman R, Aronson M, Fuld P, Kawas C, Brown T, Morgenstern H, Frishman W, Gidez L, Eder H, Ooi WL: Development of dementing illnesses in an 80-year-old volunteer cohort. *Ann. Neurol. 25*, 317 – 324, 1989.

Kessler II: Epidemiologic studies of Parkinson's disease. III. A community-based survey. *Am. J. Epidemiol.: 96,* 242 – 254, 1972a.

Kessler II: Epidemiologic studies of Parkinson's disease. II. Hospital-based survey. *Am. J. Epidemiol.: 95,* 308 – 318, 1972b.

Kokmen E, Chandra V, Schoenberg BS: Trends in incidence of dementing illness in Rochester, Minnesota, in three quinquennial periods, 1960 – 1974. *Neurology: 38,* 975 – 980, 1988.

Kondo K: Epidemiological clues for the etiology of Parkinson's disease. *Adv. Neurol: 40,* 345 – 351, 1984.

Kurland LT. Epidemiology: incidence, geographic distribution and genetic consideration. In Fields WS (Editor), *Pathogenesis and Treatment of Parkinsonism.* Springfield: Charles C Thomas, pp. 5 – 49, 1958.

Kurland LT, Kurtzke JF, Goldberg ID, Choi NG, Williams G: Parkinsonism. In Kurland LT, Goldberg ID (Editors), *Epidemiology of Neurological and Sense Organ Disorders.* Cambridge, MA: Harvard University Press, pp. 50 – 55, 1979.

Langston JW, Ballard P, Tetrud JW, Irwin I: Chronic parkinsonism in humans due to a product of epinephrine-analog synthesis. *Science: 219,* 979 – 980, 1983.

Levick SE: Dementia from aluminum pots? *N. Engl. J. Med.: 303,* 164, 1980.

Li SC, Schoenberg BS, Wang CC, Cheng XM, Rui DY, Bolis CL, Schoenberg DG: A prevalence survey of Parkinson's disease and other movement disorders in the People's Republic of China. *Arch. Neurol.: 42,* 655 – 657, 1985.

Mardsen CD, Harrison MJG: Outcome of investigation of patients with presenile dementia. *Br. Med. J.: 2,* 249, 1972.

Marttila RJ: Epidemiology. In Koller WC (Editor), *Handbook of Parkinson's disease.* New York: Marcel Dekker, 1987.

Marttila RJ, Rinne UK: Epidemiology of Parkinson's disease in Finland. *Acta Neurol. Scand.: 53,* 81 – 102, 1976a.

Marttila RJ, Rinne UK: Arteriosclerosis, heredity, and some previous infections in the etiology of Parkinson's disease. A case-control study. *Clin. Neurol. Neurosurg.: 79,* 46 – 56, 1976b.

Marttila RJ, Rinne UK: Epidemiology of Parkinson's disease – an overview. *J. Neurol. Transm.: 51,* 135 – 148, 1981.

Mas JL, Alperovitch A, Derouesné C: Epidémiologie de la démence de type Alzheimer. *Rev. Neurol.: 3,* 161 – 171, 1987.

Mayor GH, Keiser JA, Makdani D, Ku PK: Aluminum absorption and distribution: effect of parathyroid hormone. *Science: 197,* 1187 – 1189, 1987.

Mckhann G, Drachman D, Folstein M, Katzman R, Price D, Stadlan EM: Clinical diagnosis of Alzheimer's disease: report of the NINCDS-ADRDA Work Group under the auspices of Department of Health and Human Service Task Force on Alzheimer's disease. *Neurology: 34,* 939 – 944, 1984.

Molsa PK, Marttila RJ, Rinne UK: Epidemiology of dementia in a Finnish population. *Acta Neurol. Scand.: 65,* 541 – 552, 1982.

Mortimer JA, French LR, Hutton JT, Schuman LM: Head injury as a risk factor for Alzheimer's disease. *Neurology: 35,* 264 – 267, 1985.

Mortimer JA: Epidemiology of dementia: cross-cultural comparisons. In Wurtman RJ, Corkin S, Growdon JH, Ritter-Walker E (Editors), *Advances in Neurology, Vol. 51: Alzheimer's Disease.* New York: Raven Press, 1990.

Mutch W, Dingwall-Fordyce I, Downie AW, Paterson JG, Roy SK: Parkinson's disease in a Scottish city. *Br. Med. J.: 192,* 535 – 536, 1986.

National Institutes of Health Consensus Development Conference Statement: Differential diagnosis of dementing diseases. *Alz. Dis. Assoc. Disorders: 2,* 4 – 28, 1988.

Nielsen J: Geronto-psychiatric period-prevalence investigation in a geographically delimited population. *Acta Psychiat. Scand.: 38,* 307 – 330, 1963.

Nilsson LV: Incidence of severe dementia in an urban sample followed from 70 to 79 years of age. *Acta Psychiat. Scand.: 70,* 478 – 486, 1984.

Pearce F: Acid rain may cause senile dementia. *New Sci.: 25,* 7, 1985.

Rajput AH: Epidemiology of Parkinson's disease. *Can. J. Neurol. Sci.: 11,* 156 – 160, 1983.

Rajput AH, Offord KP, Beard M, Kurland LT: Epidemiology of parkinsonism: incidence, classification, and mortality. *Ann. Neurol.: 16,* 278 – 282, 1984.

Reef HE: Prevalence of Parkinson's disease in a multiracial community. In Jager HWA, Bruyn GW, Heijstee APJ (Editors), *Proceedings of the 11th World Congress of Neurology.* Amsterdam: Excerpta Medica, p. 125, 1977.

Rocca WA, Amaducci L: The familial aggregation of Alzheimer's disease: an epidemiological review. *Psychiat. Dev.: 1,* 23 – 36, 1988.

Rocca W, Amaducci LA, Schoenberg BS: Projected demographic trends for the elderly population between 1980 and 2000: implications for senile dementia prevalence. In Schoenberg BS (Editor), *Proceedings of the Meeting of the Research Committee on Neuroepidemiology, World Federation of Neurology.* Boston: WFN Research Committee on Neuroepidemiology, p. 5, 1984.

Rocca WA, Bonaiuto S, Lippi A, Luciani L, Turtu' F, Cavarzeran F, Amaducci L: Prevalence of clinically diagnosed Alzheimer's disease and other dementing disorders: a door-to-door survey in Appignano, Macerata province, Italy. *Neurology: 40,* 626 – 631, 1990.

Rocca WA, Fratiglioni L, Bracco L, Pedone D, Groppi C, Schoenberg B: The use of surrogate respondents to obtain questionnaire data in case-control studies of neurological diseases. *J. Chron. Dis.: 39,* 907 – 912, 1986.

Rosati G, Granieri E, Pinna L, Aiello I, Tola R, De Bastiani P, Pirisi A, Devoto MC: The risk of Parkinson disease in Mediterranean people. *Neurology: 30,* 250 – 255, 1980.

Roth M: Epidemiological studies. In Katzman R, Terry RD, Bick KL (Editors), *Alzheimer's Disease: Senile Dementia and Related Disorders.* New York: Raven Press, pp. 337 – 339, 1978.

Roth M, Tym E, Mountjoy CQ, Huppert FA, Hendrie H, Verma S, Goddard R: CAMDEX, A standardized instrument for the diagnosis of mental disorder in the elderly with special reference to the early detection of dementia. *Br. J. Psychiatry: 149,* 698 – 709, 1986.

Schellenberg GD, Bird TD, Wijsman EM, Moore DK, Boehnke M, Bryant EM, Lampe TH, Nochlin D, Sumi SM, Deeb SS, Beyreuther K, Martin GM. Absence of linkage of chromosome 21q21 markers to familial Alzheimer's disease. *Science: 241*, 1507 – 1510, 1988.

Schlesselman JJ: *Case-Control Studies: Design, Conduct, Analysis.* New York: Oxford University Press, 1982.

Schoenberg BS: Analytic, experimental, and theoretical epidemiology. In Schoenberg BS (Editor), *Advances in Neurology, Vol. 19: Neurological Epidemiology: Principles and Clinical Applications.* New York: Raven Press, 1978.

Schoenberg BS, Anderson DW, Haerer AF: Prevalence of Parkinson's disease in the biracial population of Copiah county, Mississippi. *Neurology: 35*, 841 – 845, 1985.

Schoenberg BS, Anderson DW, Haerer AF: Severe dementia. Prevalence and clinical features in a biracial US population. *Arch. Neurol.: 42*, 740 – 743, 1985.

Schoenberg BS, Kokmen E, Okazaki H: Alzheimer's disease and other dementing illnesses in a defined United States population: incidence rates and clinical features. *Ann. Neurol.: 22*, 724 – 729, 1987.

Shalat SL, Seltzer B, Pidcock C, Baker EL Jr: Risk factors for Alzheimer's disease: a case-control study. *Neurology: 37*, 1630 – 1633, 1987.

Shen YC, Li G, Chen CH, Zhao YW: An epidemiological survey on age-related dementia in an urban area of Beijing, presented at the WHO International Workshop on Epidemiology of Mental and Neurological Disorders of the Elderly, Beijing, November 16 – 20, 1987.

Sluss TK, Gruenberg EM, Kramer M: The use of longitudinal studies in the investigation of risk-factors, for senile dementia-Alzheimer type. In Mortimer JA, Schuman LM (Editors), *The Epidemiology of Dementia.* New York: Oxford University Press, pp. 132 – 154, 1981.

Soininen H, Heinonen OP: Clinical and etiological aspects of senile dementia. *Eur. Neurol.: 21*, 401 – 410, 1982.

St George Hyslop PH, Tanzi RE, Polinsky RJ, Haines JL, Nee L, Watkins PC, Myers RH, Feldman RG, Pollen D, Drachman D, Growdon J, Bruni A, Foncin JF, Salmon D, Frommelt P, Amaducci L, Sorbi S, Piacentini S, Stewart GD, Hobbs WJ, Conneally PM, Gusella JF: The genetic defects causing familial Alzheimer's disease maps on chromosome 21. *Science: 235*, 885 – 890, 1987.

Sulkava R, Erkinluntti T, Palo J: Head injuries in Alzheimer's disease and vascular dementia. *Neurology: 35*, 1804, 1985a.

Sulkava R, Wikstrom J, Aromaa A, Raitasalo R, Lehtinen V, Lahtela K, Palo J: Prevalence of severe dementia in Finland. *Neurology: 35*, 1025 – 1029, 1985b.

Tanner CM: Influence of environmental factors on the onset of Parkinson's disease. *Neurology: 36* (Suppl 1), 215, 1986.

Tomlinson BE, Blessed G, Roth M: Observations on the brains of demented old people. *J. Neurol. Sci.: 11*, 205, 1970.

Treves T, Korczyn A, Zilber N, Kahana E, Leibowitz Y, Alter M, Schoenberg BS: Presenile dementia in Israel. *Arch. Neurol.: 43*, 26 – 29, 1986.

United Nations: Report of the Interregional Seminar to Promote the Implementation of the International Plan of Action on Aging, United Nations Publication Sales No. E. 86. IV. 5, 1986.

Ward CD, Duvoisin RC, Ince SE, Nutt JD, Eldridge R, Calne DB, Dambrosia J: Parkinson's disease in twins. *Adv. Neurol.: 40*, 341 – 345, 1984.

Wells CE: *Dementia.* Philadelphia: Davis, 1979.

Whalley LJ, Carothers AD, Colleyr S, De Mey R, Frackiewicz: A study of familial factors in Alzheimer's disease. *Br. J. Psychiatry: 140*, 249 – 256, 1982.

Yesalis CE, Lemke J, Wallace RB, Kohout FJ, Morris MC: Health status of the rural elderly according to farm work history: The Iowa 65 + rural health study. *Arch. Environ. Health: 40*, 245 – 253, 1985.

Zhang M, Katzman R, Salmon D, Jin H, Cai G, Wang Z, Qu G, Grant I, Yu E, Levy P, Klauber RM, Liu TW: The prevalence of dementia of Alzheimer's disease (AD) in Shanghai, China: impact of age, gender, and education. *Ann. Neurol.: 27*, 428 – 437, 1990.

© 1991 Elsevier Science Publishers B.V.
Handbook of Neuropsychology, Vol. 5
F. Boller and J. Grafman (Eds)

CHAPTER 2

Subgroups of dementia: methodological issues and applications to Alzheimer's disease

Helena Chang Chui

Department of Neurology, University of Southern California, School of Medicine, Los Angeles, CA, U.S.A.

The wealth of diversity spawned by medical illness poses both a nosological and a scientific challenge. Phenotypic heterogeneity may originate from several sources, including differences in etiology, pathogenesis, distribution of lesions, stage of illness, socio-demographic characteristics, as well as the method of experimental observation. For the purposes of primary therapy, differences in etiology and pathogenesis are paramount. For understanding brain – behavior relationships, the anatomic distribution of lesions is critical. Finally, for the day-to-day management of individual patients, stage of illness and socio-demographic differences are germane. Thus, the relevance of specific types of heterogeneity varies, depending upon the context of investigation.

For illnesses that cause dementia, understanding of phenotypic diversity is in its infancy. For several diseases, information is available regarding etiology. For example, Huntington's disease is caused by an abnormal gene located on the distal short arm of chromosome 4. For this genetically defined disease, phenotypic diversity may be substantial. Most commonly, clinical symptoms such as personality changes, chorea and dementia develop in the fourth and fifth decades of life. In a juvenile variant, however, symptoms appear much earlier, and rigidity rather than chorea is the most prominent extrapyramidal sign (Shoulson, 1986). Since all forms of Huntington's disease are attributed to a single gene mutation, these phenotypic variations presumably represent differences in pathogenesis rather than etiology.

In contrast to Huntington's disease, both etiology and pathogenesis are unknown for the most prevalent dementing disorders. Accordingly, illnesses are often classified by clinico-pathological phenotype. This is true in the case of Alzheimer's disease (AD), a syndrome currently defined as a progressive dementia associated with neurofibrillary tangles and senile plaques in many areas of the brain. Within this clinico-pathological definition, rich clinical and pathological diversity can be appreciated, and the entire spectrum of subgroup determinants (including differences in etiology and pathogenesis) may be hidden. If pathogenetic differences do exist, their discovery might be significantly delayed by the failure to consider the possibility of subgroups. Thus, when a dementing disorder can only be defined based on clinical-pathological phenotype, subgroup research may be the most challenging and potentially rewarding.

The purpose of this chapter is two-fold. Aside from several critical reviews (Jorm, 1985; Chui, 1987), little has been written regarding conceptual issues in dementia subgroups research. Thus, conceptual and methodological issues underlying such investigations will be considered first. Methods to increase the likelihood of identifying pathogenetically-relevant subgroups and to decrease the likelihood of proliferating trivial, non-pathogenetic subgroups will be suggested. Second, the range

15

of clinical-pathological diversity associated with AD will be reviewed. The possible significance of subgroups will be considered.

Conceptual and methodological issues in subgroups research

Significance of subgroups

The relationship between various sources of heterogeneity and clinical-pathological phenotype can be clarified by structural diagrams. Such diagrams have previously been developed (Jorm, 1985) and modified (Chui, 1987) to examine the evidence for subtypes of Alzheimer dementia. Further modifications of this heuristic device are presented here (see Figs. 1 and 2). In the hypothetical chain of events leading from etiology to clinical and pathological phenotype (Fig. 1), non-observable constructs are depicted as circles, while manifest characteristics are shown as boxes. A pathological disturbance (etiological cause, A), produces a pathogenetic cascade, which results in manifest pathology (X). In turn, pathological changes produce a functional disorder (B), which

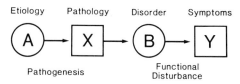

Fig. 1. Hypothetical chain of events leading from etiology to clinical and pathological phenotype.

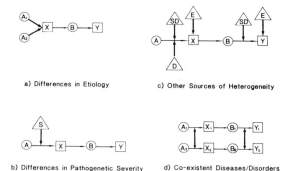

a) Differences in Etiology

c) Other Sources of Heterogeneity

b) Differences in Pathogenetic Severity

d) Co-existent Diseases/Disorders

Fig. 2. Variation in clinical-pathological phenotype (X-Y) arising from multiple sources.

results in clinical signs and symptoms (Y).

Variation in clinical-pathological phenotype (X-Y) could arise from multiple sources (see Fig. 2). These might include differences in: (1) etiological cause (A), (2) factors which modulate severity of disease pathogenesis (S), (3) factors which influence the anatomic distribution of lesions, (4) duration, which determines stage of illness (D), (5) the concurrent presence of co-existent disease (A2), (6) socio-demographic profile (SD), and (7) experimental methodology (E). Factors 1 – 3 appear to be most closely related to primary disease pathogenesis and therefore most relevant for understanding treatment, prognosis and brain – behavior relationships.

Two processes are involved in subgroup research: (1) the development of a subgroup nosology, and (2) the identification of responsible subgroup determinant(s). The former process provides associative information and may suggest possible subgroup determinants. The actual identification of determinants, on the other hand, is beyond the scope of subgroups research and requires the alliance of modern neurobiology. From the standpoint of scientific relevance, research efforts should focus on those subgroups most likely to reflect differences in etiology and pathogenesis (so-called pathogenetic subgroups). Conversely, factors deemed to be of less scientific interest (i.e., spurious sources of heterogeneity that give rise to non-pathogenetic subgroups) should be explicitly controlled.

Definition of subgroups

A 'subgroup' is generally understood to represent a subordinate group of members sharing a 'common differential quality' (Webster's Dictionary). Subgroups can be defined in several ways. In the context of dementia, subgroups can be differentiated based on (1) demographic characteristics (e.g., sex, race, age), (2) clinical-pathological phenotype, or (3) family history of dementia. Clinical phenotype refers to disease-related parameters that can be measured in living subjects (e.g., neuropsychological, behavioral, physiological); pathological phenotype refers to parameters measured in brain tissue (e.g., neuropathological, neurochemical, molecular). Subgroups can be pre-defined using univariate parameters such as age at symptom onset or psychometric performance. Alternatively, they may be defined post-hoc, using variables empirically derived from multi-variate statistics. The first approach tends to generate unidimensional, but usually understandable, subgroups. By contrast, the second method tends to produce multi-dimensional, although less intuitive, subgroups.

A subgroup nosology is based on associations between predictor and criterion variables. Depending upon the experimental and statistical design, one variable serves as an independent or predictor variable while the other serves as a dependent or criterion variable. For example, correlations are frequently sought between age at onset (independent or predictor variable) and rate of progression (dependent or criterion variable). It is important to note that in subgroups research, the term 'independent or predictor' and 'dependent or criterion' do not necessarily imply causation. While the ultimate purpose of subgroups research is to facilitate a neurobiological and dynamic understanding of pathogenesis, the nature of subgroups research by itself is relational, not causal.

In the literature, subgroups have been categorized as qualitative or quantitative depending on the nature of the features which differentiate them (Jorm, 1985; Chui, 1987). For example, differences in *rate* of progression may be used to define quantitative subgroups, while the *presence* or *absence* of Pathology X or Symptom Y may define qualitative subgroups. Several difficulties, however, are associated with this dichotomization. First, the apparent absence of a feature may not indicate qualitative differences, but merely reflect lack of sensitivity of the experimental measure. More importantly, the qualitative versus quantitative distinction is irrelevant to the nature of the underlying determinants. Important differences in etiology and pathogenesis may be associated with quantitative or qualitative differences in pheno-

type. For these reasons, the differentiation between qualitative and quantitative subgroups is not emphasized in this chapter.

Prospective sample selection
When non-pathogenetic variables are controlled across subgroups, the probability that these factors will become subgroup determinants is minimized. Such factors would include: (1) duration or stage of illness (D), (2) the presence of co-existent disease and medication (O), (3) socio-demographic characteristics, such as age, sex, race, education, occupation, socio-economic class (SD), and (4) experimental methodology, including diagnostic criteria (E). Obviously, control over such confounding factors is best realized with prospective (as opposed to retrospective) sampling. Selection of matched subjects and explicit inclusion/exclusion criteria help in addressing these issues.

Matching subjects   Matching subjects offers one method for controlling spurious sources of heterogeneity. Because dementia usually results from progressive neurological disease, substantial clinical heterogeneity evolves as the disease progresses. In order to control for this source of diversity, patients in each subgroup should be initially matched for stage or severity of illness. Similarly, changes associated with aging (Finch, 1990), as well as other demographic factors such as race, sex, education and socio-economic status, can influence and interact with disease expression. Thus, patients in comparison subgroups should be matched for age, as well as other demographic factors. When matching for age is precluded, such as when age at onset is used as a predictor variable (for example, in a comparison of early versus late onset subgroups), age-matched controls should be included in parallel studies.

Inclusion and exclusion criteria
In order to control other unwanted sources of heterogeneity, inclusion and exclusion criteria (rather than matching) are appropriate. Coexistent illnesses and medications that may affect the cen-

tral nervous system are highly prevalent in the elderly. For example, in several pathological studies of dementia, a combination of vascular lesions and Alzheimer's disease was diagnosed in 15% of cases (Katzman et al., 1988a). To the extent possible, coexistent illness and medications with prominent central nervous system side-effects should be excluded from the sample selection.

Uniform application of diagnostic criteria   In the absence of specific biological markers, the methods of diagnosing various dementing disorders are limited in accuracy and may vary regionally. For example, NINCDS/ADRDA criteria (McKhann et al., 1984) are used in the United States for the clinical diagnosis of AD, while a variety of diagnostic criteria are favored in other countries (for review see Boller and Saxton, 1990). Differences in diagnostic criteria may complicate the international comparison of subgroups research. At least for individual studies, diagnostic criteria should be clearly operationalized and uniformly applied in order to equalize the contribution of misdiagnosis across subgroups.

Longitudinal design
Longitudinal design allows: (1) examination of subgroup stability, (2) assessment rate of progression and (3) post-mortem confirmation of clinical diagnosis. Longitudinal stability of predictor – criterion relationships *decreases* the likelihood that subgroup differences are related to developmental stage of illness. It is important to keep in mind, however, that when a criterion can no longer be measured (i.e., the variable reaches the floor of the measuring tool) subgroup stability may not be demonstrable. When rate of progression is the criterion of interest, a longitudinal rather than cross-sectional design is clearly preferred. In cross-sectional studies, rate of progression is inferred by relating stage of illness to reported duration of illness. In longitudinal studies, both dementia severity and time can be quantified more accurately. Rate of progression may be assessed as the change in dementia severity divided by the time interval.

Alternatively, actuarial or survival methods may be applied. In the latter instance, the predictor variable is studied in relation to the probability that a discrete event (e.g., death, institutionalization, or decline to a fixed psychometric score) will occur over time. An advantage of survival analyses is the ability to utilize censored observations or incomplete data which occur when a patient has not yet reached end-point or is lost to follow-up. Finally, longitudinal follow-up is required for postmortem confirmation of clinical diagnosis. In many dementing disorders this may be the sole means to recognize and correct misdiagnoses. Thus, a longitudinal, as well as prospective, experimental design is essential for subgroups research.

Independent validation of subgroups
The likelihood of identifying pathogenetic subgroups is increased when subgroupings are validated both with new measures and by independent investigators. The cumulative association of new clinical and pathological markers with various subgroups may help to clarify their biological determinants. The effects of selection bias are minimized when subgroupings are reproduced by different investigators and new patient samples. Independent validation is relevant to experimental methodologies in general, but is particularly important in dementia subgroups research, where it is often difficult to control multiple confounding variables.

Identification of subgroup determinant
The ultimate goal of subgroups research is to facilitate the understanding of disease pathogenesis. The pattern of variable-clusters may suggest possible underlying determinants. The identification of these biological determinants themselves, however, falls outside the province of subgroups research. For example, an association between early symptom onset and faster rate of progression may suggest a relative excess or deficiency of Factor Z, which modulates pathogenetic severity. The identification of Factor Z, however,

would require other tools of modern neurobiology. In an ideal and perhaps unrealizable scenario, manipulation of Factor Z would result in a predictable alteration of subgroup phenotype. Thus, subgroup research can be viewed as an important ally of neurobiology.

In summary, for disorders currently classified by clinical-pathological phenotype, the possibility of pathogenetic subgroups is an important concept. Control of spurious sources of heterogeneity (for example, standardization of diagnostic and experimental protocols, prospective and matched sample selection, and longitudinal follow-up), as well as an attempt to validate subgroups independently, will maximize the likelihood of identifying pathogenetic subgroups. The significance of clinical pathological diversity in AD can now be considered within this conceptual framework.

Subgroups of Alzheimer's disease

Because etiology and pathogenesis are unknown, Alzheimer's disease (AD) is currently defined as a clinical-pathological entity: clinically, by a history of progressive dementia; pathologically, by widespread neurofibrillary tangles and senile plaques (McKhann et al., 1985). At present there is no means (other than cortical biopsy) to ascertain the presence of tangles and plaques in living subjects. Thus, the accuracy of the clinical diagnosis of AD is limited. This uncertainty is recognized by clinical designations such as probable AD or senile dementia of the Alzheimer type (SDAT). In clinical-pathological series, the sensitivity and specifity of the clinical diagnosis of AD has ranged between 64 and 87% (Bowen et al., 1982; Sulkava et al., 1983; Wade et al., 1987; Joachim et al., 1968; Boller et al., 1989). Thus, until more accurate diagnostic tests become available, a proportion of apparent clinical diversity may represent misdiagnosis. However, even when diagnostic accuracy has not been an issue, rich diversity in demography, clinical-pathological phenotype and familial aggregation pattern has been associated with AD. The significance of this heterogeneity is unknown

and could include the range of possibilities discussed earlier.

Demographics

Little information is available regarding differences in AD based on race or sex. In an epidemiological study of a bi-racial population, the prevalence of SDAT was similar in blacks and whites (Schoenberg et al., 1985). The gender-specific incidence and the prevalence of SDAT are higher in women than men (Rocca et al., 1986). The differences in prevalence, at least, can be explained by lower absolute and relative survival of men compared with women (Barclay et al., 1985a). Greater neuronal loss in the locus ceruleus was reported in a group of younger female SDAT cases (Bondareff et al., 1982), but has not been confirmed. These findings suggest that sex may play a modulating influence upon disease expression. At present, however, virtually nothing is known about the possible mechanisms.

Age at onset
Alois Alzheimer described a 55-year-old woman with progressive dementia and widespread neurofibrillary tangles and senile plaques (Alzheimer, 1907). The eponym, Alzheimer's disease, was initially reserved for clinical-pathological cases with similar presenile symptom onset. Subsequently, it became apparent that many patients who develop progressive dementia late in life show qualitatively identical tangles and plaques (Tomlinson, 1970). Thus, the diagnosis of Alzheimer's disease is currently applied regardless of age at symptom onset (for review, see Amaducci et al., 1986).

Nonetheless, age-at-onset appears to be associated with *quantitative* differences in clinical and pathological phenotype. Bondareff (1983) has proposed that AD is composed of two subtypes. AD-1 begins in old age and runs an insidious course, while AD-2 begins in middle age and takes a more rapid course. Parietal involvement, motor signs, ventricular enlargement, tangles, plaques, neuronal loss and neurotransmitter loss are all said to be greater in AD-2 (early onset) compared to AD-1 (late onset) (Bondareff, 1983). More detailed review suggests that, although quantitative differences exist, dichotomization of AD into two subtypes probably represents an oversimplification.

In several cross-sectional studies, differences between early and late onset SDAT have been shown based on: (1) the severity of neuropsychological deficits, especially in concentration (Loring and Largen, 1985; Selnes et al., 1988) and possibly language, (2) the frequency of myoclonus (Mayeux et al., 1985; Chui et al., 1985) and (3) the estimated degree of gray matter atrophy (Prohovnik et al., 1989). The relationship between age at onset and language disorder is controversial. More severe language disturbance has been linked to early symptom onset by some investigators (Seltzer and Sherwin, 1983; Chui et al., 1985; Faber-Langendoen et al., 1988), but has not been confirmed by others (Selnes et al., 1988; Becker et al., 1988). Thus, cross-sectional data regarding age-at-onset and clinical severity have been inconsistent.

Prospective longitudinal studies are far more powerful than cross-sectional studies for examining the issue of differential rates of progression. No group differences were demonstrated in two studies which used change scores of the Blessed Dementia Scale (Blessed et al.,1968) to assess rate of decline in early versus late onset subgroups (Huff et al., 1987b; Katzman et al., 1988b). Similarly, in a study of three community cohorts, age-at-onset did not predict change scores in the Blessed Information-Memory-Concentration Test (Katzman et al., 1988b). Finally, Boller et al. (1990) could find no relationship between age-at-onset and change scores on the Mini-Mental State Exam. Thus, several longitudinal studies have failed to support the hypothesis that early onset is associated with faster clinical progression.

These negative studies do not preclude the possibility that specific cognitive abilities (e.g., language rather than memory) decline faster in early versus late onset AD. For example, principal components analysis of a neuropsychological test battery, followed by multiple stepwise regression analysis, showed age-at-onset to be predictive of some but not all neuropsychological factors (Brandt et al., 1989). Early onset was associated with greater decline in 'naming' but not 'visual-spatial' or other 'language' weighted abilities. Additional studies of this nature are required to determine whether age-at-onset might be associated with differential decline in specific cognitive abilities.

Actuarial analyses have also been used to examine differential progression. Relative survival was found to be significantly decreased in early onset patients (Barclay et al., 1985a; Heyman et al., 1987). On the other hand, in a 66-month study of 43 patients with mild SDAT, age-at-onset was not found to be predictive of either institutionalization or death (Berg et al., under review). Although institutionalization and death are discrete outcome measures, they may not be the most appropriate indicators of disease progression. Nursing-home placement depends on the characteristics of the care-giver, as well as the patient (Colerick and George, 1986). Death is often due to extraneous, non-AD related causes (Heyman et al., 1987). In one study which used a measure of dementia severity (MMSE $\leq$ 5) as an alternative end-point (Brandt et al., 1989), more malignant progression was found in early onset SDAT. These differences suggest that the choice of outcome measures may be important in applying actuarial methods to AD.

Significant differences between early and late onset have been described in neuropathological studies of AD (for review, see Bondareff, 1983; Roth, 1986). For example, early symptom onset has been associated with greater numbers of cerebral cortical neurofibrillary tangles (Sourander and Sjogren, 1970; Mountjoy et al., 1984; Hansen et al., 1988), subcortical neuronal loss (Bondareff et al., 1982; Tagliavini and Pilleri, 1983; Mann and Yates, 1984; Bondareff et al., 1987), and depression of cortical choline acetyltransferase and dopamine β-hydroxylase activity (Rossor et al., 1981, 1984; Bird et al., 1983; Mountjoy et al.,

1984). In this regard, the neuropathological data have been more consistent than the clinical.

Neuropathological studies are, however, necessarily cross-sectional, making it difficult to match cases for stage and duration of illness. Longer duration of illness occurs in early onset cases (Barclay et al., 1985a; Chui et al., under review) and could at least partially account for differences in pathological severity. Therefore, duration and stage of illness should be included as co-variates in neuropathological studies of AD.

We recently used stepwise multiple regression to examine the relative contributions of age-at-onset, duration of illness and severity of dementia to measures of pathological severity. Early onset was associated with more severe neurofibrillary degeneration in several subcortical and neocortical association areas, but not in the hippocampal complex (Chui et al., under review). These findings support the hypothesis that, at least in certain brain regions, early onset is associated with more severe pathology. These differences in regional pathology are reminiscent of differential patterns of cognitive dysfunction: more prominent concentration (Selnes et al., 1988) and language impairment (Faber-Langendoen et al., 1988; Brandt et al., 1989), but not necessarily memory impairment (Huff et al., 1987a; Katzman et al., 1988b) in early onset SDAT. Thus, both pathological and clinical differences related to age-at-onset may be regionally and behaviorally selective.

In summary, although two subtypes of early (AD-2) and late onset (AD-1) have been postulated, consistent differences have not been demonstrated. The inconsistencies in the literature may possibly be related to the specific outcome measures, cognitive factors or regions of the brain chosen for study. Some evidence suggests that quantitative (severity) and possibly qualitative (regional distribution) differences may be associated with age-at-onset. The direction of these associations cannot be explained by the combined effects of normal aging, which would tend if anything to increase the clinical-pathological severity in late onset AD. The underlying factors responsible for such associations are unknown, but may be related to differences in pathogenetic severity or selective vulnerability.

Clinical-pathological phenotype

Simple senile dementia

A syndrome known as 'simple senile dementia' has been described in the European literature (Constantinidis, 1978). This syndrome is described in older patients as a prominent disturbance of recent memory, with subsequent impoverishment of language and constructional apraxia. Aphasia, ideomotor apraxia and agnosias are absent and clinical progression is relatively slow. More recent reports of a subset of mildly demented patients who progress very little, if at all, over several years (see Pearce and Pearce, 1962; Mayeux et al., 1985; Berg et al., 1984; Botwinick et al., 1986) appear to fit this syndrome.

In correlative neuropathological studies of patients with simple senile dementia, neurofibrillary tangles were mainly found in the hippocampus and the temporal lobes (Constantinidis, 1978). On the other hand in patients with dementia associated with aphasia, apraxia, or agnosia, neurofibrillary tangles were dispersed throughout the cerebral cortex. Ulrich and Stahelin (1984) also described AD cases with pathological changes restricted to the mediobasal temporal lobe, but were unable to clinically differentiate these patients based on severity of dementia. Additional clinical-pathological correlations are needed which relate specific patterns of clinical symptoms to regional pathology. These studies may help to elucidate brain – behavior relationships as well as the factors that determine regional-selective vulnerability.

Focal and asymmetric presentations

Although memory loss characteristically precedes the appearance of aphasia and visual spatial loss in SDAT, significant variations in the pattern of symptom development have been described. In some patients the presenting symptom has been aphasia (Mesulam, 1982; Kirschner et al., 1984;

Pogacar and Williams, 1984) or visual-spatial disturbance (Crystal et al., 1982; Martin et al., 1986; Sullivan et al., 1986). Disproportionate impairment in lexical-semantic or visuoconstructive tasks has also been identified (Martin et al., 1987; Becker et al., 1988). Unusually rapid clinical deterioration has been reported in a small subset of middle-aged patients with severe spatial disorientation, aphasia, apraxia and agnosia (Brion and Plas, 1989). These examples of focal and asymmetric psychological function are reminiscent of the common asymmetry in tremor and rigidity in Parkinson's disease.

Cerebral metabolic studies, using positron emission tomography (PET), have also shown hemispheric asymmetries in SDAT (Duara et al., 1986; Rapoport et al., 1986). These asymmetries correlate with patterns of neuropsychological performance (Foster et al., 1983; Haxby et al., 1985; Grady et al., 1986). For individual patients, stability of neuropsychological and metabolic asymmetry has been demonstrated over a period of 15 months (Grady et al., 1986), making differences in stage an unlikely explanation for these asymmetries.

These neuropsychological and metabolic asymmetries would be expected to correspond to differences in hemispheric pathology (Rapoport et al., 1986). Intra-hemispheric differences in AD pathology are substantial, due to the differential pattern of selective vulnerability in AD. Inter-hemispheric differences have been less prominent (Arendt et al., 1985; Moossy et al., 1988). In one clinical-pathological correlation, however, excellent correspondence was found between neuropsychological findings and regional abnormalities shown by CT, MRI, PET and neuropathological studies (McGeer, 1986). A case approach may therefore be necessary to demonstrate consistent clinical-pathological correlations in hemispheric asymmetry.

The biological significance of these focal and hemispheric asymmetries remains as obscure in SDAT as in Parkinson's disease. The asymmetries may reflect pre-existing individual differences or superimposed biological factors that facilitate or inhibit the evolution of pathology. Although it seems unlikely that these asymmetries represent distinct underlying etiologies, elucidation of the biological factors that determine the symmetry of hemispheric pathogenesis is an intriguing and important scientific problem.

Depression and psychosis

Behavioral changes are as frequent as cognitive changes in SDAT and include alterations in personality, motor activity, affect and motivation (Gustafson, 1975; Reisberg et al., 1986, 1987). Depression occurs in up to a third of patients with SDAT, usually in the mild to moderate stages of dementia (Knesevich et al., 1983; Reifler et al., 1986; Ross et al., in press). Depression in patients with autopsy-confirmed AD has been correlated with neuronal loss in the locus ceruleus (Zweig et al., 1989), and in both locus ceruleus and substantia nigra (Zubenko and Moossy, 1988), and with a higher incidence of familial affective disorder (Ross et al., in press). Thus, neuroanatomical, neurochemical and familial correlates of depression in AD may be similar to those associated with major depression occurring in other clinical settings.

Hallucinations and delusion may also occur in some patients, usually in the middle stages of disease. Schneider et al. (1989) found significantly lower platelet [^{3}H]imipramine binding in SDAT patients with behavioral agitation or delusions, compared to other SDAT patients without symptomatic behaviors or normal controls. In addition, increases in monoamine oxidase have been reported in SDAT patients without agitation (Schneider et al., 1989). The presence of psychosis has also been associated with more rapid progression of dementia (Stern et al., 1987; Drevets and Rubins, 1989). Thus the presence of either depression or psychosis may identify subgroups of SDAT, but requires longitudinal verification of stability.

Myoclonus and extrapyramidal disorder

In a retrospective study, the presence of extrapyramidal disorder and myoclonus was associated with greater initial severity of dementia and faster rates of decline (Mayeux et al., 1985). Similarly, in a cross-sectional study, dementia was more severe in SDAT patients with non-iatrogenic extrapyramidal disorder (33%) or myoclonus (6%) than in those without these motor signs (Chui et al., 1985).

Prospective rates of progression have not yet been reported for patients with myoclonus, perhaps because of its lower prevalence and relatively late appearance in the evolution of AD. The presence of extrapyramidal disorder, on the other hand, has been linked to a faster rate of progression. In a longitudinal study of 43 patients initially entered with mild SDAT, the development within five years of parkinsonian signs was associated with more frequent progression to moderate and severe dementia (Morris et al., 1987). Using actuarial methods, extrapyramidal signs were associated with faster progression from estimated year of onset to a cognitive, but not functional, end-point (Stern et al., 1987).

Despite these prognostic implications, the longitudinal stability and the pathological basis of subgroups defined by extrapyramidal signs and myoclonus remain unclear. Extrapyramidal signs (e.g., akinesia, cogwheel rigidity, paratonic rigidity and gait disturbance) are not a unitary phenomenon, but may result from disturbances in the substantia nigra, basal ganglia, supplementary motor area, or their interconnections. These various forms of extrapyramidal symptomatology/pathology should be distinguished in future longitudinal studies.

Cerebral amyloid angiopathy

Cerebral amyloid angiopathy (CAA) refers to the deposition of β-amyloid in cerebral blood vessels (Scholz, 1938; Glenner and Wong, 1984). CAA has been associated with parenchymal hemorrhage (Jellinger, 1972; Gilles et al., 1984), micro-infarcts (Okazaki et al., 1979; Ferreiro et al., 1989) and subcortical anteriosclerotic encephalopathy (Bogucki et al., 1988). CAA occurs to some extent in normal aging, but it is significantly increased in AD (Pantelakis, 1954; Wright et al., 1969; Stam et al., 1986). AD cases often appear to have some vascular deposits of amyloid (Mandybur, 1975; Glenner, 1983; Esiri and Wilcock, 1986), but the degree of deposition is highly variable (Joachim et al., 1988). The variability in the prevalence of CAA may reflect differences in the age of the patient studied and the methods of sampling the blood vessels, as well as the severity of disease (Esiri and Wilcock, 1986). Differences in the reported prevalence of CAA (60 – 92%) could also be explained if significant CAA occurred in only a subset of AD patients. In the latter case, the development of CAA may reflect the presence of a second pathogenetic process.

Familial aggregation

Although the risk of dementia is increased in first-degree relatives of patients with SDAT (Heston et al., 1981; Heyman et al., 1983; Breitner et al., 1984; Mohs et al., 1987; Huff et al., 1988; Farrer et al., 1989), this risk varies widely between individual kindreds, ranging from sporadic cases (Sporadic AD or SAD) to multiply affected pedigrees suggestive of autosomal dominant inheritance (Familial AD or FAD). Depending upon the pedigree, environmental or genetic (polygenic, or dominant modes of inheritance with delayed and limited penetrance) factors have been proposed as causes for AD (for review, see Davies 1988; Fitch et al., 1988). The heterogeneity observed in familial aggregation patterns provides the most promising evidence for pathogenetic subgroups of AD.

Interestingly, however, no consistent correlation between FAD or SAD and clinical-pathological phenotype or genetic linkage has emerged. Age-at-onset tends to be similar within a family (Heston, 1971; Powell and Folstein, 1984), but varies considerably between families. Heston et al. (1977, 1978) reported an increased prevalence of trisomy 21 and myeloproliferative disorder in early onset familial AD, an association not found by others

(Whalley et al., 1982; Nee et al., 1983). A family history of dementia has been related to agraphia or aphasia by some (Breitner and Folstein, 1984) but not all investigators (Heyman et al., 1984; Chui et al., 1985; Knesevich et al., 1985). Increased fluidity of the platelet membrane has been found in familial SDAT relative to sporadic SDAT (Zubenko et al., 1987), but this report awaits wider confirmation. Thus, associations between family history and clinical phenotype have been inconsistent.

Similarly no pathological distinctions between FAD and SAD have been found. In fact considerable neuropathological heterogeneity exists even between FAD pedigrees (Bird et al., 1989). Linkage analyses in FAD have also been inconsistent: evidence for linkage disequilibrium on chromosome 21 has been found by some investigators (St. George Hyslop et al., 1987) and excluded by others (Schellenberg et al., 1988; Pericak-Vance et al., 1988). This variability in clinical, pathological and genetic findings suggests that FAD is itself heterogeneous and should not be considered a unitary entity.

Despite this complexity, the polarization of familial aggregation patterns continues to provide the strongest candidates for pathogenetic subgroups of AD. In FAD and SAD, genetic and environmental influences may play differential roles. No consistent differences in clinical or pathological features can be attributed to FAD versus SAD. Thus, apparently diverse genetic and environmental etiologies may activate a similar pathogenetic cascade, leading to indistinguishable clinical-pathological phenotypes.

Summary

The identification of pathogenetic subgroups is a challenging objective for dementia research. By definition, pathogenetic subgroups are based upon differences in either etiology or pathogenesis. Methods of enhancing the likelihood of identifying pathogenetic subgroups, such as a prospective-longitudinal design and subgroup validation with new criterion variables, have been discussed. While the evolution of a subgroup may suggest its underlying determinant, the identification of this determinant requires other neurobiological tools. Thus, subgroups research can be viewed as a useful and perhaps necessary but not a sufficient method of clarifying etiology and pathogenesis.

Potential candidates for pathogenetic subgroups of AD have been reviewed. These include subgroups defined by age-at-onset, clinical-pathological phenotype and family history of dementia. In many cases, subgroup associations have been inconsistent and the relevance of proposed AD subgroups remains unclear. Clinical-pathological subgroups have potential relevance for day-to-day patient management, understanding brain — behavior relationships and elucidating principles of selective vulnerability. Subgroups defined by age-at-onset (early versus late) and family history (FAD or SAD) offer the most promising candidates for pathogenetic subgroups. Thus, in the neurobiological pursuit of the pathogenesis of AD, these factors warrant special consideration.

Acknowledgements

This work was supported by an NIH Teacher Investigator Award (1K07NS00794), the Estelle Doheny Foundation and the State of California Department of Health Services.

References

Alzheimer A. Ueber eine eigenartige Erkrankung der Hirnrinde: *Allg. Zeitshr. fur Psychiat.: 64,* 146 – 148, 1907.

Amaducci LA, Rocca WA, Schoenberg BS: Origin of the distinction between Alzheimer's disease and senile dementia. *Neurology: 36,* 1497 – 1499, 1986.

Arendt T, Bigl V, Tennstedt A, Arendt A: Neuronal loss in different parts of the nucleus basalis is related to neuritic plaque formation in cortical target areas in Alzheimer's disease. *Neuroscience: 14,* 1 – 14, 1985.

Barclay LL, Zemcov A, Blass J, McDowell FH: Factors associated with duration of survival in Alzheimer's disease *Biol. Psychiatry: 20,* 86 – 93, 1985a.

Barclay LL, Zemcov, A, Blass JJ, Sansone J: Survival in Alzheimer's disease and vascular dementias. *Neurology: 35,* 834 – 840, 1985b.

Becker JT, Huff J, Nebes R, Holland A, Boller F: Neuro-psychological function in Alzheimer's disease: Pattern of impairment and rates of progression. *Arch. Neurol.: 45,* 263 – 268, 1988.

Berg L, Danziger WL, Storandt M, Coben L, Gado M, Hughes CP, Knesevich JW, Botwinick J: Predictive features in mild senile dementia of the Alzheimer type. *Neurology: 34,* 563 – 569, 1984.

Berg L, Miller JP, Storandt M, Duchek J, Morris J, Rubin EH, Burke WJ, Coben LA: Mild senile dementia of the Alzheimer type: 2. Longitudinal assessment. *Ann. Neurol.: 23,* 477 – 484, 1988.

Bird TD, Stranahan S, Sumi SM, Raskind M: Alzheimer's disease: choline acetyltransferase activity in brain tissue from clinical and pathological subgroups. *Ann. Neurol.: 14,* 284 – 293, 1983.

Bird TD, Lampe TH, Nemens EJ, Miner GW, Sumi SM, Schellenberg GD: Familial Alzheimer's disease in American descendents of the Volga Germans: probable genetic founder effect. *Ann. Neurol.: 23,* 23 – 31, 1988.

Bird TD, Sumi SM, Nemens EJ, Nochlin D, Schellenberg G, Lampe TH, Sadovnick A, Chui H, Miner GW, Tinklenberg J: Phenotypic heterogeneity in familial Alzheimer's disease: a study of 24 kindreds. *Ann. Neurol.: 25,* 12 – 25, 1989.

Blessed G, Romlinson BE, Roth M: The association between quantitative measures of dementia and senile change in the cerebral grey matter of elderly subjects. *Br. J. Psychiatry: 114,* 797 – 811, 1968.

Bogucki A, Papierz W, Szymanska R, Staniaszcyk R: Cerebral amyloid angiopathy with attenuation of the white matter on CT scans: subcortical anteriosclerotic encephalopathy (Binswanger) in a normotensive patient. *J. Neurol.: 235,* 435 – 437, 1988.

Boller F, Saxton J. Comparison of criteria for diagnosing Alzheimer's disease in the United States and Europe. In Wurtman RJ et al (Editors), *Advances in Neurology, Vol. 51: Alzheimer's Disease.* New York: Raven Press., 1990. pp. 1 – 5.

Boller F, Lopez OL, Moossy J: Diagnosis of dementia: clinicopathologic correlations. *Neurology: 39,* 76 – 79, 1989.

Boller F, Becker JT, Holland AL, Forbes MF, Hood P, McGonigle-Gibson K: Predictors of decline in Alzheimer's disease. *Neurology: 40* (Suppl. 1), 448, 1990.

Bondareff W: On the relationship between age and Alzheimer's disease. *Lancet: i,* 1447, 1982.

Bondareff W, Mountjoy CQ, Roth M: Loss of neurons of origin of the adrenergic projection to cerebral cortex (nucleus locus ceruleus) in senile dementia. *Neurology: 32,* 164 – 168, 1982.

Bondareff W, Mountjoy CQ, Roth M, Rossor MN, Iversen LL, Reynolds GP: Age and histopathologic heterogeneity in Alzheimer's disease. *Arch. Gen. Psychiatry: 44,* 412 – 417, 1987.

Botwinick J, Storandt M, Berg, L: A longitudinal behavioral study of senile dementia of the Alzheimer type. *Arch. Neurol: 43,* 1124 – 1127, 1987.

Bowen DM, Benton JS, Spillane JA, Smith CCT, Allen SJ: Choline acetyltransferase activity and histopathology of frontal neocortex from biopsies of demented patients. *J. Neurol. Sci.: 57,* 191 – 202, 1982.

Brandt J, Mellits ED, Rovner B, Gordon B, Selnes OA, Folstein M: Relation of age of onset and duration of illness to cognitive functioning in Alzheimer's disease. *Neuropsychiatry, Neuropsychol. Behav. Neurol.* in press.

Breitner JCS, Folstein MF: Familial Alzheimer dementia: a prevalent disorder with specific clinical features. *Psychol. Med.: 14,* 63 – 80, 1984.

Brion S, Plas J: the French view. In Hovaguimian T, Henderson S, Khachaturian Z, Orley J (Editors): *Classification and Diagnosis of Alzheimer's Disease. An International Perspective* Toronto: Hogrefe and Huber, pp. 31 – 36, 1989.

Chui HC: The significance of clinically defined subgroups of Alzheimer's disease. *J. Neural Transmission (Suppl): 24,* 57 – 68, 1987.

Chui HC, Teng EL, Henderson VW, Moy AC: Clinical subtypes of dementia of the Alzheimer type. *Neurology: 35,* 1544 – 1550, 1985.

Chui HC, Sobel E, Hsu E, Zarow C, Slager UT: Age-onset and neurofibrillary degeneration in Alzheimer's disease (under review).

Colerick EJ, George LK: Predictors of institutionalization among caregivers of patients with Alzheimer's disease. *J. Am. Geriatrics Soc.: 34,* 493 – 498, 1986.

Corsellis JAN, Brierly GB: An unusual type of pre-senile dementia (atypical Alzheimer's disease) with amyloid changes. *Brain: 77,* 571 – 587, 1954.

Crystal HA, Horoupian DS, Katzman R, Jorkowitz S: Biopsy-proved Alzheimer disease presenting as a right parietal lobe syndrome. *Ann. Neurol.: 12,* 186 – 188, 1982.

Davies P: The genetics of Alzheimer's disease: a review and a discussion of the implications. *Neurobiol. Aging: 7,* 459 – 466, 1986.

Drevets WC, Rubins EH: Psychotic symptoms and the longitudianl course of senile dementia of the Alzheimer type. *Biol. Psychiatry: 25,* 39 – 48, 1989.

Duara R, Grady C, Haxby J, Sundaram M, Cutler NR, Heston L, Moore A, Schlageter N, Larson S, Rapoport SI: Positron emission tomography in Alzheimer's disease. *Neurology: 36,* 879 – 887, 1986.

Esiri MM, Wilcock GK: Cerebral amyloid angiopathy in dementia and old age. *J. Neurol. Neurosurg. Psychiatry: 49,* 1221 – 1226, 1986.

Faber-Langendoen K, Morris JC, Knesevich JW, LaBarge E, Miller JP, Berg L: Aphasia in senile dementia of the Alzheimer type. *Ann. Neurol.: 23,* 365 – 370, 1988.

Farrer LA, O'Sullivan DM, Cupples LA, Growdon JH, Myers R: Assessment of genetic risk for Alzheimer's disease among first degree relatives. *Ann. Neurol.: 25,* 485 – 493, 1989.

Ferreiro JA, Ansbacher LE, Vinters HV: Stroke related to cerebral amyloid angiopathy; the significance of systemic vascular disease. *J. Neurol.: 236,* 267 – 272, 1984.

Finch CE: The relationships of aging changes in the basal ganglia to manifestations of Huntington's chorea. *Ann. Neurol.: 7,* 406 – 411, 1980.

Finelli PF, Kessimian N, Berstein PW: Cerebral amyloid angiopathy manifesting as recurrent intracerebral hemorrhages. *Arch. Neurol.: 41,* 330 – 333, 1984.

Fitch N, Becker R, Heller A: The inheritance of Alzheimer's disease: a new interpretation. *Ann. Neurol.: 23,* 14 – 19, 1988.

Foster NL, Chase TN, Fedio P, Patronas NJ, Brooks R, DiChiro G: Alzheimer's disease: focal cortical changes shown by positron emission tomography. *Neurology: 33,* 961 – 965, 1983.

Gilles C, Brucher JM, Khoubesserian P, Vanderhaegen JJ: Cerebral amyloid angiopathy manifesting as recurrent intracerebral hemorrhages. *Neurology: 34,* 730 – 735, 1984.

Glenner GG: Alzheimer's disease: multiple cerebral amyloidosis. In *Banbury Report 15.* Cold Spring Harbor Symposium on Biological Aspects of Alzheimer's disease. Cold Spring Harbor, NY, pp. 137 – 144, 1983.

Glenner GC, Wong CW: Alzheimer's disease: initial report of the purification and characterization of a novel cerebrovascular amyloid protein. *Biochem. Biophys. Res. Commun.: 120,* 885 – 890, 1984.

Grady CL, Haxby JV, Schlageter NL, Berg G, Rappoport SI: Stability of metabolic and neuropsychological asymmetries in dementia of the Alzheimer type. *Neurology: 36,* 1396 – 1392, 1986.

Hansen LA, DeTeresa R, Davies P, Terry TD: Neocortical morphometry, lesion counts, and choline acetyltransferase levels in the age spectrum of Alzheimer's disease. *Neurology: 38,* 48 – 54, 1988.

Haxby JV, Duara R, Grady CL, Cutler NR, Rapoport SI: Relations between neuropsychological and cerebral metabolic asymmetries in early Alzheimer's disease. *J. Cerebral Blood Flow Metab.: 5,* 193 – 200, 1985.

Heston LL: Alzheimer's disease, trisomy 21, and myeloproliferative disorders: associations suggesting a genetic diathesis. *Science: 196,* 322 – 323, 1977.

Heston LL, White J: Pedigrees of 30 families with Alzheimer's disease: associations with defective organization of microfilaments and microtubules. *Behav. Genet.: 8,* 315 – 331, 1978.

Heston LL, Mastri AR, Anderson VE, White J: Dementia of the Alzheimer type. *Arch. Gen. Psychiatry: 38,* 1085 – 1090, 1981.

Heyman A, Wilkinson WE, Hurwitz BJ, Schmechel D, Sigmon A, Weinberg R, Helms MJ, Swift M: Alzheimer's disease: genetic aspects and associated clinical disorders. *Ann. Neurol.: 14,* 507 – 515, 1983.

Heyman A, Wilkinson WE, Hurwitz BJ, Helms MJ, Haynes CS, Utley CM, Gwyther LP: Early-onset Alzheimer's disease: clinical predictors of institutionalization and death. *Neurology; 37,* 980 – 984, 1987.

Huff FJ, Becker JT, Belle SH, Nebes RD, Holland AL, Boller F: Cognitive deficits and clinical diagnosis of Alzheimer's disease. *Neurology: 37,* 1119 – 1124, 1987a.

Huff FJ, Growdon JH, Corkin S, Rosen TJ: Age at onset and rate of progression of Alzheimer's disease. *J. Am. Geriatrics Soc.: 35,* 27 – 30, 1987b.

Huff FJ, Auerbach J, Chakravarti A, Boller F: Risk of dementia in relatives of patients with Alzheimer's disease. *Neurology: 38,* 780 – 790, 1988.

Jellinger K: Zur atiologie und pathogenese der spontanen intra zerebralen blutung. *Therapie woche: 2,* 1440 – 1450, 1972.

Jellinger K: Cerebrovascular amyloidosis with cerebral hemorrhage. *J. Neurol.: 214,* 195 – 206, 1977.

Joachim CL, Morris JH, Selkoe DJ: Clinically diagnoses Alzheimer's disease: autospy results in 150 cases. *Ann.*

Neurol.: 24, 50 – 56, 1988.

Jorm AF: Subtypes of Alzheimer's dementia: a conceptual analysis and critical review. *Psychol. Med.: 15,* 543 – 553, 1985.

Katzman R, Lasker B, Bernstein N: Advances in the diagnosis of dementia: accuracy of diagnosis and consequences of misdiagnosis of disorders causing dementia. In Terry R (Editor), *Aging and the Brain.* New York: Raven Press, p. 33, 1988a.

Katzman R, Brown T, Thal LJ, Fuld PA, Aronson M, Butters N, Klauber M, Wiederholt W, Pay M, Renbing X, Ooi WL, Hofstetter R, Terry R: Comparison of rate of annual change of mental status score in four independent studies of patients with Alzheimer's disease. *Ann. Neurol.: 24,* 384 – 389, 1988b.

Kemper T: Neuroanatomical and neuropathological changes in normal ageing and dementia. In Albert ML (Editor), *Clinical Neurology of Aging.* Oxford: Oxford University Press, pp.9 – 52, 1984.

Khachaturian ZS: Diagnosis of Alzheimer's disease. *Arch. Neurol.: 42,* 1097 – 1105, 1985.

Kirschner HS, Webb WG, Kelly MP, Wells CE; Language disturbance: an initial symptom of cortical degenerations and dementia. *Arch. Neurol.: 41,* 491 – 496, 1984.

Knesevich JW, Martin RL, Berg L, Danziger W: Preliminary report on affective symptoms in the early stages of senile dementia of the Alzheimer type. *Am. J. Psychiatry: 140,* 233 – 235, 1983.

Knesevich JW, Toro FR, Morris JC, LaBarge E: Aphasia, family history, and the longitudinal course of senile dementia of the Alzheimer type. *Psychiatry Res.: 14,* 255 – 263, 1985.

Loring DW, Largen JW: Neuropsychological patterns of presenile and senile dementia of the Alzheimer's type. *Neuropsychologia: 23,* 351 – 357, 1985.

Mandybur TI: The incidence of cerebral amyloid angiopathy in AD. *Neurology: 25,* 120 – 126, 1975.

Mann DMA, Yates PO, Marcyniuk B: A comparison of changes in the nucleus basalis and locus ceruleus in Alzheimer's disease. *J. Neurol. Neurosurg. Psychiatry: 47,* 201 – 203, 1984.

Martin A, Brouwers P, Lalonde F, Cox C, Teleska P, Fedio P, Foster N, Chase T: Toward a behavioral typology of Alzheimer's patients. *J. Clin. Exp. Neuropsychol.: 8,* 549 – 610, 1986.

Mayeux R, Stern Y, Spanton S: Heterogeneity in dementia of the Alzheimer type: evidence for subgroups. *Neurology: 35,* 453 – 461, 1985.

McGeer PL, Kamo H, Harrop R, McGeer EG, Martin WRW, Pate BD, Li DKB: Comparison of PET, MRI and CT with pathology in a proven case of Alzheimer's disease. *Neurology: 36,* 1569 – 1574, 1986.

McKhann G, Drachman D, Folstein M, Katzman R, Price D, Stadlan E: Clinical diagnosis of Alzheimer's disease: report of the NINCDS-ADRDA Work Group under the auspices of Department of Health and Human Services Task Force on Alzheimer's Disease. *Neurology: 34,* 939 – 944, 1984.

Mesulam M-M: Slowly progressive aphasia without generalized dementia. *Ann. Neurol.: 11,* 592 – 598, 1982.

Mohs RC, Breitner JCS, Silverman JM, Davis KL: Alzheimer's disease: morbid risk among first degree relatives approximates 50% by age 90. *Arch. Gen. Psychiatry: 44,* 405 – 408, 1987.

Moossy J, Zubenko G, Martinez J, Rao GR: Bilateral symmetry of morphologic lesions in Alzheimer's disease. *Arch. Neurol.: 45,* 251 – 254, 1988.

Morris JC, Drazner M, Fulling K, Berg L: Parkinsonism in senile dementia of the Alzheimer type. In Wurtman RJ, Corkin SH, Gowdon JH (Editors), *Alzheimer's Disease: Advances in Basic Research and Therapies.* Proceedings of the Fourth Meeting of the International Study Group on the Pharmacology of Memory Disorders Associated with Aging. Zurich, Switzerland, January, 1987.

Mountjoy CQ, Rossor MN, Iversen LL, Roth M: Correlation of cortical cholinergic and GABA deficits with quantitative neuropathological findings in senile dementia. *Brain: 107,* 507 – 518, 1984.

Nee LE, Polinsky RJ, Eldridge R, Weingartner H, Smallberg S, Ebert M: A family with histologically confirmed Alzheimer's disease. *Arch. Neurol.: 40,* 203 – 208, 1983.

Pantelakis: Un type particular d'angiopathic senile du systeme nerveax central: l'angiopathic congophile, topographie et frequence. *Monatschr. Psychiatrie Neurol.: 128,* 219 – 256, 1954.

Pearce JMS, Pearce I: The nosology of Alzheimer's Disease. In Glen AIM, Whalley LJ (Editors), *Alzheimer's disease – Early Recognition of Potentially Reversible Deficits.* New York: Churchill Livingstone, pp. 93 – 96, 1979.

Pericak-Vance MA, Yamaoka LH, Haynes CS, Speer MC, Haines JL, Gaskell PC, Hung W-Y, Clark CM, Heyman AL, Trofatter JA, Eisenmenger JP, Gilbert JR, Lee JE, Alberts MJ, Dawson DV, Bartlett RJ, Siddique ET, Vance JM, Conneally M, Roses AD: Genetic linkage in Alzheimer's disease families. *Exp. Neurol.: 102,* 271 – 279, 1988.

Pogacar S, Williams RS: Alzheimer's disease presenting as slowly progressive aphasia. *R. I. Med. J.: 67,* 181 – 185, 1984.

Powell D, Folstein MF: Pedigree study of familial Alzheimer disease. *J. Neurgenet. 1,* 189 – 197, 1984.

Rapoport SI, Horwitz B, Haxyby JV, Grady CL: Alzheimer's disease: metabolic uncoupling of associative brain regions. *Can. J. Neurol. Sci.: 13,* 540 – 545, 1986.

Reifler BV, Larson E, Tei L, Poulsen M: Dementia of the Alzheimer's type and depression. *J. Am. Geriatrics Soc.: 34;* 855 – 859, 1986.

Reisberg B, Borenstein J, Franssen E, Shulman E, Steinberg G, Ferris SH: Remediable behavioral symptomatology in Alzheimer's disease. *Hosp. Community Psychiatry: 37,* 1199 – 1201, 1986.

Reisberg B, Borenstein J, Salob SP, Ferris SH, Franssen E, Georgotas A: Behavioral symptoms in Alzheimer's disease: phenomenology and treatment. *J. Clin Psychiatry: 48* (5, Suppl), 9 – 15, 1987.

Ross CA, Zweig RM, Hedreen JC, Whitehouse PJ, Steele C, Folstein MF, Price DL: Depression and cell loss in the locus ceruleus in Alzheimer's disease. *Biol. Psychiatry:* in press.

Rossor MN, Iversen LL, Johnson AJ, Mountjoy CQ, Roth M: Cholinergic deficit in frontal cerebral cortex in Alzheimer's disease is age dependent. *Lancet: ii,* 1422, 1981.

Rossor MN, Iversen LL, Reynold GP, Mountjoy CQ, Roth M: Neurochemical characteristics of early and late onset types of

Alzheimer's disease. *Br. Med. J.: 288,* 961 – 964, 1984.

Roth M: The association of clinical and neurological findings and its bearing on the classification and etiology of Alzheimer's disease. *Br. Med. Bull.: 42,* 42 – 50, 1986.

St George Hyslop PH, Tanzi RE, Polinsky RJ, Haines JL, Nee L, Watkins PC, Myers RH, Feldman RG, Pollen D, Drachman D, Growdon J, Bruni A, Foncin J-F, Salmon D, Frommelt P, Amaducci L, Sorbi S, Piacentini S, Stewart GD, Hobbs WJ, Conneally M, Gusella JF: The genetic defect causing familial Alzheimer's disease maps on chromosome 21. *Science: 235,* 885 – 235, 1987.

Schneider LS, Severson JA, Chui HC, Pollock VE, Sloane RB, Frederickson ER: Platelet tritiated imipramine binding and MAO activity in Alzheimer patients with agitations and delusions. *Psychiatry Res.: 25,* 311 – 322, 1988.

Scholz W: Studien zur Pathologic der Hirngetasse II: Die drusige entartung der Hirnarterien und Capilluren. *Z. Ges. Neurol. Psychiatrie: 162,* 694 – 715, 1938.

Schellenberg GD, Bird TD, Wijsman EM, Moore DK, Boehnke M, Bryant EM, Lampe TH, Nochlin D, Sumi SM, Deeb SS, Beyreuther K, Martin GM: Absence of linkage of chromosome 21q21 markers to familial Alzheimer's disease. *Science: 241,* 1507 – 1510, 1988.

Selnes OA, Carson K, Rovner B, Gordon B: Language dysfunction in early- and late-onset possible Alzheimer's disease. *Neurology: 38,* 1053 – 1056, 1988.

Selzter B, Sherwin I: A comparison of clinical features in early- and late-onset primary degenerative dementia. *Arch. Neurol.: 40,* 143 – 146. 1983.

Shoulson I. Huntington's disease. In Asbury AK, McKhann G, McDonald WI (Editors), *Diseases of the Nervous System: Clinical Neurobiology.* Philadelphia: Ardmore Medical Books, pp. 1258 – 1267, 1986.

Sourander P, Sjogren H: The concept of Alzheimer's disease and its clinical implications. In Wolstenholmes GEW, O'Connor M (Editors), *Alzheimer's Disease and Related Disorders.* A CIBA Foundation Symposium. London: Churchill, pp. 11 – 36, 1970.

Stam FC, Wigboldus JM, Smeulders AWM: Age incidence of senile brain amyloidosis. *Pathol. Res. Practice: 181,* 558 – 562, 1986.

Stern Y, Mayeux R, Sano M, Hauser WA, Bush T: Predictors of disease course in patients with probable Alzheimer's disease. *Neurology: 37,* 1649 – 1653, 1987.

Sulkava R, Haltia M, Paetau A, Wikstrom J, Palo J: Accuracy of clinical diagnosis in primary degenerative dementia: correlation with neuropathological findings. *J. Neurol. Neurosurg. Psychiatry; 46,* 9 – 13, 1983.

Sullivan EV, Corkin S, Growdon JH: Verbal and nonverbal short-term memory in patients with Alzheimer's disease and in healthy elderly subjects. *Dev. Neuropsychol.: 2,* 387 – 400, 1986.

Tagliavini F, Pilleri G: Neuronal counts in basal nucleus of Meynert in Alzheimer's disease and in simple senile dementia. *Lancet: i,* 469 – 470, 1983.

Tomlinson BE, Blessed G, Roth M: Observations on the brains of demented old people. *J. Neurol. Sci. 11,* 205 – 242, 1970.

Ulrich J, Stahelin HB: The variable topography of Alzheimer type changes in senile dementia and normal old age. *Gerontology: 30,* 210 – 214, 1984.

Wade JP, Mirsen TR, Hachinski VC, Fisman M, Lau C, Merskey H: The clinical diagnosis of Alzheimer's disease. *Arch. Neurol.: 44,* 24 – 29, 1987.

Webster's Seventh New Collegiate Dictionary. Springfield: G & C Merriam Company, Publishers, pp 874, 1967.

Wright JR, Calkins E, Breen WJ, Stolte G, Schultz RT: Relationship of amyloid to aging. *Medicine: 48,* 39 – 60, 1969.

Zubenko GS, Moossy J: Major depression in primary dementia: clinical and neuropathologic correlates. *Arch. Neurol.:*
45, 1182 – 1186, 1988.

Zubenko GS, Wusylko M, Cohen BM, Boller F, Teply I: Family study of platelet membrane fluidity in Alzheimer's disease. *Science: 238,* 539 – 542, 1987.

Zweig RM, Ross C, Hedreen JC, Steele C, Cardillo JE, Whitehouse P, Folstein M, Price DL: The neuropathology of aminergic nuclei in Alzheimer's disease. *Ann. Neurol.: 24,* 233 – 242, 1988.

© 1991 Elsevier Science Publishers B.V.
Handbook of Neuropsychology, Vol. 5
F. Boller and J. Grafman (Eds)

CHAPTER 3

Pathological and chemical correlates of dementia

Peter J. Whitehouse[1], Massimo Tabaton[2] and Douglas Lanska[3]

[1]Case Western Reserve University School of Medicine and Alzheimer Center, University Hospitals of Cleveland, [2]Departments of Pathology and Neurology, Case Western Reserve University and University Hospitals of Cleveland, and [3]Neurobehavior Section, Department of Neurology, Case Western Reserve University and Alzheimer Center, University Hospitals of Cleveland, Cleveland, OH 44106, U.S.A.

Introduction

Approximately 150 years ago the essential clinical feature of dementia, progressive loss of previously intact cognitive abilities, was differentiated from static mental retardation and psychiatric conditions in which disorders of thought content predominated. Some 50 years later, sectioning and staining techniques were developed which allowed identification of pathological features of the degenerative and vascular dementias. Using these approaches, Alois Alzheimer described the disease which came to bear his name and also contributed to understanding the neuropathology of vascular dementia, Pick's disease and Huntington's disease. The neurochemical characterization of dementia began approximately 25 years ago with the characterization of the dopaminergic abnormalities in Parkinson's disease (PD). Today, we are faced with the complex task of integrating these different levels clinical characterization, neuropathological assessment and neurochemical analysis. In this paper we will review studies of autopsy tissue which attempt to establish relationships between clinical features and biological variables. Cerebrospinal fluid and brain imaging studies will not be systematically considered although they can contribute to understanding brain – behavior relationships. We will begin with a brief consideration of the brain regions which

may play a role in normal intellectual activity and conclude with a discussion of the conceptual and methodological issues in attempts at clinical – pathological correlation.

Biological basis of normal cognition

Normal cognitive activities are dependent on the interaction between many different brain regions as well as on metabolic and hormonal systems in the rest of the body. Functions such as language, praxis, executive abilities and perception are most closely associated with neocortex; memory and emotions with the limbic system; attention with diffuse projecting systems including the basal forebrain nuclei, locus coeruleus, raphe nucleus and ventral tegmental area. The roles of other structures such as striatum, thalamus and cerebellum in cognition are particularly poorly understood. All these brain regions demonstrate pathology in one dementia or another. The study of dementias can contribute to an understanding of the biological basis of cognition, because these disorders involve selective, albeit complex, lesions in different brain structures that underlie intellectual activity. By relating the clinical heterogeneity present in life in different dementias to the biological variability found after death, the roles of different neural systems in cognition can be delineated.

In order to understand the cellular and chemical bases of dementia, we need to understand normal age-related cognitive changes. Neuronal loss and concomitant neurochemical changes occur in normal aging in many of the same systems affected in the degenerative dementias (Whitehouse et al., 1985). Thus, the biology of age-associated memory impairment shares features with the biology of memory dysfunction in dementia (Bartus et al., 1982). Whether degenerative dementias are qualitative or quantitative variations on the themes found in normal aging needs to be established.

Clinical pathological studies of dementia

Alzheimer's disease

Neuropathology

Alzheimer's disease (AD) is characterized pathologically by neuronal loss in neocortex, hippocampus, amygdala and several subcortical projecting systems including cholinergic basal forebrain, noradrenergic locus coeruleus and serotonergic raphe nuclei. Recently neuronal loss in areas previously not well studied such as retina and hypothalamus has also been demonstrated in some cases (Saper, 1988). Neuritic plaques, neurofibrillary tangles and granulovacuolar degeneration also occur, although their relationships to neuronal dysfunction are not clear. In 1968, Blessed et al. confirmed earlier impressions (Grünthal, 1927) that the severity of pre-mortem dementia correlated positively with the density of neocortical plaques found at autopsy. Fuld et al. (1982) found a correlation between the occurrence of word intrusion errors in memory tests and density of cortical plaques. A significant association between plaques and cognitive impairment was also reported in biopsy tissue from left frontal cortex (Martin et al., 1987). Not all studies have confirmed this relationship, however. Neary et al. (1986) did not find a correlation between plaques and dementia in a study of right temporal biopsy specimens. Mölsa et al. (1987) reported high correlations between dementia and plaque counts only

when their control and demented subjects were analysed together. Correlations were not significant when the more appropriate examination of the AD group alone was performed. Interestingly, Fuld et al. (1987) found a correlation between memory dysfunction and the number of plaques in non-demented elderly people. Morimatsu et al. (1975) and Wilcock and Esiri (1982) found stronger correlations between density of cortical neurofibrillary tangles and cognitive impairment than betweeen density of plaques and dementia. Terry (unpublished observations) has claimed that plaques and tangles may be epiphenomena and that the key biological marker which best relates to cognition is the number of synapses. Certainly dysfunction and eventual death of cells must relate to the dementia. For example, the extent of neuronal loss in the cholinergic basal forebrain has also been associated with the severity of dementia in AD (McGeer et al., 1984). Recently we have found preliminary evidence that neuronal loss in locus coeruleus and raphe nuclei may correlate with depression but not dementia (Zweig et al., 1987). Neurochemical evidence supporting this view has recently been reported (Zubenko et al., 1990).

Neurochemistry

Several different neurotransmitter systems are affected in different brain regions in AD (Price et al., 1986). Loss of choline acetyltransferase activity (ChAT) in the neocortical areas has been most strongly and consistently correlated with the severity of the dementia (Perry et al., 1978; McGeer et al., 1984). Reductions in ChAT have also been reported to correlate with the number of intrusion errors in memory testing (Fuld et al., 1982). Intrusion errors represent the recurrence of items in a memory test from a previous trial. Reductions in the concentration of nicotinic receptors are a consistent feature of AD and PD, whereas the reports of changes in muscarinic receptors are inconsistent (Kellar et al., 1987). No receptor alteration has been directly associated with clinical features, although reduction in nicotinic receptors tends to correlate with reduction in ChAT activity.

Alterations in the bioaminergic markers have not been consistently related to dementia (Perry et al., 1981). One study of hippocampus (Burke et al., 1987) related reductions in phenylethanolamine *N*-methyltransferase, a marker for epinephrine neurons, to dementia, however. Cortical somatostatin concentrations are fairly consistently reduced in AD (Davies et al., 1980; Rossor et al., 1980). In CSF, lower somatostatin concentrations have been correlated with dementia (Tamminga et al., 1987), although brain levels have not been consistently linked to cognitive impairment (Beal et al., 1986). Reductions in corticotropin-releasing factor immunoreactivity in AD and PD correlate with reductions in ChAT activity but have not been directly linked to cognitive impairment (DeSouza et al., 1988; Whitehouse et al., 1987; Bisette, 1985).

Parkinsons's disease (PD)

Neuropathology
Perhaps one-third of patients with PD will eventually develop dementia (Mortimer et al., 1985; Mayeux et al., 1981). A larger percentage of patients have cognitive impairment (such as bradyphrenia, or slowed thinking) not severe enough to be considered dementia (Pirrozolo et al., 1982). The neuropathological substrate of dementia in PD is variable. Early studies (Boller et al., 1980; Hakim and Mathieson, 1979) suggested that the dementia in PD was pathologically similar to that found in AD, but other forms such as Lewy body (Yoshimura, 1983) and simple atrophy occur. Cell loss in the cholinergic basal forebrain has been observed in PD (Whitehouse et al., 1983) and related to the presence of dementia (Candy et al., 1983). In our study, the magnitude of cell loss was greater in the PD patients with dementia but was also present to a small degree in apparently nondemented cases as well. Similarly, pathology in the dopaminergic ventral tegmental area (Uhl et al., 1985), noradrenergic locus coeruleus and serotonergic raphe nuclei (Alvord, 1968) has been reported.

Neurochemistry
Abnormalities in many of the same classic and peptide neurotransmitters affected in AD have also been reported in PD (Price et al., 1986), although differences exist (Hornykiewicz and Kish, 1984; Agid and Javoy-Agid, 1985). As in AD, the neurotransmitter marker most strongly correlated with dementia in PD is choline acetyltransferase (Ruberg, 1982). Based primarily on data from studies of cerebrospinal fluid, Mayeux and colleagues believe that alterations in serotonergic systems may be a substrate for depression in PD (Mayeux et al., 1981). Some evidence (Cash et al., 1987) suggests that noradrenergic markers in locus coeruleus are more affected in demented PD patients than in nondemented patients. Not all workers have been able to relate pathology in this system to cognitive impairment, however (D'Amato et al., 1987).

Multi-infarct dementia

Neuropathology
Multi-infarct dementia is considered to be the second most common cause of dementia and can often be differentiated from AD by abrupt onset, stepwise course, the presence of focal neurological signs and symptoms, accompanied by other signs of vascular disease on neurological exam (Hachinski et al., 1975). Blessed et al. (1986) compared two groups of patients with multiple cerebral infarcts; one with, and one without, dementia. They found that volume of infarcted tissue correlates positively with the severity of dementia in life. Interestingly, infarcts in the hippocampus were associated with dementia, although the laterality and location of the infarcts did not otherwise correlate strongly with dementia. Mixed cases of AD and vascular dementia also are not uncommon.

Neurochemistry
Relatively few neurochemical studies of multi-infarct dementia have been reported. Clearly the chemical changes may vary as a function of where the infarcts are located. No consistent alterations

31

in cholinergic markers have been reported (Perry et al., 1981).

Methodological and conceptual issues

It is obvious from this brief review that our understanding of the biological basis of dementia is rudimentary. In these next sections, we will review some of the problems of establishing clinico-pathological correlations and suggest how future studies may be improved. We will outline some of the problems with clinical tools used to assess dementia, consider attempts to quantify biological changes, and finally discuss specific problems relating clinical and pathological data.

Clinical assessment

Standard lengthy neuropsychological batteries present difficulties when used to assess demented patients (Lezak, 1985; Cummings and Benson, 1983). Many shorter cognitive screening tests, sensitive to a fairly wide range of cognitive abilities, are now available. These tests have been used to study the progression of the cognitive impairment in dementia, as well as to correlate the degree of behavioral dysfunction with pathology measures (Blessed et al., 1968; Perry et al., 1978; Martin et al., 1987).

These brief mental status tests present several difficulties in clinico-pathological studies, however.

(1) Several aspects of cognition are combined into one score. As a result, two patients with similar scores may have very different levels of function in specific areas (visuospatial, memory, language, etc.). The multimodal nature of the scales precludes precise clinico-pathological correlation.

(2) Brief mental status examinations are insensitive to early changes in cognitive function and cannot accurately measure a wide range of changes in any one cognitive skill. Severely demented patients may also show floor effects.

(3) Often, no adjustment is made in scoring for premorbid level of functioning (Kittner, 1986).

(4) Mental status tests are not true numerical (interval) scales. For example, a score of 30 does not mean twice as much cognitive function as a score of 15 (Kurtzke, 1986). Depending on the characteristics of the distribution of scores, statistical tests based on analysis of variance and regression procedures may yield misleading results (Kurtzke, 1986).

By partitioning cognitive functions into their basic components, it is possible to make a more precise anatomical and clinical correlation. Indeed, recent studies correlating clinical and pathological measures have avoided simplistic screening rating scales (Fuld et al., 1987; Tamminga et al., 1987). Instead, they have chosen tests of specific behavioral functions and compared these with various pathological measures.

Pathological analysis

Assessment of biological changes in the brains of patients with dementia is complex. Many pre- and post mortem variables may affect the measurement of biological alterations in autopsy tissue. For example, the cause of death, drug history of the patient at death, post mortem delay in refrigerating and freezing tissues and length of time of storage of tissues may cause alterations in biological markers and affect interpretation of the relationship between these markers and the clinical symptoms (Whitehouse et al., 1984).

Neuropathological assessments of the severity of neuronal loss, neurofibrillary tangle and senile plaque formation are often only semi-quantitative. A wide variety of new neuroscientific techniques can now be applied to autopsy brain tissue, including receptor autoradiography, immunocytochemistry, and in situ hybridization. Receptor autoradiography employs radioactively labelled drugs or neurotransmitters themselves which bind to neurotransmitter receptors to map the distribution of receptors in frozen animal or human autopsy tissue. Receptors are the protein molecules which respond to release of neurotransmitters into the synapse and can be located pre- or post-synaptically. Immunocytochemistry uses antibodies to label specific cytoskeletal or neurotransmitter-related (e.g. metabolic enzymes) proteins in tissue. In situ hybridization also depends on radioactively labelled probes (RNA or DNA) which interact (hybridize) with native RNA or DNA in the specimen and thus allows mapping of the location (and amount) of these nucleic acids in particular neurons. Images produced by these techniques are exceedingly rich in information about the distribution of proteins and nucleic acids in brain tissues. New computer analysis systems should be able to improve assessment of these images. The systems allow more precise definition of the biological features to be assessed. Large fields can be studied by computer control of the microscope stage. Sampling strategies can be well defined to avoid observer bias. Measurements can be made of neurons, almost literally impossible by manual techniques, such as size and shape using Fourier analysis. Statistical models can be applied to understanding the distribution of biological markers in a field and the alterations that may occur in the distribution as a function of the disease.

Relating clinical and pathological data

Valid correlations of disordered behavior and pathological change require consideration of a large number of factors (Damasio and Geshwind, 1985): the nature, extent and rapidity of the pathological process; variations in the way mental functions are mapped onto cerebral substance (Mesulam, 1981); the timing of the anatomical and behavioral observations; and the sex, age, education and premorbid psychological and social background of the individuals under study. Some of these factors will be considered below.

Since the brain, like other organs, has a certain amount of functional reserve, the extent of pathological change may relate to level of cognitive function only after some critical threshold is reached. This threshold level may vary considerably among individuals. As a result, extensive pathological change may occur in some persons with apparently intact cognitive function prior to death, whereas some demented individuals may have relatively little evidence of pathological change (Rothschild, 1937). Given the inter-individual variation in the functional reserve of the brain, the degree of cognitive dysfunction cannot be predicted precisely from the extent of pathological change alone.

Precise clinico-pathological correlation is further hampered by our limited knowledge of the way mental functions are mapped onto the brain. Divergent opinions on this subject have led to several theories of localization (see this series, Volume 1, Chapter 7). The centrist approach proposes that complex functions are integrated by specific cortical areas devoted exclusively to those functions. In contrast, the holistic approach minimizes local variations and assumes that each complex function is represented widely in the cortex. An intermediate view, the network approach, suggests that complex functions are subserved by an integrated network of specific cortical regions, each with a unique functional role that reflects its profile of anatomic connectivity. All these approaches may have validity, depending on the function under consideration. For example, vision may be more organized in a centrist fashion, intelligence and personality may be represented by a holistic model, and directed attention may be integrated in a network of specific subcortical and cortical regions.

Another problem in establishing clinico-pathological correlations in dementia is that the dynamic view of the disease established clinically from the onset of cognitive dysfunction is usually only correlated with a static pathological view of the disease at its terminal stage. In many dementias the cognitive functions initially affected and the clinical course are varied (this volume, Chapter 2). Variable early signs and symptoms of dementia probably reflect differences in the areas of the brain first affected. As the disease progresses, the patient's abilities become more limited and the clinical picture becomes more stereotyped. Indeed, the pathological correlations that may have reflected early differences may not be apparent by the time of autopsy. Serial neurochemical analyses of CSF, computed tomography, magnetic resonance imaging and positron emission tomography can provide dynamic functional or structural views of the progressive changes in dementia during life (this series, volume 4, Chapter 9).

Avoiding artifactual associations

Claimed associations between biological data and behavioral measures may be artifactual, resulting from chance occurrences, failure to control for confounding factors, or other systematic biases. Tests of statistical significance determine the likelihood that chance alone could produce the observed effects. The fewer the number of study subjects, the more likely the observations are to be influenced by chance sampling fluctuation (and the harder it will be to detect true differences). Furthermore, as the number of independent statistical tests increases, so does the probability of obtaining at least one spuriously significant result. The investigator should try to specify a select limited number of contrasts in advance. Adjustments for multiple comparisons can be made by requiring tests to meet very rigorous significance levels (i.e. at a small probability level) (Tukey, 1977) or by using special statistical procedures.

Even if a statistically significant association is demonstrated, extraneous factors or systematic biases may account for the observed relationship. Confounding refers to the effect of extraneous factors that wholly or partially account for the apparent effect of the study variable or that mask an underlying true association. Factors which may confound apparent clinico-pathological correlations in studies of dementia include clinical variables such as age or premorbid characteristics, and biological measurements relating to tissue handling, such as delay in tissue processing, etc. Knowledge of the pathophysiology of the disease under investigation and previous study results may suggest other potential confounding variables that must be considered to prevent spurious associations.

A study may be designed to prevent certain extraneous variables from producing misleading group differences. For example, cases and controls may be matched for age so that differences in age distribution will not lead to spurious associations. However, it may not be possible to 'control' all pertinent variables from the outset, and potentially confounding variables may only be considered in the analysis phase of the study. Fortunately, it is possible to analyse data in ways that take extraneous factors into account. The simplest method involves examining the data separately for each level of the variable to be controlled (stratification). More complex statistical procedures (analysis of covariance, multiple regression, logistic regression) are also available for exploring the effects of confounding variables on statistical associations.

Systematic biases must also be carefully considered as an explanation for an apparent association. Bias can be introduced during any phase of the study. Symmetry between comparison groups must be ensured in all operational aspects of the study, including history-taking, recording of observations, staging, treatment, and follow up — hence, the value of blinding and randomization. Finding the same association in several different studies provides some assurance that the association is not an artifact of the way a particular study was carried out or of an unusual group of study subjects.

Establishing causal associations

Once a significant association is established, the next step is to determine whether this association represents a causal or noncausal (indirect) association. Etiological associations exist when a change in a pathological variable is directly followed by a change in a behavioral variable. Noncausal associations occur when a pathological change and a behavioral change both result from some common underlying process. Alteration of the indirectly associated pathological factor does not necessarily produce a change in behavior.

Statistical associations derived from well-controlled experimental (interventional) studies can usually be interpreted as cause-and-effect relationships: a treatment is applied and a result is observed. Direct experiments to establish a cause-and-effect relationship between biological and behavioral changes in dementing illnesses are limited. The deleterious or beneficial effects of drugs may provide some evidence to support an association between a neural system and cognition, e.g., anticholinergic drugs can impair memory; cholinomimetics under some circumstances may improve memory. Better animal models of dementia which permit interventional studies would obviously be helpful.

Establishing a causal relationship in the absence of direct experimental action is not easy. Additional knowledge, external to the particular study, is typically required. Differences of opinion resulting from the interpretation and assembly of evidence are common. Nevertheless, several criteria can be helpful in distinguishing causal and indirect associations suggested by observational studies (Friedman, 1974; Evans, 1978):

(1) Strength of the association;
(2) Coherence with existing knowledge (biological plausibility);
(3) Temporality of the anatomical and behavioral observations;
(4) Gradient of effect (dose – response relationship);
(5) Modification of effect;
(6) Experimental reproduction of the association.

None of these criteria is either necessary or sufficient for making a causal interpretation (Friedman, 1974; Evans, 1978). Other statistical techniques, such as path analysis, allow determination of likely sequential relationships among variables that intercorrelate.

Conclusion

The development of new powerful methods to analyse brain tissue and a resurgence of activity in cognitive science portend well for improved understanding of brain – behavior relationships in dementia. If we are to improve upon the simplistic notions of clinical – pathological correlation that have been used so far in the study of dementia, more care will need to be given to the process of integrating clinical and biological data.

References

Agid Y, Javoy-Agid: Peptides and Parkinson's disease. *Trends Neurosci.: 8,* 30 – 35, 1985.

Alvord EC Jr: The pathology of parkinsonism. In Minckler J (Editor), *Pathology of the Nervous System, Vol. 1.* McGraw-Hill, New York: pp. 1152 – 1161, 1968.

Amaducci LA, Rocca WA, Schoenberg BS: Origin of the distinction between Alzheimer's disease and senile dementia: how history can clarify nosology. *Neurology: 36,* 1497 – 1499, 1986.

Bartus RT, Dean RL III, Beer B, Lippa AS: The cholinergic hypothesis of geriatric memory dysfunction. *Science: 217,* 408 – 417, 1982.

Beal MF, et al: Somatostatin alterations in the central nervous system in neurological disease. In Martin JB, Barchas JD (Editors), *Neuropeptides in Neurologic and Psychiatric Disease, Vol. 64,* p. 215. New York: Raven Press, 1986.

Bissette G, Reynolds GP, Kilts CD, Widerlov E, Nemeroff CB: Corticotropin-releasing factor-like immunoreactivity in senile dementia of the Alzheimer type. *JAMA: 254,* 3067 – 3069, 1985.

Blessed G, Tomlinson BE, Roth M: The association between quantitative measure of dementia and of senile change in the cerebral grey matter of elderly subjects. *Br. J. Psychiatry: 114,* 797 – 811, 1968.

Boller F, Mizutani T, Roessmann U, Gambetti P: Parkinson disease, dementia, and Alzheimer disease: clinicopathological correlations. *Ann. Neurol.: 7,* 329, 1980.

Brun A: An overview of light and electron microscopic changes. In Reisberg B (Editor), *Alzheimer's Disease: The Standard Reference.* New York: Free Press, 1983.

Burke WJ, Chung HD, Nakra BRS, Grossberg GT, Joh TH: Phenylthanolamine *N*-methyltransferase activity is decreased in Alzheimer's disease brains. *Ann. Neurol.: 22,* 278 – 280, 1987.

Candy JM, Perry RH, Perry EK, et al: Pathological changes in the nucleus of Meynert in Alzheimer's and Parkinson's Disease. *J. Neurol. Sci.: 59,* 277 – 289, 1983.

Cash R, Dennis T, L'Heureux R, et al: Parkinson's disease and dementia: norepinephrine and dopamine in locus ceruleus. *Neurology: 37,* 42 – 46, 1987.

Cummings JL, Benson DF: *Dementia: A Clinical Approach.* Boston: Butterworth, 1983.

Damasio AR, Geschwind N: Anatomical localization in clinical neuropsychology. In Frederiks JA (Editor), *Handbook of Clinical Neurology: Vol. 1(45): Clinical Neuropsychology.* Amsterdam: Elsevier Science Publishers, 1985.

D'Amato RJ, Zweig RM, Whitehouse PJ, et al: Aminergic systems in Alzheimer's disease and Parkinson's disease. *Ann. Neurol.: 22,* 229 – 236, 1987.

Davies P, Katzman R, Terry RD: Reduced somatostatin-like immunoreactivity in cerebral cortex from cses of Alzheimer disease and Alzheimer senile dementia: *Nature (London): 288,* 279, 1980.

Desouza EB, Whitehouse PJ, Price DL, Vale WW: Abnormalities in corticotropin-releasing hormone (CRH) in Alzheimer's disease and other human disordes. In DeSouza EB, Nemeroff C (Editors), *Corticotropin-Releasing Factor: Basic and Clinical Studies of a Neuropeptide.* Annals of the New York Academy of Sciences (Proceedings of the Hypothalamic-Pituitary-Adrenal Axis Revisited). Boca Raton: CRC Press, 1988.

Evans AS: Causation and disease: a chronological journey. *Am. J. Epidemiol.: 108,* 249 – 258, 1978.

Friedman GD: *Primer of Epidemiology.* St. Louis: McGraw-Hill, 1974.

Fuld PA, Katzman R, Davies P, Terry RD: Intrusions as a sign of Alzheimer dementia: chemical and pathological verification. *Ann. Neurol.: 11,* 155 – 159, 1982.

Fuld PA, Dickson D, Crystal H, Aronson MK: Primitive plaques and memory dysfunction in normal and impaired elderly persons. *N. Engl. J. Med.: 316,* 756, 1987.

Grünthal E: Klinisch-anatomisch vergleichende Untersuchungen über den Greisenblodsinn. *Z. gest. Neurol. Psychiat.: 111,* 736 – 817, 1927.

Hakim AM, Mathieson G: Dementia in Parkinson disease: a neuropathologic study. *Neurology: 29,* 1209 – 1212, 1979.

Hachinski VS, Iliff LD, Zilhka E, et al: Cerebral blood flow in dementia. *Arch. Neurology: 32,* 632 – 637, 1975.

Hornykiewicz O, Kish S: Neurochemical basis of dementia in Parkinson's disease. *J. Can. Sci. Neurol.: 11,* 185 – 190, 1984.

Kalaria RN, Harik SI: Increased α_2- and β_2- adrenergic receptors in cerebral microvessels in Alzheimer's disease. *Neurosci. Lett: 106,* 233 – 238, 1989a.

Kalaria RN, Harik SI: Reduced glucose transporter at the blood-brain barrier in cerebral cortex in Alzheimer's disease. *J. Neurochem.: 53,* 1083 – 1088, 1989b.

Kellar KJ, Whitehouse PJ, Martino Barrows AM, Marcus K, Price DL: Muscarinic and nicotinic cholinergic binding sites in Alzheimer's disease cerebral cortex. *Brain Res.: 436,* 62 – 28, 1987.

Kennedy JS, Whitehouse PJ: Alzheimer's disease. In Barclay L (Editor), *Clinical Geriatric Neurology,* in press.

Kittner SJ, White LR, Farmer ME, et al: Methodological issues in screening for dementia: the problem of education adjustment. *J. Chron. Dis.: 39,* 163 – 170, 1986.

Kurtzke JF: Neuroepidemiology. Part II: Assessment of therapeutic trials. *Ann. Neurol.: 19,* 311 – 319, 1986.

Lezak MD: *Neuropsychological Assessment.* New York: Oxford University Press, 1983.

Lezak MD: Neuropsychological assessment. In Frederiks JA (Editor), *Handbook of Clinical Neurology, Vol. 1(45): Clinical Neuropsychology.* Amsterdam: Elsevier Science Publishers, 1985.

Luxenberg MD, Haxby JV, Creasey H, Sundaram M, Rapoport SI: Rate of ventricular enlargement in dementia of the Alzheimer type correlates with rate of neuropsychological deterioration. *Neurology: 37,* 1135 – 1140, 1987.

Martin EM, Wilson RS, Penn RD, Fox JH, Clasen RA, Savoy

SM: Cortical biopsy results in Alzheimer's diseases correlation with cognitive results. *Neurology: 37,* 1201 – 1204, 1987.

Mayeux R, Stern Y, Rosen J, Leventhal J: Depression, intellectual impairment and Parkinson's disease. *Neurology: 31,* 645 – 650, 1981.

McGeer PL, McGeer EG, Suzuki J, et al: Aging, Alzheimer's disease, and the cholinergic system of the basal forebrain. *Neurology: 34,* 741 – 745, 1984.

Mesulam M-M: A cortical network for directed attention and unilateral neglect. *Ann. Neurol.: 10,* 309 – 325, 1981.

Mölsa PK, Sako E, Paljarvi, Rinne JO, Rinne UK: Alzheimer's disease: neuropathological correlates of cognitive and motor disorders. *Acta Neurol. Scand.: 75,* 376 – 384, 1987.

Morimatsu M, Hirai S, Muramatsu A, Yoshikawa M: Senile degenerative brain lesions and dementia. *J. Am. Gerontol. Soc.: 23,* 390 – 406, 1975.

Mortimer JA, Christensen KJ, Webster DD: Parkinsonian dementia. In Frederiks JAM (Ed) *Handbook of Clinical Neurology, Vol. 2.* Amsterdam: Elsevier, 1985.

Neary D, Snowden JS, Bowen DM, et al: Neuropsychological syndromes in presenile dementia due to cerebral atrophy. *J. Neurol. Neurosurg. Psychiatry: 49,* 163 – 174, 1986.

Perry EK, Tomlinson BE, Blessed G, et al: Correlation of cholinergic abnormalities with senile plaques and mental test scores in senile dementia. *Br. Med. J.: ii,* 1457 – 1459, 1978.

Perry EK, Tomlinson BE, Blessed G, et al: Neuropathological and biochemical observations on the noradrenergic system in Alzheimer's disease. *J. Neurol. Sci.: 51,* 279 – 287, 1981.

Pirozzolo FJ, Hansch EC, Mortimer JA, et al: Dementia in Parkinson disease: a neuropsychological analysis. *Brain Cognition: 1,* 71 – 83, 1982.

Price DL, Whitehouse PJ, Struble RG: Cellular pathology in Alzheimer's and Parkinson's disease. *Trends Neurosci.: 9,* 29 – 22, 1986.

Rossor MN, Emson PC, Mountjoy CQ, et al: Reduced amounts of immunoreactive somatostatin in the temporal cortex in senile dementia of Alzheimer type. *Neurosci. Lett.: 20,* 373 – 377, 1980.

Roth M: The diagnosis of dementia in late and middle life. In Mortimer JA, Schuman LM (Editors), *The Epidemiology of Dementia.* New York: Oxford University Press, pp. 24 – 61, 1981.

Rothschild D: Pathologic changes in senile psychoses and their psychobiologic significance. *Am. J. Psychiatry: 93,* 757, 1937.

Ruberg M, Ploska A, Javoy-Agid F, Agid Y: Muscarinic binding and choline acetyltransferase activity in parkinsonian subjects with reference to dementia. *Brain Res.: 232,* 129 – 139, 1982.

Saper CP: Chemical neuroanatomy of Alzheimer's disease. In Iversen SD, Iversen LL, Sanyo SH (Editors), *Handbook of Psychopharmacology, Vol. 20. Biology of Alzheimer's Disease.* New York: Plenum Press, 1988.

Tamminga CA, Foster NL, Fedio P, Bird ED, Chase TN: Alzheimer's disease: low cerebral somatostatin levels correlate with impaired cognitive function and cortical metabolism. *Neurology: 37,* 161 – 165, 1987.

Tomlinson BE, Irving D, Blessed G: Cell loss in the locus coeruleus in senile dementia of Alzheimer type. *J. Neurol. Sci.: 49,* 419 – 428, 1981.

Tukey JW: Some thoughts on clinical trials, especially problems of multiplicity. *Science: 19*, 679 – 684, 1977.

Uhl GR, Hedreen JC, Price DL: Parkinson's disease: loss of neurons from the ventral tegmental area contralateral to therapeutic surgical lesions. *Neurology: 35*, 1215 – 1218, 1985.

Weiss NS: Inferring causal relationships. Elaboration of the criterion of 'Dose-response'. *Am. J. Epidemiol.: 113*, 487 – 490, 1981.

Whitehouse PJ: The concept of subcortical and cortical dementia: another look. *Ann. Neurol.: 19*, 1 – 6, 1986.

Whitehouse PJ, Unnerstall JR: Neurochemistry of dementia. *Eur. Neurol.: 28*, Suppl 1, 36 – 41, 1988.

Whitehouse PJ, Hedreen JC, White CL, Price DL: Basal forebrain neurons in the dementia of Parkinson disease. *Ann. Neurol.: 13*, 243, 1983.

Whitehouse PJ, Lynch D, Kuhar MJ: Effects of postmortem delay and temperature on neurotransmitter receptor binding in a rat model of the human autopsy process. *J. Neurochem.: 43*, 553 – 559, 1984.

Whitehouse PJ, Struble RG, Hedreen JC, Clark AW, Price DL: Alzheimer's disease and related dementias: selective in-volvement of specific neuronal systems *Crit. Rev. Clin. Neurobiol.: 1(4)*, 319 – 339, 1985.

Whitehouse PJ, Vale WW, Zweig RM, Singer HS, Mayeux R, Kuhar MJ, Price DL, DeSouza EB: Reductions in cor-ticotropin releasing factor-life immunoreactivity in cerebral cortex in Alzheimer's disease, Parkinson's disease, and pro-gressive supranuclear palsy. *Neurology: 37*, 905 – 909, 1987.

Whitehouse PJ, Martino AM, Marcus KA, Zweig RM, Singer HS, Price DL, Kellar KJ: Reductions in acetylcholine and nicotine binding in several degenerative diseases. *Arch. Neurol.: 45*, 722 – 724, 1988.

Wilcock GK, Esiri MM: Plaques, tangles, and dementia. *J. Neurol. Sci.: 56*, 343 – 356, 1982.

Yoshimura Y: Cortical changes in the parkinsonian brain: a contribution to the delineation of 'diffuse Lewy body disease.' *J. Neurol.: 229*, 17 – 32, 1983.

Zubenko GS, Moossy J, Kopp U: Neurochemical correlates of major depression in primary dementia. *Arch. Neurol.: 47*, 209 – 214, 1990.

Zweig RM, Ross CA, Hedreen JC, et al: The neuropathology of aminergic nuclei in Alzheimer's disease. *Ann. Neurol.: 24*, 233 – 242, 1988.

© 1991 Elsevier Science Publishers B.V.
Handbook of Neuropsychology, Vol. 5
F. Boller and J. Grafman (Eds)

CHAPTER 4

Nuclear magnetic resonance: principles and applications to neuroscience research

Jay W. Pettegrew

Neurophysics Laboratory, Department of Psychiatry, University of Pittsburgh, Pittsburgh, PA, U.S.A.

Historical perspective

In 1924 Pauli suggested that hydrogen nuclei might possess a magnetic moment. This was confirmed in 1939 by Rabi, who demonstrated that a beam of hydrogen molecules in a magnetic field absorbed a discrete radio frequency energy which presumably was the resonance frequency.

The first successful NMR experiments were conducted independently in late 1945 by Purcell, Torrey and Pound (Purcell et al., 1946) and by Bloch, Hansen and Packard (Bloch et al., 1946). The Purcell group detected proton NMR in solid paraffin; the Bloch group detected proton NMR in liquid water. Bloch and Purcell received the Nobel Prize for Physics in 1952 for their observations. Until about 1952, studies of solids dominated the field of NMR. However, the reports of observations of chemical shifts of ^{31}P resonances in several compounds (Knight, 1949), of ^{14}N resonances in several ions (Proctor and Yu, 1950) and of ^{19}F resonances in several compounds (Dickinson, 1950) led to the development of high-resolution NMR in liquids. Since the molecular motions in liquids result in very narrow lines compared to those in solids, much smaller chemical shifts could be detected. This resulted in the domination of high-resolution NMR of liquids for the past 30 years.

In 1957 Lowe and Norberg demonstrated that the NMR spectrum in the frequency domain, as obtained by a continuous-wave (cw) experiment, was the Fourier transform (FT) of the NMR free-induction decay obtained in the time domain. This important observation led to the development of pulsed FT NMR. The increased efficiency of FT NMR over cw NMR was demonstrated in 1966 by Ernst and Anderson. Other NMR techniques were developed to remove the effect of inhomogeneity in the applied field. These were called spin-echo techniques and were first proposed by Hahn in 1950. Spin-echo techniques have been of particular importance in measuring relaxation times. These techniques have been described by Carr and Purcell (1954) and have been further modified by Meiboom and Gill (1958).

The first potential medical application of NMR was described by Damadian in 1971 for the detection of tumors. A patent for this application of NMR was awarded to Damadian in 1972. In 1973 Lauterbur proposed the potential imaging capabilities of NMR.

Elementary theory of nuclear magnetic resonance

(1) Atomic nuclear properties relevant to NMR

Atomic nuclei are composed of protons and neutrons, both of which have intrinsic spin and a spin quantum number of 1/2. Another important nuclear property is the nuclear distribution of positive charge. This charge distribution is given by the nuclear quadrupole, eQ, where e is the unit of electrostatic charge and Q is a measure of the deviation of the charge distribution from spherical symmetry. If all the nuclear particle spins are paired, there will be no net spin and the nuclear spin quantum number, I, will be zero. This will be the case for atomic nuclei with even numbers of protons and neutrons. The distribution of positive charge will be spherical and the nuclear quadrupole movement, eQ, will also be zero. A spherical non-spinning nucleus is an example of a nucleus in which $I = 0$ and $eQ = 0$. A nucleus may have $I = 1/2$ (presence of an unpaired spin), and $eQ = 0$, in which case the nucleus will be spherical and spinning. The presence of an unpaired spin also gives rise to a nuclear magnetic moment μ_m.

Nuclei which have $I > 1$ will not only have a nuclear spin, but also will have a non-spherical distribution of positive charge. The charge distribution will in this case be ellipsoidal. A positive value for Q indicates that the ellipsoid major axis will be oriented along the direction of an applied magnetic field H_o. Atomic nuclei which have negative values for Q will orient themselves in an applied magnetic field so that the ellipsoid long axis is perpendicular to the applied magnetic field (Fig. 1).

(2) Nuclear spin angular momentum and allowed spin transitions

Atomic nuclei also have nuclear spin angular momentum quantum numbers, m_I, which indicate the allowed orientations of the nuclear magnetic moment μ_m with respect to an applied magnetic field (H_o). The quantum number m_I has values: I, $(I-1), \ldots -(I-1), -I$. For $I = 1/2$, m_I has the values of $+1/2$ or $-1/2$. For $I = 1$, m_I has values of $+1$, 0 and -1. For $I = 3/2$, m_I has values of $3/2$, $1/2$, $-1/2$, $-3/2$. In the absence of a magnetic field, all orientations of the nuclear magnetic moment are degenerate. In the presence of an applied magnetic field the degeneracy is removed. For nuclei with spin quantum number

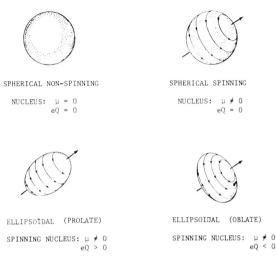

SPHERICAL NON-SPINNING

NUCLEUS: $\mu = 0$
$eQ = 0$

SPHERICAL SPINNING

NUCLEUS: $\mu \neq 0$
$eQ = 0$

ELLIPSOIDAL (PROLATE)

SPINNING NUCLEUS: $\mu \neq 0$
$eQ > 0$

ELLIPSOIDAL (OBLATE)

SPINNING NUCLEUS: $\mu \neq 0$
$eQ < 0$

Fig. 1. Different types of nucleus.

$I = 1/2$ in the presence of an applied magnetic field, $m_I = +1/2$ corresponds to the nuclear magnetic moment aligned with the applied magnetic field and $m_I = -1/2$ corresponds to the nuclear magnetic moment aligned opposed to the applied magnetic field. One possible transition exists between the $m_I = +1/2$ and $m_I = -1/2$ quantum states. For nuclei with $I = 1$, the presence of an applied magnetic field gives rise to m_I values of $+1$, 0 and -1 corresponding respectively to alignments of the ellipsoid major axis with, perpendicular to and opposed to the applied magnetic field. Two possible transitions now exist: one between the $m_I = +1$ and $m_I = 0$ quantum states and another between the $m_I = 0$ and $m_I = -1$ quantum states. For nuclei with $I = 3/2$, the presence of an applied magnetic field gives rise to four possible orientations of the nuclear magnetic moment with respect to the applied field. This in turn gives rise to three possible transitions: $m_I = 3/2$ to $m_I = 1/2$, $m_I = 1/2$ to $m_I = -1/2$ and $m_I = -1/2$ to $m_I = -3/2$ (Fig. 2). Examples of atomic nuclei with $I = 1/2$ are ^{1}H, ^{13}C, ^{19}F and ^{31}P; with $I = 1$ are ^{2}H and ^{14}N; and with $I = 3/2$ are ^{7}Li, ^{23}Na, ^{35}Cl and ^{39}K.

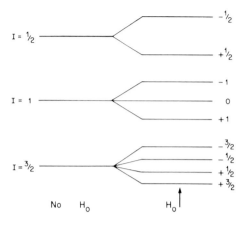

Fig. 2. Angular moment quantum levels.

(3) Effect of applied static magnetic field

In the presence of an applied magnetic field H_0, a nuclear magnetic moment will precess (rotate) around H_0. The precessional frequency is referred to as the Larmor frequency (ω_0) and is given by

$$\omega_0 = \gamma H_0$$

where γ is the gyromagnetic ratio of the atomic nucleus. Therefore ω_0 is linearly dependent on H_0. The values of ω_0 are in the radio frequency range (Fig. 3).

(4) Effect of pulsed radio frequency field

In order to induce transitions between different quantum states (m_I), one needs to apply a magnetic field (H_1) which has the same frequency as the Larmor frequency ω_0. This is accomplished by pulsing a radio frequency field (H_1) along an axis orthogonal to H_0. The atomic nucleus will then absorb energy and go from one spin angular momentum quantum state (m_I) to another.

(5) Sensitivity of NMR

The major limitation of NMR is the lack of sensitivity. The reason for this is readily apparent by

considering the equilibrium populations for the nuclear ground and excited spin states. According to the Boltzmann distribution law, the population of nuclear spins in the upper spin state β (N_β) divided by the population in the lower spin state α ($N\alpha$) is

$$N_\beta / N_\alpha = e^{-\Delta E/kT}$$

where

$$
\begin{aligned}
\Delta E &= \gamma h H_o \\
\hbar &= \text{Planck's constant } h \text{ divided by } 2\pi \\
&= 6.6242 \times 10^{-27} \text{ erg} \cdot \text{s}/2\pi \\
&= 1.0543 \times 10^{-27} \text{ erg} \cdot \text{s} \\
k &= \text{Boltzmann's constant} \\
&= 1.3805 \times 10^{-16} \text{ erg} \cdot \text{degree}^{-1} \\
H_o &= \text{static field in gauss} \\
T &= \text{temperature in degrees Kelvin} \\
&= 273.15 + {}^\circ C \\
\gamma &= \text{magnetogyric constant}
\end{aligned}
$$

The difference in the population of the β and α nuclear spin states relative to the total number of spins present is given by

$$\frac{N_\alpha - N_\beta}{N_\alpha + N_\beta} = \gamma \hbar H_o / 2kT$$

At 1.5 Tesla and room temperature (300°K) this calculates to be only 2.6×10^{-6} for protons. This

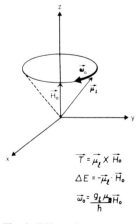

Fig. 3. Effect of an external magnetic field.

value will, of course, be smaller for other nuclei with smaller γ values. Since the radio frequency field stimulates emission as well as absorption, the net absorption is very weak at this field strength and frequency since almost the same number of nuclear spins are available for emission as absorption. However, at a field of 10 Tesla, the population difference is nearly seven times greater and the net absorption is correspondingly more intense. Therefore, the sensitivity increases with the field strength (H_o), and the nuclear magnetogyric ratio (γ). One also can increase the signal intensity by enriching the sample with those nuclei whose NMR observable isotope is not 100% naturally abundant.

It has been shown that at constant H_o and under extreme narrowing conditions (i.e., $\omega_o^2 \tau_c^2 << 1$, $T_1 = T_2$) the signal intensities obtained in continuous-wave NMR experiments are proportional to $\gamma^3 NI(I + 1)$ (the receptivity). The receptivity of a given nucleus (x) may be determined relative to ^1H by the expression (Harris, 1978)

$$D_x^P = \frac{\gamma_x^3 N_x I_x (I_x + 1)}{\gamma_p^3 N_p I_p (I_p + 1)}$$

$$= 6.9664 \times 10^{-28} \, \gamma_x^3 \, N_x \, I_x \, (I_x + 1)/\text{rad}^3$$

$$T^{-3} S^{-3} \, \%$$

The relative receptivities and other NMR properties of biologically useful nuclei are given in Table 1.

(6) Chemical shift

When atomic nuclei are covalently bonded together, the electron distribution surrounding a given nuclide will be different for different types of chemical moieties. For example, the electron cloud surrounding a phosphorus atom will be different for the phosphorus in sugar phosphates (such as glucose 6-P), inorganic orthophosphate, the γ, α, β phosphates of ATP, etc. In the presence of an applied magnetic field H_o, there will be an induced motion in the electron cloud such that the moving electrons will generate a magnetic field opposed to the applied field H_o. This is referred to as diamagnetic shielding. The magnitude of the shielding will depend on the nature of the electron cloud surrounding the nucleus in question. Therefore, the magnitude of the effective field experienced by a nucleus is given by

$$H_{\text{eff}} = H_o - H_o \sigma = H_o(1 - \sigma)$$

where σ is a non-dimensional shielding constant. The resonance frequency will therefore be decreas-

TABLE I

Isotope	Spin	Natural abundance ($N\%$)	Magnetic moment (μ/μ_n)	Magnetogyric ratio ($\gamma/10^7$ rad $\cdot T^{-1} \cdot S^{-1}$)	NMR frequency (MHz)	Relative receptivity
^1H	1/2	99.985	4.8371	26.7510	100.000	1.000
^2H	1	0.015	1.2125	4.1064	15.351	1.45×10^{-6}
^{13}C	1/2	1.108	1.2162	6.7263	25.145	1.76×10^{-4}
^{14}N	1	99.63	0.5706	1.9324	7.224	1.00×10^{-3}
^{19}F	1/2	100	4.5506	25.166	94.093	0.8328
^{29}Si	1/2	4.70	-0.9609	-5.3141	19.867	3.69×10^{-4}
^{31}P	1/2	100	1.9581	10.829	40.480	0.0663
^{23}Na	3/2	100	2.8610	7.0760	26.451	9.25×10^{-2}
^7Li	3/2	92.58	4.2035	10.396	38.864	0.272
^{27}Al	5/2	100	4.3051	6.9706	26.057	0.206
^{35}Cl	3/2	75.53	1.0598	2.6212	9.798	3.55×10^{-3}
^{39}K	3/2	93.1	0.5047	1.2484	4.666	4.73×10^{-4}
^{55}Mn	5/2	100	4.075	6.598	24.67	0.175
^{59}Co	7/2	100	5.2344	6.3171	23.614	0.277

ed by the shielding. It is because of this diamagnetic shielding contribution that atoms in different chemical moieties come into resonance at different pulsed H_1 field frequencies. Because of this phenomenon, NMR can be used as an analytical tool. Under appropriate instrumental conditions, the integrated area under an NMR signal peak corresponds to the number of atoms of that particular chemical moiety in the sample. The strength of the secondary magnetic field and, consequently, the chemical shift (measured as a frequency) are both proportional to H_0. Therefore, chemical shift dispersion is expected to increase with increases in H_0.

(7) Spin relaxation

Once a particular nucleus has been excited to a higher quantum state by an applied radio frequency field H_1, the nucleus can lose its excited state potential energy by two different relaxation processes. The first is called spin-lattice relaxation (T_1) and is produced by *rapidly* fluctuating magnetic fields directed along the x and y axes of a coordinate system which is rotating about the z axis at the Larmor frequency (rotating frame). The other relaxation mechanism is called spin-spin relaxation (T_2) and is produced by *both rapidly* and *slowly* fluctuating magnetic fields directed along the x, y and z axes of the rotating frame. Therefore, there are more potential interactions giving rise to T_2 relaxation as compared to T_1 relaxation and, consequently, $T_2 \leq T_1$. The interaction mechanisms involved in relaxation processes include dipole-dipole, quadrupole, chemical shift anisotropy, scalar coupling and spin-rotation. Space does not permit a full discussion of these mechanisms (see Farrar, 1989, and Woessner, 1989). In all these relaxation mechanisms, however, two molecular parameters determine the rate of the relaxation. The first is the magnitude of the particular type of interaction and the other is the correlation time, τ_c, which can be defined as the 'average' time between molecular collisions for a molecule in some state of motion. More

specifically is the importance of the magnitude of τ_c in relation to ω_0. From these considerations one can define ranges of molecular motion as fast (extreme narrowing limit, $\omega_0^2 \tau_c^2 << 1$), intermediate ($\omega_0^2 \tau_c^2 = 1$) or slow (high-field limit, $\omega_0^2 \tau_c^2 >> 1$). It is also apparent that the range of molecular motions available for study will depend on the strength of the applied field H_0, since $\omega_0 = \gamma H_0$ (Fig. 4).

Safety

Many studies have been done investigating the safety of NMR. These studies have been numerous and the vast majority have failed to demonstrate any deleterious effect of NMR on a wide variety of organisms. A few of these studies include:

(1) No effect of 30 MHz (20 min, 7.05 kgauss) continuous-wave irradiation on frog spermatozoa, fertilized eggs or embryos (Prasad et al., 1982).

(2) No effect of 30 MHz (1 h, 7.05 kgauss) con-

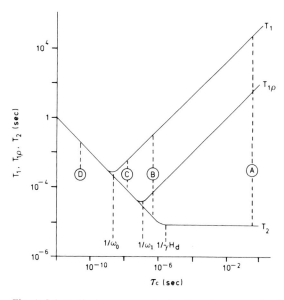

Fig. 4. Schematic dependence of relaxation times on molecular correlation time, τ_c, for relaxation determined by dipole–dipole interactions. A = rigid lattice; B = nonrigid solid; C = viscous liquid; D = nonviscous liquid.

tinuous irradiation on mouse bone marrow chromosomes (Prasad et al., 1984).

(3) Pulsed fields with peak rates of change of 60 Tesla/s have no effect on the cardiac or respiratory function or the brain activity of anesthetized rabbits (Gore et al., 1982).

(4) Static fields (0.15 Tesla) have no effect on morphine-induced analgesia in adult male rats. However, radio frequency fields of 2 ms (90° pulse) and 4 ms (180° pulse) significantly reduced morphine-induced analgesia, and time-varying magnetic fields (0.4 – 0.6 Tesla/s with 2 – 3 ms rise times) abolish morphine-induced analgesia (Prato et al., 1987).

(5) Static fields of 0.15 Tesla have no effect on the open-field behavior and passive avoidance in rats (Ossenkopp et al., 1986) or the spatial memory tests in rats (Innis et al., 1986).

(6) MRI at 0.15 Tesla has no significant effect on human cognitive functioning (Sweetland et al., 1987).

(7) Neonatal and adult mice exposed to a 1.89 Tesla magnetic field have no gross morphological, histological, hematological or blood chemistry alterations (Osbakken et al., 1986).

Because of the apparent safety of NMR imaging, it would appear to be the imaging method of choice in children. In fact, studies in children have demonstrated increased resolution and sensitivity of MRI over CT scanning in post-infectious encephalomyelitis (Dunn et al., 1986a), grey matter heterotopia (Dunn et al., 1986b), intracranial masses (Barnes et al., 1986) and various diseases of the central nervous system (Pennock et al., 1986; Zimmerman and Bilanicik, 1986). MRI has even been extended to the human fetus in utero to monitor fetal and placental aging and function (Smith et al., 1984; McCarthy, 1986). MRI has also demonstrated brain abnormalities in patients with psychotic behavior in whom CT scans were normal and in whom a metabolic abnormality was subsequently found such as Wilson's disease (Lukes et al., 1983; Lawler et al., 1983), adrenoleukodystrophy (James, 1984) and systemic lupus erythematosus (Vermess, 1983).

Comparison of CT and MRI

MRI is frequently compared with CT scanning in terms of resolution and sensitivity. At this time, MRI has a decided advantage for imaging the central nervous systems. These advantages include:

(1) Better resolution: MRI resolutions of approximately 0.03 mm^3 voxels are now being reported.

(2) MRI has higher sensitivity to soft tissue contrast, which is particularly important in brain imaging.

(3) MRI is capable of multiplanar imaging (axial, sagittal, coronal, oblique), which is very important for brain imaging.

(4) MRI monitors the chemical structure of biological water through the water T_1 and T_2 relaxation times. Therefore, this important biological parameter is being assessed.

(5) MRI has no bone artifact and is not as susceptible to brain – CSF edge effects as CT and is, therefore, quantitatively more accurate for brain volume measurements. This is particularly important for use in conjunction with PET studies so that accurate tissue volumes can be obtained for metabolic rate calculations.

(6) MRI has no ionizing radiation.

The sensitivity of MRI to the intracellular chemical structure of water may have significant implications for future applications of MRI. The potential for ^{23}Na imaging (Moseley et al., 1985; Lee et al., 1986) with a 4.0 mm resolution has also been demonstrated, as has ^{19}F imaging (Nunnally et al., 1985) with an in-plane resolution of 0.6 mm. Recently, preliminary studies have also demonstrated the feasibility of ^{7}Li NMR imaging in brain (Renshaw, 1986). Although the ^{23}Na, ^{19}F and ^{7}Li NMR imaging capabilities are intriguing and should be researched vigorously, none of these nuclei has the sensitivity or resolution capabilities at present that ^{1}H possesses.

Future directions of MRI

New approaches are being rapidly developed to enhance the resolution and sensitivity of MRI even further. One rapidly developing area is the area of image enhancers. Image enhancers are, in general, molecules that contain either paramagnetic or ferromagnetic atoms, which secondarily influence the relaxation properties of any molecules the image enhancers come in close contact with.

The first type of image-enhancing agent is paramagnetic cations, which increase the relaxation rate for nuclei which undergo dipole-dipole interactions with the paramagnetic cation. The two types of paramagnetic image enhancers most commonly employed are either transition metals such as Mn^{2+} or lanthanides such as Gd^{3+}. The other class of paramagnetic contrast agents is based on organic nitroxide spin-labels such as derivatives of piperidine. A general review of this topic was carried out by Brown et al. (1985).

The paramagnetic metals are too toxic to be used as free cations for image enhancement. Therefore, the paramagnetic cations are usually chelated to organic molecules. The use of paramagnetic cations as image enhancers was first suggested by Lauterbur in 1978 (Lauterbur, 1978). Iron (Carr et al., 1984), manganese (Huberty, 1983), chromium and gadolinium chelates (Brasch et al., 1984; Carr et al., 1984) have all been demonstrated to be effective image-enhancing agents in animals. Gadolinium-DPTA also has been successfully used as an image enhancer in human brain (Carr, 1985; Runge, 1985).

The magnetic resonance properties of 12 paramagnetic piperidine nitroxyls have been reviewed (Lovin et al., 1985). One nitroxide spin label has been demonstrated to be a hypoxia-sensitive NMR image enhancer (Swartz et al., 1986). Immunospecific NMR image enhancers have also been described (Renshaw et al., 1986). The potential application of immunospecific NMR image enhancers to neuroscience research is tremendous.

It has been demonstrated that the relaxation properties of image enhancers depends on the magnetic field strength (H_o) and the correlation time of the paramagnetic or nitroxyl spin-label. These relationships are well-known extensions of relaxation theory as given in the Solomon-Bloembergen equation (Bloembergen, 1957; Solomon, 1955). When the correlation time (τ_c) of the paramagnetic atom molecular complex is approximately equal to the inverse of the observed frequency, $1/\omega_o$, the relaxation rate enhancement will be maximal. These relationships have recently been demonstrated for monoclonal antibodies labeled with polymeric paramagnetic ion chelates (Shreve and Aisen, 1986) and nitroxyl spin labels (Slane et al., 1986).

Potential of MRS

NMR spectroscopy holds great promise for the investigation of molecular structure/dynamics and metabolic processes both in vitro and in vivo. The potential role of in vivo NMR spectroscopy in clinical medicine has been reviewed (Radda et al., 1984; Bore, 1985a,b; Radda and Taylor, 1985; Iles, 1982; Evanochko et al., 1984). The available experience, to date, suggests that in vivo NMR spectroscopy has been most successfully applied to disorders of skeletal muscle, followed by liver, heart and kidneys. The application of in vivo NMR spectroscopy to human brain is not as well developed, but certainly holds tremendous potential for the future. This potential appears to be the greatest for those neurological and psychiatric disorders whose pathologies are at a sub-cellular and molecular/metabolic level. What follows is a brief review of the capabilities and biological applications of ^{31}P, ^{13}C, ^{1}H, ^{23}Na, ^{7}Li high-resolution and ^{31}P solid-state NMR spectroscopy. Following this the newer techniques of two-dimensional NMR and NMR microimaging will be introduced.

(1) ^{31}P NMR spectroscopy

The ^{31}P NMR spectrum of mammalian brain can be conveniently separated into three regions (Glonek et al., 1982): (i) orthophosphate (5 to −1.5 ppm), (ii) guanidophosphate (−3.5 to −5 ppm) and (iii) polyphosphate (−5 to −23 ppm). The orthophosphate region can be further subdivided into ionized ends (−5 to −8 ppm), esterified ends (−8 to −14 ppm) and middles (−18 to −23 ppm).

Contributing to the phosphomonoester region are hexose 6-phosphates, triose phosphates, pentose phosphates, phosphoethanolamine, phosphocholine, inorganic orthophosphate (P$_i$), anomeric sugar phosphates and several signals that have not been characterized as to the source phosphate. Contributing to the phosphodiester region are glycerol phosphodiesters (primarily glycerol 3-phosphoethanolamine and glycerol 3-phosphocholine), a broad resonance from phosphorylated glycolipids and glycoproteins and several uncharacterized resonances. The guanidophosphate region contains resonances from phosphocreatine (PCr) and phosphoarginine.

In the polyphosphate part of the spectrum, the ionized ends region contains resonances from the

γ-phosphate of nucleotide triphosphates and the β-phosphate of nucleotide diphosphates. The esterified ends region contains resonances for the α-phosphate of nucleotide triphosphates, the α-phosphate of nucleotide diphosphates, the nicotinamide adenine dinucleotides and the uridine diphospho-sugars (galactose, glucose, mannose). The only resonance that makes a contribution to the middle region is the β-phosphate of nucleotide triphosphates. In mammalian brain, the predominant contributors to the nucleotide triphosphate and nucleotide diphosphate resonances are ATP and ADP (Fig. 5).

From a metabolic viewpoint, the ^{31}P NMR spectrum contains information about the energy status of the brain from the resonances for PCr, ATP, ADP and P$_i$. Resonances related to phospholipid metabolism are contained in the phosphomonoester and phosphodiester regions (Pettegrew et al., 1987a). In mammalian brain, the phosphomonoester region contains resonances

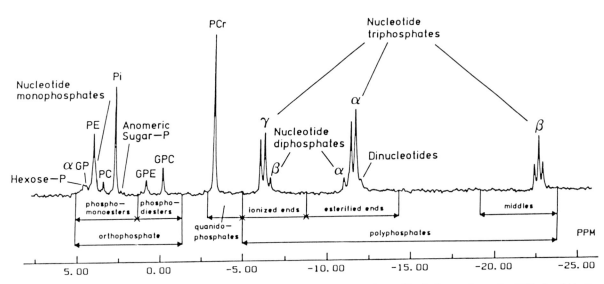

Fig. 5. High-resolution ^{31}P NMR spectrum of a perchloric acid extract of freeze-clamped brain from a 3-month-old Fischer 344 rat. The easily identifiable resonances and their chemical shifts (δ) include the phosphomonoesters (PME): α-glycerol phosphate (α-GP, 4.29δ), L-phosphoserine (PS, 3.89δ), phosphoethanolamine (PE, 3.84δ) and phosphocholine (PC, 3.33δ); inorganic orthophosphate (Pi, 2.63δ); the phosphodiesters (PDE); glycerol 3-phosphoethanolamine (GPE, 0.81δ) and glycerol 3-phosphocholine (GPC, −0.13δ); phosphocreatine (PCr, −3.12δ); the nucleotide triphosphates (especially ATP; γ −5.80δ, α −10.92δ, β −21.45δ); the nucleotide diphosphates (especially ADP; β −6.11γ, α −10.61γ); dinucleotides such as nicotinamide adenine dinucleotide (NAD) (−11.37δ) and a complex resonance band centered on −12.89δ which is composed of nucleoside diphospho-derivatives such as uridine diphospho-sugars and cytidine diphospho-derivatives such as cytidine diphosphocholine and cytidine diphosphoethanolamine.

predominantly from α-glycerol phosphate, phosphoethanolamine and phosphocholine. These three metabolites in mammalian brain are found predominantly in the anabolic pathway of membrane phospholipid metabolism. The phosphodiester region contains predominantly the resonances of glycerol 3-phosphoethanolamine and glycerol 3-phosphocholine, which, in mammalian brain, are catabolic breakdown products of phospholipid metabolism (Dawson, 1985; Porcellati and Arienti, 1983). Therefore the steady-state turnover of brain phospholipids (anabolism/catabolism) can be assessed by ^{31}P NMR spectroscopy (Pettegrew et al., 1987b). Since neural membrane (especially synaptosomal) structure, dynamics and function are of vital importance to normal neurochemical, neurophysiological and neuropharmacological function, ^{31}P NMR has the potential to provide important insights into normal and altered brain function.

The in vitro ^{31}P NMR studies provide chemical conditions more favorable to ^{31}P NMR analysis than occur in the living brain and, therefore, a greater sensitivity and resolution is achieved as compared to in vivo analytical approaches. The enhanced sensitivity and resolution of in vitro extract studies permit the characterization and quantitation of many different phosphorus-containing compounds. Previous in vitro ^{31}P NMR studies demonstrated a remarkable correlation with more classical assay procedures and, in addition, revealed previously uncharacterized metabolites and unrecognized metabolic relationships (Pettegrew et al., 1982, 1984, 1986, 1987a,b; Glonek et al., 1982; Cohen et al., 1984).

In order to correctly interpret ^{31}P NMR spectra, the identities of the individual resonance signals must be carefully verified through the use of appropriate biochemical and spectroscopic procedures. The importance of this verification was recently demonstrated for a prominent ^{31}P NMR resonance at 3.84 ppm in mammalian brain which has now been identified as phosphoethanolamine (Pettegrew et al., 1986). The identification was based on ^{1}H and ^{31}P NMR findings (including pH titrations) at 4.7 and 14.1 Tesla, as well as thin-layer chromatography studies.

Pettegrew and co-workers previously demonstrated an elevated phosphomonoester resonance in rapidly dividing neuroblastoma clonal lines (Pettegrew et al., 1979) and have recently shown the elevation of a prominent phosphomonoester resonance in developing and degenerating brain (Pettegrew et al., 1985, 1986, 1987a). The prominent phosphomonoester resonance has been identified as phosphoethanolamine (Pettegrew et al., 1986). These previous studies and the present study are in agreement with earlier studies which demonstrated a relative abundance of phosphoethanolamine in developing rabbit brain (Cohen and Lin, 1962). A relatively prominent phosphomonoester resonance exhibiting the appropriate ^{31}P chemical shift has also been reported in human neonatal brain (Cady et al., 1983; Younkin, 1984) and childhood neuroblastoma (Maris et al., 1985) using an in vivo MRS surface coil technique.

Effects of brain development and aging in the Fischer 344 rat on energy and phospholipid metabolism

^{31}P NMR studies have been conducted in the Fischer 344 rat from 12 hours of age (newborn) to 24 months of age (aged) (Pettegrew et al., 1985, 1987a, 1990). These studies demonstrate a marked influence of brain development and a less marked influence of brain aging on high-energy phosphate and membrane phospholipid metabolism. In brief, phosphocreatine (PCr) is low in newborn rat brain and then rapidly increases through the stage of dendritic proliferation (10 – 20 days of age) and then remains stable until senescence (>12 months) when small increases in PCr are observed. The levels of phosphodiesters (PDE) follow a similar developmental and aging time course. In contrast, the levels of phosphomonoesters (PME) are high in the newborn rat brain and rapidly decrease to reach their adult levels at the end of dendritic proliferation. In aged rats (>12 months) the levels of PME again increase slightly.

The PME/PDE ratio, which is an estimate of membrane phospholipid turnover, is high in the newborn period, rapidly decreases up to 3 months of age and then remains relatively constant up to 12 months of age. The high PME levels in the developing brain probably reflect the active synthesis of membranes associated with the development of neuritic processes. After 12 months of age the PME/PDE ratio decreases slightly, suggesting that membrane phospholipid breakdown is proceeding slightly faster than membrane phospholipid synthesis. The changes are probably the molecular/metabolic processes underlying the loss on neuritic processes observed in normal aging.

The PCr/P_i ratio provides a convenient measure of the energy status of the brain. The PCr/P_i ratio is quite low in the newborn period until 5 days of age, after which time the PCr/P_i ratio rapidly increases up to 3 months of age. After 3 months of age the PCr/P_i ratio remains relatively constant until 12 months of age, when the ratio again slowly increases up to 24 months of age. These findings suggest either that the aging brain synthesizes PCr at an increased rate or that there is a decreased utilization of PCr.

Effect of aging on human brain metabolism
It is important to determine whether similar developmental and aging changes occur in humans and their time course. In vivo ^{31}P NMR studies have been conducted on normal, healthy, young and elderly subjects. Compared to young adults ($n = 10$, 27.6 ± 1.7 years), normal elderly subjects ($n = 6$, 72.3 ± 3.1 years) have decreased levels of PME ($p = 0.05$) and nucleoside diphospho-derivatives (NPD-D) (such as UDP-sugars and CDP-choline or CDP-ethanolamine, $p = 0.0002$) and increased levels of PDE ($p = 0.0004$) without changes in PCr, ATP or intracellular pH. The decreased levels of PME and increased levels of PDE suggest decreased synthesis and increased breakdown of membrane phospholipids in normal elderly human cerebral cortex. The decreased levels of NDP-D suggest decreased glycosylation of membrane proteins and

lipids (UDP-S) or decreased synthesis of membrane phospholipids (CDP-choline). Both of these aging-related changes in membrane metabolism are not surprising given the histological evidence for changes in dendritic spines in aged human brain. However, for the first time these changes can be non-invasively followed in living human subjects. These findings provide in vivo molecular insights into normal brain aging processes.

Membrane phospholipid changes in Alzheimer's disease
^{31}P NMR studies demonstrate significant changes in membrane phospholipid metabolism in Alzheimer's disease (AD) brain obtained at autopsy and biopsy (Pettegrew et al., 1984, 1985, 1987a,b). These membrane alterations have now been observed in antemortem in vivo studies (Gdowski et al., 1988; Brown et al., 1989). The changes in phospholipid metabolism are in essentially the same cortical areas of the AD brain where others have shown decreased glucose utilization and abnormal electrophysiological responses to event-related evoked potentials (Cutler et al., 1985; Duara et al., 1986; Jagust et al., 1987; Haxby et al., 1987; Beradi et al., 1987; Friedland et al., 1987; Horwitz et al., 1987; Rapoport et al., 1986; Fletcher and Sharpe, 1986, 1988). AD brains contain significantly elevated levels of phosphomonoesters (PME), which are precursors to membrane phospholipids or products of phospholipase C or phosphodiesterase activity, without significant elevations of phosphodiesters (PDE), which are phospholipase A-mediated breakdown products of membrane phospholipids. In contrast, non-AD diseased control brains contain significant elevations of PDE.

Further in vivo ^{31}P NMR results (Pettegrew et al., unpublished results) demonstrate a negative correlation between the levels of PDE and the Mattis scores ($r = 0.97$; $p = 0.01$) and a positive correlation between the PCr levels and the Mattis scores ($r = 0.95$; $p = 0.01$). The PME levels do not correlate with the Mattis scores ($r = 0.61$, $p = NS$). There are no within-group or between-group differences in the intracellular pH. Therefore, the PCr changes are not due to a pH-induced alteration in the creatine kinase equilibrium.

These in vivo findings are consistent with the findings in AD autopsy brain and suggest that the alterations in PME perhaps antedate the onset of cognitive changes. The PDE-Mattis correlation suggests that the cognitive decline is closely associated with neuronal degeneration which occurs later in the course of the disease. The PCr-Mattis correlation suggests either decreased synthesis or increased utilization of PCr as the disease progresses.

It should be noted that these findings in AD are distinctly different from the findings in normal aging in the Fischer 344 rat and in humans. It is of some considerable interest that the AD findings are strikingly similar to the findings in normal brain development. It is also of interest that the PME levels observed in AD brain are similar to those observed in developing brain coincident with normal programmed cell death (Pettegrew et al., 1990). These metabolic insights taken together could prove valuable in advancing our understanding of the molecular basis of AD. In vivo ^{31}P NMR could also prove valuable non-invasively following metabolic responses to therapeutic interventions.

The findings of increased PME in AD brain cannot be explained simply by degeneration of brain tissue; with degeneration, the PDE should be elevated and not PME. Increased turnover of membrane phospholipids should result in elevations of both PME and PDE as observed in normal aging in Fischer 344 rats (Pettegrew et al., 1987b, 1990). The PDE elevations in non-AD diseased brain could be consistent with increased phospholipid turnover or degeneration of brain tissue. The finding of increased PME in AD brain could be due to one or more of the following mechanisms (Pettegrew et al., 1989): (1) increased synthesis of membrane phospholipids; (2) a relative metabolic block in the synthetic pathway;

(3) a decreased breakdown of PME secondary to decreased phospholipase D activity in AD brain (Kanfer and McCartney, 1987); (4) stimulation of phopholipase C by neuromodulators and growth factors (Nishizuka, 1986) or oncogenes (Lacal et al., 1987); or stimulation of phosphodiesterase activity (Kanfer et al., 1990).

As previously noted, elevated levels of PME occur in the normal immature developing brain, particularly during the period of elaboration of dendritic processes. Therefore, the findings of elevated PME in the AD brain could suggest an increase in membrane phospholipid synthesis, as it can occur during the formation of membranous structures such as dendritic processes. There is evidence from previous reports indicating that elaboration of dendritic processes does occur in both AD (Scheibel, 1979; Geddes et al., 1985) and normal aged brain (Buell and Coleman, 1979, 1981; Pettegrew et al., 1988b).

Recent computer molecular model studies (Pettegrew et al., 1988a; McClure and Pettegrew, 1989) have demonstrated conformational similarities between the neurotransmitter *N*-methyl-D-aspartate (NMDA) and L-glutamate with those of PME phosphocholine (PC), phosphoethanolamine, (PE) and L-phosphoserine (PS). In hippocampal slice studies, it has been shown that low concentrations of PME depresses the electrophysiological activity of CA1 pyramidal cells which contain L-glutamate receptors and appears to block the Ca^{2+}-activated K^+ channel (Pettegrew et al., 1989). At higher concentration, PME activates the L-glutamate receptors, which could lead to a series of membrane changes resulting in increased phospholipase C (PL-C), which, in turn, would enhance protein kinase C (PK-C) activity. Stimulation of protein kinase C could have a cascade of consequences such as increasing the cytoplasmic levels of inositol 1,4,5-triphosphate leading to activation of the extracellular Ca^{2+}-mediated second messenger system and the hyper-phosphorylation of cytoskeletal and membrane bound proteins.

(2) ^{13}C NMR spectroscopy of mammalian brain

Natural abundance ^{13}C NMR   The natural abundance ^{13}C NMR spectrum of rat brain has been obtained and demonstrates ^{13}C NMR chemical shifts of brain metabolites very similar to the chemical shifts of the pure chemical (Barany et al., 1985). Readily identifiable resonances for amino acids and their derivatives include glutamate, glutamine, glycine, taurine, alanine, aspartate, *N*-acetylaspartate and γ-aminobutyrate; for the phospholipid metabolites phosphoethanolamine, inositol and glycerol 3-phosphocholine and for the energy-related metabolites creatine and lactic acid. Therefore, the natural abundance ^{13}C NMR spectrum contains significant information about brain amino acid metabolism and some information about phospholipid and energy metabolism.

^{13}C NMR using ^{13}C-enriched substrates ^{13}C NMR in combination with ^{13}C-enriched substrates has proven to be a powerful and elegant analytical method to study selected areas of metabolism (Cohen, 1983, 1987a,b,c; Cohen and Shulman 1982). The advantage of the ^{13}C NMR studies is that all metabolites that have been adequately labeled are simultaneously detected, allowing flux through metabolic pathways to be analysed.

(3) ^{1}H NMR spectrum

^{1}H NMR spectra have been obtained for tissues and tissue extracts (Behar et al., 1983, 1984; Evanochko et al., 1984; Tanaka, 1986; Rosenberg et al., 1989). Identifiable resonances include those from amino acids and their derivatives such as glutamate, glutamine, aspartate, *N*-acetylaspartate, glycine, alanine, valine, taurine, leucine, phenylalanine, tyrosine, proline, γ-aminobutyrate and histidine; metabolites related to energy metabolism such as glucose, phosphocreatine, creatine, lactate and acetate; metabolites related to phospholipid metabolism such as phosphocholine and phosphoethanolamine; and metabolites related to nucleotide metabolism such as adenine, guanine,

uracil and cytosine. Because of the inherent sensitivity of ^{1}H NMR and since methods exist to suppress the large water signal, ^{1}H NMR studies of brain should be very informative.

(4) ^{23}Na and ^{7}Li NMR

^{23}Na NMR   Fundamentally important to human biological processes are sodium trans-membrane fluxes and intracellular sodium concentrations, including their modulation by means of exchange processes operating among the ion-coordinated ligands. These exchange processes serve to alter the chemical state of the ion and, hence, the position of delicately poised equilibria. Alterations in trans-membrane sodium unidirectional rate constants with resultant alterations in intracellular sodium concentration have been implicated in a number of human diseases. A few such diseases which are diverse in clinical phenotype include manic-depressive disease, essential hypertension and cystic fibrosis, as well as cellular proliferative responses during mitogenesis and oncogenesis. Since sodium trans-membrane fluxes are clearly dependent on the physiological integrity of the living cell and its membrane, the advantage of a non-invasive, non-perturbing technique for monitoring tissue sodium is obvious. ^{23}Na NMR spectroscopy is such a technique.

A recent ^{23}Na NMR study has demonstrated that a significant fraction of the sodium inside human erythrocytes is relatively immobilized (Pettegrew et al., 1984). This immobilization of intracellular sodium probably results from a transient coordination of the cation to functional groups of proteins or lipids. This observation has two immediate implications. The intracellular immobilization of sodium is likely to be genetically regulated and the degree of sodium immobilization will significantly affect sodium trans-membrane flux and secondarily cellular physiology.

^{7}Li NMR   Lithium ion has a demonstrated efficacy in the prophylactic treatment of manic depressive illness, the acute treatment of mania

and the treatment of some patients with schizophrenia. The molecular basis for the biological action of Li^+ is unknown, although it has been postulated that Li^+ competes for the binding sites of biological cations such as Na^+, K^+, Mg^{2+} and/or Ca^{2+} and that Li^+ interacts with membrane phospholipids. Li^+ has been demonstrated to inhibit the conversion of inositol phosphate to inositol + phosphate in the phosphatidylinositol second messenger pathway (Hallacher and Sherman, 1980). In addition, a recent ^7Li NMR study provided evidence that Li^+ interacts with the membrane-associated cytoskeleton in human erythrocytes (Pettegrew et al., 1987c). These observations taken together suggest that Li^+ interacts with important regulatory sites on the cytoplasmic surface of cellular membranes. These regulatory sites may be phosphorylated sites of polymers or enzymes. Therefore, ^7Li NMR would appear to be a very informative analytical approach to the intracellular chemistry of Li^+.

(5) Solid-state NMR of model membranes and brain tissues

Solid-state ^{31}P NMR spectroscopy In recent years there has been increasing interest in NMR of solids. This interest is the result of a series of instrument advances including mini-computer-based digital techniques, high-power radio frequency pulse sequences, high-power proton decoupling, cross-polarization and magic-angle sample spinning (for reviews see Maciel, 1984; Frye, 1989). For many years, the main applications of NMR were molecular structure analyses of liquid samples. The increasing applications of NMR of solid samples represents, however, a return to the early experiments in the field of NMR. Since the molecular motions in liquids result in very narrow lines compared to those in solids, much smaller chemical shifts could be detected. This led to the domination of high-resolution NMR in liquids. The broad NMR lines in solids generally precluded the detailed chemical shift measurements possible in liquids until the recent advances, mentioned

above, enabled the spectroscopist to mimic for solids the line-narrowing molecular motions in liquids.

^{31}P NMR studies of selected membranes To date, numerous solid state ^{31}P NMR studies have been performed on model membranes and biological membranes (for reviews, see Smith and Ekiel, 1984; Smith, 1989). These studies demonstrate that solid-state ^{31}P NMR can clearly differentiate the bilayer and hexagonal II phases. Calcium has been shown to induce bilayer to hexagonal II phase transitions in model membranes (Cullis and Hope, 1978; Hope et al., 1983). A recent study has also demonstrated that Al^{3+} can induce the bilayer to hexagonal II phase transition in model membranes and mammalian brain (Pettegrew, 1989, in press). These findings are of particular biological importance as the hexagonal II phase structure has been shown to enhance membrane fusion (Poste and Allison, 1973; Cullis and DeKruijff, 1979; Hope and Cullis, 1981; Nayar et al., 1982), and similar membrane alterations may contribute to the pathogenesis of Alzheimer's disease (Pettegrew and Panchalingam, 1989; Pettegrew et al., 1990, in press).

The application of solid-state NMR to the study of brain tissue will undoubtedly provide insights into membrane organization and function that are not available with any other technology. The solid-state NMR studies will be complementary to freeze-fracture electron microscopy studies of membranes.

(6) Two-dimensional Fourier transform NMR

Two-dimensional Fourier transform NMR (2D-FT NMR) techniques are powerful analytical approaches for determining molecular structure and conformation in solution (for reviews see Bax, 1984; Turner, 1985; Hutton, 1984; Bothner-By, 1989). A few examples to which these techniques have been successfully applied include the 65-residue protein hirudin (Sukumaran et al., 1987), the alkaloid gephyrotoxin ($C_{19}H_{29}NO_4$) (Edwards and Bax, 1986), coenzyme B_{12} ($M_r = 180$) (Summers et al., 1986) the antibiotic desertomycin ($M_r = 1192$) (Bax et al., 1986), the polynucleotide d(C-G-C-A-G-A-G-C-T-C-G-C-G) duplex (Hare et al., 1986a), the polynucleotide duplex d(C-G-T-G-A-A-T-T-C-G-C-G) (Hare et al., 1986b), and encephalon analogues (Hassan and Goodman, 1986; Mummi and Goodman, 1986). In addition, the molecular conformations derived from the 2D-FT NMR experiments can be used as starting points for computer-calculated energy-minimization studies yielding refined molecular conformations (Hare et al., 1986a,b; Hassan and Goodman, 1986). The application of artificial-intelligence techniques to 2D-FT NMR also has great potential for protein structure determination (Duncan et al., 1989). Therefore, it seems certain that 2D-FT NMR techniques will continue to make major contributions to understanding molecular conformation in solution. The determination of molecular conformation by 2D-FT NMR techniques is likely to find many applications in future neuroscience research.

(7) NMR microscopy (micro-imaging)

The first NMR image of a single cell was reported by Aguayo et al. (1986). This experiment was performed on a Bruker 9.4 Tesla NMR spectrometer in a collaborative effort between Johns Hopkins and Bruker Medical Instruments. This initial attempt yielded a resolution of 10×13 μm for a slice width of 250 μm, which was sufficient to identify intracellular structures in ova obtained from *Xenopus laevis*. The research possibilities that this accomplishment opens up are immense. Cellular structures and metabolic processes can now be investigated at single-cell level with NMR.

References

Aguayo J, Blackband S, Schoeninger J, Mattingly M, Hentermann M: Nuclear magnetic resonance imaging of a single cell. *Nature: 322,* 190 – 191, 1986.

Barany M, Yen-Chung C, Arus C, Rustan T, Frey W: Increased glycerol-3-phosphorylcholine in post-mortem Alzheimer's brain. (Letter) *Lancet: i,* 517, 1985.

Barnes PD, Lester PD, Yamanaski WS, Woosley RE, Wheatley KK: Magnetic resonance imaging in childhood intracranial masses. *Magnetic Resonance Imaging: 4,* 41 – 50, 1986.

Bax A: *Two-dimensional Nuclear Magnetic Resonance in Liquids.* Dordrecht: Delft University Press, 1984.

Bax A, Aszalos A, Dinya Z, Sudo K: Structure elucidation of the antibiotic desertomycin through the use of new two-dimensional NMR techniques. *J. Am. Chem. Soc.: 108,* 8056 – 8063, 1986.

Behar K, Hollander J, Stromski M, Ogino T, Shulman R: High resolution ^{1}H NMR studies of cerebral hypoxia in vivo. *Proc. Natl. Acad. Sci. USA: 80,* 4945 – 4948, 1983.

Behar K, Rothman D, Shulman R, Petroff O, Prichard J: Detection of cerebral lactate in vivo during hypoxemia by ^{1}H NMR at relatively low field strengths (1.9T). *Proc. Natl. Acad. Sci. USA: 81,* 2517 – 2519, 1984.

Beradi A, Haxby JV, Grady CL, Rapoport SI: Asymmetrics of brain glucose consumption and memory performance in mild dementia of the Alzheimer type and in healthy aging. *Neurology: 37,* 160, 1987.

Berent S, Foster NL, Gilman S, Hichwa R, Lehtinen S: Patterns of cortical ^{18}F-FDG metabolism in Alzheimer's and progressive supranuclear palsy patients are related to the types of cognitive impairments. *Neurology: 37,* 172, 1987.

Bloch F, Hansen WW, Packard ME: Nuclear induction. *Physics Rev.: 69,* 127, 1946.

Bloembergen N: Proton relaxation times in paramagnetic solutions. *J. Chem. Phys.: 27,* 572 – 573, 1957.

Bore PJ: The role of magnetic resonance spectroscopy in clinical medicine. *Magnetic Resonance Imaging: 3,* 407 – 413, 1985a.

Bore PJ: Principles and applications of phosphorus magnetic resonance spectroscopy. *Magnetic Resonance Annu.:* 45 – 69, 1985b.

Bothner-By AA: Two-dimensional fourier transform NMR: homonuclear and heteronuclear couplings-multiple quantum filtering. In Pettegrew JW (Editor), *NMR: The Principles and Applications of NMR Spectroscopy and Imaging to Biomedical Research.* New York: Springer-Verlag, Ch. 3, pp. 68 – 78, 1989.

Brasch R, Weinmann H, Wesbey G: Contrast-enhanced NMR imaging: animal studies using gadolinium-DTPA complex. *Am. J. Roentgenol.: 142,* 625 – 630, 1984.

Brown M, Stenzel T, Ribeiro A, Drayer B, Spicer L: NMR studies of combined lanthanide shift and relaxation agents for differential characterization of ^{23}Na in a two-compartment model system. *Magnetic Resonance Med.: 3,* 289 – 295, 1985.

Brown GG, Levins SR, Gorell JM, Pettegrew JW, Gdowski JW, Bueri JA, Helpern JA, Welch KMA: In vivo ^{31}P NMR profiles of Alzheimer's disease and multiple subcortical infarct dementia. *Neurology: 39,* 1423 – 1427, 1989.

Buell SJ, Coleman PD: Dendritic growth in the aged human brain and failure of growth in senile dementia. *Science: 206,* 854 – 856, 1979.

Buell SJ, Coleman PD: Quantitative evidence for selective dendritic growth in normal human aging but not in senile dementia. *Brain Res.: 241,* 23 – 41, 1981.

Cady EB, Dawson MJ, Hope PL, Tofts P, Costello A, Delpy

D, Reynolds E, Wilkie D: Non-invasive investigation of cerebral metabolism in newborn infants by phosphorus nuclear magnetic resonance spectroscopy. *Lancet: i,* 1059–1062, 1983.

Carr DH: The use of proton relaxation enhancers in magnetic resonance imaging. *Magnetic Resonance Imaging: 3,* 17–26, 1985.

Carr HY, Purcell EM: Effects of diffusion on free precession in NMR experiments. *Phys. Rev.: 94,* 630–638, 1954.

Carr DH, Brown J, Bydder G, Weinmann H, Speck U, Thomas D, Young I: Intravenous chelated gadolinium as a contrast agent in NMR imaging of cerebral tumors. *Lancet: i,* 484–486, 1984.

Cohen M, Lin S: Acid soluble phosphates in the developing rabbit brain. *J. Neurochem.: 9,* 345–352, 1962.

Cohen MM, Pettegrew JW, Kopp SJ, Minshew N, Glonek T: P-31 nuclear magnetic resonance analysis of brain. Normoxic and anoxic brain slices. *Neurochem. Res.: 9,* 785–801, 1984.

Cohen SM: The molecular organization of the red cell membrane skeleton. In Miescher P, Jaffe E (Editors), *Seminars in Hematology.* New York: Grune and Stratton, pp. 141–158, 1983.

Cohen SM: ^{13}C and ^{31}P NMR study of gluconeogenesis: utilization of ^{13}C-labeled substrates by hyperfused liver from streptozotocin-diabetic and untreated rats. *Biochemistry: 26,* 563–572, 1987a.

Cohen SM: Effects of insulin on perfused liver from streptozotocin-diabetic and untreated rats: ^{13}C NMR assay of pyruvate kinase flux. *Biochemistry: 26,* 573–580, 1987b.

Cohen SM: ^{13}C NMR study of effects of fasting and diabetes on the metabolism of pyruvate in the tricarboxylic acid cycle and of the utilization of pyruvate and ethanol in lipogenesis in perfused rat liver. *Biochemistry: 26,* 563–572, 1987c.

Cohen SM, Shulman RG: ^{13}C NMR studies of gluconeogenesis in hepatocytes from euthyroid and hyperthyroid rats in perfused mouse liver: in situ measurements of pyruvate kinase flux and pentose cycle activity. In Cohen J (Editor), *Noninvasive Probes of Tissues Metabolism.* New York: Wiley-Interscience, pp. 119–147, 1982.

Cullis PR, Hope MJ: Effects of fusogenic agent on membrane structure of erythrocyte ghosts and the mechanism of membrane fusion. *Nature: 271,* 670–672, 1978.

Cullis PR, De Kruijff B: Lipid polymorphism and the functional roles of lipids in biological membranes. *Biochim. Biophys. Acta: 559,* 399–420, 1979.

Cutler NR, Haxby JV, Duara R, Grady CL, Moore AM, Parisi JE, White J, Heston L, Margolin RM, Rapoport SI: Brain metabolism as measured with positron emission tomography: serial assessment in a patient with familial Alzheimer's disease. *Neurology: 35,* 1556–1561, 1985.

Damadian R: Tumor detection by NMR. *Science: 171,* 1151–1153, 1971.

Damadian R: Apparatus and method for detecting cancer in tissue. U.S. Patent no. 378983. Filed March, 1972.

Dawson RMC: Enzymatic pathways of phospholipid metabolism in the nervous system. In Eichberg J (Editor), *Phospholipids in Nervous Tissues.* New York: Wiley, pp. 45–78, 1985.

Dickinson WC: Collisions of the second order and their effect on the field of the positive column of a glow discharge and

mixture of the rare gases. *Phys. Rev.: 77,* 736, 1950.

Duara R, Grady C, Haxby J, Sundaram J, Cutler NR, Heston L, Moore A, Schlageter N, Larson S, Rapoport SI: Positron emission tomography in Alzheimer's disease: [^{18}F] 2-fluoro-2-deoxy-D-glucose study in the resting state. *Neurology: 36,* 879–887, 1986.

Duncan BS, Brinkley JF, Altman RB, Buchanan BG, Jardetzky O: Artificial intelligence techniques and NMR spectroscopy: application to the structure of proteins in solution. In Pettegrew JW (Editor), *NMR: The Principles and Applications of NMR Spectroscopy and Imaging to Biomedical Research.* New York: Springer-Verlag, Ch. 5, pp. 99–118, 1989.

Dunn V, Bale J Jr, Zimmerman RA, Purdue Z, Bell WE: MRI in children with post infectious disseminated encephalomyelitis. *Magnetic Resonance Imaging: 4,* 25–32, 1986a.

Dunn V, Mock T, Bell WE, Smith W: Detection of heterotopic gray matter in children by magnetic resonance imaging. *Magnetic Resonance Imaging: 4,* 33–39, 1986b.

Edwards M, Bax A: Complete proton and carbon-13 NMR assignment of the alkaloid gephyrotoxin through the use of homonuclear Hartmann-Hahn and two-dimensional NMR spectroscopy. *J. Am. Chem. Soc.: 108,* 918–923, 1986.

Ernst RR, Anderson WA: Application of fourier transform spectroscopy to magnetic resonance. *Rev. Sci. Instrum.: 37,* 93–102, 1966.

Evanochko W, Ng T, Glickson J: Application of in vivo NMR spectroscopy to cancer. *Magnetic Resonance Imaging: 1,* 508–534, 1984.

Farrar TC: Principles of pulse NMR spectroscopy. In Pettegrew JW (Editor), *NMR: Principles and Applications to Biomedical Research.* New York: Springer-Verlag, Ch. 1, pp. 1–36, 1989.

Fletcher WA, Sharpe JA: Saccadic eye movements dysfunction in Alzheimer's disease. *Ann. Neurol.: 20,* 464–471, 1986.

Fletcher WA, Sharpe JA: Smooth pursuit dysfunction in Alzheimer's disease. *Neurology: 38,* 272–276, 1988.

Friedland RP, Jagust WJ, Budinger TF, Koss E, Ober BA: Consistency of temporal parietal cortex hypometabolism in probable Alzheimer's disease (AD): relationships to cognitive decline. *Neurology: 37,* 224, 1987.

Frye JS: High-resolution NMR of solids. In Pettegrew JW (Editor), *NMR: The Principles and Applications of NMR Spectroscopy and Imaging to Biomedical Research.* New York: Springer-Verlag, Ch. 4, pp. 79–98, 1989.

Gdowski JW, Brown GG, Levine SR, Smith M, Helpern J, Bueri J, Gorell J, Welch KMA: Patterns of phospholipid metabolism differ between Alzheimer's and multi-infarct dementia. *Neurology: 38,* 286, 1988.

Geddes JW, Monaghan DT, Cotman CW, Lott IT, Kim RC, Chui HC: Plasticity of hippocampal circuitry in Alzheimer's disease. *Science: 230,* 1179–1181, 1985.

Glonek T, Kopp SJ, Kott E, Pettegrew JW, Harrison WH, Cohen MM: P-31 Nuclear magnetic resonance analysis of brain. I. The perchloric acid extract spectrum. *J. Neurochem.: 39,* 1210–1219, 1982.

Gore JC, McDonnell MJ, Pennock JM, Steinbrook HS: An assessment of the safety of rapidly changing magnetic fields in the rabbit: implications for NMR imaging. *Magnetic Resonance Imaging: 1,* 191–195, 1982.

Hahn EL: Spin echoes. *Phys. Rev.: 80,* 580–594, 1950.

Hallacher LM, Sherman WR: The effects of lithium ions and other agents on the activity myo-inositol-1-phosphatase from bovine brain. *J. Biol. Chem.: 255,* 896 – 910, 1980.

Hare D, Shapiro L, Patel D: Extrahelical adenosine stacks into right-handed DNA: solution conformation of the d(c-g-t-g-a-a-t-t-c-g-c-g) duplex deduced from distance geometry analysis of nuclear overhauser effect spectra. *Biochemistry: 25,* 7456 – 7464, 1986a.

Hare D, Shapiro L, Patel D: Wobble DG · DT pairing in right-handed DNA: solution conformation of the d(c-g-t-g-a-a-t-t-c-g-c-g) duplex deduced from distance geometry analysis of nuclear overhauser effect spectra. *Biochemistry: 25,* 7445 – 7456, 1986b.

Harris RK: Introduction. In Harris RK, Mann BE (Editors), *NMR and the Periodic Table.* New York: Academic Press, Ch. 1, pp. 1 – 19, 1978.

Hassan M, Goodman M: Computer simulations of cyclic encephalon analogues. *Biochemistry: 25,* 7596 – 7606, 1986.

Haxby JV, Grady CL, Ross E, Friedland RP, Rapoport SI: Heterogenous metabolic and neuropsychological patterns in dementia of the Alzheimer type: cross-sectional and longitudinal studies. *Neurology: 37,* 159, 1987.

Hope MJ, Cullis PR: The role of nonbilayer lipid structures in the fusion of human erythrocytes induced by lipid fusogens. *Biochim. Biophys. Acta: 640,* 82 – 90, 1981.

Hope MJ, Walker DC, Cullis PR: Ca^{2+} and pH induced fusion of small unilamellar vesicles consisting of phosphatidylethanolamine and negatively charged phospholipids: a freeze fracture study. *Biochem. Biophys. Res. Commun.: 110,* 15 – 22, 1983.

Horwitz B, Grady CL, Schlageter NL, Duara R, Rapoport SI: Intercorrelations of regional cerebral glucose metabolic rates in Alzheimer's disease. *Brain Res.: 407,* 294 – 306, 1987.

Huberty J: NMR contrast enhancements of the kidneys and liver with paramagnetic metal complexes. *Soc. Magnetic Resonance:* 175 – 176, 1983.

Hutton WC: Two-dimensional phosphorus-31 NMR. In: Gorenstein DG (Editor), *Phosphorus 31 NMR.* Orlando: Academic Press, pp. 479 – 510, 1984.

Iles RA: NMR studies of metabolites in living tissues. *Prog. NMR Spectrosc.: 15,* 49 – 200, 1982.

Innis NK, Ossenkopp KP, Prato FS, Sestini E: Behavioral effects of exposure to nuclear magnetic resonance imaging: II. Spatial memory tests. *Magnetic Resonance Imaging: 4,* 281 – 284, 1986.

Jagust WJ, Friedland RP, Koss E, Ober BA, Mathis CA, Huseman RH, Budinger TF: Progression of regional cerebral glucose metabolic abnormalities in Alzheimer's disease. *Neurology: 37,* 156, 1987.

James ACD: Schizophrenia psychosis and adrenomyeloneuropathy. *J. R. Soc. Med.: 77,* 882 – 884, 1984.

Kanfer JN, McCartney DG: Phosphatase and phospholipase activity in Alzheimer brain tissues. In Wurtman RJ, Corkin S, Growden JH (Editors), *Topics in the Basic and Clinical Science of Dementia.* Wien, New York: Springer-Verlag, Suppl. 24, J. Neural Transmission, pp. 183 – 188, 1987.

Kanfer JN, Pettegrew JW, Moossy J et al.: Possible enzymatic causes for elevated phosphomonoesters in Alzheimer's brain. Presented at the Academy of Neurology Annual Meeting April 30 – May 6, (Abstract) 1990.

Knight WD: Nuclear magnetic resonance shifts in metals. *Phys. Rev.: 76,* 1259, 1949.

Lacal JC, Moscat J, Aaronson S: Novel source of 1,2-diacylglycerol elevated in cells transformed by Ha-ras oncogene. *Nature: 330,* 19, 269 – 271, 1987.

Lauterbur PC: Augmentation of tissue water proton spin-lattice relaxation rates by in vivo addition of paramagnetic ions. *Front. Biol. Energet.: 1,* 752 – 759, 1978.

Lawler GA, Pennock J, Steiner R, Jenkins W, Sherlock S, Young I: NMR imaging in Wilson's disease. *J. Comput. Assist. Tomogr.: 7,* 1 – 8, 1983.

Lee SW, Hilal SK, Cho ZH: Multinuclear magnetic resonance imaging technique – simultaneous proton and sodium imaging. *Magnetic Resonance Imaging: 4,* 343 – 350, 1986.

Lovin J, Wesbey G, Englestad B, Sosnovsky G, Moseley M, Tuck D, Brasch R: Magnetic field dependence of spin-lattice relaxation enhancement using piperdinyl nitroxyl spin-labels. *Magnetic Resonance Imaging: 3,* 73 – 82, 1985.

Lowe IJ, Norberg RE: Free-induction decays in solids. *Phys. Rev.: 107,* 46 – 61, 1957.

Lukes SA, Aminoff M, Crooks L: NMR imaging in movement disorders. *Ann. Neurol.: 13,* 690 – 691, 1983.

Maciel GE: High-resonance NMR in solids. *Science: 226,* 282 – 287, 1984.

Maris JM, Audrey B, Evans E: ^{31}P NMR spectroscopic investigation of human neuroblastoma in situ. *N. Engl. J. Med.: 312,* 1500 – 1505, 1985.

McCarthy S: Magnetic resonance imaging in obstetrics and gynecology. *Magnetic Resonance Imaging: 4,* 59 – 66, 1986.

McClure RJ, Pettegrew JW: Computer molecular modeling of L-glutamate agonists and antagonists. (Abstract) *Neurology: 39,* 398, 1989.

Meiboom S, Gill D: Modified spin-echo method for measuring nuclear relaxation times. *Rev. Sci. Instrum.: 29,* 688 – 691, 1958.

Moseley ME, Chew WM, Nishimura MC, Richards TL, Murphy-Boesch J, Young GB, Marschner TM, Pitts LH, James TL: In vivo sodium-23 magnetic resonance surface coil imaging: observing experimental cerebral ischemia in the rat. *Magnetic Resonance Imaging: 3,* 383 – 387, 1985.

Mummi NJ, Goodman M: Conformational analysis of cyclical partially modified retro-inversion encephalon analogues by proton NMR. *Biochemistry: 25,* 7607 – 7614, 1986.

Nayar R, Hope MJ, Cullis PR: Phospholipids as adjuncts for calcium ion stimulated release of chromaffin granule contents: implications for mechanisms of exocytosis. *Am. Chem. Soc.: 82,* 4583 – 4589, 1982.

Nishizuka Y: Studies and perspectives of protein kinase C. *Science: 233,* 305 – 312, 1986.

Nunnally RL, Babcock EE, Horner SD, Peshach RM: Fluorine-19 NMR spectroscopy and imaging investigations of myocardial perfusion and cardiac function. *Magnetic Resonance Imaging: 3,* 399 – 405, 1985.

Osbakken M, Griffith J, Taczanowsky P: A gross morphologic, histologic and blood chemistry study of adult and neonatal mice chronologically exposed to high magnetic fields. *Magnetic Resonance Imaging: 3,* 502 – 517, 1986.

Ossenkopp KP, Innis NK, Prato FS, Sestini E: Behavioral effects of exposure to nuclear magnetic resonance imaging: I. Open-field behavior and passive avoidance learning in rats.

Magnetic Resonance Imaging: 4, 275 – 280, 1986.

Pauli W: Coordination of the complete structure terms in strong and weak external fields. *Z. Physics: 20*, 371 – 387, 1924.

Pennock JM, Bydder GM, Dubowitz IMS, Johnson MA: Magnetic resonance imaging of the brain in children. *Magnetic Resonance Imaging: 4*, 1 – 9, 1986.

Pettegrew JW, Panchalingam K: Solid state ^{31}P and ^{27}Al NMR studies of model membranes and mammalian brain possible implications for Alzheimer's disease. In Pettegrew JW (Editor), *NMR: Principles and Applications to Biomedical Research*. New York: Springer-Verlag, Ch. 10, pp. 310 – 354, 1989.

Pettegrew JW: Molecular insights into Alzheimer's disease. In Khachaturia Z, Cotman C, Pettegrew JW (Editors), *Calcium, Membranes, Aging and Alzheimer's Disease*. New York: New York Academy of Sciences. 1989; in press.

Pettegrew JW, Glonek T, Baskin F, Rosenberg RN: Phosphorus-31 NMR of neuroblastoma clonal lines: effect of cell confluency state and dibutyryl cyclic AMP. *Neurochem. Res.: 4*, 795 – 801, 1979.

Pettegrew JW, Minshew NJ, Glonek T, Kopp SJ, Cohen MM: Phosphorus-31 Nuclear Magnetic Resonance analysis of Huntington and control brain. *Ann. Neurol.: 12*, 91, 1982.

Pettegrew JW, Kopp SJ, Dadok J, Minshew NJ, Feliksik JM, Glonek T, Cohen MM: Chemical characterization of a prominent phosphorylmonoester resonance in animal, Huntington's and Alzheimer's brain: ^{31}P and ^{1}H NMR analysis at 4.7 and 14.1 Tesla. *Ann. Neurol.: 16*, 136 – 137, 1984.

Pettegrew JW, Kopp SJ, Minshew NJ, Glonek T, Feliksik JM, Tow JP, Cohen MM: ^{31}P NMR studies of phospholipid metabolism in developing and degenerating brain. *Neurology: 35*, 257, 1985.

Pettegrew JW, Kopp SJ, Dadok J, Minshew NJ, Feliksik JM, Glonek T, Cohen MM: Chemical characterization of a prominent phosphomonoester resonance from mammalian brain: ^{31}P and ^{1}H NMR analysis at 4.7 and 14.1 Tesla. *J. Magnetic Resonance: 67*, 443 – 450, 1986.

Pettegrew JW, Kopp SJ, Minshew NJ, Glonek T, Feliksik JM, Tow JP, Cohen MM: ^{31}P nuclear magnetic resonance studies of phosphoglyceride metabolism in developing and degenerating brain: preliminary observations. *J. Neuropathol. Exp. Neurol.: 46*, 419 – 430, 1987a.

Pettegrew JW, Withers G, Panchalingam K, Post JFM: ^{31}P Nuclear Magnetic Resonance (NMR) spectroscopy of brain in aging and Alzheimer's disease. *J. Neur. Transm.: 24*, 261 – 268, 1987b.

Pettegrew JW, Post JFM, Panchalingam K, Withers G, Woessner DE: ^{7}Li NMR study of normal human erythrocytes. *J. Magnetic Resonance: 71*, 504 – 519, 1987c.

Pettegrew JW, Moossy J, Withers G, McKeag D, Panchalingam K: ^{31}P Nuclear magnetic resonance study of brain in Alzheimer's disease. *J. Neuropathol. Exp. Neurol.: 47*, 235 – 248, 1988a.

Pettegrew JW, Panchalingam K, Moossy J, Martinez J, Rao G, Boller F: Correlation of Phosporus-31 magnetic resonance spectroscopy and morphologic findings in Alzheimer's disease. *Arch. Neurol.: 45*, 1093 – 1096, 1988b.

Pettegrew JW, Panchalingam K, Withers G, McKeag D, Strychor S: Changes in brain energy and phospholipid

metabolism during development and aging in the Fischer 344 Rat. *J. Neuropathol. Exp. Neurol.:* 1990 in press.

Porcellati G, Arienti G: Metabolism of phosphoglycerides. In Lajtha J (Editor), *Handbook of Neurochemistry, Vol. 3*. New York: Plenum Press, pp. 133 – 61, 1983.

Poste D, Allison AC: Membrane fusion. *Biochim. Biophys. Acta: 300*, 421 – 465, 1973.

Prasad N, Wright DA, Forster JD: Effect of NMR on early stages of amphibian development. *Magnetic Resonance Imaging: 1*, 35 – 38, 1982.

Prasad N, Bushang C, Thornby JE, Bryan RN, Hazlewood CF, Harrell JE: Effect of nuclear magnetic resonance on chromosomes of mouse bone marrow cells. *Magnetic Resonance Imaging: 2*, 37 – 39, 1984.

Prato FS, Ossenkopp KP, Kavaliers M, Sestini E, Teskey GC: Attentuation of morphine-induced analgesia in mice by exposure to magnetic resonance imaging: separate effects of the static, radiofrequency and time-varying magnetic fields. *Magnetic Resonance Imaging: 5*, 9 – 14, 1987.

Proctor WG, Yu FC: The disorder of NMR frequency in chemical compounds. *Phys. Rev.: 77*, 717, 1950.

Purcell EM, Torrey HC, Pound RV: Resonance absorption by nuclear magnetic moments in solids. *Phys. Rev.: 69*, 37, 1946.

Rabi I: The gyromagnetic properties of the hydrogens. *Phys. Rev.: 50*, 472 – 481, 1939.

Radda GK, Taylor DJ, Styles P, Matthews P, Arnold D, Gadian D, Bore P: Exercise-induced ATT depletions in normal muscle. *Magnetic Resonance Med.: 1*, 229, 1984.

Radda GK, Taylor DJ: Energetics of human muscle: exercise-induced ATP depletion. *Magnetic Resonance Med.: 3*, 44 – 54, 1985.

Rapoport SI, Horwitz B, Haxby J, Grady CL: Alzheimer's disease: metabolic uncoupling of associative brain regions. *Can. J. Neurol. Sci.: 13*, 540 – 545.

Renshaw PF: Ferromagnetic contrast agents: a new approach. *Magnetic Resonance Med.: 3*, 217 – 225, 1986.

Renshaw PF, Owen CS, Evans AE, McLaughlin A, Leigh JS Jr: Immunospecific NMR contrast agents. *Magnetic Resonance Imaging: 4*, 351 – 357, 1986.

Rosenberg GA, Kyner E, Gasparovic C, Griffey RH, Matwiyoff NA: ^{1}H-NMR spectroscopy of brain. In Pettegrew JW (Editor), *NMR: Principles and Applications to Biomedical Research*. New York: Springer-Verlag, Ch. 14, pp. 468 – 484, 1989.

Runge VM: The use of DTPA as a perfusion agent and marker of bloodbrain barrier disruption. *Magnetic Resonance Imaging: 3*, 43 – 45, 1985.

Scheibel AB: Dendritic changes in senile and presenile dementias. In Katzman R (Editor), *Congenital and Acquired Cognitive Disorders*. Based on Proceedings of the 57th Annual Meeting of the Association for Research in Nervous and Mental Diseases, 2 – 3 December 1977. New York: Raven Press (Research Publication Volume 57), pp. 107 – 124, 1979.

Shreve P, Aisen MA: Monoclinical antibodies labeled with polymeric paramagnetic ion chelates. *Magnetic Resonance Imaging: 3*, 336 – 340, 1986.

Slane JMK, Lai C, Hyde J: A proton relaxation enhancement investigation of the binding of fatty acid spin labels to human serum albumin. *Magnetic Resonance Imaging: 3,* 699 – 706, 1986.

Smith F, Runge V, Permezel M, Smith C: NMR imaging in the diagnosis of spinal osteomyelitis. *Magnetic Resonance Imaging: 2,* 53 – 56, 1984.

Smith I, Ekiel I: ^{31}P NMR of phospholipids in membranes. In Gorenstein DG (Editor), *Phosphorus 31-NMR.* New York: Academic Press, pp. 447 – 474, 1984.

Smith ICP: Application of solid state NMR to the lipids of model and biological membranes. In Pettegrew JW (Editor), *NMR: The Principles and Applications of NMR Spectroscopy and Imaging to Biomedical Research.* New York: Springer-Verlag, Ch. 6, pp. 124 – 156, 1989.

Solomon I: Relaxation processes in a system of two spins. *Phys. Rev.: 99,* 559 – 565, 1955.

Sukumaaran DK, Clore G, Preuss A, Zarbock J, Gronenborn A: Proton NMR study of hirudin: resonance assignment and secondary structure. *Biochemistry: 26,* 332 – 338, 1987.

Summers M, Marzilli L, Bax A: Complete ^{1}H and ^{13}C assignments of coenzyme B_{12} through the use of new two-dimensional NMR experiments. *J. Am. Chem. Soc.: 108,* 4285 – 4294, 1986.

Swartz HM, Chen K, Pals M, Sentjurc M, Morse P: Hypoxia-sensitive NMR contrast agents. *Magnetic Resonance Imaging: 3,* 169 – 174, 1986.

Sweetland J, Kertesz A, Prato FS, Nantua K: The effect of magnetic resonance imaging on human cognition. *Magnetic Resonance Imaging: 5,* 129 – 135, 1987.

Tanaka C: Proton nuclear magnetic resonance spectra of brain tumors. *Magnetic Resonance Imaging: 4,* 503 – 508, 1986.

Turner DL: Basic two-dimensional NMR. *Prog. NMR Spectrosc.: 17,* 281 – 358, 1985.

Vermess M: NMR imaging of the brain in systemic lupus erythematosus. *J. Comput. Assist. Tomography: 7,* 461 – 467, 1983.

Woessner DE: Relaxation theory with applications to biological studies. In Pettegrew JW (Editor), *NMR: Principles and Applications to Biomedical Research.* New York: Springer-Verlag, Ch. 2, pp. 37 – 67, 1989.

Younkin DP: Unique aspects of human newborn cerebral metabolism evaluated with phosphorus NMR spectroscopy. *Lancet: i,* 1059 – 1062, 1984.

Zimmerman RA, Bilanicik LT: Applications of magnetic resonance imaging in diseases of the pediatric central nervous system. *Magnetic Resonance Imaging: 4,* 11 – 24, 1986.

© 1991 Elsevier Science Publishers B.V.
Handbook of Neuropsychology, Vol. 5
F. Boller and J. Grafman (Eds)

CHAPTER 5

Treatment strategies in primary degenerative dementias

Erich Mohr[1] and Thomas N. Chase[2]

[1]*Royal Ottawa Hospital, Neuropsychology Service, University of Ottawa, School of Psychology and Faculty of Medicine, Ottawa, Ontario, Canada, and* [2]*Experimental Therapeutics Branch, National Institute of Neurological Disorders and Stroke, Bethesda, MD, U.S.A.*

Primary degenerative dementia is one of the major health problems in the world today. Social and medical costs are staggering and are likely to rise further, as medical advances continue to increase longevity. Development of effective treatment strategies is therefore an increasingly important research goal. Primary degenerative dementia is defined as a deterioration in intellectual functioning, severe enough to interfere significantly with work or usual social activities or relationship with others (American Psychiatric Association, 1987). Intellectual deterioration mainly involves deficits in memory (Katzman, 1986a,b), but may include abnormalities in language functioning and in visuospatial abilities or present as a global cognitive decline (Martin et al., 1986). Various factors have been implicated in the clinical features of these disorders, including age at onset (Filley et al., 1986), rate of progression (Mann et al., 1989), neurotransmitter characteristics (Agid et al., 1986) or molecular genetic factors (Tanzi et al., 1989). Most individuals with primary degenerative dementia are now diagnosed as having Alzheimer's disease (Thal, 1988). Other diagnostic entities subsumed within the rubric of primary degenerative dementia include the dementing sequelae of Parkinson's disease (Brown and Marsden, 1984, 1987; Mohr et al., 1991), Huntington's disease (Goldberg et al., 1990; Starkstein et al., 1988; Weinberger et al., 1988), progressive supranuclear palsy (Maher and Lees, 1986) and Pick's disease (Poppe et al., 1985). Although many of the characteristics of these disorders tend to be distinct, there are several features which they may have in common. In particular, commonalities may include variable involvement of monoaminergic, cholinergic and peptidergic transmitter systems (Carlsson, 1987; Whitehouse et al., 1988), and characteristic neuronal pathological changes (Probst et al., 1988). While Alzheimer's disease will serve as the focus of discussion here, some of the approaches outlined may have applications for all primary degenerative dementias. Excluded will be the cognitive loss associated with normal aging, i.e., age-associated memory impairment (Crook et al., 1986b), as well as pseudodementia occurring in patients with depression (Lishman, 1987) or related to other etiological factors (Roberts, 1984).

Diagnostic accuracy for Alzheimer's disease during life depends at present entirely on clinical criteria, since there is no known biological marker for this disorder (McKhann et al., 1984). Alzheimer's disease is a dementing disorder of insidious onset and inexorable progression, with usual onset in later adult life. Its etiology remains unknown. It is now recognized as a major public health problem (5 – 15% of those over 65 and 20% of those over 80 years of age suffer from dementia, approximately half of those from Alzheimer's disease; Katzman, 1986a). Clinical features include characteristic changes in memory and in verbal and visuospatial cognitive function mainly reflecting abnormalities in the hippocampus and parietotemporal association cortex (Chase et al., 1984, 1985; Foster et al., 1984) as well as variable changes in frontal lobe mediated behaviors (Chase et al., 1987; Mann et al., 1989). Restlessness, mood alterations, hallucinations, delusions and altered sleep – waking cycle may also be present (Katzman, 1986a).

Experimental design issues

Preclinical models

The development of satisfactory preclinical models for primary degenerative dementia is still an elusive goal. While present animal models may provide critical clues, in particular with respect to neurochemical changes, their general reliance on static central nervous system lesions tends to limit their usefulness as models of the dynamic, diffuse lesions which develop as a consequence of primary degenerative dementia (Mohr et al., 1990a). A further complication in the use of animal models is related to their enormous diversity (Bartus, 1988). One of the main problems cited in this context is the lack of consensus with respect to the brain structures which are involved in normal and abnormal memory processes (Kordower and Gash, 1988). Pharmacological reversal trials, such as the reversal of scopolamine-induced amnesia with cholinomimetics (Bartus and Johnson, 1976; Smith, 1988) in the experimental animal, on the other hand, have led to increased refinement in clinical trial methodology (Sunderland et al., 1985b, 1986). Furthermore, clinical trials at present frequently occur as a consequence of preclinical findings, such as the recent trials of various noradrenomimetic agents (Mohr et al., 1989b; Schlegel et al., 1989), where experimental rationale was largely based on work in the experimental animal. In spite of present limitations, preclinical models, particularly pharmacological reversal, will continue to provide valuable information with respect to treatment strategies. In particular, reversal models might allow for the development of 'drug screens' predictive of the antidementia efficacy of a particular compound in an individual patient (sensitivity to pharmacological blockage would predict response to a pharmacological enhancer).

Clinical trials

Studies assessing the effects of a treatment by comparing outcome measures of a patient group either with itself while on control treatment or with an alternative group receiving control therapy (Bornstein, 1991) are the bench mark of efficacy evaluation (McKhann, 1989). A whole host of factors need to be considered when conducting clinical trials, such as patient inclusion criteria and affective state as well as choice of outcome measures and statistical considerations (Albert, 1991; Altshuler et al., 1991; Brouwers and Mohr, 1991; Larrabee and Crook, 1991; Mohr et al., 1991b).

Patient selection in particular is of critical importance (Morris and Thompson, 1990). More than 60 causes of dementia have been identified to date (Moos et al., 1988). Diagnostic screening, which should include as a minimum a careful history, general physical examination, neurological examination, neuropsychological work-up as well as extensive laboratory testing (Table 1) (Mohr et al., 1991b), should be the norm at the onset of any clinical trial.

The selection of appropriate outcome measures, while seemingly obvious, is often given too little attention. General guidelines include careful con-

TABLE 1

Diagnostic assessment for dementia

1. History
2. Physical examination
3. Neurological examination
4. Neuropsychological examination
5. Chest X-ray
6. Computer tomography or magnetic resonance imaging scan
7. Cerebrospinal fluid
8. Electrocardiogram
9. Laboratory testing:
    – full blood count and film, erythrocyte sedimentation rate
    – serology for syphilis
    – thyroid function test, liver function tests
    – electrolytes, calcium, urea
    – vitamin B12, folate
10. Electroencephalogram

ideration of the length and complexity of the test battery with respect to range of cognitive impairment levels of the target population, availability of multiple test forms as well as standardization of the tests in question (Albert, 1991; Gamzu and Gracon, 1988; Morris and Thompson, 1991). Furthermore, few empirical data exist to date on the question of learning effects with multiple test forms in demented populations. Of specific import might be the concept of 'testing toward the deficit' in clinical trials. This would entail concentrating neuropsychological outcome measures on those domains known to be affected by a particular compound or compound family. For example, testing of noradrenomimetic agents in primary degenerative dementia should take into account what is known thus far on the role of noradrenaline in learning and memory (Mohr et al., 1989b). Furthermore, given the neuroanatomical projections of the noradrenergic system from locus coeruleus to the frontal lobe, a cognitive test battery might at the very least include measures sensitive to frontal lobe function. Careful selection of non-cognitive measures such as the ease with which demented patients might adjust to test failure (which is necessary to avoid ceiling effects) needs to be considered as well (Albert, 1991; Altshuler et al., 1991). Cognitive improvement as a direct consequence of ameliorated central nervous system function has to be differentiated from secondary effects of neuropsychological test performance due to an alteration in affective state related to pharmacological or environmental factors. Accurate assessment of mood state and other affective variables is therefore crucial to the clinical evaluation of antidementia compounds (Altshuler et al., 1991). Finally, behavioral observations with respect to patients' social and communication skills, as well as self-care (activities of daily living) need to form an integral part of any drug efficacy evaluation in dementia (Growdon, in press).

Clinical trial design

Since early stages of drug development (Phase I studies) are often performed with young subjects, potential age-related differences in drug metabolism, bioavailability and pharmacokinetics have to be carefully evaluated. One of the widely accepted standards for clinical trials is the double-blind, placebo-controlled randomized cross-over design (Gracon et al., 1991; McKhann, 1989). However, novel study designs, including enrichment through selection of patients who respond to treatment, can reduce the number of subjects needed to evaluate a particular compound, while increasing the ability to identify a true drug response (Gracon et al., 1991). Furthermore, actual replacement characteristics of given drugs need to be considered. For example, in patients with long-term cognitive disability it may be important to replace defective neurotransmitter function continuously rather than intermittently, and chronically rather than acutely. Moreover, the lack of efficacy of antidementia drugs may indicate either that the hypothesis which generated the clinical trial was incorrect or that the drug failed to exert its intended pharmacological action within the central nervous system. Analyses of cerebrospinal fluid constituents or positron emission tomography scanning results often appear helpful in making these distinctions.

Ethical considerations

Three ethical principles are of particular importance in the development of clinical research protocols in general and drug trials in particular. (1) Respect for the individual, which pertains to the notion of autonomy, the control over one's own body and mind (Schwartz, 1981). This concept gives rise to the legal requirement of 'truly competent, voluntary, and informed consent' before participation as a subject in clinical research (Dept. Health Hum. Serv., 1981). (2) The principle of beneficence, which requires that the risk benefit ratio of any proposed research is acceptable (Schwartz, 1981). (3) The principle of justice, which stipulates that research subjects are selected equitably and that no group (e.g. the poor, the elderly, the institutionalized) are over-represented (Schwartz, 1981). One of the most difficult principles to deal with in the context of development of efficacious therapies in primary degenerative dementias is the provision for 'truly

AUGUSTANA UNIVERSITY COLLEGE
LIBRARY .

competent, voluntary and informed consent' (Dept. Health Hum. Serv., 1981; Med. Res. Council Can., 1987). The mere fact that a patient suffers from primary degenerative dementia is not sufficient to render him or her legally incompetent to consent (Schwartz, 1981). Even if a person is not found legally incompetent to provide informed consent, the clinician might still act both illegally and unethically to accept as competent a consent from a subject who cannot weigh the risks and benefits of participation in a particular investigation (Rosoff, 1981; Schwartz, 1981). Present guidelines do not provide a final, definitive answer as to who is to be considered sufficiently competent to consent. The consent process must therefore take into account individual needs and ensure that pertinent information is imparted, in terms of both content and timing, so that it will maximize the patient's ability to provide truly competent, voluntary and informed consent (Schwartz, 1981). Whenever possible clinical trials should avoid inclusion of: (1) the most severely demented; (2) mainly aged individuals; and (3) nursing home or other institutionalized patients. In all cases individual patient needs must be carefully considered and accommodated (Schwartz, 1981).

Symptomatic (palliative) therapies

Transmitter replacement strategies

Attempts to develop such therapies are based on the successful palliation of Parkinson's disease with dopaminomimetic compounds (Cotzias et al., 1969; Hornykiewicz, 1966). In the primary degenerative dementias, however, it remains unclear which transmitter system or systems are critically involved.

Despite numerous attempts to develop effective palliative treatments for primary degenerative dementias in general and Alzheimer's disease in particular, next to no success has been reported to date (Ashford et al., 1981; Drachman et al., 1982; Litvan et al., 1989; Mohr et al., 1986,1989b; Schlegel et al., 1989; Stern et al., 1987). This relative failure might be related to several factors: central among these are the uncertain predictive values of existing animal models. In addition, inadequate assurance of cen-

tral pharmacological activity may play a role, including length of exposure to pharmacological compounds (reliance on brief and/or intermittent therapy rather than long-term infusion to ensure continuous bioavailability of compound). Finally, there are considerable doubts about the possibilities for success of the transmitter replacement approach in the face of the multisystem abnormalities characteristic of these disorders.

The current lack of consensus as to what constitutes appropriate outcome measures provides further obstacles. Minimum requirements for successful trials of palliative treatment strategies in primary degenerative dementias would include matching individual patient's transmitter deficits (see Table 2) with a particular drug's pharmacological action ('treating toward the deficit'). Postsynaptic receptor integrity (e.g. through cerebral imaging or pharmacological challenge approaches) would have to be ensured. The provision of chronic, steady-state replacement, with concomitant monitoring of central drug levels and pharmacological effects, can be of import in the initial testing phases of a compound. Suppression of peripheral deleterious side-effects with peripheral antagonists (e.g. glycopyrrelate with cholinomimetics) helps identify centrally mediated effects. Finally, use of neuropsychological measures based on the principle of 'testing toward the deficit' may aid in the identification of efficacious compounds.

TABLE 2

Transmitter system selective biochemical assays and pharmacological agents[a]

System	CSF	Antagonist	Agonist
ACh	–[a]	Scopolamine	Physostigmine
NE	MHPG	Yohimbine	Clonidine
5-HT	5-HIAA	Ketanserin	5-Hydroxytryptophan
SRIF	SRIF	Cysteamine	Sandostatin
GLUT	GLU	MK-801	Milacemide

[a]These limited examples ignore the complexities of transmitter receptor subtypes.

Acetylcholine

The cholinergic hypothesis of intellectual dysfunction in Alzheimer's disease (Perry, 1986, 1988; Perry et al., 1978) as well as certain other primary degenerative dementias (e.g. some demented parkinsonian patients) (Agid et al., 1986) reflects the most consistently implicated transmitter deficit. Several sources of empirical evidence support this notion: first, the loss of cholinergic cortical terminals due to degeneration of projections from the basal nucleus of Meynert and other ventral forebrain nuclei (Bruno et al., 1986; Coyle et al., 1983; Davies and Maloney, 1976; Mouradian et al., 1988b; Whitehouse et al., 1982), and, second, the close relation between the decline in cortical choline acetyltransferase and the degree of cognitive impairment (Perry et al., 1978). Pharmacological studies have demonstrated impairment of intellectual and memory functions with cholinergic antagonists in normal individuals (Drachman, 1977; Drachman and Leavitt, 1974; Sunderland et al., 1987) as well as demented patients (Sunderland et al., 1985a,b, 1987). The observation that postsynaptic muscarinic receptor sites remain largely unaltered in Alzheimer's disease (Holman et al., 1985; Mash et al., 1985; Whitehouse and Kin Sing Au, 1986) gave rise to three main conceptual approaches to the experimental treatment of Alzheimer's disease: (1) attempts to increase synthesis of acetylcholine through administration of metabolic precursors such as choline or phosphatidylcholine (Etienne et al., 1981); (2) efforts to elevate intrasynaptic acetylcholine by inhibiting its enzymatic degradation with drugs such as physostigmine or tetrahydroaminoacridine (THA) (Beller et al., 1985; Christie et al., 1981; Davis and Mohs, 1982; Summers et al., 1986); (3) use of direct cholinergic agonists such arecoline (Christie et al., 1981; Tariot et al., 1988) and RS-86 (Bruno et al., 1986; Mouradian et al., 1988b) to stimulate acetylcholine receptors situated postsynaptic to the degenerating cortical projections.

Metabolic precursors of acetylcholine, such as choline or phosphatidylcholine, have been administered alone or in combination with inhibitors of the transmitter's degradation. Use of these compounds as monotherapies has failed to produce promising results in either acute (Brinkman et al., 1982; Dysken et al., 1982; Smith et al., 1978; Sullivan et al., 1982; Weintraub et al., 1983) or relatively long-term studies (Etienne et al., 1981; Little et al., 1985). Combined administration of cholinergic precursors and metabolic degradation blockers has not, as yet, been found to substantially improve the value of precursor monotherapy (Kaye et al., 1982).

Numerous studies have attempted to evaluate the therapeutic efficacy of drugs that block acetylcholine degradation. All act by inhibiting the enzyme, acetylcholinesterase, which metabolizes acetylcholine and contributes to the regulation of transmitter levels in the synaptic cleft. While some reports claimed improvement of circumscribed aspects of cognitive function with these acetylcholinesterase inhibitors (e.g. Beller et al., 1985; Christie et al., 1981; Davis and Mohs, 1982; Moos et al., 1985; Summers et al., 1986), overall results remain equivocal, since many others found no significant changes (e.g. Ashford et al., 1981; Drachman et al., 1982; Jotkowitz, 1983; Schwartz and Kohlstaedt, 1986; Stern et al., 1987). Physostigmine therapy may in fact be limited by several properties specific to this compound, which could theoretically be overcome by other cholinesterase-inhibiting agents. Among these are erratic absorption after oral ingestion, short duration of action and pronounced cholinergic side effects (Growdon, in press). THA (tacrine) and the pharmacologically related compound HP-029 reportedly have fewer limitations and are now the focus of several multicenter trials. Nevertheless, early claims of dramatic improvement in cognitive status in demented patients with THA treatment (Summers et al., 1986) have yet to be substantiated. While neuropsychological test results suggest improvement in some patients, the gains of safely administered dose levels now appear generally modest and of uncertain clinical value.

Therapeutic attempts with directly acting cholinergic agonists such as RS-86 (Bruno et al., 1986; Mouradian et al., 1988b), arecoline (Christie et al., 1981; Wettstein and Spiegel, 1984) or bethanechol (Davous and Lamour, 1985) have also failed to produce consistent therapeutic benefits. These negative results occurred despite experiments with administration routes (intraventricular infusion pump to improve entry into the central nervous system and minimize peripheral side-effects (Harbaugh et al., 1984; Penn et al., 1988) as well as multiple-dose approaches) (Bruno et al., 1986; Mouradian et al., 1988b).

Notwithstanding these generally disappointing results, it would be premature to discard the cholinergic hypothesis of memory dysfunction in dementia. Technically, there may be several shortcomings in the testing of this hypothesis: present agents have little (most cholinergic agonists used to date) or no (acetylcholine precursors or degradation inhibitors) specificity for subgroups of cholinergic receptors. While the practical significance of this lack of specificity is still unclear, there is evidence that most central M1 receptors are postsynaptic and M2 receptors are largely presynaptic. The failure of RS-86 to ameliorate dementia may relate to the fact that this is a weak, partial and mixed M1 and M2 agonist (Mouradian et al., 1988b). The recent cloning of five subtypes of cholinergic receptors can be expected to assist in the development of agonists that selectively interact with the optimal set of cholinergic receptors and thus have a vastly improved therapeutic index. Adverse effects due to hyperstimulation of peripheral cholinergic functions, as well as toxic effects on other organ systems, continue to limit definitive tests of the cholinergic hypothesis. Increasing evidence also suggests that other transmitter systems contribute to the pathophysiology of dementia of the Alzheimer type. Conceivably, cholinomimetic treatment might thus be a necessary but not sufficient therapeutic intervention.

Monoamines

Deficiencies in central noradrenergic (Crook et al., 1983; Gottfries et al., 1983; Narang and Cutler, 1986), serotonergic (Adolfsson et al., 1978; Palmer et al., 1987; Whitford, 1986) and possibly dopaminergic (Cavagnaro, 1986; Gottfries et al., 1983) systems have been described in Alzheimer's disease. Reports of small but consistent improvement in circumscribed aspects of cognitive function with dopaminergic therapy in Parkinson's disease (Delis et al., 1982; Mohr et al., 1987, 1989a) raise the possibility of reduced intellectual deficits with dopamine replacement therapy in dementia in general. Unfortunately, therapeutic attempts to improve cognition in dementing disorders with dopaminomimetics have been largely unsuccessful (Adolfsson et al., 1982; Ferris et al., 1982; Kristensen et al., 1977). A partial exception to this disappointing record arises from a single report that deprenyl, which at lower doses acts as a selective inhibitor of monoamine oxidase B and thus blocks dopamine catabolism, improves some cognitive functions in patients with Alzheimer's disease (Tariot et al., 1987).

Reductions in cortical noradrenergic innervation, due to degeneration of the locus coeruleus (Adolfsson et al., 1979; Berger, 1984; Bondareff et al., 1982; Moore and Bloom, 1979; Vijayashankar and Brody, 1979), the source of noradrenergic innervation to the cerebral cortex and hippocampus (Marcyniuk et al., 1986), may play a more important role in the pathophysiology of Alzheimer's disease. Considerable preclinical evidence implicates the noradrenergic system in certain aspects of learning and memory (Haroutunian et al., 1986; Kety, 1972; Mohr et al., 1989b; Randt et al., 1971; Stein et al., 1975). In fact, the noradrenergic alpha 2 receptor agonist clonidine reportedly improved delayed response deficits in aged primates with low noradrenaline levels as well as in young primates whose noradrenergic projections had been lesioned chemically (Arnsten and Goldman-Rakic, 1985; Goldman-Rakic and Brown, 1981). Nevertheless, clinical trials with clonidine and the second-generation alpha 2 receptor agonist guanfacine in patients with Alzheimer's disease failed to improve cognitive function (Mohr et al., 1989b; Schlegel et al., 1989). Recent evidence of a slow versus fast progressive variant of Alzheimer's disease (Mann et al., 1989), which might have some relation to differential noradrenergic involvement, supports the hypothesis that a priori patient selection on the basis of biochemical profiles might be important for rational testing of efficacy of these compounds.

Serotonin, which also contributes to certain aspects of arousal and mood (Maas, 1975) as well as learning and memory (Altman and Normile, 1986, 1988), is reportedly deficient in many patients with Alzheimer's disease (Arai et al., 1984; Quirion et al., 1986). Serotonin receptor reduction has been observed (Cross et al., 1984) in frontal and temporal cortical areas as well as in the hippocampus (Bowen et al., 1983). Serotonergic replacement strategies have included the administration of tryptophan, alaproclate, zimeldine and *m*-chlorophenylpiperazine, but results have been disappointing at best (Cutler et al., 1985; Dehlin et al., 1985; Lawlor et al., 1988; Smith et al., 1984). Monoaminergic replacement therapy by itself has thus shown little promise, making it necessary to further explore alternative hypotheses.

Glutamate

There is now considerable evidence that glutamate functions as a neurotransmitter in cortical association fibers, perforant pathway inputs to hippocampus and several corticofugal projection systems which have been shown to degenerate in Alzheimer's disease (Beal et al., 1987). Glutamate receptors, especially the *N*-methyl-D-aspartate (NMDA) subtype, appear to remain relatively intact in this disorder (Mouradian et al., 1988a), which raises the possibility that glutamate replacement might confer symptomatic benefit. However, all currently known NMDA receptor agonists are neurotoxic and glutamate itself is unable to penetrate the blood – brain barrier. Recent evidence suggests, however, that activation of strychnine-insensitive glycine receptors positively modulates adjacent NMDA receptors and accordingly enhances the effects of glutamate-mediated synaptic transmission (Johnson and Ascher, 1987). Compounds capable of increasing brain glycine or stimulating the glycinergic receptor (e.g. milaci-

mide) thus may have the potential for modulating central action of the glutamate system.

Gamma-aminobutyric acid

Cortical gamma-aminobutyric acid (GABA) interneurons receive terminals from cholinergic basal forebrain nuclei (Coyle et al., 1983). Cerebrospinal fluid levels of GABA are typically reduced in Alzheimer's disease (Enna et al., 1977; Kuroda, 1983; Manyam et al., 1980; Zimmer et al., 1984), and postmortem studies have revealed reductions in cerebral GABA levels as well as in the activity of its synthesizing enzyme glutamic decarboxylase (Davies, 1979; Perry et al., 1977; Rossor et al., 1982). Based on the rationale that GABA-containing neurons located postsynaptically to cholinergic projections might contribute to the intellectual deterioration in Alzheimer's disease, a clinical trial with the relatively selective GABA agonist THIP (4, 5, 6, 7-tetrahydroisoxalo (5, 4-*c*) pyridine-3-ol) was undertaken. Although dose levels were high enough to produce centrally mediated adverse effects similar to those of other GABA agonists, no systematic benefit to cognitive function was discerned (Mohr et al., 1986). While further multiple transmitter replacement approaches may well need to further investigate the GABA hypothesis, present evidence indicates that the GABA system deficit is not a critical primary link in Alzheimer's dementia.

Neuropeptides

Changes in central neuropeptide concentrations have been reported in Alzheimer's disease (Beal et al., 1987). Nevertheless, clinical trials with peptidergic agents have been complicated by the fact that naturally occurring neuropeptides have a very limited ability to penetrate the blood – brain barrier (Davies et al., 1980; Gomez et al., 1986; Raskind et al., 1986; Tamminga et al., 1985; Wood et al., 1982). Attempts with synthetic analogues, particularly for the vasopressin system (Peabody et al., 1985, 1986), have been unsuccessful to date. Trials with opiate receptor antagonists (based on the rationale that endogenous opioids interfere with memory in the experimental animal) (Izquierdo, 1980; Izquierdo et al., 1980) also produced no measurable benefit (Blass et al., 1983; Hyman et al., 1985; Pomara, 1985; Reisberg et al., 1983; Serby et al., 1986; Steiger et al., 1985).

Somatostatin reductions in the cerebral cortex are one of the consistent transmitter abnormalities in Alzheimer's disease (Beal et al., 1987; Cutler et al., 1985; Gomez et al., 1986; Tamminga et al., 1985). In addition, diminution in somatostatin spinal fluid levels reportedly correlate with certain dementia severity measures (Tamminga et al., 1985). Depletion appears most concentrated in the parietotemporal cortical regions, an area which has most consistently been implicated in the pathophysiology of Alzheimer's disease (Chase et al., 1984, 1985; Foster NL et al., 1984; Mann et al., 1989). In addition to blood – brain barrier penetration problems, naturally occurring somatostatin is unsuitable for clinical use, due to its extremely short half-life. However, the development of synthetic analogues with considerably longer half-lives (i.e. SMS 201-995, sandostatin) have made clinical trials possible. The efficacy of such approaches may be compromised if cortical somatostatin receptors are lost.

Empirical strategies

Current approaches to the treatment of primary degenerative dementias frequently employ compounds with unknown pharmacological mechanisms but well-established cognitive activation profiles in the experimental animal.

Vasodilators

The original rationale for use of the vasodilating agents was based on the assumption that there is a causal link between decreased blood flow and dementia (Cook and James, 1981; Crook et al., 1986a). Agents with primary vasodilating properties include papaverine, cyslandelate, isoxsuprine, cinnarizine and betahistine (Crook et al., 1986a). Vasodilators with metabolic activation are dihydroergotoxine (hydergine), nafronyl and pyritinol

(Crook et al., 1986a). While limited improvement in intellectual function was reported in some of the more than 100 clinical trials performed with these compounds, none proved to be a reliable cognition enhancer (Drachman and Swearer, 1989). Nevertheless, hydergine, in spite of its lack of proven efficacy, remains one of the most widely prescribed treatments for dementia in the world today (Hollister and Yesavage, 1984).

Nootropics

This term was proposed in 1972 by Giurgea (Giurgea, 1981) and is based on the concept of 'noos' (mind) and 'tropein' (forward). Nootropics ordinarily have no measurable effect on transmitter system function and their mechanism of action remains unknown (Waters, 1988). The rationale for the use of these agents is entirely based on cognitive and physiological effects on experimental animals. Nootropics were developed with the aim of producing compounds with cognition-enhancing characteristics, without sedative, neuroleptic or analgesic properties (Waters, 1988). The principal example of these compounds is 2-pyrrolidine acetamide (piracetam). Early positive findings (e.g. Chouinard et al., 1981) could not be substantiated later, when piracetam was given either alone or in combination with choline or lecithin (Friedman et al., 1981; Growdon et al., 1986; Smith et al., 1984). Subsequently, more potent nootropics like aniracetam and oxiracetam have also shown promising results in the experimental animal (Cumin et al., 1982; Schwam et al., 1985; Sourander et al., 1987; Vincent et al., 1985), but no definite clinical efficacy (e.g. Moglia et al., 1986; Sourander et al., 1987; Villardita et al., 1987).

Ancillary symptom relief

The crippling effects of the intellectual and memory impairment in primary degenerative dementias naturally focus most therapeutic efforts on the alleviation of these cognitive sequelae, but restlessness, aggression, hallucination, paranoia, mood disturbances and disruptions in the sleep – wake cycle frequently accompany these disorders (Cohen-Mansfield, 1986; Rubin et al., 1987; Swearer et al., 1988). In contrast to therapeutic interventions in the cognitive domain, these ancillary symptoms are usually amenable to drug therapy.

Neuroleptics

Restlessness and aggression, hallucination and paranoia are most commonly treated with anti-psychotic medications (Birkett and Boltuch, 1972; Helms, 1985; Raskind et al., 1987; Risse et al., 1987; Salzman, 1987; Small, 1988; Steele et al., 1986; Wragg and Jeste, 1988). It is important to stress that Alzheimer's patients may be particularly susceptible to developing extrapyramidal side-effects associated with neuroleptica (Growdon, in press). Furthermore, treatment decisions need to carefully balance the need to control patients' behavior with the necessity to leave the individual maximally intact and mobile, thus minimizing the risks of sedation and extrapyramidal dysfunction.

Anxiolytics

These compounds appear particularly useful in treating the agitation and minor depression occurring in some demented patients. However, few rigorous clinical trials have been undertaken and clinical utility is again limited by potential side-effects. Even low doses of anxiolytic drugs can produce excessive sedation and impair cognition. A further troubling effect of benzodiazepines is that, due to long half-lives and active degradation products, some of these compounds tend to accumulate in older patients (Greenblatt et al., 1982). A benzodiazepine with a short half-life (oxazepam) has been observed to decrease agitation and anxiety in elderly psychiatric patients in general (Beber, 1965; Sanders, 1965) but this compound's utility is less well documented in patients who are demented. As a global guideline, it appears that benzodiazepines with single-stage degradation and short half-lives may be the treatment of choice, to avoid excessive systemic accumulation over time (Drachman and Swearer, 1989).

Antidepressants

The diagnosis of depression in primary degenerative dementia is often exceedingly difficult, since many symptoms common to depressive disorders are in fact part of the dementia syndrome (e.g. no interest in surroundings, lack of energy and appetite and sleep disturbance) (Growdon, in press). Treatment decision with antidepressants again have to be carefully weighed, since many of these compounds, particularly the tricyclics, have anticholinergic effects, and thus may potentially aggravate memory deficits. Treatment with trazodone, an antidepressant chemically unrelated to other compounds in this class, reportedly improved agitation and screaming in dementia (Simpson and Foster, 1986; Tingle, 1986). As is the case with antipsychotics and anxiolytics, judicious use of antidepressants can symptomatically improve the day-to-day functioning of the demented patients.

Psychostimulants

The observation of declining performance speed with aging led to the hypothesis that central nervous system stimulation might improve intellectual function (Kaplitz, 1975). Initially encouraging results with methylphenidate in a geriatric population (Kaplitz, 1975) could not be substantiated subsequently (Crook et al., 1977). Present evidence suggests that psychostimulants are of no benefit to the core symptoms of dementia (Prien, 1983) and may in fact pose substantial risks to these patients. Among these are the induction of agitation and paranoid ideation, as well as sudden and precipitous increases in blood pressure and heart rate (Crook, 1979). For these reasons, psychostimulants have largely been discarded as ancillary treatments in dementia.

Hypnotics

Disruptions in the sleep – waking cycle are a common concomitant of dementing disorders. These can be treated with hypnotics, such as temazepam, chloral hydrate or clonazepam (Leishman et al., 1989). Use of triazolam, while effective in initiating sleep, has not been shown to provide good sleep maintenance, due to its short-acting nature (Leishman et al., 1989). Moreover, possible side-effects of hypnotics, such as motor incoordination, postural instability and aggravation of intellectual deficits, have to be balanced against potential benefits of these agents in the demented patient (Growdon, in press).

Definitive therapies

General consideration

An alternative strategy for the treatment of Alzheimer's disease is to attempt interdiction of pathogenetic mechanisms operative in this disorder. The advantage of this approach is obvious: in contrast to palliative treatments, which address only symptom suppression, these strategies attempt to retard disease progression or even to restore disordered neuronal function. The effective implementation of these approaches requires some knowledge of the pathogenesis of the disorder, if only to the extent needed to make a heuristic assumption. Supposing that a cascade of events links the initial etiological factor with the ultimate loss of nerve cells, the success of this approach depends on the identification of only one step in the pathogenetic chain. At present, most work in the realm of definitive interdictions takes place at the preclinical level, and the hypotheses currently being considered remain highly speculative and rapidly evolving. A review of the current status of these efforts can do little more than hint at the possibilities available for future exploration.

Excitotoxin blockade

Glutamate, aspartate and certain other excitatory amino acids are synthesized within the mammalian central nervous system and play an important role in neuronal development and cognitive function (Rothman and Olney, 1986). Receptors mediating the actions of these transmitters are currently divided into three pharmacologically distinct subtypes: *N*-methyl-D-aspartate (NMDA), kainate and quisqualate (Watkin and Olverman, 1982). It has been suggested that clinical conditions may arise where one or more of these amino acids could act as an excitotoxin and contribute to neuronal death (Schwarcz, 1989). This possibility is based on the finding that endogenous excitatory amino acids, especially quinolinic acid, can induce selective neuronal degeneration within the central nervous system. Indeed, neuropathological changes occurring in certain neurodegenerative disorders, including Alzheimer's disease, resemble excitotoxic lesions produced in the experimental animal (Greenamyre et al., 1988). Conceivably, a pathological hyperabundance of excitotoxins, such as an extracellular accumulation of endogenous excitatory amino acids, might excessively stimulate glutamate receptors (Benveniste et al., 1984). In Alzheimer's disease, for example, the reported loss of cortical glutamate uptake sites (Cowburn et al., 1988) could expose postsynaptic glutamatergic receptors to potentially excitotoxic glutamate levels. Although preclinical studies reveal marked elevations in extracelluar concentrations of excitatory amino acids in various models of selective neuronal death (Benveniste et al., 1984), it has yet to be established just how hyperstimulation of glutamate receptors leads to nerve cell destruction. Current evidence points to the crucial role of intracellular calcium accumulations as a consequence of NMDA receptor activation (Choi, 1988). In any case, the characteristic regional and cellular changes found in Alzheimer's disease might relate to the metabolic state of neurons at risk, the density and location of NMDA receptors, and local tissue factors, especially mechanisms that clear extracellular excitotoxins.

The hypothesis that excitotoxins serve as a link in the pathogenetic cascade culminating in neuronal degeneration of the Alzheimer type derives support from preclinical experiments demonstrating the neuroprotective effects of excitatory amino acid antagonists. These studies have largely focused on the NMDA receptor complex, which possesses multiple modulatory sites in addition to those responsible for the binding of classical agonists such as glutamate and NMDA. Several relatively potent and selective non-competitive (for example, MK 801 and ketamine) and competitive (CPP and CGS 19756) inhibitors of the NMDA complex are available for experimental use (Choi, 1987; Rothman and Olney, 1987; Wong et al., 1988). These drugs characteristically block neuronal damage occurring as a consequence of ischemia or hypoglycaemia (Meldrum, 1988). Drugs, such as 7-chlorokynurenic acid and HA 966, which inhibit glycine enhancement of NMDA-mediated mechanisms expectably exhibit a similar neuroprotective potential (Thompson, 1989). Compounds that stimulate kynurenic acid synthesis have also been reported to have neuroprotective activity, possibly related to the ability of this naturally occurring brain metabolite to function as a non-specific competitive antagonist at all three classically defined excitatory amino acid receptors as well as to function as a glycine antagonist at the NMDA receptor complex (Foster AC et al., 1984). Some calcium channel antagonists, such as flunarizine, have been found to limit hypoxic-ischemic damage in the experimental animal as well as in patients with subarachnoid hemorrhage (Silverstone et al., 1986). If the influx of extracellular calcium is a requisite of excitotoxin cell damage, then these drugs may be expected to confer therapeutic benefit in situations involving excitatory amino acid-induced neuronal degeneration. Other drugs receiving investigative attention with respect to the excitotoxin hypothesis include cytosolic calcium release inhibition (e.g., IP-3) and calpain inhibitors (i.e., calcium-activated proteases) which appear to limit free intracellular calcium, a factor implicated in the production of free radicals and the stimulation of phospholipase activity that may lead to cell death. In addition, gangliosides, a group of naturally occurring glycosphingolipids, reportedly protect against excitatory amino acid neurotoxicity, possibly by affecting intracellular protein kinase C (Favaron et al., 1988).

NMDA receptor mediated mechanisms appear crucial for a host of normal brain functions (Smith et al., 1988). Thus it is not surprising that the initial clinical use of the more potent NMDA receptor antagonists like MK 801 has been associated with behavioral disturbances including confusion and hallucinations. This toxic potential has clearly tended to limit clinical trials of the excitotoxin hypothesis, while at the same time stimulating the search for drugs with greater selectivity for hyperstimulated excitatory amino acid receptors and thus the potential for a more favorable therapeutic index.

Abnormal fibrillary protein inhibitors

The major histopathological features of Alzheimer's disease are senile (neuritic) plaques, neurofibrillary tangles and amyloid angiopathy. Both plaques and tangles increase with normal aging and can occur in other dementing disorders, but are both particularly abundant in patients with Alzheimer's disease. Indeed, the pathological diagnosis of this disorder depends on an exceptionally high cortical density of these abnormal filamentous deposits. Plaques are almost exclusively found in hippocampus, amygdala and association areas for frontal, temporal and parietal cortex, especially in cortical laminae dominated by corticocortical associative relations (Pearson et al., 1985; Rogers and Morrison, 1985); they occur at a much lower density in primary visual, somatosensory and motor cortical regions (Pearson et al., 1985; Rogers and Morrison, 1985). They are found at sites of intense proteolytic activity. Tangles occur in the same cortical regions as plaques and also in subcortical nuclei projecting to the cortex (Brun, 1983; Ishil, 1966). The amount of cytoplasm, size of the nucleus, amount of rough endoplasmic reticulum and ribosomes all diminish in tangle-bearing cells; such cells thus seem to undergo a progressive reduction in metabolic capability likely to result in death (Hardy et al., 1986). It is thus not surprising that the density of plaques and tangles tends to correlate with dementia severity and neuronal loss (Blessed et al., 1968; Dayan et al., 1970; Mountjoy et al., 1983; Wilcock and Esiri, 1982).

Both senile plaques and neurofibrillary tangles are generally assumed to arise as a consequence of the primary degenerative process. On the other hand, it is not inconceivable that one or both structures or their major constituents are a part of the pathogenetic chain that ultimately gives rise to neuronal destruction. As already noted, plaques are the foci of proteolytic cell damage, while tangles appear to distort intracellular structures. Inhibiting the formation of these deposits might thus be expected to retard disease progression. This possibility has helped stimulate considerable research directed towards a more comprehensive understanding of the origin and composition of both plaques and tangles.

Senile plaques are characterized by an extracellular area of disorganized neuropil up to 150 nm across, consisting of 4 – 8-nm filaments that are not twisted in pairs. Plaque cores contain a 42-amino-acid peptide, usually termed A4-amyloid (also known as A4-protein, beta amyloid or beta protein), which appears very similar to the amyloid isolated from cerebral blood vessels of Alzheimer's disease and Down's syndrome patients (Masters et al., 1985). A4-amyloid derives from a precursor glycoprotein of 695 amino acids, usually termed amyloid precursor protein, which has three domains: (a) a relatively long extracellular portion containing the recognition site and the N-terminus; (b) a transmembrane portion containing most of A4-amyloid; and (c) a short intracellular portion with the C-terminus. Excessive amyloid deposition occurs not only in Alzheimer's disease but also in aged normal brain and in Down's syndrome, where it reflects a genetically determined overproduction of the amyloid precursor protein. The gene coding for A4-amyloid has been mapped to the proximal portion of the long arm of chromosome 21, and the sequence of amyloid precursor protein has been determined (Goldgaber et al., 1987; Kang et al., 1987; Wong et al., 1985). The mRNA encoding amyloid precursor protein appears normal and thus abnormalities in the processing of gene products presumably accounts for the excessive deposition of A4-amyloid in brain tissue.

Amyloid precursor protein is largely hydrophilic, in contrast to the cleaved amyloid fragment, which tends to polymerize into highly insoluble, beta-pleated sheets under physiological conditions (Gorevic et al., 1986; Kirshner et al., 1987; Masters

et al., 1985). Extensive proteolysis of the precursor protein must take place before A4-amyloid deposition can occur. Interestingly, two alternative transcripts for amyloid precursor protein are known, one containing a 56-amino-acid insert near the N-terminus of the extracellular domain which possesses serine protease inhibitory activity of the Kunitz type (Kitaguchi et al., 1988). Moreover, another protease inhibitor, alpha-antichymotrypsin, has been found to surround the amyloid core of senile plaques (Abraham et al., 1988). The functional significance of these inhibitors is not yet known. Conceivably, either inhibitor might affect internal proteolytic events, while the Kunitz-type inhibitor might simply be released from the amyloid precursor protein to modulate proteolysis elsewhere. Although it is not yet clear which A4 sequence is processed to form amyloid deposits, the necessary intermediates presumably vary in accordance with the local presence of protease inhibitors. A more precise elucidation of relevant proteolytic events could potentially lead to the development of an effective pharmaceutical intervention. Direct biological studies of Alzheimer's disease have heretofore been limited by the lack of animal or cellular models. Recently, the over-expression of A4-amyloid had been reported in a line of genetically transformed cells (Marotta et al., 1989), opening the possibility for tests of pharmaceutical means to modify amyloid production at the transcriptional, translational, post-translational and degradatory levels.

Neurofibrillary tangles are composed of two 10 nm filaments twisted about each other at 80 nm intervals (Wischik et al., 1985). These paired helical filaments are hardly unique to Alzheimer's disease but occur in various unrelated brain disorders. They are found not only in tangles within the neuronal perikarya but also in the dendritic and axonal processes at the periphery of the senile plaque. A family of microtubule-associated tau proteins now appears to be the major structural component of the paired helical filaments. Tau proteins are required to stabilize microtubules and maintain normal cytoskeletal function; their incorporation into paired helical filaments could reflect a loss from normal function and account for the disturbance in axoplasmic flow reported in Alzheimer's disease (Brion et al., 1986). Under such circumstances it might be beneficial to retard an accelerated rate of tau disposition. Since calpains mediate normal tau degradation, one approach to this goal might be to inhibit these calcium-activated enzymes. On the other hand, abnormal phosphorylation of tau not only appears to interfere with normal degradation, but also seems to be necessary for tau incorporation into paired helical filaments (Grundke-Iqbal et al., 1988) or possibly even to trigger their incorporation (Filament and Delacourte, 1989). If true, pharmaceutical intercessions that retard tau phosphorylation or accelerate normal degradation might slow the formation of paired helical filaments.

Based on the foregoing considerations it might be hypothesized that neuronal degeneration in Alzheimer's disease arises as a consequence of the abnormal processing of a protein such as tau, leading to neurofibrillary tangle deposition intracellularly, or such as A4-amyloid, leading to senile plaque formation extracellularly, either or both of which might alter the structural integrity of neurons and ultimately contribute to their demise. Alternatively, the synthesis of the fibrous protein components of plaques and tangles might reflect the operation of an aberrant pathway, diverting crucial cellular constituents and thus compromising cellular function. The development of drugs that selectively modify the processing of these proteins might then allow testing of the hypothesis that they are participants in the pathogenetic cascade, rather than a mere consequence of it. In addition, this might allow for evaluation of their neuroprotective activity.

Oxy-radical scavengers

Hydrogen peroxide (H_2O_2) as well as its associated free oxy-radicals, namely the superoxide radical (O_2^-) and the hydroxy radical (OH·), are generated as a result of normal cellular metabolism or exposure to certain external agents such as radiation. These oxidative stressors clearly pose a threat to the structural integrity of the central nervous system due to its high rate of oxygen consumption and copious amounts of unsaturated lipids susceptible to oxy-radical toxicity. The exact mechanism of cellular damage has yet to be established, although DNA modification, protein denaturation or lipid peroxidation appear involved. Several scavenger systems normally operate to prevent the cerebral accumulation of oxygen-based neurotoxic compounds. These systems include superoxide dismutase, catalase and the glutathione scavengers (glutathione and associated enzymes, including glutathione synthetase, glutathione peroxidase and glutathione reductase). In neurodegenerative disease, the possibility exists that these systems become defective or are overcome by an excess of oxy-radicals, thus allowing cell membrane damage.

The activity of the free radical scavenging enzymes, superoxide dismutase (Marklund et al., 1985) and glutathione peroxidase (Kish et al., 1986), appears normal in sporadic Alzheimer's disease, although superoxide dismutase abnormalities have been observed in those with the familial form of this disorder (Zemlan et al., 1989). Indirect evidence provides some support for the suggestion that an increase in cerebral lipid peroxidation may accelerate the neuronal death underlying Alzheimer's dementia (Adolfsson et al., 1980; Harman, 1985; Sinet, 1982). Indeed, abnormal peroxidation with the formulation of free radicals is known to increase with age as well as with exposure to ischemia, trauma and organic solvents, all possible risk factors for Alzheimer's disease (Henderson, 1988).

Reports of the apparent ability of deprenyl (selegiline) to slow progression of Parkinson's disease (Birkmeyer et al., 1983; Tetrud and Langston, 1989; The Parkinson Study Group, 1989) have stimulated attempts to develop similar agents for those with Alzheimer's disease. Preclinical studies indicate that deprenyl prevents 1-methyl-4-phenyl-1,2,3,6-tetrahydropyridine (MPTP)-induced dopamine neuron destruction, presumably by blocking the monoamine oxidase-dependent conversion of MPTP into its putative toxic metabolite, the 1-methyl-4-phenylpyridinium ion (MPP+)

(Cohen et al., 1984; Langston et al., 1984). Although deprenyl was initially tested in parkinsonian patients because of its ability to inhibit monoamine oxidase-B, the drug has other pharmacological actions within the central nervous system, including a possible free-radical-scavenging effect (Cohen, 1987; Knoll, 1987). The mechanism of its putative neuroprotective action is thus uncertain, and the possibility that deprenyl-like compounds might exert a salutary effect in patients with other selective neuronal degenerative disorders remains to be evaluated. The acute administration of deprenyl has, however, been reported to improve performance on some tests of learning and memory in patients with Alzheimer's disease, possibly owing to the drug's ability to block degradation of monoaminergic neurotransmitters (Tariot et al., 1987).

Several studies are now in progress to test the neuroprotective efficacy of drugs believed to influence oxy-radical toxicity. In addition to clinical trials with deprenyl, alphatocopherol (vitamin E), a well known free-radical-scavenging agent (Tappel, 1962), is currently being tested for neuroprotective activity in Parkinson's disease (The Parkinson Study Group, 1989). Acetyl-L-carnitine, which reportedly elevates the cerebral content of reduced glutathione (Fariello et al., 1988), a presumptive scavenger of reactive metabolites depleted by MPTP (Ferraro et al., 1986; Meister, 1983), has received recent clinical attention. Lipid peroxidase inhibitors, including the lazeroid series of compounds, are also being assessed for efficacy in various neurodegenerative disorders.

Growth and regeneration stimulants
Numerous preclinical studies are currently attempting to evaluate the therapeutic potential of agents and procedures that stimulate growth or regeneration of damaged neural elements within the mammalian central nervous system. The possibility of restoring normal neuronal function or retarding the degenerative process in Alzheimer's disease is suggested by preclinical studies indicating that cholinergic neurons in the septal-diagonal band

area, nucleus basalis and corpus striatum are sensitive to nerve growth factor (Hefti et al., 1985). Specifically, the intraventricular administration of this neurotrophic protein prevents retrograde neuronal death and promotes behavioral recovery following lesions of the septohippocampal pathway in young adult rats (Kromer, 1987; Will and Hefti, 1985). Perhaps more relevant to Alzheimer's disease, continuous intracerebral infusions of nerve growth factor partially reverse cholinergic cell body atrophy and improve spatial memory performance in behaviorally impaired aged rats (Fischer et al., 1987). Nerve growth factor is normally synthesized in cerebral cortex and hippocampus and transported retrogradely to cholinergic neurons in the nucleus basalis, where it contributes to the regulation of choline acetyltransferase activity. Brain levels and receptors for nerve growth factor appear normal in Alzheimer's disease.

Various other putative central nervous system survival and/or growth factors, in addition to nerve growth factor, are now receiving intense investigative scrutiny. These include GM_1 gangliosides (Crino et al., 1989), heparan sulphate proteoglycan (Lander et al., 1982), vasoactive intestinal peptide (Brenneman and Eiden, 1986), thy-1 glycoprotein (Leifer et al., 1984; Williams, 1982), and various peptide mitogens (e.g., substance P, vasopressin, bombesin). The clinical evaluation of these compounds presents special challenges, since most penetrate the blood – brain barrier poorly, if at all. Thus the use of carrier systems may have to be considered, to permit systemic rather than intrathecal administration. A partial exception to this generality is GM_1 ganglioside, one of several gangliosides reportedly depleted in Alzheimer's disease brain (Crino et al., 1989) and now in clinical trials.

Genetic approaches
An increased prevalence of dementia among first-degree relatives of Alzheimer's disease patients has been reported, suggesting polygenetic heritability or an autosomal dominant disorder with age-dependent penetrance. Several large families who

appear to inherit Alzheimer's disease as an autosomal dominant trait have now been identified (Tanzi et al., 1989). All have a disease phenotype essentially indistinguishable from that of sporadic Alzheimer's disease. Evidence currently points to the proximal half of the long arm of chromosome 21 as the site of familial Alzheimer's gene. The fact that both the familial Alzheimer's disease and amyloid precursor protein genes are located on chromosome 21 is presumably coincidental, since the two are not closely linked. Moreover, twin studies, indicating discordance, suggest the need for caution regarding relatively simplistic pathogenetic hypotheses for Alzheimer's disease relying on a single autosomal dominant gene (Nee et al., 1987). Nevertheless, isolation and characterization of familial Alzheimer's disease gene(s) should facilitate identification of the gene product and elucidation of pathogenetic mechanisms relevant to both forms of the illness. Unfortunately, genetic approaches to cloning the gene for familial Alzheimer's disease will be relatively difficult and alternative strategies may have to be pursued. Moreover, since homogeneity for the familial Alzheimer's disease gene locus has not been conclusively established, the application of linkage analysis techniques for presymptomatic testing and genetic counselling in this disorder has yet to be attempted.

Conclusion

Impressive strides are now being made towards the goal of developing effective therapeutic approaches to the primary degenerative dementias. Nevertheless, diagnostic uncertainties continue to plague these efforts. Agreement on outcome measures (testing toward the deficit) and development of pharmacological profiling approaches will advance palliation. Especially in the context of definitive intercessions, it would be helpful to know whether the clinical-pathological condition now termed Alzheimer's disease encompasses a single disease entity or a group of disorders. Future progress in the development of rational therapeutic interventions, especially those which seek to slow disease progression, will increasingly depend on an improved understanding of the neurobiology of this disorder. This fundamental research is now progressing rapidly. In the meantime, advances in the treatment of Alzheimer's disease and other primary degenerative dementias would appear most likely to derive from the continuing application of transmitter pharmacological strategies to the development of pharmaceuticals able to palliate dementia symptoms.

Acknowledgement

The valuable contribution of Margaret Sampson, Margaret Gearing, Joanne Gallagher and Eva Hill in the technical preparation of this chapter is gratefully acknowledged.

References

Abraham CR, Selkoe DJ, Potter H: Immunochemical identification of the serine protease inhibitor alpha 1-antichymotrypsin in the brain amyloid deposits of Alzheimer's disease. *Cell: 52,* 487 – 501, 1988.

Adolfsson R, Gottfries C, Oreland L, Roos B, Winblad B: Reduced levels of catecholamines in the brain and increased activity of monoamine oxidase in platelets in Alzheimer's disease: therapeutic implications. In Katzman R, Terry R, Bick K (Editors), *Alzheimer's Disease: Senile Dementia and Related Disorders.* New York: Raven Press, 1978.

Adolfsson R, Gottfries CG, Roos BE, Winblad B: Changes in brain catecholamines in patients with dementia of the Alzheimer type. *Br. J. Psychiat.: 135,* 216 – 223, 1979.

Adolfsson R, Gottfries CG, Wiberg A, Winblad B: Increased activity of brain and platelet monoamine oxidase in dementia of the Alzheimer's type. *Life Sci. 27,* 1029 – 1034, 1980.

Adolfsson R, Brane G, Bucht G, Karlsson I, Gottfries CG, Persson S, Winblad B: A double-blind study with levodopa in dementia of Alzheimer type. In Corkin S, Davis K, Growdon J, Usdin E, Wurtman R (Editors), *Alzheimer's Disease: a Report of Progress.* New York: Raven Press, pp. 469 – 473, 1982.

Agid Y, Ruberg M, Dubois B, Pillon B, Cusimano G, Raisman R, Cash R, Lhermitte F, Javoy-Agid F: Parkinson's disease and dementia. *Clin. Neuropharmacol.: 9 (Suppl. 2),* S22 – S36, 1986.

Albert M: Criteria for the choice of neuropsychological tests. In Mohr E, Brouwers P (Editors), *Handbook of clinical trials: The neurobehavioral approach.* Lisse: Swets Publishing Service, 1991.

Altman HJ, Normile HJ. Serotonin, learning, and memory: Implications for the treatment of dementia. In Crook T, Bartus R, Ferris S, and Gershon S (Editors), *Treatment Development Strategies for Alzheimer's Disease.* Madison: Mark Powley Associates, Inc., pp. 361 – 383, 1986.

Altman HJ, Normile HJ: What is the nature of the role of the serotonergic nervous system in learning and memory: prospects for development of an effective treatment strategy for senile dementia. *Neurobiol. Aging:* 9, 627 – 638, 1988.

Altshuler L, Post R, Fedio P: Affective variables in clinical trials. In Mohr E, Brouwers P (Editors), *Handbook of Clinical Trials: The Neurobehavioral Approach.* Lisse: Swets Publishing Service, 1991.

American Psychiatric Association: *Diagnostic and Statistical Manual of Mental Disorders: revised,* Edn. 3. Washington, DC: American Psychiatric Association, 1987.

Arai H, Kosaka K, Iizuka R: Changes of biogenic amines and their metabolites in post-mortem brains from patients with Alzheimer-type dementia. *J. Neurochem.:* 43, 388 – 393, 1984.

Arnsten AFT, Goldman-Rakic PS: Alpha adrenergic mechanisms in prefrontal cortex associated with cognitive decline in aged nonhuman primates. *Science:* 230, 1273 – 1276, 1985.

Ashford JW, Soldinger S, Schaeffer J, Cochran L, Jarvik LF: Physostigmine and its effect on six patients with dementia. *Am. J. Psychiatry:* 138, 829 – 830, 1981.

Bartus RT: The need for common perspectives in the development and use of animal models for age-related cognitive and neurodegenerative disorders. *Neurobiol. Aging:* 9, 445 – 451, 1988.

Bartus RT, Johnson HR: Short-term memory in the rhesus monkey: disruption from the anti-cholinergic scopolamine. *Pharmacol. Biochem. Behavi.:* 5, 39 – 46, 1976.

Beal MF, Kowall NW, Mazurek MF: Neuropeptides in Alzheimer's disease. *J. Neural Transm.: 24 (Suppl),* 163 – 174, 1987.

Beber CR: Management of behavior in the institutionalized aged. *Dis. Ner. Sys.:* 26, 591 – 595, 1965.

Beller SA, Oversall JE, Swann AC: Efficacy of oral physostigmine in primary degenerative dementia. *Psychopharmacology:* 87, 147 – 151, 1985.

Benveniste J, Drejer J, Schousboe A, Diemer NH: Elevation of the extracellular concentrations of glutamate and aspartate in rat hippocampus during transient cerebral ischemia monitored by intracerebral microdialysis. *J. Neurochem.:* 43, 1369 – 1374, 1984.

Berger B: Anomalies of neurotransmitters in Alzheimer's disease. *Rev. Neurol. (Paris):* 140, 539 – 552, 1984.

Birkett DP, Boltuch B: Chlorpromazine in geriatric psychiatry. *J. Am. Geriat. Soc.:* 20, 403 – 406, 1972.

Birkmeyer W, Knoll J, Reiderer P, Youdim MB: (–) Deprenyl leads to prolongation of L-Dopa efficacy in Parkinson's disease. *Mod. Probl. Pharmacopsychiatry:* 19, 170 – 176, 1983.

Blass JP, Reding MJ, Drachman DA, Mitchell A, Glosser G, Katzman R, Thal LJ, Grenell S, Spar JE, Larue A, Liston E: Effects of naloxone in senile dementia: a double-blind trial: a reply. *N. Engl. J. Med.:* 309, 556, 1983.

Blessed G, Tomlinson BE, Roth M: The association between quantitative measures of dementia and of senile change in the cerebral grey matter of elderly subjects. *Br. J. Psychiat.:* 114, 797 – 811, 1968.

Bondareff W, Mountjoy CQ, Roth M: Loss of neurons of origin of the adrenergic projection to cerebral cortex (nucleus locus ceruleus) in senile dementia. *Neurology:* 32, 164 – 168, 1982.

Bornstein R: The role of neuropsychological assessment in clinical trials. In Mohr E, Brouwers P (Editors), *Handbook of Clinical Trials: The Neurobehavioral Approach.* Lisse: Swets Publishing Service, 1991.

Bowen DM, Allan SJ, Benton JS, Goodhardt MJ, Haan EA, Palmer AM, Sims NR, Smith CCT, Spillane JA, Esiri MM, Neary D, Snowdon JS, Wilcock GK, Davison AN: Biochemical assessment of serotonergic and cholinergic dysfunction and cerebral atrophy in Alzheimer's disease. *J. Neurochem.:* 41, 266 – 272, 1983.

Brenneman DE, Eiden LE: Vasoactive intestinal peptide and electrical activity influence neuronal survival. *Proc. Natl. Acad. Sci. USA: 83,* 1159 – 1162, 1986.

Brinkman SD, Smith RC, Meyer JS, Vroulis G, Shaw T, Gordon JR, Allen RH: Lecithin and memory training in suspected Alzheimer's disease. *J. Gerontol.: 37,* 4 – 9, 1982.

Brion J-P, Flament-Durand J, Dustin P: Alzheimer's disease and tau proteins. *Lancet: 2,* 1098, 1986.

Brouwers P, Mohr E: Design of clinical trials. In Mohr E, and Brouwers P (Editors), *Handbook of Clinical Trials: The Neurobehavioral Approach.* Lisse: Swets Publishing Service, 1991.

Brown RG, Marsden CD: How common is dementia in Parkinson's disease? *Lancet: 2,* 1262 – 1265, 1984.

Brown RG, Marsden CD: Neuropsychology and cognitive function in Parkinson's disease: an overview. In Marsden CD and Fahn S (Editors), *Movement Disorders Vol 2.* London, Butterworths, pp. 99 – 123, 1987.

Brun A: An overview of light and electron microscopic changes. In Reisberg B (Editor), *Alzheimer's Disease: The Standard Reference.* New York: The Free Press, pp. 37 – 47, 1983.

Bruno G, Mohr E, Gillespie M, Fedio P, Chase TN: Muscarinic agonist therapy in Alzheimer's disease: a clinical trial of RS-86. *Arch. Neurol.:* 43, 659 – 661, 1986.

Carlsson A: Brain neurotransmitters in aging and dementia: similar changes across diagnostic dementia groups. *Gerontology: 33,* 159 – 167, 1987.

Cavagnaro J: Possible immunological treatments for Alzheimer's disease. In Crook T, Bartus R, Ferris S, Gershon S (Editors), *Treatment Development strategies for Alzheimer's Disease.* Madison: Mark Powley Assoc, pp. 267 – 291, 1986.

Chase TN, Foster NL, Fedio P, Brooks R, Mansi L, Di Chiro G: Regional cortical dysfunction in Alzheimer's disease as determined by positron emission tomography. *Ann. Neurol.: 15 (Suppl),* S170 – S174, 1984.

Chase TN, Brooks RA, Di Chiro G, Fedio P, Foster NL, Kessler RA, Mansi L, Manning RG, Patronas NJ: Focal cortical abnormalities in Alzheimer's disease. In Greitz T, Ingvar DH and Widen L (Editors), *The Metabolism of The Human Brain Studied with Positron Emission Tomography.* New York: Raven, pp. 433 – 440, 1985.

Chase TN, Burrows GH, Mohr E: Cortical glucose utilization patterns in primary degenerative dementias of the anterior and posterior type. *Arch. Gerontol. Geriatr.: 6,* 289 – 297, 1987.

Choi DW: Dextrorphan and dextromethorphan attenuate glutamate neurotoxicity. *Brain Res.: 403,* 333 – 336, 1987.

Choi DW: Glutamate neurotoxicity and diseases of the nervous system. *Neuron: 1,* 623 – 634, 1988.

Chouinard G, Annable L, Ross-Chouinard A, Olivier M, Fontaine F: A double-bind placebo-controlled study of piracetam in elderly psychiatric patients. *Psychopharmacol. Bull.: 17,* 129, 1981.

Christie JE, Shering A, Ferguson J, Glen AI: Physostigmine and arecoline: effects of intravenous infusions in Alzheimer presenile dementia. *Br. J. Psychiat.: 138,* 46 – 50, 1981.

Cohen G: Monoamine oxidase, hydrogen peroxide, and Parkinson's disease. *Adv. Neurol.: 45,* 119 – 125, 1987.

Cohen G, Pasik P, Cohen B, Leist A, Mytilineou C, Yahr MD: Pargyline and deprenyl prevent the neurotoxicity of 1-methyl-4-phenyl-1,2,3,6-tetrahydropyridine (MPTP) in monkeys. *Eur. J. Pharmacol.: 106,* 209 – 210, 1984.

Cohen-Mansfield J: Agitated behaviors in the elderly: II. Preliminary results in the cognitively deteriorated. *J. Am. Geriatr. Soc.: 34,* 722 – 727, 1986.

Cook P, James I: Cerebral vasodilators. *N. Engl. J. Med.: 305,* 1508 – 1513, 1981.

Cotzias GC, Papavasiliou PS, Gellene R: Modification of Parkinsonism – chronic treatment with L-Dopa. *N. Engl. J. Med.: 280,* 337 – 345, 1969.

Cowburn R, Hardy J, Roberts P, Briggs R: Presynaptic and postsynaptic glutamatergic function in Alzheimer's disease. *Neurosci. Lett.: 86,* 109 – 113, 1988.

Coyle JT, Price DL, Delong MR: Alzheimer's disease: a disorder of cortical cholinergic innervation. *Science: 219,* 1184 – 1190, 1983.

Crino P, Ullman MD, Vogt B, Bird E, Volicer L: Brain gangliosides in dementia of the Alzheimer type. *Arch. Neurol.: 46,* 398 – 401, 1989.

Crook T: Central-nervous-system stimulants: appraisal of use in geropsychiatric patients. *J. Am. Geriatr. Soc.: 27,* 476 – 477, 1979.

Crook T, Ferris S, Sathananthan G, Raskin A, Gershon S: The effect of methylphenidate on test performance in the cognitively impaired aged. *Psychopharmacology: 52,* 251 – 255, 1977.

Crook T, Ferris S, Bartus R: *Assessment in Geriatric Psychopharmacology,* New Canaan, CT: Mark Powley Associates, 1983.

Crook T, Bartus RT, Ferris S, Gershon S: *Treatment Development Strategies for Alzheimer's Disease.* Madison: Mark Powley Associates, Inc., 1986a.

Crook T, Bartus RT, Ferris SH, Whitehouse P, Cohen GD, Gershon S: Age-associated memory impairment: proposed diagnostic criteria and measurement of clinical change-report of a NIMH work group. *Dev. Neuropsychol.: 2,* 261 – 276, 1986b.

Cross AJ, Crow TJ, Ferrier IN, Johnson JA, Bloom SR, Corsellis JAN: Serotonin receptor changes in dementia of the Alzheimer type. *J. Neurochem.: 43,* 1574 – 1581, 1984.

Cumin R, Bandle EF, Gamzu E, Haefely WE: Effects of the novel compound aniracetam (Ro 13-5057) upon impaired learning and memory in rodents. *Psychopharmacology: 78,* 104 – 111, 1982.

Cutler N, Haxby J, Narang PK, May C, Barg C: Evaluation of an analogue of somatostatin (L363,586) in Alzheimer's disease. *N. Engl. J. Med.: 312,* 725, 1985.

Cutler NR, Haxby J, Kay AD, Narang PK, Lesko LJ, Costa JL, Ninos M, Linnoila M, Potter WZ, Renfrew JW, Moore AM: Evaluation of zimeldine in Alzheimer's disease: cognitive and biochemical measures. *Arch. Neurol.: 42:* 744 – 748, 1985.

Davies P: Neurotransmitter-related enzymes in senile dementia of the Alzheimer type. *Brain Res.: 171,* 319 – 327, 1979.

Davies P, Maloney AJF: Selective loss of central cholinergic neurons in Alzheimer's disease. *Lancet: 2,* 1403, 1976.

Davies P, Katzman R, Terry RD: Reduced somatostatin-like immunoreactivity in cerebral cortex from cases of Alzheimer disease and Alzheimer senile dementia. *Nature: 288,* 279 – 280, 1980.

Davis KL, Mohs RC: Enhancement of memory processes in Alzheimer's disease with multiple dose intravenous physostigmine. *Am. J. Psychiatry: 139,* 1421 – 1424, 1982.

Davous P, Lamour Y: Bethanechol decreases reaction time in senile dementia of the Alzheimer type. *J. Neurol. Neurosurg. Psychiatry: 48,* 1297 – 1299, 1985.

Dayan AD: Quantitative histological studies on the aged human brain: II. Senile plaques and neurofibrillary tangles in senile dementia (with an appendix on their occurrence in cases of carcinoma). *Acta Neuropathol. (Berl.): 16,* 95 – 102, 1970.

Dehlin O, Hedenrud B, Jansson P, Norgard J: A double-blind comparison of alaproclate and placebo in the treatment of patients with senile dementia. *Acta Psychiatr. Scand.: 71,* 190 – 196, 1985.

Delis D, Direnfeld LK, Alexander MP, Kaplan E: Cognitive fluctuations associated with the on-off phenomenon in Parkinson disease. *Neurology: 32,* 1049 – 1052, 1982.

Department of health and human services. Final regulations amending basic HHS policy for the protection of human subjects. *Fed. Register: 46,* 8366 – 8391, 1981.

Drachman DA: Memory and cognitive function in man: does the cholinergic system have a specific role? *Neurology: 27,* 783 – 790, 1977.

Drachman DA, Leavitt J: Human memory and the cholinergic system. *Arch. Neurol.: 30,* 113 – 121, 1974.

Drachman DA, Swearer JM: The therapy of Alzheimer's disease. In Porter R, Schoenberg B (Editors), *Controlled Clinical Trials in Neurologic Disease.* Norwell, MA: Kluwer Academic Publishers, 1989.

Drachman DA, Glosser G, Fleming P, Longenecker G. Memory decline in the aged: treatment with lecithin and physostigmine. *Neurology: 32,* 944 – 950, 1982.

Dysken MW, Fovall P, Harris CM, Davis JM: Lecithin administration in Alzheimer dementia. *Neurology: 32,* 1203 – 1204, 1982.

Enna SJ, Stern LZ, Wastek GJ, Yamamura HI: Cerebrospinal fluid gamma-aminobutyric acid variations in neurologic disorders. *Arch. Neurol.: 34,* 683 – 685, 1977.

Etienne P, Dastoor D, Gauthier S, Ludwick R, Collier B: Alzheimer disease: lack of effect of lecithin treatment for three months. *Neurology: 31,* 1552 – 1554, 1981.

Fariello RG, Ferraro TN, Golden GT, Demattei M: Systemic acetyl-L-carnitine elevates nigral levels of glutathione and GABA. *Life Sci.: 43,* 289 – 292, 1988.

Favaron M, Manev H, Alho H, Bertolino M, Ferret B, Guidotti A, Costa E: Gangliosides prevent glutamate and kainate neurotoxicity in primary neuronal cultures of neonatal rat cerebellum and cortex. *Proc. Natl. Acad. Sci. USA: 85,* 7351 – 7355, 1988.

Ferraro TN, Golden GT, Demattei M, Hare TA, Fariello RG: Effect of 1-methyl-4-phenyl-1,2,3,6-tetrahydropyridine (MPTP) on levels of glutathione in the extrapyramidal system of the mouse. *Neuropharmacology: 25,* 1071 – 1074, 1986.

Ferris SH, Reisberg B, Crook T, Friedman E, Schneck MK, Mir P, Sherman KA, Corwin J, Gershon S, Bartus RT: Pharmacologic treatment of senile dementia: choline, L-Dopa, piracetam and choline plus piracetam. In Corkin S, Davis K, Growden J, Usdin E, Wurtman R (Editors), *Alzheimer's Disease: A Report of Progress.* New York: Raven Press, pp. 475 – 494, 1982.

Filament S, Delacourte A: Abnormal tau species are produced during Alzheimer's disease. *FEBS Lett.: 247,* 213 – 216, 1989.

Filley CM, Kelly J, Heaton RK: Neuropsychologic features of early- and late-onset Alzheimer's disease. *Arch. Neurol.: 43,* 574 – 576, 1986.

Fischer W, Wictorin K, Bjorklund A, Williams LR, Baron S, Gage FH: Amelioration of cholinergic neuron and spatial memory impairment in aged rats by nerve growth factor. *Nature: 329,* 65 – 68, 1987.

Foster AC, Vezzani A, French ED, Schwarcz R: Kynurenic acid blocks neurotoxicity and seizures induced in rats by the related brain metabolite quinolinic acid. *Neurosci. Lett.: 48,* 273 – 278, 1984.

Foster NL, Chase TN, Mansi L, Brooks R, Fedio P, Patronas NJ, De Chiro G: Cortical abnormalities in Alzheimer's disease. *Ann. Neurol.: 16,* 649 – 654, 1984.

Friedman E, Sherman KA, Ferris SA, Reisberg B, Bartus RT, Schneck MK: Clinical response to choline plus piracetam in senile dementia: relation to red-cell choline levels. *N. Engl. J. Med.: 304,* 1490 – 1491, 1981.

Gamzu ER, Gracon SI: Drug improvement of cognition: hope and reality. *Psychiatr. Psychobiol.: 3,* S115 – S123, 1988.

Giurgea CE: *Fundamentals to a Pharmacology of the Mind.* Springfield, IL: Charles C. Thomas, 1981.

Goldberg TE, Berman KF, Mohr E, Weinberger D: Regional cerebral blood flow and cognitive function in Huntington's disease and schizophrenia: a comparison of patients matched for performance on a prefrontal task. *Arch. Neurol.: 474,* 418 – 422, 1990.

Goldgaber D, Lerman MI, McBride OW, Saffiotti U, Gajdusek DC: Characterization and chromosomal localization of the cDNA encoding brain amyloid of Alzheimer's disease. *Science: 235,* 877 – 880, 1987.

Goldman-Rakic PS, Brown RM: Regional changes of monoamines in cerebral cortex and subcortical structures of aging rhesus monkeys. *Neuroscience: 6,* 177 – 187, 1981.

Gomez S, Puymirat J, Valade P, Davous P, Rondot P, Cohen P: Patients with Alzheimer's disease show an increased content of 15Kdalton somatostatin precursor and a lowered level of tetradecapeptide in their cerebrospinal fluid. *Life Sci.: 39,* 623 – 627, 1986.

Gorevic PD, Goeni F, Pons-Estel B, Alvarez F, Peress NS, Frangione B: Isolation and partial characterization of neurofibrillary tangles and amyloid plaque core in Alzheimer's disease: immunohistological studies. *J. Neuropath. Exp. Neurol.: 45,* 647 – 664, 1986.

Gottfries CG, Adolfsson R, Aquilonius S-M, Carlsson A, Eckernas S-A, Nordberg A, Oreland L, Svennerholm L, Wiberg A, Winblad B: Biochemical changes in dementia disorders of Alzheimer's type (AD/SDAT). *Neurobiol. Aging: 4,* 261 – 271, 1983.

Gracon SI, Gamzu ER, Mancini ADJ: Multicenter clinical trials. Design considerations, standardization and implementation. In Mohr E, Brouwers P (Editors), *Handbook of Clinical Trials: The Neurobehavioral Approach.* Lisse: Swets Publishing Service, 1991.

Greenamyre JT, Maragos WF, Albin RL, Penney JB, Young AB: Glutamate transmission and toxicity in Alzheimer's disease. *Prog. Neuro-Psychopharmacol. Biol. Psychiatry: 12,* 421 – 430, 1988.

Greenblatt DJ, Sellers EM, Shader RI: Drug therapy: drug disposition in old age. *N. Engl. J. Med.: 306,* 1081 – 1088, 1982.

Growdon JH: Biological therapies for Alzheimer's disease. In Whitehouse P (Editor), *Dementia.* Philadelphia: F.A. Davis (in press) 1990.

Growdon JH, Corkin S, Huff FJ, Rosen TJ. Piracetam combined with lecithin in the treatment of Alzheimer's disease. *Neurobiol. Aging: 7,* 269 – 276, 1986.

Grundke-Iqbal I, Vorbrodt AW, Iqbal K, Tung Y-C, Wang GP, Wisniewski HM: Microtubule-associated polypeptides tau are altered in Alzheimer paired helical filaments. *Mol. Brain Res.: 4,* 43 – 52, 1988.

Harbaugh RE, Roberts DW, Coombs DW, Saunders RL, Reeder TM: Preliminary report: intracranial cholinergic drug infusion in patients with Alzheimer's disease. *Neurosurgery: 15,* 514 – 518, 1984.

Hardy JA, Mann DM, Wester P, Winblad B: An integrative hypothesis concerning the pathogenesis and progression of Alzheimer's disease. *Neurobiol. Aging: 7,* 489 – 502, 1986.

Harman D: Role of free radicals in aging and disease. In Johnson HA (Editor), *Relations Between Normal Aging and Disease.* New York, Raven Press: pp. 45 – 84, 1985.

Haroutunian V, Kanof PD, Tsuboyama GK, Campbell GA, Davis KL: Animal models of Alzheimer's disease: behavior pharmacology, transplants. *Can. J. Neurol. Sci.: 13,* 385 – 393, 1986.

Hefti F, Hartikka J, Eckenstein F, Gnaha H, Heumann R, Schwab M: Nerve growth factor increases choline acetyltransferase but not survival or fiber outgrowth of cultured fetal septal cholinergic neurons. *Neuroscience: 14,* 55 – 68, 1985.

Helms PM: Efficacy of antipsychotics in the treatment of behavioral complications of dementia: a review of the literature. *J. Am. Geriat. Soc.: 33,* 206 – 209, 1985.

Henderson AS: The risk factors for Alzheimer's disease: a review and a hypothesis. *Acta Psychiatr. Scand.: 78,* 257 – 275, 1988.

Hollister LE, Yesavage J: Ergoloid mesylates for senile dementias: unanswered questions. *Ann. Intern. Med.: 100,* 894 – 898, 1984.

Holman BL, Gibson RE, Hill TC, Eckelman WC, Albert M, Reba RC: Muscarinic acetylcholine receptors in Alzheimer's disease: in vivo imaging with iodine 123-labeled 3-quinuclidinyl-4-lodobenzilate and emission tomography. *JAMA: 254,* 3063 – 3066, 1985.

Hornykiewicz O: Dopamine (3-hydroxytyramine) and brain function. *Pharmacol. Rev.: 18,* 925 – 964, 1966.

Hyman BT, Eslinger PJ, Damasio AR: Effect of naltrexone on senile dementia of the Alzheimer type. *J. Neurol. Neurosurgery. Psychiatry: 48,* 1169 – 1171, 1985.

Ishil T: Distribution of Alzheimer's neurofibrillary changes in the brain stem and hypothalamus of senile dementia. *Acta Neuropathol.: 6,* 181 – 187, 1966.

Izquierdo I: Effect of β-endorphin and naloxone on acquisition, memory and retrieval of shuttle avoidance and habituation learning in rats. *Psychopharmacology: 69,* 111 – 115, 1980.

Izquierdo I, Paiva ACM, Elisabetsky E: Post-training intraperitoneal administration of leu-enkephalin and beta-endorphin causes retrograde amnesia for two different tasks in rats. *Behav. Neural Biol.: 28,* 246 – 250, 1980.

Johnson JW, Ascher P: The specificity of NMDA receptors in mouse brain. *Nature: 325,* 529, 1987.

Jotkowitz S: Lack of clinical efficacy of chronic oral physostigmine in Alzheimer's disease. *Ann. Neurol.: 14,* 690 – 691, 1983.

Kang J, Lamaire HG, Unterbeck A, Salbaum JM, Masters CL, Grzeschik KH, Multhaup G, Beyreuther K, Mueller-Hill B: The precursor of Alzheimer's disease amyloid A4 protein resembles a cell-surface receptor. *Nature: 325,* 733 – 736, 1987.

Kaplitz SE: Withdrawn, apathetic geriatric patients responsive to methylphenidate. *J. Am. Geriatr. Soc.: 23,* 271 – 276, 1975.

Katzman R: Alzheimer's disease. *N. Engl. J. Med.: 314,* 964 – 973, 1986a.

Katzman R: Differential diagnosis of dementing illnesses. *Neurol. Clin.: 4,* 329 – 340, 1986b.

Kaye W, Sitaram N, Weingartner H, Elbert M, Smallberg S, Gillin J: Modest facilitation of memory in dementia with combined lecithin and anticholinesterase treatment. *Biol. Psychiatry: 17,* 275 – 280, 1982.

Kety SS: The possible role of the adrenergic systems of the cortex in learning. *Res. Publ. Assoc. Res. Nerv. Ment. Dis.: 50,* 376 – 389, 1972.

Kirshner DA, Inouye H, Duffy LK, Sinclair A, Lind M, Silkoe DJ: Synthetic peptide homologous to protein from Alzheimer's disease forms amyloid-like fibrils in vitro. *Proc. Natl. Acad. Sci. USA: 84,* 6953 – 6957, 1987.

Kish SJ, Morito CL, Hornykiewicz O: Brain glutathione peroxidase in neurodegenerative disorders. *Neurochem. Pathol.: 4,* 23 – 28, 1986.

Kitaguchi N, Takahashi Y, Tokushima Y, Shiorjiri S, Ito H: Novel precursor of Alzheimer's disease amyloid protein shows protease inhibitory activity. *Nature: 331,* 530 – 532, 1988.

Knoll J: R-(–)-deprenyl (Selegiline, Movergan) facilitates the activity of the nigrostriatal dopaminergic neuron. *J. Neural Transm.: 25 (Suppl),* 45 – 66, 1987.

Kordower JH, Gash DM: Animal models of age- and disease-related cognitive decline: perspectives on the models and therapeutic strategies. *Neurobiol. Aging: 9,* 685 – 689, 1988.

Kristensen V, Olsen M, Theilgaard A. Levodopa treatment of presenile dementia. *Acta Psychiatr. Scand.: 55,* 41 – 51, 1977.

Kromer LF: Nerve growth factor treatment after brain injury prevents neuronal death. *Science: 235,* 214 – 216, 1987.

Kuroda H: Gamma-aminobutyric acid (GABA) in cerebrospinal fluid. *Acta Med. Okayama: 37,* 167 – 177, 1983.

Lander AD, Fujii DK, Gospodarowicz D, Reichardt LF: Characterization of a factor that promotes neurite outgrowth: evidence linking activity to a heparan sulfate proteoglycan. *J. Cell Biol.: 94,* 574 – 585, 1982.

Langston JW, Irwin I, Langston EB, Forno LS. Pargyline prevents MPTP-induced parkinsonism in primates. *Science: 225,* 1480 – 1482, 1984.

Larrabee G, Crook T. Computerized memory testing in clinical trials. In Mohr E, Brouwers P (Editors), *Handbook of Clinical Trials: The Neurobehavioral Approach.* Lisse: Swets Publishing Service, 1990.

Lawlor BA, Mellow AM, Sunderland T, Hill JL, Murphy DL. A pilot study of serotonergic system responsivity in Alzheimer's disease. *Psychopharmacol. Bull.:* 24, 127 – 129, 1988.

Leifer D, Lipton SA, Barnstable CJ, Masland RH. Monoclonal antibody to Thy-1 enhances regeneration of processes by rat retinal ganglion cells in culture. *Science:* 224, 303 – 306, 1984.

Leishman D, Ancill R, MacEwan W: Sleep disturbance in cognitively impaired elderly persons. *Am. J. Psychiatry: 146,* 1078 – 1079, 1989.

Lishman WA: *Organic Psychiatry: The Psychological Consequences of Cerebral Disorder:* Edn. 2. Oxford: Blackwell Scientific Publications, 1987.

Little A, Levy R, Chauqui-Kidd P, Hand D: A double-blind, placebo controlled trial of high-dose lecithin in Alzheimer's disease. *J. Neurol. Neurosurgery Psychiatry: 48,* 736 – 742, 1985.

Litvan I, Gomez C, Atack JR, Gillespie M, Kask AM, Mouradian MM, Chase TN: Physostigmine treatment of progressive nuclear palsy. *Ann. Neurol.: 26,* 404 – 407, 1989.

Maas JW: Biogenic amines and depression – biochemical and pharmacological separation of two types of depression. *Arch. Gen. Psychiatry: 32,* 1357 – 1361, 1975.

Maher ER, Lees AJ: The clinical features and natural history of the Steele-Richardson-Olszewski syndrome (progressive supranuclear palsy). *Neurology: 36,* 1005 – 1008, 1986.

Mann UM, Mohr E, Chase TN: Rapidly progressive Alzheimer's disease. *Lancet: 2,* 799, 1989.

Manyam NV, Katz L, Hare TA, Gerber JC, Grossman MH: Levels of gamma-aminobutyric acid in cerebrospinal fluid in various neurologic disorders. *Arch. Neurol.: 37,* 352 – 355, 1980.

Marcyniuk B, Mann DMA, Yates PO: The topography of cell loss from locus caeruleus in Alzheimer's disease. *J. Neurol. Sci.: 76,* 335 – 345, 1986.

Marklund SL, Adolfsson R, Gottfries CG: Superoxide dismutase isoenzymes in normal brains and in brains from patients with dementia of Alzheimer type. *J. Neurol. Sci.: 67,* 319 – 325, 1985.

Marotta CA, Chou WG, Majocha RE, Watkins R, Labonne C, Zain SB: Overexpression of amyloid precursor protein A4 (beta-amyloid) immunoreactivity in genetically transformed cells: implications for a cellular model of Alzheimer amyloidosis. *Proc. Natl. Acad. Sci. USA: 86,* 337 – 341, 1989.

Martin A, Brouwers P, Lalonde F, Cox C, Teleska P, Fedio P, Foster NL, Chase TN: Towards a behavioral typology of Alzheimer's patients. *J. Clin. Exp. Neuropsychol.: 8,* 594 – 610, 1986.

Mash DC, Flynn DD, Potter LT: Loss of M2 muscarine receptors in the cerebral cortex in Alzheimer's disease and experimental cholinergic denervation. *Science: 228,* 1115 – 1117, 1985.

Masters CL, Simms G, Weinman NA, Multhaup G, McDonald BL, Beyreuther K: Amyloid plaque core protein in Alzheimer disease and Down syndrome. *Proc. Natl. Acad. Sci. USA: 82,* 4245 – 4249, 1985.

McKhann GM: The trials of clinical trials. *Arch. Neurol.: 46,* 611 – 614, 1989.

McKhann G, Drachman D, Folstein M, Katzman R, Price D, Stadlan EM: Clinical diagnosis of Alzheimer's disease: report of the NINCDS-ADRDA working group under the auspices of Department of Health and Human Services Task Force on Alzheimer's Disease. *Neurology: 34,* 939 – 944, 1984.

Medical Research Council of Canada. *Guidelines on Research Involving Human Subjects:* Ottawa: Ministry of Supply and Services Canada, 1987.

Meister A: Selective modification of glutathione metabolism. *Science: 220,* 472 – 477, 1983.

Meldrum B: Excitatory amino acids in neurological disease. *Curr. Opinion Neurol. Neurosurg.: 1,* 563 – 568, 1988.

Moglia A, Sinforiani E, Zandrini C, Gualtieri S, Corsico R, Arrigo A: Activity of oxiracetam in patients with organic brain syndrome: a neuropsychological study. *Clin. Neuropharmacol.: 9 (Suppl 3),* S73 – S78, 1986.

Mohr E, Bruno G, Foster N, Gillespie M, Cox C, Hare TA, Tamminga C, Fedio P, Chase TN: GABA-agonist therapy for Alzheimer's disease. *Clin. Neuropharmacol.: 9,* 257 – 263, 1986.

Mohr E, Fabbrini G, Ruggieri S, Fedio P, Chase TN: Cognitive concomitants of dopamine system stimulation in Parkinsonian patients. *J. Neurol. Neurosurgery. Psychiatry: 50,* 1192 – 1196, 1987.

Mohr E, Fabbrini G, Williams J, Schlegel J, Cox C, Fedio P, Chase TN: Dopamine and memory function in Parkinson's disease. *Movement Disorders: 4:* 113 – 120, 1989a.

Mohr E, Schlegel J, Fabbrini G, Williams J, Mouradian MM, Mann UM, Claus JJ, Fedio P, Chase TN: Clonidine treatment of Alzheimer's disease. *Arch. Neurol.: 46,* 376 – 378, 1989b.

Mohr E, Carter C, Wallin A: Neurochemical substrates of dementing processes. *Pharmacopsychiatry: 23:* 53 – 56, 1990a.

Mohr E, Claus JJ, Mann UM, Chase TN: Dementing disorders. In Mohr E, Brouwers P (Editors), *Handbook of Clinical Trials: The Neurobehavioral Approach.* Lisse: Swets Publishing Service, 1991.

Mohr E, Litvan I, Williams J, Fedio P, Chase TN: Selective deficits in Alzheimer and Parkinsonian dementia: visuospatial function. *Can. J. Neurol. Sci.: 17,* 292 – 297, 1990b.

Moore RY, Bloom FE: Central catecholamine neuron systems: anatomy and physiology of the norepinephrine and epinephrine systems. *Annu. Rev. Neurosci.: 2,* 113 – 168, 1979.

Moos RC, Davis BM, Johns CA, Mathe AA, Greenwald BS, Horvath TB, Davis KL: Oral physostigmine treatment of patients with Alzheimer's disease. *Am. J. Psychiatry: 142,* 28 – 33, 1985.

Moos WH, Davis RE, Schwarz RD, Gamzu ER: Cognition activators. *Med. Res. Rev.: 8,* 353 – 391, 1988.

Morris RD, Thompson NJ: Patient screening and inclusion criteria. In Mohr E, Brouwers P (Editors), *Handbook of Clinical Trials: The Neurobehavioral Approach.* Lisse: Swets Publishing Service, 1990.

Mountjoy CQ, Roth M, Evans NJ, Evans HM: Cortical neuronal counts in normal elderly controls and demented patients. *Neurobiol. Aging: 4,* 1 – 11, 1983.

Mouradian MM, Contreras PC, Monahan JB, Chase TN: [^{3}H]-MK-801-binding in Alzheimer's disease. *Neurosci. Lett.: 93,* 225 – 230, 1988a.

Mouradian MM, Mohr E, Williams JA, Chase TN: No response

to high-dose muscarinic agonist therapy in Alzheimer's disease. *Neurology: 38,* 606 – 608, 1988b.

Narang PK, Cutler NR: Pharmacotherapy in Alzheimer's disease: basis and rationale. *Prog. Neuro-Psychopharmacol. Biol. Psychiatry: 10,* 519 – 531, 1986.

Nee LE, Eldridge R, Sunderland T, Thomas CB, Katz D, Thompson KE, Weingartner H, Weiss H, Julian C, Cohen R: Dementia of the Alzheimer's type: clinical and family study of 22 twin pairs. *Neurology: 37,* 359 – 363, 1987.

Palmer AM, Francis PT, Benton JS, Sims NR, Mann DMA, Neary D, Snowden JS, Bowen DM: Presynaptic serotonergic dysfunction in patients with Alzheimer's disease. *J. Neurochem.: 48,* 8 – 15, 1987.

Peabody CA, Thiemann S, Pigache R, Miller TP, Berger PA, Yesavage J, Tinklenberg JR: Desglycinamide-9-arginine-8-vasopressin (DGAVP, Organon 5667) in patients with dementia. *Neurobiol. Aging: 6,* 95 – 100, 1985.

Peabody CA, Davies H, Berger PA, Tinklenberg JR: Desamino-D-arginine-vasopressin (DDAVP) in Alzheimer's disease. *Neurobiol. Aging: 7,* 301 – 303, 1986.

Pearson RCA, Esiri MM, Hiorns RW, Wilcock GK, Powell TP: Anatomical correlates of the distribution of the pathological changes in the neocortex in Alzheimer disease. *Proc. Natl. Acad. Sci. USA: 82,* 4531 – 4534, 1985.

Penn RD, Martin EM, Wilson RS, Fox JH, Savoy SM: Intraventricular bethanechol infusion for Alzheimer's disease: results of double-blind and escalating-dose trials. *Neurology: 38,* 219 – 222, 1988.

Perry E: Acetylcholine and Alzheimer's disease. *Br. J. Psychiat.: 152,* 737 – 740, 1988.

Perry EK: The cholinergic hypothesis - ten years on. *Br. Med. Bull.: 42,* 63 – 69, 1986.

Perry EK, Gibson PH, Blessed G, Perry RH, Tomlinson BE: Neurotransmitter enzyme abnormalities in senile dementia. Choline acetyltransferase and glutamic acid decarboxylase activities in necropsy brain tissue. *J. Neurol. Sci.: 34,* 247 – 265, 1977.

Perry EK, Tomlinson BE, Blessed G, Bergmann K, Gibson PH, Perry RH: Correlation of cholinergic abnormalities with senile plaques and mental test scores in senile dementia. *Br. Med. J.: 2,* 1457 – 1459, 1978.

Pomara N, Roberts R, Rhiew HB, Stanley M, Gershon S: Multiple, single-dose naltrexone administration fail to effect overall cognitive functioning and plasma cortisol in individuals with probable Alzheimer's disease. *Neurobiol. Aging: 6,* 233 – 236, 1985.

Poppe W, Lauter H, Tibilowna AU: Über den Wahrscheinlichkeitscharakter der klinischen Diagnosen Morbus Pick und Morbus Alzheimer. *Psychiat. Neurol. Med. Psychol.: 37,* S518 – S528, 1985.

Prien RF: Psychostimulants in the treatment of senile dementia. In Reisberg B (Editor), *Alzheimer's Disease.* New York: Free Press, pp. 381 – 386, 1983.

Probst A, Langui D, Lautenschlager C, Ulrich J, Brion JP, Anderton BH: Progressive supranuclear palsy: extensive neuropil threads in addition to neurofibrillary tangles. *Acta Neuropathol.: 77,* 61 – 68, 1988.

Quirion R, Martel JC, Robitaille Y, Etienne P, Wood P, Nair NPV, Gauthier S: Neurotransmitter and receptor deficits in senile dementia of the Alzheimer type. *Can. J. Neurol. Sci.:*

13, 503 – 510, 1986.

Randt CT, Quartermain D, Goldstein M, Anagnoste B: Norepinephrine biosynthesis inhibition: effects on memory in mice. *Science: 172, 498 – 499, 1971.*

Raskind MA, Peskind ER, Lampe TH, Risse SC, Taborsky GJ, Dorsa D: Cerebrospinal fluid vasopressin, oxytocin, somatostatin, and beta-endorphin in Alzheimer's disease. *Arch. Gen. Psychiatry: 43, 382 – 388, 1986.*

Raskind MA, Risse S, Lampe TH: Dementia and antipsychotic drugs. *J. Clin. Psychiatry: 48 (suppl), 19 – 22, 1987.*

Reisberg B, Ferris S, Anand R, Mir P, Geibel V, De Leon MJ: Effect of naloxone in senile dementia: a double-blind trial. *N. Engl. J. Med.: 308, 721 – 722, 1983.*

Risse SC, Lampe TH, Cubberley L: Very low-dose neuroleptic treatment in two patients with agitation associated with Alzheimer's disease. *J. Clin. Psychiatry: 48, 207 – 208, 1987.*

Roberts JKA: *Differential Diagnosis in Neuropsychiatry.* Chichester: John Wiley & Sons, 1984.

Rogers J, Morrison JH: Quantitative morphology and regional and laminar distributions of senile plaques in Alzheimer's disease. *J. Neurosci.: 5, 2801 – 2808, 1985.*

Rosoff AJ: *Informed Consent: A Guide for Health Care Providers.* Rockville: Aspen Systems Corporation, 1981.

Rossor MN, Garrett NJ, Johnson AL, Mountjoy CQ, Roth M, Iverson LL: A post-mortem study of the cholinergic and GABA systems in senile dementia. *Brain: 105, 313 – 330, 1982.*

Rothman SM, Olney JW: Glutamate and the pathophysiology of hypoxic-ischemic brain damage. *Ann. Neurol.: 19, 105 – 111, 1986.*

Rothman SM, Olney JW: Excitotoxicity and the NMDA receptor. *Trends Neurosci.: 10, 299 – 302, 1987.*

Rubin EH, Morris JC, Storandt M, Berg L: Behavioral changes in patients with mild senile dementia of the Alzheimer's type. *Psychiatry Res.: 21, 55 – 62, 1987.*

Salzman C: Treatment of the elderly agitated patient. *J. Clin. Psychiatry: 48 (5, Suppl), 19 – 22, 1987.*

Sanders JF: Evaluation of oxazepam and placebo in emotionally disturbed aged patients. *Geriatrics: 20, 739 – 746, 1965.*

Schlegel J, Mohr E, Williams J, Mann U, Gearing M, Chase TN: Guanfacine treatment of Alzheimer's disease. *Clin. Neuropharmacol.: 12, 124 – 128, 1989.*

Schwam E, Keim K, Cumin R, Gamzu E, Sepinwall J: The effect of aniracetam on primate behavior and EEG. *Ann. N. Y. Acad. Sci.: 444, 482 – 484, 1985.*

Schwarcz R: Excitotoxic and anti-excitotoxic mechanisms in neurologic disease. *Curr. Opinion Neurol. Neurosurg.: 2, 504 – 508, 1989.*

Schwartz AS, Kohlstaedt EV: Physostigmine effects in Alzheimer's disease: relationship to dementia severity. *Life Sci.: 38, 1021 – 1028, 1986.*

Schwartz R: Some ethical and legal considerations. *Psychopharmacol. Bull.: 17, 64 – 73, 1981.*

Serby M, Resnick R, Jordan B, Alder J, Corwin J, Rotrosen JP: Naltrexone and Alzheimer's disease. *Prog. Neuro-Psychopharmacol. Biol. Psychiatry: 10, 587 – 590, 1986.*

Silverstone FS, Buchanan K, Hudson C, Johnston MV: Flunarizine limits hypoxia-ischemia induced morphologic injury in immature rat brain. *Stroke: 17, 477 – 482, 1986.*

Simpson D, Foster D: Improvement in organically disturbed

behavior with Trazodone treatment. *J. Clin. Psychiatry: 47, 191 – 193, 1986.*

Sinet PM: Metabolism of oxygen derivatives in Down's syndrome. *Ann. N. Y. Acad. Sci.: 396, 83 – 94, 1982.*

Small G: Psychopharmacological treatment of elderly demented patients. *J. Clin. Psychiatry: 49 (suppl), 8 – 13, 1988.*

Smith C, Swash M, Exton-Smith AN, Phillips MJ, Overstall PW, Piper ME, Bailey MR: Choline therapy in Alzheimer's disease. (Letter) *Lancet: 2, 318, 1978.*

Smith DF, Stromgren E, Petersen HN, Williams DG, Sheldon W: Lack of effect of tryptophan treatment in demented gerontopsychiatric patients. *Acta Psychiatr. Scand.: 70, 470 – 477, 1984.*

Smith G: Animal models of Alzheimer's disease: experimental cholinergic denervation. *Brain Res.: 472, 103 – 118, 1988.*

Smith JC, Feldman JL, Schmibt BJ: Neural mechanisms generating locomotion studied in mammalian brain stem-spinal cord in vitro. *FASEB J.: 20, 2283 – 2288, 1988.*

Smith RC, Vroulis G, Johnson R, Morgan R: Comparison of therapeutic response to long-term treatment with lecithin versus piracetam plus lecithin in patients with Alzheimer's disease. *Psychopharmacol. Bull.: 20, 542 – 545, 1984.*

Sourander LB, Portin R, Molsa P, Lahdes A, Rinne UK: Senile dementia of the Alzheimer's type treated with aniracetam: a new nootropic agent. *Psychopharmacology (Berlin): 91, 90 – 95, 1987.*

Starkstein SE, Brandt J, Folstein S, Strauss M, Berthier ML, Pearlson GD, Wong D, McDonnell A, Folstein M: Neuropsychological and neuroradiological correlates in Huntington's disease. *J. Neurol. Neurosurgery. Psychiatry: 51, 1259 – 1263, 1988.*

Steele C, Lucas MJ, Tune L: Haloperidol versus thioridazine in the treatment of behavioral symptoms in senile dementia of the Alzheimer type: preliminary findings. *J. Clin. Psychiatry: 47, 310 – 312, 1986.*

Steiger WA, Mendelson M, Jenkins T, Smith M, Gay R: Effects of naloxone in treatment of senile dementia. *J. Am. Geriatr. Soc.: 33, 155, 1985.*

Stein L, Belluzzi JD, Wise CD: Memory enhancement by central administration of norepinephrine. *Brain Res.: 84, 329 – 335, 1975.*

Stern Y, Sano M, Mayeux R: Effects of oral physostigmine in Alzheimer's disease. *Ann. Neurol.: 22, 306 – 310, 1987.*

Sullivan EV, Shedlack KJ, Corkin S, Growdon JH: Physostigmine and lecithin in Alzheimer's disease. In Corkin S, Davis K, Growdon J, Usdin E, Wurtman R (Editors), *Alzheimer's Disease: A Report of Progress in Research.* New York: Raven Press, 1982.

Summers WK, Majovski LV, Marsh GM, Tachiki K, Kling A: Oral tetrahydroaminoacridine in long-term treatment of senile dementia, Alzheimer type. *N. Engl. J. Med.: 315, 1241 – 1245, 1986.*

Sunderland T, Tariot P, Murphy DL, Weingartner H, Mueller EA, Cohen RM: Scopolamine challenges in Alzheimer's disease. *Psychopharmacology: 87, 247 – 249, 1985a.*

Sunderland T, Tariot PN, Mueller EA, Murphy DL, Weingartner H, Cohen RM: Cognitive and behavioral sensitivity to scopolamine in Alzheimer patients and controls. *Psychopharmacol. Bull.: 21, 676 – 679, 1985b.*

Sunderland T, Tariot PN, Weingartner H, Murphy DL,

Newhouse PA, Mueller EA, Cohen RM: Pharmacologic modelling of Alzheimer's disease. *Prog. Neuro-Psychopharmacol. Biol. Psychiatry: 10,* 599 – 610, 1986.

Sunderland T, Tariot PN, Cohen RM, Weingartner H, Mueller EA, Murphy DL: Anticholinergic sensitivity in patients with dementia of the Alzheimer type and age-matched controls. *Arch. Gen. Psychiatry: 44,* 418 – 426, 1987.

Swearer JM, Drachman DA, O'Donnell BF, Mitchell AL: Troublesome and disruptive behaviors in dementia: relationships to diagnosis and disease severity. *J. Am. Geriatr. Soc.: 36,* 784 – 790, 1988.

Tamminga CA, Foster NL, Chase TN: Reduced brain somatostatin levels in Alzheimer's disease. *N. Engl. J. Med.: 313,* 1294 – 1295, 1985.

Tanzi RE, St George-Hyslop PH, Gusella JF: Molecular genetic approaches to Alzheimer's disease. *Trends Neurosci.: 12,* 152 – 158, 1989.

Tappel AL: Vitamin E as the biological lipid antioxidant. *Vitamins Hormones: 20,* 493 – 510, 1962.

Tariot P, Cohen R, Welkowitz J, Sunderland T, Newhouse PA, Murphy H, Weingartner H: Multiple-dose arecoline infusion in Alzheimer's disease. *Arch. Gen. Psychiatry: 45,* 901 – 905, 1988.

Tariot PN, Sunderland T, Weingartner H et al. Cognitive effects of L-Deprenyl in Alzheimer's disease. *Psychopharmacology (Berlin): 91,* 489 – 495, 1987.

Tetrud JW, Langston JW: The effect of deprenyl (selegiline) on the natural history of Parkinson's disease. *Science: 245,* 519 – 522, 1989.

Thal, LJ: Dementia update: diagnosis and neuropsychiatric aspects. *J. Clin. Psychiatry: 49:5 (Suppl),* 5 – 7, 1988.

The Parkinson Study Group. Effect of deprenyl on the progression of disability in early Parkinson's disease. *N. Engl. J. Med.: 321,* 1364 – 1371, 1989.

Thompson AM: Glycine modulation of the NMDA receptor/channel complex. *Trends Neurosci.: 12,* 349 – 353, 1989.

Tingle D: Trazodone in dementia. *J. Clin. Psychiatry: 47,* 482, 1986.

Vijayashankar N, Brody H: A quantitive study of the pigmented neurons in the nuclei locus coeruleus and subcoeruleus in man as related to aging. *J. Neuropath. Exp. Neurol.: 38,* 490 – 497, 1979.

Villardita C, Parini J, Grioli S, Quattropani M, Lomeo C, Scapagnini U: Clinical neuropsychological study of oxiracetam in patients with mild to moderate degree dementia. *J. Neural Transm.: 24 (Suppl),* 293 – 298, 1987.

Vincent G, Verderese A, Gamzu E: The effects of aniracetam (Ro 13-5057) on the enhancement and protection of memory. *Ann. N. Y. Acad. Sci.: 444,* 489 – 491, 1985.

Waters C. Cognitive enhancing agents: Current status in the treatment of Alzheimer's disease. *Can. J. Neurol. Sci.: 15,* 249 – 256, 1988.

Watkin JC, Olverman HJ: Agonist and antagonists for excitatory amino acid receptors. *Trends Neurosci.: 10,* 265 – 272, 1982.

Weinberger DR, Berman KF, Iadarola M, Driesen N, Zec RF: Prefrontal cortical blood flow and cognitive function in Huntington's disease. *J. Neurol. Neurosurgery. Psychiatry: 51,* 94 – 104, 1988.

Weintraub S, Mesulam M, Auty R, Baratz R, Cholakos BN, Kapust L, Ransil B, Tellers JG, Albert MS, Locastro S, Moss M: Lecithin in the treatment of Alzheimer's disease. *Arch. Neurol.: 40,* 527 – 528, 1983.

Wettstein A, Spiegel R: Clinical trials with the cholinergic drug RS 86 in Alzheimer's disease (AD) and senile dementia of the Alzheimer type (SDAT). *Psychopharmacology (Berlin): 84,* 572 – 573, 1984.

Whitehouse PJ, Kin Sing Au: Cholinergic receptors in aging and Alzheimer's disease. *Prog. Neuro-Psychopharmacol. Biol. Psychiatry: 10,* 665 – 676, 1986.

Whitehouse PJ, Price DL, Struble RG, Clarke AW, Coyle JT, Delong MR: Alzheimer's disease and senile dementia: loss of neurons in the basal forebrain. *Science: 215,* 1237 – 1239, 1982.

Whitehouse PJ, Martino AM, Marcus KA, Zweig RM, Singer HS, Price DL: Reductions in acetylcholine and nicotine binding in several degenerative diseases. *Arch. Neurol.: 45,* 722 – 724, 1988.

Whitford GM: Alzheimer's disease and serotonin: a review. *Neuropsychobiology: 15,* 133 – 142, 1986.

Wilcock GK, Esiri MM: Plaques, tangles and dementia. *J. Neurol. Sci.: 56,* 343 – 356, 1982.

Will B, Hefti F: Behavioural and neurochemical effects of chronic intraventricular injections of nerve growth factor in adult rats with fimbria lesions. *Behav. Brain Res.: 17,* 17 – 24, 1985.

Williams AF: Neuronal cell Thy-1 glycoprotein: homology with immunoglobulin. *Science:* 216, 696, 1982.

Wischik CM, Crowther RA, Stewart M, Roth M. Subunit structure of paired helical filaments in Alzheimer's disease. *J. Cell Biol.: 100,* 1905 – 1912, 1985.

Wong CW, Quaranta V, Glenner GG: Neuritic plaques and cerebrovascular amyloid in Alzheimer disease are antigenically related. *Proc. Natl. Acad. Sci. USA: 82,* 8729 – 8732, 1985.

Wong EHF, Kemp JA, Priestley T, Knight AR, Woodruff GN, Inversen LL: The anticonvulsant MK-801 is a potent N-methyl-D-aspartate antagonist. *Proc. Natl. Acad. Sci. USA: 83,* 7104 – 7108, 1988.

Wood PL, Etienne P, Lal S, Gauthier S, Cajal S, Nair NP: Reduced lumbar CSF somatostatin levels in Alzheimer's disease. *Life Sci.: 31,* 2073 – 2079, 1982.

Wragg RE, Jeste DV: Neuroleptics and alternative treatments: management of behavioral symptoms and psychosis in Alzheimer's disease and related conditions. *Psychiatr. Clin. North Am.: 11,* 195 – 213, 1988.

Zemlan FP, Thienhaus OJ, Bosmann HB: Superoxide dismutase activity in Alzheimer's disease: possible mechanism for paired helical filament formation. *Brain Res.: 476,* 160 – 162, 1989.

Zimmer R, Teelken AW, Trieling WB, Weber W, Weihmayr T, Lauter H: Gamma-aminobutyric acid and homovanillic acid concentration in the CSF of patients with senile dementia of Alzheimer's type. *Arch. Neurol.: 41,* 602 – 604, 1984.

© 1991 Elsevier Science Publishers B.V.
Handbook of Neuropsychology, Vol. 5
F. Boller and J. Grafman (Eds)

CHAPTER 6

The role of attention disorders in the cognitive deficits of dementia

Hans Spinnler

First Neurological Department, University of Milan, Milan, Italy

Introduction

When dealing with 'attention', it may be convenient to report how Pillsbury, as late as 1908, tried to outline the predominantly introspective evidence of this psychological construct: 'The manifestations of the state which we commonly call attention are protean. No part of the individual is untouched by them. They extend to every part of the physical organism, and are amongst the most profound facts of mind. So numerous and varied are the ramifications of attention, that we find it defined by competent authorities as a state of muscular contraction and adaptation, as a pure mental activity, as an emotion or feeling, and as a change in the clearness of ideas.'

The general purpose of this chapter is to reinstate the neglected issue of attentional control in neuropsychological reasoning. The dementing process allows the longitudinal following of the interplay between attentional and cognitive breakdown and its influence on everyday coping and test performance of demented patients. In line with the neuropsychological tradition, neuropsychologists are far more attracted by the clinically apparent failures stemming from the disruption of unitarily conceived processes (i.e., basic or 'instrumental' cognitive abilities or mechanisms) and from the damage to circumscribed brain regions, leaving to the psychologist the study of clinically vaguer disorders such as those consequent on disruption of control functions (Caird and Inglis, 1961). The latter mainly surface through ecological and introspective experience, both qualifications viewed with suspicion by the clinical neuropsychologist (Neisser, 1987). Actually, ecological and introspective experiences start by accepting at face value the existence of phenomena and effects rather than producing them by hypothesis-driven experiments. The apparently low interest in attention shown by neuropsychologists (Flicker et al., 1986) is further reduced when the issue at study is the dissection of the processes that are impaired by a dementing disease. Deterioration of behavior because of dementia is generally held to follow either multifocal or widespread anatomical and/or neurotransmitter impairments: both conditions are not very appealing for straightforward correlations of behavior with the underlying neuronal network. Moreover, particularly when dealing with diffusely brain-damaged people, deciding whether poor cognitive performance on an apparently attention-demanding task is due predominantly to attention or to other currently associated basic cognitive defects remains, given the present state of the art, often a mere matter of opinion. Finally, because attention plays a broad and nonspecific role in brain activities, the cerebral conditions affecting its efficiency are extremely heterogeneous. Actually, attention defects may follow structural damage of the central nervous system or metabolic and drug-induced alterations of it. Purely psychological modifications may give rise to attention disorders (Ottmans, 1978; Byrne, 1976; Martin and Jones, 1984) that are basically indistinguishable from those caused by structural modifications of the brain. So, attention defects are by no means a characteristic only of the demential syndromes. Possibly, however, neurotransmitter disorders are involved in all attention defects.

Section 1. The definitional framework of attention: from normal to demented subjects

Neuropsychologists' approach to attentional disorders relies on the conceptual framework of healthy working attention that is sketched below and that will guide review of the contributions of the attention disorders to the breakdown of cognition observed in dementia.

Kinsbourne's (1986) general suggestion of a 'systematizing cognitive psychology' under the jacksonian organizing principle of the 'differentiation of the neuronal system subserving cognition' is a particularly well-suited recommendation. There is speculation that at one extreme, attention with a predominantly subcortical anatomical linkage (Saper and Plum, 1985) acts similarly to phasic arousal, promoting Head's (1923) 'efficiency' of the brain, whereas at the other extreme attention with a prevailing cortical rostral linkage acts more selectively, supervising complex ongoing behavior and planning. As it is still a tentative contribution to a formal neurospychological construct of attention, it remains bound to several operational aspects, that is, to the tasks employed to reveal its role in cognitive computing and performance. The actual attention load of a given task is, however, seldom verified, being instead more often based on a reasonable guess. Hence the risks of circularity are particularly high when dealing with attention and discussing cognitive experiments related to it.

Although it has been studied for a century (Ribot, 1889; James, 1890; Titchner, 1903; Pillsbury, 1908) the role of attention in behavior still remains in a preparadigmatic stage, making a detailed definition, albeit still mainly descriptive in nature, mandatory. To fulfill this, one must resort to the concepts produced by psychologists, unfortunately without any neuropsychological goal in mind.

(i) Definition

Attention is viewed as a wide set of processes encompassing the regulation of actions from before they start up until they end. Hebb, as late as 1949, noted cautiously that there was no way to escape accepting the wide set of controlling activities ascribed to attention. He wrote: 'When an experimental result makes it necessary to refer to 'set' or 'attention' the reference means, precisely, that activity that controls the form, speed, strength, or duration of the response is not immediately preceding excitation of the receptor cells alone.' Hence, it appears to be convenient to conceive of attention as the 'central process involved in the control and execution of performance' (Hockey, 1984).

When dealing with attention disorders in dementia it is reasonable to refer to the work of Kahneman (1973), Shiffrin and Schneider (1977) and Kahneman and Treisman (1984), who reconsidered previous 'capacity' hypotheses. Reference is then made to Hasher and Zacks' (1979) model of automatic and effortful processing, to Reason's (1984a) unlimited automatic and attention-restricted model of production of actions, as well as to Norman and Shallice's (1980, 1986) supervisory attentional system.

At present, the supervisory attentional model appears closest to meeting the neuropsychologist's needs. It assumes (Fig. 1) a two-level control of behavior; hence it belongs to the class of hierarchical models. The first level involves parallel-running, possibly very refined programs (or action and thought schemata), operating by means of 'horizontal threads'. The second level − a higher device, the supervisory system itself − deals with modulation of first-level programs in order to start organizing new activities, to change ongoing activity, to stop more automatically already running activities, and

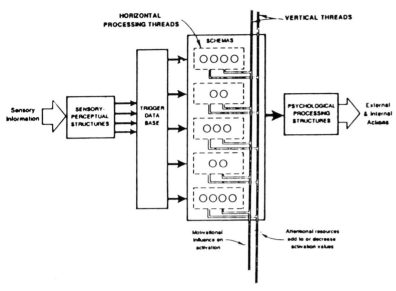

Fig. 1. Norman and Shallice's (1980, 1986) attention model. (Reproduced from Consciousness in Contemporary Sciences, Oxford, Claridon Press, 1988).

to render different and parallel running activities not reciprocally interfering with each other. The supervisory system allows a flexible (i.e., adaptive) approach to coping. Its operation it run by means of the 'vertical threads'. The dichotomy of the model is based on the automatic/effortful tradeoff. Norman and Shallice (1986) state that 'attentional processes can modulate the selection process only by adding activation or inhibition'. Attentional processes are in fact independent of the actual content of the performance at issue. This functionalistic statement is close to Luria's (1966) neuropsychological views on the unitary role of the prefrontal cortex, namely that it regulates, irrespectively of its contents, the execution of any kind of action sequence. As already maintained by Flechsig (1896), the execution per se belongs to other (more posterior) regions of the brain, and, accordingly, to different (so-called 'instrumental') cognitive functions or mechanisms; they are strictly linked to the content of the actions produced.

Possibly akin to the neuropsychological viewpoint is also Wickens' (1984) multiple-resources hypothesis: Specific capacity-limited resources are envisaged therein to be coupled with specific cognitive computations. There can be some conceptual overlap between Wickens' (1984) special resources and Norman and Shallice's (1980, 1986) sets of schemata.

There is a recurring psychological concept in discussing attention, namely that of 'attentional resources'. It permits one to frame cognitive reasoning in a functionalistic perspective and refers to an amount of available control activity in a given moment, irrespective of the task under course. However, its biological counterpart is by no means obvious. In any case, it cannot be straightforwardly identified with the biological dynamics and presently loose cognitive links of specific neurotransmitters or transient synaptic modifications, as could be suggested when dealing with AD and attempts at its symptomatic treatment. At present, such equations must be conceived of as nothing more than possibly provocative metaphors.

In order to become acquainted with the issues credited to the attention domain and their relevance to the coping defects of demented patients, some instances of attentional control are listed below. One issue is the protection brought about against interference when perceptually and mnestically dealing with incoming information, or when producing a new strategy to cope with novelty (Luria, 1973), or when setting a criterion in advance (viz., threshold) for the success of an action about to be produced, or when reassembling in a new way notions or procedures in order to solve problems. The ability to foresee from an existing context actions that are not actually under way (e.g., Gibson's, 1979, 'affordances') as well as to forecast their plausible consequences is another feature pertaining to the highest levels of the attentional control. This aspect of attentional control is possibly crucial for any kind of adaptation to the environment, and would possibly have a phylogenetic counterpart. The forecasting ability implicit in the attentional control of actions is driven by the interaction of an external context (or a specific experience) with an internal, possibly semantic, frame: this allows the subject to prepare to fulfill a task in the most convenient way.

Kahneman (1973) and Hasher and Zacks (1979) maintain that attention capacity varies within and across individuals. A common-sense approach labels, in fact, as more or less attention-dependent a performance whose accuracy is more or less unpredictably variable, given that the underlying instrumental function is assumed not to vary its processing capability. Actually, attention is conceived – admittedly somewhat elusively – as an energetic and dynamic supplement (Parasuraman and Nestor, 1986) associating the processing of each basic cognitive activity with the goal of optimizing the corresponding performance. This function is somehow accomplished in a fluctuating way by reallocating nonspecific energy resources to overcome internal and external interferences. 'Resource allocation' is another oft-recurring metaphor when discussing how attention dynamically controls psychological activity.

The list of the most convincing attention-loaded activities is long and, as expected (Pillsbury, 1908), very heterogeneous. An example is Titchner's (1903) apparently exhaustive list (reported in Moray, 1970), which first of all confirms the peculiar nature of attention, namely its essentially introspective nature (James, 1890). The items related to both laboratory and everyday settings set forth by Moray himself (1970) form a more updated attentive checklist. It includes mental concentration, watchkeeping, facing the 'cocktail party' problem, searching for signals, 'getting ready to deal with whatever happens next', as well as preparing to give a predisposed answer.

Common-sense qualifies a given task as 'difficult' insofar as the task calls for such a great amount of attentional resources that the corresponding performance appears to be hindered by any other concomitant activity or stream of thought. The neuropsychologist should become acquainted with the conceptually two-edged origin of task difficulty, namely that which is intrinsic to the task itself for a number of specific reasons (e.g., the combination of more than one instrumental ability specifically involved therein) and that belonging to its attentional demand.

Attention is a proteiform control system. It interacts both with input and output processes as well as with the representations involved in the related computing systems, but it is not specific to any of those components. The interaction between attention-shifting and gaze direction in stimulus-driven and concept-driven eye movements (Groner and Groner, 1989) is an enlightening instance of the moment-to-moment input and output control. Another particular example comes from unilateral neglect. Here the attentional disorder affects several of the levels involved when a spatially cued performance is carried out. It impairs mechanisms of overtly or covertly directing 'attention' (Posner and Boies, 1971; Posner et al., 1984; Mesulam, 1985; Baynes et al., 1986) up to a lacunar exploration of the external space (Chedru, 1976, following Kleist, 1934). At the same time, it impairs focusing on internal representations (Mesulam, 1981; Bisiach and Berti, 1986) or on the ability to retrieve them from remote memory into a working memory system. In this way it seems to impair computations involving the spatial use of representations. Accordingly, some of the failures in spatially coded orthographic representations in acquired dyslexia and dysgraphia have been reported (Hills and Caramazza, 1983) as convincingly fitting a unilateral disruption of focusing and shifting ability of attention.

Probably there are also many behavioral activities carried out nearly without any attentional control. Examples of automatic activities are those ruled by the 'Gestalt principles of perception' envisaged and still thought of as belonging to the visual (Wertheimer, 1923; Weizsaecker, 1950) and also the musical (Deutsch, 1982; Sloboda, 1985) domains. Other automatically running activities might be those related to the procedural learning of new skills (Eslinger and Damasio, 1986) or to most procedural retrievals (Saint-Cyr et al., 1988). Stopping costless, automatic activities is an effortful enterprise. The effort expended, for instance, by a continental citizen when safely crossing a British road to overcome continental scanning habits provides an example. The cost of the nonhabit action involved is shown by the slowing down or even stopping of concomitant speech.

(ii) Taxonomy

A widely agreed and intuitive taxonomy of attention features useful to the understanding of current tasks and experiments is framed in the automatic/controlled processing dichotomy (Shiffrin and Schneider, 1977; Schneider et al., 1984). The interaction of the two allows 'a limited-capacity processor to accomplish very complex tasks' (Schneider and Fisk, 1982). There is a tendency to limit the meaning of the word 'attention' only to the effortful control of actions and thought. Notwithstanding, it is more convenient for the aims of this overview to follow Kahneman's (1973) and Hasher and Zaks' (1979) automatic/effortful distinction as useful for encompassing the overall role of attention, by including its automatic aspect.

Automatic processing is defined operationally, that is, it runs without reducing the available control processing resources, thus providing the opportunity for mixed types (i.e., automatic and controlled) of parallel processings (Duncan, 1980). Controlled processes evolve in automatized computations (Hasher and Zacks, 1979) as a function of the amount of training and degree of consistency across

trials (Shiffrin and Dumais, 1981; Schneider et al., 1984). Automatic processing is capable of facing even extremely complex operations. Examples are those underlying intelligence differentiation (Hunt, 1978), low-level schemata (Norman and Shallice, 1980), automatic complex processing (Fisk and Schneider, 1983), board schemata activities (Reason, 1984a), and decentralized control of categorization (Brooks, 1987). Automatic control exerts its function in a quick, errorless and capacity-independent manner. One may suggest that the automaticity of some actions and thoughts reflects a sort of function-related intrinsic control (along the lines of Wickens, 1984), which acts in a completely independent way with respect to the general pool of attentional resources (Kahneman, 1973).

From a general biological viewpoint, automatic action routines must be conceived as top-level achievements. Perfectly automatic actions, though running without attentional effort, can be switched into conscious and controlled ones, usually as soon as they become part of a more complex plan of action sequence. However, the speed and accuracy that characterize automatically running skills are disrupted as soon as low-speed conscious control is forced into play.

Automatic computing is not a necessarily conscious or aware activity or, according to Reason (1984a), the performance is often aware whereas the underlying schemata are usually not. There is an ongoing vivid debate about the degree to which complex information-processing systems have access to their own internal states, and thus are able to give an explicit account of them. An enlightening discussion dealing with the relationship between consciousness and attention may be found in Shallice (1988). Some of the best candidates to allow the surfacing of consciousness in ongoing psychological processes are isolated paths of general functions (i.e., some processing subsystems) such as episodic memory (Tulving, 1983), lexical choices (Dennett, 1969), short-term stores involved in perception (Atkinson and Shiffrin, 1972; Marcel, 1983), and 'contention-scheduling' of attentional control (discussed by Shallice, 1988).

Along the lines of Rozin's (1976) proposals, Medin and Wattenmaker (1987) maintain that 'the evolution of cognitive systems is associated with a gradual increase in accessibility': amongst the prominent features of the most complex cognitive systems are increased flexibility and consciousness. Being conscious of at least some steps of a given processing routine is likely to enable the cognitive system to find, to make explicit and finally to put to test new, apparently more convenient, computing routines and models of knowing. Thus 'cognitive consciousness' greatly enhances sophistication of adaptation. The demented patients' adaptation to unforeseen environmental changes from an early stage of the disease is very poor. The demented patients' ability to produce and to handle new abstract sets of information is nearly absent. One can speculate that demented patients are bereft at an early stage of the possibly very great amount of attentional resources needed so that new situations are not dealt with by overpractised modes of representing the world in the computing system. Testing AD patients' creativity would possibly produce data helpful to the general understanding of their worsening coping competence, which in turn is shared by many frontally damaged patients. The issue of consciousness of cognitive deterioration will be raised later on with reference to AD (section 2.i).

Good examples of a basically automatized and overlearned complex behavior include piano- and chess-playing. The professional chess-player's ability to reproduce after a brief glance the meaningful arrangement of the pieces (de Groot, 1965) or to retain a listing of legal chess constellations of a dimension comparable to that of most people's lexicon (Chase and Simon, 1973) is a pertinent instance. There are, of course, plenty of other extremely refined automatic sequences of response, such as reading and writing (La Berge and Samuels, 1974) and gestural habits. Together, they make up the bulk of our everyday cognitive and noncognitive activities. By and large, one of the fundamental functions of the central nervous system, namely that of homeostatic maintenance − both physiological and psychological in nature, and on the pathological side of homeostasis − are carried out by means of complex, automatically running sets of responses. Most of them escape awareness.

Controlled activities should be considered as the first-step approach to novelty, with the aim of maturing into a less expensive (viz., more automatized) set of responses. Control processes require resources and efforts that are capacity-limited. They basically improve responsiveness to selected information. It is usually thought that controlled activities are intentional and aware, at least in the stage of initiation or breakdown (but see the discussion by Shallice, 1988). Following this line, consciousness seems to be more likely to surface precisely when effortful approaches are going to mature into automatic routines or the latter regress to controlled activities.

The tasks corresponding to controlled processes can be classified operationally on a duration basis into *selective attention versus sustained attention tasks*. The former refer to *focused and divided attention* (Schneider et al., 1984). Both ways of operating of selective attention need the unified functioning of the hemispheres, which requires an intact corpus callosum (Wale and Geffen, 1989).

Focused attention is directed to one source (or quality) of information (or cognitive processing) by ignoring others. Hence, focused attention involves the ability to establish the focus of computing, to maintain it as long as needed and to shift it in order to establish a new one (Davies et al., 1984). An often recurring instance of focused attention is that of extracting relevant from nonrelevant information. An example of such an activity is seen in the perceptual focused attention experiment with Gottschaldt's hidden figures carried out by Capitani et al. (1988) on AD patients and discussed later on. Even if healthy old age is believed to involve a reduction of selective attentional resources (Craik and Byord, 1982; Rabbit, 1979), focused attention, as opposed to divided attention (Salthouse, 1982; Salthouse et al., 1985), is believed to be among the least-impaired attentional activities in elderly subjects (Wright and Elias, 1979; Nebes and Madden, 1983; Gilmore et al., 1985; Nebes and Brady, 1989). Another example of focused attention settings are those provided by go/no-go tasks, used for the purpose of inquiring into frontal lobe function, in both animals and humans (Leimkuhler and Mesulam, 1985). Finally, a neuropsychologically important task, usually classed as focused attention, is that involved in Stroop's (1935) test (Golden, 1978).

It is, however, apparent that not all prima facie effortful actions easily fit the focused/divided distinction. Together with the go/no-go and Stroop (1935) tasks, an example of incomplete fitting is letter or digit random generation tasks (Skinner, 1942; Baddeley, 1966; Tune, 1964; Evans, 1978; Wagenaar, 1972). Such tasks show how poorly even normal individuals master the attentional load involved in producing series of unrelated items. They require shifting the focus of attention (Weiss, 1964) from a just given item to a new one, at the same time checking their unrelatedness, when they are temporarily stored in a buffer device (Baddeley, 1966; Wolitzky and Spence, 1968). Possibly, the complexity of such tasks underlies their high sensitivity to a heterogeneous set of diffuse cerebral damages (metabolic, psychiatric or degenerative in nature). The requirement to inhibit the easiest (viz., context- and habit-driven) answer makes go/no-go, Stroop and random generation tasks likely to involve the highest levels of control, possibly linked to prefrontal cortex.

Divided (or distributed) attention is the other face of selective attention. The division or distribution is between two or more sources of information or cognitive processings. Distributed attention is more likely to explain everyday successes and lapses than purposefully focused attention (Martin and Jones, 1984), which in turn is more often involved in laboratory testing. Divided attention requirements are usually embedded in all problem-solving tasks as well as in the ongoing checking activity of a multistep planned behavior. Test conditions calling for processing of two sources of stimuli (e.g., experiments on AD patients by Baddeley et al., 1986, and Grady et al., 1989), are good examples of divided attention testing.

It is apparent that the focusing aspect of selective attention is linked to rapid shifting in successive moments from one to another stimulus or computation, whereas the distributed or divided aspect of selective attention is linked to the simultaneous use of more than one stimulus or computation.

Sustained attention (Swets and Kristofferson, 1970; Stroh, 1971) chiefly refers to vigilance tasks that require focusing or dividing abilities over long (conventionally more than 30 minutes in healthy subjects) and unbroken periods of time in order to react to small and seldom occurring changes in the stream of the information being presented (Mackworth, 1957, 1969; Bakan, 1959; Buckner et al., 1966; Davies and Parasuraman, 1982; Parasuraman, 1984; Davies et al., 1984). The corresponding experimental settings necessarily impose a memory component. The long-duration work of a radar operator is an example of a subject who has to keep track of seldom occurring variations against a visual noise in a vigilance test condition: his activity basically fits a focused attention requirement.

None of the attentional models so far provides a satisfying explanation of the inconsistency, even in healthy subjects, over short times of the resources supplied to actions and thoughts, even when task instructions or the ecological setting do not undergo any variation. Quickly recurring lapses of attentional control increase the risk of random capture of thoughts and actions by unselected environmental cues. This is commonly labelled as 'distraction'. 'Capture errors' and slips of action in healthy people (Norman, 1976; Reason and Mycielska, 1982; Reason, 1984; Reason and Lucas, 1984b) are trivial examples of the intrinsic unsteadiness of the attentional control. This inconsistency is particularly enhanced in demented and frontal patients. Moreover, present attentional models do not take into account the 'awareness of fatigue', which at a certain moment in carrying out a controlled action is a universal experience. It is apparent that awareness of 'attentional fatigue' crops up in demented patients very early while they are trying to cope with every kind of controlled performance. One has to be aware that fatigue per se can add further impairment to the patients' cognitive performance, unduly introducing biases in the interpretation of test scores.

(iii) Attention tests

The psychometric tradition devised tests whose attentional load was held to predominate with respect to any other processing component involved: they were labelled 'attentional tests' (Leszak, 1983). Such tests range from mainly response-speed assessing tasks (e.g., simple reaction times), to tests of speed/accuracy trade-off (e.g., complex reaction times), to more elaborate tasks involving the focusing or the dividing or the sustained use of selective attention, up to testing procedures of withdrawal from automatic acting and of optimization of a limited amount of resources (viz., planning).

One can list some of the most popular instances of tests currently employed to provide measures of the available attentional resources: backward counting, serial subtraction by seven (Smith, 1967) or by three, digit spans forward (Spitz, 1972), backward, or their difference, the digit-symbol WAIS subtest, trail-making tests 'A' and 'B' (Reitan, 1958), one of the several variations of Mirski et al.'s (1960) continuous performance test, the Stroop test (Perret, 1974), cancellation tests (Lezak, 1983) go/no-go and random generation tasks of digits, letters or scrawls.

The psychometric tradition of attention tests deserves, however, some criticism in the light of the widely agreed functionalistic approach (Norman and Shallice, 1980, 1986; Reason, 1984a) to the issue of attentional control. Actually, considering a given test device as a reliable measure per se of some aspects of attentional control is liable to be a conceptually wrong belief, since it considers attention as a content-dependent ability comparable with that of 'instrumental' functions. It is reasonable to claim that almost every test − even the most 'instrumentally' directed one − is capable of providing attention-dependent scores whenever its administration has been framed in an attention-demanding experimental design. The attentional de-

mand may be increased by different testing conditions, such as facing two − even if completely heterogeneous and both strictly 'instrumental' − tasks at the same time, or inhibiting overpractised (i.e., automatic) responses on behalf of a strictly decisional performance. Admittedly, in some single tests (e.g., random generation of letters) multiple processing demands, such as those sketched above, are built in in the same device. It is likely, however, that crediting a single performance as attentive in nature independently from the experimental context of administration risks being to an unpredictable extent misleading. Actually, if doing so, one collapses the instrumental and the attentional component together, lending importance to one of them − thereby giving the qualifying label to the test − following a face-value (viz., introspective) criterion. Introspective shortcomings can of course be avoided by exploring preliminarily the attentional cost of a task performance, for instance plotting the hit and error trade-off of two pertinent performances in a divided-attention setting.

By the above considerations one does not claim that the attentional cost of every cognitive performance is exclusively context (viz., experiment-) dependent. In fact, there are tasks whose underlying mechanisms are for a number of reasons more or less prone to distraction or call for a continuous checking of the ongoing computation or combine the action of different cognitive abilities in sequence, and so on. There is therefore a subjective, albeit vague, possibility of ranking tests for their basic attentional load, and these feelings add to the opinions about the 'difficulty' of a given test.

In brain-damaged patients with a functional impairment somewhere in the psychological mechanism underlying a specific performance, the normal requirement of attentional resources is greatly increased to overcome the noise and inconsistency of the damaged working processor. It is for this reason that one experiences particularly great difficulty when trying to separate the instrumental from the attentional component in a test performance of a brain-damaged patient. This difficulty becomes especially great in the case of demented patients' cognitive performances inasmuch as the functional impairment of their psychological processing is reasonably held to affect more than one step in a computing system. In general, one must be extremely cautious when taking for granted in brain-damaged patients the psychological construct of a test (viz., its predominant cognitive features) which has been ascertained only in healthy controls. This particularly applies to attention testing in AD patients (Capitani et al., 1988).

(iv) Relationship of attention to intelligence and motivation

One must take into consideration the relationship between traditional control functions such as intelligence, motivation and attention. Dementia is universally agreed to impair all these functions from a certain stage of its progression. Thus, it is often necessary in experiments on demented people to distinguish the consequences of their concomitant breakdown.

It has been said (Edwards, 1974) that one of the earliest definitions of 'intelligence' by Wechsler himself was: 'a kind of energy which is neither definable nor measurable'. His later position (Wechsler, 1974) is reminiscent of Boring's (1923) well-known dictum that 'measurable intelligence is simply what tests of intelligence test, until further scientific observation allows us to extend the definition'. In its circularity, this strictly operational approach applies to attention, to motivation and to any other construct, provided that there is evidence for a common empirical trait. Unfortunately, however, a variety of factor analysis approaches have proved rather unsuccessful in measuring the psychometric construct of intelligence (Schoenemann, 1981). In a goldsteinian vein, performances can possibly still be labelled as 'intelligence' when the corresponding tasks call for an 'abstract attitude', such as the ability to discriminate in a factual context new problems or general features. Another solution is to restrict to intelligence those performances which call for new assembling of a variety of sophisticated routines laid down in the

semantic (or even procedural) repertoire. The latter position applies to the construct of 'crystallized intelligence', whereas the former refers to 'fluid intelligence' (Cattell, 1963; Horn and Cattell, 1967; Horn, 1976). Both aspects envisaged are possibly among the first impairments of AD patients (Spinnler and Della Sala, 1988), although everyday coping requirements seldom pose 'intelligent' demands and, consequently, clinical histories of demented patients are often for a long time negative for strict intelligence failures.

Following Norman and Shallice (1986), 'motivation' can be viewed as a slow-acting system, attentional in nature, that biases through steady 'vertical thread activation' the selection of contention-scheduling mechanisms (see Fig. 1). Hence, motivation lends consistency to the style of everyday coping. Motivational control is chiefly driven by inner needs and desires (Mesulam, 1985) and its traits are possibly determined very early in life by the social environment, possibly under some genetic determinism. An example is the motivationally driven improvement in retrieving to awareness and even in remembering for a long time dreams by subjects living in a particular existential period, such as, for instance, psychotherapy. Motivational differences play possibly the most sensitive role in bringing about interindividual differences in the coping style, a major component of personality. Blurred motivational control (viz., inconsistent drive) hampers access to semantic knowledge and autobiographical traces (Baddeley and Wilson, 1986; Reiser et al., 1986; Dall'Ora et al., 1989). Such defects are in turn crucial in bringing about the 'impoverishment of personality', one of the most universal hallmarks of the demential breakdown as well as of prefrontal damage. Over and above this, motivation is conceived of as the most consistent facet of the control functions. It is likely that the encroachment upon motivation occurs in the dementing process at a later stage with respect to intelligence.

Somehow at variance with intelligence and even more with motivation, the present status of attention modelling has completely grown away from operative or content-linked definitions. Nevertheless, its hierarchical control role is far from being sharply separated from several aspects embodied in intelligence models, from Spearman's (1927) two-factor theory to Sternberg's (1980) multicomponential model. In our opinion, recent models of attention (e.g., Norman and Shallice, 1980, 1986; Shallice 1988b; Reason, 1979, 1984a), which are free from contextual constraints and support their coping flexibility with every kind of cognitive computation, embrace the operations on which intelligence and motivation are thought to exert a specific imprinting. This impression crops up in James' (1890) and Pillsbury's (1908) descriptive outlines of the concept of attention. Attention is expected to assume more and more an expanding and subsuming role for all control activities coupled with cognitive computing. However, in order to base on empirical evidence the terminological issue of what phenomena and traditional items in the array of the psychological functions can be labelled as 'attentional in nature', one needs contributions from the classical psychometric approach in normals (e.g., factor analysis) and from brain-damaged patients (e.g., dissociated cases). The enlarged concept of attention still waits for such, or for other kinds of experimental, ecological or clinical proofs. Interestingly, however, attention, motivation and intelligence are currently believed to be linked to the same prefrontal circuits.

(iv) Anatomical correlates: role of frontal lobes in attentional control

The anatomical correlates of attention still remain an ill-defined topic that overlaps with the traditional frontal localization of the control functions (see Faglioni's review, 1990). Further, one can think of attention in general as one of the functions related to the nervous network (Mesulam, 1981) of the prefrontal and paralimbic forebrain (Feuchtwanger, 1923; Rylander, 1939; Mesulam, 1986). One ought, however, to regard such localizations as still provisional. Actually, whenever one takes into account the increasing array of operations encompassed by the label of 'control function' which are, more

or less, tacitly embodied in the concept of attention, the obvious question arises whether the fronto-rostral areas are really of pivotal importance for all control functions, or whether, on the other hand, fronto-rostral areas are only linked to the attentional aspects involving planning of future and modulation of ongoing actions. There is no convincing evidence supporting any correlation between different operational aspects of attention and topographical landmarks of the nervous network.

Tracing attention disorders back to damage of the frontal lobes (Pribram and McGuinness, 1975) is based on very old clinical observations of tumor patients (Welt, 1888; Oppenheim, 1896; Jastrowitz, 1897) and on every other etiological kind of (possibly massive and bilateral) damage to that region (in traumatic and vascular patients, Kleist, 1934; Rylander, 1939; Angelergues et al., 1955; Hècaen, 1964; Lhermitte et al., 1972; in demented patients, Delay and Brion, 1962; Neary et al., 1988; Knopman et al., 1989). However, when testing frontal patients for attention, there is often a contrast between clinically apparent attentional and motivational disorders and the normal outcome of formal testing. This discrepancy is one component of the 'paradox of the frontal lobe' (Mesulam, 1986). Attention testing of frontal patients (meant here as patients with neurosurgically or neuroradiologically ascertained frontal lesions) mostly concerns concentration tasks. They have repeatedly produced inconsistent findings in frontal patients (cf. the review by Stuss et al., 1981), leaving open the question whether prefrontal regions are as crucial as had been believed for attention, or whether the tests used were not sufficiently specific or sensitive to detect any attentional involvement. It is also possible that such a large brain region needs, for correlative purposes, to be broken down into much greater anatomical detail than has been done (Stuss and Benson, 1986).

So called 'frontal' disorders of behavior (Rylander, 1939) — chiefly, inertia and disinhibition — become more and more frequent among AD patients in their mid- or end-stages (Gilley et al., 1989). Given the role of frontal involvement in most demented patients at a certain stage of their disease for metabolic assessments, cf. Frackowiack et al., 1981; Grady et al., 1988; Pawlik and Heiss, 1989; and others), a neuropsychologically minded review of the relationship between attention and dementia must go into some detail about the anatomical correlates of attention. The present neuropsychological constructs of attention (e.g., Norman and Shallice, 1980, 1986; Reason, 1984) stem in part from animal and human experiments and in part from clinical anecdotes gathered over a span of more than a hundred years, starting with Harlow's (1868) case of Phineas Gage. The role of the frontal lobes in performance that prima facie requires an attentional control of action and thought dates back as far as Ferrier (1876), Bianchi (1895), Flechsig (1905) and Bechterew (1907), after Gratiolet's (1861) first statement. The top position tentatively assigned to the rostral cortical regions of the frontal lobes, linking them to the leadership in the will and consciousness for any kind of behavior, stems from Jackson (1868) and Flechsig (1896). The former speculated that prefrontal cortex was amongst the phylogenetically (and myelogenetically; Flechsig, 1896) later portions of the brain to mature and, for that reason, remained the topographically and functionally least differentiated one. Henceforth, the prefrontal region was considered to be the best candidate to exert its action without any constraint on a particular type of processing and performance, and without any spatial limitation.

The frontal lobes, however, seem no longer to be the only cortical structure related to attention. Following Sokolov's (1960) schema, selective attention to incoming stimuli (viz., 'selective sensory' attention) finds its hierarchically highest areas in the supramodal, posterior parietal cortex (Hyvaerinen, 1982). Attentive control driven by inner needs (motivation) is held to be linked to the cingulate gyrus (Mesulam, 1985). Attentive control in execution (viz., 'selective motor' attention, in its planning, modulating and checking components: Luria, 1966) is currently agreed (Benson and Geschwind, 1975; Heilman et al., 1987) to be anchored to the anterior cingular, premotor and prefrontal areas. It seems apparent that less rostral frontal areas (i.e.,

oculomotor and premotor) are involved in the intentional control of activities, chiefly motor in nature, carried out in the contralateral space (Kennard and Ectors, 1938; Welch and Stuteville, 1958; Watson et al., 1977). On the other hand, the most rostral areas of the laterodorsal aspects of the prefrontal cortex are devoted to the attentional control of every kind of action without any spatial constraint.

The dopaminergic supply to the rostral frontal network from the mesencephalic nigral and reticular systems (Simon, 1981; Heilman et al., 1987) may be involved in the motivational and intentional drive of selective attention (Newman et al., 1984).

The rostral location of attentional control fits both into the descriptive frame of Fuster's (1980) sensorimotor *Gestaltkreis* (Weizsaecker, 1950) and into the functionalistic interpretation of Norman and Shallice's (1980, 1986) cognitive model. Shallice (1982) himself collected some empirical evidence, using a test version of the Tower of Hanoi game, in support of the role of the prefrontal network (particularly of the left hemisphere) in the functioning of the supervisory system. Data from our laboratory (Spinnler, Della Sala and Marchetti, unpublished findings) fail to support the sensitivity of a simplified version of the Hanoi Towers test for the presence of uni- and bilateral frontal lesions. Another candidate for a supervisory test could be the Wisconsin Card Sorting test (Milner, 1963): its sensitivity in telling apart frontal patients from controls as well as its specificity for revealing the consequences of frontal damage appear, however, to hold true no longer (Anderson et al., 1990). Thus great doubt is cast on the Hanoi and Wisconsin tests as valuable tools to reveal the frontal linkage of the highest aspects of the attentional control on cognitive coping. On the other hand, Wilkins et al.s' (1987) data on a slow-paced numerosity judgement, in line with Salmaso and Denes' (1982) novel stimulus detection in a monotonous vigilance task, point to the frontorostral areas (particularly of the right hemisphere) as playing an important role in sustained attention.

In the light of PET investigations of the topographical subdivisions of the associative frontal cortex (Duara et al., 1986), it turns out (Haxby et al., 1988) in AD that, when the frontal region was metabolically already involved, the premotor areas were the most and the orbitofrontal the least impaired; the polar areas had an intermediate degree of hypometabolism. One should, however, be cautious when equating regional PET discrepancies across subdivisions of the rostral cerebral surface defined geometrically on scan views with the traditional cytomyeloarchitectonic and functional divisions of the frontal multimodal associative cortex. In any case, from correlative studies on AD patients (Haxby et al., 1988) the bulk of the attentional and metabolic impairment is not as straightforwardly linked to the polar areas as expected from previous findings on animals (Fuster, 1980) and on neurological patients not affected by AD (viz., so-called 'frontal lobe dementia'; Neary et al., 1988).

It has been stated by Denny-Brown and Chambers (1958) that prefontral areas relate to inner needs of the organism (emotional as well as cognitive in nature), whereas supramodal posterior parietal areas have the opposite, environmentally directed role. This 'janusian view of fronto-parietal interactions' (Mesulam, 1986) can explain how 'prefrontal lesions could promote not only an excessive approach to the environment, leading to distractibility and concreteness, but perhaps also an excessive distance from intrapsychic processes necessary for insight, foresight and abstraction. In contrast, lesions in the parietal network could promote an avoidance of the extrapersonal world and perhaps an excessive reliance on intrapsychic data, even when these are in conflict with external reality' (Mesulam, 1986). Many neuropsychological symptoms and their parietotemporo-to-frontal evolution (viz., the parallel, even if temporally discrepant, progression of the metabolic and histopathological impairment; see section 3) in AD patients fit into the just quoted 'janusian view of fronto – parietal interactions'.

Along the lines of the long-standing neurological debate on the differentiation of Pick's disease from AD (Munos-Garcia et al., 1984; Tissot et al., 1985; Knopman et al., 1989), there has recently been a reappraisal of histopathologically non-AD dementias, in some of which the bulk of the degenerative lesions is located in the frontal cortex (Gustafson, 1987; Neary et al., 1988). Most of them are marked from the onset by personality change and social breakdown, and pathologically show up with a predominant frontal lobe degeneration (Neary et al., 1988). The progressive demential picture of such patients is characterized by cognitive impairment in regulating behavior (Knopman et al., 1989): literally, 'in directing and maintaining attention to a task, implementing effective strategies for achieving a solution and checking of responses' (Neary et al., 1988). It should, however, be noted that, even if not so early and selectively in their course (Grady et al., 1988), attentional control disorders are an obvious component also of the Alzheimer cognitive disorders. Thus, from the neuropsychological viewpoint of dementias, there is some evidence for a predominantly frontal location of the attentional control.

Finally, there are interesting contributions from blood-flow studies. They show that so-called 'hyperfrontality' in the resting state (Ingvar, 1976; Prohovnik et al., 1980) is highly variable across the same individual, with a clearcut consistent reduction (i.e., 'habituation') when parallel forms of cognitive tasks have been administered over time (Risberg et al., 1977; Maximilian et al., 1980). It is thought that the effort to establish a learning standard entails, in blood-flow terms, an increase of the frontal baseline, whereas frontal habituation takes place as soon as that notion or that procedure consolidates in a steady trace (Ingvar, 1979; Wood, 1987).

Section 2. Attention disorders in demented patients

This section is subdivided into four topics. The underlying assumption is that the performances considered can be ranked according to their attentional demands. Moreover, it is held that this variable is relevant to the understanding of the progressive neuropsychological impairment during the course of the dementing process. Such a strategy of meta-analysing the available data is in keeping with that adopted by Hasher and Zacks (1979) in their review of several attentional facets of memory-processing in healthy people, and by Jorm (1986) in his review of cognitive failures in demented people.

The first heading (i) will go quickly through scattered neurological remarks on attention disorders in demented patients, derived from clinical settings. The second heading (ii) reviews neuropsychological findings mostly derived from formal experimental settings, whose purpose, however, was not to investigate attention directly. The third heading (iii) deals with a handful of experiments done in order to tackle specific issues related to the attentional behavior of demented people. The last heading (iv) is devoted to attentional disorders underlying pseudodementias. With the exception of heading (iii) the main focus of section 2 is to take into account clinical claims ((i) and (iv)) and experimental outputs (ii) on the assumption that they have something in common. We recognize the obvious risk of arbitrarily forcing into the thought system of attention a welter of otherwise heterogeneous phenomena, most of which had not been originally described as an instance of attention-controlled behavior.

(i) 'Attention disorders' mentioned by neurologists

Clinical neurologists often simply adopt for some patients the uninformative description 'attentionally impaired', whenever during examination the patient appears easily distractable or confused, and, because of that, poorly cooperative. The psychological construct of reference is implicitly that of Head's (1923) definition of what by that time was meant by 'vigilance', namely 'a state of high-grade efficiency of the central nervous system'. Here 'efficiency' indicates chiefly the goal-directed processing and answering capacity of the brain when dealing with incoming stimuli.

A more precise neurological approach to attention disorders is the jacksonian approach of Benson and Geschwind (1975). These authors organize

hierarchically the consequences of the lesions to the upper brainstem activating system, to the thalamic projection system, and to the forebrain-frontal region. The lesions to the most caudal level, when not (or before) resulting in structural stupor and coma (Plum and Posner, 1980; Saper and Plum, 1985), give rise to disorders of ongoing alertness. Benson and Geschwind (1975) call it 'drifting attention', that is, a paramount defect of sustained attention. Lesions to the intermediate level, which is often embedded in the metabolic, pharmacological or psychiatric delirium syndrome, give rise to an extreme distractibility, often without clouded alertness. The resulting condition of 'wandering attention' is a profound defect of selective attention. Impairment of the most rostral level brings about the disorders of planned behavior (Stuss and Benson, 1984), again without clouding of alertness. The present review deals with the latter two sets of attention disorders, since brainstem lesions are a marginal component of the neuropathology of the dementing processes.

Neurologists emphasize the difficulty that demented patients have in focusing attention, what Delay and Brion (1962) called a defect of 'voluntary attention'. Actually, demented patients poorly withstand distraction when engaged in the rather informal tasks involved in a neurological examination. Clinicians are struck by the fragility and shortness of demented people's sustained attention.

Complaints of 'difficulties in seeing' are often an early symptom of AD patients (Cogan, 1985; Sadun et al., 1987). Hutton et al. (1989) maintain that the AD seeing disorders are, when not agnosic in nature (cf. review by Harin, 1987), disorders of the automatic looking mechanisms, that is, of gaze movements. Visual coping of AD patients appears hampered by slowness in initiating saccades (Fletcher and Sharpe, 1986), poor compensation with large corrective saccades, failures of smooth pursuits (Hutton et al., 1984), and poor general organization of environmental scanning (Hutton et al., 1987). Progressive disorders of the automatic control of the interplay of motor and perceptual feedback, with a poorly efficient regression to effortful control, seem to be at work at a certain point of the dementing course. One can trace back to a particular kind of attention disorder, namely the shifting capacity of attention, the poor visual (and possibly auditory) behavior of some severely deteriorated Alzheimer patients (Hutton et al., 1985). Some of them show up with so severe a visual scanning defect as to almost fit into the Balint-Holmes syndrome (De Renzi, 1982). In fact, once a target has been selected, or is happened upon by chance, an impairment in disengaging focused attention in order to shift to a new target in a complex visual environment sometimes becomes paramount. Such a condition causes the demented patient to behave as if they were affected by Wolpert's simultaneoagnosia. Whereas fully fledged 'locked gaze' is a seldom apparent defect, one forms the impression that many AD patients suffer an overall reduction of the visual attentional field without having any campimetric narrowing. Both defects of spatial exploration can be framed in Denny-Brown and Chamber's (1958) and Mesulam's (1986) already mentioned hypothesis on the fronto-parietal tradeoff of attentional control.

AD patients are very frequently reported to fail in maintaining over short periods an intentionally achieved, contextually unprimed, posture such as protrusion of the tongue, closure of the eyes, etc. This disorder, which is surely far from specific to demented subjects, can be looked on as the impairment of a short-lasting sustained attention task. The resulting 'motor impersistence' (Joynt et al., 1962) has, however, up to now not been defined as a formal item in the clinical evaluation of demented patients.

In this theoretically poorly directed vein, De Mol (1986) found that nearly all his patients suffering normotensive hydrocephalus had preoperatively an attention disorder, presenting as poor concentration apparent during verbal learning and mental calculation. An attention involvement has also been suggested in Binswanger's subcortical arteriosclerotic encephalopathy (Derix et al., 1987). Another instance of vaguely defined claims of attention disorders is that of Vitaliano et al. (1986), who at-

tached a predictive power to attention measures in AD patients: attention was, however, ascertained only by means of some isolated items of Mattis' (1976) dementia rating scale.

Collecting the stories relating to the early steps of the dementing course of intellectually still active AD patients, one of the apparently paradoxical and common features is the dissociation between the still well-preserved professional coping and the severely deteriorated ability to cope with the domestic trivial activities. In explaining the 'facade-phenomenon' (reevaluated by Spinnler, 1985) one can maintain that fewer resources are needed to master even a sophisticated, but overpractised, intellectual activity than to face possibly less trained sets of domestic requests. This frequent observation is reminiscent of Jackson's (1868) 'automatic-voluntary dissociation' apparent in many left-brain damaged patients within the verbal and praxic domains, which, however, remains inapparent in everyday behavior and occurs nearly only in testing settings on comparable tasks. To my knowledge this is the first time that different behaviors were traced back to different degrees of attention control. 'Automatic' is here chiefly meant as an environmentally driven response, that is, a long consolidated procedure to respond in a fixed way given a specific, albeit complex, context or set of stimuli. The post hoc explanation attributes to the damage of the brain a propensity to impair far more the effortful activities and to leave nearly untouched quasi-automatic responses, as if the former called for a larger amount of attentional resources.

It is worth stressing that patients with subcortical dementia (Albert et al., 1974; Cummings and Benson, 1984; Cummings, 1986), characterized by a task-independent psychomotor slowing, may be distinguished from AD patients, who, instead, very often appear to be in a hyperaroused state. Yerks and Dodson's (1908) inverted 'U' function, relating arousal and cognitive capacity (Kahneman, 1973; Mandler, 1975), may provide a descriptive frame for the nonaware emergence of an automatic, though poorly appropriate, response (Norman, 1976), both in hypoaroused subcortical patients and in hyperaroused AD patients. Moreover, such opposite styles of coping might have a particularly narrow window in AD, being likely to occur in the same individual with very short time lags.

Most neurological accounts of attention disorders in demented patients refer to orientation defects. Attention is reasonably held to be involved therein (Chedru and Geschwind, 1972; Seltzer and Mesulam, 1988). Orientation refers to the ability to give instantaneously a full account of the several links between the self, one's surrounding, and one's own past (Berrios, 1983). 'Disorientation' and 'confusion' refer, respectively, to the test (viz., inquiry) assessed condition and to the general clinical syndrome of impaired orientation (Lipowski, 1985). Orientation is, of course, not a unitary ability and it breaks down into different content-related inquiries, such as spatial, temporal, personal, familiar items, and so on. This heterogeneity may account for the poor correlations across orientation scores for different contents in normals as well as in AD patients (Cossa, Della Sala and Spinnler, unpublished findings). The process underlying orientation may be conceived of as a recollection activity integrating automatically acquired ongoing information (Hasher and Zacks, 1979) with actively retrieved semantic notions about the self. The assessment of issues of orientation is currently embodied into mental status examinations aiming to evaluate the overall severity of dementia. Efficient perception, intelligence and, of course, memory (Daniel et al., 1987) are required for appropriately encoding, organizing and retrieving packages of associated context- and biography-related information in order to have full knowledge and awareness of one's own identity. Active (i.e., controlled) search is generally held to play a significant role in the converging processes of orientation (Goody, 1969). This effort increases enormously when it is brought into play by brain-damaged patients, possibly emphasizing the attentional dependence of many orientation tasks. Given the link of orientation with so many different cognitive activities, its high sensitivity to the presence of the most heterogeneous structural and metabolic brain damage and psychological

disorders is not surprising (Lezak, 1983). Attention-impairing drugs, such as alcohol, benzodiazepines and anticholinergics, often induce clearcut confusional states, and the opposite may occur with other drugs, such as amphetamine and cocaine. In any case, Yerkes and Dodson's (1908) 'law' also describes the variability of orientation performances, because they are similarly impaired at both extremes of 'arousal'.

One can raise the question here that often crops up in the clinical wards and institutions, namely how conscious AD patients are of their cognitive deficits. One of the underlying general questions is to what extent 'consciousness' is a property of attentional control (Shallice, 1988). At least for definitional purposes, as far as concerns the vexed concept of awareness (equated here with consciousness), we agree with Schacter's (1990) view, namely that of 'ongoing representation of specific mental activities' as well as their partial defects.

One must agree that AD patients, as well as frontal patients, are surely not fully bereft of consciousness of their cognitive incompetence, although their attentional control has become clearly inefficient. If we take as a pertinent behavioral, albeit anecdotal, index the degree of anosognosia of dementia, AD patients retain (at least intermittently) up to rather severe stages of the disease the ability to make fairly explicit their knowledge about their own poor cognitive coping. The role of the damage to the frontal lobes in bringing about anosognosia of neurological and cognitive deficits is discussed in Stuss and Benson's (1986) review. As far as amnesia is concerned, it seems as if patients with frontal lobe damage coupled with amnesic deficits are unaware of having memory problems, and often present with confabulations. This is said (e.g., Schachter, 1990) not to be the case with temporal lobe amnesic patients. A difference of possibly similar importance can be seen when comparing awareness of autobiographical defective recall of thalamic versus widespread anoxic amnesics: respectively perfect versus dim awareness (Dall'Ora et al., 1989). In this study AD patients appeared to be unaware of their poor autobiographical recall. Whereas strict anosognosia of specific cognitive defects is a rare occurrence, a vague feeling of poor cognitive coping is instead very frequent in the early and middle stages of AD. In everyday settings AD patients often claim that there is 'something wrong in their heads', that they are 'confused', that, at variance with their past, every question appears now to be too hard to be answered, but the critical complaint of a specific memory or language or spatial breakdown crops up rather seldom, and in the same patient inconsistently. This blurred knowledge may be simply a consequence of an impaired episodic learning and it is mere speculation to trace it back to the frontal lobe involvement by the AD process.

Finally, it is worth pointing out that among the neuropsychological deficits rendering an AD patient no longer testable for experimental purposes (viz., for the assessment of her/his residual cognitive abilities), attention disorders possibly play an important role. It is the extreme momentary unsteadiness of selective attention – resulting in proneness to inner and outer triggered distractibility – or a steady motivational loss (i.e., inertia) that enhances the cognitive incompetence, causing the patient to become inaccessible to any testing procedure. The same possibly underlies the severity of the ecological incompetence that leads the patient to an institution. For the reason above, samples of AD patients suited to neuropsychological research are biased toward the presence of some residual control efficiency (Capitani et al., 1990) This is one of the biases that make them not straightforwardly representative of the whole AD population.

(ii) Cognitive defects of demented patients that could allow ordering along the automatic/effortful dimension

Cognitive decline in the demential process clearly runs an uneven course and it is assumed that the attentional component involved in each instrumental performance can provide a cue to the understanding of the degree of its failure. Put in other words, the forecast posed here is that the more attention-demanding a task is, the more and earlier will the

corresponding performance be disrupted in AD patients (Jorm, 1986). The plan of the meta-analysis that follows is drawn from the above assumption, which will in turn be discussed in section 3 of this chapter.

Attentional disorders in the language domain
Recent data (Kertesz et al., 1986; Spinnler and Della Sala, 1988) frequently show an early language impairment in AD patients. For instance, in Gavazzi's et al. (1986) series of mildly deteriorated Alzheimer patients, 90% of them turned out to be 'aphasic' following the strictly probabilistic criteria provided by the Aachener Aphasie Test (De Blesser et al., 1986). In the follow-up (Gavazzi, Luzzatti, Spinnler and Willmes, 1990) all patients were classified – in keeping with Rapacszak et al.'s (1989) data – as 'aphasic'.

It is universally agreed that the most salient language defect of Alzheimer patients is their word-finding impairment (Irigaray, 1973). Cued generation of words became a standardized test as early as the Simon-Binet examination for intelligence (Terman and Merrill, 1937), from which later derived the formal word-fluency test of Spreen and Benton (1969) and, in recent times, tests standardized for age and education (Spinnler and Tognoni, 1987, for categorically cued fluency; Novelli et al., 1986, for alphabetically cued fluency; Bandera et al., in press, for free word generation. In a recent study (Capitani, Della Sala, Lorenzi and Spinnler, unpublished data) on 66 mild AD patients and 66 healthy matched elderly it turned out that categorically cued fluency ranked at the 3rd place among 4 tests, the nonverbal ones being, respectively, of visual selective attention, supra-span spatial learning, and spatial cognition (constructional apraxia); the fluency test achieved an overall predictive power of 86.4%.

Modern studies on language disorders of demented patients usually collect data derived from test batteries. Studies administering verbal batteries permit one to contrast patients' individual performance on different language tasks. This approach established that there is a consistent, and longitudinally enhancing, contrast between the early name-finding impairment (as assessed in test settings or in spontaneous speech; Appel et al., 1982; Martin and Fedio, 1983) as opposed to preserved repetition (Rochford, 1971; Bayles and Tomoeda, 1983; Gavazzi et al., 1987) up to echolalia in the most severely deteriorated patients. In fact, access to the inner lexicon (or perhaps to the organized semantic knowledge per se; Martin and Fedio, 1983) appears to be impaired far more and earlier.

It is agreed that the active search involved makes access to the inner lexicon different from the automatic use of syntax and phonology (Whitaker, 1976; Schwartz et al., 1979; Bayles and Boone, 1982; Gewirth et al., 1984). As a consequence, it appears that in AD patients' everyday conversation the morphological structure of language is well-preserved for a long time. Thus, propositional everyday talking remains formally correct but, for communication purposes, almost completely 'empty' (Benson, 1979). Emphasis is put on the attentional cost of word-searching activity as well as of planning discourse, whereas even the complex routines of morphology are nearly automatic, at least for the native speaker.

One can suggest that it is for attentional reasons that all access tasks to the lexicon (viz., lexical retrieval by means of generative and confrontation naming; Bonsfield and Sedgewick, 1944) and to discourse-planning prove highly sensitive to the presence of dementia, even before an overt aphasic disorder of language has become apparent. It must, however, be pointed out that even among healthy elderly subjects, word-finding and discourse-planning during intentional communication become progressively harder (viz., more control-demanding) as witnessed by the frequent occurrence of extremely inconsistent 'tip-of-the-tongue' (viz., anomic) phenomena, even if aging results in a progressively more refined, though nearly costless, morphological building of the sentences (Obler and Albert, 1981; Huff, 1990, pp. 251 – 253). So a rather normal event may be overemphasized in demented patients. In fact, demented elderly fail more dramatically on tasks which nondemented elderly

rank among the hardest. These tasks may be harder either because they simply compel the subject to search in a wider range of alternatives, or because they reflect differences in the demand for focusing control (Reason and Lukas, 1984) that allows linking thought to the appropriate words and discourse plan.

Visual word identification during reading – in clear contrast with confrontation naming to visual stimuli or to verbal definition – is another example of an ability that is preserved in AD patients (Jorm and Share, 1983; La Berge and Samuels, 1984). For the same well-reading patient comprehension of the written test can, however, be severely reduced up to 'transcortical alexia'. This discrepancy in AD patients to read between their ability, and to comprehend is one of the more surprising pieces of evidence for some kind of preserved automatic access to very particular functional aspects of procedural knowledge (Nebes et al., 1984; Nebes and Boller, 1986; Nebes and Madden, 1988). In fact, while these patients poorly understand what they are reading, at the same time they automatically correct the morphological errors built into the text. The finding of preserved slavish reading is such a robust finding that it gave rise to formal procedures aiming at reliably estimating premorbid intelligence in demented patients (Nelson and McKenna, 1975; Nelson and O'Connell, 1978; Ruddle and Bradshaw, 1982). The phonological-lexical discrepancy of impairment is also apparent in Rapacsak's et al. (1989) study on AD patients (all affected by anomic or transcortical sensory aphasia). All of them end up with lexical agraphia (sometimes coupled with apraxic agraphia), while their phonological system appears to be almost untouched. Here again the role of attentional defects needs to be evaluated in future goal-directed studies.

While single-word comprehension is only mildly impaired, at least in the early stages of AD, it is apparent in ecological and experimental settings (Gavazzi et al., 1986; Gavazzi, Luzzatti, Spinnler and Willmes, 1990) that language comprehension becomes more and more hampered as the amount of information increases (viz., from word to sentence and prose comprehension). Sentence and prose comprehension in demented patients is likely to require more than only language abilities: besides short-term memory, selection and organization of information to be stored for further processing involve an attentional demand. Focusing on lexical and syntactic comprehension and dividing attention between working memory and semantic processing to grasp the overall meaning involve attentional demands that have hitherto not been elucidated in AD patients.

'Semantics' was conceived of as the study of the 'relationship between linguistic signs and the world'; its definition is now generalized to 'the relationship between any object and event (not only linguistic objects) and the general knowledge we have of those objects and events' (Caramazza et al., in press). One has to believe that a good deal of the cognitive deterioration of dementia is rooted in the progressive impoverishment of the above-mentioned, very sophisticated, relationships. Many of the issues raised when discussing semantic disorders usually of left-hemisphere damaged patients (cf. Gainotti, 1988; Vignolo, 1989), are now growing into a vivid debate also with respect to AD. A line of studies (Martin and Fedio, 1983; Huff et al., 1986) supports the view that a degradation of the semantic information in AD patients' knowledge causes the breakdown of the ability to establish or reject rapidly membership in a category (Bayles and Tomoeda, 1983; Huff et al., 1984; Grober et al., 1985; Nebes et al., 1986; Nebes and Brady, 1988). These studies point to a particular access disorder in AD, namely a failure in picking out the salient attributes and in generating useful semantic features of a given concept. Mildly deteriorated AD patients in Nebes and Brady's (1988) study continue to maintain a rather rich network of semantic associations (viz., lexical semantic fields). Such findings emphasize the working of the active way in which some tasks require access to semantic associations. The poor drive to recollection (see next heading of this section) from remote memory appears to be a general characteristic of AD patients. Such a disorder is possibly more akin to a supervisory,

plan-generation defect than to a trace degradation. There is, however, a complete lack of any information about the natural history of the semantic amnesia in AD: it may well be that the controversial conclusions of the studies above stem from sampling differences, namely more deteriorated patients in Martin and Fedio's (1983) and less severely deteriorated patients in Nebes' studies.

As already mentioned, impairment of verbal semantic abilities of AD patients comprises, besides defects in confrontation naming, the inability to grasp the semantic relationships between a set of stimuli and to pick out from lexical-semantic remote memory members of a given category. Two significant papers on this topic (Nebes et al., 1986, 1989) depended upon semantic priming tasks. They show that AD patients use controlled process to access semantic information, as well as the automatic spreading activation of a fragment of the semantic net (Stanovich and West, 1983), which Neeley (1977) found to be at work in normals. The former way 'involves the subject consciously directing a limited capacity processor to a location in the semantic memory' (Nebes et al., 1986) by means of a sentence-generated expectancy. Nebes et al. (1989) suggested that the poor versus relatively well-preserved semantic access in different AD patients rests on the inability versus ability to generate from the context a new searching strategy (a task accomplished by the supervisory system).

There are other facets of semantic processing possibly dependent upon attentional supervision. Mention is made once more of word comprehension as well as of identification of objects (Ratcliff and Newcombe, 1982; Glucksberg, 1984; Snodgrass, 1984; Caramazza and Berendt, 1987; Martin, 1987), capacities that are impaired less, or more seldom, or later on during the course of the disease, in comparison to any kind of active searching in the remote memory repertoire (e.g., accessing lexicon to generate words under given constraints). The discrepancy above is likely to find future explanation in terms of different and selective access and output disorders from (possibly unitary; Caramazza, Hillis, Rapp and Romani, unpublished findings) semantic representation(s) (Seymour, 1979). In any case, longitudinal studies of semantic disorders in AD patients, besides potentially influencing the semantic modelling debate, should include some kind of assessment of the attentional cost of each test (or each step in a processing model) in order to check possible attentional biases involved in discrepant performances (e.g., language comprehension or object recognition versus word generation or object naming).

AD patients have language deficits that tentatively could be traced back to each of the levels of control postulated by Norman and Shallice's (1980, 1986) model (see Fig. 1). Let us give for each level an example related to the most trivial language impairments of AD patients. In the model, 'horizontal threads' give an account of how 'trigger conditions' – provided they match the contents of a 'trigger database' – start an overlearned, habitual action that does not demand any sensitive attentional cost. Often many clumsy, non-echolalic, utterances of demented patients who are asked to express personal or common information appear to be the output of isolated single verbal schemas. The sentences are often inappropriate because there is a faulty matching with the corresponding database. Moreover, they fail to stimulate a strand of processing capable of completing even a small fragment of a sentence. This condition of an extremely poor external activation of uncontrolled schemas usually characterizes severe deterioration. Let us now approach a slightly higher level in the model at issue. A disorder of the 'vertical threads' controlling 'contention-scheduling' would result in a defect of cooperative, well-timed, activation/inhibition of a set of schemas. The 'source-schema', given its fragility and inconsistency in the AD patient, no longer controls sequences of actions, bereft as it is of superimposed modulation. This is the failure of the actions directed to achieve a communicative goal following a definite discourse strategy. Actually, 'empty' and circumlocutory speech can be conceived of as the consequence of failures in organizing a communicative plan. The defect of this attentional level applies currently to moderately deteriorated

patients. Finally, when the 'supervisory system' is unable to bias autonomously sets of schemas by the 'contention-scheduling' mechanisms, the patient is no longer able to initiate untriggered communicative plans, such as a spontaneous narration that involves discourse planning. Such an onset condition comes to the fore in everyday settings only from time to time, a common instance being the so-called 'demential episodes' (Spinnler, 1985). These failures occur with full awareness on the part of the mildly deteriorated patient.

It is worth underscoring that for each of the levels of disordered attentional control putatively involved in the previous listed examples, the patients are still able to produce the corresponding instrumental performance per se. Reference is made, respectively, to word production by repetition, to the ability to complete stereotyped ways of saying with preserved morphology, and to high-quality environmentally triggered communicative routines. The preservation of the latter performances closely mimics the often accurate fixed habit performances of frontal patients (Rylander, 1939; McFie, 1960; Lhermitte et al., 1972). Luria (1966) stated that such frontal patients are sometimes able to answer, albeit laconically, but are unable to give an organized narrative account. This behavioral discrepancy is an early finding in AD patients too. More in general, a two-component hypothesis could throw light also on the verbal communication disorders of AD patients and on their natural history. Capitani, Della Sala, Lorenzi and Spinnler (unpublished data) suggest that language disorders of AD are due both to instrumental (viz. retrorolandic and truely 'aphasic' in nature) and control (viz., prefrontal and attention in nature, such as hampered discourse planning) impairments.

It would, of course, be interesting to push the longitudinal analysis of AD patients further along the frames of a detailed attentional model. Actually, such an enterprise could lend support to a hierarchical deterioration of the attentional system throughout the course of AD (Jorm, 1986). After all, some language testing can be performed until relatively late in the course of AD patients.

Attentional disorders in the memory domain

The presence of some kind of memory disorder is an essential feature for the diagnosis of AD (cf. Bannister, 1978; Lishman, 1978; Eisdorfer and Cohen, 1980; McKhann et al., 1984; Spinnler and Della Sala, 1988). Detailed information, however, on the degree of impairment of the various facets of memory-processing in AD patients is still rather scanty.

Memory should be regarded as a non-unitary function especially in discussing the role of attention. Recent data from a neuropsychological survey (Spinnler and Della Sala, 1988) that administered only tests yielding age, education and sex-adjusted scores, comparable to healthy baselines and across themselves (Spinnler and Tognoni, 1987; Capitani and Laiacona, 1988), show the following frequencies of definitely impaired scores in mild AD patients: forward verbal span 40% of the patients, forward spatial span 48%, supra-span verbal learning (LTS) 58%, supra-span spatial learning 57%; prose memory 91%; autobiographical memory 88%. (Dall'Ora et al., 1989). These findings confirm that during the first steps of the dementing disease none of the classical memory facets examined in a laboratory setting remains preserved. No patient, diagnosed on external criteria to be affected by probable AD, passed all the tests, although very few fail on all of them. This evidence – at variance with the results of language-testing above – renders the allocation of single tasks along the automatic/effortful continuum even more arbitrary.

Moreover, in most studies on AD patients several facets of memory-processing have been left out. This is the case with semantic memory. Recent preliminary findings of ours regarding memory for semantic information point to an impairment in AD comparable to that suggested for episodic memory: Bressi, Della Sala and Spinnler (unpublished data) found impaired subjects in a series of mild AD patients ranging from 40 to 88% for verbal and from 35 to 45% for nonverbal semantic tests. There is a particular dearth in Alzheimer studies on the topic of 'automatic memory' (Hasher and Zacks, 1979), which is somehow preserved in healthy aging

(Kausler and Puckett, 1980). A similar dearth exists regarding procedural memory, with the exceptions of Butters' (1984) and Butters et al.'s (1988) studies. Moreover, there is scanty information on AD patients' ability in uncued remembering (Weingartner et al., 1981; Kopelman, 1985), such as 'memory for intentions', or 'prospective memory' (Levy and Loftus, 1984; Harris, 1984), an attention-related fundamental component of patients' paramount everyday absentmindedness and forgetfulness.

Interestingly, the evolution of memory models from separate 'boxes' (Atkinson and Shiffrin, 1971, 1972), to in-depth processing (Craik and Lockhart, 1972), and to the working memory model (Baddeley and Hitch, 1974), increasingly stresses the role of attention. The working memory model explicitly embodies control systems therein, such as Baddeley's (1986) 'central executive'. Broadbent's (1984) 'Maltese cross' hypothesis of memory processing is another example of the general trend to organize access and use of special functional devices, by means of a supraordinated allocator of resources that is explicitly conceived of as attentive in nature. In connection with this tendency, one must be aware of the risk of crediting as attentive all that escapes clearcut understanding about memory processing. Such a generalizing trend would unduly imply that attention becomes a sort of deus ex machina for an increasing number of cognitive computations. The memory processes for which attention has been claimed to play an important role will be now considered in some detail.

Learning is a classical token of controlled processing in Shiffrin and Schneider's (1977) paradigm. The stored information eventually becomes part of a net of automatically linked elements, a condition that facilitates retrieval. Huppert and Piercy (1978) and many others suggested that the impairment of long-term consolidation in the net of the stored information is responsible for the classical short-term/long-term memory dissociation of global amnesia. A great variety of tasks provide evidence that every type of learning becomes impaired in AD both in the verbal and in the nonverbal domain. Examples in the verbal domain are recall tasks such as paired-associated (Kaszniack et al., 1979), serial learning (Weingartner et al., 1981), learning of definitions (Irving et al., 1970), supraspan digit strings (Miller, 1973) as well as the recognition tasks (Morris et al., 1983; Wilson et al., 1983a). Impairment on nonverbal learning has been found by Miller and Lewis (1977) and Wilson et al. (1982). If storage and retrieval efficiency is to a high degree linked to the active and conscious processing of incoming information (Craik and Lockhart, 1972) it would be reasonable to trace the efficiency of this memory-processing back to the control operated by sustained focused attention. Hasher and Zacks (1979) regarded the activities characterizing encoding (such as imagery, elaborative mnemonic devices, organization and clustering) to be good examples of effortful activities that enhance long-term memory efficiency. Hasher and Zacks' (1979) conclusions implicitly point to the possibility of an impairment of learning performance that is predominantly based on insufficient attention control during encoding, an event that in a number of instances occurs also in healthy people.

Learning deficits of demented patients can in part be traced back to their attentional impairment (Becker, 1987); this argument will be raised again later on. Possibly the other critical component in long-term storage, particularly in the verbal domain, is semantic coding (Baddeley, 1982b), and, as discussed above, it is universally agreed that AD patients are also impaired at the lexical semantic level of verbal processing.

Short-term memory is thought to require a high attentional component to overcome the deleterious consequences of distraction. Parkinson et al. (1980) pointed out that the difference in short-term memory between young and adult healthy individuals is linked to the division of attention between the two or more cognitive operations possibly involved therein (Craik, 1977; Wright, 1981; Salthouse et al., 1985). This statement underscores more a control than a strict memory-processing difference.

Miller (1973), Pierce and Miller (1973), Kaszniak et al. (1979) and Morris (1984) found a slight impair-

ment of digit span in mildly deteriorated AD patients. Attentionally impaired delirious patients typically fail at this task (Spitz, 1972; Lipowski, 1985). Wilson et al. (1983b) and Spinnler et al. (1988) showed that mildly deteriorated AD patients have a normal recency component in a free-recall serial position curve experiment, being instead severely impaired in the primacy component, as are global amnesics. This finding has been interpreted (Capitani, Logie, Della Sala and Spinnler, unpublished data), within Baddeley and Hitch's (1974) working memory model, as a rather selective impairment of the 'central executive' combined with preserved articulatory rehearsal mechanisms as well as preserved passive phonological store (Morris, 1984, 1987). The latter are responsible for the relatively preserved 'instrumental' aspects of STM such as short-term memory measure.

Sullivan et al. (1986) and Morris (1986) showed that early AD patients are more severely hindered than healthy controls when requested to store short-term information while simultaneously processing a heavy cognitive load (i.e., the Brown-Peterson task, a typical short-term divided attention task). In a similar vein, Baddeley et al. (1986) found that combining forward digit span (with length of spans corresponding to the actual basal level of the subject at study) with visuomotor tracking (again, at the basal performance of the patient at study) increases the number of faulty sequences. Such an increase is significantly higher in the mild AD patients involved in the study than in the comparable healthy elderly (respectively, 43% versus 20%). Baddeley et al. (1986) argued that such findings reflect a selective attentional drop in AD patients, which crops up when resources must be divided between different activities (Wright, 1981; Nebes and Brady, 1989). In general, one can assume that divided attention findings in short-term memory-processing are likely to support the impairment in AD patients of the 'vertical threads' in Norman and Shallice's (1980, 1986) supervisory system (see Fig. 1). These devices may be involved in the operations attached to the 'central executive' of the working memory model.

Finally, *retrieval processes* are very often held to

be (Shiffrin and Schneider, 1977) an active instance of a process resembling that of problem-solving. It is termed 'recollection' by Williams (1978) and Baddeley (1982a). Hasher and Zacks (1979) claim that the active development of retrieval strategies is another convincing instance of an effortful memory activity. Put in a wide sense, recollection can be conceived of as the active process allowing one to reexperience in full awareness a unitary fragment of the past, or to trigger faithfully the conscious representation of its meaning. In fact, the operation of recollection applies to the episodic use of memory-processing (Tulving, 1985; Kinsbourne, 1987) as well as to the conscious retrieval of a meaning from semantic and autobiographical knowledge (Reiser et al., 1986). Events and concepts stored in long-term memory become available for current purposes only when they are retrieved and allocated in a working memory system where they become sensitive (henceforth, possibly unfaithfully modified) to the inner and outer context of that moment.

'Implicit knowledge' (Hirst, 1989; Schacter, 1990) refers to unawareness of a specific bit of knowledge that in fact proves to be used in ecological and test settings. Unaware perceptual and motor skill learning has been a well-known phenomenon of severely amnesic patients since Milner's et al. (1968) observation (cf., review by Schacter et al., 1988). Implicit knowledge can be conceived of as a severe disorder of recollection, viz. of aware search and reexperience of stored information. Unaware and blurred knowledge is possibly a major cognitive defect of AD patients, though it has not been formally studied, with the exception of procedural learning (Eslinger and Damasio, 1986) and semantic priming (Nebes and Boller, 1987; Nebes and Brady, 1988; Nebes et al., 1989).

The activity of recollection has more in common with attention control than with a pure memory mechanism. Recollection is a double-faced activity encompassing both planning of appropriate retrieval strategies (i.e., generating a 'context', Williams and Hollan, 1981; assembling operatively appropriate sets of schemata) and crosschecking the plausibility and usefulness of the information

retrieved (Baddeley, 1982a). With reference to autobiographical retrieval, Reiser et al. (1986) suggested that the searching process can be conceived of as actively building 'a plausible scenario' triggering – in terms of an appropriate instruction – a set of autobiographical schemata. This explanation has also been accepted by Dall'Ora et al. (1989) for AD patients' poor autobiographical retrieval. Cueing by the examiner reduces patients' retrieval defects (Miller, 1975; Morris et al., 1983) by providing them with a solution to the problem (the adequate trigger condition or instruction) as well as a reference for crosschecking the plausibility of the retrieved information. Plausibility checking can involve either autobiographical traces or general (semantic) knowledge, giving rise, when disrupted, to the various types of confabulation (cf. the frontal patient R.J. described by Baddeley and Wilson, 1980).

While encouraging very mildly deteriorated AD patients to recollect autobiographical traces (Borrini et al., 1989), Dall'Ora et al. (1989) found that the emotional experience of the patient was surprisingly flat. When she/he occasionally succeeded in retrieving a past event of her/his life, this primed very poorly the normally almost automatically running piecemeal reconstruction of other related details of that past event (cf. Stanovich and West, 1983, for the verbal semantic domain). It is as if in AD patients the usually appropriate triggers fail to match the corresponding database and thus to start a fruitful routine for most of the remote memory-related information. Poor 'contention scheduling' acts unsuccessfully to overcome poor schemata triggering (see Fig. 1). Similarly, poor results in the autobiographical achievement also occurred for 'pure' (viz., non-demented) amnesics whose brain pathology was due to a widespread damage (viz., anoxia). Such patients are, like AD patients, manifesting a flat, driveless searching activity. Their performance clearly differed from the rather good autobiographical scores earned by focally damaged (chiefly, thalamic) amnesics included in the same study (Dall'Ora et al., 1989). The discrepancy possibly fits Jacoby's (1984) distinction between intentional and incidental retrieval. The former implies processing of information in a way that is capable of providing self-generated retrieval cues (e.g., semantic relationships between stimuli), whereas the latter relies only on the cues offered by the context and the task (Nebes et al., 1989). One can argue that AD and anoxic amnesic patients' autobiographical retrieval relies only on the incidental occurrence of remembering a fragment of a past event, whereas focal amnesics are capable of an active, intentional retrieving, thus achieving a nearly normal performance. It is worth mentioning that a driveless recollective activity led 4 out the 10 CT-assessed, nondemented frontal patients studied recently by Della Sala, Laiacona, Spinnler and Trivelli (umpublished data) to poor autobiographical retrieval as well as to a poor performance on a short set of 'executive' tests.

The particular role of attention envisaged in the retrieval processes from remote memory – that is, forcing the brain into an active and strategic searching effort – possibly interacts with the question of access or store disorders specifically raised with respect to the traces of this facet of memory (Shallice, 1987). One can argue cautiously that access disorders are predominantly of an attentive nature and that, for modal and category-specific defects (Warrington and McCarthy, 1983; Warrington and Shallice, 1984; Shallice, 1987; Shallice, 1988a), specific attentive resources (Wickens, 1984) may be selectively impaired.

It is held that some function of the rostral frontal network specifically contributes to episodic and semantic retrieval (Baddeley and Wilson, 1988). Parts of the frontally located network are thought to activate some kind of strategy, such as Reiser et al.'s (1986) 'plausible scenario' for autobiographical memory, or the attention-dependent sentence-generated expectancies described by Nebes et al. (1986). Such a function organizes the goal-directed searching activity along the kaleidoscopic aspects of the memory traces (e.g., event, context, item sequence, sensory modality, general meaning and personal feeling and so on). This strategic function can be conceived of as relating outer needs (the task) to the goal-directed reorganization (or even new

modelling) of the inner representations of the world in order to master an experimental or ecological problem in the most successful way. Setting in advance the criterion of 'success' and the strategies to achieve it, as well as continuous checking of both during processing, are strictly interlaced with the available amount of control flexibility. In fact, poor creativity and poor flexibility are amongst the most pervasive traits of patients and animals bereft of the most rostral portions of their frontal lobes. There is a tendency (Baddeley and Wilson, 1988) to ascribe such activity to the highest levels of control functions: the 'central executive' in Baddeley and Hitch's (1974) working memory model, or the supervisory system in Norman and Shallice's (1980, 1986) model. This highest attentional level may control most retrieving processes from remote memory, and in AD it may be progressively disrupted. Careful goal-directed experiments are needed to lend support to these attractive speculations above: unfortunately, there is a great dearth of them.

Looking at memory processing as a set of somehow independent information-computing systems, autonomously accessible according to differently triggering purposes and contingencies, allows one to distinguish (cf. Tulving, 1987 and Squire 1990, for a review) between *episodic, semantic* and *procedural memory* or, following Cohen and Squire's (1980) dichotomy, between *conscious declarative* and an *unconscious procedural memory*. These are only the most popular classifications suggested for memory phenomena and underlying processes. Let us consider the apparently nonrandom memory deterioration that follows the course of selective AD encroachment on the neuronal network (Oyanagi et al., 1987). There is a maximal disruption at the episodic (Kopelman, 1985), less at the semantic, and least at the procedural level (Eslinger and Damasio, 1986; Heindel et al., 1989). One may envisage post hoc support for the speculation that the impairments of the most credited long-term systems during the demential process follow rather strictly an effortful/automatic line of evolution, with the semantic memory located in between the most controlled episodic and the least controlled procedural memory. Procedural memory, although still rather vaguely defined, refers to fixed links between stimulus and response (Squire, 1982): it is preserved in pure amnesia, and is said to remain untouched for a long time in AD patients as well (Martone et al., 1984; Heindel et al., 1989). It may be that the great impact of attention on encoding and retrieval of declarative memory contents (both episodic and semantic) and, in contrast, the apparently minimal impact of attention on procedural memory phenomena is mainly linked to the conscious/unconscious features of the computing activities at work (Tulving, 1987; Shallice, 1988b).

Given the very different memory processes of episodic learning and recalling, of semantic retrieving and of the use of overlearned procedures, as well as of the conscious/unconscious surfacing of memory processing, one is led to predict that independent attentive resources (Wickens, 1984) may be involved in each of the above processes. The tradeoff of separate resources with the general attentive pool (Kahneman, 1973; Wickens, 1984) may become closer when, during the course of AD, the mechanisms for memory have reached a very deteriorated state.

Of course, it would be unwise indeed to reduce all memory deficits in demented behavior to disorders of attention availability. It may well be that dementia implies an increase of effortful demands in memory processing – particularly if episodic in nature for involving recollection from remote memory – possibly due to its direct encroachment upon the hippocampal network (Heyman et al., 1984; Hamos et al., 1989). This increase of demands simply becomes more apparent for those performances which, even in healthy people, are intrinsically more 'difficult', i.e., they need strong protection against interference. One can describe the amnesic syndrome of AD as a consequence of predominant hippocampal bilateral lesions hampering directly the mechanisms of memory processing, or as a consequence of (possibly prefrontally located) damage that produces Baddeley and Wilson's (1986, 1988) 'dysexecutive syndrome',

with its predominant attentional defective traits (Shallice, 1982). Such a view is put forward by Becker (1987, 1988), and it assumes that both sites of lesions can produce a similar result, namely an everyday amnesic behavior. In a search for purely dysexecutive and purely amnesic AD patients, following statistically validated psychometric criteria, we found one patient for each category out of a series of 55 unselected mild-to-moderately deteriorated Alzheimer patients (Baddeley et al., 1991). These findings lend some empirical support to Becker's (1987) two-component (i.e., amnesic plus dysexecutive) view of the AD episodic amnesia and to his attempt to dissociate AD patients. Becker and Smith (unpublished findings) in a longitudinal study further supported the multifactorial nature of AD's memory loss, surprisingly finding new dissociating cases that developed during the one-year follow-up period of their study.

One could go on listing other cognitive impairments of AD patients, discussing for each of them the putative role played by attentional disorders. An attentional role may be envisaged in brain-damaged patients, including AD patients, for problem-solving tasks, for verbal and nonverbal intelligence performance (Gainotti, 1988; Vignolo, 1989), and for spatial cognition and perception (Wilson et al., 1982) abilities. Such an enterprise seems, however, worthless inasmuch as the examples given above for language and memory defects of AD patients cast enough light on the possible role of attention in the cognitive impairment of dementia, thereby supporting the need to turn cognitive speculations about impairment of attention in AD into goal-directed experimental findings.

(iii) Neuropsychological experiments on attention

Studies on reaction time (RT) and on selective attention in AD patients will now be reviewed.

Reaction time studies

The basic relevance of RT assessment stems from the strict relationship between speed and accuracy in almost all complex performances. Alzheimer patients appear to be severely impaired when asked to react in a complex testing condition, such as choice RT (Pirozzolo et al., 1981; Tecce et al., 1983) as well as in simple acoustic RT when associated with a visuomotor tracking task (Baddeley et al., 1986) or a letter cancellation task (Parasuraman and Nestor, 1986). Vrtunski et al.'s (1983) conclusions emphasize the AD patients' pervading disorganization and the inconsistency of the components that produce the global long latency in their choice RT. These features are thought to point to the basic failure of the central control in the planning of a response. It is well-known that even simple RTs are influenced by the attentional shift that is involved in preparation to respond during the prestimulus period. This was part of Moray's (1970) introspective evidence of the role of attention. Slight lengthening and enhanced variability of RT in AD patients can very likely be traced back to the reduction of their attentional shifting capability.

Naville's (1922) concept of 'bradyphrenia' is that of a psychomotor slowing, independent of the nature of the task at issue, due to central slowing of processing. The concept clearly belongs to the neurological frame of Head's (1923) views of 'vigilance impairments' of brain-damaged patients. It corresponds in fact to a rather aspecific attentional deficit consisting of a reduced response speed with a less affected response accuracy. Slowing of RT and reduced sustained attention (Heilman et al., 1976; Evarts et al., 1981; Stern et al., 1984) are common findings in many parkinsonian patients. Comparing simple to choice RT, their slowing has been related to the most controlled (central) component of the response latency (Mahurin et al., 1984). The degree of the parkinsonian slowing is, however, comparable to that registered in AD patients with a 'cortical' dementia (Mahurin et al., 1986) and a transmitter unbalance that is not as straightforward as that of parkinsonian patients. One can, however, object that bradyphrenia is only roughly expressed by slowing of the central component of RT. A more detailed review of bradyphrenia is found elsewhere in this volume (Dubois et al.).

Experiments on selective attention

A handful of recent studies devoted to AD patients' selective attention disorders will be reviewed.

Reporting signals presented against a distracting background (visual or auditory) is a task of selective attention often impaired in the early stages of 'presenile dementia' patients (Lawson et al., 1967). Digit or letter cancellation tasks are other selective (focused) attention instances which can reveal a control impairment in AD patients (Allender and Kaszniak, 1985; Mattis, 1976; Spinnler and Della Sala, 1988, who employed the standardized test described in Spinnler and Tognoni, 1987; for a new version, cf Della Sala, Laiacoma, Spinnler and Ubezio, unpublished data)

Capitani et al. (1988) administered Gottschaldt's hidden (or embedded) figure test (Gottschaldt, 1926, 1929) to mildly deteriorated AD patients and healthy age- and education-matched controls. The task was reasonably held to be highly demanding on the selectivity and shifting components of focused attention in order to prevent perceptual intrusions. In normal subjects Gottschaldt's test yields scores that are highly correlated with those of one of the most widely used selective attention tasks, namely Stroop's (1935) color-word interference test (Jensen and Rohmer, 1966). Performance on Stroop's task was independently shown to be impaired in Alzheimer patients by Golden (1978). Gottschaldt's test works as a sensitive tool in detecting the presence of brain damage (Teuber, 1951, 1956), particularly when frontal (Yarcorzyuski and Davis, 1945) or unilateral focal hemisphere damage (with aphasia or with posterior right lesion) is present (Russo and Vignolo, 1967). The aim of Capitani's et al. (1988) experiment was to find out whether this easily understandable Gestalt-featured task discriminates healthy from demented elderly subjects. This prediction was upheld, with 82% of AD patients and 98% of control subjects discriminated correctly. Performance on Gottschaldt's test in AD patients was directly related to that of another selective attentional task, namely a cancellation test (crossing out of digits in a matrix; Spinnler and Tognoni, 1987), which similarly tackled resistance to distraction and focus shifting. The Gottschaldt test's discriminant power was, however, only marginally related to intelligence, language, spatial and visuoperceptual capabilities of AD patients. Confirming Nissen et al.'s (1985) findings in a visual detection task, the authors took this experimental evidence as supporting the notion that even mildly deteriorated AD patients have a reduced availability of selective attentional resources.

A rather similar issue was considered by Cossa et al. (1989) by means of a computerized experiment aiming at verifying in healthy elderly, nondemented parkinsonian patients and mildly deteriorated AD patients predictions stemming from Norman and Bobrow's (1975) selective attention model. This model envisages that the information-processing system is capable of varying its input sensitivity, and thus its processing efficiency, according to the stimulus context. Priming recurrence (the data-driven process), topographical recurrence (the memory-driven process) and random recurrence of the visual target are predicted to give rise, in the ranked order, to progressive lengthenings of RT in ceiling accuracy experiments. The results for the healthy group and for the parkinsonian group perfectly fit Norman and Bobrow's (1975) predictions, whereas the result for AD patients did not.

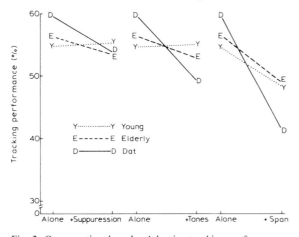

Fig. 2. Cross-sectional study. Adaptive tracking performances of Alzheimer patients (DAT) and elderly and young controls when tracking is performed alone and when it is combined with concurrent articulatory suppression, RT to a tone or digit span. (Reproduced from Baddely et al., 1986; by courtesy of Quart. J. Exp. Psychol.)

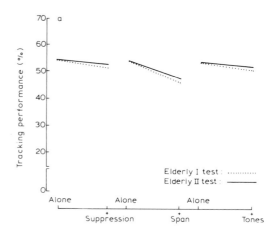

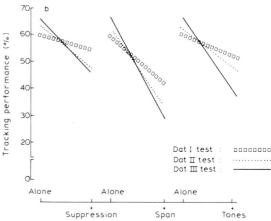

Fig. 3. (a) Follow-up study of elderly controls with a 6-month interval. Tracking performance when tracking is performed alone or combined with the three secondary tasks of the cross sectional study (see Fig. 1). (b) Follow-up study of Alzheimer patients (DAT) with a 6- and a 12-month interval. Test conditions are as in panel (a).

Actually, the latter group was insensitive to both facilitatory conditions, without any significant difference between the two, possibly because of the lack of available attentional resources.

Recent findings by Nebes and Brady (1989) suggest that AD patients 'benefited as did normals from the presence of the color cue' in a visual search experiment, that is, without any hint of a modified speed/accuracy tradeoff. The authors concluded that the focusing capacity of AD patients is in the range of that of comparable healthy elderly. Like all other cognitive findings that suggest a substantial similarity of performance between comparable normals and AD patients, the above data are very important. In fact, they underscore the neuropsychological heterogeneity of the progression of AD: in this case (viz., these patients and this experiment) an attentional facet shows resistance for a longer time than other cognitive performances to the degenerative process.

The conclusion of Nebes and Brady about AD patients' focused attention is, however, at variance with Cossa et al.'s (1989) aforementioned findings. Here again the general difficulty emerges of coping with interpatient variability when comparing different experiments. Actually this variability is particularly high when collecting neuropsychological scores of AD patients. Ideal interexperiment comparability would be achieved if reliable, cognitive-independent, information were available with respect to the degree of the degenerative encroachment upon different brain regions and, particularly, on the degree of the retrorolandic, mechanism-oriented, and the anterior frontal, control-oriented, involvement.

Nebes and Brady (1989), in the same paper quoted above, provide evidence for a divided attention impairment in AD patients, a finding in line with Baddeley et al.'s (1986) data, which will now be taken into consideration.

An already mentioned study of working memory by Baddeley et al. (1986) points to a specific impairment in mildly deteriorated AD patients of the 'central executive' component in Baddeley and Hitch's (1974) working memory model. AD patients appear to fail when dealing simultaneously with two heterogeneous concurrent tasks. This study was made up of a series of computerized experiments of divided attention between a primary visuomotor tracking task and different secondary tasks (viz., articulatory suppression, reacting to tones, digit span). Fig. 2 sets out the results of the research.

The prediction of greater tracking impairment in AD patients due to the concurrence of each of the secondary tasks was statistically upheld. This was particularly apparent for the most demanding of the secondary tasks, namely digit span. Longitudinal data (Fig. 3; Baddeley, Bressi, Della Sala, Logie and Spinnler, unpublished data) are fully consistent with the findings shown in Fig. 2. These data have been interpreted as an early and selective worsening of the central allocator device in AD patients. These findings can be viewed as a consequence of the involvement of the 'vertical threads' by dementia in Norman and Shallice's (1986) model.

It is worth making a general comment on headings (ii) and (iii). Our knowledge concerning the attention breakdown of AD remains rather incomplete, inasmuch as there are extremely few studies (Alexander, 1973) tackling 'vigilance' decrement following Wittenborn's (1943), Mackworth's (1950) and Bakan's (1955) pioneering guidelines on healthy people. Moreover, to the best of our knowledge, the crucial longitudinal dimension has only seldom been included in experiments on attentive disorders of AD patients, with the exception of Nestor and Parasuraman's (1987) and Baddeley et al.'s (unpublished data) studies. Experiments with selective attentive tasks risk producing a somewhat misleading inference because they tackle only those performances in AD patients which are likely to be amongst the most demanding on attentive control in healthy elderly as well. Therefore the differences between healthy and demented elderly are strictly quantitative in nature, with the possibility that they hide an interesting qualitative difference, as Cossa et al.'s (1989) data (referring to Norman and Bobrow's 1975 model) may suggest. In general, attentional differences between healthy elderly and AD patients are, however, likely to be quantitative in nature, in line with the concept of 'attentional resources' and related classical capacity theories of attention (Kahneman, 1973). Qualitative differences, if any, would probably stem from the impairment either of an instrumental processing threshold or of a threshold related to its unavoidable attentional demand. Hence, it is predicted that qualitative differences are likely to be of quantitative origin.

Research devoted to 'automatic processing' could produce a deeper insight into the cognitive style of computing information in demented subjects by showing, for instance, the progressive transformation of normally automatic into controlled performance, or the intrusion of no longer inhibited environment-driven actions. Sustained selective attentional paradigms involving stopping an automatic routine may provide helpful sources of knowledge. Possibly valuable tests could be the random number (Baddeley, 1966; Wagenaar, 1972) and pattern (i.e., scrawls) generation tests (Jones-Gotman and Milner, 1977; Ruff et al., 1987). Nestor and Parasuraman's (1987) recent data indicate that in early AD patients the preservation of simple cognitive operations is accomplished by means of a greater attentional cost, also for automatic performances, i.e. they no longer behave fully automatically. Other examples of automatic processing come from the memory domain, such as the tasks listed by Hasher and Zacks (1979). They generally involve retrieving marginal features of a series of memoranda, such as the frequency of occurrence of some stimuli (Jackson, 1985). They are said to require small amounts of sustained attention (Hirst and Volpe, 1984) and to be only marginally interfered with by associated effortful processing (Hasher and Zacks, 1979). There have been no experiments on this topic in demented patients, even if the dense amnesic syndrome of AD patients possibly leaves intact this type of automatic processing.

The 'distraction' effect on any performance can be considered to follow the introduction into any primary cognitive processing of task-irrelevant stimuli (Graydon and Eysenck, 1989), which per se are not expected to be processed. Thus distraction is the consequence of focused rather than divided attention failure. Several factors increase the distraction effect in normals, such as the memory (Baddeley, 1986) or the transformational load characterizing the primary task, the difficulty in discriminating task from distracting stimuli (e.g., phonological similarity; Salame and Baddeley, 1982) and practice in carrying out the primary task. Insofar as the probability of distraction is held to vary according to the total processing demands (Graydon and Eysenck, 1989), one can forecast that demented patients are more prone than healthy elderly to

ecologically or experimentally induced distraction effects. In demented patients distraction may, in fact, follow both an increased demand of attentional control for bringing about any performance, and a decreased overall availability of attentional resources, according to the stage reached by AD (cf. section 3). To the best of our knowledge, there are unfortunately no studies directly inquiring into this pervasive disorder of cognitive coping of demented patients. Actually, one can presume that one component of the difficulty AD patients have in upholding adequate control of any directed sequence of actions precisely consists of the likelihood of being distracted.

Although the experiments reviewed under headings (i) and (iii) directly support the existence of attentional disorders in AD patients, they, with the exception of Baddeley et al.'s study (1986), do not assess the extent to which failures in attention produce cognitive failures. This is the crucial question of the relationship between attention and cognition. It is necessary to look for discrepancies across tests (attention versus instrumental functions), possibly correlating them with brain landmarks of maximal/minimal metabolic impairment, in order to ascertain whether attention insufficiency and instrumental cognitive failure run different courses in the same or different AD patients or at different stages of their disease. This goal has been approached by the seminal study of Grady et al. (1988), who gained, by means of a longitudinal parallel study of positron emission tomography and neuropsychological assessment, experimental evidence confirming that in early AD patients the chronologically first non-memory consequence of the parietal-to-frontal spread of metabolic involvement is a reduced availability of attentional resources. The latter have been assessed with a divided attention test (trail making B) and a go/no-go paradigm of focused attention.

(iv) Attentional disorders in pseudodementias

Pseudodementias (Kiloh, 1961; Post, 1965; Caine, 1981) are here considered (Della Sala et al., 1986) as demented behaviors in everyday settings without the course and the evidence of the underlying nervous damage characterizing the histopathological processes encroaching upon the brain in organic dementias. Most of the pseudodementias have a defined etiology, thereby being sometimes pharmacologically reversible (surgically reversible dementias, such as found in normotensive hydrocephalus, are kept apart). Pseudodemented patients usually show up with the subcortical traits of bradyphrenia and with rapid fluctuations of their processing efficiency over time and across different cognitive performances. The prevailing opinion is that most of these fluctuations as well as slowing of cognitive activities are linked to attention modifications. Pseudodementias may, in fact, provide one of the most valuable opportunities for testing cognitive processing hindered nearly exclusively by attentional disorders. Actually, on formal testing of their instrumental abilities pseudodemented patients very frequently perform surprisingly well.

So-called 'functional' (i.e., psychiatric) cognitive disorders of behavior resembling dementia, such as those associated with schizophrenia (Crow, 1982) – particularly if of late onset (Roth, 1987) – or in aged subjects, have been suggested (Mesulam and Geschwind, 1978) to be to some extent disorders of selective (Ottmanns, 1978) or sustained (Byrne, 1976) attention, or of motivation. Cognitive data (Seidman, 1983; Harrow et al., 1987; Heaton and Drexler, 1987; Niederhe and Rusin, 1987) point to a bi- or only left frontal (and/or temporal) impairment; they chiefly consist in impaired problem-solving (Goldberg et al., 1986), episodic memory (Cutting, 1979), attribute and rule learning (Bourne et al., 1977; Goldberg et al., 1987). Defective instrumental performances can be tentatively traced back to an underlying attentional disorder, as has been verified in schizophrenics and patients with major affective disorders by Taylor and Abrams (1987). A similar position is upheld by Granholm et al.'s (1989) findings on the reduced controlled activities of nondemented schizophrenics. Cognitive defects pointing to frontal lobe dysfunction in chronic nondemented schizophrenics are mainly those observed by means of the Wisconsin Card Sorting Test (Fey, 1951; Malmo, 1974; Kolb and Wishaw, 1983; Weinberger et al., 1986), one of the most credited 'frontal' tests (Milner, 1963; Drewe, 1974; Robinson et al., 1980). There have been, however, some reports (e.g. Anderson et al.'s, 1990) questioning the specificity and sensitivity of the WCST with respect to frontal damage. It remains unclear whether patients fail on the WCST because they are not able to learn the task instructions (Goldberg et al., 1987), or because, even if perceiving 'the mistakes they make', they 'are unable to use the formation to modify their behavior' (Teuber, 1957), similarly to patients with frontal lobe damage. The latter condition would be akin to a high-order attentional defect.

Fluctuating attention disorders are claimed to be associated with neurotic disorders and with mood disturbances (Miller, 1975; Spring, 1980). Cognitive failures of anxious people have been ascribed to a supplementary load of their distributed attentional resources (Martin and Jones, 1984), yielding a tendency to attend to the variations of both external stimuli and their internal state (Eysenck, 1982).

Depression occurring in the elderly not affected by AD may be responsible for an everyday abnormal behavior that appears to mimic dementia and is sometimes surprisingly dense in severity. This pseudodemential behavior becomes apparent from time to time in nearly a fifth of depressed old subjects. The clinical picture is that of 'depressive pseudodementia of the elderly', which, together with extracerebral metabolic encephalopathies (Wells, 1979), is the most frequent instance of a reversible dementia-like behavior.

Lack of motivation appears to be associated with a reduced availability of sustained attention (Cohen et al., 1982) or, in general, with an involuntary attentional fixedness (Reason, 1984a). Particularly reliable indicators of reduced sustained attention are some complex tasks with a selective attentional component such as random digit or letter generation tests (Wagenaar, 1972; Horne et al., 1982). What random generation tasks test is the ability to overcome an automatic routine under strict, goal-directed conscious control: the subject is asked to organize the most random output sequence he can while calling out letters or digits (Baddeley, 1966). Reduced random generation of meaningless drawings has been shown by Jones-Gotman and Milner (1977) to parallel reduced verbal generation in frontally lobectomized patients. The line of investigation fostered by such tests of sustained attention can also be fruitful in pseudodemented and AD patients, provided that the difficulty of explaining the task to the deteriorated subjects, namely to refrain from doing what appears to everyone to be 'natural' to do, has been overcome. Recent findings of Bigler (1989) on different types of dementia confirm the drawing fluency (standardization in Ruff et al., 1987) impairment.

Memory lapses occurring while reading and TV-watching as well as in conversation and in work are trivial complaints of depressed and anxious people (Watts and Sharrock, 1985). They are currently attributed to poorly sustained focused attention (so called 'mind wandering' while attending to new information; Watts and Sharrock, 1985). There is, in fact, ample test evidence of episodic supraspan learning defects in depressed people (McAllister, 1981), especially when high organizational demands of the information to be encoded and retrieved are required, as with memory for the prose (Kopelman, 1986). Moreover, disorders of planning and recollecting from semantic memory appear to affect the behavior of depressed people (Silbermann et al., 1983), possibly to a degree comparable to that in AD patients. It is surprising to what a great extent coping and test impairments of the depressed sometimes overlap with AD patients' cognitive deficits: it is likely that disorders of attention represent the common trait of the two types of patient.

Whether the defect underlying attentional disorders shared by depressed and AD patients has similar neurotransmitter and/or anatomic correlates in the brain is one of the most challenging issues. Hyoscine cholinergic blockade in healthy volunteers induces several attentional defects that are also frequent in AD patients (Kopelman and Corn, 1988). A similarly challenging question is whether drug effects on memory disorders of depressed, demented and even normal subjects may reflect only (or predominantly) transmitter-mediated modifications of attentive control (Newman et al., 1984; Wolkowitz et al., 1985). Positron emission tomography studies employing imaging of transmitter regional use will help on understanding of this potentially enlightening issue. Moreover, pharmacological studies comparing healthy and depressed elderly are likely to provide clearer evidence when the dependent variable is attentional in nature than when less flexible instrumental scores are the only ones considered.

Section 3. Concluding remarks on the natural history of attentional breakdown of dementia

It has been suggested that one of the first consequences of the dementing process is an increasing failure to initiate quickly and allocate properly attentional resources in support of a given cognitive activity about to start or already under way. Consequently, progressive deterioration of instrumental performances should show a quasiordered sequence, from the most controlled performances (in the early stages of the disease) to the least controlled performances (in subsequent stages) (Jorm, 1984). This view implies that the behavior of the demented patient becomes more and more characterized by a nearly fixed array of residual automatic actions. This forecast is supported by the belief that automatic activities call for a reduced amount of attentional and neuronal resources with respect to controlled ones (cf. Jackson's, 1868, 'automatic/voluntary dissociation'). Given this frame of reference, the stress is, however, only on the attentional component of an action, with the implicit assumption that the instrumental aspect of the corresponding performance remains nearly untouched, at least for a certain time. Of course, this would be an attractive viewpoint (Jorm, 1986) as it would provide a single systematic explanation of the apparently very unsystematic course of the cognitive defects arising during the dementing process. It would attach to the attentional breakdown of dementia the role of primum movens in the cognitive deterioration of demented patients. This hypothesis would refer to a putatively beginning stage of the dementing process, and the patient would be considered a healthy individual minus a certain amount of attentional resources. It is, however, apparent that such a description is almost completely devoid of any resemblance to a person who is clinically affected by AD. At best, this description may fit that of a frontal lobe dementia, a blurred, often single case, syndrome (Gustafson, 1987; Neary et al., 1988; Knopman et al., 1989).

In reality, the encroachment of the degenerative process gives rise to predominantly posterior (parietal, temporal and hippocampal damage) as well as to slighter, possibly somehow anterior (prefrontal and cingular) damage (Duara et al., 1986; Pawlik et al., 1989). Admittedly, the typical posterior-to-anterior gradient of glucose hypometabolism changes widely across AD patients, possibly as a consequence of the stage and the tempo of evolution (Duara et al., 1986). The gradient ranges from a clearcut parietal major (viz., quasi-selective) involvement (Duara et al., 1986; Kuhl et al., 1985; Friedland et al., 1985), to an anterior/posterior equivalence (Benson et al., 1983), and even to an opposite gradient in single AD cases (Chase et al., 1984). Recent PET data of Haxby et al. (1988) indicate that mildly deteriorated AD patients differ from controls on glucose hypometabolism only in the parietal and laterotemporal areas. Premotor and prefrontal metabolic involvement adds to the parieto-temporal hypometabolism only when a moderately to severely deteriorated stage has been reached. Evidence from Haxby et al.'s (1988) data – following Duara et al.'s (1986) suggestion – points to a later development of the anterior metabolic reduction in the course of AD when it is compared with the early involvement of the parietal and temporolateral areas.

However, the neuropsychological counterpart of PET findings in Haxby et al.'s (1988) correlative study is not fully consistent with the prediction of a later onset of attentional disorders with respect to deficits in instrumental functions. Actually, mildly

demented patients are impaired not only in episodic memory, but also in tasks of sustained attention and focus-shifting. There are, however, methodological difficulties in the psychometric safety of intertest comparisons in Haxby et al.'s (1988) study. Reed et al.'s (1989) recent correlative data (viz., regional blood flow measurements and neuropsychological scores) broadly agree with the aforementioned PET data and point to a subsequent occurrence of attentional defects with respect to some memory and language impairments. On the other hand, recent data of ours, based on a cross-sectional and longitudinal study (Della Sala, Laiacona, Spinnler and Ubezio, unpublished findings), did not succeed in dividing mild to moderately deteriorated AD patients in a group with only instrumental defects (in the episodic memory, language, visuo-perceptual and spatial domains) from another group with attentional defects too. These were assessed by a new version of Spinnler and Tognoni's (1987) digit cancellation test. Whereas the former of the abovementioned groups would have referred to an earlier (only posterior) stage of AD encroachment, the latter would have referred to a subsequent (also anterior) stage. It is very likely that the psychometric assessment of attention resources cannot be safely achieved by single tests (such as a cancellation test; Lezak, 1983), but, as pointed out in a previous section (1.iii), attention in order to be reliably measured needs complex experimental designs that for instance, take into account the performance trade-off of concurrent activities. Perhaps such an approach may succeed in producing neuropsychological data that parallel PET findings (Pawlik et al., 1989) and suggest also at a cognitive level the directional staging of AD encroachment.

The relationship of the posterior towards anterior biological sequence to the instrumental versus control impairment is clearly in a very provisional state. Grady et al.'s (1989) recent study provides some hint that impairment on a dichotic task in AD patients (greater than the impairment on corresponding monotic tasks) stems from a perception disorder and also from a general imbalance of selective attention. The former seems to be related to temporal lobe atrophy with glucose hypometabolism (Grimes et al., 1985) and the latter to the encroachment of the dementing process upon extra-temporal (viz., premotor and prefrontal) regions. Existing data, however, are insufficient to untangle the test consequences of attentional from instrumental breakdown.

The present aim is to push the speculations on the attention/cognition relationship in AD a bit further. It is thought in general that coping with environmental changes is normally accomplished by a healthy adult individual through resort to a welter of quasiautomatic skills, notions and procedures making up the bulk of remote memory. This way of coping does not mean that everyday behavior is rigidly fixed. Actually, nearly cost-free feedback adjustments are embedded in every complex processing system, adding to each mechanism's complexity and flexibility (Medin and Wattenmaker, 1987). Reference is made here to the complex intelligent behaviors envisaged by Hunt (1978), to complex sets of schemata in Norman and Shallice's (1980, 1986) model, to Fisk and Schneider's (1983) complex abilities, as well as to Reason's (1984a) autonomous operating schemata and to the decentralized control of categorization (Brooks, 1987). All these instances of extremely sophisticated and largely automatic processing have much in common with the current notion of the 'crystallized' stock of the 'intelligent' abilities set out by Cattell (1963, revised by Horn, 1976). The sophistication of fine-grained routines is likely to benefit from a lifelong amelioration along the traditional effortful-towards-automatic trend of evolution. By and large, the shift towards automatic control of actions allows a quick, low in cost and in errors, adaptation to most cognitive habitual needs.

Thus a healthy old person can be considered as someone with a very rich and promptly accessible repertoire of automatic sets for actions and thoughts. Mastering the facilities of social and emotional survival for the elderly is possibly strictly related to availability and access to many well-suited, preprogrammed, cooperative routines. These routines clearly master the vast majority of

actions normally displayed by the central nervous system. Only some of them, possibly as a consequence of the condition under which they are brought into play, benefit from the feedback of consciousness. The welter of preprogrammed routines range from emotional and vegetative rigidly stereotyped response, to more complex and flexible motivational (Mesulam, 1985; Norman and Shallice, 1986) outputs, adding to the normal consistency of judgements, beliefs and behaviors in the cognitive, esthetic, ethical, religious, gastronomic domains, and so on. The most critical point at risk during healthy aging is possibly the prompt matching between the triggering external condition and the trigger database detailed by Norman and Shallice's (1986) 'horizontal threads' (see Fig. 1). Such a crucial malfunctioning of the attentional system could be at the origin of the universal senile query about 'the world that has changed too much' to continue to be coped with effectively.

Because of the topographical (i.e., associative areas) and microstructural (i.e., horizontal connectivity) peculiarities of its cortical damage (Oyanagi et al., 1987), the AD dementing process curtails interneuronal interplay, perhaps hindering for this reason access to the abovementioned quasiautomatic routines. Due to these defects, demented patients are compelled to resort very early in their coping to planning, controlling and checking almost every activity they undertake, as if routine activities had all become novel. Such a condition triggers the nonrandom longitudinal emergence of failures (Jorm, 1986) beginning with the most and ending with the least controlled performances in healthy brains, insofar as the former reasonably call for a larger amount or more exclusive allocation of attentional resources. Actually, whenever an overwhelming amount of resources is devoted to now costly activities which imply dealing with novelty and calling for the effortful focusing or dividing of selective or sustained attention one will be confronted with an attentional breakdown. Intrusions of environment-driven fragments of activity (Lhermitte, 1983, 1986) have the same effect, namely that of an attentional insufficiency surfacing. Such phenomena of distraction and unsteadiness of control give rise to the misleading impression of an increased automaticity of AD patients in a severe stage of the disease. In our opinion, actually the opposite condition is at work, namely that of a demand on attentional control even for the most trivial actions, which overwhelms the possibly almost normal amounts of attentional resources in the beginning stages of the AD dementing process.

One could go on to argue that the regression from once efficient and automatic activities to effortful activities is, in turn, a consequence of the presymptomatic breakdown of the instrumental functions. It is conceivable that each instrumental function will go on producing performances in a healthy brain by resorting to specific amounts of resources (along the lines of Wickens, 1984) without needing to access the general attentional pool. In this sense, instrumental functions run from the viewpoint of the general economy as if they work automatically when an adequate stimulus triggers them (see Fig. 1). After breaking through the threshold of neuronal degeneration of the retrorolandic associative areas, environmental triggers no longer fit the trigger database and fail to promote instrumental actions, henceforth requiring supervisory control, even for routine actions. In this line of speculation the increasing call upon control ought to be conceived of as a compensatory phenomenon (Spinnler, 1989), which tries to master a progressively more noisy and flawed working of instrumental functions.

Thus, increasing damage to neuronal horizontal connectivity of the parietal and temporal regions (Frackowiak et al., 1981; Duara et al., 1986; Grady et al., 1988; Haxby et al., 1988; cf. review in Pawlik et al., 1989) should be credited as the primum movens of the progression of the dementia behavior (Spinnler, 1989). If the predominant sequence is that just sketched, attentional insufficiency ranks as a second-stage disorder, at least in the AD type of dementia.

The attentional economy will move from a shortlasting functional insufficiency (viz., too great a burden even for a healthy brain) to a direct reduction of its general availability, due to the prefrontal

extension of the neuronal disease (Spinnler, 1989). Thus AD poses for the patient's brain the dramatic problem of a hopeless evolution of its attention economy, namely that of facing more and more overwhelming requests for attentional control in order to continue maintaining coping standards while the production of attentional resources drops more and more. The longitudinal behavioral sequence can thus be sketched from intermittent focal (Capitani et al., 1986) neuropsychological defects (such as failures in prospective and ongoing episodic memory, in word or route finding, in familiar-face recognition and so on) often elicited by trivial attentional extra demands (e.g., a noisy context, an emotional stress, a transient extracerebral metabolic imbalance and so on) to a condition of severe and steady instrumental disorders mixed up with an associated confusional state.

This course may run in the opposite direction in dementias due primarily to frontal lobe degeneration (Neary et al., 1988). However, the state of the frontal lobe dementias and in particular that in Pick's disease still remains elusive, even in their psychometric and imaging distinction from classical AD patients (Knopman et al., 1989).

Section 4. Future trends in research

Going through the above scattered notions from demented patients along the continuum of concepts, experiments, findings and opinions, from RT up to the sophistications of action optimization and plan generation, one develops the feeling that future cognitive models in each domain of information-processing and decision-making must organize two conceptually independent components, namely distinguishing between instruments (or mechanisms) producing a specific array of performances, and the set of control systems acting upon them (Pillsbury, 1908; Hebb, 1949; Luria, 1966; Moray, 1970; Norman and Shallice, 1980, 1986). We think that costless and flawless high-speed automatic performance corresponds to the best optimization of resources for the greatest part of the working-life of a healthy brain. However, the large amount of attentional expense required in coordinating a rich ar-ray of high-order cognitive routines and using them in parallel to face the current ecological requests can hardly be afforded when the available nervous structure is extensively damaged and, for this reason, is attention-consuming. This condition is believed to be the case in AD patients.

Future research on AD patients can no longer escape the burden of complex cooperative ex-perimental designs. To take all the heuristic advan-tage potentially offered by the natural experiment of a process selectively encroaching on the multimodal associative areas, future studies need to embark on longlasting longitudinal surveys, starting from the earliest stages of the clinically apparent disease. Such groups of carefully selected AD patients ought thereafter to undergo standardized subgrouping ac-cording to their predominant cognitive onset features (Capitani et al., 1986; Martin et al., 1986; Capitani et al., 1990) and to the degree of their overall deterioration in order to build up reasonably homogeneous samples of experimental subjects. Routine cognitive assessments as well as indepen-dent biological measures (first of all, regional PET assessments, extended from glucose metabolism to local transmitter supply) necessarily must resort to scores with available age-, education- and sex-adjusted healthy baselines. Psychometrical workup of scores has to allow full intertest comparability (Capitani and Laiacona, 1988).

It is within such a framework that one can distinguish two lines for future study on attentional modifications in dementing patients, namely (i) that of exploring in detail the demential involvement of the several attentional facets envisaged by the psychologists, and (ii) that of aiming at verifying the general notion that a two-component model ac-counts for possibly every neuropsychological activi-ty.

(i) Characterization of attention

First, experiments require defined operative mea-sures for each aspect of the attentional control. Moreover, they ought to be suitable for longitudinal

follow-ups through most of the long course of dementing disorders. In this set of experiments, specific cognitive loads should be reduced to the smallest possible amount in order to obtain the most well-distilled attentional measures. Examples for same aspects of selective attention are studies by Baddeley et al. (1986) and Nebes and Brady (1989). Exploring automatic behaviors may also be pro-fitably carried out in ecological settings and perhaps on severely and institutionalized demented patients as well. In these patients, an approach worthy of ex-ploration would be that of conditioned responses. The aim of such a line of studies would be two-fold, namely to validate and refine by means of a neuro-psychological approach attentional models devised by psychologists, and to lay down a general atten-tional natural history of AD. One must admit that a longitudinal assessment of attentional defects in AD is still waiting to be carried out by means of a satisfying, strictly attentive, psychometric ap-proach. Moreover, when describing the general psychometric pattern of AD patients, much more attention should be paid to their normal (Spinnler and Della Sala, 1988) and their dissociated perfor-mances (Baddeley, Della Sala and Spinnler, 1991).

(ii) Experimental design

A second line of future study calls for the develop-ment of original approaches in order to separate in healthy elderly subjects and AD patients the defects of performances due to instrumental damage from that due to insufficiency of attentional control, in order to gain insight into the interplay of the two components underlying performance. Put in other terms and following Tulving's (1983) distinction for memory processing, the time seems ripe to associate attention 'testing', with its valuable psychometric descriptive outputs, with attention 'experimenting', with the goal in mind of understanding the role of at-tention in cognitive behavior. The most trivial ap-proach could be that of assessing a well-defined neuropsychological performance under varying at-tention loads in a divided attention design (Baddeley et al., 1986). Possibly, however, the most automatic behaviors are the most enlightening targets of attentional studies in demented people. The outcome of attention experimenting may be the neuropsychological defining of different attentional systems, their link with consciousness of planning and ongoing activity and the contribution to the access/store debate for mental representations.

It is believed that such studies can throw light on the obscure interplay between information-processing and task performance on one side, and the nervous structure on the other, yielding (along the lines of Kinsbourne, 1986) the opportunity to define convergently dissociations between extra- and intra-attentional performances and PET-assessed regions of maximal/minimal metabolic encroachment. First steps in this approach are Grady et al.'s (1988) and Haxby et al.'s (1988) correlative studies. In general, the impairment of performances and the disorders of the processes related to them — some of which being more and some others much less specific to the activities at issue — now begin to appear to be interrelated in an increasingly complex way. The case of attention is paramount in this sense. It is likely that functionalistic modelling of the neuropsychological interaction between nervous machinery and psychological computing up to the identification of a clear-cut, measurable performance will in the future provide a more comprehensive insight into human brain activity than that afforded in the past by the fragmentary approach of psychometric experimentation. Single-case longitudinal studies can possibly introduce more systematic approaches with carefully selected groups of AD patients.

Attractive though it is, it may be, however, that the envisaged two-component experiments will merely prove to be an effort to schematize without reliably fitting (viz., explaining) the biological complexity of the working brain and its demential destruction.

Acknowledgements

Detailed criticism and encouragement by François Boller, Erminio Capitani, Suzanne Corkin, Sergio Della Sala, Ennio De Renzi and Guido Gainotti are warmly acknowledged. I am grateful for the editorial assistance of Rosalba Occhetti. Preparation of this manuscript was partly supported by a grant to H.S. by the Consiglio Nazionale delle Ricerche, No. 8700.233.04.115.12234.

References

Albert ML, Feldman RG, Willis AL: The 'subcortical dementia' of progressive supranuclear palsy. *J. Neurol. Neurosurg. Psychiatry: 37*, 121 – 130, 1974.

Alexander DA: Some tests of intelligence and learning for elderly psychiatric patients: a validation study. *Br. J. Soc. Clin. Psychol.: 12*, 188 – 193, 1973.

Alexander DA: Attention dysfunction in senile dementia. *Psychol. Rep.: 32*, 229 – 230, 1973.

Allender J, Kaszniak AW: Processing of emotional cues and personality change in dementia of the Alzheimer's type. Paper presented at the 13th Annual Meeting of the International Neuropsychological Society. San Diego, 1985.

Anderson SW, Jones RD, Tranel AP, Tranel D, Damasio H: Is Wisconsin Card Sorting Test an index of frontal lobe damage? (Abstract: 18th Annual INS Meeting, February 1990, Hyatt Orlando, USA). *J. Clin. Exp. Neuropsychol.: 12*, 80, 1990.

Angelergues R, Hécaen H, Ajuriaguerra J: Les troubles mentaux au cours des tumeurs du lobe frontal; à propos de 80 observations dont 54 avec troubles mentaux. *Ann. Méd. Psichol.: 113*, 577 – 642, 1955.

Appell J, Kertesz A, Fisman M: A study of language functioning in Alzheimer patients. *Brain Lang.: 17*, 73 – 91, 1982.

Atkinson RC, Siffrin RM: The control of short-term memory. *Sci. Am.: 224*, 82 – 90, 1971.

Atkinson RC, Shiffrin RM: Human memory: a proposed system and its control processes. In Spence KW, Taylor Spence J (Editors), *Psychology of Learning and Motivation*. London: Academic Press, 1972.

Baddeley AD: The capacity for generation information by randomization. *Q. J. Exp. Psychol.: 18*, 119 – 129, 1966.

Baddeley AD: Domains and recollection. *Psychol. Rev.: 89*, 708 – 729, 1982a.

Baddeley AD: Amnesia: a minimal model and an interpretation. In: Cermak LS (Editor), *Human Memory and Amnesia*. Hillsdale: Lawrence Erlbaum, 1982b.

Baddeley AD: *Working Memory*. London: Oxford University Press, 1986.

Baddeley AD, Hitch G: Working memory. In: Bower GH (Editor), *The Psychology of Learning and Motivation, Vol. 8*. New York: Academic Press, pp. 47 – 89, 1974.

Baddeley AD, Wilson B: Amnesia, autobiographical memory and confabulation. In: Rubin DC (Editor), *Autobiographical Memory*. Cambridge: Cambridge University Press, pp. 225 – 252, 1986.

Baddeley AD, Wilson B: Frontal amnesia and the dysexecutive syndrome. *Brain Cognition: 7*, 212 – 230, 1988.

Baddeley AD, Logie R, Bressi S, Della Sala S, Spinnler H: Dementia and working memory. *Q. J. Exp. Psychol.: 38A*, 603 – 618, 1986.

Baddeley AD, Della Sala S, Spinnler H: The two-component

hypothesis of memory dificit in Alzheimer's Disease. *J. Clin. Exp. Neuropsychol.:* 13, 1991.

Bakan P: Extroversion-introversion and improvement in an auditory vigilance task. *Br. J. Psychol.:* 50, 325 – 332, 1959.

Bandera L, Della Sala S, Laiacona H, Luzzatti C, Spinnler H: Generative associative naming in Alzheimer's dementia. *Neuropsychologia:* in press, 1991.

Bannister R: Brains clinical neurology. New York: Oxford University Press, pp. 479 – 485, 1978.

Bayles KA, Boone DR: The potential of language tasks for identifying senile dementia. *Brain Language: 19*, 98 – 114, 1982.

Bayles KA, Tomoeda CK: Confrontation naming impairment in dementia. *Brain Language: 19*, 98 – 114, 1983.

Baynes K, Holtzman JD, Volpe BT: Components of visual attention. Alterations in response pattern to visual stimuli following parietal lobe infarction. *Brain: 109*, 99 – 114, 1986.

Bechterew VM, quoted by Luria AR: *Le funzioni corticali superiori nell'uomo (trans.* from Russian by Bisiach E). Firenze: CE Giunti, p. 239, 1907.

Becker JT: A two component model of the memory deficit in Alzheimer's disease. In: Corkin SH, Growdon JH (Editors), *Alzheimer's Disease: Advances in Basic Research and Therapies.* Cambridge: Center for Brain Sciences and Metabolism Charitable Trust, pp. 343 – 348, 1987.

Becker JT: Working memory and secondary memory deficits in Alzheimer's disease. *J. Clin. Exp. Neuropsychol.: 10*, 739 – 753, 1988.

Benson DF: Aphasia, alexia and apraxia. New York: Churchill Livingstone, 1979.

Benson DF, Geschwind N: Psychiatric conditions associated with focal lesions of the central nervous system. In Arieti S, Reiser M (Editors), *American Handbook of Psychiatry: Organic Disorders and Psychosomatic Medicine, Vol. 4*, 2nd Edition. New York: Basic Books, 1975.

Benson DF, Kuhl DE, Hawkins RA, Phelps ME, Cummings JL, Tsai SY: The fluorodesoxyglycose scan in Alzheimer's disease and multi-infarct dementia. *Arch. Neurol.: 40*, 711 – 714, 1983.

Berrios GE: Orientation failures in medicine and psychiatry: discussion paper. *J. R. Soc. Med.: 76*, 379 – 385, 1983.

Bianchi L: The functions of the frontal lobes. *Brain: 18*, 497 – 530, 1895.

Bigler ED, Schultz R, Grand M, Knight G, Lucas J, Roman M, Hall S, Sullivan M: Design fluency in dementia of the Alzheimer's type. *Neuropsychologia:* in press.

Bisiach E, Berti A: Dyschiria: an attempt at its systemic explanation. In: Jeannerod M (Editor), *Neuropsychological and Physiological Aspects of Spatial Neglect.* Amsterdam: Elsevier, pp. 183 – 202, 1987.

Boring EG: Intelligence as the tests test it. *New Republic: 35*, 355 – 337, 1923.

Borrini G, Della Sala S, Dall'Ora P, Martinelli L, Spinnler H: Autobiographical memory: sensitivity to age and education of a standardized inquiry. *Psychol. Med.: 19*, 215 – 224, 1989.

Bourne LE, Justesen DR, Abraham T, Becker C, Branchi JT, Whitaker LC, Yaroush RA: Limits to conceptual rule-learning by schizophrenic patients. *J. Clin. Psychiatry: 33*, 324 – 334, 1977.

Bonsfield WA, Sedgewick CH: An analysis of sequence of restricted associative responses. *J. Gen. Psychol.: 30*, 149 – 165, 1944.

Broadbent DE: The Maltese cross: a new simplistic model for memory. *Behav. Brain Sci.: 7*, 55 – 94, 1984.

Brooks LR: Decentralized control of categorization: the role of prior processing episodes. In: Neisser H (Editor), *Concepts and Conceptual Development. Ecological and Intellectual Factors in Categorization.* Cambridge: Cambridge University Press, pp. 141 – 1744, 1987.

Buckner DN, Harabedian A, McGrath JJ: A study of individual differences in vigilance performance. *Technical Report No. 2*, Los Angeles: Human Factors Research Inc., 1966.

Butters N: The clinical aspects of memory disorders: contributions from experimental studies of amnesia and dementia. *J. Clin. Neuropsychol.: 9*, 17 – 36, 1984.

Butters N, Salmon DP, Heindel W, Granholm E: Episodic, semantic and procedural memory: some comparisons of Alzheimer and Huntington disease patients. In: Terry RD (Editor), *Aging and the Brain.* New York: Raven Press, 1988.

Byrne DG: Vigilance and arousal in depressive states. *Br. J. Soc. Clin. Psychol.: 15*, 267 – 274, 1976.

Caine ED: Pseudodementia. Current concepts and future directions. *Arch. Gen. Psychiatry: 38*, 1359 – 1364, 1981.

Caird WK, Inglis J: The short-term storage of auditory and visual two-channel (digits by elderly patients with memory disorder). *Mental Sci.: 107*, 1062 – 1069, 1961.

Capitani E, Laiacona M: Aging and psychometric diagnosis of intellectual impairment: some considerations on test scores and their use. *Dev. Neuropsychol.: 4*, 325 – 330, 1988.

Capitani E, Della Sala S, Spinnler H: Neuropsychological approach to dementia. In Poeck K, Freund HJ, Gaenschirt H (Editors), *Neurology.* Berlin: Springer, pp. 61 – 69, 1986.

Capitani E, Della Sala S, Lucchelli F, Soave P, Spinnler H: Gottschaldt's Hidden Figure text: sensitivity to age and education of perceptual attention. *J. Gerontol. Psychol. Sci.: 43*, 157 – 163, 1988.

Capitani E, Della Sala S, Spinnler H: Controversial neuropsychological issues in Alzheimer's disease: Influence of onset-age and hemispheric asymmetry of impairment. *Cortex: 26*, 133 – 145, 1990.

Caramazza A, Berendt RS: Semantic and syntactic processes in aphasia: a review of the literature. *Psychol. Bull.: 85*, 898 – 918, 1978.

Caramazza A, Berndt RS, Brownell HH: The semantic deficit hypothesis. Perceptual parsing and subject classification by aphasic patients. *Brain Lang.: 15*, 161 – 189, 1982.

Caramazza A, Hills AE, Rapp BC, Romani C: The multiple semantics hypothesis: multiple confusions? Preprint, report No. 42, Johns Hopkins University Cognitive Neuropsychology Laboratory.

Cattell RB: Theory of fluid and crystallized intelligence: an initial experiment. *J. Educ. Psychol.: 105*, 105 – 111, 1963.

Chase WG, Simon HA: The mind's eye in chess. In: Chase WG (Editor), *Visual Information Processing.* London: Academic Press, pp. 18 – 34, 1973.

Chase TN, Foster NL, Fedio P, Brooks R, Mansi L, Di Chiro G: Regional cortical dysfunction in Alzheimer's disease as determined by positron emission tomography. *Ann. Neurol.: 15* (suppl), 170 – 174, 1984.

Chedru F: Space representation in unilateral spatial neglect. *J. Neurol. Neurosurg. Psychiatry: 39*, 1057 – 1061, 1976.

Chedru F, Geschwind N: Disorders of higher cortical functions in acute confusional states. *Cortex: 8*, 395 – 411, 1972.

Cogan DG: Visual disturbances with focal progressive dementing disease. *Am. J. Ophthalmol.: 100*, 68 – 72, 1985.

Cohen NJ, Squire LR: Preserved learning and retention of pattern analyzing skills in amnesia: dissociation of knowing how and knowing what. *Science: 210*, 207 – 210, 1980.

Cohen RM, Weingartner H, Smallberg SA, Pickor D, Murphy DL: Effort and cognition in depression. *Arch. Gen. Psychiatry: 39*, 593 – 597, 1982.

Cossa F, Della Sala S, Spinnler H: Alzheimer's and Parkinson's patients' selective attention. Their sensitivity to memory and data-driven control. *Neuropsychologia: 27*, 887 – 892, 1989.

Craik FIM, Byrd M: Aging and cognitive deficits: the role of attentional resources. In Craik FIM, Trehub S (Editors), *Aging and Cognitive Processes*. New York: Plenum Press, pp. 191 – 212, 1982.

Craik FIM, Lockhardt RS: Levels of processing: a framework for memory research. *J. Verbal Learn. Verbal Behav.: 11*, 671 – 689, 1972.

Craik FIM: Age differences in human memory. In Birren JE, Schaie W (Editors): *Handbook of Psychology of Aging*. New York: Van Nostrand-Reinhold, pp. 384 – 420, 1977.

Crow TJ: The biology of schizophrenia. *Experientia: 38*, 1275 – 1282, 1982.

Cummings JL, Subcortical dementia. Neuropsychology, neuropsychiatry and pathophysiology. *Br. J. Psychiatry: 149*, 682 – 697, 1986.

Cummings JL, Benson DF: Subcortical dementia. Review of an emerging concept. *Arch. Neurol.: 41*, 874 – 879, 1984.

Cuttings J: Memory in functional psychosis. *J. Neurol. Neurosurg. Psychiatry: 42*, 1031 – 1037, 1979.

Dall'Ora P, Della Sala S, Spinnler H: Autobiographical memory. Its impairment in amnesic syndromes. *Cortex: 25*, 197 – 217, 1989.

Daniel WF, Crovitz HF, Weiner RD: Neuropsychological aspects of disorientation. *Cortex: 23*, 169 – 187, 1987.

Davies AR, Jones DM, Taylor A: Selective and sustained attention tasks: individual and group differences. In Parasuraman R, Davies DR (Editors), *Varieties of Attention*. Orlando: Academic Press, pp. 395 – 448, 1984.

Davies DR, Parasuraman R: *The Psychology of Vigilance*. London: Academic Press, 1982.

De Bleser R, Denes GF, Luzzatti C, Mazzucchi A, Poek F, Spinnler H, Willmes K: L'Aachener Aphasie test (AAT). Problemi e soluzioni per una versione italiana del testo e per uno studio crosslinguistico dei disturbi afasici. *Arch. Psicol. Neurol. Psichiatria: 47*, 209 – 237, 1986.

De Groot AD: *Thought and Choice in Chess*. The Hague: Mouton, 1965.

Delay J, Brion S: *Les Démences Tardives*. Paris: Masson, 1962.

Della Sala S, Nichelli P, Spinnler H: An Italian series of patients with organic dementia. *Ital. J. Neurol. Sci.: 7*, 27 – 41, 1986.

De Mol J: Sémiologie neuropsychologique dans l'hydrocéphalie à pression normale. *Arch. Suisses Neurol. Psychiatrie: 137*, 33 – 45, 1986.

Dennett DC: *Content and Consciousness*. Andover: Routledge and Kegan Paul, 1969.

Denny-Brown D, Cambers RA: The parietal lobe and behavior. *Assoc. Res. Nerv. Mental Dis. Proc.: 36*, 35 – 117, 1958.

Drewe EA: The effect of type and area of brain lesion on Wisconsin Card Sorting performance. *Cortex: 10*, 159 – 170, 1974.

De Renzi E: *Disorders of Space Explanation and Cognition*.

Chichester: Wiley, pp. 57 – 125, 1982.

Derix MMA, Hijdra A, Verbeeten JR, BW Jr: Mental changes in subcortical arteriosclerotic encephalopathy. *Clin. Neurol. Neurosurg.: 89*, 71 – 78, 1987.

Deutsch D: Grouping mechanisms in music. In: Deutsch D (Editor), *The Psychology of Music*. New York: Academic Press, pp. 46 – 61, 1982.

Duara R, Grady CL, Haxby JV, Sundaram M, Cutler NR, Heston L, Moore A, Schlageter NL, Larson S, Rapaport SI: Positron emission tomography in Alzheimer's disease. *Neurology: 36*, 879 – 887, 1986.

Duncan J: The locus of interference in perception of simultaneous stimuli. *Psychol. Rev.: 87*, 272 – 330, 1980.

Edwards AJ: Introduction. In Edwards AJ (Editor), *Selected Papers of David Wechsler*. New York: Academic Press, pp. 3 – 10, 1974.

Eisdorfer C, Cohen D: Diagnostic criteria for primary neuronal degeneration of the Alzheimer's type. *J. Family Practitioner: 11*, 553 – 557, 1980.

Eslinger PJ, Damasio AR: Preserved motor learning in Alzheimer's disease. Implications for anatomy and behavior. *J. Neurol. Sci.: 6*, 3006 – 3009, 1986.

Evans JF: Monitoring attention deployment by random number generation: an index to measure subjective randomness. *Bull. Psychonom. Soc.: 12*, 35 – 38, 1978.

Evarts EV, Teravainen H, Calne DB: Reaction time in Parkinson disease. *Brain: 104*, 167 – 186, 1981.

Eysenck MW: *Attention and Arousal*. Berlin: Springer, 1982.

Faglioni P: Il lobo frontale. In Pizzamiglio L, Denes F (Editors), *Manuale di Neuropsicologia*. Bologna: Zanichelli, pp. 1117 – 1184, 1990.

Ferrier D: *Functions of the Brain*. Smith, London: Elder and Co., 1876.

Feuchtwanger E: Die Funktionen des Stirnhirns: ihre Pathologie und Psychologie. *Monatsschr. ges. Neurol. Psychiatrie: 38*, 1 – 193, 1923.

Fey ET: The performance of young schizophrenics and young normals on Wisconsin Card Sorting Test. *J. Consult. Psychiatry: 15*, 311 – 319, 1951.

Fisk A, Schneider W: Category and word search: generalizing search principles to complex processing. *J. Exp. Psychol. Learn. Memory Cognition: 9*, 177 – 194, 1983.

Flechsig P: *Gehirn und Seele*. Leipzig: Viet, 1896.

Flechsig P: Hirnpathologie und Willens theorie. Proceedings of the 'Congresso Internazionale di Psicologia' (quoted by Bianchi L: *The Mechanisms of the Brain and the Functions of the Frontal Lobes*. New York: Wood, 1922), 1905.

Fletcher WA, Sharpe JA: Saccadic eye movement dysfunction in Alzheimer's disease. *Ann. Neurol.: 20*, 464 – 4471, 1986.

Flicker C, Ferris SH, Crook RT, Bartus RT, Reisberg B: Cognitive decline in advanced age: future directions for the psychometric differentiation of normal and pathological age changes in cognitive function. *Dev. Neuropsychol.: 2*, 309 – 322, 1986.

Flicker C, Ferris SH, Crook T, Reisberg B, Bartus RT: Implications of memory and language dysfunction in the naming deficit of senile dementia. *Brain Lang.: 31*, 187 – 200, 1987.

Frackowiak RSJ, Pozzili C, Legg WJ, Du Boulay GH, Marshall J, Lenzi G, Jones T: Regional cerebral oxygen supply and utilization in dementia. A clinical and physiological study with oxygen-15 and positron tomography. *Brain: 104*, 753 – 778, 1981.

Friedland RP, Budinger TF, Koss E, Ober BA: Alzheimer's disease: anterior-posterior and lateral hemispheric alterations in cortical glucose utilization. *Neurosci. Lett.: 553*, 235 – 240, 1985.

Fuster JM: *The Pre-frontal Cortex. Anatomy, Physiology and Neuropsychology of the Frontal Lobe.* New York: Raven Press, 1980.

Gainotti G: Neuropsychological features of normal aging and of degenerative dementia. In Pilleri G, Tagliavini F (Editors), *Brain Pathology, Vol. 1.* Bern: Anathomisches Institut der Universitaet, pp. 11 – 37, 1984.

Gainotti G: Nonverbal cognitive disturbances in aphasia. In Whitaker HA (Editor), *Contemporary Reviews in Neuropsychology.* Berlin: Springer, pp. 127 – 153, 1988.

Gavazzi P, Luzzatti C, Spinnler H: La patologia del linguaggio nella demenza di Alzheimer. *Ric. Psicolog.: 4*, 91 – 135, 1986.

Gavazzi P, Luzzatti C, Spinnler H, Willmes K: Disturbi di linguaggio e loro evoluzione nella demenza di Alzheimer. In: Salmaso D, Caffarra P (Editors) *Normalitá e patologia della funzioni cognitive nel l'invecchiamento.* Milano: F. Angeli, 1990.

Gewirth LR, Shindler AG, Hier DR: Altered patterns of word associations in dementia and aphasia. *Brain Lang.: 21*, 307 – 317, 1984.

Gibson JJ: *The Ecological Approach to Visual Perception.* Boston: Houghton Mifflin, 1979.

Gilley DW, Wilson RS, Fox JH: Relationship between behavioral disturbances and demential severity in Alzheimer's disease (abstract). *J. Clin. Exp. Neuropsychol.: 11*, 20 (INS, Vancouver Workshop, February, 1989), 1989.

Gilmore GC, Tabios TR, Rayer FL: Aging and similarity grouping in individual search. *J. Gerontol.: 40*, 586 – 592, 1985.

Glucksberg S: The functional equivalence of common and multiple codes. *J. Verbal Learn. Verbal Behav.: 23*, 100 – 104, 1984.

Goldberg TE, Weinberger DR: Methodological issues in the neuropsychological approach to schizophrenia. In Nasrallah HA, Weinberger DR (Editors), *Handbook of Schizophrenia, Vol. 1.* Amsterdam: Elsevier, pp. 141 – 156, 1986.

Goldberg TE, Weinberger DR, Berman KF, Pliskin NH, Podd MH: Further evidence for dementia of the prefrontal type in schizophrenia? *Arch. Gen. Psychiatry: 44*, 1008 – 1014, 1987.

Golden CJ: *The Stroop Color and Word Test: A Manual for Clinical and Experimental Uses.* Chicago: Stoelting, 1978.

Goody W: Disorders of the time sense. In Vinken PJ, Bruyn GW (Editors), *Handbook of Clinical Neurology.* Amsterdam: Elsevier, pp. 229 – 250, 1969.

Gottschaldt K: Ueber den Einfluss der Erfahrung auf die Wahrnehmung von Figuren. *Psychol. Forsch.: 8*, 261 – 317, 1926.

Gottschaldt K: Ueber den Einfluss der Erfahrung auf die Wahrnehmung von Figuren. *Psychol. Forsch.: 12*, 1 – 87, 1929.

Grady CL, Grimes AM, Patronas N, Sunderland T, Foster NL, Rapoport SI: Divided attention, as measured by dichotic speech performances, in dementia of the Alzheimer type. *Arch. Neurol.: 46*, 317 – 320, 1989.

Grady CL, Haxby JV, Horowitz RB, Sundaram M, Berg G, Shapiro M, Friedland RP, Rapoport SI: Longitudinal study of the early neuropsychological and cerebral metabolic changes in dementia of the Alzheimer type. *J. Clin. Exp. Neurospychol.: 10*, 576 – 596, 1988.

Granholm EL, Asarnow RF, Marder SR: Resource limmitations and the development of automatic information processing in schizophrenia (abstract). *J. Clin. Exp. Neuropsychol.: 11*, 82 (INS Vancouver Workshop, February, 1989), 1989.

Graydon J, Eysenck MW: Distraction and cognitive performance. *Eur. J. Cognitive Psychol.: 1*, 161 – 179, 1989.

Gratiolet: Observations sur la forme et le poids du cerveau. Paris (quoted by AR Luria: *Le Funzioni Corticali Superiori nell'Uomo.* Translation by Bisiach E, Firenze: Giunti, p. 237, 1961).

Grimes AM, Grady CL, Foster NL: Central auditory function in Alzheimer's disease. *Neurology: 35*, 352 – 358, 1985.

Grober E, Buschke H, Kawas C, Fuld P: Impaired ranking of semantic attributes in dementia. *Brain Lang.: 26*, 276 – 286, 1985.

Groner R, Groner MT: Attention and eye movement control: an overview. *Eur. Arch. Psychiatry Neurol. Sci.: 239*, 9 – 16, 1989.

Gustafson L: Frontal lobe degeneration of non-Alzheimer type. Clinical picture and differential diagnosis. *Arch. Gerontol. Geriatrics: 6*, 209 – 223, 1987.

Hamos JE, De Gennaro LJ, Drachman DA: Synaptic loss in Alzheimer's disease and other dementias. *Neurology: 39*, 355 – 361, 1989.

Harlow JM: Recovery from the passage of an iron bar through the head. *Massachussets Med. Soc. Publ.: 2*, 327 – 346, 1868.

Harris JE: Remembering to do things: a forgotten topic. In Harris JE, Morris PE (Editors), *Everyday Memory, Actions and Absent-Mindedness.* London: Academic Press, pp. 71 – 92, 1984.

Harrow M, Marengo J, Poque-Geile M, Pawelski TJ: Schizophrenic deficit in intelligence and abstract thinking: influence of aging and long-term institutionalization. In: Miller NE, Cohen GD (Editors), *Schizophrenia and Aging.* New York: Guildford Press, pp. 134 – 144, 1987.

Haxby JV, Grady CL, Koss E, Horowitz RB, Schapiro M, Friedland RP, Rapoport SI: Heterogeneous anterior-posterior metabolic patterns in dementia of Alzheimer type. *Neurology: 38*, 1853 – 1863, 1988.

Hasher L, Zacks RT: Automatic and effortful processes in memory. *J. Exp. Psychol. (General): 108*, 356 – 388, 1979.

Head H: The conception of nervous and mental energy and vigilance: a psychological state of the nervous system. *Br. J. Psychol.: 14*, 126 – 147, 1923.

Heaton RK, Drexler M: Clinical neuropsychological findings in schizophrenia and aging. In: Miller NE, Cohen GD (Editors), *Schizophrenia and Aging.* New York: Guildford Press, pp. 145 – 161, 1987.

Hebb DO: *The organization of behaviour. A neuropsychological theory.* New York: Wiley, p. 4, 1949.

Hécaen H: Mental symptoms associated with tumors of the frontal lobe. In Warren JM, Akert K (Editors), *The Frontal Granular Cortex and Behaviour.* New York: McGraw-Hill, pp. 335 – 352, 1964.

Heilman K, Bowers D, Watson RT, Greer M: Reaction time in Parkinson disease. *Arch. Neurol.: 33*, 139 – 140, 1976.

Heilman KM, Watson RT, Valenstein E, Goldberg ME: Attention: behavior and neuronal mechanisms. In Mountcastle VB, Plum F (Editors), *Handbook of Physiology, Section 1, Vol. 5, Part 2.* Bethesda: American Physiological Society, pp. 461 – 481, 1987.

Heindel WC, Butters N, Salmon DP: Impaired learning of a motor skill in patients with Huntington disease. *Behav. Neurosci.:* 1988, in press.

Hills AE, Caramazza A: The effects of attentional deficits on reading and spelling. Report N. 44. Reports of the cognitive neuropsychology laboratory, 1989.

Hirst W: On consciousness, recall, recognition and the architecture of memory. In: Lewandowsky S, Dunn C, Kirsner K (Editors), *Implicit memory. Theoretical issues.* Hillsdale: LEA, pp. 33 – 46, 1989.

Hirst W, Volpe BT: Automatic and effortful encoding in amnesia. In Gazzaniga MS (Editor), *Handbook of Cognitive Neuroscience.* New York: Plenum Press, pp. 309 – 386, 1984.

Hockey R: Varieties of attentional state: the effects of environment. In Parasuraman R, Davies DR (Editors), *Varieties of Attention,* Orlando: Academic Press, pp. 449 – 484, 1984.

Horn JL: Human abilities: a review of research and theory in the early 1970. *Annu. Rev. Psychol.:* 27, 437 – 463, 1976.

Horn JL, Cattell RB: Age differences in fluid and crystallized intelligence. *Acta Psychol.:* 26, 107 – 129, 1967.

Horne RL, Evans FJ, Arne MT: Random number generation, psychopathology and therapeutic change. *Arch. Gen. Psychiatry:* 39, 680 – 683, 1982.

Huff FJ, Corkin S, Growdon JH: Semantic impairment and anomia in Alzheimer's disease. *Brain Lang.:* 28, 225 – 249, 1986.

Hunt E: Mechanics of verbal ability. *Psychol. Rev.:* 85, 109 – 130, 1978.

Huppert F, Piercy M: The role of trace strength in recency and frequency judgements by amnesics and control subjects. *Q. J. Exp. Psychol.:* 30, 346 – 354, 1978.

Hutton JT: Eye movements and Alzheimer's disease: significance and relationship to visuospatial confusion. In: Hutton JT, Kenny AD (Editors), *Senile Dementia of the Alzheimer Type.* New York: Liss. pp. 3 – 33, 1985.

Hutton JT, Morris JL: Looking and seeing with age-related neurologic disease and normal aging. *Semin. Neurol.:* 9, 31 – 38, 1989.

Hutton JT, Nagel JA, Loewenson RB: Eye tracking dysfunction in Alzheimer type dementia. *Neurology:* 34, 99 – 102, 1984.

Hutton JT, Albrecht JW, Shapiro I, Johnston C: Visual information processing and dementia. *Neuro-Ophthalmology:* 7, 105 – 112, 1987.

Hyman BT, Van Hoesen GW, Damasio AR, Barnes CL: Alzheimer's disease: cell-specific pathology isolates the hippocampal formation. *Science:* 255, 2268 – 2270, 1984.

Hyvaerinen J: *The Parietal Cortex of Monkey and Man.* Berlin: Springer, pp. 156 – 159, 1982.

Inglis J: Learning, retention and conceptual usage in elderly patients with memory disorder. *J. Abnormal Soc. Psychol.:* 59, 210 – 215, 1959.

Inglis J: Psychological investigations of cognitive deficit in elderly psychiatric patients. *Psychol. Bull.:* 55, 197 – 214, 1958.

Ingvar DH: Functional landscapes of dominant hemisphere. *Brain Res.:* 107, 181 – 197, 1976.

Ingvar DH: Hyperfrontal distribution of cerebral grey matter shown in resting wakefulness on the functional anatomy of conscious state. *Acta Neurol. Scand.:* 60, 12 – 25, 1979.

Irigaray L: *Le Language des Déments.* The Hague: Mouton, 1973.

Irving G, Robinson RA, McAdam W: The validity of some cognitive tests in the diagnosis of dementia. *Br. J. Psychol.:* 117, 149 – 156, 1970.

Jackson JL: Is the processing of temporal information automatic or controlled? In Michon JA, Kackson JL (Editors), *Time, Mind and Behavior.* Berlin: Springer, pp. 179 – 190, 1985.

Jackson JH: *Selected Writings,* 1868 (reprinted by Taylor J). London: Hodder and Stoughton, 1968.

Jacoby LL: Incidental versus intentional retrieval: remembering and awareness of separate issues. In: Squire LR, Butters N (Editors), *Neuropsychology of Memory.* New York: Guilford, pp. 145 – 156, 1984.

James W: *Principles of Psychology.* New York: Holt, 1890.

Jastrowitz M: *Die Geschwuelste des Nervensystems.* Leipzig: Barth, 1897.

Jensen AR, Rohwer WD, Jr.: The Stroop color-word test: a review. *Acta Psychol.:* 25, 36 – 93, 1966.

Jones-Gotman M, Milner B: Design fluency: the invention of nonsense drawings after frontal lesions. *Neuropsychologia:* 15, 653 – 674, 1977.

Jorm AF: Controlled and automatic information processing in senile dementia: a review. *Psychol. Med.;* 16, 77 – 88, 1986.

Jorm AF, Share DI: Phonological recording and reading acquisition. *Appl. Psycholing.:* 4, 103 – 147, 1983.

Joynt RJ, Benton AL, Fogel ML: Behavioral and pathological correlates of motor impersistence. *Neurology:* 12, 876 – 881, 1962.

Kahneman D: *Attention and Effort.* Englewood Cliffs, NJ: Prentice-Hall, 1973.

Kahneman D, Treisman A: Changing views of attention and automaticity. In: Parasuraman R, Davis DR (Editors), *Varieties of Attention.* Orlando: Academic Press, pp. 29 – 62, 1984.

Kaszniack AW, Garron D, Fox J: Differential effects of age and cerebral atrophy upon span of immediate recall and paired-associate learning in older patients suspected of dementia. *Cortex:* 15, 285 – 295, 1979.

Kausler D, Puckett J: Frequency judgments and correlated cognitive abilities in young and elderly adults. *J. Gerontol.:* 3, 376 – 382, 1980.

Kennard MA, Ectors L: Forced circling movements in monkeys following lesions of the frontal lobes. *J. Neuropsychol.:* 1, 45 – 54, 1938.

Kertesz A, Appel J, Fisman M: The dissolution of language in Alzheimer's disease. *Can. J. Neurol. Sci.:* 13, 415 – 418, 1986.

Kiloh LG: Pseudodementia. *Acta Psychiatr. Scand.:* 37, 336 – 357, 1961.

Kinsbourne M: Systematizing cognitive psychology. *Behav. Brain Sci.:* 9, 556, 1986.

Kinsbourne M: Brain mechanisms and memory. *Hum. Neurobiol.:* 6, 81 – 92, 1987.

Kleist K: *Kriegsverletzungen des Gehirns in ihrer Bedeutung fuer Hirnlokalisation und Hirnpathologie.* Leipzig: Barth, 1934.

Knopman DS, Christensen KJ, Schut LJ, Harbaugh RE, Reeder RN, Ngo T, Frey W: The spectrum of imaging and neuropsychological findings in Pick's disease. *Neurology:* 39, 362 – 368, 1989.

Kolb B, Wishaw IQ: Performance of schizophrenic patients on tests sensitive to left or right frontal, temporal, parietal function in neurologic patients. *J. Nerv. Mental Dis.:* 171, 435 – 443, 1983.

Kopelman MD: Multiple memory deficits in Alzheimer type

dementia: implications for pharmacotherapy. *Psychol. Med.: 15*, 527 – 541, 1985.

Kopelman MD: Clinical test of memory. *Br. J. Psychiatry: 148*, 517 – 525, 1986.

Kopelman MD, Corn TH: Cholinergic 'blockade' as a model for cholinergic depletion. A comparison of the memory deficits with those of Alzheimer-type dementia and the alcoholic Korsakoff syndrome. *Brain: 111*, 1079 – 1110, 1988.

Kuhl DE, Metter EJ, Riege WH: Patterns of cerebral glucose utilization in depression, multiple infarct dementia and Alzheimer's disease. In Sokoloff L (Editor), *Brain Imaging and Brain Function.* New York: Raven Press, pp. 24 – 226, 1985.

La Berge D, Samuels SJ: Toward a theory of automatic information processing in reading. *Cognitive Psychol.: 6*, 293 – 323, 1974.

Lawson JS, McGhie A, Chapman J: Distractivity in schizophrenics and organic cerebral desease. *Br. J. Psychiatry: 113*, 527 – 535, 1967.

Leimkuhler ME, Mesulam MM: Reversible go – no go deficits in a case of frontal lobe tumor. *Ann. Neurol.: 18*, 617 – 619, 1985.

Levy RL, Loftus GR: Compliance and memory. In Harris JE, Morris PE (Editors), *Everyday Memory, Actions and Absent-Mindedness.* London: Academic Press, pp. 93 – 112, 1984.

Lezak MD: *Neuropsychological Assessment*, 2 nd Edition. New York: Oxford University Press, pp. 533 – 575, 1983.

Lhermitte F: 'Utilization behavior' and its relation to lesions of the frontal lobes. *Brain: 106*, 237 – 255, 1983.

Lhermitte F: Human autonomy of the frontal lobes. II. Patient behavior in complex and social situations: the 'environmental dependency syndrome'. *Ann. Neurol.: 19*, 335 – 343, 1986.

Lhermitte F, Derouesne J, Signoret JL: Analyse neuro-psychologique du syndrome frontal. *Rev. Neurol.: 127*, 415 – 440, 1972.

Lipowski ZJ: Delirium: acute confusional state. In Frederiks JAM (Editor), *Handbook of Clinical Neurology (Neurobehavioral Disorders)* (Revised series, No. 46) *Vol. 2.* Amsterdam: Elsevier, pp. 523 – 560, 1985.

Lishman WA: *Organic Psychiatry: The Psychological Consequences of Cerebral Disorder.* Oxford: Blackwell Scientific Publications, 1978.

Luria AR: *Human Brain and Psychological Processes.* New York: Harper and Row, 1966.

Luria AR: *Le Funzioni Corticali Superiori Nell'Uomo* (translated from Russian by Bisiach E.) Firenze: Giunti, pp. 236 – 247, 1967.

Luria AR: *The Working Brain. An Introduction to Neuropsychology* (translated from Russian by Haigh B). New York: Basic Books, 1973.

Mackworth NH: *Research on the measurement of human performance.* Medical Research Council Special Report, No. 268, H.M.S.O., London, 1950.

Mackworth NH: Some factors affecting vigilance. *Adv. Sci.: 53*, 389 – 393, 1957.

Mackworth NH: *Vigilance and Habituation.* Baltimore, Penguin, 1969.

Malmo HP: On frontal lobe functions: psychiatric patient controls. *Cortex: 10*, 231 – 237, 1974.

Mahurin RK, Pirozzolo F: Chronometric analysis: clinical applications in aging and dementia. *Dev. Neuropsychol.: 2*, 345 – 362, 1986.

Mahurin RK, Pirozzolo FJ, Jahkovic J: Choice reaction times in Parkinson disease and Alzheimer disease. Houstong: International Neuropsychological Society, 12th Annual Meeting, 1984.

Mandler JM: *Mind and Emotion.* New York: Wiley, 1975.

Maratone M, Butters N, Paynde M, Sax DS: Dissociations between skill learning and verbal recognition in amnesia and dementia. *Arch. Neurol.: 41*, 965 – 970, 1984.

Marcel AJ: Conscious and unconscious preception: an approach to the relations between phenomenal experience and perceptional processes. *Cognitive Psychol.: 15*, 238 – 300, 1983.

Marin OSM: Dementia and visual agnosia. In Humphreys GW, Riddoch MJ (Editors), *Visual Object Processing: a Cognitive Neuropsychological Approach.* Hillsdale: Lawrence Erlbaum Associates, pp. 261 – 280, 1987.

Martin A, Fedio P: Word production and comprehension in Alzheimer's disease: the breakdown of semantic knowledge. *Brain Lang.: 19*, 124 – 141, 1983.

Martin M, Jones CV: Cognitive failure in everyday life. In Harris JE, Morris PE (Editors), *Everyday Memory, Actions and Absent-Mindedness.* London: Academic Press, pp. 173 – 190, 1984.

Mattis S: Dementia rating scale. In Bellack R, Karasu B (Editors), *Geriatric Psychiatry.* New York: Grune and Stratton, pp. 77 – 122, 1976.

Maximillian VA, Prohovnik I, Risberg J, Hakausson K: Regional blood flow changes in the left hemisphere during word pair learning and recall. *Brain Lang.: 6*, 22 – 31, 1980.

McAllister TW: Functioning in affective disorders. *Comp. Psychiatry: 22*, 572 – 586, 1981.

McFie J: Psychological testing in clinical neurology. *J. Nerv. Mental Dis.: 131*, 383 – 393, 1960.

McKhann G, Drachman D, Folstein M, Katzman R, Prize D, Stadlan EM: Clinical diagnosis of Alzheimer's disease. *Neurology: 34*, 939 – 944, 1984.

Medin DL, Wattenmaker WD: Category cohesiveness, theories, and cognitive archeology. In H. Neisser (Editor), *Concepts and Conceptual Development. Ecological and Intellectual Factors in Categorization.* Cambridge: Cambridge University Press, pp. 255 – 262, 1987.

Mesulam MM: A cortical network for directed attention and unilateral neglect. *Ann. Neurol.: 19*, 309 – 325, 1981.

Mesulam MM: Attention, confusional states, and neglect. In MM Mesulam (Editor), *Principle of Behavioral Neurology.* Philadelphia: FA Davis Company, pp. 81 and 125 – 168, 1985.

Mesulam MM: Frontal cortex and behavior. *Ann. Neurol.: 19*, 320 – 325, 1986.

Mesulam MM, Geschwind N: On the possible role of the neocortex and its limbic connections in attention in schizophrenia. In Wynne LC, Cromwell RL, Mattyse S (Editors), *The Nature of Schizophrenia.* New York: Wiley, pp. 161 – 166, 1978.

Miller E: Short and long term memory in presenile dementia (Alzheimer's disease). *Psychol. Med.: 3*, 221 – 224, 1973.

Miller E: Impaired recall and memory disturbance in presenile dementia. *Br. J. Soc. Clin. Psychol.: 14*, 73 – 79, 1975.

Miller E, Hague F: Some characteristics of verbal behavior in presenile dementia. *Psychol. Med.: 5*, 255 – 259, 1975.

Miller E, Lewis P: Recognition memory in elderly patients with depression and dementia: a signal detection analysis. *J. Ab-*

normal Psychol.: 86, 84 – 86, 1977.

Milner B: Effects of different brain lesions on card sorting. *Arch. Neurol.: 9*, 90 – 100, 1963.

Milner B, Corkin S, Teuber HL: Further analysis of the hippocampal amnesic syndrome: 14 year follow-up study of H.M. *Neuropsychologia: 6*, 215 – 234.

Mirsky AF, Primac DW, Ajmone-Marsan C, Rosvald HE, Stevens JR: A comparison of psychological test performance of patients with focal and non focal epilepsy. *Exp. Neurol.: 2*, 75 – 89, 1960.

Moray N: *Attention. Selective Processes in Vision and Hearing.* New York: Academic Press, pp. 1 – 9, 1970.

Morris RC: Dementia and the functioning of the articulatory loop system. *Cognitive Neuropsychol.: 1*, 143 – 157, 1984.

Morris RC: Short-term forgetting in senile dementia of the Alzheimer's type. *Cognitive Neuropsychol.: 3*, 77 – 97, 1986.

Morris RC: Articulatory rehearsal in Alzheimer type dementia. *Brain Lang.: 30*, 351 – 362, 1987.

Morris RC, Weatley J, Britton P: Retrieval from long-term memory in senile dementia: cued recall revisited. *Br. J. Clin. Psychol.: 22*, 141 – 142, 1983.

Munor-Garcia D, Ludwin SK: Classic and generalized variants of Pick's disease: a clinicopathological, ultrastructural, and immunocytochemical comparative study. *Ann. Neurol.: 16*, 467 – 480, 1984.

Naville F: Complications et les sequelles mentales de l'encéphalite épidémique. *Encéphale: 17*, 369 – 375; 423 – 436, 1922.

Neary D, Snowdon JS, Northen B, Goulding P: Dementia of frontal lobe type. *J. Neurol. Neurosurg. Psychiatry: 51*, 353 – 361, 1988.

Nebes RD, Boller F: The use of language structure by demented patients in a visual search task. *Cortex: 23*, 87 – 98, 1987.

Nebes RD, Brady CB: Integrity of semantic fields in Alzheimer's disease. *Cortex: 24*, 291 – 299, 1988.

Nebes RD, Brady CB: Focused and divided attention in Alzheimer's disease. *Cortex: 25*, 305 – 315, 1989.

Nebes RD, Madden DJ: The use of focused attention in visual search by young and old adults. *Exp. Aging Res.: 9*, 139 – 143, 1983.

Nebes RD, Madden DJ: Different patterns of cognitive slowing produced by Alzheimer's disease and normal aging. *Psychol. Aging: 3*, 102 – 104, 1988.

Nebes RD, Martin DC, Horn LC: Sparing of semantic memory in Alzheimer's disease. *J. Abnormal Psychol.: 93*, 321 – 330, 1984.

Nebes RD, Boller F, Holland A: Use of semantic context by patients with Alzheimer's disease. *Psychol. Aging: 1*, 261 – 269, 1986.

Nebes RD, Brady CB, Huff FJ: Automatic and attentional mechanisms of semantic priming in Alzheimer's disease. *J. Clin. Exp. Neuropsychol.: 11*, 219 – 230, 1989.

Neely JH: Semantic priming and retrieval from lexical memory: roles of inhibitionless spreading activation and limited capacity attention. *J. Exp. Psychol. Gen.: 106*, 226 – 254, 1977.

Neisser H (Editor): From direct perception to conceptual structure. In *Concepts and Conceptual Development. Ecological and Intellectual Factors in Categorization.* Cambridge: Cambridge University Press, pp. 11 – 24, 1987.

Nelson HE, McKenna P: The use of current reading ability in the assessment of dementia. *Br. J. Soc. Clin. Psychol.: 22*,

141 – 142, 1975.

Nelson HE, O'Connell A: Dementia: The estimation of premorbid intelligence levels using the New Adults Reading Test. *Cortex: 14*, 234 – 244, 1978.

Nestor P, Parasuraman R: Learning and attention in aging and early Alzheimer's dementia. Washington: Paper presented to Gerontology Society of America, 1987.

Newman RP, Weingartner H, Shallberg S, Calne D: Effortful and automatic memory processes: effects of dopamine. *Neurology: 34*, 805 – 807, 1984.

Niederehe G, Rusin MJ: Schizophrenia and aging: information processing patterns. In Miller NE, Cohen GD (Editors), *Schizophrenia and Aging.* New York: The Guildford Press, pp. 162 – 179, 1987.

Nissen MJ, Corking S, Growdon JH: Attentional focusing in amnesia and Alzheimer's disease. Unpublished manuscript: 1985.

Norman DA: *Memory and Attention: An Introduction to Human Information Processing.* New York: Wiley, 1976.

Norman DA, Bobrow DG: On data-limited and resource-limited processes. *Cognitive Psychol.: 7*, 44 – 67, 1975.

Norman DA, Shallice T: *Attention and action: willed and automatic control of behavior.* Center for Human Information Processing, Technical Report No. 99, 1980.

Norman DA, Shallice T: Attention and action. Willed and automatic control of behavior. In Davidson RJ, Schwartz GE, Shapiro D (Editors), *Consciousness and Self-Regulation. Advances in Research and Theory.* New York: Plenum Press, pp. 1 – 18, 1986.

Novelli G, Papagno C, Capitani E, Laiacona M, Vallar G, Cappa SF: Tre test clinici di ricerca e produzione lessicale. Taratura su soggetti normali. *Arch. Psicol. Neurol. Psichiatria: 47*, 477 – 506, 1986.

Ober BA, Dronkers NF, Koss E, Delis DC, Friedland RP: Retrieval from semantic memory in Alzheimer-type dementia. *J. Clin. Exp. Neuropsychol.: 8*, 75 – 92, 1986.

Obler LK, Albert ML: Language and aging: a neurobehavioral analysis. In Beaseley DS, Davis GA (Editors), *Aging: Communications Processes and Disorders.* New York: Grune and Stratton, pp. 107 – 121, 1981.

Oppenheim, H: *Die Geschwuelste des Gehirns,* Wien, 1896: quoted by Hécaen H: Mental symptoms associated with tumors of the frontal lobe. In Warren JM, Akerd K (Editors), *The Frontal Granular Cortex and Behavior.* New York: McGraw Hill, pp. 335 – 352, 1964.

Ottmanns T: Selective attention in schizophrenia and manic psychoses: the effects of distraction on information processing. *J. Abnormal Psychol.: 87*, 221 – 225, 1978.

Oyanagi K, Takahashi H, Wakabayashi K, Ikuta F: Selective involvement of large neurons in the neostriatum of Alzheimer's disease and senile dementia: a morphometric investigation. *Brain Res.: 411*, 205 – 211, 1987.

Parasuraman R: Sustained attention in detection and discrimination. In Parasuraman R, Davies DR (Editors), *Varieties of Attention.* Orlando: Academic Press, pp. 243 – 272, 1984.

Parasuraman R, Davies DR: Preface. In: Parasuraman R, Davies DR (Editors), *Varieties of Attention.* Orlando: Academic Press, pp. 11 – 16, 1984.

Parasuraman R, Nestor P: Energetics of attention and Alzheimer's disease. In Hockey GRJ, Faillard A, Coles MGH (Editors), *Energetics and Human Information Processing.*

Dordrecht: Martinus Nijhoff, 1986.

Parasuraman R, Nestor P, Haxby J: *Patterns of attentional loss in aging and early Alzheimer's disease.* Technical Report CNL 85 – 1: Cognitive Neuroscience Laboratory, Catholic University, Washington, 1985.

Parkinson SR, Lindholm JM, Urell T: Aging, dichotic memory and digitspan. *J. Gerontol.: 35*, 87 – 95, 1980.

Pawlik G, Heiss WD: Positron Emission Tomography and neuropsychological function. In Bigler ED, Yeo RA, Turkheimer E (Editors), *Neuropsychological Function and Brain Imaging.* New York, Plenum Press, pp. 109 – 129, 1989.

Pearce J, Miller E: *Clinical Aspects of Dementia.* London: Baillière Tindall, pp. 112 – 124, 1973.

Perret E: The left frontal lobe of man and the suppression of habitual responses in verbal categorical behaviour. *Neuropsychologia: 12*, 323 – 330, 1974.

Pillsbury WB: *Attention.* New York: Macmillan, 1908.

Pirozzolo FJ, Christensen KJ, Ogle KM, Hansch EC, Thompson WG: Single and choice reaction time in dementia: clinical implications. *Neurobiol. Aging: 2*, 113 – 117, 1981.

Plum F, Posner JB: *The Diagnosis of Stupor and Coma*, 3rd edition. Philadelphia: Davis, 1980.

Posner MI, Boies SJ: Components of attention. *Psychol. Rev.: 78*, 391 – 408, 1971.

Posner MI, Walker J, Friedrich F, Rafal R: Effects of parietal lobe injury on covert orienting and visual attention. *J. Neurosci.: 47*, 1874 – 1983, 1984.

Post F: *Clinical Psychiatry of Late Life.* Oxford: Pergamon Press, 1965.

Pribram KH, McGuinness D: Arousal, activation and effort in the control of attention. *Psychol. Rev.: 82*, 116 – 149, 1975.

Prohovnik I, Hakansson K, Risberg J: Observations on the functional significance of regional cerebral blood flow in 'resting' normal subjects. *Neuropsychologia: 18*, 203 – 217, 1980.

Rabbitt P: Some experiments and a model for changes in attentional selectivity with old age. In Hoffmeister F, Muller C (Editors), *Brain Function in Old Age.* Berlin: Springer, pp. 82 – 94, 1979.

Rapsak SZ, Arthur SA, Bliklen DA, Rubens, AD: Lexical agraphia in Alzheimer's disease. *Arch. Neurol.: 46*, 65 – 68, 1989.

Ratcliff G, Newcombe F: Object recognition: some deductions from the clinical evidence. In Ellis AW (Editor), *Normativity and Pathology in Cognitive Function.* London: Academic Press, pp. 147 – 171, 1982.

Reason J: Actions not as planned. In Handerwood G, Stevens R (Editors), *Aspects of Consciousness, Vol. 1.* London: Academic Press, pp. 67 – 89, 1979.

Reason J: Lapses of attention. In Parasuraman R, Davies R, Beatty J (Editors), *Varieties of Attention.* New York: Academic Press, pp. 515 – 549, 1984a.

Reason J: Absentmindedness and cognitive control. In Harris JE, Morris PE (Editors), *Everyday Memory, Actions and Absent-Mindedness.* London: Academic Press, pp. 113 – 132, 1984b.

Reason J, Lucas D: Cognitive diaries to investigate naturally occurring memory blocks. In Harris JE, Morris PE (Editors), *Everyday Memory, Actions and Absent-Mindedness.* London: Academic Press, pp. 553 – 570, 1984.

Reason JT, Mycielska K: *Absent-minded? The Psychology of Mental Lapses and Everyday Errors.* Englewood Cliffs: Prentice Hall, 1982.

Reed BR, Seab JP, Ober BA, Jagust WJ: Neuropsychological and regional cerebral blood flow (rCBF) abnormalities in patients with extremely mild Alzheimer's disease (AD) (abstract). *J. Clin. Exp. Neuropsychol.: 11*, 20 (INS Vancouver Workshop, February 1989), 1989.

Reiser BJ, Black JB, Kalamarides P: Strategic memory search processes. In Rubin DC (Editor), *Autobiographical Memory.* Cambridge: Cambridge University Press, pp. 100 – 121, 1986.

Reitan RM: Validity of trail-making test as an indicator of organic brain damage. *Percept. Motor Skills: 8*, 271 – 276, 1958.

Ribot TA: *The Psychology of Attention.* New York: Humboldt, 1889.

Risberg J, Maximillian A, Prohovnik I: Changes of cortical activity patterns during habituation to a reasoning task: a study with 133-xenon inhalation technique for measurement of regional cerebral blood flow. *Neuropsychologia: 15*, 793 – 798, 1977.

Robinson AL, Heaton RK, Lehman RAW, Stilson DW: The utility of the Wisconsin Card Sorting Test in detecting and localizing frontal lobe lesions. *J. Consult. Psychol.: 48*, 605 – 614, 1980.

Rochford G: A study of naming errors in dysphasic and in demented patients. *Neuropsychologia: 9*, 437 – 443, 1971.

Roth M: Late paraphrenia: phenomenology and etiological factors and their bearing upon problems of the schizophrenic family of disorders. In Miller NE, Cohen GD (Editors), *Schizophrenia and Aging.* New York: The Guildford Press, pp. 217 – 234, 1987.

Rozin P: The evolution of intelligence and access to the cognitive unconscious. In Sprague JH, Epstein AN (Editors), *Progress in Psychology and Physiological Psychology.* New York: Academic Press, pp. 245 – 280, 1976.

Ruddle HV, Bradshaw CM: On the estimation of premorbid intellectual functioning: validation of Nelson and McKenna's formula and some new normative data. *Br. J. Clin. Psychol.: 21*, 159 – 165, 1982.

Ruff RM, Light RH, Evans RW: The Ruff Figural Fluency test: a normative study with adults. *Dev. Neuropsychol.: 3*, 37 – 51, 1987.

Russo M, Vignolo LA: Visual figure ground discrimination in patients with unilateral cerebral disease. *Cortex: 3*, 113 – 127, 1967.

Rylander G: Personality changes after operations on the frontal lobes: a clinical study of 32 cases. *Acta Psychiatr. Neurol. Scand. Suppl.: 20*, 3 – 327, 1939.

Sadun AA, Borchert M, De Viva E, Hinton DR, Bassi GJ: Assessment of visual impairment in patients with Alzheimer's disease. *Am. J. Ophthalmol.: 104*, 113 – 120, 1987.

Saint-Cyr JA, Taylor AE, Lang AE: Procedural learning and neostriatal dysfunction in man. *Brain: 111*, 941 – 959, 1988.

Salame P, Baddeley AD: Disruption of short-term memory by unattended speech: implications for the structure of working memory. *J. Verbal Learn. Verbal Behav.: 21*, 150 – 164, 1982.

Salmaso D, Denes G: Role of the frontal lobes on an attentional task: a signal detection analysis. *Percept. Motor Skills: 55*, 127 – 130, 1982.

Salthouse TA: *Adult Cognition: An Experimental Psychology of Human Aging.* New York: Springer, 1982.

Salthouse TA: Rogan JD, Prill KA: Division of attention: age differences on a visually presented memory task. *Memory Cognition: 12*, 613 – 620, 1985.

Saper CB, Plum F: Disorders of consciousness. In Vinken PJ, Bruyn GW, Klawans HL (Eds.), *Handbook of Clinical Neurology, Vol. 1* (Rev. Ser.). Amsterdam: Elsevier, Ch. 45, 1985.

Schacter DL, McAndrews MP, Moscovitch M: Access to consciousness: dissociations between implicit and explicit knowledge in neuropsychological syndromes. In Weiskrantz L (Editor), *Thought Without Knowledge*. Oxford: Oxford University Press, pp. 242 – 277, 1988.

Schacter DL: Toward a cognitive neuropsychology of awareness: implicit knowledge and anosognosia. *J. Clin. Exp. Neuropsychol.: 12*, 155 – 178, 1990.

Schneider W, Dumais ST, Shiffrin RM: Automatic and control processing and attention. In Parasuraman R, Davis DR (Editors), *Varieties of Attention*. Orlando: Academic Press, pp. 1 – 28, 1984.

Schneider W, Fisk AD: Degree of consistent training: improvements in search performance and automatic process development. *Percept. Psychophys.: 31*, 160 – 168, 1982.

Schoenemann PH: Factorial definitions of intelligence: dubious legacy of dogma in data analysis. In Borg I (Editor), *Multidimensional Data Representations: When and Why*. Ann. Arbor: Mathesis Press, pp. 325 – 379, 1981.

Schwartz MF, Marin OSM, Saffran EM: Dissociations of language functions in dementia: a case study. *Brain Lang.: 7*, 277 – 306, 1979.

Seidman LF: Schizophrenia and brain dysfunction. *Psychol. Bull.: 97*, 195 – 238, 1983.

Seltzer B, Mesulam MM: Confusional states and delirium as disorders of attention. In Boller F, Grafman J (Editors), *Handbook of Neuropsychology, Vol. 1*. Amsterdam: Elsevier, pp. 165 – 174, 1988.

Seymour PHF: *Human Visual Cognition*. London: Collier Macmillian, 1979.

Shallice T: Specific impairments of planning. *Phil. Trans. R. Soc. Lond.: 298*, 199 – 209, 1982.

Shallice T: Impairments of semantic processing: multiple dissociations. In Coltheart M, Sartori G, Job R (Editors), *The Cognitive Neuropsychology of Language*. London: Erlbaum, pp. 112 – 128, 1987.

Shallice T: Specialization within the semantic system. *Cognitive Neuropsychol.: 5*, 133 – 142, 1988a.

Shallice T: Information-processing models of consciousness: possibilities and problems. In Marcel AJ, Bisiach E (Editors), *Consciousness in Contemporary Sciences*. Oxford: Clarendon Press, pp. 305 – 333, 1988b.

Shiffrin RM, Dumais ST: The development of automatism. In R. Anderson (Editor), *Cognitive Skills and their Acquisition*. Hillsdale: Lawrence Erlbaum, pp. 111 – 140, 1981.

Shiffrin RM, Schneider W: Controlled and automatic human information processing: II. Perceptual learning, automatic attending and a general theory. *Psychol. Rev.: 84*, 127 – 190, 1977.

Silberman EK, Weingartner H, Post RM: Thinking disorder in depression. Logic and strategy in an abstract reasoning task. *Arch. Gen. Psychiatry: 40*, 775 – 780, 1983.

Simon H: Neurones dopaminergiques A10 et système frontal. *J. Physiol.: 77*, 81 – 95, 1981.

Skinner BF: The processes involved in the repeated string of alternatives. *J. Exp. Psychol.: 30*, 495 – 503, 1942.

Sloboda JA: *The Musical Mind. The Cognitive Psychology of Music*. Oxford: Clarendon Press, 1985.

Smith A: The serial sevens subtraction test. *Arch. Neurol. Psychiatry: 17*, 78 – 80, 1967.

Snodgrass JC: Concepts and their surface representations. *J. Verbal Learn. Verbal Behav.: 23*, 3 – 22, 1984.

Sokolov EN: Neuronal models and the orienting reflex. In Brazier MAB (Editor), *The Central Nervous System and Behavior*. Madison: Madison Printing, pp. 187 – 276, 1960.

Spearman C: *The Abilities of Man*. New York: Macmillan, 1927.

Spinnler H: *Il Decadimento Demenziale. Inquadramento Neurologico e Neuropsicologico*. Roma: Il Pensiero Scientifico, 1985.

Spinnler H: *Ruolo neuropsicologico della compromissione delle aree pre-frontali nelle demenze primarie*. Atti del XXVI Congresso Nazionale della Società Italiana di Neurologia, pp. 63 – 69. Ferrara, 28/11 – 2/12/1989.

Spinnler H, Della Sala S: The role of clinical neuropsychology in the neurological diagnosis of Alzheimer's disease. *J. Neurol.: 235*, 258 – 271, 1988.

Spinnler H, Tognoni G: Standardizzazione e taratura italiana di test neuropsicologici. *Ital. J. Neurol. Sci.: 6 (Suppl. 7)*, 1987.

Spinnler H, Della Sala S, Bandera R, Baddeley A: Dementia in aging and the structure of human memory. *Cognitive Neuropsychol.: 5*, 193 – 211, 1988.

Spitz HH: Note on immediate memory for the difits; invariance over the years. *Psychol. Bull.: 78*, 183 – 185, 1972.

Spreen O, Benton AL: *The Neurosensory Center Comprehensive Examination for Aphasia*. Victoria BC: Neuropsychology laboratory, University of Victoria, 1969.

Spring BJ: Shift of attention in schizophrenics, siblings of schizophrenics and depressed patients. *J. Nerv. Mental Dis.: 168*, 133 – 140, 1980.

Squire LR: The neuropsychology of memory. *Annu. Rev. Neurosci.: 5*, 241 – 273, 1982.

Stanovich KE, West RF: On priming by sentence context. *J. Exp. Psychol. Gen.: 112*, 1 – 36, 1983.

Stern Y, Mayeux R, Cote L: Reaction time and vigilance in Parkinson's disease. Possible role of altered norepinephrine metabolism. *Arch. Neurol.: 41*, 1086 – 1089, 1984.

Sternberg R: Sketch of a componential subtheory of human intelligence. *Behav. Brain Sci.: 3*, 573 – 614, 1980.

Stroh CM: *Vigilance: The Problem of Sustained Attention*. Oxford: Pergamon Press, 1971.

Stroop JR: Studies of interference in serial verbal reactions. *J. Exp. Psychol.: 18*, 643 – 662, 1935.

Stuss DT, Benson DF: Neuropsychological studies of the frontal lobes. *Psychol. Bull.: 95*, 3 – 28, 1984.

Stuss DT, Benson DF: *The Frontal Lobes*. New York: Raven Press, 1986.

Stuss DT, Benson DF, Kaplan EF, Weir WS, Della Malva C: Leucotomized and non-leucotomized schizophrenics; comparison on tests of attention. *Biol. Psychiatry: 16*, 1085 – 1100, 1981.

Sullivan EV, Corkin S, Growdon JH: Verbal and nonverbal short-term memory in patients with Alzheimer's disease and in healthy elderly subjects. *Dev. Neuropsychol.: 2*, 387 – 400, 1986.

Swets JA, Kristofferson AB: Attention. *Annu. Rev. Psychol.: 21*, 339 – 366, 1970.

Taylor MP, Abrams R: Cognitive impairment patterns in

schizophrenia and affective disorders. *J. Neurol. Neurosurg. Psychiatry: 50*, 895 – 899, 1987.

Tecce JJ, Cattanach L, Boehuer-Davis MB, Brauconnier RJ, Cole JO: Etude neuropsychologique de la baisse de l'attention et traitement médicamentaux chez les malades atteints de maladie d'Alzheimer.*Presse Méd.: 12*, 3155 – 2162, 1983.

Terman LM, Merrill U, MA: *Measuring Intelligence.* Boston: Houghton Mifflin, 1937.

Teuber HL: Neuropsychology: effects of focal brain lesions. *Neurosci. Res. Prog. Bull.: 10*, 381 – 384, 1972.

Teuber HL, Weinstein S: Ability to discover hidden figures after cerebral lesion. *Arch. Neurol. Psychiatry: 76*, 369 – 379, 1956.

Teuber HL, Battersby WS, Bender MR: Performance of complex visual tasks after cerebral lesion. *J. Nerv. Mental Dis.: 11*, 413 – 429, 1951.

Tissot R, Constantinidis J, Richard J: Pick's disease. In Vinken PJ, Bruyn GW, Klawans HL, Fredericks JAM (Eds.), *Handbook of Clinical Neurology. Neurobehavioral Disorders, Vol. 46*, (Rev. Ser.). Amsterdam: Elsevier, pp. 233 – 246, 1985.

Titchner E: *The Psychology of Feeling and Attention.* London: MacMillan, 1903.

Tulving E: *Elements of Episodic Memory.* New York: Oxford University Press, 1983.

Tulving E: Memory and consciousness. *Canad. Psychol.: 26*, 1 – 12, 1985.

Tulving E: Multiple memory systems and consciousness. *Hum. Neurobiol.: 6*, 67 – 80, 1987.

Tune GS: A brief survey of variables that influence random generation. *Percept. Motor Skills: 18*, 705 – 707, 1964.

Vignolo LA: Non-verbal conceptual impairment in aphasia. In Boller F, Grafman J (Editors), *Handbook of Neuropsychology, Vol. 2.* Amsterdam: Elsevier, pp. 185 – 206, 1989.

Vitaliano PP, Russo J, Breen AR, Vitiello MV, Prinz PN: Functional decline in early stages of Alzheimer's disease. *Psychol. Aging: 1*, 41 – 46, 1986.

Vrtunski PB, Patterson MB, Mack JL, Hill GO: Microbehavioral analysis of the choice reaction time response in senile dementia. *Brain: 106*, 929 – 947, 1983.

Wagenaar WA: Generation of random sequences by human subjects: a clinical survey of literature. *Psychol. Bull.; 77*, 65 – 72, 1972.

Wale J, Geffen G: Focused and divided attention in each half of space with disconnected hemispheres. *Cortex: 25*, 33 – 45, 1989.

Warrington EK, McCarthy R: Category specific access dysphasia. *Brain: 106*, 859 – 878, 1983.

Warrington EK, Shallice T: Category-specific semantic impairment. *Brain: 107*, 829 – 854, 1984.

Watson RT, Miller BD, Heilman KM: Evoked potentials in neglect. *Arch. Neurol.: 34*, 224 – 227, 1977.

Watts FN, Sharrock R: Description and measurement of concentration problems in depressed patients. *Psychol. Med.: 15*, 317 – 326, 1985.

Wechsler D: Rationale of children's scale. What intelligence tests test. In Edwards AJ (Editor), *Selected Papers of David Wechsler.* New York: Academic Press, 1974.

Weinberger DR, Berman KF, Zec RF: Physiologic dysfunction of dorsolateral prefrontal cortex in schizophrenia: I. Regional cerebral blood flow evidence. *Arch. Gen. Psychiatry: 43*,

114 – 125, 1986.

Weingartner H, Kaye W, Smallberg SA, Ebert MH, Gillin JC, Sitaram N: Memory failures in progressive idiopathic dementia. *J. Abnormal Psychol.: 90*, 187 – 196, 1981.

Weiss RL: On producing random responses. *Psychol. Rep.: 14*, 931 – 941, 1964.

Weizsaecker V, Von: *Der Gestaltkreis.* Thieme, Stuttgart, 1950.

Welch K, Stuteville P: Experimental production of unilateral neglect in monkeys. *Brain: 81*, 341 – 347, 1948.

Wells CH: *Dementia*, 2nd edition. Philadelphia: Davis, 1977.

Welt L: Ueber Charackterveraenderungen des Menschen in Folge der Laesionen des Stirnhirns. *Deutsches Archiv Klin. Med.: 42*, 334 – 362, 1888.

Wertheimer M: Untersuchungen zur Lehre von der Gestalt (II). *Psychol. Forsch.: 4*, 301 – 350, 1923.

Whithaker H: A case of isolation of the language function. In Whithaker H, Whithaker HA (Editors), *Perspectives in Neurolinguistics and Psycholinguistics. Studies in Neurolinguistics, Vol. 2.* Orlando: Academic Press, pp. 1 – 58, 1976.

Wickens CD: Processing resources in attention. In Parasuraman R, Davies DR (Editors), *Varieties of Attention.* Orlando: Academic Press, pp. 63 – 102, 1984.

Wilkins AJ, Shallice T, McCarthy R: Frontal lesions and sustained attention. *Neuropsychologia: 255*, 359 – 365, 1987.

Williams DM: The process of retrieval from very long-term memory: *Tech. Report 75.* La Jolla, University of California at San Diego.

Williams DH, Hollan JD: The process of retrieval from very long-term memory. *Cognitive Sci. 5:* 87 – 119, 1981.

Wilson RS, Bacon LD, Kramer RL, Fox JH, Kaszniak AW: Word frequency effect and recognition memory in dementia of the Alzheimer type. *J. Clin. Neuropsychol.: 5*, 97 – 104, 1983a.

Wilson SAK: Progressive lenticular degeneration; a familial nervous disease associated with cirrhosis of the liver. *Brain: 34*, 295 – 509, 1912.

Wilson RS, Kaszniack AN, Bacon LD, Fox JH, Kelly MP: Facial recognition memory in dementia. *Cortex: 18:* 329 – 336, 1982.

Wittenborn JR: Factorial equations for tests of attention. *Psychometrika: 8*, 19 – 35, 1943.

Wolitzky D, Spence DP: Individual consistency in the random generation of choices. *Percept. Motor Skills: 26*, 1211 – 1214, 1968.

Wolkowitz OM, Tinklenberg JR, Weingartner H: A psychopharmacological perspective of cognitive functions. Theoretical overview and methodological considerations. *Neuropsychobiologia: 14*, 88 – 96, 1985.

Wood F: Focal and diffuse memory activation assessed by localized indicators of CNS metabolism: the semantic-episodic distinction. *Hum. Neurobiol.: 6*, 141 – 151, 1987.

Wright RE: Aging, divided attention and processing capacity. *J. Gerontol.: 36*, 605 – 614, 1981.

Wright LL, Elias JW: Age differences in the effect of perceptual noise. *J. Gerontol.: 34*, 704 – 708, 1979.

Yacorzynski GK, Davis L: An Experimental study of frontal lobes in man. *Psychosom. Med.: 7*, 97 – 107, 1945.

Yerkes RM, Dodson JD: The relation of strength of stimulus to rapidity of habit-formation. *J. Comp. Neurol. Psychol.: 18*, 459 – 482, 1908.

1991 Elsevier Science Publishers B.V.
Handbook of Neuropsychology, Vol. 5
F. Boller and J. Grafman (Eds)

CHAPTER 7

Age-related changes in memory: learning and remembering new information

Felicia A. Huppert

University of Cambridge, Department of Psychiatry, Addenbrooke's Hospital, Cambridge, U.K.

Introduction

Much has been written about memory in the elderly and there have been some excellent reviews of the subject (e.g. Craik, 1977, 1984; Kaszniak et al., 1986; Light and Burke, 1989; Poon, 1985; Poon et al., 1980). Rather than attempting to summarize this vast literature, this chapter will focus on those areas which seem particularly relevant to neuropsychology; that is, on data and theories which may shed light on the relationship between memory processes and brain function. Nor will this chapter attempt to cover all areas of memory function. Although there is much current research interest in memory for remote events and memory for general knowledge (see Handbook of Neuropsychology, Vol. 4, Ch. 15), this chapter will be concerned mainly with memory for recently acquired information.

With most neuropsychological disorders, the need is to understand the nature and neurobiological mechanisms underlying the functional deficit. In the case of memory and aging, we need first to establish that there *is* a functional deficit, before proceeding to analyse its nature and causes. For this reason, research on memory and aging has long incorporated a psychometric or individual differences component. This has advanced alongside a cognitive/neuropsychological approach similar to the approach employed in studies of amnesic disorders. It is theory-driven, and indeed employs the same explanatory models as in amnesic research. To obtain a complete picture of memory impairment in the elderly, it is necessary to draw together these two research traditions. Some attempts to do so have recently been made (e.g. Craik et al., 1987) and will be reviewed below.

The conventional wisdom is that memory declines with age, and this is related to the loss of brain cells as we grow older. However, both assumptions have been seriously challenged. There is much evidence that when younger and older subjects are matched on education, IQ, health or other variables which may affect memory, the evidence for age differences is greatly reduced and in some cases disappears. Similarly, when post-mortem studies exclude potentially confounding variables such as the presence of neurological disease, there is little evidence for loss of cortical cells in the elderly (Terry et al., 1987).

This leaves us with a number of important questions to answer:

1. Are there true age differences in the ability to learn and retain new information? That is, are there age differences when other variables are as equal as possible?
2. What is the nature of any true age differences?
3. Since there clearly are age-*related* differences in memory, what variables are responsible for producing these secondary effects?
4. What is the neurobiological basis of true or of secondary age differences in memory?

Evidence for age differences in memory

There are two main reasons for supposing that there are age differences in memory. First, older people generally complain more than younger people about memory problems in daily life. Second, older people perform more poorly than younger people on most memory tests. I shall discuss each of these types of evidence in turn.

Self-report
Subjective complaints about failing memory can be assessed by means of standardized self-report questionnaires (e.g. Sunderland et al., 1983; Zelinski et al., 1980). Recent examinations of questionnaire findings raise doubts about whether such data provide a reliable guide to actual memory performance. Aside from the obvious point that people with memory problems may not have an accurate memory for their problems, other difficulties with these data are listed below.

(a) Memory complaints are not well correlated with performance on laboratory tests of memory (e.g. paired associate learning) or everyday tests of memory (e.g. face recognition, story recall) (Sunderland et al., 1986).

(b) Self-report of memory impairment is more highly correlated with depression scores than with performance on laboratory or clinical memory tests (Kahn et al., 1975; Roth et al., 1986).

(c) Fifty-year-olds complain more about their memory than older adults, although the former perform better on memory tests (Abson and Rabbitt, 1988). The authors suggest that this may be a contextual effect, with 50-year-olds having higher expectations and coming more into contact with younger individuals, thereby being more aware of their memory failures.

(d) Examination of the nature and frequency of memory complaints indicates that name-finding difficulties of the 'tip of the tongue' variety are by far the most common problem (Sunderland et al., 1986). Since memory tests are rarely concerned with name finding, it is little wonder that complaints and test results are poorly correlated.

We must therefore conclude that existing self-report data about memory problems are of little assistance in establishing the presence of age differences in memory for newly acquired information. Gilewski and Zelinski (1986) advocate the development of a second generation of memory questionnaires to overcome some of these difficulties.

Laboratory tests
On most laboratory tests of memory, older adults in general perform more poorly than younger adults. One approach to determining whether such differences reflect true age differences is to examine memory changes in a longitudinal design. In two longitudinal studies using subtests from the Wechsler Memory Scale (Wechsler, 1945), performance on the visual retention test was found to decrease as subjects aged, while performance on the verbal subtests showed little change (McCarty et al., 1982; Wilkie et al., 1976). This cannot be interpreted as evidence that visual-spatial memory is more impaired in the aging process, since in the Duke longitudinal study (McCarty et al., 1982) subject drop-out was related to initial verbal memory scores. There was less attrition among subjects who initially obtained high scores on verbal memory tests, so subsequent verbal memory scores may have underestimated change with age. There was no relationship between subject attrition and scores on the visual retention test. A cross-sequential design of the type espoused by Schaie and his colleagues (e.g. Schaie, 1983) would be preferable, since it is possible to separate cohort and aging effects and different members of a cohort can be sampled at different points in time. Unfortunately Schaie's own studies did not examine memory.

The vast majority of research on age differences in memory uses a cross-sectional approach. The method for determining whether observed age differences reflect true age differences is to match older and younger groups as closely as possible on variables which may influence memory performance. Such matching cannot, of course, take account of variables which are cohort-specific, such as ype of education, past health and nutrition, at-itudes towards testing and many more. However, when age groups have been matched and the esulting differences in memory are small, it can be ssumed that the role of cohort-specific variables is minimal.

Although findings continue to be published where here has been no attempt to match old and young ubjects, the importance of matching has been demonstrated in a number of studies. For example, Bowles and Poon (1982) examined the relationship etween verbal IQ (WAIS vocabulary) and word ecognition memory in young and old subjects. Low-IQ elderly recognized significantly fewer of the previously presented words than low-IQ young sub-ects, but there was no difference between young nd old subjects with a high IQ. These authors also analysed similar studies in the literature, and eported that where IQ or education data were available, results consistently indicated no age dif-erence in recognition memory for well-educated or igh-IQ groups. Thus, there do not appear to be true ge differences in conventional tests of word ecognition memory. The question of why such age differences are found for poorly educated or low-IQ lderly will be considered later.

Measures of free recall and paired associate learn-ng generally demonstrate age differences in reten-ion even when groups are matched (e.g. Schonfield nd Robertson, 1966; see Poon, 1985, for a review). Although age differences appear under standard onditions, various manipulations such as instruc-ion in verbal elaboration and visual imagery or the presentation of cues at acquisition and retrieval ave been reported to diminish or eliminate age dif-erences. For example, no age differences in free ecall of a 48-word list were found when subjects ad to sort the words into categories of their own hoosing prior to recall (Worden and Meggison, 984). The subjects in this task were all healthy and well-educated. One study has reported superior ecall by older adults as a function of familiarity of material (Hanley-Dunn and McIntosh, 1984). The ists consisted of 14 male names which were elderly-elevant, young-relevant or both-relevant. Elderly

subjects recalled more names than young subjects in the elderly-relevant and both-relevant lists. In this study, young subjects had 13 years of education compared with 12 years for the elderly. Recall and recognition have also been examined following in-cidental learning. That is, subjects carry out an orienting task (e.g., producing a rhyme or assigning a category) for each word in a list and are then unex-pectedly given a memory test. In my view the in-cidental learning paradigm comes closer to assessing everyday memory performance than do standard laboratory tests of intentional learning because most of what we remember in daily life is informa-tion which we did not deliberately try to remember; it is information which we acquired in the course of reading, listening to conversations, watching televi-sion, etc. Within this paradigm a number of in-vestigations have shown that age differences in free recall persist, although both old and young benefit from an orienting task which requires more elaborative processing, e.g., semantic category judgement (Eysenck, 1974; Perlmutter, 1978; White, cited by Craik, 1977).

Memory in an adult community sample

A recent study has examined the role of individual differences in recall following incidental learning. A British survey of the health and lifestyle of several thousand community residents aged 18+ (Cox et al., 1987) included a list of 10 common foods, and subjects were asked to decide which foods contained dietary fibre. There were no age differences in per-formance on the orienting task. Following this semantic orienting task, an unexpected recall test was given after a short distraction. Ceiling effects did not occur on this test, presumably because learn-ing was incidental. As expected, recall decreased with age across the adult lifespan (Huppert, 1987). However, further analysis of memory was under-taken for selected sub-groups matched for educa-tion, estimated IQ (based on reasoning ability) and health (Huppert and Elliott, 1988). The results are presented in Fig. 1. There is no age difference for high-IQ subjects with some educational qualifica-tion who are in good health, but a significant age difference for those in poor health. For low-IQ subjects with less education there are significant age differences even in the healthy group, and performance decreases further in the unhealthy group. These data suggest that adverse factors (poor health, low education/ intelligence) produce an additive effect on memory performance.

Further analysis of performance within the retired elderly group revealed an interesting interaction between memory and participation in leisure activities. Fig. 2 shows that the number of leisure ac-

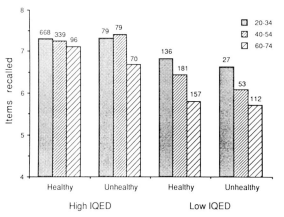

Fig. 1. Mean number of items recalled in an incidental memory test for respondents in three discrete age groups matched for health, educational qualifications and performance on a reasoning test. The numbers at the top of the columns represent the number of individuals in each group (from Huppert and Elliott, 1988).

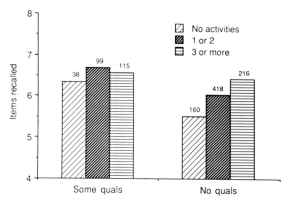

Fig. 2. Mean number of items recalled in an incidental memory test by retired respondents between the ages of 60 and 74, showing the relationship between leisure activities, education and memory (from Huppert and Elliott, 1988).

tivities is related to memory performance in subjects with no educational qualifications but not in the educationally qualified group. Indeed, the low education group that participated in three or more leisure activities performed as well as the educationally qualified group. This effect is independent of IQ. These findings provide some support for the popular belief that keeping oneself busy and stimulated might have a beneficial effect on cognitive function in the elderly. It is particularly interesting that the disadvantage associated with low education is offset by participation in leisure activities.

Tests of everyday memory

All the above tests have been concerned with memory for word lists. There is a growing interest in memory for materials which are more congruent with everyday memory performance, i.e. are 'ecologically valid'. These materials include spoken discourse, prose texts, faces and routes. Age differences are generally reported in the recall of prose or discourse, but the pattern of results depends on the individual, the task and the nature of the material. For example, Spilich (1983) and Hultsch et al. (1984) showed that older adults with low verbal IQ had poor recall of both the main ideas and the details in short texts, whereas older adults with high verbal IQ showed poor recall only of the details. Age differences have been reported in a variety of other tests of everyday memory (see Poon, 1985, for a review). These include face recognition (Smith and Winograd, 1978) and name – face matching (Ferris et al., 1980), but the role of education or IQ in these tasks does not appear to have been examined.

A useful battery of everyday memory tests, the Rivermead Behavioural Memory Test (Wilson et al., 1985), has been constructed for use with brain-damaged patients, but normal age differences have recently been reported (Cockburn and Smith, 1988). The battery includes such tests as recognition of unfamiliar faces, recalling a prose passage, re-tracing a route around the room, remembering to take and deliver a message on the route, remembering to ask for a hidden belonging and remembering to make an appointment. Two groups of normal subjects were compared: a 'young' group aged 52 to 67 and an older group aged 68 +. A significant effect of age was found in two of the tests, both measuring prospective memory; remembering to deliver a message and remembering to make an appointment. Performance on these tests was not related to IQ. No significant age effects were found for any other test in the battery, although a few tests suffer from ceiling effects. It would also be valuable to know whether this pattern of results remains when younger subjects are included in the analysis.

The prospective memory tasks in the Rivermead Behavioural Memory Test (RBMT) are all of one kind; that is, the subject has to remember to carry out an action on a single occasion. In contrast to the age differences found on these tasks, Moscovitch (1982) reported that older subjects performed *better* than younger subjects on a recurrent prospective memory task. Moscovitch required subjects to telephone once a day for two weeks at a time of day of their choosing. Only 1 of 10 elderly subjects omitted a call, whereas 8 of 10 young subjects omitted at least one call and some omitted several. Questioning revealed that all the elderly subjects and those young subjects who performed well, used external memory aids, while the more forgetful subjects relied on their memories. The age differences reported for the episodic prospective memory tasks of the RBMT may be related to the unavailability of external cues (see below).

The nature of memory impairment in elderly people

Where age differences in memory appear, these differences are greater on some tasks than on others. Age differences are large on tasks requiring free recall or remembering to carry out an instruction when external aids are not available. Age differences are small on tests of cued recall, recognition or priming (e.g. Light and Singh, 1987; Burke et al., 1987). A straightforward interpretation of this pattern of results is that some tasks are more difficult, demanding and 'effortful' (Hasher and Zacks, 1979) than others and that older people are at a

disadvantage the more complex or difficult the task (e.g. Salthouse, 1982). However, the situation is not as straightforward as this, since some sources of task difficulty or types of complexity produce a deleterious effect on older people compared with younger subjects, while others do not (see Gick et al., 1988; Morris et al., 1988). What is required is a better understanding of the nature of complexity and the particular processing difficulties associated with advancing age.

The functional approach

One approach to answering these questions is the functional account of Craik (1986). Craik suggests that remembering, like perception, should be regarded as an interaction between environmental and organismic factors. Where environmental support (i.e. cues and context) is weak, as in free recall, successful remembering relies more on the self-initiated activities of the rememberer. Self-initiated retrieval processes are described as voluntary, intentional and effortful, and are hypothesized to become increasingly more difficult to execute with advancing age. It would follow from this account that age differences should be least where there is substantial external support, as in recognition, cued recall and priming. Table 1 shows Craik's ordering of various memory tasks with respect to the balance they involve between environmental support and self-initiated activities. In this table, remembering

TABLE 1

Memory tasks showing differential effects of aging

Task	Environmental support	Self-initiated activity	Age-related decrement
Remembering to remember	increases	↑	↑
Free recall			
Cued recall			
Recognition			
Relearning			
Procedural memory (priming tasks)	↓	increases	increases

From Craik, 1986.

to remember (prospective memory) refers to tasks where external cues are not available.

It could be argued that this ordering reflects task difficulty rather than the increasing involvement of self-initiated processes, but an experiment by Craik and McDowd (1987) suggests otherwise. They compared the recall and recognition performance of young and older subjects while performing a concurrent four-choice reaction time (RT) task. The memory tests were designed so that the recall test was easy and the recognition test difficult. In both cases, the to-be-remembered items were 120 phrases and target words (e.g. 'a body of water – pond'), where the target word was not the most probable response. Half the words were tested by cued recall with the original phrases repeated, and half by yes/no recognition with the target words interspersed among matched distractors. The RT task was practised until the subjects performed to a certain level of reliability before the memory testing began. For the dual task, subjects were instructed to consider the memory task as the primary task and to perform the RT task as quickly as they could without disrupting memory performance. The subjects were all in good health, and although the elderly had fewer years of education (12 vs. 15) they had higher vocabulary scores than the young.

The results of the experiment are presented in Fig. 3. Despite the fact that cued recall yielded higher levels of performance than recognition in both age groups, cued recall was more disruptive of concurrent task performance in the elderly, but not in the young group. Craik and McDowd conclude that: (a) self-initiated activity makes greater demands on processing resources, and (b) the elderly have a smaller pool of processing resources at their disposal and are therefore disproportionately penalized in the recall condition.

Memory structures and systems

In contrast to the functional approach, which emphasizes the active processing component of memory tasks, a structural or system approach has also been used to explain age-related memory deficits. A number of memory dichotomies proposed by cognitive psychologists (e.g., primary vs. secondary memory, episodic vs. semantic memory, implicit vs. explicit remembering) have been widely employed in neuropsychology. It has been suggested that elderly people, like amnesic patients, may show impairment in one structure or system but not another. For example, normal aging is said to have its most marked effect on secondary memory, with primary memory relatively spared (Craik, 1977; Fozard, 1980; Kaszniak et al., 1986; Poon, 1985). Alternatively, older adults are said to have impaired episodic memory and intact semantic memory (e.g. Perlmutter, 1978), or to show deficits on explicit memory tasks but not implicit memory tasks (e.g. Light and Singh, 1987).

Although these dichotomies have some heuristic value, memory processes are so complex that any dichotomy is bound to be at best an oversimplification, and may be positively misleading. Considering the distinction between primary and secondary memory, Craik (1986) has pointed out that although performance on many primary memory tasks, including forward digit span and the Brown-Petersen task, is usually preserved in the elderly, other measures of primary memory show consistent impairment. These include dichotic listening (Craik, 1977), backward digit span and alpha span (Craik, 1986), where words have to be reported in the correct alphabetical order. Likewise, within secondary memory, we have already referred to studies show-

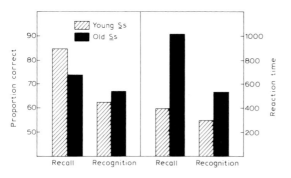

Fig. 3. Left panel: cued recall scores (proportion correct) and recognition scores (hits minus false alarms) as a function of age. Right panel: mean RT in milliseconds (mean dual-task RT minus mean baseline RT) as a function of age. From Craik and McDowd, 1987.

ing that recall is impaired in subjects whose recognition performance is unimpaired (e.g. Schonfield and Robertson, 1966). The recall/recognition difference also operates within episodic memory and within explicit memory. Similarly some forms of semantic memory, e.g. knowledge of facts, are unimpaired while other forms, e.g. the ability to generate words beginning with a specific letter, show dramatic aging effects in longitudinal studies (e.g. Schaie, 1983). A functional approach to identifying the nature of age differences in memory, such as that described above, therefore appears far more useful than a classificatory approach concerned with memory structures and systems.

Reinterpreting age differences in memory systems
Applying a functional approach to primary memory, we can ask why some tasks do show age-related deficits, while others do not (when young and old subjects have been appropriately matched). The tasks which do not show age differences involve the simple holding of information in a temporary store prior to its recall (e.g. forward digit span, Brown-Petersen task). The tasks which show age-related decrements involve the manipulation of information held in short-term memory (e.g. backward digit span, alpha span, dichotic listening). The need to carry out further operations while holding information in short-term memory has been labelled 'working memory' (Baddeley and Hitch, 1974). Age differences have also been shown in other working memory paradigms, e.g., retaining digits while simultaneously carrying out a verbal reasoning task (Wright, 1981) or recalling the final words of sentences after completing a sentence verification task (Morris et al., 1988). Salthouse (1982) pointed out that working memory tasks are more complex than span-type tasks, but since complexity is not reliably associated with age differences (see above) an explanation should be sought elsewhere. It appears that working memory tasks involve a component of divided attention, where attention is divided between the processes of maintaining information in an active state and carrying out other mental operations. Each of these makes demands on the finite pool of processing resources. If, as Craik and Byrd (1982) suggest, the elderly have a smaller pool of processing resources at their disposal, they will be disproportionately penalized in divided attention tasks. There is certainly evidence that older people are more vulnerable than the young to interference in ongoing processing tasks that involve divided attention (e.g. Salthouse et al., 1984; Welford, 1958). It is likely that retention will be impaired when information has been encoded under conditions of divided attention. If divided attention is more disruptive for the elderly, their subsequent retention is likely to be more impaired than for young people. The rare failures to find an age difference in memory following a divided attention task (Gick et al., 1988; Morris et al., 1988) may be attributable to the use of subspan memory lists which presumably make little demand on attentional resources.

The functional approach to understanding age-related memory deficits readily emcompasses a dichotomy recently proposed by Schacter et al. (1984), which distinguishes between memory for items and memory for source (context). Using a methodology similar to that developed by Schacter et al. for amnesic patients, McIntyre and Craik (1987) showed that whereas young people remembered the source of newly acquired facts after a one-week delay, older adults showed 'source amnesia'. That is, correctly recalled facts were attributed to the wrong source (i.e. not to the experiment) and to the wrong modality (auditory vs. visual) within the experiment. Janowsky et al. (1989) have also reported impaired source memory in older adults in an incidental learning paradigm. It has been suggested that the process of integrating events with their context demands a considerable amount of processing resources and older people, like amnesics, are impaired because they have less processing capacity. A general failure to integrate events with their context could also play a role in the relative deficit of recall compared with recognition tasks. Free recall of new information relies on the subject accessing the correct context; the frequent presence of intrusion errors indicates that the wrong context has been accessed. Integrating events with their context and engaging in self-initiated retrieval are two requirements for good free recall. The age-related decrement in free recall may reflect the high demand placed on processing resources by each of these requirements.

Reduced processing resources or greater demands?
To summarize the above findings, age-related memory deficits mainly appear under conditions of high processing demands, e.g., following divided attention tasks, and when retrieval requires self-initiated activity. They do not appear reliably simply as a function of task complexity. The most widely held explanation for age-related memory deficits is the suggestion of Craik and his colleagues that older adults have less 'mental energy', or a smaller pool of processing resources.

However, an alternative interpretation of the data is possible. Rather than the 'pool' of processing resources being reduced, or processing capacity being decreased, it could be argued that resources/capacity are unchanged in the elderly, but there are more demands made upon these resources. Throughout the lifespan, environmental demands, including family, work, social and community activities, tend to increase, making it increasingly difficult to focus attention or be as single-minded as young adults. Although environmental demands may be greater in middle life than in later life, the habits of middle-age may persist. Fewer mental resources may be available for a given task, because more are occupied with other concerns. In effect, divided attention is the normal state for older adults. This hypothesis is consistent not only with the introspection of older adults (e.g. anecdotal reports of friends and colleagues), but with experimental findings. Craik (1982) reports that young adults show memory impairments resembling those of older adults when the young are performing under conditions of divided attention. Decreased physical energy, poorer health and depressed mood may also reduce the amount of mental energy available for learning and remembering. Although this hypothe-

sis can explain the available data, further research is required to test its validity.

Acquisition, retention or retrieval deficit?
When a memory deficit is apparent, it is reasonable to enquire at what stage of processing the deficit is operating. The preceding account of memory impairment in terms of reduced processing resources is usually thought to operate at the time of acquisition. Effective encoding is believed to require 'deep' or elaborative processing which may be compromised where processing resources are limited. When encoding has been ineffective, the resulting memory trace will be difficult to retrieve. A primary defect of acquisition might therefore result in an apparent retrieval defect (as suggested by Huppert and Piercy, 1977, and Arenberg, 1980). On the other hand, a processing resource deficit could have a direct effect on retrieval, if the retrieval task requires self-initiated activities (e.g. Rabinowitz, 1986).

What is the evidence in support of either an acquisition or a retrieval defect when memory impairment is observed in the elderly? The fact that cued recall or recognition may eliminate age differences found on free recall is sometimes offered as evidence for a retrieval defect. However, the same finding would be expected if there was a poor memory representation due to inadequate encoding (an acquisition defect) or to defective storage in spite of adequate encoding (a retention deficit). Likewise, evidence that age differences are reduced when the elderly are encouraged to undertake elaborative encoding does not necessarily mean that they have an acquisition defect. The additional encoding may offset the effect of a weak memory trace or a faulty retrieval system.

How, then, can we pinpoint at what stage the memory deficit is operating? If memory was impaired on one occasion for information which had been effectively acquired, and on a subsequent occasion that information could be readily remembered, this would constitute clear evidence for a retrieval deficit. By this criterion, older people undoubtedly have a retrieval deficit. Evidence comes from diary studies of name-finding difficulties and the prevalence of 'tip-of-the-tongue' (TOT) phenomena in the elderly (e.g. Burke et al., 1988). These are genuine retrieval failures, because the affected words may be very familiar and generally 'pop up' after a time. Although TOTs represent failure to retrieve phonological rather than semantic information, Burke and Harrold (1989) have suggested that a general failure of retrieval processes may be a source of memory problems in old age.

There is growing doubt about the presence of acquisition problems in the elderly, and of impaired semantic coding in particular. It has been widely held that older subjects encode information less effectively because they do not spontaneously employ semantic encoding strategies (Craik, 1982; Craik and Rabinowitz, 1985). This has been termed the 'production deficiency' hypothesis (Kausler, 1970). Studies of language comprehension in the elderly which are run 'on-line', i.e. without involving a memory component, suggest that older adults engage in the same types of linguistic and semantic analysis as young adults (Burke and Harrold, 1989). Evidence is accumulating that older adults show memory deficits for material that they have semantically encoded in a similar manner to the young (e.g. Burke and Yee, 1984; Howard et al., 1986). Cohen and Faulkner (1981) showed that while younger and older adults have similar semantic representations of sentences after a brief delay, the older adults lose their representation over longer delays. In their experiment, older subjects were able to detect changes of meaning in a text after 10 seconds but failed to detect such changes after a 40-second delay. This has led to the conclusion that 'the age deficit lies mainly in the retention of semantic information rather than its acquisition' (Cohen and Faulkner, 1981, p. 265). It is interesting to note that in the same experiment, there was no age difference in the retention of non-semantic information, i.e. in the ability to detect text changes which did not alter meaning (synonym substitution, active-passive shift); both groups performed very poorly after a 40-second delay.

This is not the only study to show rapid forgetting by elderly subjects of material which was initially encoded effectively at a semantic level. Worden and Meggison (1984) showed no age differences in recall of a 48-word list after a short delay, following a category-sorting task. However, after a longer delay (at the conclusion of the test session) the age difference was significant, with young adults recalling twice as many words as older adults. McIntyre and Craik (1987) also report faster forgetting of newly acquired 'facts' by older subjects after a one-week retention interval, when old and young subjects were matched for fact knowledge.

The recent evidence that older adults forget newly acquired information more rapidly than young adults appears to be at variance with earlier reports that older and younger subjects forget verbal material at the same rate (e.g. Craik, 1977; Talland, 1967; Wickelgren, 1975). The results of Cohen and Faulkner (1981) offer a possible insight into this discrepancy. Older subjects showed fast forgetting in their semantic condition, but both groups forgot equally rapidly in their non-semantic conditions. It may be that tasks such as the Brown-Petersen test (used by Talland, 1967) or a continuous recognition paradigm such as that used by Wickelgren (1975) can be regarded as non-semantic, producing fast forgetting in young and old subjects alike. This is consistent with Craik and Lockhart's (1972) statement that these paradigms do not encourage 'deep' or semantic processing.

Additional evidence that the elderly have a retention deficit comes from a study of picture recognition (Huppert and Kopelman, 1989) using the Huppert and Piercy (1978) paradigm. Yes-no recognition of a set of 120 coloured, holiday-type slides was tested at three retention intervals, 10 min, 1 day, and 1 week. Older subjects showed significantly faster forgetting than younger subjects, even when matched on initial level of performance (Fig. 4). In this study, there was no age difference in guessing rate, and performance was unrelated to level of education. It is reasonable to assume that the information had been semantically encoded, since subjects provided a brief description of each picture when it was first presented.

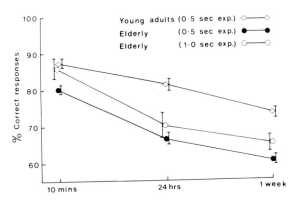

Fig. 4. Mean percentage of correct responses (± 1 SE) on a recognition memory test as a function of retention interval and duration of stimulus exposure (0.5 s or 1.0 s per picture) (from Huppert and Kopelman, 1989).

Thus, there is growing evidence for a storage defect in elderly subjects. Retrieval deficits undoubtedly occur in large numbers of elderly people, as exemplified by name finding problems, but the deficit may be specific to the ability to access phonological codes without affecting semantic representations. There is little convincing evidence at present of a semantic encoding deficit in the elderly.

Capacity for learning in older aldults

For the most part, researchers in the field of aging and cognition have focused on age-related *deficits*. A very few have emphasized the *potential* of older adults for learning and remembering new information. The names most associated with this approach are Harwood and Naylor, and more recently Baltes and his colleagues. Naylor and Harwood (1975), working in Queensland, Australia, gave a group of 80 adults (aged 63 to 91) one German lesson a week. At the end of three months, over half the group passed an examination at a level which schoolchildren normally reach after three years. In the same study, the investigators successfully taught their elderly subjects to play the recorder. The group continued to play the instruments for pleasure long after the conclusion of training. The assumption can no longer be held that learning a language and learning

a musical instrument are skills which cannot be acquired late in life.

Baltes and his colleagues also believe that for most normal elderly people there is a great reserve capacity and potential for new learning. They report impressive mnemonic skills in intelligent, elderly volunteers following intensive training. For example, after 30 training sessions, subjects increased their digit spans to 40 or more when presentation was self-paced. One elderly lady achieved a span of 120 (Baltes and Kliegl, 1986).

Neither Baltes nor Harwood and Naylor claim that the elderly perform as well as young adults on these tasks. Indeed, Baltes has shown that the majority do not. The important point is that even if there is age-related memory decline, the reserve capacity is such that older adults are far more capable of learning and remembering than has hitherto been realized. This tremendous human potential represents a largely untapped resource.

Dementia and normal age-related memory changes

Evidence of memory impairment is required for a diagnosis of dementia (e.g. DSM-III-R, American Psychiatric Association, 1987; ICD-10, World Health Organization, 1990). The memory impairment must clearly be greater than that expected for a normal individual of the same age and background. The question we need to ask is what is the nature of the memory deficit in senile dementia which is beyond that seen in many normal elderly people?

Most studies have been conducted on patients with a diagnosis of senile dementia of the Alzheimer type (SDAT). SDAT is one of the most prevalent forms of dementia, the other being vascular or multi-infarct dementia (MID). Prevalence figures for dementia vary widely, but are roughly around 5% for moderate and severe dementia in those aged 65 plus, rising to around 20% for those aged 80 plus (e.g. Henderson, 1986). If one includes mild dementia the figures may be double this. There is no evidence that the memory impairment in the two main forms of dementia is different, although this has not been systematically investigated and neuropathological studies suggest that a high proportion of cases diagnosed as MID have only Alzheimer changes (Molsa et al., 1985). Thus the term dementia will be used here to refer to both of these common forms of dementia. It will not include the rarer forms of dementia (e.g. Huntington's chorea), where the memory impairment appears to be qualitatively different (Butters et al., 1987).

In general, it can be stated that demented subjects, even those whose dementia is said to be mild (though there are no internationally agreed criteria for severity), perform worse than controls on virtually all standard tests of paired-associate learning, free recall, cued recall and recognition of both verbal and non-verbal material (see reviews by Corkin, 1982; Morris and Kopelman, 1986). Unlike the normal elderly, they are usually impaired on tests of primary memory, including span tests (e.g. Corkin, 1982; Kaszniak et al., 1986; Kopelman, 1985; Miller, 1973) and working memory (Morris, 1984; Baddeley et al., 1986). These findings are consistent with the view that demented patients have a severe acquisition deficit. This does not appear to be a 'production deficiency', i.e. a failure to use strategies which they have at their disposal, since, unlike controls, the performance of demented patients fails to improve when good encoding strategies are encouraged by means of semantic orienting tasks (Corkin, 1982) or list organization (e.g. Weingartner et al., 1981).

The nature of the memory deficit

Jorm (1986) has proposed that the memory deficit in senile dementia can be understood in terms of the continuum from automatic to controlled processing. Controlled or effortful processes are said to be impaired early in the course of dementia, with automatic processes becoming affected late in the disease. The same continuum has been employed by Craik (1986) to describe normal age differences in memory. The greater the requirement for self-initiated activities (controlled processes), the greater the age difference; the more support provided by the context, the more automatic the activity becomes,

resulting in minimal age differences. Both Jorm and Craik propose that the underlying problem is limited processing resources or 'mental energy'. If the same theory is to explain the memory deficits of dementia and normal aging, we would predict that the environmental support continuum (see Table 1) would have a similar effect on demented and normal elderly. Any differences between them should be quantitative rather than qualitative.

In a study examining a wide range of laboratory and everyday memory tasks, Huppert and Beardsall (1991 in preparation) found that the greatest difference between demented patients and normals appeared on the tests which had the least amount of environmental support, viz. prospective memory tests. At the other end of the continuum, a number of investigators have reported that AD patients are unimpaired on verbal priming tasks (e.g. Christenson, 1991; Huppert and Beardsall, 1988; Miller, 1975; Morris et al., 1983; Moscovitch, 1982; Nebes, 1984). The only exception is the reports from San Diego using a word-stem completion task (Salmon et al., 1988; Shimamura et al., 1987). The main difference between the many reports of preserved priming and the two conflicting reports is that the latter used an incidental learning paradigm, which may have produced different effects on subsequent retention in normal and demented groups.

A major difficulty with examining the effortfulness or environmental support continuum is that very different tasks are used to represent different points along the continuum. In an attempt to overcome this problem, Huppert and Beardsall (1988, 1991 in preparation) used the same stimulus presentation to examine performance at six different points along the continuum. Normal and demented elderly subjects studied a list of 16 words and were tested in six ways, which in order of increasing environmental support were: free recall, cued recall (category name), four-choice recognition, initial-letter priming, word-stem completion and perceptual priming. The list was designed so that it contained four semantic categories and the words began with one of four initial letters. For initial-letter priming, subjects were presented with the four letters one at a time and asked to generate as many words as they could think of. For the stem completion task, subjects were presented with the first 3 letters of 8 target words and 8 non-target words and asked to say the first word they could think of. The 8 remaining target words and 8 new non-target words were used in the perceptual priming task. For perceptual priming, the computer monitor was blank at first and a list word or distractor was progressively built up from random fragments until the whole word appeared. Results show that the demented subjects performed significantly more poorly than the normal group on free recall, cued recall and recognition; unlike the normals, their performance did not improve across the three conditions. In contrast, there was no difference between the groups on the three priming measures. In the initial letter and word-stem completion tasks, both groups produced list words which they had not already retrieved and produced significantly more list words than controls who had not seen the list (Table 2). In the perceptual priming task, all groups identified list words in a more fragmented form than distractors, although the demented subjects needed more time (more information) to identify both list and distractor words.

These findings do not support a continuum hypothesis of memory impairment in dementia. Rather, they demonstrate a dissociation between explicit and implicit memory similar to that shown in

TABLE 2

Performance of elderly subjects on two measures of priming

	n	Percentage of words produced which are targets	
		Initial letter priming	Word-stem Word-stem completion
Demented	20	12.5	47.5
Normal	42	12.3	57.5
Control	26	1.0	20.0

T-tests showed no significant difference between normal and demented groups, but both differed significantly from controls. From Huppert and Beardsall, in preparation.

amnesic patients (see Squire, 1987). This dissociation is akin to the distinction made by Mishkin et al. (1984) between memories and habits. Memories encompass associative learning and the ability to recognize something as familiar. Habits refer to conditioning and response adaptation. Mishkin postulates that these represent two quite separate memory systems subserved by different neuroanatomical structures. It is possible that dementia selectively affects one of these systems, leaving the other intact. The neuropathological evidence for this is discussed below.

Such selectivity does not imply that explicit memory is totally obliterated in dementia. In the early stages, the loss may be partial. In cases where explicit memory is impaired but not absent, it is reasonable to ask at what stage of processing the memory deficit is operating. There is no doubt that demented subjects have a retrieval problem. This is seen in their striking impairment on tests of word fluency. However, a retrieval deficit alone does not explain their severe impairment on tests of cued recall and recognition.

Two studies have investigated whether Alzheimer patients have a storage defect, i.e. whether they forget information more rapidly than controls. Both studies employed the technique developed by Huppert and Piercy (1978, 1979), which involves matching the recognition performance of patient and control groups as closely as possible at a short retention interval and examining the subsequent rate of forgetting. The test materials are 120 coloured slides of holiday-type photographs, tested by yes/no recognition using 120 distractors. Kopelman (1985) reported parallel forgetting over a 1-week interval, for SDAT patients and controls. Corkin et al. (1984) also reported a normal rate of forgetting over a 72-hour retention interval. In both these studies, the SDAT group required a longer stimulus presentation than controls to attain the same level of performance at the initial retention interval (10 min). These findings are identical to those obtained in studies of alcoholic Korsakoff patients (Huppert and Piercy, 1978; Kopelman, 1985). It may be concluded that SDAT patients have defective acquisition, but once information has been acquired it is retained no less efficiently than by age-matched controls.

Parkinson's disease, memory impairment and dementia

The prevalence of Parkinson's disease (PD) increases with age and there is some evidence that PD may cause cognitive impairment, including memory deficits (see reviews by Brown and Marsden, 1988; Sagar and Sullivan, 1988). PD is also associated with an increased risk of dementia. Recent estimates put the increased risk at $15 - 20\%$ above the general population (Brown and Marsden, 1984) and even lower $(7 - 15\%)$ when only studies using DSM-III criteria for dementia are accepted (Lees, 1985; Mayeux et al., 1988). When one considers that the prevalence of PD is only about 0.5% of those aged $60+$ (Sutcliffe et al., 1985) memory impairment associated with PD could account for only a small fraction of the memory impairment in old age. Parkinson's disease is discussed here not because it is a major problem for the elderly, but because it is currently arousing much research interest.

Research in this field is bedevilled by a number of methodological problems. One is the heterogeneity of PD groups, which may include patients with different etiologies (idiopathic, arteriosclerotic, postencephalitic, drug-induced PD), patients with unilateral as well as those with bilateral symptoms, and patients who may have undergone stereotaxic surgery. A second problem is determining whether cognitive deficits, if they are found, are the consequence of the disease, the medication or the high risk in PD patients of concomitant depression, physical disability and acute confusional states. Third, failure to take account of the mental slowing in PD, which is in excess of the motor slowing (e.g. Evarts et al., 1981), may give a misleading impression of memory impairment if tests are timed or the examiner lacks patience. Finally, the literature abounds with studies where PD and comparison groups have not been adequately matched. Control groups need to be matched for IQ and/or education as well as age and sex. Demented and non-demented

PD groups should be kept separate. Where comparisons are made between demented PD patients and other dementia groups, these must be matched for severity of cognitive disorder. This requires a quantitative assessment of cognitive impairment, not merely a crude categorization of mild, moderate or severe dementia.

Memory in non-demented Parkinson's patients

In spite of the difficulties inherent in this research, some tentative conclusions have been reached. Non-medicated PD patients who are also generally in the early stage of the disease do not reliably show memory impairment. Lees and Smith (1983) examined 30 cases with normal CT and no evidence of ischemia or depression. Although PD patients were impaired on some cognitive tests, there was no impairment on the memory tests, which comprised a recognition test of words and unknown faces. Sahakian et al. (1988) found that 4 out of 13 non-medicated PD patients failed to learn the hardest of a list of abstract visual stimuli (8 items) tested after a delay, but there was no evidence of impairment on a variety of other memory tests.

In medicated PD patients, who are usually at a later stage of the disease, there is evidence of impaired memory for recently acquired information, but the deficits are quite mild. Taylor et al. (1986) undertook a very thorough investigation of 40 non-demented PD patients. Compared to well-matched controls, the patient group was significantly impaired on only 2 out of 8 memory tests. These were immediate recall of a prose passage and recall of the Ray Auditory Verbal Memory Test (RAVMT). No impairment was found on delayed recall of the prose passage, recognition in the RAVMT, visual reproduction (immediate or delayed), or paired associate learning (immediate or delayed, either hard or easy pairs). The investigators suggest that the observed differences may be a rate of presentation effect rather that a true memory impairment. Information was presented at the same rate to PD and control subjects, and may have exceeded the slow processing rate of the PD patients, thereby resulting in a spurious memory deficit.

This is an important point and may account for many of the positive findings in the literature. For example, the claim that PD patients benefit less than controls from semantic cues (Tweedy et al., 1982) may be an artefact of the very rapid rate at which words were presented (1 per second). Memory tests for PD patients should probably be self-paced to avoid such problems.

Canavan et al. (1989) tested 19 early PD patients on two tests of associative learning, one a visual-motor task (associating a movement with a colour), the other a visual-visual task (associating a shape with a colour). The testing procedure was essentially self-paced. Half the patients were unmedicated and half were on anticholinergic medication. These investigators found no overall difference between PD patients and controls and there was no significant effect of medication. Indeed, there was a tendency for the medicated group to perform better than the non-medicated. However, a minority of patients performed poorly, as in the study by Sahakian et al. (1988). These tended to be the older patients. Canavan et al. also compared the performance of PD patients with a group of patients with frontal lobe lesions. In contrast to the PD group, the frontal group made significantly more errors than their controls on both learning tasks.

Thus, studies which have examined non-medicated or non-demented PD patients leave unclear the role of the basal ganglia and dopamine depletion in cognitive impairment. The few patients who were impaired in these groups may have had a greater dopamine deficiency or greater cell loss. Alternatively, the cognitive impairment may be associated with damage to other subcortical structures which are commonly affected in Parkinson's disease, notably locus ceruleus (Hornykiewicz, 1982) and the basal nucleus of Meynert (Perry et al., 1985).

The basal nucleus is the origin of the cholinergic projections to the cortex and has been implicated in Alzheimer's disease (e.g. Davies and Maloney, 1976). By comparing the cognitive deficits seen in PD and AD, it might be possible to assess the role of the cholinergic deficit in these two disorders.

Memory deficits in demented Parkinson's patients

Comparisons between PD and AD patients are only meaningful if the groups are matched for severity of cognitive impairment or if the less impaired group performs a particular task more poorly than the more impaired group. Pillon et al. (1986) found that AD patients performed more poorly than PD patients on all subtests of the Wechsler Memory Scale when the two groups were matched for severity. A recent study (Sahakian et al., 1988) reports qualitative differences in memory between PD and AD patients. AD patients showed rapid forgetting in a delayed matching-to-sample task, while PD patients, like controls, showed little effect of delay. However, the patient groups were not matched on severity of cognitive impairment.

A qualitative difference in memory has also been reported by Sagar et al. (1988). They employed a continuous verbal recognition task and compared content recognition (deciding which of two words had been presented previously) with recency discrimination (deciding which of two words had been presented more recently). AD patients were impaired on both tasks while PD patients were impaired mainly on the recency discrimination. However, the AD group was more cognitively impaired, so the effect may be quantitative rather than qualitative; recency discrimination may be more vulnerable than content recognition to the effects of cognitive impairment.

The hypothesis that PD patients have a selective impairment of memory for temporal information receives some support from studies of remote memory, where they have particular difficulty with dating events (Sagar et al., 1988; and see Handbook of Neuropsychology, Vol. 4, Ch. 15). This is consistent with the hypothesis of frontal lobe involvement in Parkinson's disease. There is a general consensus that PD patients are impaired on tests associated with frontal lobe function, such as Wisconsin Card Sorting and verbal fluency (e.g. Lees and Smith, 1983; Pillon et al., 1986; Taylor et al., 1986), although there are reports that this only occurs in a minority of cases (e.g. Canavan et al., 1989).

An advance in understanding cognitive impairment in PD has come from the work of Freedman and Oscar-Berman (1986). They compared the performance of PD and AD patients matched for severity of dementia on delayed alternation and delayed response tasks, which are both sensitive to frontal lobe impairment. AD patients were severely impaired on both tasks, while PD patients were impaired only on the delayed response tasks. Since the two tasks are subserved by different parts of the frontal lobes, the authors were able to conclude that dorsolateral frontal systems are primarily implicated in Parkinson's disease, while the frontal cortex is more diffusely affected in Alzheimer's disease.

In summary, there is as yet inconclusive evidence of memory impairment associated with Parkinson's disease per se. The significant differences which have been found between non-demented PD patients and properly matched controls may in many cases be the result of medication or of parkinsonian slowing rather than true memory impairment. Comparisons of demented PD patients with AD patients suggest that there may be qualitative differences in memory, the PD deficits possibly reflecting frontal lobe involvement of a more restricted kind than that seen in AD. Attractive as the frontal lobe hypothesis is for explaining the particular memory and other cognitive deficits in Parkinson's disease, there remains the problem that some severely parkinsonian patients show little evidence of cognitive deficit (e.g. Mayeux et al., 1981). This issue will not be resolved until far more is known about the relationship between pathology and cognition in individual cases. One cannot at present rule out the suggestion that cognitive impairment and dementia occur in PD only in those cases which have superimposed pathology of the type associated with AD (Quinn et al., 1986) or vascular dementia.

The aging brain

The neurobiology of aging is discussed elsewhere in this volume (Ch. 3). Only a brief outline is presented here in order that relationships between neurobiology and memory in the elderly may be examined.

With respect to brain morphology, early studies reported dramatic loss of neurons in cerebral cortex associated with normal aging (e.g. Brody, 1955). However, these studies have been criticized since they failed to take account of cohort differences in brain size or the confounding effects of neurological disorders other than dementia. Recent studies indicate only small age-related decrements in cortical volume (e.g. Hubbard and Anderson, 1981) when cranial capacity is taken into account. Of particular importance is the evidence of no neocortical neuronal loss in normal aging; the significant change appears to be a shrinkage of large cells particularly in frontal and temporal cortex (Terry et al., 1987).

In contrast to neocortex, there does appear to be neuronal loss in hippocampus and amygdala. A reduction of around 20% has been reported in the density of hippocampal pyramidal cells from about age 40 to age 80, correcting for hippocampal size (Mouritzen, 1979). There also appears to be neuronal loss in some subcortical structures, notably the hypothalamus, the locus ceruleus and the substantia nigra (see Coleman and Flood, 1987). The latter two structures contain the cells of origin of the catecholaminergic and dopaminergic neurotransmitter systems respectively. Neuronal loss in these regions, estimated at around 35 – 40% of pigmented cells in older adults (Tomlinson et al., 1981; Vijayashankar and Brody, 1979), appears to be associated with age-related neurotransmitter depletion. The situation regarding the cholinergic system is less clear. While there is some evidence for an age-related depletion of choline acetyltransferase (e.g. Rossor et al., 1984), some studies report age-related neuronal loss in the basal nucleus where the cholinergic projections originate, while other studies do not (see Coleman and Flood, 1987). Of course neuronal numbers, even if they could be counted accurately, would not indicate whether neuronal function is normal.

There is also evidence that the dendritic tree is reduced in extent in normal aging (e.g. Scheibel et al., 1975), although there are reports of age-related dendritic growth in the parahippocampal gyrus (Buell and Coleman, 1981). An important task for future research is to determine whether such findings reflect regional structural differences or individual differences. It is worth noting that in a study of aged rodents, dendritic sprouting was found in a group that underwent 3 weeks of training in a maze, but not in an untrained group of littermates whose lifestyle was identical up to that point (Cummins et al., 1973).

In Alzheimer's disease, there is substantial neuronal loss in the basal nucleus, locus ceruleus and substantia nigra associated with major depletion of cholinergic, noradrenergic and dopaminergic neurotransmitter systems (see Coleman and Flood, 1987). There is also loss of cortical neurons, particularly in temporal lobe and hippocampus in late-onset cases, but involving frontal cortex in younger cases (e.g. Rossor et al., 1984). Although the direction of causality is not known for certain, it has been suggested that cell loss or degeneration rather than neurochemical depletion is likely to be the primary change in Alzheimer's disease as well as normal aging (Roth, 1986). Recent work suggests that possible mechanisms for neuronal degeneration may be the age-related decreases in glucose and energy metabolism (e.g. Hoyer, 1985) or calcium mobilization and permeation across membranes (Gibson and Peterson, 1987), although the relationship between calcium-dependent processes and brain pathology is speculative at present.

Neuritic ('senile') plaques and neurofibrillary tangles are pathological changes which are the hallmarks of Alzheimer's disease. They are also present in the brains of most normal elderly people (Tomlinson, 1972). The major differences appear to be a smaller density of plaques in normal brains, and the tangles being restricted to the hippocampus rather than extending into neocortical areas as in Alzheimer's disease. There are, however, a number of difficulties with these findings: (a) the AD cases are usually in a late stage of the disease; (b) 'normals' have rarely been adequately assessed prior to death, and (c) pathological changes in 'normals' may be the consequence of chronic or terminal ill-

ness. In a recent series of post-mortems on nursing home residents who were carefully monitored prior to death, Katzman and his colleagues (1988) identified two groups of patients in whom the density and distribution of plaques was similar, but one group was demented while the other was not. The groups were found to differ significantly in brain weight, and one hypothesis which the authors advanced was that the non-demented group may have started with larger brains and thus had greater reserve capacity. However, compared with the non-demented group, the demented group had many more neurofibrillary tangles throughout the cortex and hippocampus, so it is difficult to assess the significance of differential brain weight in this study.

While most studies show that certain pathological changes occur in 'normal' brains, there are scattered reports in the literature indicating that for some cognitively intact individuals there is no sign of Alzheimer-type pathology.

Tomlinson (1985) has reported that tangles were completely absent from the brains of elderly people functioning at a very high level prior to death. In an autopsy series, Miller et al. (1984) mention an elderly lady who had no plaques or tangles. Although she had not been cognitively assessed, enquiry revealed that she had been functioning well in the community until she was knocked down by a bus. The classic paper of Blessed et al. (1968), which showed high correlations between cognitive test scores, activities of daily living and plaque counts, reported that eight out of 26 non-demented elderly had no plaques.

Usual vs. successful aging

Findings such as these make it clear that it is premature to generalize about the pathological changes in the brains of normal elderly people. Although certain changes may be statistically normal and representative of 'usual' agings, there is growing evidence that they are not representative of 'successful' aging, to use Rowe and Kahn's (1987) terminology. More information is required about the relationship between neurobiological changes and individual differences in cognitive function and sociodemographic and lifestyle variables such as education, occupation, recent participation in mentally stimulating activity and the like. There are undoubtedly many conditions which affect brain morphology or chemistry. These may include conditions which produce cerebral hypoxia, such as chronic obstructive lung disease, which is relatively common in the elderly. The hippocampus is known to be particularly vulnerable to the effects of hypoxia. Memory impairment has been reported in patients with hypoxic disease (e.g. Grant et al., 1982), and the degree of memory impairment has been shown to correlate with the degree of oxygen saturation in arterial blood samples (Huppert, 1982). There are probably many other 'usual' conditions in the elderly which influence both brain function/morphology and memory, of which investigators need to be aware if we are to understand successful aging.

Considerations such as these have implications for the new concept of 'age-associated memory impairment' (AAMI), which has recently been proposed by an NIMH workgroup. An essential criterion for AAMI is the exclusion of dementia, delirium, depression and other conditions which may impair memory. Yet in one recent paper, individuals were identified as being potential cases of AAMI, but no information about health status was provided (Buschke and Grober, 1986).

There can be no justification for giving individuals a diagnostic label such as AAMI, until: (1) far more is known about the conditions which produce poor memory in individuals of any age, and (2) the reliability of performance measures has been properly established.

Hypotheses concerning the relationship between memory impairment and the aging brain

Drawing together the evidence we have presented on age-associated neurobiological changes and age-related memory impairment, the following conclusions emerge, some more speculative than others.

Cerebral atrophy and information processing To the extent that there is an age-related reduction in the 'pool' of processing resources, the biological basis could conceivably be age-related cerebral atrophy, reduced dendritic extent, decreases in major neurotransmitters, or, more generally, reduced energy metabolism. However, functional psychological interpretations of an apparent reduction in processing resources are at least as plausible. Namely, normal older adults may have the same amount of processing resources as younger adults, but have more demands competing for these resources.

Regional specificity of pathological changes and memory impairment Evidence that age-related neocortical neuronal changes are specific to temporal and frontal cortex may provide a neurological basis for evidence and theories of age-related memory impairment. Studies of focal brain lesions implicate the temporal cortex in memory impairment, although deficits are very mild unless hippocampal structures are also damaged (Milner, 1968). McIntyre and Craik (1987) have suggested that the particular difficulties experienced by older adults on tasks requiring self-initiated activities may implicate the frontal lobes. Indeed, Janowsky et al. (1989) found that older subjects performed as poorly as patients with frontal lobe lesions on recalling the source of material which had been presented in an incidental learning paradigm. The authors suggest that in the older subjects the impaired memory for temporal context is attributable to the pathological changes which have been described in the frontal lobes of the normal elderly.

However, before accepting the conclusions of McIntyre and Craik, and of Janowsky et al., the following evidence should be borne in mind. First, Janowsky et al. (1989) found that their older subjects performed as well as younger subjects in recalling the source of information where items were presented in an intentional learning paradigm, although the patients with frontal lobe lesions were markedly impaired in both the intentional and the incidental paradigm. This implies that to the extent that frontal pathology underlies this form of memory impairment in the elderly, it is only apparent under conditions (e.g. incidental learning) where a limited amount of processing resource has been deployed in the memory task. Second, while there are some similarities between the cognitive deficits of frontal lobe patients and the normal elderly, the many differences should not be ignored. Patients with focal lesions in the frontal cortex are not only impaired on tasks requiring the initiation of behaviour and discrimination of temporal context, they are also severely impaired on tasks which require abstraction, set-shifting ability and motor programming (e.g. Walsh, 1978). In fact there is scant evidence that the normal elderly are impaired on the tasks classically associated with frontal lobe lesions (e.g. Albert and Kaplan, 1980). On the other hand, frontal lobe lesions do not produce memory deficits on standard recall and recognition tasks (see Squire, 1987) even when judgement of recency is impaired (Milner, 1971). This implies that if frontal pathology is involved at all in memory deficits in the elderly, it is not sufficient to explain the memory deficits. It is worth adding that Kopelman (1989) has shown that the memory impairment for temporal context found in both Korsakoff and Alzheimer patients bears no relationship to the degree of frontal atrophy and little relationship to tests of frontal lobe function.

This points to the difficulties inherent in applying neuropsychological models derived from research on focal brain damage to the study of aging, where pathology is more diffuse. We simply do not know what effects diffuse lesions of, say, temporal lobes exert on cognitive function. Standard neuropsychological models of localization of function may be the wrong models for understanding aging and dementia.

There is little doubt that hippocampal structures are involved in the acquisition of new information (e.g. Mahut and Moss, 1984). The presence of neurofibrillary tangles and cell loss in the hippocampi of most 'normal' elderly subjects is a possible biological basis for impaired memory for new information. Using an identical experimental paradigm, it has been found that older adults, like the patient HM who had bilateral hippocampal removal (Scoville and Milner, 1957), show fast forgetting on a picture recognition test (Huppert and Piercy, 1978; Huppert and Kopelman, 1989).

The anatomy of implicit and explicit memory Mishkin has proposed two anatomically distinct memory systems. One system is termed 'memories', and refers to the ability to recognize something as familiar (Mishkin et al., 1984; Mishkin and Appenzeller, 1987). There is evidence that it is subserved by the cortico-limbic system. The other type of memory is termed 'habits' and refers to conditioning and response adaptation. Mishkin proposes that this is subserved by the other major cortical-subcortical pathway, the cortico-striatal system. The evidence for the second system at present comes mainly from animal studies, but selectively impaired learning of a habit (pursuit rotor) has recently been demonstrated in patients with Huntington's chorea who have lesions in one of the striatal nuclei, the caudate nucleus (Heindel et al., 1988).

There is a close parallel between explicit memory and Mishkin's 'memories' on the one hand, and implicit memory and 'habits' on the other. A functional dissociation between explicit and implicit memory on the same task was described above, in mildly to moderately demented patients. Their severely impaired explicit memory contrasted with normal implicit memory (Huppert and Beardsall, 1988, and manuscript in preparation). There is also an anatomical dissociation, since limbic structures (particularly the hippocampus) show large neuronal loss in AD while the striatum remains intact (Coleman and Flood, 1987) at least in the early stages of the disease. It could be argued that the involvement of the striatum in Parkinson's disease may imply that habits should be relatively more impaired than memories. The literature is not at present clear on this point (e.g. Saint-Cyr et al., 1988). One problem may be that very different tasks have been used to examine explicit and implicit memory in PD patients.

Neurochemical changes and memory impairment Biochemical rather than morphological changes may underlie memory impairment in aging and dementia. The main contender is the cholinergic deficit which is severe in Alzheimer's disease and frequently present in Parkinson's disease (Perry et al., 1985). A cholinergic deficit also appears to be present in normal aging though it is not yet known whether it is present in successful aging. Kopelman has carried out an extensive review of the memory deficits produced by cholinergic blockade (Kopelman, 1987). He concludes that the deficits in secondary memory seen in the early stages of Alzheimer's disease (and presumably those in some normal elderly and PD cases) resemble the deficits produced by cholinergic blockade, but the AD deficits in primary memory, remote memory and the severe secondary memory deficits in later stages cannot be accounted for simply by cholinergic depletion. It is also unlikely that cholinergic depletion is a major contributor to the memory impairment in patients with vascular dementia.

Memory, intelligence and the brain Memory in the elderly is related to intelligence/education and the question arises whether this reflects neurobiological differences. Poor education is associated with low social class and there is abundant evidence of a higher prevalence of chronic diseases and reduced life expectancy in lower social classes (e.g. Cox et al., 1987). For this reason alone, it would not be surprising if there was more brain pathology in this group. A higher percentage of poorly educated subjects may have incipient dementia (Henderson, 1986) or the cognitive decline associated with 'terminal drop' (Riegel and Riegel, 1972).

There may also be education/IQ differences in intellectual stimulation, which may have neurobiological consequences. Studies of aged rodents have demonstrated increased brain weight and cortical thickness in animals reared in enriched environments compared with littermates raised in deprived environments (e.g. Cummins et al., 1973). On the other hand, the differential between these groups was eliminated following a few weeks of intellectual stimulation (learning a maze). Cummins et al. found dendritic sprouting in the restricted group following

the learning experience. The findings described above, that education-related differences in human memory are eliminated when groups are matched for high levels of leisure activities (Huppert and Elliott, 1988), is consistent with these data. Of course education/IQ differences in psychological variables such as motivation and familiarity with tests may play a role in performance on memory tests. However, in the present context, the possibility has been considered that education/IQ-related differences in memory may stem from neurobiological differences which may in some cases be reversible.

The raised prevalence of dementia reported in people with little education or low social class (reviewed by Henderson, 1986) could be a diagnostic artefact (these groups perform poorly on cognitive tests) or a genuine effect for which a neurobiological basis should be sought. To date, no study appears to have examined the relationship between social class and type of dementia. However, vascular disease is more common among low socioeconomic groups, and it would therefore not be surprising if the prevalence of vascular dementia was higher in these groups. But what might explain differences in the prevalence of Alzheimer's disease? If education/IQ or a stimulating environment is associated with increased brain size or dendritic arborization, the resulting reserve capacity may provide protection against pathology unless it is extreme.

Summary and future directions

Although memory deficits are common among the elderly, some groups of older adults show little evidence of impairment. Education and IQ have previously been identified as important variables. Current research on individual differences is beginning to uncover other relevant variables. With the rapid growth in the size of the elderly population, the identification of factors associated with preserved memory is a valuable goal. Similarly, although degenerative brain changes are common among the elderly, evidence is accumulating that these changes may be absent in individuals who are cognitively intact prior to death. Rowe and Kahn's (1987) terminology 'usual' versus 'successful' aging encapsulates this distinction.

Memory deficits in 'usual' aging are greatest on tasks such as free recall, which require self-initiated activity, because there is little environmental support for the required response. Memory deficits have been attributed to reduced processing capacity but could equally well reflect an alteration in the allocation of processing resources.

Recent experimental paradigms demonstrate that older adults do not have a problem in semantic encoding when tasks are free of a memory load. Indeed, there is little evidence for an acquisition defect in the normal elderly. On the other hand there is growing evidence for a retention defect. A variety of studies show that older adults forget well-encoded information more rapidly than younger adults.

The most interesting finding with respect to dementia is that there is some selectivity of the memory deficit, at least in the early stages. First, acquisition is severely impaired but retention appears normal; present evidence suggests that rate of forgetting is no faster than for age-matched controls when initial levels of performance have been equalized. Second, performance on explicit memory tasks is severely impaired, while performance on comparable implicit memory tasks is usually unimpaired.

Comparisons of patients with Alzheimer's disease and patients whose dementia is associated with Parkinson's disease suggest that there may be some qualitative differences in memory impairment, but confirmation is required. There is scant evidence for memory impairment in non-demented PD patients.

Some attempt has been made in this chapter to relate the memory deficits observed in 'usual' aging and AD to what is known at present about the relevant neuroanatomical and neurochemical changes. This attempt has been based on the familiar neuropsychology of localization of function. However, the author believes that this may be the wrong model

for understanding aging and dementia, where the pathological changes are known to be diffuse. If aging and AD result in the selective shrinkage of large neurons, as suggested by Terry et al. (1987), we might, for example, wish to consider developing a neuropsychological model which relates cognitive function to cell size.

Although some of the biological evidence may provide a plausible explanation for some of the memory impairment, far more research is required to establish these relationships on a sound footing. In particular, the overwhelming evidence cited above of the role of education or IQ in memory performance makes it essential for future post-mortem and neurobiological studies generally to take account of these variables. Further, in view of the evidence that dendritic growth occurs in aged rodents following a short period of training (Cummins et al., 1973), it may be necessary for studies to obtain information about the extent to which the individual was recently involved in mentally stimulating activity. A related view has been expressed by Coleman and Flood (1987, p. 521): 'the static, post-mortem status of brain morphology may not adequately reflect the functional capabilities of the dynamic morphology of the living brain'. Advances in our understanding of the relationship between memory and the aging brain are most likely to come from the combination of cognitive/lifestyle research and dynamic techniques such as PET studies and possibly new developments in magnetic resonance spectroscopy.

Acknowledgements

I would like to thank Drs. Deborah Burke and Carol Brayne for their helpful comments on the manuscript, and Carol Holmes and Roberta Patterson for their help in preparing the manuscript. Discussions with Drs. R. Brown, M. Kopelman, C.Q. Mountjoy and R. Passingham are gratefully acknowledged. This work was undertaken while Dr. Huppert was funded by the Medical Research Council and the Health Promotion Research Trust.

References

Abson V, Rabbitt P: What do self-rating questionnaires tell us about changes in competence in old age? In Gruneberg MM, Morris PE, Sykes RN (Editors), *Practical Aspects of Memory: Current Research & Issues.* Chester: John Wiley & Sons, pp. 188–191, 1988.

Albert SM, Kaplan E: Organic implications of neuropsychological deficits in the elderly. In Poon WL, Fozard LJ, Carmak LS, Arenberg D, Thompson WL (Editors), *New Directions in Memory and Aging.* Proceedings of the George A Talland memorial conference, Boston 1978. Hillside, NJ: Lawrence Erlbaum Associates, Ch. 23, pp. 403–432, 1980.

American Psychiatric Association: *Diagnostic and Statistical Manual of Mental Disorders (third edition) DSM-III-R.* Washington, DC: American Psychiatric Association, 1987.

Arenberg D: Comments on the processes that account for memory declines with age. In Poon LW, Fozard JL, Cermak LS, Arenberg D, Thompson LW (Editors), *New Directions in Memory and Aging.* Proceedings of the George A Talland memorial conference, Boston 1978. Hillside, NJ: Lawrence Erlbaum Associates, Ch. 3, pp. 67–71, 1980.

Baddeley AD, Hitch GJ: Working memory. In Bower GH (Editor), *The Psychology of Learning and Motivation, Vol. 8:* New York: Academic Press, pp. 47–90, 1974.

Baddeley AD, Logie R, Bressi S, Della Sala S, Spinnler H: Dementia and working memory. *Q. J. Exp. Psychol. 38,* 603–618, 1986.

Baltes PB, Kliegl R: On the dynamics between growth and decline in the aging of intelligence and memory. In Poeck K, Freund HJ, Ganshirt H (Editors), *Neurology.* Heidelberg: Springer-Verlag, pp. 1–17, 1986.

Blessed G, Tomlinson BE, Roth M: The association between quantitative measures of dementia and of senile change in the cerebral grey matter of elderly subjects. *Br. J. Psychiatry: 114,* 797–811, 1968.

Bowles NL, Poon LW: An analysis of the effect of aging on memory. *J. Gerontol.: 37,* 212–219, 1982.

Brody H: Organisation of the cerebral cortex. III. A study of aging in the human cerebral cortex. *J. Comp. Neurol.: 102,* 511–556, 1955.

Brown RG, Marsden CD: How common is dementia in Parkinson's disease? *Lancet: 2,* 1262–1265, 1984.

Brown RG, Marsden CD: Subcortical dementia: the neuropsychological evidence. *Neuroscience: 28,* 363–387, 1988.

Buell SJ, Coleman PD: Quantitative evidence for selective dendritic growth in normal human aging but not in senile dementia. *Brain Res.: 214,* 23–41, 1981.

Burke DM, Harrold RM: Automatic and effortful semantic processes in old age: experimental and naturalistic approaches: In Light L, Burke DM (Editors), *Language, Memory and Aging.* New York: Cambridge University Press, 1989.

Burke DM, Yee PL: Semantic priming during sentence processing by young and older adults. *Dev. Psychol.: 20,* 903–910, 1984.

Burke DM, White H, Diaz DL: Semantic priming in young and older adults: evidence for age constancy in automatic and attentional processes. *J. Exp. Psychol.: 13,* 79–88, 1987.

Burke DM, Worthley J, Martin J: I'll never forget what's-her-name: adults' tip-of-the-tongue experience in everyday life. In Gruneberg MM, Morris PE, Sykes RN (Editors), *Practical Aspects of Memory: Current Research Issues.* Chichester: John Wiley & sons, pp. 113–118, 1988.

Buschke H, Grober E: Genuine memory deficits in age-associated memory impairment. *Dev. Neuropsychol.: 2,* 287–307, 1986.

Butters N, Salmon DP, Granholm E, Heindel W, Lyon L: Neuropsychological differentation of amnesic and dementing states. In Stahl SM, Iversen SD, Goodman EC (Editors), *Cognitive Neurochemistry.* Oxford: Science Publications, Ch. 1, pp. 3–20, 1987.

Canavan AGM, Passingham RE, Marsden CD, Quinn N, Wyke M, Polkey CE: The performance on learning tasks of patients in the early stages of Parkinson's disease. *Neuropsychologia: 27,* 141–156, 1989.

Christensen H: Explicit and implicit memory in dementia and normal ageing. *Psychological Res.* (in press).

Cockburn J, Smith PT: Effects of age and intelligence on everyday memory tasks. In Gruneberg MM, Morris PE, Sykes RN (Editors), *Practical Aspects of Memory: Current Research & Issues:* Chichester: John Wiley & Sons, pp. 132–136, 1988.

Cohen G, Faulkner D: Memory for discourse in old age. *Disc. Processes: 4,* 253–265, 1981.

Coleman PD, Flood DG: Neuron number and dendritic extent in normal aging and Alzheimer's Disease. *Neurobiol. Aging: 8,* 521–545, 1987.

Corkin S: Some relationships between global amnesias and the memory impairments in Alzheimer's disease. In Corkin S, Davis KL, Growdon JH, Usdin E, Wurtman RJ (Editors), *Alzheimer's disease: A Report of Progress in Research.* New York: Raven Press, pp. 149–164, 1982.

Corkin S, Growdon JH, Nissen MJ, Huff FJ, Freed DM, Sagar HJ: Recent advances in the neuropsychological study of Alzheimer's disease. In Wurtman RJ, Corkin S, Growdon JH (Editors), *Alzheimer's Disease: Advances in Basic Research and Therapies.* Proceedings of the third meeting of the International Study Group: On the treatment of memory disorder associated with aging. Cambridge, MA: Centre for Brain Sciences and Metabolism Trust, 1984.

Cox BD, Blaxter M, Buckle ALJ, Fenner NP, Golding JF, Gore M, Huppert FA, Nickson J, Roth M, Stark JE, Wadsworth MEJ, Whichelow M: *Health and Lifestile Survey: preliminary report of a nationwide survey of the physical and mental health, attitudes and lifestyle of a random sample of 9003 British adults.* London: Health Promotion Research Trust, 1987.

Craik FIM: Age differences in human memory. In Birren JE, Schaie KW (Editors), *Handbook of the Psychology of Aging.* New York: Van Nostrand Reinhold, Ch. 17, pp. 384–420, 1977.

Craik FIM: Selective changes in encoding as a function of reduced processing capacity. In Kokx, Hoffman, Van der Meer (Editors), *Cognitive Research in Psychology.* Berlin: DVW, pp. 152–161, 1982.

Craik FIM: Age differences in remembering. In Squire LR, Butters N (Editors), *Neuropsychology of Memory.* New York: Guilford Press, Ch. 1, pp. 3–12, 1984.

Craik FIM: A functional account of age differences in memory.

In Klix F, Hagendord H, (Editors), *Human Memory and Cognitive Capabilities: Mechanisms and Performances.* Amsterdam: Elsevier Science Publishers, pp. 409 – 422, 1986.

Craik FIM, Byrd M: Aging and cognitive deficits: The role of attentional resources. In Craik FIM, Trehub SE (Editors), *Ageing and Cognitive Processes.* New York: Plenum Press, pp. 191 – 211, 1982.

Craik FIM, McDowd MJ: Age differences in recall and recognition. *J. Exp. Psychol. Learn. Mem. Cognition: 13,* 1 – 6, 1987.

Craik FIM, Rabinowitz JC: The effects of presentation rate and encoding tasks on age-related memory deficits. *J. Gerontol.: 40,* 309 – 315, 1985.

Craik FIM, Byrd M, Swanson JM: Patterns of memory loss in three elderly samples. *Psychol. Aging: 2,* 79 – 86, 1987.

Craik FIM, Lockhart RS: Levels of processing: a framework for memory research. *J. Verbal Learn. Verbal Behav.: 11,* 671 – 684, 1972.

Cummins JL, Walsh RN, Budtz-Olsen OE, Konstantinos T, Horsfall CR: Environmentally-induced changes in the brains of elderly rats. *Nature: 243,* 516 – 518, 1973.

Davies P, Maloney AJF: Selective loss of central cholinergic neurons in Alzheimer's disease. *Lancet: ii,* 1403, 1976.

Evarts EV, Teravainen H, Calne DB: Reaction time in Parkinson's disease. *Brain: 104,* 167 – 186, 1981.

Eysenck MW: Age differences in incidental learning. *Dev. Psychol.: 10,* 936 – 941, 1974.

Ferris SH, Crook T, Clark E, McCarthy M, Rae D: Facial recognition memory deficits in normal and senile dementia. *J. Gerontol.: 35,* 707 – 714, 1980.

Fozard JL: The time for remembering. In Poon LW (Editor), *Aging in the 1980s: Psychological Issues.* Washington, DC: American Psychological Association, Ch. 20, pp. 273 – 290, 1980.

Freedman M, Oscar-Berman M: Selective delayed response deficits in Parkinson's and Alzheimer's disease. *Arch. Neurol.: 43,* 886 – 890, 1986.

Gibson GE, Peterson C: Calcium and the aging nervous system. *Neurobiol. Aging: 8,* 329 – 343, 1987.

Gick ML, Craik FIM, Morris RG: Task complexity and age differences in working memory. *Mem. Cognition: 16,* 353 – 361, 1988.

Gilewski MJ, Zelinski EM: Questionnaire assessment of memory complaints. In Poon KW (Editor), *Handbook of Clinical Memory Assessment for Older Adults.* Washington, DC: American Psychological Association, Ch. 11, pp. 93 – 107, 1986.

Grant I, Heaton R, McSweeney A, Adams K, Timms R: Neuropsychological findings in chronic obstructive pulmonary disease. *Arch. Internal Med.: 142,* 1470 – 1476, 1982.

Hanley-Dunn P, McIntosh JL: Meaningfulness and recall of names by young and old adults. *J. Gerontol.: 39,* 538 – 585, 1984.

Hasher L, Zacks RT: Automatic and effortful processes in memory. *J. Exp. Psychol.: 108,* 356 – 388, 1979.

Heindel WC, Butters N, Salmon DP: Impaired learning of a motor skill in patients with Huntingdon's disease. *Behav. Neurosci.: 102,* 141 – 147, 1988.

Henderson AS: The epidemiology of Alzheimer's disease. *Br. Med. Bull.: 42,* 3 – 10, 1986.

Hornykiewicz O: Brain transmitter changes in Parkinson's disease. In Marsden CD, Fahn S (Editors), *Movement Disorders.* London: Buttertworths, pp. 41 – 58, 1982.

Howard DV, Shaw RS, Heisey JG: Aging and the time course of semantic activation. *J. Gerontol.: 41,* 195 – 203, 1986.

Hoyer S: The effect of age on glucose and energy metabolism in brain cortex of rats. *Arch. Gerontol. Geriatrics: 4,* 193 – 203, 1985.

Hubbard BM, Anderson JM: A quantitative study of cerebral atrophy in old age and senile dementia. *J. Neurol. Sci.: 50,* 135 – 145, 1981.

Hultsch DF, Hertzog C, Dixon RA: Test recall in adulthood: the role of intellectual abilities. *Dev. Psychol.: 20,* 1193 – 1209, 1984.

Huppert FA: Memory impairment associated with chronic hypoxia in man. *Thorax: 37,* 858 – 860, 1982.

Huppert FA: Cognitive function. In Cox B, Blaxter M, Buckle ALJ, Fenner NP, Golding JF, Gore M, Huppert FA, Nickson J, Roth M, Stark J, Wadsworth MEJ, Whichelow M (Editors), *Health and Lifestyle Survey: preliminary report of a nationwide survey of the physical and mental health, attitudes and lifestyle of a random sample of 9003 British adults.* London: Health Promotion Research Trust, Ch. 5, pp. 43 – 50, 1987.

Huppert FA, Beardsall L: Revealing the concealed: multiple measures of memory in dementia. In Gruneberg MM, Morris PE, Sykes RN (Editors), *Practical Aspects of Memory: Current Research & Issues.* Chichester: John Wiley & Sons, pp. 34 – 39, 1988.

Huppert FA, Beardsall L: Dissociation beteen explicit and implicit memory in dementia. In preparation.

Huppert FA, Elliott BJ: The contribution of health and lifestyle variables to cognitive function. Paper presented at the XXIV International Congress of Psychology, Sydney, August 1988.

Huppert FA, Kopelman M: Rates of forgetting in normal ageing: a comparison with dementia. *Neuropsychologia: 27,* 849 – 860, 1989.

Huppert FA, Piercy M: Recognition memory in amnesic patients: a defect of acquisition? *Neuropsychologia: 15,* 643 – 652, 1977.

Huppert FA, Piercy M: Dissociation between learning and remembering in organic amnesia. *Nature: 275,* 317 – 318, 1978.

Huppert FA, Piercy M: Normal and abnormal forgetting in amnesia: effect of locus of lesion. *Cortex: 15,* 385 – 390, 1979.

Janowsky JS, Shimamura AP, Squire LR: Source memory impairment in patients with frontal lobe lesions. *Neuropsychologia: 27,* 1043 – 1056, 1989.

Jorm AF: Controlled and automatic information processing in senile dementia: a review. *Psychol. Med.: 16,* 1569 – 1573, 1986.

Kahn RL, Zarit SH, Hilbert NM, Niderehe G: Memory complaint and impairment in the aged: the effect of depression and altered brain function. *Arch. Gen. Psychiatry: 32,* 1569 – 1573, 1975.

Kaszniak AW, Poon LW, Riege W: Assessing memory deficits: an information processing approach. In Poon LW (Editor), *Handbook of Clinical Memory Assessment of Older Adults.* Washington, DC: American Psychological Association, Ch. 17, pp. 168 – 188, 1986.

Katzman R, Terry R, DeTeresa R, Brown T, Davies P, Fuld P, Renbing X, Peck A: Clinical, pathological and neurochemical changes in dementia: A subgroup with preserved mental status and numerous neocortical plaques. *Ann. Neurol.: 23,* 138 – 144, 1988.

Kausler DH: Retention-forgetting as a nomological network for developmental research. In Goulet LR, Baltes PB (Editors), *Lifespan Developmental Psychology.* New York: Academic Press, pp. 305 – 353, 1970.

Kopelman MD: Rates of forgetting in Alzheimer-type dementia and Korsakoff's syndrome. *Neuropsychologia: 23,* 623 – 638, 1985.

Kopelman MD: How far could cholinergic depletion account for the memory deficits of Alzheimer-type dementia or the alcoholic Korsakoff syndrome? In Stahl SM, Iversen SD, Goodman EC (Editors), *Cognitive Neurochemistry.* Oxford: Oxford University Press, Ch. 16, pp. 306 – 326, 1987.

Kopelman MD: Remote and autobiographical memory, temporal context memory and frontal atrophy in Korsakoff and Alzheimer patients. *Neuropsychologia: 27,* 437 – 460, 1989.

Lees AJ: Parkinson's disease and dementia. *Lancet: i,* 43 – 44, 1985.

Lees AJ, Smith E: Cognitive deficits in the early stages of Parkinson's disease. *Brain: 106,* 257 – 270, 1983.

Light LL, Burke DM: Patterns of language and memory in old age. In Light LL, Burke DM (Editors), *Language, Memory and Aging.* New York: Cambridge University Press, 1989.

Light LL, Singh A: Implicit and explicit memory in young and older adults. *J. Exp. Psychol. Learn. Mem. Cognition: 13,* 531 – 541, 1987.

Mahut M, Moss M: Consolidation of memory: the hippocampus revisited. In Squire LR, Butters N (Editors), *Neuropsychology of Memory.* New York: Guilford Press, Ch. 29, pp. 297 – 315, 1984.

Mayeux R, Stern Y, Rosen J, Lenathal J: Depression, intellectual impairment, and Parkinson's disease. *Neurology: 31,* 645 – 650, 1981.

Mayeux R, Stern Y, Rosenstein R, Marder K, Hauser A, Cote L, Fahn S: An estimate of the prevalence of dementia in idiopathic Parkinson's disease. *Arch. Neurol.: 45,* 260 – 262, 1988.

McCarty SM, Siegler C, Logue PE: Cross-sectional and longitudinal patterns of three Wechsler Memory Scale subtests. *J. Gerontol.: 37,* 2: 169 – 175, 1982.

McIntyre JS, Craik FIM: Age differences in memory for item and source information. *Can. J. Psychol.: 41:* 175 – 192, 1987.

Miller E: Short and long-term memory in presenile dementia (Alzheimer's disease). *Psychol. Med.: 3,* 221 – 224, 1973.

Miller E: Impaired recall and the memory disturbance in presenile dementia. *Br. J. Soc. Clin. Psychol.: 14,* 73 – 79, 1975.

Miller FD, Hicks SP, A'Amato CJ, Landis JR: A descriptive study of neuritic plaques and neurofibrillary tangles in an autopsy population. *Am. J. Epidemiol.: 3,* 331 – 341, 1984.

Milner B: Disorders of memory after brain lesions in man. *Neuropsychologia: 6,* 175 – 179, 1968.

Milner B: Interhemispheric differences in the localization of psychological processes in man. *Br. Med. Bull.: 27,* 272 – 277, 1971.

Mishkin M, Malamut B, Bachevalier J: Memories and habits: two neural systems. In Lynch G, McGaugh JL, Weinberger NM (Editors), *Neurobiology of Learning and Memory.* New York: Guilford Press: Ch. 2, pp. 65 – 77, 1984.

Mishkin M, Appenzeller T: The anatomy of memory. *Sci. Am.: 256,* 62 – 71, 1987.

Molsa PK, Paljerir L, Rinne JO, Ruine VK, Sako E: Validity of clinical diagnosis in dementia: a prospective clinicopathological study. *J. Neurol. Neurosurg. Psychiatry: 78,* 1085 – 1090, 1985.

Morris RG: Dementia and the functioning of the articulatory loop system. *Cognitive Neuropsychol.: 1,* 143 – 157, 1984.

Morris RG, Kopelman MD: The memory deficits in Alzheimer-type dementia. *Q. J. Exp. Psychol.: 38,* 575 – 602, 1986.

Morris RG, Wheatley J, Britton PG: Retrieval from long-term memory in senile dementia: cued recall revisited. *Br. J. Clin. Psychol.: 22,* 141 – 142, 1983.

Morris RG, Gick ML, Craik FIM: Processing resources and age differences in working memory. *Mem. Cognition: 16,* 362 – 366, 1988.

Moscovitch M: A neuropsychological approach to perception and memory in normal and pathological aging. In Craik FIM, Trehub S (Editors), *Aging and Cognitive Processes.* New York: Plenum Press, Ch. 4, pp. 55 – 78, 1982.

Mouritzen Dam A: The density of neurons in the human hippocampus. *Neuropathol. Appl. Neurobiol.: 5,* 249 – 264, 1979.

Naylor G, Harwood E: Old dogs, new tricks: age and ability. *Psychol. Today: 1,* 29 – 33, 1975.

Nebes RD, Martin DC, Hoin LC: Sparing of semantic memory in Alzheimer's disease. *J. Abnorm. Psychol.: 93:* 321 – 330, 1984.

Perlmutter M: What is memory aging the aging of? *Dev. Psychol.: 14,* 330 – 345, 1978.

Perry EK, Curtis M, Dick DJ, Candy JM, Ratack J, Bloxham CA, Blessed G, Fairbairn A, Tomlinson BE, Perry RH: Cholinergic correlates of cognitive impairment in Parkinson's disease: comparisons with Alzheimer's disease. *J. Neurol. Neurosurg. Psychiatry: 48,* 413 – 421, 1985.

Pillon B, Dubois B, L'hermite F, Agid Y: Heterogeneity of cognitive impairment in progressive supranuclear palsy, Parkinson's disease, and Alzheimer's disease. *Neurology: 36,* 1179 – 1185, 1986.

Poon LW: Differences in human memory with aging: nature, causes, and clinical implications. In Birren JE, Schaie KW (Editors), *Handbook of the Psychology of Aging* (2nd edn.). New York: Van Nostrand Reinhold, pp. 427 – 462, 1985.

Poon LW, Walsh-Sweeney L, Fozard JL: Memory skill training for the elderly: salient issues on the use of imagery mnemonics. In Poon LW, Fozard JL, Cermak LS, Arenberg D, Thompson LW (Editors), *New Directions in Memory and Aging.* Proceedings of the George A Talland memorial conference, Boston 1978. Hillsdale, NJ: Erlbaum, Ch. 26, pp. 461 – 484, 1980.

Quinn NP, Rossor MN, Marsden CD: Dementia and Parkinson's disease-pathological and neurochemical consideration. *Br. Med. Bull.: 42,* 86 – 90, 1986.

Rabinowitz JC: Priming in episodic memory. *J. Gerontol.: 41,* 204 – 213, 1986.

Riegel KF, Riegel RM: Development, drop and death. *Dev. Psychol.: 6,* 306 – 319, 1972.

Rossor MN, Iversen LL, Reynolds GP, Mountjoy CQ, Roth M: Neurochemical characteristics of early and late onset types of Alzheimer's disease. *Br. Med. J.: 288,* 961 – 963, 1984.

Roth M: The association of clinical and neurobiological findings and its bearing on the classification and aetiology of Alzheimer's disease. *Br. Med. Bull.: 42,* 42 – 50, 1986.

Roth M, Tym E, Mountjoy CQ, Huppert FA, Hendrie H, Verma S, Goddard R: CAMDEX: a standardized instrument for the diagnosis of mental disorder in the elderly with special reference to the early detection of dementia. *Br. J. Psychiatry: 149,* 698 – 709, 1986.

Rowe JW, Kahn RL: Human aging: usual and successful. *Science: 237,* 143 – 149, 1987.

Sagar HJ, Sullivan EV: Patterns of cognitive impairment in dementia. In Kennard C (Editor), *Recent Advances in Clinical Neurology.* London: Churchill Livingstone, Ch. 3, pp. 47 – 86, 1988.

Sagar HJ, Sullivan EV, Gabrieli JDE, Corkin S, Gerowdon JH: Temporal ordering and short-term memory deficits in Parkinson's disease. *Brain: 111,* 525 – 539, 1988.

Sahakian BJ, Morris RG, Evenden JL, Heald A, Levy R, Philpot M, Robbins TW: A comparative study of visuospatial memory and learning in Alzheimer-type dementia and Parkinson's disease. *Brain: 111,* 695 – 718, 1988.

Saint-Cyr JA, Taylor AE, Lang AE: Procedural versus declarative memory impairment in Parkinson's disease. Paper given at 9th International Symposium on Parkinson's disease, Jerusalem, 1988.

Salmon DP, Shimamura AP, Butters N, Smith S: Lexical and semantic priming deficits in patients with Alzheimer's disease. *J. Clin. Exp. Neuropsychol.: 10,* 477 – 494, 1988.

Salthouse TA: *Adult Cognition: An Experimental Psychology of Human Aging.* New York: Springer-Verlag, 1982.

Salthouse TA, Rogan JD, Prill K: Division of attention: Age differences on a visually presented memory task. *Mem. Cognition: 12,* 613 – 620, 1984.

Schacter DL, Harbluk JL, McLachlan DR: Retrieval without recollection: an experimental analysis of source amnesia. *J. Verbal Learn. Verbal Behav.: 23,* 593 – 611, 1984.

Schaie KW (Editor): The Seattle longitudinal study: a 21-year exploration of psychometric intelligence in adulthood. In *Longitudinal Studies of Adult Psychological Development.* New York: Guilford Press, Ch. 4, pp. 64 – 135, 1983.

Scheibel ME, Lindsay RD, Tomiyasu U, Scheibel AB: Progressive dendritic changes in aging human cortex. *Exp. Neurol.: 47,* 392 – 403, 1975.

Schonfield D, Robertson BA: Memory storage and aging. *Can. J. Psychol.: 20,* 228 – 236, 1966.

Scoville WB, Milner B: Loss of recent memory after bilateral hippocampal lesions. *J. Neurol. Neurosurg. Psychiatry: 20,* 11 – 21, 1957.

Shimamura AP, Salmon DP, Squire LR, Butters N: Memory dysfunction and word priming in dementia and amnesia. *Behav. Neurosci.: 101,* 347 – 351, 1987.

Smith AD, Winograd E: Age differences in recognising faces. *Dev. Psychol.: 14,* 443 – 444, 1978.

Spilich GJ: Life-span components of text processing: structural and procedural differences. *J. Verbal Learn. Verbal Behav. 22,* 231 – 244, 1983.

Squire LR: *Memory and Brain.* New York: Oxford University Press, 1987.

Stine EL, Wingfield A, Poon LW: How much and how fast: rapid processing of spoken language in later adulthood. *Psychol. Aging: 1,* 303 – 311, 1986.

Sunderland A, Harris JE, Baddeley AD: Do laboratory tests predict everyday memory? A neuropsychological study. *J. Verbal Learning Verbal Behav.: 22,* 341 – 357, 1983.

Sunderland A, Watts K, Baddeley AD, Harris JE: Subjective memory assessment and test performance in elderly adults. *J. Gerontol.: 41,* 376 – 384, 1986.

Sutcliffe RLG, Prior R, Mawby B, McQuillan WJ: Parkinson's disease in the district of the Northampton health authority, United Kingdom: a study of prevalence and disability. *Acta Neurol. Scand.: 72,* 363 – 379, 1985.

Talland GA: Age and the immediate memory span. *Gerontologist: 7,* 4 – 9, 1967.

Taylor AE, Saint-Cyr JA, Lang AE: Frontal lobe dysfunction in Parkinson's disease. *Brain: 109,* 845 – 883, 1986.

Terry RD, DeTeresa R, Hanse LA: Neocortical cell counts in normal human adult aging. *Ann. Neurol.: 21,* 530 – 539, 1987.

Tomlinson BE: Morphological brain changes in non-demented old people. In VanPraag HM, Kalverbove AF (Editors), *Aging of the Central Nervous System, Biological and Psychological Aspects.* Haarlem: De Erven F. Bohn, pp. 38 – 57, 1972.

Tomlinson BE: Neuropathology of aging. Sandoz Lecture, Institute of Neurology, Queen Square, London, 1985.

Tomlinson BE, Irving D, Blessed G: Cell loss in the locus coeruleus in senile dementia of Alzheimer type. *J. Neurol. Sci.: 49,* 419 – 428, 1981.

Tweedy JR, Langer KG, McDowell FH: The effect of semantic relations in the memory deficit associated with Parkinson's disease. *J. Clin. Neuropsychol.: 4,* 235 – 247, 1982.

Vijayashankar N, Brody H: A quantitative study of the pigmented neurons in the nuclei locus coeruleus and subcoeruleus in man as related to aging. *J. Neuropathol. Exp. Neurol.: 38,* 490 – 497, 1979.

Walsh KW: *Neuropsychology: A Clinical Approach.* Edinburgh: Churchill Livingstone, 1978.

Wechsler DA: A standardized memory scale for clinical use. *J. Psychol.: 19,* 87 – 95, 1945.

Weingartner H, Kaye W, Smallberg SA, Ebert MH, Gillan JC, Sitaram N: Memory failures in progressive idiopathic dementia. *J. Abnorm. Psychol.: 90,* 187 – 196, 1981.

Welford AT: *Aging and Human Skill.* London: Oxford University Press, 1958.

Wickelgren WA: Age and storage dynamics in continuous recognition memory. *Dev. Psychol.: 11,* 165 – 169, 1975.

Wilkie FJ, Eisdorfeer C, Nowling JB: Memory and blood pressure in the aged. *Exp. Aging Res.: 2,* 3 – 16, 1976.

Wilson B, Cockburn J, Baddeley AD: *The Rivermead Behavioural Memory Test.* Reading: Thames Valley Test Company, 1985.

Worden PE, Meggison DL: Aging and the category-recall relationship. *J. Gerontol.: 39,* 322 – 324, 1984.

World Health Organization. ICD-10. Draft of Chapter V.

Categories F00 – F99. Mental Behavioural and Developmental Disorders. Geneva, 1990.

Wright R: Aging, divided attention, and processing capacity. *J. Gerontol.: 36,* 605 – 614, 1981.

Zelinski EM, Gilewski MJ, Thompson LW: Do laboratory tests relate to self-assessment of memory ability in the young and old? In Poon LW, Fozard JL, Cermak LS, Arenberg D, Thompson LW (Editors), *New Directions in Memory and Aging.* Proceedings of the George A Talland memorial conference, Boston 1978. Hillsdale, NJ: Lawrence Erlbaum Associates, Ch. 30, pp. 519 – 544, 1980.

© 1991 Elsevier Science Publishers B.V.
Handbook of Neuropsychology, Vol. 5
F. Boller and J. Grafman (Eds)

CHAPTER 8

Differential effects of aging and age-related neurological diseases on memory subsystems of the brain

John D.E. Gabrieli

Department of Brain and Cognitive Sciences and Clinical Research Center, Massachusetts Institute of Technology, Cambridge, MA, U.S.A.

Introduction

The ability to learn new information dwindles with age, is at risk in Parkinson's disease (PD), and is impaired markedly in Alzheimer's disease (AD). Understanding age-related mnemonic disabilities in terms of specific brain functions is an important step in the rational search for treatments that could ameliorate or even cure disturbances of memory. Such an understanding, however, is difficult to achieve because the declines in memory are accompanied by complex patterns of age- and disease-related reductions in nonmnemonic mental capacities, such as attention, language and motor control. Further, neuropathology in these diseases and changes in brain function associated with aging are multifocal in nature, and it is difficult to relate multiple sites of neuropathology to multiple disturbances of cognition and memory.

One strategy for investigating the neural basis of memory loss in aging and age-related neurological diseases is to take advantage of what is known about the relatively pure losses of memory seen in patients with global amnesia. This chapter first summarizes what is known about learning capacities in global amnesia and how research with amnesic patients has led to the idea of memory subsystems. The second section raises significant interpretive issues that are part-and-parcel of a subsystems analysis of memory loss. The next sections apply memory subsystems analyses to disabilities in learning new information in AD, PD and typical aging. The final section presents a putative neural architecture of human memory built upon associations between specific learning impairments and characteristic neuropathology in amnesia, AD and PD.

Global amnesia and memory subsystems

Global amnesia is a neurological syndrome characterized by a deficit in learning new information that does not appear to be secondary to any other behavioral incapacity, as demonstrated by the integrity of attentional, perceptual, motor, motivational, language and reasoning capacities (Milner in Milner and Teuber, 1968). Immediate or short-term memory is relatively spared. Amnesic patients typically retain knowledge acquired in the remote past, although they do have retrograde amnesias that are most evident for the time just before the onset of their anterograde amnesia (e.g., Marslen-Wilson and Teuber, 1975; Albert et al., 1979). Global amnesia results from bilateral lesions of the limbic system, specifically medial temporal-lobe structures (including the hippocampus, amygdala and entorhinal cortex) (Scoville and Milner, 1957; Zola-Morgan et al., 1986), diencephalic structures (including the mediodorsal nucleus of the thalamus and mammillary bodies) (Victor et al., 1971), or basal forebrain structures (Damasio et al., 1985). Although there remains some uncertainty about the specific roles of the various limbic structures in new learning, there is a good correspondence between the sites of brain lesions that lead to amnesia in humans and the sites of experimental lesions that produce analogous memory deficits in monkeys (e.g., Mishkin, 1978; Mahut et al., 1982; Zola-Morgan and Squire, 1985, 1986).

Amnesic patients are impaired on *direct tests* of memory, tests in which subjects are asked explicitly to recall or recognize a particular event, such as a list of words that had been read aloud (the distinction between direct and indirect tests of memory comes from Johnson and Hasher, 1987, and Richardson-Klavehn and Björk, 1988). Direct tests of memory, in order of typical decreasing difficulty, include free recall, cued recall, yes/no recognition, and multiple-choice recognition. Severely amnesic patients exhibit a deficit on direct tests of memory regardless of the type of direct test employed (e.g., recall or recognition), the nature of stimulus materials (e.g., verbal or nonverbal), the modality of stimulus presentation (e.g., visual or auditory), or the nature of an event (e.g., a public or personal event). Others have termed this deficit as one in declarative (Cohen and Squire, 1980) or explicit (Graf and Schacter, 1985) memory. Experimental analysis of the amnesic syndrome has revealed that patients forget not only particular events (such as personal experiences or materials presented in experimental episodes) but also the sorts of knowledge that people acquire in everyday life, such as the meanings of words that newly enter the language (Gabrieli et al., 1988). Thus, amnesic patients have a deficit in the kind of memory that not only records events but also transforms the knowledge gained in those events into the sort of facts about the world (generic or semantic information) that people learn without necessarily remembering the events in which they encountered that information. It may be said, therefore, that amnesic patients have a deficit in *event-fact memory* and that the limbic structures damaged in amnesia constitute important parts of an event-fact memory subsystem.

Amnesic patients appear unable to gain any sort of new knowledge normally. Experimental research, however, has revealed some sorts of learning

that are nearly or entirely normal in even the most amnesic patients. The preserved learning capacities are manifest on *indirect tests* of memory, tests in which no explicit reference is made to a prior event. Instead, learning is inferred by experiment-induced changes in the speed, accuracy or bias with which subjects perform a task. Indirect testing of memory is not a sufficient condition to detect preserved learning in amnesia (e.g., Cermak et al., 1988; Gabrieli et al., 1988), but it does appear to be a necessary condition. Amnesic patients have shown preserved learning on indirect tests of memory in three broad domains: *skill learning, repetition priming* and *perceptual aftereffects.* Cases of preserved learning in amnesia have been considered to reflect procedural (Cohen and Squire, 1980) or implicit (Graf and Schacter, 1985) memory.

In skill-learning tasks, subjects perform a challenging task on repeated trials in one or more sessions. The (indirect) measure of learning is the improvement in speed or accuracy achieved by a subject across trials and sessions. Amnesic patients have shown normal or near-normal acquisition and retention of *sensorimotor skills* on such tasks as mirror tracing (Milner, 1962), rotary persuit (Corkin, 1968; Cermak et al., 1973; Brooks and Baddeley, 1976; Cohen, 1981) and serial reaction time (Nissen and Bullemer, 1987). They have also learned some *perceptual skills,* such as reading mirror-reversed text (Cohen and Squire, 1980; Martone et al., 1984), and some *problem-solving skills,* such as solving the Tower-of-Hanoi problem (Cohen and Corkin, 1981; Saint-Cyr et al., 1988; but see Butters et al., 1985; Gabrieli et al., 1987) and learning an algorithm to square two-digit numbers mentally (Charness et al., 1988; Milberg et al., 1988). Amnesic patients gain and maintain mastery on these difficult tasks despite being unable to recall the episodes in which they learned their skill, unable to recognize the materials they encountered in those episodes, and unaware of their newly acquired prowess.

The second major class of tasks on which amnesic patients have shown spared learning are *repetition priming* tasks. Priming experiments typically consist of two phases: a study phase in which subjects are presented with a series of stimuli and a test phase in which subjects process the same stimuli again. Changes in the speed, accuracy or bias with which the repeated stimuli are reprocessed (relative to their initial processing or an appropriate baseline measure) provide a measure of learning called repetition priming. A different sort of priming is semantic priming, which probes the structure and function of long-term semantic memory (e.g., that 'doctor' and 'nurse' are related words), and which dissipates quickly even in young, healthy subjects (e.g., Dannenbring and Briand, 1982). Because this chapter focuses on the learning of information that enters long-term memory, semantic priming is not reviewed and the term priming refers only to repetition priming (see Nebes, 1989, for a review of semantic priming in AD).

Most repetition priming tasks used with amnesic patients may be classified as being primarily percept-limited or concept-limited. *Percept-limited* tasks pose problems in the identification of visually degraded stimuli, such as incomplete figures, incomplete words or very briefly presented words. *Concept-limited* tasks require subjects to retrieve a word from a category of words on the basis of a conceptual criterion, such as producing a word that begins with three particular letters (e.g., STA__) or that belongs to a particular semantic category (e.g., BIRDS). Performance on these tasks is constrained by the ability of subjects to retrieve an appropriate response from their knowledge of words and their meanings. Amnesic patients have shown normal or near-normal levels of repetition priming on percept-limited tasks (Milner et al., 1968; Warrington and Weiskrantz, 1968, 1970; Cermak et al., 1985; Gabrieli, 1986) and on concept-limited tasks (e.g., Warrington and Weiskrantz, 1970; Graf et al., 1984; Shimamura and Squire, 1984; Gabrieli, 1986). It is striking when an amnesic patient exhibits normal repetition priming following one exposure to a word but cannot recall or recognize the word.

Finally, amnesic patients exhibit long-lasting tactual and visual perceptual aftereffects despite their poor memory for the perceptual experience that produced the aftereffect (Benzing and Squire, 1989; Savoy and Gabrieli, in press). For example, the McCollough effect (McCollough, 1965) is a long-lasting pattern-contingent color aftereffect. In one version of this aftereffect, subjects are exposed for five minutes to two alternating adapting patterns: a green-and-black square wave pattern with bars oriented at $+45°$ and a magenta-and-black square wave pattern with bars oriented at $-45°$. Subsequently, subjects perceive a neutral pattern with black bars oriented at $+45°$ as a magenta pattern and a neutral pattern with black bars oriented at $-45°$ as a green pattern. An amnesic patient who could not recall either the patterns or the colors seen in the adapting phase nevertheless exhibited a McCollough effect of normal magnitude and duration (Savoy and Gabrieli, in press).

The presence of preserved and compromised learning capacities in amnesia provides strong evidence for the separability of the neural circuits mediating those learning capacities. The separable neural circuits constitute distinct memory subsystems, a memory subsystem being defined as the minimal neural circuit needed to record, retain and retrieve a form of knowledge. Indeed, the evidence for distinct memory subsystems is so compelling that most theories about the neural organization of human memory processes are founded upon dissociations between preserved and compromised learning abilities in amnesic patients (e.g., procedural/ declarative (Cohen and Squire, 1980) and implicit/explicit (Graf and Schacter, 1985)). The development of theories about the neural architecture of human memory, however, demands that a distinction be made between tests of memory and kinds of memory. A test of memory is composed of the task that a subject is asked to do (e.g., instructions, stimulus materials) and the measure of performance on that task (e.g., percentage correct or speed of response). A kind of memory refers to a class of computations that support one aspect of memory performance across tests or tasks. When a specific kind of memory can be linked to a particular neural substrate, one has identified a putative memory subsystem.

Applying memory subsystems analyses to normal aging and age-related neurological diseases

A number of interpretive problems may arise in the effort to relate test performance to the integrity of putative memory subsystems. At present, there are no formal solutions to these problems. Rather, any particular finding must be evaluated in the context of prior patient research as well as converging evidence from the cognitive sciences and from the basic neurosciences.

One problem follows from the fact that different sorts of measurement scales are often used to measure performance on direct versus indirect tests of memory. Direct measures of memory are expressed typically as the number or percentage correct (e.g., performance on recall or recognition tests). Indirect measures are expressed typically as changes in speed (e.g., performance on mirror tracing, rotary pursuit, serial reaction time or lexical decision tests). The different measurement scales are likely to differ in sensitivity and be differentially susceptible to floor or ceiling effects. Consequently, an apparent dissociation between impaired and intact learning could reflect differences in measurement scales rather than differences in the integrity of neurally distinct memory subsystems. The use of different measurement scales may be unavoidable because different measures may be needed to assess the different forms of learning mediated by neurally distinct memory subsystems.

Evidence for the existence of a memory subsystem comes from preserved learning in memory-disordered patients. It is difficult to specify, however, what degree of learning is required to provide such evidence. In some instances, patients have shown entirely normal learning on a particular test, providing unambiguous evidence in favor of the existence of a distinct memory subsystem. In other instances, patients have shown less learning on a task than normal control subjects but more learning than might have been expected by virtue of their amnesia. Such instances of relatively intact learning require careful interpretation because they raise two possibilities that have quite different implications

for the identification of memory subsystems. One possibility is that the indirect measure obtained is a more sensitive index of event-fact memory than the direct measure that was employed. In this instance, no evidence for a subsystem has been garnered. Such a finding is far from meaningless. For example, it may be useful in quantifying a memory subsystem's degree of impairment in a group of subjects. The second possibility is that a task is evoking two memory subsystems, one that is intact and one that is impaired. To the extent that the task taps the intact subsystem, the memory-disordered subjects will approach the learning shown by control subjects. In that instance, the indirect test of memory is an impure measure of the kind of learning mediated by the intact memory subsystem.

Another issue of interpretation arises because AD, PD and normal aging affect a variety of behavioral domains, and these subject groups often have significant nonmnemonic deficits. Most skill-learning and some repetition-priming tasks compare an initial or baseline measure of performance to a performance after repeated trials. The nonmnemonic deficits of the patient or older groups may make their baseline performance worse than that of control or younger groups. For example, many patients with early AD have difficulties with naming (e.g., Huff et al., 1986) that may result in an impaired baseline score on a perceptual learning task that uses naming as a response. In such cases, there are two possible criteria for establishing the presence of 'normal' learning: a normal change in the absolute magnitude or a normal change in the percentage relative to baseline. One candidate solution to this scoring problem is to equate or normalize baseline performance by making the task easier for the patient or the older group (e.g., Heindel et al., 1988, 1989). This approach, however, poses as substantial an interpretive problem as different baselines because the two groups are actually performing different tasks that may or may not involve the same psychological processes and neural substrates.

Two other issues arise in memory subsystems studies in AD, PD or normal aging that do not pertain to studies with amnesic patients. The most common strategy in exploring the status of memory subsystems in AD, PD or healthy older subjects is to use a memory test that previously revealed intact learning in amnesic patients. However, the only way to know for certain that a test of memory given in a particular way reveals preserved learning in amnesia is to administer that test to amnesic patients. Thus, a study of AD, PD or normal aging that includes amnesic patients as a control group can provide strong evidence that a skill learning or priming protocol being used does not draw upon event-fact memory (e.g., Corkin, 1982; Gabrieli, 1986; Shimamura et al., 1987; Saint-Cyr et al., 1988). Because global amnesia occurs rarely, however, many studies may not have amnesic patients available as a control group. For those studies, methodological details (e.g., instructions, stimulus materials, delays) need to be considered carefully if the performance of AD, PD or normal older subjects is to be compared to that of amnesic patients in other studies.

A second factor that differentiates memory subsystem analyses in AD, PD and normal aging from those done with amnesic patients is that amnesic patients are selected for studies on the basis of a behavioral syndrome rather than a disease or an age. Indeed, it is common to have amnesic patients with different etiologies of amnesia (e.g., alcoholism versus anoxia) and different sites of lesions (e.g., diencephalic versus medial temporal) included in the same study. Although differences in etiology and locus of lesion are important for some aspects of amnesia (e.g., Squire, 1982), most patients with severe global amnesia show the same pattern of impaired recall and recognition and spared skill learning, priming and perceptual aftereffects (Gabrieli, 1986). For studies of normal aging and of age-related neurological diseases, however, subject selection is not usually conducted on the basis of behavioral criteria but rather on the basis of age or diagnosis. Thus, three quite different aims of such studies may be differentiated. One aim is to characterize the pattern of memory functions and dysfunctions associated with a disease or a certain

age. A second and different aim is to characterize memory functions in a select subgroup of subjects, e.g., untreated PD patients who are not demented or healthy subjects who are in their eighties. Subgroups of AD, PD and normal older subjects are more likely to be homogeneous in terms of brain functions than unselected groups, and such studies may be of particular value in establishing brain – behavior relations. A third aim is to search for dissociations among memory functions and thus identify memory subsystems. It may be that atypical cases of PD, for example, could provide strong evidence about memory subsystems despite being unrepresentative of PD. It is useful to remember the different aims of studies examining memory in AD, PD or normal aging when generalizing across studies.

Potential interpretive problems in the identification of memory subsystems ought not to obscure the considerable appeal of subsystems analyses of memory loss in humans. Memory subsystems analyses of amnesia are founded upon a stringent behavioral criterion: the experimental demonstration of preserved learning in patients with severe memory disorders. The demonstration of preserved learning may be even more remarkable (albeit more prone to interpretive problems) in groups who have the widespread disturbances of cognition associated with aging and age-associated neurological diseases. Also, memory subsystems analyses of human amnesia have shown strong concordances with animal research with regard to impaired and preserved learning capacities (e.g., Zola-Morgan and Squire, 1984). Consequently, such analyses provide important links between diseases of human memory and animal models of those diseases. Finally, there have been surprising parallels between dissociations of spared and compromised learning in amnesia and the apparent organization of normal human memory (e.g., Graf et al., 1982). These parallels suggest that the neural organization of memory subsystems creates strong constraints upon the operations of normal memory, constraints that may have to a play a role in a deep understanding of human learning and memory.

Memory subsystems in Alzheimer's disease

AD patients become increasingly demented; severely demented patients can perform only the simplest tasks, if any. Therefore, memory subsystems analyses are applicable primarily to patients in the early stages of AD, i.e., patients with mild or moderate dementia.

Event-fact memory

Patients must have a deficit in event-fact memory in order to meet the DSM-III (1980) diagnostic criteria for dementia. Many studies have documented the event-fact memory deficit in AD patients (e.g., Corkin, 1982; Shimamura et al., 1987; Heindel et al., 1988, 1989; Sagar et al., 1988; Sullivan et al., 1989; Gabrieli et al., submitted; Keane et al., submitted). Mildly and moderately demented AD patients demonstrate recall and recognition deficits that are comparable quantitatively to those of most patients with global amnesia (e.g., Corkin, 1982; Gabrieli, 1986; Shimamura et al., 1987; Heindel et al., 1988). It is likely, however, that memory test scores of AD patients reflect a combination of mnemonic and nonmnemonic (e.g., attention, language) disturbances whereas the scores of amnesic patients reflect more pure mnemonic dysfunction.

Skill learning

Sensorimotor tasks The first formal examination of skill learning in AD patients used the rotary pursuit task (Eslinger and Damasio, 1986). AD and control subjects were asked to maintain contact between a hand-held stylus and a target metal disk, the size of a nickel, on a revolving turntable. With practice, normal subjects increased the time per trial that they were able to maintain contact with the disk. Despite an initial level of performance that was 45% below that of normal control subjects, the AD patients exhibited normal improvement and retention, over a delay of 30 minutes, of a skill for rotary pursuit. After training, the AD patients had a level of performance only 10% below that of control subjects. In order to equate initial performance on the rotary pursuit task, Heindel et al. (1988) adjusted the speed of the rotor for each subject to that speed at which the subject came closest to an initial time-on-target of 5 seconds (in a 20-second trial). In that study (and in a subsequent replication, Heindel et al., 1989), the learning exhibited by the AD patients was indistinguishable from that of normal control subjects. Moreover, there is evidence that AD patients retain their rotary pursuit skill almost normally over a 24-hour period (Corkin et al., 1986).

Gabrieli (1986) examined the performance of AD patients on a second sensorimotor skill learning task, mirror tracing. AD patients and normal control subjects had to trace a five-pointed star with a stylus without seeing their hand, the stylus, or the star except as reflected in a mirror. They did so in three sessions on three consecutive days. Patients and control subjects made successively fewer errors (i.e., tracing departed from the star fewer times) and decreased the time needed to trace the star. Some of the AD patients were unable to do the task. Those AD patients who did do the task, however, demonstrated normal improvement across sessions despite 24-hour intervals between each of three sessions. Further, the AD patients (and amnesic patients) were able to transfer normally their mirror-tracing skill from one pattern to another.

Knopman and Nissen (1987) tested the performance of 28 AD patients on a serial reaction time task. On each trial, a light appeared at one of four possible locations on a computer monitor. Responses were made by pressing one of four keys, with each key placed directly below one of the four monitor locations. As soon as a light appeared, the subject pressed the corresponding key. Subjects made few errors, and the measure of performance was the speed of response. Subjects were given 5 blocks of 100 trials each. Unbeknownst to the subjects, the trials in the first four blocks were arranged in a repeating 10-trial sequence. The trials in the last block appeared randomly in the four locations (i.e., without any repeating pattern). Control subjects improved the speed of their reaction times across the four blocks of repeating trials. The increased speed of response was attributed to subjects learning the sequence, because their reaction times slowed sharply in the fifth, random block of trials. AD patients were slower than control subjects. The patients, however, improved their speed of response across the repeating-sequence blocks and showed the typical slowing when the block of random trials was administered. Examination of the individual performances of the AD patients revealed that 9 of the 28 AD patients failed to show evidence of learning the sequence in that those patients had response times in the fifth, random block that were as fast as or faster than shown in the last block of the repeating sequence trials. There were no evident differences between the 19 'learners' and 9 'nonlearners' in terms of age, sex, severity of dementia, or scores on standard tests of memory and language. There were, however, significant differences between the two groups of AD patients on two tests: WAIS block design (raw score) and Porteus Mazes. The especially poor performance of the 'nonlearner' AD patients on these two visuospatial attention-demanding tasks provides a clue about the functional basis of learning the repeating sequence (see also Nissen and Bullemer, 1987). The Knopman and Nissen result also underscores the importance of testing a large number of AD patients on a task if the aim of the study is to characterize the status of a particular learning capacity in AD. Had they examined a small number of subjects, their results could have been taken to be evidence that AD patients can learn the sequence (if the sample had been composed of mostly 'learners') or that AD patients cannot learn the sequence (if the sample had been composed mainly of 'nonlearners').

Priming

Concept-limited tasks   Most studies examining priming in AD have used a concept-limited priming task, word completion. Subjects saw words in a study phase (e.g., STAMP). Then, they were presented with the three-letter stems of those words (e.g., STA__) and additional stems that served as a baseline measure. Every stem had 10 or more possible completions. Subjects were asked to complete each stem to the first word that they could think of; no reference was made to the fact that a possible answer had been presented in the study phase. Normal subjects are known to provide the words seen in the study phase at a rate above chance, and amnesic patients show a priming effect of normal magnitude and duration (Warrington and Weiskrantz, 1970; Graf et al., 1984). Four studies have found significantly reduced word-completion priming in AD patients (Gabrieli, 1986; Shimamura et al., 1987; Salmon et al., 1988; Heindel et al., 1989). The low level of word-completion priming was especially striking in that two of the studies (Gabrieli, 1986; Shimamura et al., 1987) included amnesic patients whose recall and recognition scores were no better than those of the AD patients but whose word-completion priming was equivalent to that of normal subjects. Reduced word-completion priming is likely to be related to the language problems evident in many AD patients, but the nature of that relation has not yet been determined.

Percept-limited tasks   Although most studies of priming in AD have examined concept-limited priming, two studies have investigated percept-limited priming in AD using tasks that have revealed substantial priming in amnesic patients: the Gollin incomplete-figures task (Milner et al., 1968; Warrington and Weiskrantz, 1968) and the identification of very briefly presented words (Cermak et al., 1985; Gabrieli and Keane, 1988). In the Gollin task, the stimulus materials consisted of simple line drawings of 20 animals and common objects, each in five degrees of fragmentation (from Gollin, 1960). On the first trial, all drawings were presented in their most fragmented version, and the subject was encouraged to guess what each one represented. This procedure continued through four more trials, with the drawings becoming more complete on each successive trial. The identification scores from the initial session provided an index of competence in visual perception and naming. The same procedure was repeated, without warning, an hour later. The reduction of identification errors from the first to the second session constituted a subject's priming score. Thirteen AD patients were given the incomplete-figures test described above in the same way that the test had been administered to an amnesic patient (Milner et al., 1968). Although they performed more poorly (i.e., had a worse baseline score) on the test than normal control or amnesic subjects, the AD patients showed the same absolute magnitude of priming (improvement between the two testing sessions) as the amnesic patients (Gabrieli et al., submitted).

In a second study of a percept-limited priming in AD, Keane et al. (submitted) used a perceptual identification paradigm that had yielded normal priming in amnesic patients (Cermak et al., 1985; their paradigm was based upon that of Jacoby and Dallas, 1981). In the study phase, AD patients and control subjects read words presented on a computer monitor. In the test phase, subjects were presented words very briefly, and the minimum presentation time needed to read a word correctly was recorded on each trial. Half of the test-phase words had been seen in the study phase and half were new words that had not been seen in the study phase. The measure of priming was the advantage subjects showed for reading previously seen versus previously unseen (new) words. The AD patients required longer presentations than the control subjects in order to read the words correctly, but they displayed the same absolute magnitude of priming as did the control subjects. Although the AD patients' impaired baseline performance precludes drawing a strong conclusion from the results of the above two studies, the normal magnitudes of priming exhibited by the patients suggest that percept-limited priming may be intact in early AD.

Perceptual aftereffects

Savoy and Gabrieli (1991, in press) examined the status of the McCollough effect (McCollough, 1965) in five mildly-to-moderate demented AD patients with the protocol described earlier. The patients exhibited an aftereffect with a magnitude and a duration (delays of 5, 25 and 60 minutes) equal to that shown by normal control subjects.

Summary

Despite their severe impairments on tests of recall and recognition, AD patients exhibit nearly normal learning on sensorimotor skill-learning tasks (although the problems of different levels of baseline performance are apparent on those tasks). Thus, most mildly-to-moderately demented AD patients exhibit the same pattern of impaired event-fact memory and intact sensorimotor skill learning as do amnesic patients. AD patients also are similar to at least one amnesic patient in that they have an intact perceptual aftereffect in the McCollough paradigm.

Unlike amnesic patients, AD patients are often impaired on word-completion priming tasks. Thus, AD patients provide evidence in favor of separable neural bases for sensorimotor skill learning, intact in most mildly demented patients, and concept-limited priming, impaired in most such patients. In fact, the dissociation been between intact skill learning and impaired priming has been demonstrated within the same groups of AD patients (Gabrieli, 1986; Heindel et al., 1989). Although Huntington's disease (HD) is not an age-related disease, it is a neurodegenerative disease that includes dementia as a cardinal feature. HD patients have shown impaired learning on the rotary pursuit task and intact word-completion priming (Heindel et al., 1988, 1989). Thus, the AD and HD studies provide a double dissociation between sensorimotor skill learning (preserved in AD but not HD) and concept-limited priming (preserved in HD but not AD). Finally, studies with AD patients suggest a possible dissociation between concept-limited priming (reduced absolute magnitude in AD) and percept-limited priming (normal absolute magnitude in AD).

Memory subsystems in Parkinson's disease

James Parkinson (1817) contrasted the 'shaking palsy' motor impairment of PD with 'the senses and intellect being uninjured'. More recent studies have come to three contradictory conclusions: PD patients are cognitively intact (e.g., Matthews and Haaland, 1979), PD patients have pervasive cognitive impairments (e.g., Pirozzolo et al., 1982), or PD patients have specific cognitive deficits (e.g., Lees and Smith, 1983; Growdon et al., 1990). Further complicating any overall conclusion about the status of cognition in PD is the fact that some, but certainly not all, PD patients evince a clinical dementia. Estimates of the prevalence of dementia in PD range from 2 to 93% (Growdon and Corkin, 1986).

Two factors may account for the remarkable range of findings about cognition and dementia in PD. First, measures of cognition and operational definitions of dementia vary from study to study. There is strong evidence that many PD patients are prone to a specific class of cognitive impairments: PD patients who score normally on many measures of cognition and memory may, nevertheless, demonstrate impaired performance on tasks that are sensitive to frontal-lobe dysfunction, such as card sorting and verbal fluency (e.g., Cools et al., 1984; Lees and Smith, 1983; Taylor et al., 1986). Consequently, studies including tests that require the class of cognitive operations supported by the frontal lobes tend to find pervasive cognitive deficits in PD patients. Further, it is unclear how such specific impairment fits in with dementia classification schemes formed primarily upon experience with AD patients who have multiple kinds of cognitive impairment (Sagar and Sullivan, 1988).

Second, there is growing evidence that patients with PD constitute a spectrum of subgroups in terms of brain – behavior relations. Some significant variables have been identified for the subgrouping of PD patients. First, there appear to be tonic and phasic cognitive consequences of drug-treatment in PD patients (e.g., Gotham et al., 1988). Second, patients vary in response to drug therapy, and there is evidence that treatment responsiveness (e.g., good, poor or variable) is associated with variable patterns of cognitive impairment, although such variation may have relatively limited influence on event-fact memory (Taylor et al., 1987). Third, some patients with PD are depressed and score significantly lower on some tests of event-fact memory than nondepressed PD patients (Taylor et al., 1986).

Fourth, age of onset appears to be an important variable. Patients with late-onset PD appear to be prone to more widespread and more severe cognitive impairments than those with early-onset PD when compared to age-matched control subjects (Wilson et al., 1980; Hietanen et al., 1988; Dubois et al., 1990).

These patient characteristics have been shown to be of sufficient importance that further studies of cognition in PD are likely to be of substantial value only if the PD patients are carefully characterized in terms of dementia, depression, disease severity, age of onset and treatment factors as measured by specific and quantitative criteria. Many early studies examining cognition in PD did not characterize patients in terms of dementia. More recent studies of PD have characterized PD patients in terms of the presence or absence of dementia in an effort to avoid a confounding influence of AD. One study included separate groups of demented and nondemented PD patients (Heindel et al., 1989). Thus, there is already a trend towards using selected PD groups, but future studies may be able to select even more biologically homogeneous PD subgroups and offer increasingly precise identification of memory subsystems. Even with careful patient characterization, some important variables may not be identifiable in vivo by current techniques. For example, post-mortem studies indicate that demented PD patients include two major subgroups: a subgroup that has PD only and whose dementia is due primarily to subcortical damage and a subgroup that has PD and AD and whose dementia reflects cortical and subcortical damage (de la Monte et al., 1989).

Event-fact memory
Many studies find event-fact memory deficits in PD patients on tests of recall and recognition (for reviews see Growdon and Corkin, 1986; Sagar and Sullivan, 1988; Growdon et al., 1990). Many, but not all, of those studies were done before the importance of the patient variables discussed above was fully appreciated. It is now clear that many PD patients have event-fact memory deficits, but some nondemented (treated or untreated) PD patients ex-

hibit normal event-fact learning when that sort of learning is assessed by Wechsler Memory Scale subtests (Logical Memory, Visual Reproduction) or other standard tests of verbal recall and recognition (e.g., Lees and Smith, 1983; Taylor et al., 1986, 1987; Saint-Cyr et al., 1988; Sagar et al., 1988; Heindel et al., 1989). It is, therefore, impossible to generalize about the status of event-fact memory in PD beyond saying that event-fact memory is at risk but may be spared in any individual or group according to a specific measure of memory. One aspect of memory performance in these patients is unique: PD patients may exhibit an impairment in immediate recall or recognition for information that they are later unimpaired in recalling and recognizing (Taylor et al., 1986; Sagar et al., 1988). Thus, short-term memory may be impaired relative to long-term memory in PD, whereas long-term memory is always impaired relative to short-term memory in global amnesia. Under some conditions, then, the influence of time upon event-fact memory performance in some PD patients is the opposite of that seen in patients with global amnesia.

Even patients with PD who are not demented and have normal long-term event-fact learning capacities often exhibit impairments on direct tests of memory that are also failed by patients with frontal-lobe lesions (Table 1). PD patients are known to have a dopaminergic cell loss in the substantia nigra, cells that are efferent to the neostriatum. The neostriatal structures, in turn, are extensively interconnected with prefrontal regions (Delong et al., 1983; Alexander et al., 1986). It is hypothesized that the dopaminergic cell loss in PD patients disturbs the normal interactions between frontal and neostriatal regions, resulting in a dysfunction of cognitive operations dependent upon the frontal lobes.

PD patients' deficits in temporal ordering (Sagar et al., 1988) are not limited to information drawn from newly gained knowledge. In one study, PD patients had to arrange pictures placed before them in the proper order to convey a meaningful story (Picture Arrangement subtest of the Wechsler Adult Intelligence Test – Revised) (Sullivan et al., 1989). The Picture Arrangement subtest could be called a test of temporal order in that the correct arrangement of the pictures displays a story that unfolds in a particular order over time. The subtest, however, does not include a long-term memory demand because all the pictures are present at all times in front of the subject. Nevertheless, nondemented PD patients were impaired on this task. It may be hypothesized that the failure of the PD patients on the temporal ordering and picture-arrangement tasks arose from a reduced *planning-selection* capacity (what Norman and Shallice (1980) have termed the supervisory attentional system and what Baddeley (1986) has termed the central executive component of working memory). The temporal ordering and picture arrangement tasks may require subjects to make novel kinds of judgments. In order to make such judgments, subjects may have to develop a plan, such as devising a plausible story line for the pictures or a way of reconstructing temporal order. Then, subjects may select their response

TABLE 1

Memory impairments common to patients with frontal-lobe lesions or Parkinson's disease

Memory impairment	Frontal-lobe lesions	Parkinson's disease
Temporal order	Milner, 1971	Sagar et al., 1988
Source	Janowsky et al., 1989	Taylor et al., 1989
Conditional associative learning	Petrides, 1985	Gotham et al., 1988[a]
Self-ordered pointing	Petrides and Milner, 1982	Gotham et al., 1988[a]
Recall relative to recognition	Jetter et al., 1986	Taylor et al., 1986

[a]On Levadopa only.

under the supvervision of the novel plan. The PD
patients may have had an impaired ability to perform such a planning-selection operation whether
the operation was applied to information drawn
from perception (picture arrangement) or from
memory (temporal ordering). By this view, the frontal lobes may not store long-term memories per se,
but could be essential for the expression of memory
in tasks that demand substantial restructuring of acquired knowledge (i.e., when a memory task cannot
be accomplished on the basis of content-addressable
memory operations).

Skill learning

Sensorimotor tasks   Nondemented PD patients
appear to acquire and retain the skill for rotary pursuit performance despite their extrapyramidal
motor disease (Heindel et al., 1989). Demented PD
patients, however, fail to show normal learning on
this task. This deficit is notable because the
demented PD patients were no more motorically impaired than the nondemented PD patients according
to rating scale estimates of tremor, rigidity or
bradykinesia. Also, the demented PD patients were
less demented according to a dementia rating scale
than the AD patients who showed normal learning
on the task.

Problem-solving tasks   Perhaps the most surprising and least well understood case of preserved learning in amnesic patients was their acquisition and
retention of the optimal solution for the complex
Tower of Hanoi problem (Cohen and Corkin,
1981). In order to examine the status of problem-
solving learning in PD, Saint-Cyr et al. (1988)
created an easier version of the Tower of Hanoi problem which they called the Tower of Toronto. At the
outset of the Tower of Toronto problem, four
different-colored disks were arranged on the leftmost of three pegs. Subjects had to move the disks
from the leftmost to the rightmost peg in as few
moves as possible and observing two rules: they
could only move one disk at a time and they could
never move a darker disk on top of a lighter one. The

optimal solution (i.e., the least number of moves) required 15 moves and there was only one optimal sequence of moves. Saint-Cyr at al.'s procedure began
with subjects performing a 3-disk version three
times in order to acquaint subjects with the task and
to establish a baseline measure of problem-solving
ability. The 3-disk version requires the same sort of
planning ability as the 4-disk version, but there is
relatively little new learning involved because most
subjects recognize the optimal 7-move solution in
the first or second trial. Subjects then proceeded to
5 trials of the more difficult 4-block problem in each
of two sessions with 90 minutes between the sessions. Twenty-four nondemented PD patients were
unimpaired on 5 tests of event-fact memory, were
unimpaired in their ability to solve the 3-disk puzzle,
but were impaired significantly in learning the 4-
disk version of the Tower of Toronto. Two amnesic
patients presented the opposite pattern of intact and
impaired learning: they were severely impaired on
the tests of event-fact memory but unimpaired in
learning the Tower of Toronto.

Priming

Heindel et al. (1989) examined the performance of
nondemented and demented PD patients on a word-
completion priming task. The nondemented patients exhibited normal levels of priming, but the
demented PD patients had significantly reduced
levels of priming.

Summary

PD patients may have intact or impaired event-fact
memory depending upon patient characteristics and
upon the measure of memory. Some PD patients appear to have preserved event-fact memory capacities
except for tests of memory that demand considerable planning, such as temporal order
discriminations. Impaired performance on such
tasks may be interpreted as a deficit secondary to impaired planning capacities that are evident on tasks
that do not require new learning. Also, PD patients
may exhibit greater short-term than long-term
memory deficits. Overall, nondemented PD patients have a pattern of memory performance that is

more similar to patients with frontal-lobe lesions than to amnesic patients (Table 1).

There have not been many priming studies done with PD patients, but the available evidence shows that nondemented PD patients have normal priming capacities. Demented PD patients are like AD patients with regard to showing reduced priming on a word-completion task. The two groups of demented patients differ, however, with respect to sensorimotor skill learning, impaired in demented PD patients but intact in AD patients.

Nondemented PD patients show normal skill learning on a sensorimotor task (rotary pursuit), and other nondemented PD patients show impaired skill learning on a problem-solving task (Tower of Toronto). The contrast in learning on these two tasks in PD suggests a dissociation between two kinds of skill learning (Gabrieli, 1989). The kind of skill learning required for learning the Tower of Toronto task involves planning ahead and selecting appropriate moves in the context of the plan. Such learning may reflect the operations of a planning-selection memory subsystem. Learning on the rotary pursuit task may depend upon the improved execution of a motor program and reflect the operations of a compilation-action subsystem. The compilation-action subsystem may be damaged in demented PD patients and in HD patients, two groups who fail to show the good rotary pursuit learning exhibited by amnesic, AD and nondemented PD patients.

Memory subsystems in aging

Studies of 'normal' or typical aging pose considerable methodological and theoretical challenges (Salthouse, 1982; Rowe and Kahn, 1987). Studies examining the effect of aging upon learning in terms of memory subsystems have been cross-sectional and have assumed a 'normal' model of aging. Cross-sectional studies compare memory performance of subjects in different age groups and are susceptible to confounding cohort effects (differences between the groups of different ages that are not due to aging itself). Longitudinal studies have shown that age-related declines in cognitive functions are considerably smaller than indicated by cross-sectional studies (Schaie and Labouvie-Vief, 1974), presumably due to confounding cohort effects. In addition, it is difficult to know what criteria ought to be used for selecting comparable groups of different ages. Most recent cross-sectional studies of aging and memory, including the studies reviewed below, have used some instrument to rule out dementia in their older subject groups. These studies, however, have subscribed to a 'normal' model of aging that does not distinguish between successful aging and usual aging (Rowe and Kahn, 1987); in the latter case extrinsic factors exaggerate the effects of aging alone. Studies that include older subjects of both kinds may fail to detect good memory performance in older subjects who are aging successfully. In the future, more attention will be paid to these important issues in the analysis of the effects of aging upon memory. These issues, however, do not invalidate the results reviewed below because cross-sectional studies of 'normal' aging enhance the probability of finding impaired memory performance in older subjects relative to younger subjects. Consequently, examples of preserved learning abilities in older subjects are all the more impressive in studies that may tend to overestimate declines in memory performance due to aging.

Event-fact memory

Many studies document a reduction in event-fact memory through the course of aging (for reviews, see Craik, 1977; Salthouse, 1982). As in the case of the far more memory-impaired amnesic patients, older subjects show less decline in short-term memory and in their fund of general knowledge. Craik (1989) has summarized a great deal of research in this area by noting that memory tasks requiring self-initiated activity (e.g., free recall) are more susceptible to the deleterious effects of aging than tasks with environmental support (e.g., recognition). Older subjects are also impaired on tests of source memory (McIntyre and Craik, 1987; Janowsky et al., 1989). It was noted earlier that, under some circumstances, patients with frontal-lobe lesions or PD exhibit impaired memory when asked to recall stimulus items or their source, despite good recognition memory (Table 1). It is likely that normal aging influences many aspects of localizable brain function, but it is striking that those aspects of memory dependent upon the frontal lobes appear to be most vulnerable in older subjects. Older subjects often have deficits relative to younger subjects on recognition tests, however, so that the difficulties with memory that accompany aging cannot be ascribed solely to frontal-lobe types of dysfunctions.

Priming

Several cross-sectional studies have compared young and old subjects on recall and recognition measures versus priming measures. Light and Singh (1987) compared the performance of younger (19 – 33 years) and older (60 – 78 years) subjects on direct tests of event-fact memory (free recall, cued recall, yes/no recognition) and on indirect tests of percept-limited priming (perceptual identification) and concept-limited priming (word completion). Older subjects performed significantly less well than younger subjects on most of the recall and recognition measures, but were not significantly impaired on either of the priming measures. Another study (Light et al., 1986) compared the performance of younger (19 – 35 years) and older subjects (61 – 81 years) on a yes/no recognition test and on a test of concept-limited priming (fragment completion). Older subjects performed significantly worse than younger subjects on the recognition test but were unimpaired on the priming test. A study (Rose et al., 1986) using a homophone spelling task (derived from Jacoby and Witherspoon, 1982) found impaired priming in the older subjects. The significance of that priming deficit is uncertain, however, because some amnesic patients also show impaired homophone spelling priming (Cermak et al., 1986).

Summary

People between 60 and 80 years old perform less well than younger people on direct tests of event-fact memory. The age-related decline in new learning is most striking on tasks that demand self-organized responses, tasks that may be especially sensitive to frontal-lobe dysfunction. Older people, however, may be unimpaired on some tests of repetition priming. Thus, they present a pattern of impaired and preserved learning, relative to younger subjects, that is somewhat similar to that seen in amnesic patients and bears an even closer resemblance to that seen in many PD patients.

Putative neural substrates of memory subsystems

A major goal of neuropsychological research is to explain human learning disabilities and abilities in terms of the operations of memory subsystems. Subsystems analyses have not only revealed intact memory capacities in older healthy people and in patients with memory disorders due to neurodegenerative diseases, but have also drawn distinctions among disease-specific forms of memory dysfunction (Table 2). PD patients without dementia, PD patients with dementia, AD patients and HD patients have each shown unique patterns of spared and compromised memory function. Moreover, there is already evidence pointing to behavioral subgroups in AD (e.g., Knopman and Nissen, 1987), PD (e.g., Taylor et al., 1987) and HD (e.g., Saint-Cyr et al., 1988) that may have clinical implications and that suggests further distinctions in brain – behavior relations within and between neurodegenerative diseases.

Subsystems analyses of memory disorders in age-related neurodegenerative disease have provided new clues about the neural architecture of human memory. The discovery of spared learning in global amnesia showed that memory is not a unitary capacity because bilateral lesions to certain limbic structures impaired event-fact learning but spared learning in a variety of other domains. Thus, studies with amnesic patients suggested the existence of a corticolimbic memory subsystem mediating event-fact learning. It was unknown, however, whether the variety of learning capacities spared in amnesia reflected the operation of one, two or many memory

TABLE 2

Status of putative memory subsystems in normal aging and in neurodegenerative diseases

Memory subsystem	PD[a]	PDD[a]	AD[a]	HD[a]	Older healthy subjects[b]
Perceptual-structural			↑		↑
Lexical-semantic	↑	↓	↓	↑	↑
Event-fact	↑	↓	↓	↓	↓
Planning-selection	↓	↓		↓	↓
Compilation-action	↑	↓	↑	↓	

PD = Parkinson's disease without dementia; PDD = Parkinson's disease with dementia; AD = Alzheimer's disease; HD = Huntington's disease; ↑ = intact learning; ↓ = impaired learning. No mark indicates a lack of experimental evidence.
[a] Relative to age-matched control subjects.
[b] Relative to younger healthy subjects.

subsystems. Further, studies documenting preserved learning in amnesia provided no evidence about the neural substrate(s) of intact forms of memory (except that the limbic structures damaged in amnesia are not necessary components of those substrates). The results of studies with AD, PD and HD patients argue strongly for a dissociation between skill learning and priming processes and provide some evidence for further dissociations among priming processes and among skill-learning processes. Knowledge about the major neuropathologies associated with each of the age-associated neurodegenerative diseases provides suggestions about the putative neural bases of some of these forms of human learning.

Perceptual-structural memory
Patients with AD are known to have a pattern of neuropathology affecting the medial temporal-lobe limbic structures damaged in global amnesia (e.g., Hyman et al., 1984; Whitehouse et al., 1982). Unlike patients with global amnesia, AD patients have compromised neocortical association areas, especially in the parietal and temporal lobes. Postmortem neuropathology and in-vivo imaging studies, however, have shown that primary sensory areas, including primary visual cortex, are relatively spared (especially in the early phase of the disease when patients are testable) (Brun and Englund, 1981; Frackowiak et al., 1981; Johnson et al., 1987).

AD patients exhibited a normal McCollough effect, and it has been hypothesized, on psychophysical and electrophysiological grounds, that the effect is mediated in part by changes in primary visual cortex (Savoy, 1985; Savoy and Gabrieli, in press). Thus, there is a suggestion of a striate learning circuit in occipital cortex that mediates plasticity in early stages of feature perception, such as color and orientation.

Further, patients with AD showed a normal absolute magnitude of priming on two percept-limited tasks. Indirect evidence from patients with agnosias (Hecaen and Albert, 1978) and direct evidence from positron emission tomography (PET) (Posner et al., 1988) with normal subjects has implicated extrastriate visual areas in early stages of meaningful form perception. These findings suggest that there may be an extrastriate learning circuit that mediates the learning of visual shapes. The striate and extrastriate learning circuits could be important constituents of a perceptual-structural memory subsystem that acquires knowledge used to support visual recognition of objects and words.

Lexical-semantic memory
The reduced word-completion priming in AD patients indicates that temporal-parietal cortex, which is especially compromised early in the disease according to physiological imaging studies (e.g., Frackowiak et al., 1981; Johnson et al., 1987), may be a critical part of the neural substrate supporting

such priming. Amnesic patients exhibit intact word-completion performance and there is now direct evidence that metabolism in temporal-parietal cortex is not selectively compromised in global amnesia (Gabrieli et al., in preparation). These findings suggest that a temporal-parietal circuit constitutes a lexical-semantic memory subsystem that acquires knowledge used to support word-retrieval components of language.

Planning-selection memory and compilation-action memory

Patients with HD are known to have major degeneration in the caudate nucleus, and patients with PD are known to have severe degeneration of dopaminergic cells in the substantia nigra. Impaired skill learning in HD and PD patients suggests a critical role of the basal ganglia in human skill learning. Some PD patients have apparently intact event-fact learning and impaired skill learning capacities, whereas amnesic patients display the reverse pattern of spared skill learning and compromised event-fact learning. The idea that there are dissociable corticolimbic and corticostriatal memory subsystems is bolstered by a parallel double dissociation of learning capacities in a recent animal study (Packard et al., 1989).

Moreover, it is tempting to relate the impaired sensorimotor skill learning in HD and the impaired problem-solving learning in PD to neurally distinct 'motor' and 'complex' frontostriatal loops, respectively (Delong et al., 1983; Alexander et al., 1986). The motor loop may be a critical component of a compilation-action memory subsystem that acquires knowledge used to support motor program execution on such tasks as rotary pursuit. The complex loop may play an important role in a planning-selection memory subsystem used to support performance on novel tasks that demand a substantial reorganization of previously known information. The functional separability of these two corticostriate memory subsystems is supported further by the finding that drug administration to newly diagnosed PD patients ameliorates motor distur-

bances without improving performance on complex cognitive tasks (Cooper et al., 1989).

Conclusions

Eventually, the multifocal changes associated with normal aging and age-related neurodegenerative disease need to be understood in terms of relations between specific neuroanatomical (or neurochemical) systems and specific components of human memory if treatment efforts are to be pursued in an effective manner. At that point, the memory difficulties of individual older people, with or without age-related diseases, will be explained in terms of particular patterns of intact and impaired memory subsystems operating interactively. Different patterns of impairment will have different therapeutic implications. Although such patterns are complex and variable, the evidence reviewed in this chapter (and summarized in Table 2) indicates that they are not random.

Memory subsystems analyses hold considerable promise as a way of investigating the functional neural architecture of normal memory and of understanding how localized damage to that architecture results in different forms of memory impairment. The putative neural architecture of human learning abilities offered above is speculative at present. More certain is that the study of memory in AD, PD and normal aging has revealed the existence of memory subsystems of the human brain that process different kinds of information, have distinct neural substrates and are differentially at risk in normal aging and in age-related neurological diseases.

Acknowledgements

I thank Suzanne Corkin, James W. Hall, Edith V. Sullivan, Margaret M. Keane, Daniel B. Willingham and Christopher F.O. Gabrieli for their valuable comments on earlier versions of this chapter and Wendy Francis for her help in the production of the manuscript. I thank also my collaboratories in studying memory disorders in age-related neurological diseases: Suzanne Corkin, John H. Growdon, Margaret M. Keane, Harvey J. Sagar, Robert L. Savoy and Edith V. Sullivan. The writing of this chapter was supported by NIH grant AGO6605 to Suzanne Corkin, by National Research Service Award AGO5450 to the author, and by NIH center grant 1P50NS26985 to the Memory Disorders Research Center at the Boston Veterans Administration Medical Center.

References

Albert MS, Butters N, Levin J: Temporal gradients in the retrograde amnesia of patients with alcoholic Korsakoff's disease. *Arch. Neurol.: 36,* 211 – 216, 1979.

Alexander GE, DeLong MR, Strick PL: Parallel organization of functionally segregated circuits linking basal ganglia and cortex. *Annu. Rev. Neurosci.: 9,* 357 – 381, 1986.

Baddeley A: *Working Memory.* Oxford: Oxford University Press, 1986.

Benzing WC, Squire LR: Preserved learning and memory in amnesia: intact adaptation-level effects and learning of stereoscopic depth. *Behav. Neurosci.: 103,* 538 – 547: 1989.

Brooks DN, Baddeley A: What can amnesic patients learn? *Neuropsychologia: 14,* 111 – 122, 1976.

Brun A, Englund E: Regional pattern of degeneration in Alzheimer's disease: neuronal loss and histopathological grading. *Histopathology: 5,* 549 – 564, 1981.

Butters N, Wolfe J, Martone M, Grandholm E, Cermak LS: Memory disorders associated with Huntington's disease: verbal recall, verbal recognition, and procedural memory. *Neuropsychologia: 6,* 729 – 744, 1985.

Cermak LS, Lewis R, Butters N, Goodglass H: Role of verbal mediation in performance of motor tasks by Korsakoff patients. *Percept. Motor Skills: 37,* 259 – 263, 1973.

Cermak LS, Talbot N, Chandler K, Wolbarst LR: The perceptual priming phenomenon in amnesia. *Neuropsychologia: 23,* 615 – 622, 1985.

Cermak LS, O'Connor M, Talbot N: Biasing of alcoholic Korsakoff patient's semantic memory. *J. Clin. Exp. Neuropsychol.: 8,* 543 – 555, 1986.

Cermak LS, Bleich RP, Blackford SP: Deficits in the implicit retention of new associations by alcoholic Korsakoff patients. *Brain Cognition: 7,* 312 – 323, 1988.

Charness N, Milberg W, Alexander MP: Teaching an amnesic a complex cognitive skill. *Brain Cognition: 8,* 253 – 272, 1988.

Cohen NJ: Neuropsychological evidence for a distinction between procedural and declarative knowledge in human memory and amnesia. Unpublished doctoral dissertation, University of California, San Diego, 1981.

Cohen NJ, Corkin S: The amnesic patient H.M.: Learning and retention of cognitive skill. *Soc. Neurosci. Abstr.: 7,* 517, 1981.

Cohen NJ, Squire LR: Preserved learning and retention of

pattern-analyzing skill in amnesia: dissociation of knowing how and knowing that. *Science: 210,* 207 – 210, 1980.

Cools AR, van den Bercken JHL, Horstink MWI, van Spaendonck KPM, Berger HJC: Cognitive and motor shifting aptitude disorder in Parkinson's disease. *J. Neurol. Neurosurg. Psychiatry: 47,* 443 – 453, 1984.

Cooper JA, Sagar HJ, Jordan N, Sullivan EV, Harvey NS: Cognitive function in untreated Parkinson's disease and the effects of treatment. *J. Clin. Exp. Neuropsychol.: 11,* 369, 1989.

Corkin S: Acquisition of motor skills after bilateral medial temporal-lobe excision. *Neuropsychologia: 6,* 255 – 265, 1968.

Corkin S: Some relationships between global amnesias and the memory impairments in Alzheimer's disease. In Corkin S, Davis KL, Growdon JH, Usdin E (Editors), *Alzheimer's Disease: A Report of Progress in Research.* New York: Raven Press, pp. 149 – 164, 1982.

Corkin S, Gabrieli JDE, Stanger BZ, Mickel SF, Rosen TJ, Sullivan EV, Growdon JH: Skill learning and priming in Alzheimer's disease. *Neurology (Suppl. 1): 36,* 296, 1986.

Craik FIM: Age differences in human memory. In Birren JE, Schaie KW (Editors), *Handbook of the Psychology of Aging.* New York: Van Nostrand Reinhold, 1977.

Craik FIM: Changes in memory with normal aging: A functional view. In Wurtman RJ, Corkin S, Growdon JH, Ritter-Walker E (Editors), *Alzheimer's Disease (Advances in Neurology, Vol. 51).* New York: Raven Press, pp. 201 – 205, 1990.

Damasio AR, Graff-Radford NR, Eslinger PJ, Damasio H, Kassell, N: Amnesia following basal forebrain lesions. *Arch. Neurol.: 42,* 263 – 271, 1985.

Dannenbring GL, Briand K: Semantic priming and the word repetition effect in a lexical decision task. *Can. J. Psychol.: 36,* 435 – 444, 1982.

De la Monte SM, Wells BS, Hedley-Whyte ET, Growdon JH: Neuropatholocial distinction between Parkinson's dementia and Parkinson's plus Alzheimer's disease. *Ann. Neurol.: 26,* 309 – 320, 1989.

DeLong MR, Georgopoulos AP, Crutcher MD: Cortico-basal ganglia relations and coding of motor performance. *Exp. Brain Res.: 49,* Supplement 7: 30 – 40, 1983.

Diagnostic and Statistical Manual of Mental Disorders, 3rd edn. Washington, DC: American Psychiatric Association, 1980.

Dubois B, Pillon B, Sternic N, Lhermitte F, Agid Y: Age-induced cognitive disturbance in Parkinson's disease. *Neurology: 40,* 38 – 41, 1990.

Eslinger PJ, Damasio AR: Preserved motor learning in Alzheimer's disease: implications for anatomy and behavior. *J. Neurosci.: 6,* 3006 – 3009, 1986.

Frackowiak RSJ, Pozzili C, Legg NJ, Du Boulay GH, Marshall J, Lenzi GL, Jones T: Regional cerebral oxygen supply and utilization in dementia: a clinical and physiological study with oxygen-15 and positron tomography. *Brain: 104,* 753 – 778, 1981.

Gabrieli JDE: Memory systems of the human brain: dissociations among learning capacities in amnesia. Unpublished doctoral dissertation, Massachusetts Institute of Technology, Cambridge, MA, 1986.

Gabrieli JDE: Dissociation of memory capacities in neurodegenerative disease. In Wurtman RJ, Corkin S, Growdon JH, Ritter-Walker E (Compilers), *Alzheimer's*

Disease: Advances in Basic Research and Therapies. Cambridge: Center for Brain Sciences and Metabolism Charitable Trust, pp. 317–327, 1989.

Gabrieli JDE, Keane MM: Priming in the amnesic patient H.M.: new findings and a theory of intact and impaired priming in patients with memory disorders. *Soc. Neurosci. Abstr.: 14,* 1290, 1988.

Gabrieli JDE, Keane MM, Corkin S: Acquisition of problem solving skills in global amnesia. *Soc. Neurosci. Abstr.: 13,* 1455, 1987.

Gabrieli JDE, Cohen NJ, Corkin S: The impaired learning of semantic knowledge following bilateral medial temporal-lobe resection. *Brain Cognition: 7,* 157–177, 1988.

Gabrieli JDE, Holman BL, Nagel JS, Corkin S: Single photon emission computed tomography in global amnesia due to bilateral medial temporal-lobe resection: in preparation.

Gabrieli JDE, Keane MM, Stanger BZ, Kjelgaard MM, Banks KS, Corkin S, Growdon JH: Dissociations among structural-perceptual, lexical-semantic, and event-fact memory subsystems in global amnesia, Alzheimer's disease, and normal memory. Submitted.

Gollin ES: Developmental studies of visual recognition of incomplete objects. *Percept. Motor Skills: 11,* 289–298, 1960.

Gotham AM, Brown RG, Marsden CD: 'Frontal' cognitive function in patients with Parkinson's disease 'on' and 'off' levodopa. *Brain: 111,* 299–321, 1988.

Graf P, Schacter DL: Implicit and explicit memory for new associations in normal and amnesic subjects. *J. Exp. Psychol. Learn. Mem. Cognition: 11,* 501–518, 1985.

Graf P, Mandler G, Haden PE: Simulating amnesic symptoms in normals. *Science: 218,* 1243–1244, 1982.

Graf P, Squire LR, Mandler G: The information that amnesic patients do not forget. *J. Exp. Psychol. Learn. Mem. Cognition: 10,* 164–178, 1984.

Growdon JH, Corkin S: Cognitive impairments in Parkinson's disease. In Yahr MD, Bergman KJ (Editors), *Parkinson's Disease (Advances in Neurology, Vol. 45).* New York: Raven Press, pp. 383–392, 1986.

Growdon JH, Corkin S, Rosen TJ: Distinctive aspects of cognitive dysfunction in Parkinson's disease. In *Parkinson's Disease (Advances in Neurology).* New York, Raven Press, in press, 1990.

Hecaen H, Albert ML: *Human Neuropsychology.* New York: John Wiley and Sons, 1978.

Heindel WC, Butters N, Salmon DP: Impaired learning of a motor skill in patients with Huntington's disease. *Behav. Neurosci.: 102,* 141–147, 1988.

Heindel WC, Salmon DP, Shults CW, Walicke PA, Butters N: Neuropsychological evidence for multiple implicit memory systems: a comparison of Alzheimer's, Huntington's, and Parkinson's disease patients. *J. Neurosci.: 9,* 582–587, 1989.

Hietanen M, Teravainen H: The effect of age of disease onset on neuropsychological performance in Parkinson's disease. *J. Neurol. Neurosurg. Psychiatry: 51,* 244–249, 1988.

Huff FJ, Corkin S, Growdon JH: Semantic impairment and anomia in Alzheimer's disease. *Brain Lang.: 28,* 235–249, 1986.

Hyman BT, Van Hoesen GW, Damasio AR, Barnes CL: Alzheimer's disease: cell-specific pathology isolates the hippocampal formation. *Science: 225,* 1168–1170, 1984.

Jacoby LL, Dallas M: On the relationship between autobiographical memory and perceptual learning. *J. Exp. Psychol. Gen.: 110,* 306–340, 1981.

Jacoby LL, Witherspoon D: Remembering without awareness. *Can. J. Psychol.: 36,* 300–324, 1982.

Janowsky JS, Shimamura AP, Squire LR: Source memory impairment in patients with frontal lobe lesions. *Neuropsychologia: 8,* 1043–1056, 1989.

Jetter W, Poser U, Freeman RB Jr., Markowitsch HJ: A verbal long term memory deficit in frontal lobe damaged patients. *Cortex: 22,* 229–242, 1986.

Johnson MK, Hasher L: Human learning and memory. *Annu. Rev. Psychol.: 38,* 631–668, 1987.

Johnson KA, Mueller ST, Walshe TM, English RJ, Holman BL: Cerebral perfusion imaging in Alzheimer's disease. *Arch. Neurol.: 44,* 165–168, 1987.

Keane MM, Gabrieli JDE, Fennema AC, Growdon JH, Corkin S: Perceptual priming in patients with Alzheimer's disease: evidence for a perceptual-structural memory subsystem. Submitted.

Knopman DS, Nissen MJ: Implicit learning in patients with probable Alzheimer's disease. *Neurology: 37,* 784–788, 1987.

Lees AJ, Smith E: Cognitive deficits in the early stages of Alzheimer's disease. *Brain: 106,* 257–270, 1983.

Light LL, Singh A: Implicit and explicit memory in young and older adults. *J. Exp. Psychol. Learn. Mem. Cognition: 13,* 531–541, 1987.

Light LL, Singh A, Capps JL: Dissociation of memory and awareness in young and older adults. *J. Clin. Exp. Neuropsychol.: 8,* 62–74, 1986.

Mahut H, Zola-Morgan S, Moss M: Hippocampal resections impair associative learning and recognition memory in the monkey. *J. Neurosci.: 2,* 1214–1229, 1982.

Marslen-Wilson WD, Teuber H-L: Memory for remote events in anterograde amnesia: Recognition of public figures from news photographs. *Neuropsychologia: 13,* 353–364, 1975.

Martone M, Butters N, Payne M, Becker J, Sax DS: Dissociations between skill learning and verbal recognition in amnesia and dementia. *Arch. Neurol.: 41,* 965–970, 1984.

Matthews CG, Haaland KY: The effect of symptom duration on cognitive and motor performance in parkinsonism. *Neurology (New York): 29,* 951–956, 1979.

McCollough C: Color adaptation of edge-detectors in the human visual system. *Science: 149,* 1115–1116, 1965.

McIntyre JS, Craik FIM: Age differences in memory for item and source information. *Can. J. Psychol.: 41,* 175–192, 1987.

Milberg W, Alexander MP, Charness N, McGlinchey-Berroth R, Barrett A: Learning of a complex arithmetic skill in amnesia: evidence for a dissociation between compilation and production. *Brain Cognition: 8,* 91–104, 1988.

Milner B: Les troubles de la memoire accompagnant des lesions hippocampiques bilaterales. In *Physiologie de l'Hippocampe.* Paris: Centre National de la Recherche Scientifique, pp. 257–272, 1962.

Milner B: Interhemispheric differences in the localization of psychological processes in man. *Br. Med. J.: 27,* 272–277, 1971.

Milner B, Teuber H-L: Alteration of perception and memory in man. In Weiskrantz L (Editor), *Analysis of Behavioral Changes.* New York: Harper and Row, pp. 268–375, 1968.

Milner B, Corkin S, Teuber H-L: Further analysis of the hippocampal amnesic syndrome: 14-year follow-up study of H.M. *Neuropsychologia: 6*, 215 – 244, 1968.

Mishkin M: Memory in monkeys severely impaired by combined but not by separate removal of amygdala and hippocampus. *Nature: 273*, 297 – 298, 1978.

Nebes RD: Semantic memory in Alzheimer's disease. *Psychol. Bull.: 106*, 377 – 394, 1989.

Nissen MJ, Bullemer P: Attentional requirements of learning: evidence from performance measures. *Cognitive Psychol.: 19*, 1 – 32, 1987.

Norman DA, Shallice T: Attention to action: willed and automatic control of behaviour. University of California CHIP Report 9, 1980.

Packard MG, Hirsh R, White NM: Differential effects of fornix and caudate nucleus lesions on two radial maze tasks: evidence of multiple memory systems. *J. Neurosci.: 9*, 1465 – 1472, 1989.

Parkinson J: *An Essay on the Shaking Palsy*. London: Sherwood, Neely, and Jones, 1817.

Petrides M: Deficits on conditional associative-learning tasks after frontal- and temporal-lobe lesions in man. *Neuropsychologia: 23*, 601 – 614, 1985.

Petrides M, Milner B: Deficits on subject-ordered tasks after frontal and temporal lobe lesions in man. *Neuropsychologia: 20*, 249 – 262, 1982.

Pirozzolo FJ, Hansch EC, Mortimer JA, Webster DD, Kuskowski MA: Dementia in Parkinson disease: a neuropsychological analysis. *Brain Cognition: 1*, 71 – 83, 1982.

Posner MI, Petersen SE, Fox PT, Raichle ME: Localization of cognitive operations in the human brain. *Science: 240*, 1627 – 1631, 1988.

Richardson-Klavehn A, Björk RA: Measures of memory. *Annu. Rev. Psychol.: 39*, 475 – 543, 1988.

Rose TL, Yesavage JA, Hill RD, Bower GH: Priming effects and recognition memory in young and elderly adults. *Exp. Aging Res.: 12*, 31 – 37, 1986.

Rowe JR, Kahn RL: Human aging: usual and successful. *Science: 237*, 143 – 149, 1987.

Sagar HJ, Sullivan EV: Patterns of cognitive impairment in dementia. In Kennard C (Editor), *Recent Advances in Clinical Neurology*. London: Churchill Livingstone, pp. 47 – 86, 1988.

Sagar HJ, Sullivan EV, Gabrieli JDE, Corkin S, Growdon JH: Temporal ordering and short-term memory deficits in Parkinson's disease. *Brain: 111*, 525 – 539, 1988.

Saint-Cyr JA, Taylor AE, Lang AE: Procedural learning and neostriatal dysfunction in man. *Brain: 111*, 941 – 959, 1988.

Salmon DP, Shimamura AP, Butters N, Smith S: Lexical and semantic deficits in patients with Alzheimer's disease. *J. Clin. Exp. Neuropsychol.: 10*, 477 – 494, 1988.

Salthouse TA: *Adult Cognition: An Experimental Psychology of Human Aging*. New York: Springer-Verlag, 1982.

Savoy RL: Extinction of the McCollough effect does not transfer interocularly. *Percept. Psychophys.: 36*, 571 – 576, 1985.

Savoy RL, Gabrieli JDE: Normal McCollough effect in Alzheimer's disease and global amnesia. *Soc. Neurosci. Abstr.: 14*, 217, 1988.

Schaie KW, Labouvie-Vief G: Generational and cohort-specific differences in adult cognitive functioning: a fourteen-year study of independent samples. *Dev. Psychol.: 10*, 305 – 320, 1974.

Scoville NB, Milner B: Loss of recent memory after bilateral hippocampal lesions. *J. Neurol. Neurosurg. Psychiatry: 209*, 11 – 19, 1957.

Shimamura AP, Squire LR: Paired-associate learning and priming effects in amnesia: a neuropsychological study. *J. Exp. Psychol. Gen.: 113*, 556 – 570, 1984.

Shimamura AP, Salmon DP, Squire LR, Butters N: Memory dysfunction and word priming in dementia and amnesia. *Behav. Neurosci.: 101*, 347 – 351, 1987.

Squire LR: Comparisons between forms of amnesia: some deficits are unique to Korsakoff's syndrome. *J. Exp. Psychol. Learn. Mem. Cognition: 8*, 560 – 571, 1982.

Sullivan EV, Sagar HJ, Gabrieli JDE, Corkin S, Growdon JH: Different cognitive profiles on standard behavioral tests in Parkinson's disease and Alzheimer's disease. *J. Clin. Exp. Neuropsychol.*: in press: 1989.

Taylor AE, Saint-Cyr JA, Lang AE: Frontal lobe dysfunction in Parkinson's disease: the cortical focus of neostriatal outflow. *Brain: 109*, 845 – 883, 1986.

Taylor AE, Saint-Cyr JA, Lang AE: Parkinson's disease: cognitive changes in relation to treatment response: *Brain: 110*, 35 – 51, 1987.

Victor M, Adams RD, Collins GH: *The Wernicke-Korsakoff Syndrome*. Philadelphia: Davis, 1971.

Warrington EK, Weiskrantz L: A new method of testing long-term retention with special reference to amnesic patients. *Nature: 217*, 972 – 974, 1968.

Warrington EK, Weiskrantz L: The amnesic syndrome: consolidation or retrieval? *Nature: 28*, 628 – 630, 1970.

Whitehouse PJ, Price DL, Struble RG, Clark AW, Coyle JT, DeLong MR: Alzheimer's disease and senile dementia: loss of neurons in the basal forebrain. *Science, 215*, 1237 – 1239, 1982.

Wilson RS, Kaszniak AW, Klawans HL, Garron DC: High speed memory scanning in parkinsonism. *Cortex: 16*, 67 – 72, 1980.

Zola-Morgan S, Squire LR: Preserved learning in monkeys with medial temporal lesion: sparing of motor and cognitive skills. *J. Neurosci.: 4*, 1072 – 1085, 1984.

Zola-Morgan S, Squire LR: Amnesia in monkeys following lesions of the mediodorsal nucleus of the thalamus. *Ann. Neurol.: 17*, 558 – 564, 1985.

Zola-Morgan S, Squire LR: Memory impairments in monkeys following lesions of the hippocampus. *Behav. Neursoci.: 100*, 155 – 160, 1986.

Zola-Morgan S, Squire LR, Amaral, D: Human amnesia and the medial temporal region: enduring memory impairment following a bilateral lesion limited to the CA1 field of the hippocampus. *J. Neurosci.: 6*, 2950 – 2967, 1986.

© 1991 Elsevier Science Publishers B.V.
Handbook of Neuropsychology, Vol. 5
F. Boller and J. Grafman (Eds)

CHAPTER 9

Motor function in aging and neurodegenerative disease

Francis J. Pirozzolo, Roderick K. Mahurin and Andrew A. Swihart

Department of Neurology, Baylor College of Medicine, One Baylor Plaza, Houston, TX 77030, U.S.A.

Introduction

Movement is the final common pathway of central nervous system activity. As such, it is a crucial behavioral function that invites scientific investigation in many areas of the neurosciences. The neurobehavioral sciences have a rich and proud tradition rooted in the study of motor control. Psychological measurement had its stirrings in the assessment of reaction time by Swiss astronomers in the early part of the nineteenth century. The nascence of empirical physiological psychology can be traced to the study of the properties of muscle contractility in the middle of the nineteenth century, and later to the contributions of Fritsch and Hitzig, who discovered that neural tissue was electrically excitable. The clinical observations of John Hughlings Jackson, with his models of the neural control of human movement, and Sir Charles Sherrington, whose laboratory investigations were profoundly significant contributors to the understanding of motor control, are even today considered to be remarkably accurate frameworks for understanding movement and movement disorders.

Neuropsychological research on the aging nervous system has tended to focus on intellectual deterioration associated with age. The age-related decline in motor function has not received as much research attention, but the study of motor control in elderly subjects may be likely to reveal important biochemical, morphological and behavioral phenomena that have implications for the etiology of certain age-related neurodegenerative diseases. There

are numerous associations among aging, age-related neurochemical alterations, the control of movement, and specific neurodegenerative disorders, which make these topics highly intriguing to the neuroscientist.

This chapter briefly reviews the neuroanatomy and biochemistry of motor function, with particular emphasis given to the basal ganglia and extrapyramidal motor systems. A discussion of the consequences of age-related decrements in motor function follows. Aging muscle, an often neglected factor in the decline of motor function in elderly subjects, is discussed in detail. Several of the most common neurodegenerative diseases seen by the neuropsychologist, again with particular attention given to the basal ganglia, are covered from the perspective of the motor control problems that exist in each disorder. In conclusion, a short discussion is presented on the potentially beneficial effects of exercise to the physical and cognitive status of elderly subjects.

Motor system structure and function

Human motor function is traditionally discussed in terms of three primary systems: pyramidal, extrapyramidal and cerebellar. Although this classification is clinically and heuristically useful, a strictly neuroanatomical division of motor function with regard to aging and pathology poses several difficulties, including co-extensive neuropathological substrates among motor disorders, uncertainties as to the roles of critical biochemical pathways, and difficulties in substantiating anatomical involvement in vivo (Joynt and Shoulson, 1985; Whitehouse et al., 1982). Additionally, intact motor production is dependent on the integrated functioning of the motor systems. Impairment in one system can negatively affect other systems, or compensatory mechanisms may be brought into play. Alterations in one system must, therefore, be considered from the perspective of overall motor organization and structure. The focus of the present chapter is on the basal ganglia and extrapyramidal system, for changes in these systems are most closely related to age-related motor dysfunction and disease. However, a brief review of age-related changes in pyramidal and cerebellar function is also included below.

Pyramidal system

The pyramidal system, which derives its name from the medullary pyramids of the descending corticospinal tract, is primarily associated with voluntary control of fine movement. Two-thirds of cortical motor output cells are located in the Brodmann's precentral areas 4 and 6 (motor and premotor areas), with postcentral somatosensory regions 1, 2, 3 also contributing to efferent production (Asanum, 1989). Other cortical motor areas, including the supplementary motor region, frontal association cortex and parietal association areas, integrate motor commands and relay information to the primary output areas (Wiesendenger et al., 1987). The motor strip itself seems to have limited control over motor functions, with the possible exception of 'fine tuning' the force, velocity and direction of voluntary movements (Asanum, 1989). Efferent tracts descend from the primary motor cortex to include the corticobulbar (head, neck, face and other brainstem nuclei), corticospinal (crossed spinal cord pathways) and anterior corticospinal (uncrossed spinal cord pathways) tracts (Kuypers, 1981).

Lesions of the primary motor area and its efferent pathways result in specific weakness and motor deficits (Ghez, 1981). Lesions in premotor regions result in less specific deficits, and affect the sequenc-ing, timing and regulation of movement (Roland, 1984). Higher-level cortical motor association areas (parietal and prefrontal regions) are associated with abstract motor activities, and lesions in these regions affect conceptual functions such as goal formation, monitoring of performance and adjustment of action plans (Luria, 1983).

Aging is associated with neuronal loss in both primary and secondary motor cortex (Brody, 1976; LeWitt and Calne, 1982), with regressive changes in dendritic structure also reported, particularly in pyramidal cells (Scheibel and Schiebel, 1975). There is accumulation of lipofuscin in both cortical pyramidal cells and spinal cord anterior horn cells (LeWitt et al., 1982). This increase in lipofuscin is associated with neuronal pathology, although functional correlates are not well established. In contrast to these decrements, there is relatively little age-related neuronal fall-off in primary visual, auditory and somatosensory cortices (Curcio et al., 1982).

Extrapyramidal system

The extrapyramidal system is usually thought of in reference to the interconnected system of basal ganglia, thalamic nuclei and midbrain regions. These structures, together with the nigrostriatal pathway, a major dopaminergic system connecting the pars compacta of the substantia nigra and corpus striatum, play an important role in complex motor and cognitive function (Marsden, 1982; Weiner and Lang, 1989). Their role in neurodegenerative disease is well documented in other chapters in this volume (e.g., Agid and colleagues; Brandt et al.).

The basal ganglia (caudate, putamen, globus pallidus and subthalamic nuclei) are implicated in the planning, initiation and timing of complex motor function (Marsden, 1982, 1984). Lesions of these structures or connecting pathways result in either negative motor signs, such as hypokinesia and rigidity, or, through release of function, positive motor signs such as tremor, chorea or hemiballismus (Mayeux, 1990). Little age-associated cell loss is evident in the basal ganglia themselves (with the exception of the putamen)

(McGeer et al., 1977), but dopamine concentrations are significantly lowered. In contrast, significant neuronal dropout is evident in two brainstem structures, the dopaminergic substantia nigra and the noradrenergic locus coeruleus (Brody, 1981; McGeer et al., 1977; Tomlinson et al., 1981).

The striatum, mainly composed of the caudate nucleus and the putamen, is the major 'receptive' area of the basal ganglia. Most regions of the cerebral cortex contain projections to this region. These projections are mediated by the excitatory neurotransmitter glutamate. The somatosensory, motor and premotor cortices project largely to the putamen, whereas cortical association fibers project largely to the caudate (Young and Penney, 1988). This anatomical arrangement suggests that the putamen is primarily concerned with motor control and that the caudate is mainly involved in more complex cognitive or 'central programming' activity, with only a minor role in the control of movement (DeLong et al., 1985; DeLong and Georgeopoulos, 1981).

Recent research has shown that the basal ganglia are components of 'circuits' or 'loops' involving the thalamus, striatum and cortex, which allow the processing of complex motor, emotional and cognitive behaviors (DeLong et al., 1983). However, while the basal ganglia are still thought to modulate and integrate cortical inputs, it is now known that there is a great deal of functional and somatotopic segregation of the pathways within these circuits. Portions of the basal ganglia previously thought to be homogeneous structures (such as the striatum) are now known to be highly heterogeneous (Graybiel and Hickey, 1982; Graybiel and Ragsdale, 1978). The subregions within the striatum, termed the striosomes and matrix, differ not only in their afferents and efferents, but also in the distribution of their receptors and neuropeptides (Gerfen, 1984; 1989; Young et al., 1988).

Young and Penney have incorporated many of these findings into a model of basal ganglia function with implications for age-related motor dysfunction (Penney et al., 1986; Penney and Young, 1983, 1986; Young and Penney, 1984; Young et al., 1988).

There are two fundamental attributes of this model. The first is the existence of the striosomes and matrix described above. The second is that dopamine has differential effects within the nigrostriatal system. For example, Pan et al. (1985) produced lesions in the medial forebrain bundle, a nigrostriatal pathway, using 6-hydroxydopamine (6-OHDA). It was hypothesized that if dopamine was inhibitory on GABAergic output cells, then the removal of this inhibitory effect should cause the striatal neurons to be overactive and result in receptor down-regulation in striatal projection areas. If dopamine was excitatory, then the opposite would be true. It was found that, after 6-OHDA lesions, GABA receptors were decreased in the striatum and lateral globus pallidus (LGP) but were increased in the medial globus pallidus (MGP) and substantia nigra pars reticulata and SNpr. These findings suggest that dopamine inhibits function in striatal projections to the LGP, but excites function in projections to the MGP and SNpr.

Age-related dopamine reductions in the extrapyramidal system thus have the potential to critically affect motor function. Biochemical assays have demonstrated the presence of two types of dopamine receptor site, D1 and D2, with different affinities for adenylate cyclase (Creese et al., 1983; Kebabian and Calne, 1979). Autoradiographic studies of postmortem tissue have revealed high density of both types of receptor in the striatum, but higher concentrations of D1 than D2 receptors in the substantia nigra (Palacios et al., 1988). Age-related D1 receptor density reductions of more than 50% have been demonstrated, consistent with previous findings of decreased dopaminergic neurons in subjects without neurological disease across the lifespan (McGeer et al., 1977). In addition, positron emission tomography (PET) studies have shown age-related decreases in both pre- and postsynaptic dopaminergic function (Martin et al., 1986; Wong et al., 1984). Progressive declines in other parameters of the dopaminergic system occur with increasing age, including reductions in substantia nigra pars compacta cell count, reduction in dopamine concentration in the caudate nucleus, and declining numbers of D2 receptors. These changes are thought to be associated with negative motor signs (chiefly bradykinesia), and are correlated with age in otherwise healthy adults (Mortimer, 1988).

Cerebellum

Intact cerebellar function is crucial to the coordination and timing of complex movements, primarily through feedback loops to vestibular nuclei, spinal cord, pons, red nucleus, inferior olive, ventrolateral thalamus and cortical motor regions (Ghez and Fahn, 1981). In conjunction with other portions of the motor system, the cerebellum contributes to maintenance of muscle tone, adjustment of stretch reflexes, synchronization of gait, postural control, regulation of speech, oculomotor integration and motor learning (Lechtenberg, 1988).

Lesions of either the cerebellum itself or these widespread connecting pathways lead to disruptions of the force, velocity and timing of coordinated muscular activity (Strata, 1989). Dyscoordination of eye movements (nystagmus), postural instability, gait disturbance, titubation of head and trunk, dysarthria and deceased muscle tone are common clinical signs of cerebellar disease (Harding, 1982; Ito, 1984). For example, intention tremor, a frequent clinical manifestation of cerebellar disease, is thought to be related to disrupted timing of activation of agonist and antagonist muscles as a limb approaches a target (Arsharsky et al., 1986).

Lesion studies reveal that cerebellar function can be broadly divided by function of midline structures and the lateral cerebellar hemispheres. Postural instability, gait ataxia and truncal titubation are thought to be associated with degeneration of the vermis, the primary midline structure. This structure integrates oculo-vestibular and proprioceptive information, and is critically involved in adjustment of balance mechanisms and postural reflexes. In contrast, dysarthria, dysmetria, limb ataxia and hypotonia have been related to lesions of lateral portions of the cerebellar cortex (Ito, 1984).

Loss of Purkinje cells, the primary output cell of the cerebellum, is consistently noted in aging, with decreases of approximately 25% over the life-span

(Hall et al., 1975). In addition, age-related pathological processes, such as spinocerebellar degeneration, involve bilaterally symmetric atrophy in the neocerebellum, particularly pronounced loss of Purkinje cells in anterior cerebellar cortex and vermis. Aging is also associated with brainstem cell loss in the inferior olives and demyelination of their projections to the cerebellar cortex (i.e., the inferior cerebellar peduncles) (Rogers, 1988). Asymmetrical gait ataxia may be associated with unequal degeneration of the hemispheres, affecting coordination of the ipsilateral lower limb. In contrast, involvement of cerebellar midline structures, particularly the anterior vermis and its connecting pathways, results in generalized gait ataxia without lateralized lower limb dyscoordination. Olivopontocerebellar atrophy, a cerebellar disease seen in the elderly, has clinical features consistent with both cerebellar and brainstem dysfunction, including ataxia, dysarthria, rigidity and akinesia. Cognitive deficits may also be apparent, especially in later stages of the disease (Berciano, 1988; Duvoisin, 1987; Feher et al., 1988).

Integration of function

Although the basic motor systems are in principle independent, smooth motor performance is dependent on integrity of interaction among them. For example, spatio-temporal characteristics, including force, velocity, amplitude and positioning, may be disrupted by lesions in cerebellum, basal ganglia, somatosensory cortical regions, efferent motor pathways or proprioceptive pathways (Bateuv, 1987). The ability to sustain arousal and concentration, working memory for the planned sequence of activities and for the motor skills themselves, and verbal self-regulation of behavior are necessary preconditions for effective motor performance. These abilities may be disrupted by lesions of the neuraxis affecting arousal, cortical or subcortical regions associated with memory, or speech areas of the frontal cortex (Luria, 1983). In addition, the feedback component of movement is also vulnerable to disruption (particularly in the kinesthetic and visual modalities), with damage to muscle and joint receptors, peripheral nerves, or the postcentral gyrus resulting in clumsy, inaccurate movements (Allum and Hulliger, 1989).

Age-related motor changes

Age-related changes in postural control and gait are well documented and have significant implications for both personal safety and mobility. Vestibular, visual and somatosensory systems are all important contributors to postural control, and each of these systems undergoes age-associated changes (Swihart and Pirozzolo, 1988). For example, primary vestibular functions are frequently impaired in the older adult, secondary to either impaired peripheral vestibular function, impaired central integrative processes, or both (Woollacott et al., 1988). These decrements in vestibular function, in turn, can have significant negative effects on balance control. Visual acuity, contrast sensitivity and multiple ocular motor functions (e.g., accommodative convergence, full upgaze, efficient pursuit and saccadic eye movements) all decline with age (Wright and Henkind, 1983; Klein and Schieber, 1985) and have detrimental affects on the postural control system (Woollacott et al., 1988).

Age-associated postural instability appears to result from changes in long-latency postural reflex motor synergies (Woollacott et al., 1982, 1988). These disturbances in the temporal organization of motor synergies directly influence both static and dynamic balance (Stelmach et al., 1989). Together, these adverse changes in primary vestibular, visual and somatosensory systems, and additional declines in the postural control system, produce a baseline of larger-amplitude body sway and decreased righting ability relative to younger adults (Lichtenstein et al., 1990; Manchester et al., 1989). Age-related increased risk for falling results from not only increased postural sway and decreased balance, but also weakness of lower extremities, visual impairment, vestibular changes, joint stiffness and increased sensitivity to medication effects (Tinetti, 1989; Nevitt et al., 1989; Ochs et al., 1985). As a consequence, it has been suggested that older individuals, particularly those who have fallen in the past, assume a cautious, wide-based stance in anticipation of a 'fear of further falling' (Tideiksaar, 1988).

Numerous changes in gait occur with aging (Sudarsky, 1990). It is reported that approximately 13% of older adults currently experience some functional disability secondary to disturbance of gait in the absence of any specific disease process (Larish et al., 1988). A decrease in preferred walking speed is the most consistently reported change in gait, with other changes including shorter stride length, decreased stride frequency, increased stance and stride width, and a decreased ratio of swing-to-stance time (Larish et al., 1988). In addition, normal elderly subjects often show slight anteroflexion of the upper torso and flexion of the arms and knees and diminished arm swing, suggestive of mild parkinsonian features (see discussion below) (Murray et al., 1969).

Larish and colleagues (1988) found no difference in the freely chosen walking speed of old (mean age 70.5 years) and young (mean age 25.6 years) subjects, but reported that the metabolic economy of walking was lower in the aged subjects than in the young subjects at all walking speeds. However, this study was performed with physically active, regularly exercising, healthy older adults, suggesting that the commonly reported detrimental effects of aging on gait may be reduced by maintenance of more optimal levels of physical fitness (see below). Further, the various parameters of gait typically measured in these studies (e.g., walking speed, stride frequency, stride length, stance width, etc.) are known to be highly interdependent. Therefore, maintenance of preferred walking speed across the life-span at levels seen in young adults may eliminate the detrimental changes reported in the other specific components of gait.

Absolute strength and speed of movement also decline with advancing age. For example, maximum strength of hand-grip, although relatively well-maintained into the fifth decade, undergoes an accelerating decline thereafter (Larsson, 1982). Between years 20 and 80 varying rates of strength decline are observed in other muscle groups, including proximal muscles of the lower extremities, shoulder strength and foot strength (44%, 32% and 21%, respectively) (Larsson, 1982; Potvin et al., 1981). The maximal speed of movement of numerous muscle groups also declines with age (Larsson et al., 1979). Such speed decrements for simple movements are generally of a 30% magnitude; more complex movements (e.g., timed digit copying) show up to 100% increases in time necessary for task completion (Welford, 1977). Changes in non-motor factors, such as visual sensory processing speed, response bias and self-monitoring time, may all contribute to age-related slowing observed in these complex motor tasks (Mahurin and Pirozzolo, 1986).

The peripheral nervous system is largely spared in the aging process (Schaumberg et al., 1983). For example, neural conduction is estimated to slow approximately 5%, which is of insufficient magnitude to account for behavioral slowing in elderly subjects (Weiss, 1965). Differences between simple RT for jaw, knee and arm have also been shown to be approximately equal for younger and older subjects, again indicating the small contribution of peripheral neural conduction to age-related slowing (Botwinick, 1978). Hugin and colleagues (1960) showed that latency of the plantar flexion reflex did not significantly change from the twenties to the nineties, but tactile-induced RT of the same foot showed significant declines. This finding supports the hypothesis of central, rather than peripheral, nervous system slowing with age.

It has been commonly accepted that there is roughly a 20% decline in RT from healthy individuals in their twenties to those in their sixties (Botwinick, 1978; Surwillo, 1973; Welford, 1985; Waugh et al., 1978). However, recent studies question this degree of decline in function. Gottsdanker (1982) examined simple RT in a large group of subjects aged from their twenties through to their nineties, and found an average 2 millisecond per decade decrease in response time. This finding argues against a significant age-related decline in simple motor speed (Smith, 1989).

In contrast to equivocal indications of increased simple RT with age, more complex movements

clearly show age-related slowing (Cerella et al., 1980; Birren et al., 1980). Components of choice RT include initial sensory signal transduction, neural transmission time from periphery to brain, signal identification, response choice, neural transmission from brain to effector muscles, and muscle activation time (Welford, 1988). This view is confirmed in RT experiments, in which the greatest age effect is noted in initial response time rather than movement time (Welford, 1985). The degree of slowing evident in choice RT tasks increases as the complexity of the relationship between signal and response increases (Mahurin et al., 1986). This association illustrates the predominant role in age-related slowing played by changes in central processing speed (slowing of the signal identification and response choice components) rather than slowing of movement time per se (Welford, 1988).

Factor analytic studies indicate that performance of healthy and neurologically impaired older adults loads on relatively independent movement factors (Mahurin and Inbody, 1989). For example, changes in simple motor tasks (such as finger tapping) show less change with age than do more complex visuomotor tasks. Tasks requiring fine motor coordination and visual monitoring (such as rotary pursuit or pegboard tasks) carry higher psychomotor demands, and are more sensitive to age and age-related dysfunction. Potvin and colleagues (Potvin and Tourtellotte, 1985) have documented a number of such changes, such as manipulating buttons, tying shoelaces and opening medication containers which show age-related declines. Complex visuomotor abilities are those most likely to be used in many activities of daily living, and even modest decrements may result in significant changes in everyday functioning (Mahurin et al., in press).

Some authorities have raised the issue of whether differences between young and old may be attributed not to neural factors but solely to criterial variables; i.e., the responses of elderly subjects are slow merely because of an inflexible psychological strategy that is overcautious and minimizes risk-taking (Botwinick, 1969; Fozard, 1981; Welford, 1985, 1988). However, studies from the verbal learing, signal detection and pain perception arenas ail to support a simple association between sychological factors and speed differences. For ex- mple, Okun and colleagues (Okun et al., 1978;)kun and DiVesta, 1976) have shown that over- autiousness does not account for the observed age ifferences in performance on serial learning tasks, finding repeated in areas of signal detection and ain perception work (e.g., Harkins and Chapman, 977). Reviews of the literature by Salthouse (1985, 988) also conclude that age differences in speed lso exist independently of the individual's bias owards speed or accuracy, lending support to the onclusion that shifts in response bias alone do not xplain all of the slowing evident in RT performance f elderly subjects.

It has also been suggested that declines in age- elated speed may not represent normal aging at all, ut rather represent a selection bias in choosing ounger, disease-free subjects. Rabbit (1983), in a road study of psychomotor and cognitive perfor- nance in younger and older subjects, reported that vhen Performance IQ was statistically controlled, ge-related differences in response time were not een. Smith (1989) has suggested that 'aging, per se, s not the cause of deterioration in performance. Rather, elderly subjects are more likely to have liseases that result in deterioration of performance' p. 71). In support of this viewpoint, the effect of ag- ng on RT has been shown to interact with car- liovascular health (Light, 1978), cerebrovascular lisease (Benton, 1977), motivation and experimen- al set (Botwinick et al., 1959) and practice effects Botwinick and Storandt, 1973). From this perspec- ive, the aging individual is slower in responding to xternal stimuli secondary to subclinical pathologi- al processes, and is less resilient in compensating or physiological and psychological insult.

Aging muscle

A number of age-related changes take place in the ohysical structure and physiological functioning of he systems that serve movement. One often notices he appearance of muscle wasting in healthy aging

persons to the extent that it is commonly accepted as normal and is expected as normal during clinical ex- amination (Schaumburg et al., 1983). Recent re- search has quantified the types of muscle loss, as well as changes in metabolism within the muscle, in the aged individual and age-related changes in muscular metabolism, reflex functioning and para- meters of movement.

Recent findings on changes in the morphology of muscle have included diminution of the number of motor units (Grimby, 1988; Lexell et al., 1983, 1988; Brown et al., 1988; Borkan et al., 1985; Grimby et al., 1982). The motor unit is the most basic element of investigation (Munsat, 1984), and consists of a single alpha motor neuron and all muscle fibers that it innervates. Grimby has recently shown that, with aging, the reduction in muscle mass is due to loss of numbers of these motor units (Grimby, 1988). Up to age 70 years, it was found that changes are more quantitative than qualitative, in that reduction in numbers of fibers took place. There was also a reduction in muscle fibers as a relationship of dif- ferences in patterns of activity and recruitment, with reduction in quadriceps, but not in other muscle groups such as upper extremity biceps (Young et al., 1985; Grimby, 1988). Another study indicated that atrophy may start as early as 25 years of age (Lexell et al., 1988) and accelerate after that. These in- vestigators found no predominant type of muscle fiber loss, but rather a steady diminution of numbers of fibers in general. In another study using electromyography as an indirect way of measuring sizes of motor units by their electrical potentials and as an estimate of the innervation zones (Brown et al., 1988), it was found that normal healthy in- dividuals over the age of 60 years have approximate- ly one-half the number of motor units of subjects under 60 years of age.

Experiments have also sought to determine whether types of muscle fiber are differentially lost or spared, and thus investigators have focused on striated muscle types known as slow twitch and fast twitch fibers. Some studies have found a greater loss of type II, or fast twitch fibers (Grimby, 1988; Oertel, 1986; Poggi et al., 1987) relative to the numbers of type I or slow twitch. Other investigators have postulated that perhaps rather than selective type II atrophy, type II fibers may possibly convert to type I fibers (Poggi et al., 1987). Other investigations have found no differential loss of the two types of fiber (Lexell et al., 1983; Grimby et al., 1982; Grimby et al., 1984). As these investigations have sampled identical muscle groups (usually the vastus lateralis) more research is necessary to determine the role of individual differences in the selectivity of this type of atrophy.

Within the muscle, age-related changes have also been found using histochemical staining for myofibrillar ATPase (Klitgaard et al., 1989). Vastus lateralis muscles in healthy aged subjects demonstrated increased amounts of type 1 myosin heavy-chain protein. The amount of calcium ATPase was also significantly lower in the aged group compared to younger controls, in an analysis of sarcoplasmic reticulum protein (Klitgaard et al., 1989). However, another two proteins localized in the lumen and junctional regions of the sarcoplasmic reticulum, calsequestrin and 350-kDa ryanodine-binding protein, did not show the same decreases across age groups (Klitgaard et al., 1989). The authors concluded that aging differentially affects extrajunctional and junctional portions of the sarcoplasmic reticulum in human skeletal muscle. These hypothesized age-related changes, however, were not observed within a group of older subjects who had enrolled in a program of strength training.

Deposition of lipid appears to shift in location (Meredith et al., 1989) as a function of age. It has been shown that lipid droplets are present in increasing numbers within muscle fibers as individuals age (Poggi et al., 1987). Additionally, these investigators found mitochondrial size and mitochondrial percentage per fiber to decrease with age. The authors concluded that the changes in mitochondrial size and percentage may represent a response to reduced metabolic demand within the muscle as activity levels change during aging. In a related process to the deposition of lipid droplets, lipid pigment (lipofuscin) granules were also detected in greater numbers within perioral muscles as age increased

(Dayan et al., 1988). In an analysis of other components of the muscle cell bodies, a planimetr method for analysing relative sizes of the cell contents indicated that the ratio of nucleus size to cytoplasm area increased significantly after the age of 60. Overall, cell diameter size decreased, as well as the aforementioned findings of numbers of muscle fibers. However, the number of muscle nuclei remained unchanged. These authors compared th finding with that seen in atrophy due to denervation (Manta et al., 1987).

Changes in motor innervation have also been investigated in human intercostal muscle fibers using silver and acetylcholinesterase staining methods and autoradiography using labeled alpha-bungarotoxin (Oda, 1984). As age increases, the number of preterminal axons entering the motor endplate and the length of the endplate were found to be increased and the endplate was composed of a greater number of conglomerates of acetylcholine receptors. This comparison was made between subjects in their fourth decade and those in their eighth decade. A linear relationship was found for each of these morphological parameters with regard to age, and the authors concluded that there are gradual changes in pre- and postsynaptic elements of the human motor endplate over the course of aging (Oda, 1984). Reasons for the age-related dropping out of motor units have been investigated. However, the etiology of 'senile muscle atrophies' remains unclear, but it is plausible that multiple causes contribute to these age-related changes (Schaumburg et al., 1983). Some hypotheses (Munsat, 1984) have been advanced that attribute atrophy to the absence of regular contraction against resistance. It is suspected that regular exertion must be performed for the muscle fibers to be preserved.

Biochemical and neurophysiological functioning of muscle appears to change little with aging. Studies have found that plasma resting values for lactic acid, pyruvic acid, serum creatine phosphokinase (CPK), electrolytes (Munsat, 1984; Moller et al., 1979), lactic acid dehydrogenase, myosinase (Aniansson et al., 1986) and phosphate metabolic products do not change with age (Taylor et al.,

1984). Phosphodiesters have been shown to increase in slow twitch muscles as age increases (Satrustegui et al., 1988). The ability to use oxygen during muscle activity has consistently been shown to undergo age-related decline (Suominen et al., 1977). Also, in response to endurance training, glycogen stores increased significantly, only in elderly subjects, whereas prior to training glycogen utilization was higher in elderly than in younger subjects (Meredith et al., 1989). Mitochondrial oxidative capacity shows a substantial fall in relation to age (Trounce et al., 1989), and this loss of mitochondrial respiratory capacity may account for reduced exercise capacity in elderly subjects.

The ability to metabolize protein has also been shown to change in elderly subjects (Uauy et al., 1978; Young, 1990). The distribution of whole body protein metabolism changes significantly with age, with muscle breakdown making a contribution of 20% or less in elderly subjects versus a mean of 27% in young adults (Uauy et al., 1978; Young, 1990). The decline in muscle protein metabolism was cited as a possible factor in the reduced capacity of elderly subjects to withstand stressful situations (Young, 1990). Additionally, this reduced ability for muscle to supply glutamine, essential for immune function, is further evidence for reduction of this vital function.

The action of muscle in subserving movement also changes with age. Motor units are summated or recruited to effect force and then derecruited. In younger subjects, recruitment and derecruitment occur in an orderly fashion, whereas in older subjects the orderliness appears to break down (Kamen and DeLuca, 1989). Movement trajectories are less accurate in elderly subjects because of occasional tonic co-contraction of agonist and antagonist fibers prior to and during movements (Darling et al., 1989), which causes greater trajectory for acceleratory and deceleratory phases of movement (Darling et al., 1989; Cooke et al., 1989).

Age-related deficits in postural control (described above) may be secondary to disturbed muscle synergy. It has been hypothesized that this phenomenon is related to reversals of the onset of proximal and distal muscles, as well as increases in latency of distal muscle activation (Woollacott et al., 1986). Substitution of larger motor units for smaller ones which may usually effect low levels of tension also occurs more often in elderly subjects (Nelson et al., 1983, 1984). With the dropout of units, the changes in respiratory activity, and the possibility of dyssynergy, it follows that reduced muscle force occurs in elderly subjects. This has been quantified in triceps surae experimentally as compared to young controls following voluntary and evoked (tetanic) contractions (Davies and White, 1983; Petrella et al., 1989). It was found that the triceps surae of men in their late sixties were weaker, more slowly contracting, and showed a greater relative force loss in a standard fatigue test than the younger subjects (Davies et al., 1983). With electrically elicited contraction, elderly subjects showed reduced amplitude but prolonged response in comparison to that of younger adults (McDonagh et al., 1984). After fatiguing contractions by tetanic stimulation, muscle of elderly subjects (mean age 66 years) showed slower return to resting levels of the rate and time course of twitch relaxation, as compared with that of physically active 25-year olds (Klein et al., 1988).

Thus, with age, overall motor activity may suffer from a variety of effects at the muscle level. Large-scale loss of fibers occurs and in those fibers that remain there is alteration in innervation, metabolism and energy utilization and recruitment of units, and their synergistic activity all serve to reduce force. However, there is some indication that a high level of activity interacts with these deteriorating trends to slow their progression or reverse them, and that regular endurance training can overcome some of this loss of motoric vigor (see discussion below).

Neurodegenerative disease and aging

Many age-related neurodegenerative disorders have motor and cognitive features. Parkinson's disease (PD), progressive supranuclear palsy (PSP), Huntington's disease (HD), normal-pressure hydrocephalus (NPH) and Alzheimer's disease (AD) are considered in this chapter. These neurodegenerative disorders are characterized by mixed cognitive and motor features. For example, HD, PD and PSP are classified as movement disorders, even though cognitive deficits are common. In contrast, AD is primarily a dementing illness; however, motor features such as bradykinesia, myoclonus and rigidity are frequently present. The cognitive aspects of many of these disorders are well described elsewhere in this volume. Therefore, the following section focuses on motor characteristics of the neurodegenerative disorders, especially with reference to extrapyramidal dysfunction.

Parkinson's disease

After essential tremor, PD is the most common movement disorder of the elderly that is seen by neurologists (Jankovic, 1989). Initial symptoms usually appear in the fifth or sixth decade, and the disease follows a variably progressive course. Diagnosis of PD is made on the basis of clinical presentation, and is based on symptoms of tremor at rest, bradykinesia, rigidity and postural instability (Zetusky et al., 1985). Associated symptoms include stooped posture, poverty of spontaneous facial and limb movement, shuffling gait, micrographia, hypophonia and weakness (Jankovic, in press; Marsden, 1990).

Cognitive impairment is a significant feature of PD (Pirozzolo et al., 1988). Estimates of the prevalence of dementia in PD populations range from 20% (Pollock and Hornabrook, 1966) to 81% (Martin et al., 1973), with the majority of studies reporting between 30% and 50% (Boller et al., 1980). Pirozzolo et al. (1982a) found intellectual deficits in 93% of a sample of 60 PD patients, with 83% of these patients performing at lower levels than controls even when tests requiring motor coordination and speed were excluded from the analysis. However, a lack of bimodality in the distribution of scores did not allow a clear-cut division into 'demented' and 'non-demented' subgroups, and suggested a limited usefulness in attaching a prevalence estimate to the occurrence of dementia in PD. Nevertheless, specific cognitive deficits are frequently reported in PD, particularly visuospatial impairment, memory deficits and deficits in temporal ordering and sequencing of new information (Growdon and Corkin, 1986).

The relative contribution of limb rigidity, as opposed to central processing limitations, in explaining bradykinesia in PD has been the focus of several RT studies (Flowers, 1976; Heilman et al., 1976; Evarts et al., 1981). When slowing is observed in PD subjects, longer RTs are positively correlated with disease severity (Cassell et al., 1973), and show a strong relationship to pattern of motor symptoms (Mahurin and Pirozzolo, 1985). It has also been demonstrated that choice RT, but not simple RT, is adversely affected by decreased L-dopa infusion rate, suggesting differential sensitivity of RT components in PD patients (Pullman et al., 1988).

A number of investigators have reported a close relation between severity of parkinsonian symptoms, primarily bradykinesia, and degree of intellectual loss (Marttila and Rinne, 1976; Mayeux et al., 1981; Mortimer et al., 1985; Pirozzolo et al., 1982a). If subcortical involvement is responsible for both intellectual and motoric dysfunction, then a high degree of correlation should exist between these two variables. Quantified measurement of severity of bradykinesia, rigidity and tremor in PD has failed to reveal high inter-correlations, suggesting their relative independence. For example, Mortimer and colleagues (Mortimer, 1988; Mortimer and Webster, 1982) report that significant negative correlations were found between the degree of bradykinesia and visuospatial performance (both timed and untimed), spatial-orientation memory and psychomotor speed. Tremor, in contrast, was found to be positively correlated with spatial-orientation memory. Rigidity was not significantly correlated with any of the neuropsychological measures. These relationships were not significantly changed when age, age at onset or degree of depression were statistically controlled (Mortimer et al., 1982). However, subsequent data from Mortimer and colleagues indicate that these relationships are not universal in PD patients, but tend to apply within more specific subgroups, perhaps defined by the extent of dopaminergic involvement (Mortimer, 1988; Pirozzolo et al., 1988).

Apraxia, the inability to carry out familiar movements correctly on command, has also been examined in patients with PD. Pirozzolo et al. (1982a) did not find significant impairment in praxis for PD patients as compared with control subjects. Nevertheless, the authors noted that the small number and relative ease of items on the apraxia tests may have created a 'ceiling effect', obscuring possible deficits. Another study of PD patients demonstrated significantly lower praxis scores for PD patients as compared with a neurological control group (Goldenberg et al., 1986). PD patients were found to be significantly worse in imitation of movements, but not in production of movements to verbal command. When results were statistically adjusted for age and general intelligence, significant correlations were still found within the PD group between imitation of movement sequences and hand positions, and measures of visuospatial construction and perception. The authors discuss the possible role of both an interaction between visuospatial abilities and the short-term memory required for imitation of movements, and an interference effect between successive components of movement sequences in contribution to the observed deficits.

Parkinsonian features are associated with a variety of etiological factors, including viral encephalitis, neuroleptic usage, manganese and carbon monoxide poisoning, and multiple infarcts. However, approximately 85% of cases of parkinsonism are of obscure etiology, and are diagnosed as 'idiopathic' PD (Jankovic, in press). Recent evidence of parkinsonian features associated with exposure to the neurotoxin MPTP suggests, in some cases, a possible environmental etiology for PD (Langston, 1988; Langston et al., 1987).

Although levodopa provides the most effective symptomatic relief of PD through replacement therapy, it does not stop the progression of the basic disease process. Alternative pharmacological therapies are employed, including anticholinergic agents, amantadine (an antiviral agent which acts to release dopamine from intact neurons) and postsynaptic dopaminergic agonists (bromocriptine, pergolide and lisuride). The efficacy of monoamine oxidase inhibitors to slow the progression of PD is also currently under investigation (Jankovic et al., in press; Tetrud and Langston, 1989). Experimental treatment involving transplantation of dopamine-producing cells from the patient's own adrenal medulla to the caudate have recently received much attention, but the long-term outcome of this procedure is as yet uncertain (Jankovic et al., 1989).

Neuropathological correlates
Neuropathological findings in PD include degeneration of pigmented brainstem nuclei, predominantly the zona compacta of the substantia nigra, but also the ventral tegmental area, locus coeruleus, dorsal vagal nucleus and sympathetic ganglia (Young et al., 1988). The histopathological appearance of Lewy bodies confirms the degenerative changes in these areas (Gibb, 1988; Growdon et al., 1986). The basal ganglia in PD show neuronal degeneration in the substantia nigra, involving predominantly ventral lateral (output) portions. Biochemical dysfunction most likely involves not only dopaminergic pathways exclusively, but also interactions with other neurotransmitter substances, including acetylcholine, GABA, monamines and various neuropeptides (Yebenes and Gomez, 1988; Agid et al., 1987). The severity of the parkinsonian disability has been shown to correlate highly with the degree of striatal dopaminergic deficiency; decreased caudate levels are associated with bradykinesia, while deficiencies in the pallidum are correlated with degree of tremor (Delwaide and Gonce, 1988).

Another biochemical pathway, that of ascending cholinergic fibers, the substantia innominata, may relate symptoms of dementia seen in PD to those of AD (Marsden, 1990; Whitehouse et al., 1982, 1983). For example, Boller et al. (1980) found clinical documentation of severe dementia in about one-third of a group of 29 parkinsonian patients. All of these patients had a quantitative predominance of histological changes suggestive of AD, and significant correlations were established between severity of recorded intellectual impairment and the presence of the neurological stigmata. Other studies have documented similar neuropathological findings in both cortex and basal forebrain of PD patients. As is the case for AD, relationships have been established between clinically determined dementia and postmortem findings of neuritic plaque formation and neurofibrillary tangling (Hakim and Mathieson, 1979; Nakano and Hirano, 1983).

However, it remains unclear whether there are common mechanisms underlying the motor and cognitive deficits in PD. For example, although neuropathological findings similar to AD have been described in PD, hippocampal levels of choline acetyltransferase and cholinesterase are reported to be no different in PD patients than those of a control group of similar age (McGeer and McGeer, 1971). It has also been shown that the presence of dementia in PD has been found to contraindicate the effectiveness of levodopa therapy, rather than paralleling it; Although cognition improves briefly following initiation of L-dopa, the effect has consistently been found to be short-lasting (Botez and Barbeau, 1975; Halgin et al., 1977). Further, the finding of diffuse Lewy disease in a high percentage of PD patients with dementia suggests that as yet unspecified mechanisms may underlie the cognitive impairments seen in the disease (Growdon et al., 1986).

Neurobehavioral disturbances such as personality changes and cognitive deficits characterize PD but, again, these deficits have been difficult to localize. Taylor and colleagues have provided evidence that some of these deficits may be due to primary frontal-lobe dysfunction (Taylor et al., 1986). Again, these deficits may be related to the 'complex' caudatofugal pathway. Some but not all of these 'frontal' deficits improve with levodopa therapy, suggesting that the relationship between these deficits and an underlying dopamine deficiency is complex.

Young and Penney's (1984, 1988; Penney and Young, 1983, 1986) model of basal ganglia function

(described above) provides a theoretical basis for describing motor dysfunction in PD. According to this model, motor behavior is maintained under normal conditions by a reinforcing feedback loop from cortex through the basal ganglia to the thalamus and back to the cortex. When a particular motor behavior is selected, the thalamic neurons are disinhibited, facilitating the motor programs. It is hypothesized that the primary feedback loop reinforcing a particular behavior is diminished in normal aging, and more significantly impaired in PD. The loss of excitatory input to striatal cells would result in slowness and poverty of movement. In addition, inhibitory dopaminergic input to striatal neurons projecting to LGP would be lost. Thus, there would be decreased activity (i.e., increased inhibition) of LGP neurons, which would result in disinhibition of STN output to MGP and SNpr, reinforcing inhibition of unwanted movements. If this suppression is excessive, then it would be difficult to switch to new behaviors in the context of additional difficulty in maintaining the ongoing behavior. Excessive negative input to striatal cells that project to MGP and SNpr may result in the gradual decrescendo pattern often seen in attempts by PD patients to maintain motor behaviors.

An alternative explanation for the bradykinesia of PD is given in the parallel circuit model of function proposed by DeLong and colleagues (Alexander et al., 1986; DeLong et al., 1983, 1984). As discussed above, movements in PD are characterized by slow RTs and slow movement times. Pullman et al. (1988) have found that RTs for simple tasks and RTs for tasks requiring choice are differently affected in PD. Both are prolonged in PD. However, simple RTs are not improved by L-dopa therapy, whereas choice RTs are restored almost to normal. Simple RT hypothesized to depend on the subject's attention and preparation to move, while choice RT is dependent on an additional cognitive factor to select an appropriate direction of movement.

Simple RT performance may be associated with the motor circuit that projects to the SMA. The motor circuit proposed by DeLong projects almost exclusively to the SMA. The SMA contains a signifiant proportion of neurons exhibiting preparatory set related activity. The attention and preparation underlying a simple RT task is analogous to the motor readiness of preparatory set behavior. The SMA and its connections are non-dopaminergic, so it is reasonable that dopamine replacement does not improve simple RT. However, choice RT is dependent on cognitive processes beyond attention and preparation alone and thus may be subserved by the 'complex' pathway that projects to the prefrontal pathway. This pathway is dopaminergic and would be restored by dopamine replacement.

The other 'negative' cardinal sign of PD, postural instability, is probably mediated by complicated physiological processes that have not been well elucidated. However, the 'positive' signs of PD, rigidity and tremor, have received some attention. While no definite conclusions have been reached from neurophysiological studies, it is hypothesized that an abnormally increased drive from MGP may be responsible for the rigidity in PD (DeLong et al., 1981, 1983). Nigrostriatal dopamine depletion may result in pallidal disinhibition and increased suprasegmental activation of normal spinal reflex mechanisms. This activation is ultimately expressed in increased muscle tone. The other 'positive' sign, tremor, is thought to be dependent on a central oscillator mechanism but also influenced by peripheral reflex mechanisms. Reports of rhythmic firing of neurons in the thalamus and basal ganglia support the existence of a central generator. Within the motor circuit, a central oscillator would determine tremor, amplitude and frequency by periodic inputs to the motor neurons through descending motor pathways (Burne, 1987).

PD and aging

The frequently observed movement patterns of 'normal' elderly subjects, including hypokinesia, tremor, shuffling gait and stooped posture, are so similar to clinical features of PD that comparisons of the two processes seem inevitable (Barbeau, 1973; McGeer et al., 1977; Mortimer et al., 1982; Teravainen and Calne, 1983).

As previously discussed, the most striking age-related biochemical alteration in the human CNS is the reduction of dopamine in the basal ganglia (Miller and DeLong, 1988). A similar, although more profound, reduction of dopamine, tyrosine hydroxylase and dopa-decarboxylase occurs in PD. PET studies comparing PD patients who have hemiparkinsonism with age-matched controls have shown decreased presynaptic dopamine levels in the contralateral striatum (Garnett et al., 1984). Presynaptic reductions have also been shown in patients with bilateral parkinsonism (Leenders et al., 1986). For patients with hemiparkinsonism, ipsilateral regions also showed decreased concentrations, suggesting subthreshold decrease of dopamine neurons prior to the presentation of clinical symptoms (Martin et al., 1986).

However, although some of the motor features of PD are seen in normal aging, they differ in severity and distribution. For example, Mortimer (1988) found no significant correlations between age and positive motor signs (rigidity and tremor) in a group of 74 healthy elderly subjects, but did find significant negative associations between age and speed of limb movement and ambulation. Significant correlations were also found between age and several motor performance tasks, including rotary pursuit, rate of pronation-supination and finger tapping. Additionally, disruptions in basic movement patterns, such as vestibulomotor integration, oculomotor control, regulation of gait and maintenance of postural tone, are frequently seen with extrapyramidal lesions, but have no direct counterparts in the normally aging adult (Mortimer, 1988).

Further, only a small percentage of elderly individuals eventually develop PD. This finding, evidence from MPTP studies, plus the lack of strong evidence for an inherited basis for PD (primarily from twin studies) suggest that environmental factors are, at least to some extent, involved in the etiology of PD (Calne and Langston, 1983). It may be that PD is caused by the normal process of aging and the existence of an endotoxin dopamine itself. The mechanism of this interaction may be the oxidation of dopamine by monoamine oxidase, which leads to free radical production. For each molecule of dopamine that is oxidized by MAO there is production of one equivalent molecule of hydrogen peroxide. Excess hydrogen peroxide and other oxyradicals may be toxic to neurons. It is possible that dopamine is toxic to nigral neurons via autoxidation to cytotoxic quinone and covalent binding of oxidized intermediates (Graham, 1978).

An alternative hypothesis has been proposed, in which PD may be associated with an environmental insult (e.g., a neurotoxin) superimposed on already existing age-related declines in dopamine function (Calne et al., 1983). It has been shown that an 80% depletion of dopamine cells in the substantia nigra is necessary for the clinical presentation of PD (Riederer and Wuketich, 1976). In addition, an age-related increased sensitivity to MPTP has been demonstrated in rats, suggesting an increased vulnerability to environmental neurotoxins that occurs with aging (Ricaurte, 1987). Finally, other, as yet poorly understood, influences may underlie the degenerative process of PD, such as lack of a trophic factor, or early insult to the substantia nigra that increases dopamine turnover in spared neurons. The latter process would accentuate the process of free radical generation leading to cell death.

Progressive supranuclear palsy

PSP was first described by Steele et al. (1964). The title of the paper serves as a capsule description of the disease: 'A heterogeneous degeneration involving the brain stem, basal ganglia and cerebellum with vertical gaze and pseudobulbar palsy, nuchal dystonia and dementia'. PSP overlaps PD in both pathology and symptoms, and it has been estimated that 4% of patients given an initial diagnosis of PD will later receive a diagnosis of PSP (Jackson et al., 1983).

The age of onset of PSP is typically between 50 and 70 years. Disease progression is variable, but is generally more rapid than in PD. The patients of Steele et al. (1964) died within 5 − 7 years of first symptoms, and most patients die within the first decade (mean of 6 years in two recent studies: Golbe and Davis, 1988; Golbe et al., 1987). The most com-

mon initial symptom is gait difficulty, often with falling (Golbe et al., 1987). Other early symptoms include vertical gaze palsy (followed later by lateral gaze palsy), dysarthria, and dysphagia (Jankovic et al., 1990). In addition to gaze paresis, a variety of other oculomotor abnormalities occur in PSP, and some patients initially present with vague visual complaints.

Several features distinguish PSP and PD. Although PSP, like PD, is characterized by bradykinesia and postural instability, the rigidity in PSP is predominantly axial with hypertonic neck extension, as opposed to the diffuse rigidity of PD (Jankovic, 1984). In contrast to PD, resting tremor is rare in PSP. Facial expression in PD is 'masked' or hypomimic; PSP patients often have a grimacing facial expression, with deep facial lines. Stutter and palilalia are more common in PSP, as are frequent blinking and apraxia of eyelid opening (Golbe et al., 1988; Lees, 1982).

Depending on the extent of involvement, the gait in PSP may appear similar to the akinetic-rigid gait in PD. However, in contrast to the bradykinetic, narrow-based, shuffling gait seen in PD, the gait in PSP is characteristically stiff and broad-based, with a halting, uncertain quality to it. Nuchal rigidity and downward gaze paresis disallow the patient complete visual information of step placement, and may contribute to the gait disturbance, particularly when the patient is required to step over objects or descend stairs. For these reasons, unsteadiness and frequent falls, both forward and backward, are often early signs of PSP, and aid in differential diagnosis. The disturbed gait seen in PSP is not thought to be associated with cerebellar-type ataxia, vestibular or proprioceptive disturbance, or limb weakness (Maagr and Lees, 1986).

Dementia was described in the initial clinical report of PSP, and since then other authors have discussed the mental changes as being prototypical of the so-called 'subcortical dementias' (Albert et al., 1974). There is no doubt that significant cognitive loss occurs in the late stages of illness, but there has been debate regarding the occurrence of a true dementia early in the disease (Hynd et al., 1982;

Pirozzolo et al., 1988). Kimura et al. (1981) and others have emphasized that oculomotor disturbance affects performance on neuropsychological testing, and that patients' performance is often within normal limits when testing is designed to take this into account (Pirozzolo et al., 1988). Recently PET studies have emphasized the existence of frontal lobe hypometabolism in PSP (Goffinet et al., 1989), and poor performance on cognitive tests associated with frontal lobe functions have also been reported (Pillon et al., 1986; Milberg and Albert, 1989). However, it is unclear from these studies at what stage of the diagnosis frontal dysfunction can first be detected (either by PET or by neuropsychological testing).

Pharmacological treatment of PSP has been less successful than that of PD. Dopamine-enhancing agents, anticholinergics and a variety of other agents have been tried with minimal results, although failure of large research studies does not preclude responsiveness in a given individual patient. Symptomatic treatment of depression and pseudobulbar affect with antidepressants is also successful in certain patients.

Neuropathological correlates

Currently, the etiology of PSP is unknown. The diagnosis has been difficult to study because of its relative rarity, and there is little evidence bearing on genetics, transmissible, toxic or other possible etiologies. The pathology of PSP suggests some commonalities with other neurodegenerative disorders. Neurofibrillary tangles (NFTs) are a hallmark of PSP and are also found in Alzheimer's disease. The tangles have twisted as well as straight filaments, and many have the same antigenic epitopes as those in AD. However, they differ in other respects from NFTs found in AD (Golbe et al., 1988), and their association with cognitive loss is still unclear. The greatest areas of cell loss in PSP are the striatum, midbrain tegmentum, superior colliculi, periacqueductal gray matter, dentate nucleus and other brainstem nuclei.

Autopsy reports as well as CT and MRI scanning may in some cases reveal disproportionate midbrain atrophy and enlargement of the third ventricle (Haldeman et al., 1981). Neuropathological findings (including NFTs, gliosis and granulovacuolar degeneration) are most pronounced in striatal regions, but also include subthalamic nucleus, substantia nigra and locus coeruleus. Degenerative changes have also been reported in the hippocampal gyri, inferior olive and dentate nuclei of the cerebellum, superior colliculi, vestibular nuclei, periaqueductal grey, pontomesencephalitic tegmentum and the nucleus basalis of Meynert (Ishino and Otsuki, 1976; Powell et al., 1974).

Biochemical studies reveal a marked reduction in dopamine and homovanillic acid in basal ganglia structures, particularly the caudate and putamen. Biochemical analysis reveals reduced levels of tyrosine hydroxylase, a precursor in catecholamine pathways (Jellinger et al., 1980). This reduction is significant throughout brainstem areas, suggesting loss of dopaminergic neurons. However, in contrast to PD, in which postsynaptic receptors remain intact, PSP is characterized by reduction in postsynaptic D-2 dopamine receptors. This finding may account for the relative ineffectiveness of levodopa in the treatment of PSP.

Huntington's disease

HD was first described in a classic paper by George Huntington in 1872. The disease is rare, occurring in 5 – 10 per 100,000 people. Inheritance is autosomal dominant with offspring at 50% risk. Usual age of onset is between 30 and 50 (Myers and Martin, 1982), but juvenile cases (Westphal variant) and elderly cases also occur. The former usually inherit the disorder from the mother. Duration of the illness is 10 – 30 years.

Chorea is the predominant motor symptom in HD (Weiner and Lang, 1989). However, initial symptoms may go unrecognized, consisting of minor tics, muscle twitches or clumsiness. In addition, coordination of upper extremities and stability of gait may undergo subtle changes. As the disease progresses, choreiform movements become more pronounced, consisting of abrupt, jerking motions of the extremities, trunk and head (Shoulson, 1990). In what appears as a semi-purposeful attempt to cover the extent of adventitious movements, the patient may incorporate involuntary motions into commonplace actions, such as brushing back the hair, adjusting clothing or coughing.

As the disease progresses, athetoid movements may become prominent, characterized by writhing, flexion-extension motions of the trunk, limbs and neck. Grimacing and tic-like movements of the face and mouth are also common (Shoulson, 1990). Decreased muscle tone may be present, and reduced motor control of the speech apparatus is frequently seen, resulting in dysarthric, slurred speech. Approximately 10% of patients present with an akinetic-rigid variation of symptoms, approximating those of classical Parkinson's disease (Bird and Paulson, 1971; Bitterbender and Quadfasel, 1962). Abnormal eye movements may also become apparent in HD, including disturbance of voluntary gaze, nystagmus and disruption of rapid-eye movements during sleep (Starr, 1967).

The gait of HD patients becomes progressively irregular and unsteady, imparting a characteristic dancelike (choreic) appearance to walking. Biomechanical analysis reveals greater variance in the gait of HD patients as compared to controls, with decreased walking velocity, stride length and cadence (Koller and Trimble, 1985). Clinical observation reveals that smoothly integrated ambulation is compromised by athetotic and choreic jerking movements of the trunk and limbs, resulting in awkward, halting forward motion. Step placement is unpredictable, and the patient assumes a wide base to maintain balance. Slow twisting movements of the trunk and abnormal head posturing contribute to the typical picture. Irregular, dystonic limb positioning disturbs attempts to find a consistent center of gravity over which to position the body, and adds to the patient's inability to maintain a well-balanced stance or gait. The physical base of the lower limbs themselves may also be compromised secondary to dystonic plantar-flexion or dorsiflexion. It has been suggested that principal motor symptoms differ according to age of onset, with

rigidity prominent in earlier years, chorea in mid-life onset, and intention tremor more pronounced in older patients (Lishman, 1978). In all cases, however, severe dystonia and near-immobility eventually render the patient incapable of self-care.

Psychological symptoms are common in HD, with some writers reporting such symptoms in over 90% of patients. Emotional disorder or personality change is often the initial symptom, before chorea or dementia. The psychiatric symptoms vary widely, ranging from anxiety, irritability and impulsivity to psychosis (Martin and Gusella, 1986). A schizophrenic-like psychosis is usually reported but mania can also occur (Sax et al., 1983). Depression is common and suicide risk is high, especially in the early stages (Schoenfeld et al., 1984). Certain psychiatric symptoms suggests frontal system dysfunction (apathy, emotional lability, impulsivity, inappropriate behavior, disregard of personal hygiene). The onset of depressive and personality changes prior to overt physical manifestations implicates specific biological substrates for these psychological symptoms, and suggest they are not completely accounted for by reactive emotional response to the disease.

Dementia is considered universal in HD, although the cognitive changes may be minimal in the early stages. Intellectual deterioration in HD typically first affects memory, with later involvement of visual-spatial, problem-solving, psychomotor and arithmetic abilities (Schoulson, 1990). It has been suggested that a characteristic cognitive profile exists in HD, distinct from other dementias (Aminoff et al., 1975; Butters et al., 1979). Although suggestive, these claims are difficult to substantiate. For example, reports of 'visuospatial abnormalities' and 'sequential planning deficits' can be said to be present in many dementias. Nonetheless, there has been consistency across studies in describing memory loss early in the diagnosis and in describing attention/concentration deficits as prominent. A 'frontal lobe syndrome' is also often reported, with decreased performance on word-generation tasks and on tasks requiring mental flexibility or shifting of cognitive set. Language is reported as preserved, but with dysnomia on formal testing and with reduced verbal output (Butters et al., 1979).

Predictive testing is now possible for HD. At-risk individuals can be told with 98% certainty that they will or will not develop the disease (Martin, 1989). To date, however, this is a highly restricted practice with significant ethical and social implications. One limitation of testing is that a number of family members must also be tested, including both affected and unaffected relatives, so the test cannot be applied in small families (Wexler et al., 1985). Predictive testing was made possible by discovery of a genetic marker on chromosome 4 (Gusella et al., 1983). However, the gene itself has so far eluded detection; until the gene and its function are known, effective intervention appears unlikely.

Treatment of HD is symptomatic. Dopamine antagonists such as haloperidol may improve the chorea. Psychiatric disturbances may also respond to pharmacotherapy, although the schizophrenia-like psychosis seen in some patients is said to be refractive to treatment. Supportive therapies and genetic counseling have a major place in treatment but are often underused.

Neuropathological correlates

Marked bilateral atrophy of the caudate nucleus and putamen are evident in pathological studies of HD patients, with resulting enlargement of the frontal horns of the lateral ventricles (VonSattel et al., 1985). Positron emission tomography reveals decreased glucose metabolism in regions of the caudate, as well as globus pallidus, thalamus and subthalamic nucleus (Benson et al., 1981; Kuhl et al., 1982). Cortical metabolism, in contrast, is generally reported as normal (Kuhl et al., 1982).

Neuropathological studies reveal reduction of GABAergic neurons that project to the substantia nigra, with only slight involvement of cholinergic neurons (Kuhl et al., 1982; Martin, 1984). Biochemical changes in the neostriatum include reductions in glutamic acid decarboxylase, an enzyme necessary for the production of GABA (Penney and Young, 1988). Disruption of the biochemical balance between neostriatum and substantia nigra potentially results in disinhibition (increase) of dopaminergic output from the substantia nigra, in turn causing the choreic movements. This model is strengthened by the observation that administration of levodopa to HD patients results in a worsening of choreic movements, while dopamine antagonists (e.g., phenothiazines, butyrophenones) partially alleviate chorea (Weiner et al., 1989). However, GABA agonists have not been proven clinically successful in the control of abnormal movements associated with HD.

Normal pressure hydrocephalus

Normal pressure hydrocephalus (NPH) was first reported as a distinct clinical entity in the mid-1960s (Adams et al., 1965). It is a disease of elderly subjects, with age of onset generally between 60 and 70 years of age. An average incidence of less than 10% has been reported across series of elderly patients presenting with dementing syndromes (Maletta et al., 1982; Wolff, 1982). Although it occurs with relatively low frequency, clinical recognition of NPH is important because it is a potentially treatable disorder.

As with the other age-related movement disorders discussed in this chapter, NPH is characterized by both motor and cognitive features. The classically recognized triad of symptoms includes dementia, gait disturbance and urinary incontinence. However, all three of these features need not be invariably present. The identifying neuroradiological feature is distension of the ventricular system in the absence of consistent increases in intraventricular and cerebrospinal fluid (CSF) pressure. Obstruction in CSF flow is thought to occur in re-uptake over the sagittal sinuses. Initial pressure-related dilation of the ventricles is followed by equilibration of the intraventricular pressure-volume relationship. This is in contrast to 'tension' hydrocephalus, in which CSF pressure is increased secondary to intraventricular obstruction (Turner and McGeachie, 1988). However, even in NPH transient elevations in CSF tension have been documented (Hartmann and Alberti, 1977).

CT scan, MRI and pneumoencephalogram reveal dilation of cerebral ventricles, particularly the lateral and third ventricles. Radioisotope cisternography may also be employed in the differential workup, with slowed re-uptake of CSF over the convexities of the cerebral hemispheres being the characterizing feature. This procedure aids in the differentiation between NPH and hydrocephalus 'ex-vacuo', in which ventricular dilation is secondary to generalized cerebral atrophy.

Disturbed gait, the prominent motor sign in NPH, is typically slow, shuffling, and consists of small, hesitant steps. However, speed of ambulation may be increased by encouraging the patient to walk faster, or by entraining the patient's steps to those of the examiner. There is difficulty stepping over obstacles, climbing stairs and turning in place. The patient may also exhibit great difficulty in initiating ambulatory movement, even though poised to begin walking, and expressing comprehension of the examiner's request to do so. The appearance given is as if the feet were stuck, or 'glued' to the floor (so-called 'magnetic' gait) (Adams et al., 1965). Once in motion, the steps may assume a 'slipping-clutch' appearance. This type of gait superficially resembles that of patients with PD, but without associated tremor or rigidity.

Etiological factors are identifiable in about two-thirds of patients presenting with NPH. Precipitating causes include subarachnoid hemorrhage, meningitis, trauma, tumor, aqueductal stenosis, basilar artery ectasia and Paget's disease. The remaining third of cases are of unknown etiology, and the mechanisms underlying such idiopathic NPH are poorly understood (Turner et al., 1988).

Many patients with NPH may show symptomatic relief following CSF shunting procedures. The improvements in symptoms following shunting is presumed to result from the arrest of episodic increases in CSF pressure in the ventricular system, resulting in the prevention of further ischemia of periventricular tissue. However, not all patients benefit from shunting, and it is currently difficult to predict who will benefit from the procedure. Despite efforts to identify good candidates for surgery, only an estimated 55% of shunted NPH patients show appreciable change in their symptoms after surgery (Katzman, 1977; Mareth and Martin, 1977). Complications following surgery add to the difficulty in prediction of outcome, with estimates of these complications varying from 10% to 40%. Improvement in cognitive test scores from pre- to post-lumbar puncture has been demonstrated to hold promise for the selection of NPH patients who may benefit from shunt placement (Turner et al., 1988).

Neuropathological correlates

Motor dysfunction in NPH is hypothesized to be associated with medial frontal lobe pathology secondary to intraventricular tension. This results in stretching of frontal-subcortical white matter fibers carrying both afferent and efferent information. It has been noted that medially descending fibers from the motor cortex control both gait and urinary function, suggesting a common mechanism of involvement (Turner et al., 1988). Stretching of corticopontine white matter tracts that connect with cerebellar structures may also be related to the ataxic gait sometimes seen in the disorder (Marsden, 1984). The similar presentation of frontal-akinetic gait disturbance in AD, NPH, MID and PD suggests common involvement of frontal-subcortical structures and pathways (Lohr and Wisniewski, 1987). The prominent cognitive slowing and memory dysfunction typically seen in NPH is possibly associated with increased intraventricular pressure, particularly on the frontal lobes and subcortical structures surrounding the third ventricle.

Alzheimer's disease

The most common cause of intellectual deterioration in elderly subjects is AD (Evans et al., 1989). Although AD is principally characterized by diffuse intellectual deterioration, motor signs commonly accompany the disorder. Clinical diagnosis of AD is based on the history of illness, presenting mental and functional status, and detailed assessment of cognitive function (Katzman et al., 1988). Symptoms vary in severity among patients, and patients may show uneven rates of decline. Most cases, however, ultimately progress to death within 5 – 10 years, usually due to secondary infection or other complications of immobility.

The well-documented cognitive features of AD include memory impairment, visuospatial disorientation, language deficits, temporal and spatial confusion, apraxia, poor problem-solving ability and personality change (Cummings and Benson, 1983; McKhann et al., 1984; Pirozzolo et al., 1989; Reisberg, 1983; Swihart et al., 1988). Rigidity, gegenhalten, paratonia, myoclonus and spasticity are documented in AD, especially in advanced stages of illness (Chui et al., 1985; Mayeux et al., 1985; Molsa et al., 1984). Chui et al. (1985) examined a series of 146 AD patients, and found 45% to have extrapyramidal features, and 6% to have myoclonus.

The relationship of age-of-onset to severity of motor features in AD is unclear. Several studies have found a positive association between the two factors, with early appearance of motor signs reported to be more frequent in the familial, or early-onset variant of AD (Pirozzolo et al., 1982b; Pomara et al., 1981; Boller et al., 1980). However, Huff et al. (1987) examined the effect of age on presence of motor signs, and failed to find significant differences between younger (below age 65 years) and older (age 65 years or greater) AD patients.

AD patients have been evaluated in comparison with age-matched control subjects on simple auditory, simple visual, and choice RT tasks, and have been found to be impaired in all conditions (Ferris et al., 1976; Pirozzolo et al., 1981; Vrtunski et al., 1983). The degree of RT slowing in AD is highly associated with the generalized severity of dementia (Pirozzolo and Hansch, 1981). In addition, cognitive and motor speed has been shown to differentiate AD patients from individuals with major depressive disorder (Pirozzolo et al., 1985), PD (Mahurin and Pirozzolo, 1984) and PSP (Pirozzolo et al., 1988).

Factor analysis of motor abilities in AD suggests that deficits are patterned in a hierarchical manner,

with simple, more automatic actions spared relative to performance on tasks with greater cognitive demand (Mahurin et al., 1989). While early- to mid-stage AD patients do not significantly differ from age-matched controls on tasks loading on a simple motor factor (rate of finger tapping, alternate tapping and grip strength), these patients are significantly impaired on complex motor tasks involving attentional, visual-spatial and motor control mechanisms (grooved pegboard, Purdue pegboard, rotary pursuit and choice RT). Performance by AD patients on these more complex motor tasks has been shown to correlate highly with performance-based test of daily living skills, indicating the importance of these abilities to everyday functional status (Mahurin et al., in press).

Several aspects of motor function are preserved in AD. For example, although the slope of the increase between simple RT and the number of alternatives in choice RT is significantly greater in AD patients, this linear trend has been shown to follow the same logarithmic ratio (Hick's Law) as that found in healthy elderly subjects (Mahurin and Pirozzolo, in press). Further, in comparison with HD patients, AD patients have been shown to significantly improve their performance on a rotary pursuit task with practice over repeated trials, demonstrating preserved motor learning ability (Heindel et al., 1988). These findings suggest that research into rehabilitation of movement deficits in AD may have significant benefit.

The etiology of AD remains to be elucidated. Neurotransmitter deficits, metal toxicity, trophic factor depletion, infectious agents, cerebrovascular protein abnormalities and genetic predisposition have all been explored as possible factors. There is at present no effective treatment for AD. Although a number of attempts have been made to alleviate symptoms through use of cholinergic agents and cerebral metabolic enhancers, none has proven more than minimally efficacious (see related chapters in this volume).

Neuropathological correlates
Characteristic neuropathological changes in AD,

including pronounced neurofibrillary tangles, cerebrovascular amyloidosis, granulovacuolar degeneration and neuritic plaques, have been well-described (Pirozzolo et al., 1989). These pathological features have a broad bilateral distribution, but are particularly prominent in parietal, temporal and prefrontal cortical areas (Kemper, 1984). In addition to diffuse cortical atrophy, neuronal loss has been demonstrated subcortically in the nucleus basalis of Meynert, the mesial-limbic system and the locus ceruleus (Tomlinson et al., 1981).

Primary motor regions (e.g., precentral and postcentral gyri) are spared of neuropathological changes, consistent with the absence of focal motor deficits in the disease. The extrapyramidal features seen in AD may be related to diffuse cortical pathology, basal ganglia pathology or disruption of frontal-subcortical pathways. Dyskinetic movements in AD have been correlated with numbers of plaques and tangles in multiple cerebral areas, suggesting association with multiple areas of pathology (Pirozzolo et al., 1989). Neuronal loss, Lewy bodies and neurofibrillary tangles are frequently reported in the substantia nigra of AD patients, suggesting a common mechanism with changes seen in PD (Leverenz and Sumi, 1986). However, as has been pointed out, the similarities in both cognitive and neuropathological features between AD and PD do not necessarily implicate common disease processes (Corkin et al., 1989). Further research is necessary to reliably establish common mechanisms in the two disorders.

Decreased neurotransmitter levels are also well-documented in AD. There is an association between degree of cognitive deficit and decreased levels of acetylcholine in basal forebrain regions (Whitehouse et al., 1982, 1983). However, unlike PD, a neurotransmitter-deficit model for motor features in AD is not clear-cut. Reduced dopamine levels have not been consistently demonstrated to be correlated with motor involvement in AD. In addition, reduction of other neurotransmitters, including GABA, somatostatin and norepinephrine, has been demonstrated in AD (Cummings and Benson, 1983; Swihart et al., 1989), and the contribution of these neurochemical deficits to motor symptoms in AD remains to be further explored.

Exercise and aging

Although aging has been discussed thus far in a uniform manner, not all individuals experience similar degrees of age-related decline in psychomotor abilities. In particular, individuals who maintain a high level of physical fitness and exercise regularly tend to be more resistant of the effects of aging on psychomotor speed (Spirduso, 1980). Elderly individuals who participate in regular aerobic exercise show less slowing in both central and peripheral components of RT than do age-matched counterparts who do not exercise regularly (Baylor and Spirduso, 1988). Spirduso (1975) reported faster RTs and movement speed in a group of physically active subjects as compared with non-active counterparts. Clarkson (1978) also compared physically active individuals in their seventh decade with sedentary subjects of the same age, and found significantly faster RTs in the active group. More recent studies have supported this association, with positive correlation between physical exercise and cognitive abilities in older adults (Clarkson-Smith and Hartley, 1989).

Although this positive association between increased neuromuscular speed and level of physical fitness in elderly subjects has been well-documented, the direction of causality remains unclear. The active subjects in both these studies reported consistently higher levels of physical activity throughout most of their adult years. Older subjects with greater physical skill may be more likely to continue to participate in activities as they age. Therefore, subsequent studies have examined whether introduction of exercise programs for elderly subjects can result in increases in performance speed (Larson and Bruce, 1987).

Panton and colleagues (Panton et al., 1990) examined the effect of a six-month training period of either aerobic or strength (resistance) training on subjects from 70 to 79 years of age. Fractionated RT measurement revealed no differences between these two groups or between either group and control subjects following the training period, and no significant change from baseline measurements. Changes in premotor time, motor time, total RT and movement speed were all nonsignificant, in spite of significant increases in aerobic capacity and strength among the training participants. The authors noted that their study employed a simple RT task, and that findings of improvement may be found in other studies using younger subjects with lower initial levels of fitness, or by employing more complex RT tasks as the dependent measure.

Other studies have looked at the results of shorter-term exercise programs for older subjects. Eight-week strength training of frail institutional volunteers with mean age of 90 years produced significant gains in muscle strength, size and functional mobility (Fiatarone et al., 1990). A twelve-week low-impact aerobic exercise program for sedentary older women (mean age 65 years) resulted in significant gains, including cardiorespiratory endurance, strength, agility and balance (Hopkins et al., 1990). Balance platform testing before and after a 16-week program of static balance, active balance and active exercise revealed reduced sway with eyes open for a group of elderly women (mean age 77 years), but no improvement in balance with eyes closed (Lichtenstein et al., 1989). Effects of exercise on cognition have not been as conclusive, with recent studies reporting absence of significant gains in either cognitive functioning or psychological well-being following 12-week exercise programs for elderly subjects (Blumenthal and Madden, 1988; Emery and Gatz, 1990).

Future directions

The clinical characteristics of motor changes in normal aging and age-related movement disorders are, at this stage, relatively well-documented. However, underlying changes in the neurological and neurophysiological substrates are not as well-elucidated. Advances in basic biochemistry will allow for better models of neurodegenerative disease, and lead to therapeutic strategies relevant to movement disorders. In addition, advances in neuroimaging, electroencephalography and real-time metabolic visualization of cerebral motor processes (e.g., positron emission tomography and cerebral blood flow) should result in better-defined correlations between theoretical models of motor function and their physiological correlates. This sophistication will enhance the accuracy of longitudinal outcome and treatment studies. Together with advances in the cognitive sciences, specific models of motor function will be developed that may change current clinical classifications of movement disorders from anatomically based schemes to a more functionally based nosology. These developments will ultimately further our understanding of basic processes underlying age-related changes and abnormalities in motor function.

Acknowledgements

We gratefully acknowledge the contributions of Joel Levy, Ph.D. Edward Feher, Ph.D. and Joseph Jankovic, M.D., in preparation of this chapter.

References

Adams RD, Fisher CM, Hakim S, Ojemann RD, Sweet WH: Symptomatic occult hydrocephalus with 'normal' cerebrospinal fluid pressure. *N. Engl. J. Med: 272,* 117 – 126, 1965.

Agid J, Javoy-Agid F, Ruberg M: Biochemistry of neurotransmitters in Parkinson's disease. In Marsden CD, Fahn S (Editors.), *Movement Disorders 2,* London: Butterworths, pp. 166 – 230, 1987.

Albert ML, Feldman RJ, Willis A: The subcortical dementia of progressive supranuclear palsy. *J. Neurol. Neurosurg. Psychiatry: 37,* 121 – 131, 1974.

Alexander GE, DeLong MR, Strick PL: Parallel organization of functionally segregated circuits linking basal ganglia and cortex. *Annu. Rev. Neurosci: 9,* 357 – 381, 1986.

Aminoff MJ, Marshall J, Smith EM, Wyke MA: Pattern of intellectual impairment in Huntington's disease. *Psychol. Med: 5,* 169 – 172, 1975.

Aniansson A, Hedberg M, Henning GB, Grimby G: Muscle morphology, enzymatic activity, and muscle strength in elderly men: a follow-up study. *Muscle Nerve: 9,* 585 – 591, 1986.

Arsharsky YI, Gilfand IM, Orlovsky GN: *Cerebellar and Rhythmical Movements.* New York: Springer-Verlag, 1986.

Asanum H: *The Motor Cortex.* New York: Raven, 1989.

Allum JHJ, Hulliger M: Afferent control of posture and locomotion. *Progress in Brain Research, Vol. 80.* New York: Elsevier, 1989.

Barbeau A: Aging and the extrapyramidal system. *J. Am. Geriatric Soc: 21,* 145 – 149, 1973.

Baskin D: Neuropathological and neuropsychological changes in Alzheimer's disease. *Clin. Geriatr. Med.: 5,* 425 – 440, 1989.

Bateuv: *Higher Integrative Systems of the Brain.* New York: Gordon & Breach, 1987.

Baylor AN, Spirduso WW: Systematic aerobic exercise and components of reaction time in older women. *J. Gerontol. Psychol. Sci: 43,* P121 – 126, 1988.

Benson DF, Kuhl DE, Hawkins RA, Phelps ME, Cummings JL, Tsai SY: Positron computed tomography in the diagnosis of dementia. *Ann. Neurol: 10,* 76, 1981.

Benton AL: Interactive effects of age and brain disease on reaction time. *Arch. Neurol: 34,* 369 – 370, 1977.

Benton AL, Joynt RJ: Reaction time in unilateral cerebral disease. *Confin. Neurol: 19,* 247 – 256, 1958.

Berciano J: In Jankovic J, Tolosa E (Editors), *Parkinson's Disease and Movement Disorders.* Baltimore, MD: Urban & Schwarzenberg, pp. 131 – 151, 1988.

Bird MT, Paulson GW: The rigid form of Huntington's chorea. *Neurology: 21,* 271 – 276, 1971.

Birren JE, Woods AM, Williams WV: Behavioral slowing with age: causes, organization, and consequences. In Poon LW (Editor), *Aging in the 1980's: Psychological Issues.* Washington, D.C., American Psychological Association, pp. 293 – 308, 1980.

Bittenbender JB, Quadfasel FA: Rigid and akinetic form of Huntington's chorea. *Arch. Neurol.: 7,* 275 – 288, 1962.

Blumenthal JA, Madden DJ: Effects of aerobic exercise training, age, and physical fitness on memory-search performance. *Psychol. Aging: 3,* 280 – 285, 1988.

Boller F, Mizutani R, Roessmann U, Gambetti P: Parkinson's disease, dementia, and Alzheimer's disease: Clinicopathological correlations. *Ann. Neurol.: 7,* 329 – 335, 1980.

Borkan GA, Hults DE, Gerzof SG et al.: Comparison of body composition in middle-aged and elderly males using computed tomography. *Am. J. Phys. Anthropol.: 66,* 289 – 295, 1985.

Botez MI, Barbeau A: Neuropsychological findings in Parkinson's disease: a comparison between various tests during long-term levodopa therapy. *Int. J. Neurol.: 10,* 222 – 232, 1975.

Botwinick J: Disinclination to venture responses vs. cautiousness in responding: age differences. *J. Gerontol.: 24,* 55 – 62, 1969.

Botwinick J: *Aging and Behavior.* New York, Springer, pp. 185 – 207, 1978.

Botwinick J, Brinley JF, Robbins JS: Maintaining set in relation to motivation and age. *Am. J. Psychol.: 72,* 585 – 588, 1959.

Botwinick J, Storandt M: Age differences in reaction time as a function of experience, stimulus intensity and preparatory interval. *J. Genet. Psychol.: 123,* 209 – 217, 1973.

Brody H: An examination of cerebral cortex and brainstem aging. In Terry RD, Gershon S (Editors), *Aging, Vol. 3.* New York: Raven, 1976.

Brody H: Cell counts in cerebral cortex and brainstem. In Katzman R, Terry RD, Bick KI (Editors), *Alzheimer's Disease, Senile Dementia and Related Disorders.* New York: Raven, 1981.

Brown WF, Strong MJ, Snow R: Methods for estimating numbers of motor units in the biceps brachialis muscles and losses of motor units with aging. *Muscle Nerve: 11,* 423 – 432, 1988.

Burne JA: Reflex origin of parkinsonian tremor. *Exp. Neurol.: 97,* 327 – 339, 1987.

Butters N, Albert MS, Sax D: Investigations of the memory disorders of patients with Huntington's disease. *Adv. Neurol.: 23,* 203 – 213, 1979.

Caine ED, Ebert MH, Weingartner H: An outline for the analysis of dementia. The memory disorder of Huntington's disease. *Neurology: 27,* 1087 – 1092, 1977.

Calne DB, Langston JW: Aetiology of Parkinson's disease. *Lancet: 2,* 1457 – 1459, 1983.

Cassell K, Shaw K, Stern G: A computerized tracking technique for the assessment of parkinsonian motor disabilities. *Brain: 96,* 815 – 826, 1973.

Cerella J, Poon LW, Williams DM: Age and the complexity hypothesis. In Poon L (Editor), *Aging in the 1980's: Psychological Issues.* Washington, DC: American Psychological Association, pp. 332 – 340, 1980.

Chui HC, Teng EL, Henderson VW, Moy AC: Clinical subtypes of dementia of the Alzheimer typse. *Neurology: 35,* 1544 – 1550, 1985.

Clarkson PM: The effect of age and activity level on simple and choice fractionated response time. *Eur. J. Appl. Physiol.: 40,* 17 – 25, 1978.

Clarkson-Smith L, Hartley AA: Relationships between physical exercise and cognitive abilities in older adults. *Psychol. Aging: 4,* 183 – 189, 1989.

Cooke JD, Brown SH, Cunningham DA: Kinematics of arm movements in elderly humans. *Neurobiol. Aging: 10,* 159 – 165, 1989.

Corkin S, Growdon JH, Desclos G, Rosen TJ: Parkinson's disease and Alzheimer's disease: differences revealed by neuropsychologic testing. In Munsat TL (Editor), *Quantification of Neurologic Deficit.* Boston: Butterworths, pp. 311 – 325, 1989.

Cresse I, Sibley DR, Hamblin HW, Leff StE: The classification of dopamine receptors: relationship to radioligand binding. *Annu. Rev. Neurosci.: 6,* 43 – 71, 1983.

Cummings JL, Benson DF: *Dementia: A Clinical Approach.* Boston, Butterworth, pp. 35 – 72, 1983.

Curcio CA, Buell SJ, Coleman PD: Morphology of the aging central nervous system: Not all downhill. In Mortimer JA, Pirozzolo FJ, Maletta GJ (Editors), *Advances in Neurogerontology, Vol. 3: The Aging Motor System.* New York: Praeger, pp. 7 – 35, 1982.

Darling WG, Cooke JD, Brown SH: Control of simple arm movements in elderly humans. *Neurobiol. Aging: 10,* 149 – 157, 1989.

Davies CT, White MJ: Contractile properties of elderly human triceps surae. *Gerontology: 29,* 1925, 1983.

Dayan D, Abrahami I, Buchner A, Gorsky M, Chimovitz N: Lipid pigment (lipofuscin) in human perioral muscles with aging. *Exp. Gerontol.: 23,* 97 – 102, 1988.

DeLong MR, Georgopoulos AP: *Motor Functions of the Basal Ganglia. Handbook of Physiology.* Bethesda, MD: American Physiological Society, pp. 1017 – 1061, 1981.

DeLong MR, Georgopoulos AP, Crutcher MD: Cortico-basal ganglia relations and coding of motor performance. *Exp. Brain Res. (Suppl. 7):* 30 – 40, 1983.

DeLong MR, Alexander GE, Georgopoulos AP, Crutcher MD, Mitchell SJ, Richardson RT: Role of basal ganglia in limb movements. *Hum. Neurobiol.: 2,* 235 – 244, 1984.

DeLong MR, Crutcher MD, Georgopoulos AP: Primate globus pallidus and subthalamic nucleus: functional organization. *J. Neurophysiol.: 53,* 530 – 543, 1985.

Delwaide PJ, Gonce M: Pathophysiology of Parkinson's signs. In Jankovic J, Tolosa E (Editors), *Parkinson's Disease and Movement Disorders.* Baltimore: Urban & Schwarzenberg, pp. 59 – 72, 1988.

DeYebenes JG, Gomez MAM: The dopaminergic brain. In Jankovic J, Tolosa E (Editors), *Parkinson's Disease and Movement Disorders.* Baltimore: Urban & Schwarzenberg, pp. 13 – 26, 1988.

Dubois B, Pillon B, Sternic N, Lhermitte F, Agid Y: Age-induced cognitive disturbances in Parkinson's disease. *Neurology: 40,* 38 – 41, 1990.

Duvoisin RC: Olivopontocerebellar atrophies. In Marsden CD, Fahn S (Editors), *Movement Disorders, 2.* Boston: Butterworths, pp. 249 – 269, 1987.

Emery DF, Gatz M: Psychological and cognitive effects of an exercise program from community-residing older adults. *Gerontologist: 30,* 184 – 188, 1990.

Evans DA, Funkenstein HH, Albert MS, Scherr PA, Cook NR, Chown MJ, Hebert LE, Hennekens CH, Taylor JO: Prevalence of Alzheimer's disease in a community population of older persons: higher than previously reported. *J. Am. Med. Assoc.: 262,* 2551 – 2556, 1989.

Evarts EV, Teravainen H, Calne DB: Reaction time in Parkinson's disease. *Brain: 104,* 167 – 186, 1981.

Feher EP, Inbody SB, Nolan B, Pirozzolo FJ: Other neurologic diseases with dementia as a sequela. *Clin. Geriatr. Med.: 4,* 799 – 814, 1988.

Ferris S, Crook T, Sathananthan G, Gershon S: Reaction time as a diagnostic measure in senility. *J. Am. Geriatr. Soc.: 12,* 529 – 533, 1976.

Fiatarone MA, Marks EC, Ryan ND, Meredith CN, Lipsitz LA, Evans WJ: High-intensity strength training in nonagenarians. *J. Am. Med. Assoc.: 263,* 3029 – 3034, 1990.

Flowers KA: Visual closed-loop and open-loop characteristics of voluntary movement in patients with parkinsonism and intention tremor. *Brain: 99,* 269 – 310, 1976.

Fozard J: Speed of mental performance and aging: costs of aging and benefits of wisdom. In Pirozzolo FJ, Maletta GJ (Editors), *Advances in Neurogerontology: Behavioral Assessment and Psycho-pharmacology.* New York: Praeger, 1981.

Garnett ES, Nahmias C, Firnau G: Central dopaminergic pathways in hemiparkinsonism examined by positron emission tomography. *Can. J. Neurol. Sci.: 11,* 174 – 179, 1984.

Gerfen CR: The neostriatal mosaic: compartmentalization of corticostriatal input and striatonigral output systems. *Nature: 311,* 461 – 464, 1984.

Gerfen CR: The neostriatal mosaic: striatal patch-matrix organization is related to cortical lamination. *Science: 246,* 385 – 388, 1989.

Ghez C: Cortical control of voluntary movement. In Kandel ER, Schwartz JH (Editors), *Principles of Neural Science.* New York: Elsevier, pp. 324 – 333, 1981.

Ghez C, Fahn S: The cerebellum. In Kandel ER, Schwartz JH (Editors), *Principles of Neural Science.* New York: Elsevier, pp. 334 – 346, 1981.

Gibb WRG: The neuropathology of parkinsonian disorders. In Jankovic J, Tolosa E (Editors), *Parkinson's Disease and Movement Disorders.* Baltimore: Urban & Schwarzenberg, pp. 205 – 223, 1988.

Goffinet AM, De Volder AG, Gillian C, Rectem D, Bol A, Michel C, Cogneau M, Labar D, Laterre C: Positron tomography demonstrates frontal lobe hypometabolism in progressive supranuclear palsy. *Ann. Neurol.: 25,* 131 – 139, 1989.

Golbe LI, Davis PH: Progressive supranuclear palsy: Recent advances. In Jankovic J, Tolosa E (Editors), *Parkinson's Disease and Movement Disorders.* Baltimore: Urban & Schwarzenberg, 1988.

Golbe LI, Davis PH, Schoenberg BS, Duvoisin RC: The natural history and prevalance of progressive supranuclear palsy. *Neurology: 37 (suppl. 1),* 121, 1987.

Goldenberg G, Wimmer A, Auff E, Schnaberth G: Impairment of motor planning in patients with Parkinson's disease: Evidence from ideomotor apraxia testing. *J. Neurol. Neurosurg. Psychiatry: 49,* 1266 – 1272, 1986.

Gottsdanker R: Age and simple reaction time. *J. Gerontol.: 37,* 342 – 348, 1982.

Graham OG: *Mol. Pharmacol.: 14,* 633 – 643, 1978.

Graybiel AM, Hickey TL: Chemospecificity of ontogenetic units in the striatum: demonstration of combining [^{3}H] thymidine neuronography and histochemical staining. *Neurobiology: 82,* 198 – 202, 1982.

Graybiel AM, Ragsdale Jr CW: Histochemically distinct compartments in the striatum of human, monkey, and cat demonstrated by acetylcholinesterase staining. *Proc. Nat. Acad. Sci.: 75,* 5723 – 5726, 1978.

Grimby G: Physical activity and effects of muscle training in the elderly. *Ann. Clin. Res.: 20,* 62 – 66, 1988.

Grimby G, Danneskiold Samse B, Hvid K, Saltin B: Morphology and enzymatic capacity in arm and leg muscles in 78 – 81 year old men and women. *Acta Physiol. Scand.: 115,* 125 – 134, 1982.

Grimby G, Aniansson A, Zetterberg C, Saltin B: Is there a change in relative muscle fibre composition with age? *Clin. Physiol.: 4,* 189 – 194, 1984.

Growdon JH, Corkin S: Cognitive impairments in Parkinson's disease. In Yahr MD, Bergman KJ (Editors), *Advances in Neurology, Vol. 45.* New York: Raven Press, 1986.

Gusella JF, Wexler NS, Conneally PM, Nayler SL, Anderson MA, Tanzi RE, Watkins PC, Ottina K, Wallace MR, Sakaguchi AY, Young AB, Shoulson I, Bonilla E, Martin JB: A polymorphic DNA marker genetically linked to Huntington's disease. *Nature: 306,* 234 – 238, 1983.

Hakim AM, Mathieson G: Dementia in Parkinson disease: A neuropathological study. *Neurology: 29,* 1209 – 1214, 1979.

Haldeman S, Goldman JW, Hyde J, Pribram HFW: Progressive supranuclear palsy, computed tomography, and response to anti-parkinsonian drugs. *Neurology: 31,* 442 – 445, 1981.

Halgin R, Rilkin M, Misiak H: Levodopa, parkinsonism, and recent memory. *J. Nerv. Mental Dis.: 164,* 268 – 272, 1977.

Hall TC, Miller AKH, Corsellis JAN: Variations in the human

Purkinje cell population according to age and sex. *Neuropath. Appl. Neurobiol.: 1,* 267–292, 1975.

Harding AE: The clinical features and classification of the late onset autosomal dominant cerebellar ataxias. *Brain: 105,* 1, 1982.

Harkins SW, Chapman RC: The perception of induced dental pain in young and elderly women. *J. Gerontol.: 32,* 428–435, 1977.

Hartmann A, Alberti E: Differentiation of communicating hydrocephalus and presenile dementia by coutinuous recording of cerebrospinal fluid pressure. *J. Neurol. Neurosurg. Psychiatry: 40,* 630–640, 1977.

Heilman KM, Bowers D, Watson RT, Greer M: Reaction times in Parkinson disease. *Arch. Neurol.: 33,* 139–140, 1976.

Heindel WC, Butters N, Salmon DP: Impaired learning of a motor skill in patients with Huntington's disease. *Behav. Neurosci.: 102,* 141–147, 1988.

Hopkins DR, Murrah B, Hoeger WWK, Rhodes RC: Effect of low-impact aerobic dance on the functional fitness of elderly women. *Gerontologist: 30,* 189–192, 1990.

Huff FJ, Boller F, Lucchelli F, Querriera R, Beyer J, Belle S: The neurological examination in patients with probable Alzheimer's disease. *Arch. Neurol.: 44,* 929–932, 1987.

Hugin F, Norris AH, Shock NW: Skin reflex and voluntary reaction time in young and old males. *J. Gerontol.: 15,* 388–391, 1960.

Hynd GW, Pirozzolo FJ, Maletta GJ: Progressive supranuclear palsy. *Int. J. Neurosci.: 16,* 87, 1982.

Ishino H, Otsuki S: Frequency of Alzheimer's neurofibrillary tangles in the cerebral cortex in progressive supranuclear palsy. *J. Neurol. Sci.: 28,* 309–316, 1976.

Ito M: *The Cerebellum and Motor Control.* New York: Springer-Verlag, 1984.

Jackson JA, Jankovic J, Ford J: Progressive supranuclear palsy: clinical features and response to treatment of 16 patients. *Ann. Neurol.: 13,* 273, 1983.

Jankovic J: Progressive supranuclear palsy: Clinical and pharmacologic update. *Neurol. Clin.: 2,* 473, 1984.

Jankovic J: Tremor, tic, & myoclonic disorders. *Curr. Opinion Neurol. Neurosurg.: 2,* 324–329, 1989.

Jankovic J: Clinical aspects of Parkinson's disease. In Marsden CD, Fahn S (Editors), *New Trends in Assessment and Therapy of Parkinsonism.* Carnforth: Parthenon, in press.

Jankovic J, Grossman R, Goodman F, Pirozzolo F, Schneider L, Zhu Z, Scardino P, Garber AJ, Jhingran SG, Martin S: Clinical, biochemical, and neuropathological findings following transplantation of adrenal medulla to the caudate nucleus for treatment of Parkinson's disease. *Neurology: 39,* 1227–1234, 1989.

Jankovic J, Friedman DI, Pirozzolo FJ, McCrary JA: Progressive supranuclear palsy: Motor, neurobehavioral and neuro-ophthalmic findings. *Adv. Neurol.: 59,* 293–304, 1990.

Jankovic J, McDermott M, Carter J, Gauthier S, Goetz C, Golbe L, Huber S, Koller W, Olanow C, Shoulson I, Stern M, Tanner, Weiner, and the Parkinson Study Group: Variable expression of Parkinson's disease: an analysis of the DATATOP database. *Neurology,* in press.

Jellinger K, Riederer P, Tomonasa M: Progressive supranuclear palsy: clinico-pathological and biochemical studies. *J.*

Neural Transmission (Suppl 16): 111–128, 1980.

Joynt RJ, Shoulson I: Dementia. In Heilman KH, Valenstein EV (Editors), *Clinical Neuropsychology* (2nd edn.). New York: Oxford University Press, pp. 453–479, 1985.

Kamen G, DeLuca CJ: Unusual motor unit firing behavior in older adults. *Brain Res.: 482,* 136–140, 1989.

Katzman R: Normal pressure hydrocephalus. In Wells CE (Editor), *Dementia* (2nd edn.)., Philadelphia: F.A. Davis, pp. 69–92, 1977.

Katzman R, Lasker B, Bernstein N: Advances in the diagnosis of dementia: accuracy of diagnosis and consequences of misdiagnosis of disorders causing dementia. In Terry RD (Editor), *Aging and the Brain.* New York: Raven Press, 1988.

Kebabian JW, Calne DB: Multiple receptors for dopamine. *Nature: 277,* 93–96, 1979.

Kemper T: Neuroanatomical and neuropathological changes in normal aging and dementia. In Albert M (Editor), *Clinical Neurology of Aging.* New York: Oxford University Press, pp. 9–52, 1984.

Kimura D, Barnett HM, Burkhart G: The psychological test pattern in progressive supranuclear palsy. *Neuropsychologia: 19,* 301, 1981.

Klein C, Cunningham DA, Paterson DH, Taylor AW: Fatigue and recovery contractile properties of young and elderly men. *Eur. J. Appl. Physiol. Occup. Physiol.: 57,* 684–690, 1988.

Klein DW, Schieber F: Vision and Aging. In Birren JE, Schaie KW (Editors), *Handbook of the Psychology of Aging* (2nd edn.). New York: Van Nostrand Reinhold, pp. 296–331, 1985.

Klitgaard H, Ausoni S, Damiani E: Sarcoplasmic reticulum of human skeletal muscle: age-related changes and effect of training. *Acta Physiol. Scand.: 137,* 23–31, 1989.

Koller WC, Trimble J: The gait abnormality of Huntington's disease. *Neurology: 35,* 1450–1454, 1985.

Kulh DE, Phelps ME, Markham CH, Metter, Riege, Winter: Cerebral metabolism and atrophy in Huntington's disease determined by FDG-18 and computerized tomographic scan. Ann. Neurol.: 12, 425, 1982.

Kuypers H: Anatomy of the descending pathways. In Brooks VB (Editor), *Motor Control (Part 1), Handbook of Physiology (Section 1: The Nervous System).* Bethesda, MD: American Physiological Society, pp. 597–666, 1981.

Langston JW: The etiology of Parkinson's disease: New directions for research. In Jankovic J, Tolosa E (Editors), *Parkinson's Disease and Movement Disorders.* Baltimore: Urban & Schwarzenberg, pp. 75–86, 1988.

Langston JW, Irwin I, Ricaurte GA: Neurotoxins, parkinsonism, and Parkinson's disease. *Pharmacol. Ther.: 32,* 19–49, 1987.

Larish DD, Martin PE, Mungiole M: Characteristic patterns of gait in the healthy old. *Ann. N. Y. Acad. Sci: 515,* 18–32.

Larson EB, Bruce EA: Health benefits of exercise in aging society. *Arch. Internal Med.: 147,* 353–356, 1987.

Larsson L: Aging in mammalian skeletal muscle. In Mortimer JA, Pirozzolo FJ, Maletta GJ (Editors), *Advances in Neurogerontology (Vol. 3): The Aging Motor System.* New York: Praeger, pp. 60–97, 1982.

Larsson L, Grimby G, Karlsson J: Muscle strength and speed

of movement in relation to age and muscle morphology. *J. Appl. Physiol.: 46*, 451–456, 1979.

Lechtenberg R: Ataxia and other cerebellar syndromes. In Jankovic J, Tolosa E (Editors), *Parkinson's Disease and Movement Disorders*. Baltimore, MD: Urban & Schwarzenberg, pp. 365–376, 1988.

Leenders KL, Palmer AJ, Quinn N, Clark JC, Firau G, Garnett ES, Nahmias C, Jones T, Marsden CD: Brain dopamine metabolism in patients with Parkinson's disease measured with PET. *J. Neurol. Neurosurg. Psychiatry: 49*, 855–860, 1986.

Lees AJ: The Steele-Richardson Olszewski syndrome (progressive supranuclear palsy). In Marsden CD, Fahn S (Editors), *Movement Disorders, 2*. Boston: Butterworths, pp. 272–287, 1982.

Leverenz J, Sumi SM: Parkinson's disease in patients with Alheimer's disease. *Arch. Neurol.: 43*, 662–664, 1986.

LeWitt PA, Calne DB: Neurochemistry and pharmacology of the aging motor system. In Mortimer JA, Pirozzolo FJ, Maletta GJ (Editors), *Advances in Neurogerontology (Vol. 3): The Aging Motor System*. New York: Praeger, pp. 36–59, 1982.

Lexell J, Hendriksson-Larsen K, Winblad B, Sjostrom M: Distribution of different fiber types in human skeletal muscles: effects of aging studied in whole muscle cross sections. *Muscle Nerve: 6*, 588–595, 1983.

Lexell J, Taylor CC, Sjostrom M: What is the cause of the aging atrophy? Total number, size and proportion of different fiber types studied in whole vastus lateralis muscle from 15 to 83-year-old men. *J. Neurol. Sci.: 84*, 276–294, 1988.

Lichtenstein MJ, Shields SL, Shiavi RG, Burger MC: Exercise and balance in aged women: a pilot controlled clinical trial. *Arch. Phys. Med. Rehabil.: 70*, 138–143, 1989.

Lichtenstein MJ, Burger MC, Shields SL, Shiavi RG: Comparison of biomechanics platform measures of balance and videotaped measures of gait with a clinical mobility scale in elderly women. *J. Gerontol.: 45*, M49–54, 1990.

Light K: Effects of mild cardiovascular and cerebrovascular disorders on serial reaction time performance. *Exp. Aging Res.: 4*, 3–22, 1978.

Lishman WA: *Organic Psychiatry: The Psychological Consequences of Cerebral Disorder*. London: Blackwell, 1978.

Lohr JB, Wisniewski A: *Movement Disorders: A Neuropsychiatric Approach*. New York: Guilford, 1987.

Luria AR: *The Working Brain*. New York: Basic Books, 1973.

Maagr ER, Lees AJ: The clinical features and natural history of the Steele-Richardson-Olszewski syndrome (progressive supranuclear palsy). *Neurology: 36*, 1005, 1986.

Mahurin RK, Inbody SB: Psychomotor assessment of the older patient. *Clin. Geriatr. Med.: 5*, 499–518, 1989.

Mahurin RK, Pirozzolo FJ: Cognitive speed in cortical versus subcortical dementia. *J. Clin. Exp. Neuropsychol.: 6*,

Mahurin RK, Pirozzolo FJ: Relative contributions of motor and cognitive demands to psychomotor performance: an analysis of bradykinetic parkinsonian patients. *J. Clin. Exp. Neuropsychol.: 6*

Mahurin RK, Pirozzolo FJ: Chronometric analysis: clinical applications in aging and dementia. *Dev. Neuropsychol.: 2*, 345–362, 1986.

Mahurin RK, Pirozzolo FJ: Preservation of Hick's Law in

dementia. *Percept. Motor Skills*, in press, 1991.

Mahurin RK, Pirozzolo FJ, Appel SH: Motor control deficits in Alzheimer's disease. *J. Clin. Exp. Neuropsychol.: 11*, 86, 1989.

Mahurin RK, DeBettingies BH, Pirozzolo FJ: The structured assessment of independent living skills: preliminary findings in Alzheimer's disease. *J. Gerontol.*: in press, 1991.

Maletta GJ, Pirozzolo FJ, Thompson G, Mortimer JA: Organic mental disorders in a geriatric outpatient population. *Am J. Psychiatry: 139*, 521–523, 1982.

Manchester D, Woollacott M, Zederbauer-Hylton N, Marin O: Visual, vestibular, and somatosensory contributions to balance control in the older adult. *J. Gerontol.: 44*, M118–M127, 1989.

Manta P, Vassilopoulos D, Spengos M: Nucleocytoplasmic ratio in ageing skeletal muscle. *Eur. Arch. Psychiatry Neurol. Sci.: 236*, 235–236, 1987.

Mareth TR, Martin WL: Normal pressure hydrocephalus: a case presentation. *Dis. Nerv. System: 38*, 635–637, 1977.

Marsden CD: The mysterious motor function of the basal ganglia: The Robert Wartenberg lecture. *Neurology: 32*, 514–539, 1982.

Marsden CD: The pathophysiology of movement disorders. *Neurol. Clin.: 2*, 435–459, 1984.

Marsden CD: Parkinson's disease. *Lancet: 335*, 948–952, 1990.

Martin JB: Huntington's disease: new approaches to an old problem. *Neurology: 34*, 1059, 1984.

Martin JB: Molecular genetic studies in the neuropsychiatric disorders. *Trends Neurosci.: 12*, 130–137, 1989.

Martin JB, Gusella JF: Huntington's disease: pathogenesis and management. *N. Engl. J. Med.: 315*, 1267, 1986.

Martin WE, Loewenson RB, Resch JA, Baker AB: Parkinson's disease: clinical analysis of 100 patients. *Neurology: 23*, 783–790, 1973.

Martin WW, Adam MJ, Bergstrom M, Ammann W, Harrop R, Laihinen A, Rogers J, Ruth T, Sayre C, Stoessl J, Pate BD, Calne DB: In vivo study of DOPA metabolism in Parkinson's disease. In Fahn S, Marsend CD, Jenner P, Teychenne P (Editors). *Recent Developments in Parkinson's Disease*. New York: Raven Press, pp. 97–102, 1986.

Martin WW, Stoessl AJ, Cumming P, Adam M, Ruth T, Pate BD: The effect of age of 6-fluorodopa metabolism. *Neurology: 36 (Suppl. 1)*: 182, 1986.

Marttila RJ, Rinne UK: Dementia in Parkinson's disease. *Acta Neurol. Scand.: 54*, 431–441, 1976.

Mayeux R: Dementia in extrapyramidal disorders. *Curr. Opinion Neurol. Neurosurg.: 3*, 98–102, 1990.

Mayeux R, Stern Y, Spanton S: Heterogeneity in dementia of the Alzheimer type: evidence of subgroups. *Neurology: 35*, 453–461, 1985.

McDonagh MJ, White JJ, Davies CT: Different effects of ageing on the mechanical properities of human arm and leg muscles. *Gerontology: 30*, 49–54, 1984.

McGeer PK, McGeer EG: Cholinergic enzyme systems in Parkinson's disease. *Arch. Neurol.: 35*, 265–268, 1971.

McGeer PL, McGeer EG, Suzuki JS: Aging and extrapyramidal function. *Arch. Neurol.: 34*, 33–35, 1977.

McKhann G, Drachman D, Folstein M, Katzman R, Price D, Stadlan EM: Clinical diagnosis of Alzheimer's disease:

report of the NINCDS-ADRDA work group under the auspices of Department of Health and Human Task Force on Alzheimer's disease. *Neurology: 34,* 939 – 944, 1984.

Meredith CN, Frontera WR, Fisher EC, Hughes VA, Herland JC, Edwards J, Evans WJ: Peripheral effects of endurance training in young and old subjects. *J. Appl. Physiol.: 66,* 2844 – 2849, 1989.

Milberg W, Albert M: Cognitive differences between patients with progressive supranuclear palsy and Alzheimer's disease. *J. Clin. Exp. Neuropsychol.: 11,* 605 – 614, 1989.

Miller WC, DeLong MR: Control determinates of age related declines in motor function. *Ann. N.Y. Acad. Sci.: 515,* 287 – 302, 1988.

Moller P, Bergstrom J, Erikson S, Furst P, Hellstrom K: Effect of aging on free amino acids and electrolytes in skeletal muscle. *Clin. Sci.: 56,* 427 – 432, 1979.

Molsa PK, Marttila RJ, Rinne UK: Extrapyramidal signs in Alzheimer's disease. *Neurology: 34,* 1114 – 1116, 1984.

Mortimer JA: Human motor behavior and aging. *Ann. N. Y. Acad. Sci.: 515,* 54 – 65, 1988.

Mortimer JA, Webster DD: Comparison of extrapyramidal motor function in normal aging and Parkinson's disease. In Mortimer JA, Pirozzolo FJ, Maletta GJ (Editors), *Advances in Neurogerontology (Vol. 3): The Aging Motor System.* New York: Praeger, pp. 217 – 241, 1982.

Mortimer JA, Kuskowski MA, Pirozzolo FJ, Webster DD: Prevalence and age distribution of intellectual deficits in Parkinson's disease. *J. Clin. Exp. Neuropsychol.: 7,* 603, 1985.

Munsat TL: Aging of the neuromuscular system. In Albert ML (Editor), *Clinical Neurology of Aging.* New York: Oxford University Press, pp. 404 – 424, 1984.

Murray MP, Kory RC, Clarkson BH: Walking patterns in healthy old men. *J. Gerontol.: 24,* 169, 1969.

Myers RH, Martin JB: Huntington's disease. *Semin. Neurol.: 2,* 365, 1982.

Nakano I, Hirano A: Neuron loss in the nucleus basalis of Meynert in parkinsonism-dementia complex of Guam. *Ann. Neurol.: 13,* 87 – 91, 1983.

Nelson RM, Soderberg GL, Urbscheit NL: Comparison of skeletal muscle motor unit discharge characteristics in young and aged humans. *Arch. Gerontol. Geriatr.: 2,* 255 – 265, 1983.

Nelson RM, Soderberg GL, Urbscheit NL: Alteration of motor-unit discharge characteristics in aged humans. *Phys. Ther.: 64,* 29 – 34, 1984.

Nevitt MC, Cummings ST, Kidd S, Black D: Risk factors for recurrent nonsyncopal falls: a prospective study. *J. Am. Med. Assoc.: 261,* 2663 – 2668, 1989.

Ochs AL, Newberry J, Lenhart ML, Harkins SW: Nerual and vestibular aging associated with falls. In Birren J, Schaie KW (Editors), *Handbook of the Psychology of Aging* (2nd edn.). New York: Van Nostrand Reinhold, pp. 378 – 399, 1985.

Oda K: Age changes of motor innervation and acetylcholine receptor distribution on human skeletal muscle fibers. *J. Neurol. Sci.: 66,* 327 – 338, 1984.

Oertel G: Changes in human skeletal muscles due to ageing. Histological and histochemical observations on autopsy material. *Acta Neuropathol.: 69,* 309 – 313, 1986.

Okun MA, DiVesta F: Cautiousness in adulthood as a function of age and instructions. *J. Gerontol.: 31,* 571 – 576, 1976.

Okun MA, Seigler I, George L: Cautiousness and verbal learning in adulthood. *J. Gerontol.: 33,* 94 – 97, 1978.

Palacios JM, Camps M, Cortes R, Sharuchinda C: Characterization and distrubution of brain dopamine receptors. In Jankovic J, Tolosa E (Editors), *Parkinson's Disease and Movement Disorders.* Baltimore: Urban & Schwarzenberg, pp. 27 – 36, 1988.

Pan HS, Penney JB, Young AB: Gamma-aminobutyric acid and benzodiazepine receptor changes induced by unilateral 6-hydroxydopamine lesions of the medial forebrain bundle. *J. Neurochem.: 45,* 3 – 15, 1985.

Panton LB, Granves JE, Pollock ML, Hagberg JM, Chen W: Effect of aerobic and resistance training on fractionated reaction time and speed of movement. *J. Gerontol.: 45,* M26 – 31, 1990.

Penney GR, Arsharpour S, Kitai ST: The glutamate decarboxylase-, leucine enkephalin-, methionine enkephalin- and substance P-immunoreactive neurons in the neustriatum of the rat and cat: evidence for partial population overlap. *Neuroscience: 17,* 1011 – 1045, 1986.

Penney Jr GR, Young AB: Speculations of the functional anatomy of basal ganglia disorders. *Annu. Rev. Neurosci.: 6,* 73 – 94, 1983.

Penney JB, Young AB: Striatal inhomogeneties and basal ganglia function. *Movement Disorders: 1,* 3 – 15, 1986.

Penney JB, Young AB: Huntington's disease. In Jankovic J, Tolosa E (Editors), *Parkinson's Disease and Movement Disorders.* Baltimore: Urban & Schwarzenberg, pp. 167 – 178, 1988.

Petrella RJ, Cunningham DA, Vandervoort AA, Paterson DH: Comparison of twitch potentiation in the gastrocnemius of young and elderly men. *Eur. J. Appl. Physiol. Occup. Physiol.: 58,* 395 – 399, 1989.

Pillon B, Dubios B, Lhermitte F, Agid J: Heterogeneity of cognitive impairment in progressive supranuclear palsy, Parkinson's disease, and Alzheimer's disease. *Neurology: 36,* 1179 – 1185, 1986.

Pirozzolo FJ, Hansch EC: Oculomotor reaction time in dementia reflects degree of cerebral dysfunction. *Science: 214,* 349 – 351, 1981.

Pirozzolo FJ, Christensen KJ, Ogle KM, Hansch EC, Thompson: Simple and choice reaction time in dementia: Clinical implications. *Neurobiol. Aging: 2,* 113 – 117, 1981.

Pirozzolo FJ, Hansch EC, Mortimer JA, Webster DD, Kuskowski MA: Dementia in Parkinson disease: a neuropsychological analysis. *Brain Cognition: 1,* 71 – 83, 1982a.

Pirozzolo FJ, Maletta G, Thompson WG, Kendall J: Motor disturbance in dementia of the Alzheimer's type. In Pirozzolo FJ, Maletta GJ (Editors), *The Aging Motor System.* New York: Praeger, 1982b.

Pirozzolo FJ, Mahurin RK, Loring DW, et al: Choice reaction time modifiability in dementia and depression. *Int. J. Neurosci.: 26,* 1 – 7, 1985.

Pirozzolo FJ, Swihart AA, Rey G, Jankovic J, Mortimer JA: Cognitive impairments associated with Parkinson's disease and other movement disorders. In Jankovic J, Tolosa E (Editors), *Parkinson's Disease and Movement Disorders.* Baltimore: Urban & Schwarzenberg, pp. 425 – 439, 1988.

Poggi P, Marchetti C, Scelsi R: Automatic morphometric

analysis of skeletal muscle fibers in the aging man. *Anatom. Rec.: 217*, 30 – 34, 1987.

Pollock M, Hornabrook RW: The prevalence, natural history, and dementia of Parkinson's disease. *Brain: 89*, 429 – 448, 1966.

Pomara N, Reisberg B, Albers S: Extrapyramidal symptoms in patients with primary degenerative dementia. *J. Clin. Psychopharmacol.: 1*, 398 – 400, 1981.

Potvin AR, Tourtellotte WW: *Quantitative Examination of Neurologic Functions, Vols. 1 & 2*. Boca Raton: CRC Press, 1985.

Potvin AR, Syndulko K, Tourtellotte WW, Goldberg A, Potvin JH, Hansch EC: Quantitative evaluation of normal age-related changes in neurologic function. In Pirozzolo FJ, Maletta GJ (Editors), *Advances in Neurogerontology (Vol. 2): Behavioral Assessment and Psychopharmacology*. New York: Praeger, pp. 13 – 57, 1981.

Powell HC, London GW, Lampert PW: Neurofibrillary tangles in progressive supranuclear palsy. *J. Neuropathol. Exp. Neurol.: 33*, 98 – 106, 1974.

Pullman SL, Watts RL, Juncos JL, Chase TN, Sanes JN: Dopaminergic effects on simple and choice reaction time performance in Parkinson's disease. *Neurology: 38*, 249 – 254, 1988.

Rabbitt P: How can we tell whether human performance is related to chronological age? In Samuel D (Editor), *Aging of the Brain*. New York: Raven, 1983.

Reisberg B (Editor): An overview of current concepts of Alzheimer's disease, senile dementia, and age-associated cognitive decline. *Alzheimer's Disease: The Standard Reference*. New York: MacMillan, pp. 3 – 20, 1983.

Ricaurte GA, Irwin I, Forno LS, DeLanney LE, Langston EB, Langston JW: Aging and MPTP-induced degeneration of dopaminergic neurons in the substantia nigra. *Brain Res.: 403*, 43 – 51, 1987.

Riederer P, Wuketich S: Time course of nigrostriatal degeneration in Parkinson's disease. *J. Neural Transmission: 38*, 277 – 301, 1976.

Rogers J: The neurobiology of cerebellar senescence. *Ann. N. Y. Acad. Sci.: 515*, 251 – 268, 1988.

Roland PE: Organization of motor control by the normal human brain. *Hum. Neurobiol.: 2*, 205, 1984.

Salthouse TA: Speed of behavior and its implications for cognition. In Birren JE, Schaie KW (Editors), *Handbook of the Psychology of Aging* (2nd edn.). New York: Van Nostrand Reinhold, pp. 400 – 426, 1985.

Salthouse TA: Cognitive aspects of motor function. *Ann. N. Y. Acad. Sci.: 515*, 33 – 41, 1988.

Satrustegui J, Berkowitz H, Boden B, Donlon E, McLaughlin A, Maris J, Warnell R, Chance B: An in vivo phosphorus nuclear magnetic resonance study of the variations with age in the phosphodiester content of human muscle. *Mech. Aging Dev.: 42*, 105 – 114, 1988.

Sax DS, O'Donnell B, Butters N, Mnezer L, Montgomery K, Kayne HL: Computed tomographic, neurologic, and neuropsychological correlates of Huntington's disease. *Int. J. Neurosci.: 18*, 21 – 36, 1983.

Schaumburg HH, Spencer PS, Ochoa J: The aging human peripheral nervous system. In Katzman R, Terry RO (Editors) *The Neurology of Aging*. Philadelphia: F.A. Davis Company, pp. 111 – 122, 1983.

Schiebel ME, Schiebel AB: Structural changes in the aging brain. In Brody H, Harman D, Ordy JM (Editors), *Aging (Vol. 1)*. New York: Raven, pp.11 – 37, 1975.

Schoenfeld M, Meyers RH, Crupples LA: Increased rate of suicide among patients with Huntington's disease. *J. Neurol. Neurosurg. Psychiatry: 47*, 1283, 1984.

Shoulson I: Huntington's disease: cognitive and psychiatric features. *Neuropsychiatry Neuropsychol. Behav. Neurol.: 3*, 15 – 22, 1990.

Smith MC: Neurophysiology of aging. *Semin. Neurol.: 9*, 68 – 81, 1989.

Spirduso WW: Reaction and movement time as a function of age and physical activity level. *J. Gerontol.: 30*, 435 – 440, 1975.

Spirduso WW: Physical fitness, aging, and psychomotor speed: a review. *J. Gerontol.: 35*, 850 – 865, 1980.

Starr A: A disorder of rapid eye movements in Huntington's chorea. *Brain: 90*, 545 – 564, 1967.

Steele JC, Richardson JC, Olszewski J: Progressive supranuclear palsy: A heterogeneous degeneration involving the brainstem, basal ganglia and cerebellum with vertical gaze and pseudobulbar palsy, nuchal dystonia and dementia. *Arch. Neurol.: 10*, 333, 1964.

Stelmach GE, Phillips J, DiFabio RP, Teasdale N: Age, functional postural reflexes, and voluntary sway. *J. Gerontol.: 44*, M100 – M106, 1989.

Strata P (Editor): *The Olivocerebellar System in Motor Control*. New York: Springer Verlag, 1989.

Sudarsky L: Geriatrics: gait disorders in the elderly. *N. Engl. J. Med.: 322*, 1441 – 1446, 1990.

Suominen H, Heikkinen E, Liesen H, Michel D, Hollman W: Effects of 8 weeks endurance training on skeletal muscle metabolism in 56-70 year old sedentary men. *Eur. J. Appl. Physiol.: 37*, 173 – 180, 1977.

Surwillo WW: Choice reaction time and speed of information processing in old age. *Percept. Motor Skills: 36*, 321 – 322, 1973.

Swihart AA, Pirozzolo FJ: The neuropsychology of aging and dementia: clinical issues. In Whitaker HA (Editor), *Neuropsychological Studies of Nonfocal Brain Damage*. New York: Springer-Verlag, pp. 1 – 60, 1988.

Swihart AA, Baskin DS, Pirozzolo FJ: Somatostatin and cognitive dysfunction in Alzheimer's disease. *Dev. Neuropsychol.: 5*, 159 – 168, 1989.

Taylor AE, Saint-Cyr JA, Lange AE: Frontal lobe dysfunction in Parkinson's disease. *Brain: 109*, 845 – 883, 1986.

Taylor DJ, Crowe M, Bore PJ, Styles P, Arnold DL, Radda GK: Examination of the energetics of aging skeletal muscle using nuclear magnetic resonance. *Gerontology: 30*, 2 – 7, 1984.

Teravainen H, Calne DB: Motor system in normal aging and Parkinson's disease. In Katzman R, Terry R (Eds.), *The Neurology of Aging*. Philadelphia: F.A. Davis, pp. 85 – 109, 1983.

Tetrud JW, Langston JW: The effect of deprenyl (Selegiline) on the natural history of Parkinson's disease. *Science: 245*, 519 – 522, 1989.

Tideiksaar R: *Falling in Old Age: Its Prevention and Treatment*. New York: Springer, 1988.

Tinetti ME: Instability and falling in older patients. *Semin. Neurol.: 9*, 39 – 45, 1989.

Tomlinson BE, Irving D, Blessed G: Cell loss in the locus coeruleus in senile dementia of the Alzheimer type. *J. Neurol. Sci.: 49,* 419 – 128, 1981.

Trounce I, Byrne E, Marzuki S: Decline in skeletal muscle mitochondrial respiratory chain function: possible factor in ageing. *Lancet: i,* 637 – 639, 1989.

Turner DA, McGeachie RE: Normal pressure hydrocephalus and dementia: evaluation and treatment. *Clin. Geriatr. Med.: 4,* 815 – 830, 1988.

Uauy R, Winterer JC, Bilmazes C, Haverberg LH, Scrimshaw NS, Munro HN, Young VR: The changing pattern of whole body protein metabolism in aging humans. *J. Gerontol.: 33,* 663 – 671, 1978.

VonSattel JP, Ferrante RJ, Stevens TJ, Richardson EP: Neuropathologic classification of Huntington's disease. *J. Neuropathol. Exp. Neurol.: 44,* 559 – 577, 1985.

Vrtunski TB, Patterson MB, Mack JL, Hill GO: Microbehavioral analysis of the choice reaction time response in senile dementia. *Brain: 106,* 929 – 947, 1983.

Waugh NC, Fozard JL, Thomas JC: Age-related differences in serial binary classification. *Exp. Aging Res.: 4,* 133 – 142, 1978.

Weiner WJ, Lang AE: *Movement Disorders: A Comprehensive Survey: An Introduction to Movement Disorders and the Basal Ganglia.* Mount Kisco, NY: Futura, pp. 1 – 22, 1989.

Weiss AD: The locus of reaction time change with set, motivation, and age. *J. Gerontol.: 20,* 60 – 64, 1965.

Welford AT: Motor performance. In Birren JE, Schaie KW (Editors), *Handbook of the Psychology of Aging.* New York: Van Nostrand Reinhold, pp. 450 – 496, 1977.

Welford AT: Motor performance. In Birren JE, Schaie KW (Editors), *Handbook of the Psychology of Aging* (2nd edn.). New York: Van Nostrand Reinhold, pp. 152 – 187, 1985.

Welford AT: Reaction time, speed of performance, and age. *Ann. N. Y. Acad. Sci.: 515,* 98 – 119, 1988.

Wexler NS, Conneally PM, Housman D, et al: A DNA polymorphism for Huntington's disease marks the future. *Arch. Neurol.: 42,* 20, 1985.

Whitehouse PJ, Price DL, Struble RG, Clark AE, Coyle JT, DeLong MR: Alzheimer's disease and senile dementia: loss of neurons in the basal forebrain. *Science: 215,* 1237 – 1239, 1982.

Whitehouse PJ, Hedreen JC, White CL, Price DL: Basal forebrain neurons in the dementia of Parkinson disease. *Ann. Neurol.: 13,* 243 – 248, 1983.

Wiesendenger M, Hummelshein H, Bianchetti M, Chen DF Hyland D, Maier V, Wiesendenger R: Input and output organization of the supplemental motor area. In *Ciba Foundation Symposium 132, Motor Areas of the Cerebral Cortex* New York: John Wiley, pp 46 – 62, 1987.

Wolff ML: Reversible intellectual impairment: An internist's perspective. *J. Am. Geriatr. Soc.: 30,* 647 – 650, 1982.

Wong DF, Wagner HN, Dannals RF, Links JM, Frost JJ, Raver HT, Wilson AA, Rosenbau AE, Gjedde A, Douglas KH Petronis JD, Folstein MF, Toung JT, Burns HD, Kuhar MS Effects of age on dopamine and serotonin receptors measured by positron emission tomography in the living human brain *Science: 226,* 1393 – 1396, 1984.

Woollacott MH, Shumway-Cook A, Nashner L: Postural reflexes and aging. In Mortimer JA, Pirozzolo FJ, Maletta GJ (Editors), *Advances in Neurogerontology (Vol. 3): The Aging Motor System.* New York: Praeger, pp. 98 – 119, 1982.

Woollacott MH, Shumway-Cook A, Nashner LM: Aging and posture control: changes in sensory organization and muscular coordination. *Int. J. Aging Hum. Dev.: 23,* 97 – 114, 1986.

Woollacott MH, Inglin B, Manchester D: Neuromuscular changes in the older adult. *Ann. N. Y. Acad. Sci.: 515,* 42 – 53, 1988.

Wright BE, Henkind P: Aging changes and the eye. In Katzman R, Terry R (Editors), *The Neurology of Aging.* Philadelphia: F.A. Davis, pp. 149 – 165, 1983.

de Yebenes JG, Gomez MAM: The dopaminergic brain. In Jankovic J, Tolosa E (Editors), *Parkinson's Disease and Movement Disorders.* Baltimore: Urban & Schwarzenberg, pp. 13 – 26, 1988.

Young VR: Protein and amino acid metabolism with reference to aging and the elderly. *Prog. Clin. Biol. Res.: 326,* 279 – 300, 1990.

Young AB, Penney JB: Neurochemical anatomy of movement disorders. *Neurol. Clin.: 2,* 417 – 433, 1984.

Young AB, Penney JB: Biochemical and functional organization of the basal ganglia. In Jankovic J, Tolosa E (Editors), *Parkinson's Disease and Movement Disorders.* Baltimore: Urban & Schwarzenberg, pp. 1 – 11, 1988.

Young A, Stokes M, Crowe M: The size and strength of the quadriceps muscles of old and young men. *Clin. Physiol.: 5,* 145 – 154, 1985.

Zetusky WJ, Jankovic J, Pirozzolo F: The heterogenity of Parkinson's disease: Clinical and prognostic implications. *Neurology: 35,* 522 – 526, 1985.

© 1991 Elsevier Science Publishers B.V.
Handbook of Neuropsychology, Vol. 5
F. Boller and J. Grafman (Eds)

CHAPTER 10

Cognitive deficits in Parkinson's disease

Bruno Dubois[1], François Boller[2], Bernard Pillon[1] and Yves Agid[1]

[1]*INSERM U 289, Hôpital de la Salpêtrière, 47 Boulevard de l'Hôpital, 75651 Paris Cedex 13, France, and* [2]*INSERM U 324, Centre Paul Broca, 2ter rue d'Alésia, 75014 Paris, France*

This chapter discusses the broad spectrum of cognitive disorders seen over the course of idiopathic Parkinson's disease (PD). Partly because of Parkinson's lapidary description of the disease almost two centuries ago (1817), PD was long considered homogeneous in its presentation, symptoms, clinical course, and in its neuropathology. Recently, however, it has become evident that PD is heterogeneous clinically and neuropathologically. It is therefore not surprising that the cognitive profiles of PD patients vary considerably. This variation occurs within the same patients at different times of the day, between patients, and between series of patients. As a result, there are wide discrepancies in the literature which have led to a great deal of sometimes passionate controversy.

The present chapter will review the history of cognitive changes in PD with emphasis on dementia defined according to DSM III criteria (APA, 1980, 1987) and on isolated cognitive changes, as well as the neuronal correlates of these changes. This chapter will show that because of its implications for several different fields, including neuropharmacology and neurochemistry, PD constitutes an interesting and so far underestimated model of brain – behavior correlations.

Historical aspects

James Parkinson's summary of the disease (1817) was unequivocal, as far as cognitive changes are concerned: 'The intellect (of patients with 'shaking palsy' is) uninjured'. However, as pointed out by Mayeux and his colleagues (Mayeux et al., 1981), careful reading of the original essay indicates an abnormal mental status, specifically depression, in at least one of the six patients he described.

Parkinson's monograph received scant attention at the time of its publication and was reviewed by only a few journals (McMenemey, 1955). In subsequent years, neurologists in Great Britain (e.g. Robert Todd, 1834) and in continental Europe (e.g. Moritz Romberg, 1840) occasionally quoted his writings, but it is fair to say that, on the whole, Parkinson's contribution was close to forgotten by the medical world. No portrait of him is known to exist and, as far as we know, no obituary was published at the time of his death. This may be because James Parkinson was in the habit of strongly expressing views that were against those of the establishment (Yahr, 1978). More importantly, in our opinion, he made astute use of what we now call the clinical method (Adams and Victor, 1989); but because this approach had not yet been sufficiently applied to neurological problems, he was definitely ahead of his time.

As pointed out by Tyler (1987), this picture changed dramatically almost half a century later, when French neurologists, particularly Trousseau, Charcot and Vulpian, brought the disorder (and Parkinson's contribution) to the attention of the medical world. These clinicians were also the first to point out that intellectual impairment can be part of PD. Trousseau (1861) stated that '. . . the intellect . . . gets weakened at last; the patient loses his memory and his friends soon notice that his mind is not as clear as it was . . .'. This statement could easily have originated from a contemporary clinician aware of the current DSM III-R definition of dementia (APA, 1987). Charcot and Vulpian (1861, 1862) thought that, 'in general, psychic faculties are definitely impaired'; in a later review Charcot (1872) added that, 'at a given point, the mind becomes clouded and the memory is lost'. Another important nineteenth-century contribution came from William Gowers (1899) of Great Britain, whose observations on paralysis agitans included the comment that in later stages of the disease, one often finds 'mental weakness' and 'loss of memory'.

In later years, papers dealing directly or indirectly with the intellectual status of PD patients can be divided into several categories. First, several authors, like Parkinson, have stated specifically that *no changes* occur in the mental status of PD patients. Boller (1980) was able to find over 20 papers where no association between dementia or other cognitive changes and PD had been found. Few of these papers used psychological tests and almost all of them were written before 1970, that is in the 'pre-L-DOPA era'. A more recent paper (Matthews and Haaland, 1979) included only patients who were not on dopaminergic medications and thus presumably were tested before L-DOPA was widely available.

Second, many other authors have described mental status changes in PD. Some of the early descriptions focused on psychiatric symptoms. These reports include the papers by Ball (1882), who is often credited with being the first to have pointed out the mental status changes in PD. Even though others had already mentioned them, he is the first to have described these changes in detail. However, in discussing *'insanity'*, Ball mainly described patients with psychiatric symptoms such as hallucinations or depression. Apparently, only one of his seven cases was demented.

Third, other papers, mostly published from the seventies to the early eighties, mention cognitive

changes and particularly *dementia* in a sometimes astonishingly high percentage of PD patients. For example Martin et al. (1973) stated that 'intellectual impairment' is found in over 80% of patients. The etiology of the dementia was unclear until, a few years later, it was found (Hakim and Mathieson, 1979; Boller et al., 1980) that, at autopsy, PD patients often showed neurohistological features resembling those of Alzheimer's disease (AD). As the present chapter will show, there are reasons to believe that there is a definite overlap between PD and AD. However, this does not imply that the cognitive deficits of PD patients *always* arise from the association of PD with AD.

In recent years there has been a surge in the number of PD patients thought to have cognitive changes. The increase may be explained by clinicians' greater awareness of dementia or as an effect of L-DOPA administration, either because of a direct CNS effect of the drug or, more likely, because, owing to L-DOPA and the compounds that followed, PD patients live longer and are therefore more likely to manifest cognitive changes.

Finally, detailed studies and the use of sophisticated neuropsychological tests have shown that a significant percentage of PD patients exhibit *isolated and specific cognitive deficits*. These deficits will be reviewed in later sections of this chapter. The papers dealing with dementia will be discussed in the following section.

Cognitive changes

Dementia

Prevalence and risk factors

Most contemporary authors agree that in an unselected population of PD patients, the prevalence of dementia is greater than in age-matched control subjects. Boller (1980) and Cummings (1988) have shown that estimates of the prevalence of dementia vary widely among different sources (Table 1). The extreme variability of the frequency of dementia shown in Table 1 may be explained by methodological differences related to the

riteria used for the definition of dementia in PD
nd the populations studied in each case. DSM III
1980) and DSM III-R (1987) provided operational
riteria to define dementia in PD and other illnesses.
Iowever, the adequacy of these criteria to PD is
robably questionable because of the severe motor
eficit which accompanies the disease. Three studies
re particularly reliable because they are based on

TABLE 1

Reference, method, number and percentage of demented
atients in studies that found an association between PD and
ementia

Reference	Method	(n) %
atrick & Levy, 1922	Clinical examination	(146) 4%
ewy, 1923	Clinical examination	(70) 63%
Jjönes, 1949	Psychological tests	(194) 40%
ollock et al., 1966	Clinical examination	(84) 20%
oehn & Yahr, 1967	Clinical examination	(802) 14%
hristensen, 1970	Psychological tests	(41) 15%
lindham, 1970	Clinical examination	(36) 33%
elesia et al., 1972	Psychological tests	(153) 40%
arron et al., 1972	Psychological tests	(30) 45%
oranger et al., 1972a	Psychological tests	(63) 37%
acks et al., 1972	Clinical examination	(72) 21%
Iartin et al., 1973	Psychological tests	(100) 81%
ajput et al., 1975	Clinical examination	(125) 28%
Iarttila et al., 1976	Psychological tests	(444) 29%
weet et al., 1976	Clinical examination	(100) 56%
ieberman et al., 1979	Clinical examination	(520) 32%
Iakim et al., 1979	Clinical examination	(34) 56%
esser et al., 1979	Clinical examination	(131) 31%
oller et al., 1980	Clinical examination	(36) 55%
roka et al., 1981	Clinical examination	(71) 15%
e Smet et al., 1982	Clinical examination	(75) 36%
lindham et al., 1982	Psychological tests	(40) 20%
irozzolo et al., 1982	Psychological tests	(60) 93%
Iershey, 1982	Psychological tests	(22) 45%
iccirilli et al., 1984	Psychological tests	(70) 33%
ortin et al., 1984	Psychological tests	(79) 42%
ajput et al., 1984	Clinical examination	(138) 9%
ees, 1985	Clinical examination	(48) 15%
aylor et al., 1985	Psychological tests	(100) 8%
etuski et al., 1985	Clinical examination	(334) 77%
lizan et al., 1986	Clinical examination	(203) 29%
Iuber et al., 1986b	Psychological tests	(48) 33%
yebode et al., 1986	Psychological tests	(43) 72%
irotti et al., 1988	Clinical examination	(147) 14%
Iayeux et al., 1988	Clinical examination	(339) 11%
illon et al., in press	Psychological tests	(164) 18%
eid et al., 1990	Psychological tests	(107) 8 to 83%

fairly large samples and because they use comparable instruments (which can be equated to the
current DSM III-R). Their estimates range from
32% to 40% (Celesia and Wanamaker, 1972;
Lieberman et al., 1979; Marttila and Rinne, 1976).
The estimates become higher if 'somewhat less impaired' patients are included (Celesia and
Wanamaker, 1972). A more recent longitudinal
study of newly diagnosed patients (Reid et al., 1990)
separated late- (> 70 years) from early-onset (< 70
years) PD and concluded that, in untreated patients,
dementia was found in 8% of the early-onset and
32% in the late-onset. At three years follow-up,
18% of the early-onset group and 83% of the late-
onset group were classified as demented, on the
basis of formal neuropsychological tests. In contrast, other recent studies estimate a lower percentage (10% to 15%) of dementia in PD (Brown and
Marsden, 1984a; Rajput et al., 1984; Lees, 1985;
Taylor et al., 1985), but generally the percentage remains greater than in control subjects (Mindham et
al., 1982).

The risk factors for dementia in PD are far from
being clearly known. Aging seems to play a role, as
suggested by the positive correlation between age of
disease onset and cognitive impairment (Garron et
al., 1972; Celesia and Wanamaker, 1972; Marttila
and Rinne, 1976; Lieberman et al., 1979; Lichter et
al., 1988; Lavernhe et al., 1989). The influence of
age of disease onset on cognition has been confirmed by studies comparing intellectual status of early-
and late-onset forms of the disease (Hietanen and
Teräväinen, 1988a; Dubois et al., 1990; Reid et al.,
1990). Severity and duration of the motor illness
may also be considered as risk factors (see review in
Mayeux and Stern, 1983). Growdon et al. (1990)
confirmed the existence of a relationship between
motor and cognitive impairment. Based on prospective data for 191 patients, they found that no PD patient in Stage 1 of Hoehn and Yahr's (1967) scale
(unilateral symptoms only) had dementia, whereas
35% of those in Stage 4 and 57% of those in stage
5 were demented. Among the motor symptoms,
rigidity and akinesia have been proposed as the best
predictors. For example Mortimer et al. (1982),

following previous suggestions based on clinical data, showed that *bradykinesia* is correlated with poor cognitive test performance, even when measured by untimed tests. Other studies have emphasized the frequency of gait disorders in demented PD patients (Pillon et al., 1989b; Lavernhe et al., 1989), and the association of tremor with better cognitive test performance (Mortimer et al., 1982). The latter findings, however, have not been universally confirmed (Boller et al., 1984; Ransmayr et al., 1986).

Storandt (1990, p. 362) has reviewed data suggesting that the progression of cognitive decline in treated PD is probably relatively slow. This is probably true if a large unselected sample of PD patients is being followed. The data presented above indicate, however, that among the patients 'at risk' such as those with late onset of the disease, the rate of cognitive decline is significantly faster than in the early-onset group (Reid et al., 1990).

While the risk factors for dementia in PD remain to be established, and while the overall question of whether demented PD patients represent a distinct subgroup of PD is not settled, one feature that does seem to separate demented from nondemented PD patients is the risk of death. Mindham et al. (1982) found that in their three-year longitudinal study, only 13% of the demented patients had survived, in contrast to 87% of the nondemented. Boller et al. (1980) found that demented PD patients had a significantly shorter survival rate than nondemented patients. These data are in keeping with older data indicating that demented patients have a lower life expectancy than do controls (Go et al., 1978). In contrast, more recent and carefully controlled studies have failed to show that dementia shortens life (Martin et al., 1987).

Clinical picture

The neuropsychological profile of demented PD patients is less clearly established than one would expect, in part because, in many papers, the diagnosis of dementia relied simply on clinical judgment or on simple, informal tests. For example, Pollock and Hornabrook (1966), who conducted one of the early epidemiological studies of dementia in PD, used no formal psychological tests and did not characterize the mental status changes found in their subjects. Lieberman et al. (1979) used a 'simple bedside evaluation' and again provided no detail. Boller et al. (1980) used a retrospective chart review and noticed that the dementia was characterized mainly by disorders of orientation, construction and memory, whereas social behavior, language and praxis were relatively less impaired.

Other authors (Celesia and Wanamaker, 1972; Hardyck and Petrinovich, 1963; Loranger et al., 1972a; Reitan and Boll, 1971) used the WAIS or other standard tests. Some found, in addition to a decreased IQ, a tendency for the Performance Scale to be significantly lower than the Verbal Scale, an exaggeration of the effect usually found in normal aging (Becker et al., 1987). Further, the clinical impression that the language impairment in PD is less severe than that in AD has been confirmed (e.g. Gainotti et al., 1980).

In more recent papers, cognitive tests scores in PD patients have been more critically examined, controlling for the severity of intellectual deterioration. In nondemented PD patients, language functions tend to be relatively spared with the exception of verbal fluency and occasionally naming (as reviewed in the section on speech and language). Demented PD patients, however, do show impairment on many verbal tasks, and on the whole resemble AD patients except that the latter group is more severely impaired. Memory impairment is characteristic of AD and demented PD patients. As pointed out by Brown and Marsden (1988c, p. 374), the ability to learn new information is impaired in both diseases and 'any differences are simply quantitative, representing different severities of intellectual impairment'. Other memory processes, however, may be differentially affected in the two diseases (as reviewed in a later section). Few studies have assessed visuospatial functions in demented PD subjects, but current evidence suggests no qualitative difference between them and AD subjects (Brown and Marsden, 1988c, pp. 376–377). However, the resemblance between the dementia of PD and that lack of specificity of the tests used. For instance, some studies suggest that demented PD patients are particularly affected on those specific tests of 'executive functions' (see below) that best discriminate non-demented PD patients from control subjects (Pillon et al., 1986; Girotti et al., 1988).

The neuronal basis of dementia and other cognitive disorders in PD will be discussed in a later section of the chapter.

Isolated ('specific') cognitive changes

The concept of specificity of cognitive changes in PD is a vexing one. First of all, the term 'specific' may not always be semantically correct since most changes are not exclusively found in PD. Also, as is often the case in 'classical' neuropsychology, there is a tendency to mix cognitive tests with the domains or 'functions' they are supposed to be testing and with the cerebral areas they are thought to be associated with. For example, in patients with focal lesions, visuospatial functions (see definition below) are often associated with lesions of the right parietal lobe. However, it does not necessarily follow that a similar impairment found in PD implies structural lesions located in the parietal lobe. Similarly, poor performance on the Wisconsin Card Sorting Test is too often automatically attributed to structural lesions of the frontal lobes. In this light, the following sections will try to weigh critically the results of particular tests. Another difficulty in attempting to interpret the literature is the frequent use of tests that are not based on a specific neuropsychological model, that have not been sufficiently validated in normal subjects, and that cannot be readily attributed to a given cognitive domain, let alone to a given neural structure. Finally the 'specificity' of cognitive deficits in PD must always be discussed keeping in mind that any disease of the central nervous system tends to impair performance compared to controls.

With these caveats in mind, this section will review the literature concerning changes in speech and language, visuospatial functions and memory. It will conclude with a review of two more nebulous concepts often discussed in PD: impairment of executive functions and bradyphrenia.

Speech and language

Parkinson in his original report (1817) noted that sometimes 'the speech was very much interrupted'. Certainly in many advanced cases, speech output becomes very limited and it is at times difficult to differentiate severe loss of voice (aphonia) and of articulatory capacities (anarthria) from 'unresponsiveness with the appearance of alertness' as found in akinetic mutism (Critchley, 1981).

In less severe cases, however, one can more easily separate the difficulties in communicative abilities that are due to impairment in speech (i.e. involving the neuro-mechanical process of articulation) from those due to aphasia-like disorders. A review of speech and language changes in PD is also found in Huff (1990, pp. 259 – 260).

Speech abnormalities are frequently observed in PD. The most typical changes include reduced variability in pitch and loudness, reduced loudness level, and decreased use of all vocal parameters for achieving stress and emphasis. Articulation is imprecise and generated at variable rates in short bursts of speech punctuated by pauses (Darley et al., 1975). This 'hypokinetic dysarthria' is sometimes accompanied by other phenomena such as marked acceleration of speech rate (tachiphemia) and, less commonly, compulsive repetition of words or phrases (palilalia; Boller et al., 1975). Experimental studies have shown that the dysarthria is related to a failure to control respiration, and to a stiffness of facial, oral, buccal and pharyngeal muscles (Luchsinger and Arnold, 1965). There is also decreased speed of articulator movement and probably a disorder in speech planning (Connor et al., 1989). These phenomena are closely akin to the movement disorder seen in other parts of the body. However, as pointed out by Critchley (1981), clinical experience shows that the rate of deterioration or recovery (during therapy) of speech does not always parallel the locomotor changes.

Some researchers have found that, unlike dysprosodies due to cortical lesions, the dysprosody of hypokinetic dysarthria found in PD is not accompanied by loss of prosody comprehension, suggesting that it is related to a disorder of motor control rather than to a loss of linguistic knowledge (Darkins et al., 1988). Scott et al. (1984), however, found that PD patients were unable to appreciate the prosodic and emotional aspects of their own and others' speech and facial expression. Blonder et al. (1989) also found impaired comprehension of prosody in PD patients with unilateral symptoms, without difference between left and right involvement. In both studies, however, the interpretation of these findings is clouded by a lack of information concerning other cognitive functions.

It is often stated that linguistic abilities remain normal in PD. For example Pirozzolo et al. (1982), in their study investigating the nature and prevalence of cognitive deficits in PD, found that in comparison to control subjects, PD patients performed significantly worse on a series of neuropsychological tests including the Vocabulary and Information subtests of the WAIS, but that they did not differ in their performance on an object-naming test. Normal confrontation naming has also been reported by Freedman et al. (1984) and by Mildworf (1978) for the Boston Naming Test (Borod et al., 1980), and by Bayles and Tomoeda (1983) for PD patients with mild impairment tested on the Peabody Picture Vocabulary Test. In a study of spontaneous speech and reading abilities in 10 male PD patients and 10 control subjects, Illes et al. (1988) showed that PD patients tended to produce temporally longer sentences, not because of increased word production or syntactic complexity (which were reduced), but mainly because of a greater number of pauses ('silent hesitations'). They concluded that the pauses represent an adaptive compensatory mechanism for the speech-motor difficulties that accompany the disease.

Many other authors, however, have found that PD patients have word-finding difficulties in tasks of visual confrontation naming. For instance, Growdon et al. (1990) reported that non-demented PD subjects are impaired on the Boston Naming Test. Matison et al. (1982) found that PD

patients benefit considerably from phonetic and semantic cueing, prompting the authors to call the disorder 'word production anomia' accompanied by a 'tip-of-the tongue' phenomenon as seen in some aphasic patients and on occasion in normal individuals (Brown and McNeill, 1966). PD patients have also been shown to be impaired in completing a sentence and in grammatical comprehension (Grossman et al., 1990), and in word fluency (Rosen, 1980). Further, verbal fluency discriminated best between PD patients and normal subjects (Bayles and Kaszniak, 1987). Interpretation of the deficit is complex because performance is thought to involve processes which are not only linguistic. These findings, therefore, will be discussed in a later section (executive functions).

When discussing language (as well as other cognitive functions) in PD, it is essential to be aware of the degree of overall cognitive deficit in each case. Cummings et al. (1988) compared the linguistic performance of three groups of patients: PD without overall intellectual impairment, PD with dementia (Mini Mental State – MMS (Folstein et al., 1975) scores between 12 and 24, mean 20.25) and AD patients whose MMS scores were slightly but not significantly below the demented PD group (mean 17.9). The tasks were derived from two standard batteries, the Boston Diagnostic Aphasia Examination (Goodglass and Kaplan, 1976) and the Western Aphasia Battery (Kertesz, 1979). The nondemented PD patients showed significant abnormalities in two tasks (Information Content of Spontaneous Speech and Comprehension of Complex Commands), whereas all other linguistic tasks, including Naming, Comprehension, Repetition, Reading and Automatic Speech, were performed normally. However, when the two PD groups were compared, PD patients with dementia showed significant impairment in several areas (naming, comprehension, repetition, with borderline impairment in reading and automatic speech). AD patients, however, had more impoverished information content of spontaneous speech, more impaired word list generation and more severe anomia than demented PD patients. In contrast, Como and Caine (1987) found no difference between demented PD and AD patients on a series of language tasks including 'higher-level' tasks such as the development of narrative.

One important consideration applies to the interpretation of the findings presented in this section as well as in some other sections (particularly memory and visuospatial deficits). According to the methodology used, and most importantly according to the particular subjects sampled, estimates of cognitive changes vary widely. It may be bewildering for those new to the field to be confronted with such diametrically opposed viewpoints. It is true that clearcut aphasia is not normally seen in PD and that other communicative disorders based on linguistic impairment are relatively minor and infrequent. However, more language impairment is seen when the sample includes demented PD patients and those in more advanced stages of the disease. Cummings and his colleagues, in the conclusion of their article comparing language output in AD and PD patients (Cummings et al., 1988), speculated that the subgroup with language disorder (which constituted over one-third of their demented PD subjects) probably reflects the simultaneous occurrence of PD and AD.

Visuospatial deficits

In Chapter 17, Volume 2 of the *Handbook*, Newcombe and Ratcliff (1989, p. 334) pointed out that virtually all visual stimuli and, one could add, all motor behaviors performed in response to these stimuli are *spatial* because they imply a position in space. However, following these two authors, we will limit our discussion of visuospatial deficits to impairment of the ability to appreciate the relative position of stimuli and objects in space, difficulty in integrating those objects into a coherent spatial framework, and difficulty in performing mental operations involving spatial concepts.

Clues about the role of the basal ganglia in visuospatial functions come from studies in animals. Rats, carnivores and subhuman primates with basal ganglia lesions perform poorly at tasks with a strong visuospatial component, such as multiple-alley mazes (Thomson, 1974), spatial

delayed alternation, and many other tests involving visual discrimination (reviewed by Teuber, 1976).

Table 2 summarizes the results of studies that have evaluated visuospatial disorders in PD. Proctor (later Bowen), was probably the first to point out an isolated visuospatial deficit in PD patients (Proctor et al., 1964) and to observe a similar change in monkeys following caudate lesions (Bowen, 1969). Since then, many authors (see Table 2A) have confirmed the presence of such deficits. The tests included such complex *visuomotor* tasks as walking on a given route, making complex gestures and drawing or copying complex figures. Boller et al. (1984b) used, in addition to these classic tests, a

TABLE 2

Summary of results obtained by studies of visuospatial functions

Reference	Task
(A) Impairment found:	
Proctor et al., 1964	Judgment of orientation
Bowen et al., 1972	Route-walking test
Danta & Hilton, 1975	Judgment of orientation
Bowen et al., 1976	Personal orientation
Villardita et al., 1982	Visuoperceptual tests
Pirozzolo et al., 1982	Spatial orientation test
Stern et al., 1983	Pattern tracing
Stern et al., 1984a	Pattern construction
Boller et al., 1984b	Visuomotor tests
	Visuoperceptual tests
Oyebode et al., 1986	Mental imagery
Hovestadt et al., 1987a	Rod orientation test
Stern et al., 1990*	Drawing test
Growdon et al., 1990	BVRT, multiple choice
(B) Mixed results:	
Goldenberg et al., 1986	Judgment of line orientation – impaired
	Mental rotation – unimpaired
Ransmayr et al., 1987	BVRT, multiple choice – impaired
	Visuospatial thinking – unimpaired
(C) No impairment found:	
Brown et al., 1986	Judgment of spatial relationships
Della Sala et al., 1986	Directional forecast
Taylor et al., 1987	Imaginary route-walking test
Stelmach et al., 1989	Judgment of spatial displacement
Hietanen et al., 1990	Mental rotation

Stern et al.'s study (*) refers to MPTP subjects

series of tasks requiring only minimal motor responses (pointing or answering yes or no), referred to as *'visuo-perceptual'* tasks. The visuospatial tasks ranged from simple to complex. The PD group demonstrated significant visuospatial impairment on both the visuomotor tasks and the visuoperceptual tasks. The visuospatial impairment was not related to a decrement in intellectual abilities because the patients performed well on standard intelligence tests. In independent research carried out at about the same time (Stern et al., 1983, 1984), PD patients performed poorly at visuospatial tasks involving tracing and construction. These authors postulated an underlying perceptual motor deficit, which may result in impaired internal representations. Villardita et al. (1982) and several other authors have obtained results compatible with that hypothesis.

In contrast, other researchers have found mixed results (Table 2B) or no evidence (Table 2C) of spatial impairment in PD. The negative studies indicate that PD does not always impair visuospatial abilities. Several factors may contribute to the apparently contradictory results.

The first is a *test bias*. As mentioned previously, some studies which found a visuospatial impairment in PD were based on tests that included a significant visuomotor component. Accordingly, Brown and Marsden (1986) rejected the idea of a generalized visuospatial deficit in PD. However, as noted above, several of the authors who found an impairment (Table 2A and B) used tests that made only minimal demand on the visuomotor aspect of performance. In addition, in several studies, simple visuospatial tasks have been found to discriminate better between PD patients and control subjects than some apparently much more complex tasks. This finding brings to mind DeRenzi's statement (1982) that 'a more definite answer to the issue concerning the relation between the locus of lesion and the breakdown of spatial functions might be obtained by employing elementary tasks, which tap the basic mechanism underlying spatial perception'.

The second possible confounding factor is a *selection* or *sample bias*. In many studies, patients who

are older, in more advanced stages of PD, or have grater motor impairment are excluded. These selection criteria may exclude subjects likely to have visuospatial deficits (Hovestadt et al., 1987b). However, while the negative studies could be criticized for what Della Sala et al. (1986) recognize as a possibly significant source of variability, they do raise the question of why some PD patients are able to complete tasks which undoubtedly require visuospatial abilities even when they are on drug therapy, are relatively old and are in a moderately advanced stage of the disease. This evidence argues in favor of the heterogeneity of PD as suggested by El Awar et al. (1987). They hypothesized that PD patients can be divided into three groups, according to cognitive changes: completely unimpaired, with 'isolated' cognitive changes, and with dementia. The answer to this and other issues raised in this chapter will come from longitudinal studies (Spinnler and Della Sala, 1987).

What are the basic nature and significance of visuospatial disorders when they are found in PD? Proctor et al. (1964) attributed the impaired judgment of visual-vertical and postural-vertical to a frontal-lobe disorder. While a considerable body of literature has shown that patients with frontal-lobe lesion do perform these tasks poorly, the tasks nevertheless fit into the definition provided above for visuospatial functions. The same is true in animal experiments, where a task with a strong visuospatial component, such as delayed alternation, is considered as paradigmatic of frontal-lobe impairment. Ogden et al. (1990) have found that high-functioning PD patients performed poorly on complex visuospatial tests when the task involved planning and sequencing, a finding which is compatible with frontal lobe involvement. Possibly, as for other types of visuospatial behavior, many of the tasks discussed here require that visuomotor mechanisms of the parietal and frontal lobes work together, in concert with subcortical visual centers (Newcombe and Ratcliff, 1989).

From a more strictly psychological viewpoint, Brown and Marsden (1990), who do not believe that a generalized visuospatial deficit exists in PD, have explained positive results such as those listed in Table 2A by proposing a depletion of central processing resources, e.g. the Central Executive of the Working Memory model (Baddeley, 1986) and the supervisory attentional system in the attentional model of Norman and Shallice (1980). It can be argued, however, that the logic on which this hypothesis is based is circular because any task on which patients are impaired could, by definition, be considered resource-demanding. Whatever the explanation, the disorders lend themselves to human and animal experiments that would improve our understanding of the phenomena.

Visuospatial disorders must be clearly differentiated from dementia, although it is not known whether they eventually evolve into dementia (Ogden, 1990, p. 274). PD patients with visuospatial deficits may not come to the attention of health personnel as often as do those with memory impairment or dementia, yet the visuospatial deficits may produce significant impairments in everyday life. In AD, it has been shown (Saxton, in preparation) that nonverbal tests with a strong visuospatial component best predict everyday capabilities (as measured by the activities of daily living (ADL) tests). PD patients with visuospatial disorders may be more impaired than those without: the combination of perceptual disorders with the motor impairment that accompanies the disease may produce an impairment many times worse than either alone, as illustrated by an anecdote from Hovestadt et al. 1987a) reminiscent of statements made by some of our patients: 'I used to walk alone in the wood, fog or no fog, but when the symptoms of Parkinson's disease appeared, I noticed that I could not orient myself any more, and in case of fog, I got lost'.

Memory

Memory disturbance is a hallmark of dementia (Boller et al., 1984) and can be considered a nonspecific sign of cognitive impairment. Indeed, the severity of the memory disorder in PD is related to the severity of the global intellectual deterioration (Huber et al., 1986; Pillon et al., in press). Memory, however, is not unitary, but must be parcelled according to underlying mechanisms and to the temporal organization of information storage (Squire, 1987; see also section 4, Volume 3 of the *Handbook*). Even in demented PD patients, some memory functions are preserved in comparison to those in patients with AD (Sagar et al., 1988). Further, nondemented patients with PD show impairment of some memory functions relative to healthy subjects (Taylor et al., 1986; Growdon et al., in press). Is there a specificity of memory disorders in PD?

Primary memory According to Squire (1987) 'primary memory' refers to the information to be remembered that is the focus of current attention 'as when one holds a telephone number in mind'. Compared to 'short-term memory', 'primary memory' places less emphasis on the duration of memory storage, and more emphasis on the role of attention, conscious processing and memory capacity (Atkinson and Shiffrin, 1968). 'Working memory' describes a workspace that maintains information while it is being processed, and consists of a number of inter-related systems, the three principal components of which are the Central Executive System (CES), the Articulatory Loop System (ALS) and the Visuospatial Scratchpad (VSSP; Baddeley, 1986). The ALS permits recycling of verbal information while it is being processed. The VSSP permits temporary storage and manipulation of visuospatial information. Finally, the CES, assumed to function like a 'limited-capacity attentional system', controls and coordinates the other subsystems by selecting strategies and integrating information.

The passive and immediate repetition of digit series (Asso, 1969; Hietanen and Teräväinen, 1988a), and the immediate tapping of a block array (Morris et al., 1988; Sullivan and Sagar, 1989) are usually preserved even in patients with late onset of the disease (Dubois et al., 1990), poor response to L-DOPA treatment (Taylor et al., 1987), or dementia (Huber et al., 1989). However, difficulties may appear with the use of interfering stimuli. In the Peterson and Peterson (1959) procedure, three consonant letters are presented and immediately followed by a distractor task, intended to prevent rehearsal of the to-be-remembered items before recall. PD patients are impaired on this task (Tweedy et al., 1982) and the extent of the impairment is similar to that observed in AD (Huber et al., 1989c). In the Sternberg (1975) paradigm, the subject must decide whether or not probe digits belong to a set of a variable number of digits held in a short-term memory. Thus, the amount of information to process varies, but the motor demands of the task are constant. Wilson et al. (1980) found that scanning accuracy was normal for the PD patient group as a whole, but that scanning speed was lower for the older patients. This phenomenon of cognitive slowing could explain why PD patients are impaired at the shortest but not at the longest intervals in recognition (Sagar et al., 1988; Sullivan and Sagar, 1989) and matching to sample (Sahakian et al., 1988) tasks, unlike patients with AD, who are impaired at the longest, but not at the shortest intervals.

A specific impairment of the visuospatial subsystem of working memory has been hypothesized by Bradley et al. (1989) in PD. In the primary visuospatial task, patients were shown a videotape of a road, and were asked to imagine that road and report the direction of all turns starting mentally from one extremity of the road. They also administered a primary verbal memory task which involved memorizing a short phrase and then making decisions about initial letters of the words in the phrases. While the control group's speed of response was stable across tasks, the PD patients' reaction times were much slower on the visuospatial than they were on the verbal task. Level of difficulty, however, cannot be excluded as a contributory factor: in the verbal task, subjects only had to make lexical desicions and were guided by well-established lexical knowledge; in the visuospatial task subjects had to switch their attention between two different representations of the same road, according to the starting point, and were cued only by their short-term memory representation; and the control group's error rate was greater on the visuospatial than on the verbal task.

Thus, it seems possible that the visuospatial nature of the task is not the crucial factor. In visuospatial tasks, PD patients are impaired relative to controls when they must generate a response, but not when they are given a multiple-choice task (Ransmayr et al., 1987). PD patients may also be impaired in purely verbal tasks, as noted in the Peterson and Peterson and the Sternberg procedures. Therefore the impairment of primary memory in PD patients may reflect a deficit in attention and therefore depend on the attentional resources required for the task.

Secondary memory   Secondary memory or long-term memory is activated when the capacity of primary or short term memory is exceeded. Secondary memory can be divided into explicit and implicit memory (Graf and Schacter, 1985).

Explicit memory. Explicit memory refers to facts and data acquired through learning processes which are accessible to conscious recollection. Recognition is the more 'passive' paradigm of declarative memory: 'a simple decision between fixed alternatives is all that is required' (Flowers et al., 1984). Normal recognition memory has been demonstrated in PD, for verbal and visuospatial material (Lees and Smith, 1983; Boller et al., 1984b; Flowers et al., 1984; Weingartner et al., 1984; Taylor et al., 1986; El-Awar et al., 1987). Recognition may be impaired, however, when tasks require PD patients to scan mentally, manipulate the material, or organize actively a response. For instance, in the study of Tweedy et al. (1982), subjects were required to signal with a hand movement either the repetition of a previously presented word or the occurrence of a synonym. PD patients recognized fewer repetitions and synonyms than control subjects, and were more impaired on synonyms than on detection of repetitions.

Recall requires sustained effort and cognitive capacity (Weingartner et al., 1984). In PD, story and paired associate recall, immediately and after a delay, are generally impaired (Bowen et al., 1976; Halgin et al., 1977; Pirozzolo et al., 1982; Stern et al., 1984; Pillon et al., 1986; El-Awar et al., 1987). The impairment is even more severe when the material to be learned is not semantically organized, as in word-list acquisition (Tweedy et al., 1982; Villardita et al., 1982; Weingartner et al., 1984; Globus et al., 1985), the Rey Auditory Verbal Learning Test (Taylor et al., 1986, 1987; Caltagirone et al., 1989), or the Buschke Selective Reminding Test (Della Sala et al., 1986; Mayeux et al., 1987; Helkala et al., 1989). PD patients' visual recall is significantly poorer than that of control subjects (Boller et al., 1984b; Sullivan et al., 1989; Growdon et al., in press). Therefore, the ability to register verbal or visuospatial material is preserved in PD, as shown by recognition tasks, but the recall deficit suggests that the processes of retrieval or functional use of memory stores are defective (Ruberg and Agid, 1988).

Interestingly, the recall deficit is present in early-onset PD (Hietanen and Teräväinen, 1988a) and is not worse in the late-onset form of the disease (Dubois et al., 1990). Thus, it cannot be interpreted as a nonspecific effect of aging. The recall deficit is also observed in early, untreated PD patients (Hietanen and Teräväinen, 1986). Therefore, it cannot be due to a nonspecific effect of treatment. Dopamine, however, has been implicated in disorders of the functional use of memory stores. Treatment with dopaminomimetics has been reported to improve effortful memory in normal individuals (Newman et al., 1984). Indeed, Huber et al. (1987, 1989) found a correlation between plasma dopamine level and acquisition rate in PD patients, whereas the absolute level of dopamine did not influence retention. Variation in plasma dopamine levels between the time of original learning and subsequent memory retrieval resulted in a state-dependent memory impairment (Huber et al., 1987). Mohr and his colleagues (Mohr et al., 1987, 1989), however, found a selective influence of dopaminomimetic therapy only on delayed verbal recall and no state-dependence.

Anticholinergics have also been implicated in memory performance (Drachmann, 1977). Indeed, Sadeh et al. (1982) observed that anticholinergics influenced explicit memory in PD patients. In contrast, Dubois et al. (1990) found that an-

ticholinergics influenced attention (digit span) and tests sensitive to frontal-lobe dysfunctions, rather than memory. These contradictory results could indicate that dopaminergic and cholinergic neuronal systems, impaired in PD, have little influence on information storage, but modify the level of active attentional control, affecting acquisition and retrieval.

Implicit memory. Neuropsychological evidence for multiple implicit memory systems has been provided by Heindel et al. (1989). Procedural learning is the ability to acquire a perceptual or motor skill or a cognitive routine through repeated exposures to a specific activity constrained by invariant rules (Cohen and Squire, 1980). Acquisition is *implicit,* acquired through practice and manifested only in significantly reduced reaction times or error scores over trials. Successful strategies cannot be consciously recalled. This kind of learning and memory is spared in amnesia (Corkin, 1965) and in AD (Knopman and Nissen, 1987). Although the anatomical substrate of procedural learning is not established, the neostriatum, especially the caudate nucleus, is thought to play a key role (Mishkin et al., 1984; Martone et al., 1984). Priming, another form of implicit memory, has been defined as the temporary facilitation of performance via prior exposure to stimuli (Butters et al., 1990). Lexical priming, which may depend upon the integrity of neocortical areas, is spared in amnesia, but impaired in AD (Butters et al., 1990).

Procedural learning, investigated with the Tower of Toronto, a simplified variant of the Tower of Hanoi puzzle, seems impaired in PD (Saint-Cyr et al., 1988). The performance of PD patients was normal on the preliminary (3-disc) phase of the tower task, but significantly impaired on the 4-disc phase. The first block of five trials, however, showed clear evidence of procedural learning in PD patients, even though it was less accurate than that of controls. Only in the second block was further acquisition impaired, indicating that the patients were unable to maintain the acquired mental set. The same results were observed in learning a new manual skill (Frith et al., 1986): the PD patients performed much worse than the control subjects, but showed clear evidence of learning, confirming previous studies (Day et al., 1984). The major difference from the controls was that patients with PD had difficulty maintaining motor sets. Therefore, the lower performance of PD patients in procedural learning may be the consequence of a more generalized behavioral impairment of the ability to maintain a set against competing alternatives (Flowers and Robertson, 1985). Heindel et al. (1989) have provided evidence showing that procedural learning and lexical priming are preserved in non-demented, but impaired in demented PD patients.

Remote memory   Representations in long-term memory are not entirely determined at the time of learning, but are affected by subsequent external events (such as repetition and other acquired information) and by internal events (such as rehearsal and efforts at reconstruction) (Squire, 1987). Remote memory refers to these old and consolidated acquisitions, learned before the onset of disease.

Remote memory for personal and public events has been found to be impaired in PD patients (Globus et al., 1985), but only if they are old (Warburton, 1967) or demented (Freedman et al., 1984; Huber et al., 1986, 1989c). Using a series of recognition and recall tests, Sagar et al. (1988a) showed that: recognition memory of content was preserved; recall was less affected for remote events than for recent ones; the magnitude and temporal extent of the retrograde loss was related to severity of dementia; and the impairment of dating capacity was relatively specific in some patients. Therefore, remote memory for events in PD illustrates the dissociation between recognition and recall observed in recent memory and a relatively specific difficulty of dating capacity.

In the section on speech and language, we indicated that PD patients are often impaired in naming and word fluency. One explanation may be that remote memory for words and their meanings, i.e. semantic memory, may be impaired in PD. Examples include confrontation naming (Matison et al., 1982; Globus et al., 1985); verbal fluency (Cools et al., 1984; Stern et al., 1984b; Pillon et al., 1986; Gurd and Ward, 1989) and synonym detection (Tweedy et al., 1982). In contrast, vocabulary remains generally intact (Asso, 1969; Matison et al., 1982; Lees and Smith, 1983).

Specificity of memory disorders in PD   In general, the above results suggest a dissociation of memory abilities, with a preserved ability to register, store and consolidate information, and a defective functional use of memory stores. Memory functions dependent upon the integrity of the temporal lobes are relatively preserved. Conversely, memory functions dependent upon the integrity of the frontal lobes (Milner and Petrides, 1984; Fuster, 1989) are impaired. They include delayed response (Freedman and Oscar-Berman, 1986), delayed alternation (Partiot et al., in preparation), recency discrimination (Taylor et al., 1986; Sagar et al., 1988b; Sullivan and Sagar, 1989), temporal ordering (Dubois et al., 1987), dating capacity (Sagar et al., 1988a), subject-ordered pointing (Gotham et al., 1988), conditional associative learning (Gotham et al., 1988; Sahakian et al., 1988; Canavan et al., 1989), and the shifting phase of an associative learning task (Goldenberg et al., 1989). All these tasks require the ability to generate spontaneously efficient strategies and to use internally guided behavior (Taylor et al., 1986). Therefore, memory disorders in PD could result from a more global behavioral impairment, not limited to memory functions. The 'frontal lobe' hypothesis is probably not sufficient, however, to explain all the memory disorders of PD patients (Growdon et al., in press). The possibility of explicit memory disorders in some subgroups of patients must be considered. El-Awar et al. (1987) suggested that several patterns of memory impairment could be discerned among PD patients: some are unimpaired relative to control subjects, some have specific difficulties, while others have a more generalized impairment of memory functions. Even in this last subgroup, however, some differences can be seen in comparison to the memory disorders observed in AD. Temporal ordering in short-term and remote memory is more impaired in PD than in AD patients (Sagar et al., 1988a and b). Conversely long-term storage of information (Helkala et al., 1989) and content of remote memory (Sagar et al., 1988a) are more impaired in AD than in demented PD patients. In contrast with declarative memory, procedural memory, preserved in AD, could be impaired in PD (Saint-Cyr et al., 1988; Heindel et al., 1989), but these preliminary results have to be confirmed.

'Executive functions'

The term 'executive functions' refers to the mental processes involved in the realization of goal-directed behavior whether expressed through a mental or motor act. They are generally thought to control formulation of goal-oriented actions, planning, carrying out of goal-directed plans, and effective performance (Lezak, 1983). Executive functions are often disturbed following frontal lobe damage (Luria, 1966; Damasio, 1979). For this reason, the trend in recent years has been to assume that the existence of executive dysfunctions, as inferred from the results of certain neuropsychological tests, implies lesions of the frontal lobes. This assumption, however, is probably not always correct. As pointed out in the introduction to this section and, in more detail, in the chapter by Vallar (this volume), performances on neuropsychological tests provide information on the cognitive processes involved in those tests rather than on the precise location of structural lesions. Recent experience shows that executive functions can be disturbed after damage either to the frontal lobes or to other related parts of the brain, particularly the basal ganglia (Laplane et al., 1989). This underscores the close relationship between the prefrontal cortex and some subcortical structures, each of which is an essential component of the anatomo-functional entity known as the 'frontal system'.

Executive functions in PD

Table 3 lists the tests most frequently used to evaluate functions in humans. The Wisconsin Card Sorting Tests (WCST; Grant and Berg, 1948; Milner, 1963) is the

most widely used, probably because it requires the participation of all the cognitive processes needed for executive functions. These include the ability to form concepts, to shift set and to regulate behavior, i.e. the ability to elaborate and reorganize behavior according to environmental cues. Accordingly, the WCST is the most sensitive test of frontal-lobe dysfunction. However, because of the number of processes involved, the interpretation of impaired performance on the WCST is often equivocal without results on other tasks. For example, Trail Making (part B) and the Stroop (part 3) tests allow one to study more specifically shifting aptitude of patients, while the Odd Man Out test and, to a lesser extent, the Word Fluency test investigate the ability to maintain a mental set. Similarly, planning and programming capacities are best studied by the Tower of London, tracking procedures and the Picture Arrangement subtest of the WAIS. Finally, temporal structuring ability, a function that is under the control of the frontal lobes (Petrides, 1989), is investigated with delayed response tasks and ordering of past public events. Each of the tasks listed above has been shown by one or more studies to be impaired in PD (Table 4). The following sections will describe in more detail the tests listed in Table 3 and the results of their application to PD patients.

Wisconsin Card Sorting Test. The WCST requires subjects to sort cards according to one criterion (color, form or number) which they must deduce from

TABLE 3

Tasks most often used for the evaluation of executive functions

Wisconsin card sorting test (WCST)
Trail-making test (part B)
Stroop test (part 3)
Odd man out test
Word association test (FAS) or word fluency task
Tower of Hanoi and its variants
Tracking procedures
Picture arrangement subtest of the WAIS
Delayed response tasks
Temporal ordering

TABLE 4

Results of studies evaluating 'executive functions'

Reference	Tests	Results	Comment
Talland, 1962	Necker cube	Increased number of reversals	Only in treated patients (anticholinergics)
Proctor et al., 1964	Judgment of orientation	Impaired	? Intellectual efficiency
	Postural task	Impaired	
Reitan & Boll, 1971	Trail-making test	Increased time (A&B)	
Danta & Hilton, 1975	Judgment of orientation	19/66 patients impaired	Control subjects younger
Bowen et al., 1975	WCST[a]	Fewer categories, more non-perseverative errors	Fewer non-perseverative errors after L-DOPA treatment
Pirozzolo et al., 1982	Trail-making test	Increased time (A&B)	Patients deteriorated
Lees & Smith, 1983	WCST[b]	Fewer categories, more perseverative errors	Untreated patients, early stage (mean duration = 2.4 years)
	Word fluency	Decreased fluency only for the 3rd letter	
Cools et al., 1984	Word fluency	Fewer responses	
	Figural sorting	Fewer correct responses	
	Finger sequences	Fewer correct responses	
Flowers & Robertson, 1985	Odd man out test	Increased number of errors	
Freedman & Oscar-Berman, 1986	Delayed alternation	Normal in both nondemented ($n = 13$) and demented ($n = 15$) patients	
	Delayed response	Normal in nondemented patients, impaired in demented patients	
Heitanen & Teräväinen 1986	Trail-making test	Increased time after control for motor slowing (B − A)	Untreated patients at early stages of the disease (mean duration of the disease = 2.3 years)
	Stroop test	Increased time	
Pillon et al., 1986	WCST[b]	Fewer categories	Patients with decreased intellectual efficiency
	Word fluency	Decreased fluency	
	Motor sequences	Impaired	
	Frontal behaviors	Impaired	
Taylor et al., 1986	WCST[a]	Fewer categories	
	Word fluency	Normal	
	Design fluency	Normal	
	Trail-making test	Normal (after control for motor slowing: B − A)	
	Delayed spatial recognition	Decreased	
Brown & Marsden, 1988a	WCST[b]	Fewer categories, more perseverative errors	
Brown & Marsden, 1988b	WCST[b]	Fewer categories, more perseverative errors	
	Stroop test	Increased time	

Gotham et al., 1988	WCST[b]	Impaired in ON and OFF state:
		  − fewer categories
		  − more perseverative and non-perseverative errors
			High mean daily dose of levodopa medication (1130 mg; range 500 – 3000 mg)

	Word fluency	Impaired in OFF state	
	Frontal memory tests	Impaired in ON state	
Morris et al., 1988	Tower of London	Normal number of moves, increased planning time	
Alberoni et al., 1988	Tower of Milano	Normal	
Sagar et al., 1988b	Verbal temporal ordering	Impaired	Patients with decreased intellectual efficiency

TABLE 4 (*Continued*)

Reference	Tests	Results	Comment
Saint Cyr et al., 1988	Tower of Toronto	Increased number of moves	
Caltagirone et al., 1989	WCST[a]	More perseverative errors in both nondemented ($n = 15$) and demented ($n = 9$) patients	
Canavan et al., 1989	WCST[b]	Normal number of categories, increased number of perseverative errors	
	Associative learning task	Normal	
Goldenberg et al., 1989	Tower of London	Normal	
	Associative learning task	Impaired only after shifting	
	Word fluency	Normal for letters; impaired for categories	
Sullivan et al., 1989	Picture arrangement	Impaired in both nondemented ($n = 8$) and demented ($n = 7$) patients	

[a] Milner (1963); [b] Nelson's (1976) procedure of administration.

the pattern of correct and incorrect responses, as indicated by the examiner. After 10 consecutive correct responses, the examiner shifts the principle of sorting without warning, requiring subjects to deduce the new criterion guided only by reinforcement for correct responses. From responses on the WCST, it is possible to determine several indices of performance: the number of *categories* or concepts achieved (a measure of the subject's concept formation ability); the number of *perseverative errors* (a measure of the patient's ability to 'get out' of the previous category and to shift from one sorting principle to another); and the number of *nonperseverative errors* (a measure of attentional disorders or difficulty in maintaining a mental set). Thus, the WCST allows one to evaluate conceptional ability and behavioral regulation, but to a different extent, according to the administration procedure. In Milner's original report (Milner, 1963), the subject had to discover the categories in a predetermined order. This procedure highlights 'concept formation' ability. In the Nelson procedure (Nelson, 1976), the order of selection of categories is freely determined by the subject. For that reason, the Nelson procedure evaluates principally the ability to shift from one category to another.

Bowen et al. (1975) were the first to study the WCST in PD patients and to demonstrate a decreased ability to form concepts, and an increased number of total and nonperseverative errors. Defective performance was considered to result from frontal-lobe dysfunction, partly because the patients could verbalize the correct categories, but seemed unable to use this information appropriately, a behavior previously observed in frontal-lobe patients (Milner, 1963; Teuber, 1966). L-DOPA therapy reduced significantly the number of errors without increasing the mean number of concepts. The action of L-DOPA was attributed to a nonspecific effect on attention or arousal. The reactivation of dopaminergic transmission had no effect on the patient's overall conceptual ability, however, because they were still unable to maintain the correct response long enough to complete a category.

The results obtained by Bowen et al. were confirmed by subsequent studies (Table 4), most of which have found a significant decrease in the number of categories or concepts achieved. These findings suggest a deficit in conceptual ability in PD. The disorder is found in the earliest stages of the disease (Lees and Smith, 1983; Canavan et al., 1989), in untreated patients (Lees and Smith, 1983), and in subjects with preserved intellectual functions (Bowen et al., 1975; Lees and Smith, 1983; Taylor et al., 1986; Brown and Marsden, 1988a,b; Gotham et al., 1988; Caltagirone et al., 1989). Thus, the difficulty encountered by PD patients seems to be a specific phenomenon related to the pathology of the disease. Indeed, the specificity of the defective performance of PD patients on the WCST was recently confirmed in a large study investigating the cognitive patterns seen in various CNS degenerative diseases, including AD, Huntington's disease (HD), progressive supranuclear palsy (PSP) and PD, with subjects matched for level of intellectual deterioration (Pillon et al., in press). Interestingly, even when the level of global intellectual efficiency was considered normal, a deficit on the WCST was the only cognitive alteration in the PD group.

Only two studies (Caltagirone et al., 1989; Canavan et al., 1989) failed to report a significant decrease in the number of sorting categories achieved, but both showed a significant increase in perseverative errors. It is known that patients with frontal lobectomies (Milner, 1963) or with selective lesions of the frontal lobes (Drewe, 1974) have a tendency to perseverate incorrect responses, associated with a marked inability to achieve categories. Perseverative errors are also increased in most studies of PD patients when Milner's criteria are used (Table 4). This emphasizes the importance of the analysis of error patterns to better understand the PD patient's difficulties.

Several arguments favor frontal system dysfunction as an explanation of the poor performance of patients in the WCST: the number of trials required to complete the *first* category, a performance which indicates selective damage of the frontal lobe, is increased in PD patients (Bowen et al., 1975; Taylor et al., 1986); PD patients often verbalize but do not execute the correct response or category (Bowen et al., 1975; Taylor et al., 1986); and PD patients are also impaired on other tests believed to assess frontal-lobe function.

The influence of dopaminergic mechanisms in WCST performance was investigated by Gotham et al. (1988). The lack of a significant effect of L-DOPA in their study is consistent with the conclusion of Bowen et al. (1975), and with the absence of

difference on WCST performance between good responders and poor responders to medications (Taylor et al., 1987). Taken together, these results indicate that the impaired WCST performance of PD patients is not responsive to the enhancement of dopaminergic transmission. This negative result, however, does not mean that the disturbance does not involve a cerebral dopaminergic mechanism. The discrepancy between the existence of a deficit specific to PD, observed in the early stages and supposed to be related to a brain dopaminergic dysfunction, and the absence of significant effect of L-DOPA therapy on this specific disorder remains to be explained. The principal characteristics of performance by PD patients at the WCST are summarized in Table 5.

Other conceptual tasks and set regulation. Other conceptual sorting tasks are impaired in PD (Tables 3 and 4). As mentioned in the Speech and Language section, verbal fluency, reported to be sensitive to frontal-lobe damage (Milner, 1964; Benton, 1968), is reduced in PD patients (Lees and Smith, 1983; Cools et al., 1984; Pillon et al., 1986; Bayles and Kaszniak, 1987; Gotham et al., 1988; Goldenberg et al., 1989). The disorder has been observed even in the early stages of the disease (Lees and Smith,

TABLE 5

Characteristic features of performance of PD patients at the WCST

---

(1) Frontal lobe-type disorder
Greater number of trials to complete the first category
   (Bowen 1975; Taylor, 1986)
More perseverative errors
   (Caltagirone, 1989; Canavan, 1989)
Dissociation between knowing and doing
   (Bowen, 1975; Taylor, 1986)
Association with impairment in other 'frontal-lobe-type' tasks (Pillon, 1986)

(2) Related to brain lesions specific to Parkinson's disease
Present in early stages
   (Lees, 1983; Canavan, 1989)
Found even in the absence of intellectual decline
   (Bowen, 1975; Taylor, 1986; Pillon, in press).

1983), but only for the third letter, for which some patients tend to revert to a previous letter category. This finding indicates that the apparent concept-formation difficulty observed in PD patients can be analysed, at least in part, in terms of difficulty in maintaining a mental set, i.e., as a deficit in behavioral regulation. This interpretation is consistent with the results of Gotham et al. (1988). These authors used an alternative fluency task, derived from Newcombe's fluency task (1969), in which subjects are asked to name alternatively examples from two different categories (e.g. boys' names and fruits). In this task, verbal fluency was impaired in PD patients during the OFF stage of L-DOPA treatment, and the impairment was more severe in the alternating condition.

The difficulty PD patients have in alternating between conceptual categories raises the question of a set-shifting deficit. This aptitude for shifting was studied by Cools et al. (1984), using motor and non-motor tasks divided into two successive phases. The first phase tests patients' concept-formation ability. The second phase evaluates the capacity to shift to new categories. The crucial measure is the second 'switch' phase. Cools et al. (1984) used three tests: a block-sorting test consisting of 27 blocks to be sorted successively according to two attributes (color and size); a test in which the names of animals had to be sorted successively according to two categories (bird – mammal; domestic – wild); and a motor test requiring two different finger-tap sequences. In these conditions, PD patients performed worse in the shifting phase. Interestingly, the decreased shifting aptitude occurred at different levels of behavioral organization, including motor aspects as indicated by the reduced capacity for shifting set from one sequence of movements to another. These results confirm the existence of a concept-utilization deficit assessed by tests other than the WCST and suggest strongly that 'shifting aptitude' is impaired in PD.

Shifting abilities have been further studied in PD patients with the Trail Making and Stroop Tests. In the Trail Making Test, part B, the subject must connect consecutively numbered and lettered circles,

thus continuously shifting from one category (letters) to another (numbers). Several studies have found that PD patients are clearly impaired on this task (Reitan and Boll, 1971; Pirozzolo et al., 1982; Hietanen and Teräväinen, 1986; Taylor et al., 1986). This finding is consistent with the set-shifting deficit reported by Cools et al. (1984). This deficit can be considered characteristic of PD, because it has been found even in early and untreated PD patients. For example, all the PD patients ($n = 67$) in the Hietanen study (1986) were de novo patients.

Results of the Stroop test (1935) are also consistent with the finding of decreased cognitive flexibility in PD patients. This test measures the ability to shift a perceptual set to conform to changing demands (Lezak, 1983). In the third condition (interference), subjects are presented with a succession of names of colors printed in a color other than the one spelled by the letters and are asked to say the color of the word as quickly as possible. The difficulty lies in the competition between the color of the ink and the meaning of the word, because the subject must inhibit the strong tendency to read the word. It has been known for some years that PD patients are significantly impaired on this test (Portin and Rinne, 1980; Hietanen and Teräväinen, 1988a; Brown and Marsden, 1988a), indicating a deficit in shifting aptitude.

Impairment in shifting ability may explain the difficulties encountered by PD patients in executing concurrent activities such as simultaneous and competing motor tasks (Schwab et al., 1954; Talland and Schwab, 1964; Taylor et al., 1986). In these tasks, difficulties occur in simple, repetitive pre-programmed operations rather than in complex manual skills (Talland and Schwab, 1964), suggesting a difficulty in serial performance rather than in elaboration of motor acts.

The root of the disorders mentioned so far probably goes beyond the ability to shift from one set to another. It may well be conceived within the larger framework of overall behavioral control as indicated by the difficulty that PD patients have trouble not only in *changing* sets, but also in *maintaining* mental sets. The Odd Man Out Test (Flowers and Robertson, 1985) is a sorting task in which subjects have to apply a concept consistently before alternating between one response 'set' and another. For example, PD patients had difficulty maintaining one response 'set' over time when two possible response modes had been suggested to them (Flower and Robertson, 1985). They tended, after the first shift, to return to the incorrect category, indicating difficulty maintaining attention to the relevant attribute. The instability of cognitive set revealed by the Odd Man Out Test brings to mind the performance of PD patients on the Necker cube (Talland, 1962), which is characterized by a high rate of spontaneous reversal of perspective. It is also reminiscent of the difficulty PD patients have in attempting to perform motor tasks with a new manual skill (Frith et al., 1986), which is thought to result from a disturbance in the acquisition and maintenance of motor sets. In summary, PD patients have reduced control over reversals on cognitive (Odd Man Out Test), perceptual (Necker test) and motor tasks, suggesting a general difficulty with set regulation.

The acquisition of a set, whether cognitive, motor or perceptual, refers to the capacity to ameliorate the processing of information through the repetition of an event. Deficit in concept formation and in behavioral regulation, i.e. shifting or maintaining a behavior, may be caused by a loss of set-elaboration abilities. Difficulty in acquisition or generation of mental sets can be demonstrated in mental, motor (planning) or even perceptual (attention) functions (Flowers and Robertson, 1985). Indeed, impaired performance of PD patients on some tests believed to assess visuospatial functions can be interpreted as a failure of elaboration of mental set (Stern, 1987). For example, the errors made by PD patients in the Aubert paradigm mentioned above (Proctor et al., 1964; Danta and Hilton, 1975) can be attributed to subjects' failure to pre-set their sensory systems to account for body tilt (Teuber, 1976).

Planning and execution of action. Planning can be defined as the definition and organization of the steps and elements needed to carry out an intention or achieve a goal (Lezak, 1983). Problem-solving tasks provide information about planning abilities.

The Tower of London task, which investigates forward planning (Shallice, 1982), has been studied in PD. The task requires moving a series of beads from a start position to a goal position with the minimum number of moves. On a computerized version of the Tower of London, PD patients solved the problem as well as controls in terms of number of moves used (Morris et al., 1988; Goldenberg et al., 1989). However, their planning time was longer, even after the actual movement time was controlled for. This indicates that PD patients are accurate but not as efficient as the control group. The increased response time evidenced in the Tower of London task could be the result either of the nonspecific slowing of processing described in PD or of a specific planning disorder. However, a planning deficit has been demonstrated by Saint-Cyr and his colleagues (1988) with the Tower of Toronto. The PD patients used significantly more moves than the normal control subjects, suggesting a procedural learning deficit as discussed in the Memory section. However, the existence of an increased number of moves by PD patients during the first block of trials favors the hypothesis of an associated problem-solving deficit in this group.

Programming and execution of motor sequences, such as graphic series and hand positions (Luria, 1966), are also disturbed in PD (Morel-Maroger, 1977; Pillon et al., 1986; Dubois et al., 1988). Deficits in motor activity programming may be understood in the light of Flowers' work (1978) on PD subjects' behavioral anticipation ability. In tracking a moving target, PD patients do not show the normal tendency to predict the immediate future movement of the target they are tracking. PD patients do not spontaneously 'use prediction as readily as normals in controlling their actions, but tend to be tied more directly to current sensory information, responding to events rather than anticipating them' (Flowers, 1978). The patients' dependency on the environment and on environmental stimulation may represent an attempt to compensate for their deficit in self-generated programming.

This dependency on the environment may have deleterious effects for PD patients, as shown by such behaviors as prehension, imitation and utilization (Pillon et al., 1986; Dubois et al., 1988). This behavior consists of spontaneously using objects presented to them. PD patients also spontaneously imitate the examiner's gestures, sometimes even when directed not to do so. This syndrome of environmental dependency, which may result in a loss of functional autonomy, is characteristic of frontal lesions (Lhermitte et al., 1986).

Temporal structuring. The critical role of the prefrontal cortex in temporal organization of behavior has been demonstrated (Fuster, 1989). Like patients with frontal-lobe lesions, PD patients have trouble in temporal-structure formation. This characteristic may explain the deficit on delayed response tasks reported in PD patients (De Lancy Horne, 1971; Freedman and Oscar-Berman, 1986; Taylor et al., 1986). Freedman and Oscar-Berman have adapted to humans the well-known experimental animal paradigms of delayed alternation and delayed response and have shown that they are specifically sensitive to frontal-lobe damage. Using the same paradigm, Partiot et al. (in preparation) have found a specific deficit in delayed response in demented and nondemented PD patients, whereas delayed alternation was not significantly impaired. These results strongly suggest an inability to maintain an association between the stimulus and the response, similar to the behavior that follows prefrontal cortex lesions in humans (Chorover and Cole, 1966) or prefrontal and striatal lesions in primates (Oberg and Divac, 1979). Taylor and her colleagues (1986) found impairment on a Delayed Recognition Test (DRT) in a series of 40 PD patients. The task was a computer-controlled test derived from a test designed by Albert and Moss (1984) to study recognition memory. It consists of sets of 14 items including words, non-sense geometric designs, or spatial positions which are presented in lists of increasing length for 15-second periods followed by a 10-second delay. Subjects must identify the new stimulus added after each delay. The novel stimulus is detected only by the recency of its addition to the pattern. This recency discrimination is altered in PD, as shown by the

significantly worse performance of patients in the spatial portion of the DRT. A temporal ordering deficit in PD has also been clearly demonstrated by Sagar et al. (1988b). Moreover, patients with PD are impaired in their capacity to date past public events despite preserved ability to recognize these events (Sagar et al., 1988a). Judgment of recency discrimination observed in the absence of deficit in recognition of stimulus content is reminiscent of frontal lobe dysfunction (Milner and Petrides, 1984).

Summary: does a fundamental disorder account for the dysexecutive syndrome of PD patients? The review of performance on executive tasks by PD patients so far shows a certain coherence. Despite the heterogeneity of PD populations, the disorders we have discussed are found in similar or complementary tasks. It is therefore reasonable to hypothesize that the deficits in executive functions result from a specific disorder of cognitive abilities. Several

TABLE 6

Neuropsychological deficits which may account for the dysexecutive syndrome in Parkinson's disease

(1) Deficit in concept formation: WCST

(2) Deficit in shifting aptitude:
Block sorting, animal sorting, finger sequences
Bi-manual performance
Trail-making test

(3) Deficit in maintaining a mental set:
Word fluency test
Odd man out
Auber effect
Necker cube
Stroop test

(4) Deficit in planning and executing:
Tower of Hanoi and its variants
Graphic series
Tracking procedures

(5) Deficit in temporal structuring:
Delayed recognition tasks
Delayed response tasks
Temporal ordering

theories have been proposed to account for these deficits (Table 6).

Decreased conceptual ability. A deficit in concept-formation ability was hypothesized by Bowen et al. (1975) to explain the WCST results. However, it may be inappropriate to equate difficulty in achieving categories with an abstract thought deficit. Alternatively, the lower performance of PD patients at the WCST may be explained by difficulty *maintaining* set (increased number of nonperseverative errors) or *shifting* set (increased number of perseverative errors). The decreased number of categories achieved by a patient is nearly always associated with a greater number of errors (Table 4).

Behavioral regulation deficit (shifting attitude and maintenance of a mental set deficit). PD patients have difficulty maintaining or shifting sets in response to environmental cues. This fundamental disorder could explain the altered performance on the WCST, because the deficit of patients with frontal-lobe lesions on this task is usually considered as an inability to modify their response sets in accordance with varying environmental cues (Milner, 1964). It would also explain performance on the Nelson procedure believed to test the 'inhibition of one mode of response in favor of another when it becomes appropriate' (Nelson, 1976).

As suggested by Cronin-Golomb (1990, p. 290), deficits in conceptual set-shifting may account for cognitive disorders and more generally for behavioral disorders encountered in PD patients. Resolution of complex neuropsychological tasks requires mental flexibility as a function of environmental cues. This theory has been criticized by Brown and Marsden (1988b) because a shifting deficit is not generalizable to all tasks. In their study, patients were not impaired in visuospatial tasks requiring the components of acquisition, maintenance and shifting of a cognitive set, although the same group of patients was impaired in all aspects of performance in the WCST. We do not believe this implies that PD patients do not have a generalized switching deficit because performance is often related to the complexity of the task. That is, the normal response of patients in visuospatial tasks found by some authors (Brown and Marsden, 1988b) may indicate either that such patients do not have difficulty in switching aptitude in visuospatial conditions or that the test used was not sensitive enough to demonstrate their underlying decreased shifting aptitude.

Programming deficit. The performance of PD patients on the Tower of London (Morris et al., 1988) and to a lesser extent on the Tower of Toronto (Saint-Cyr et al., 1988) points to a deficit in planning and programming. These deficits, however, are often mild. A programming deficit has also been suggested by Flowers and Robertson (1985) to explain the difficulties PD patients have on the Odd Man Out Test: 'Subjects can apply the rules once they are made explicit, therefore it must be in their initial formulation that the parkinsonian impairment lies'. Difficulty in self-elaboration of programmed plans may explain the strategy deficit observed in many studies (Flowers and Robertson, 1985; Taylor et al., 1986; Morris et al., 1988; Pillon et al., 1989). PD patients appear to be unable to elaborate an appropriate adaptive behavior because of a difficulty in integrating the pertinent information. This impairment, in turn, may be explained in terms of the attentional model of Norman and Shallice (1980). The Supervisory Attentional System (SAS) represents a general programming device that controls planning and decision-making in nonroutine tasks or novel situations. Disorders of PD patients may therefore result either from a deficit in the SAS itself or from a limited internal storage capacity for information needed to elaborate a response. The vulnerability of PD patients' performance to task characteristics favors the hypothesis of a limited capacity for processing resources.

Task demands and resource capacities. Whether or not performance is impaired in the PD group seems to hinge on the degree to which internally organized guidelines are required to succeed. This point was made by Taylor et al. (1986), who found that the four neuropsychological tests that distinguished PD patients from normal control subjects shared the

common feature of requiring spontaneous generation of task-specific strategies. The influence of ex-
ernal cues in PD performance was confirmed by
Brown and Marsden (1988a), who showed that patients were unimpaired in a cued version of the
Stroop test but were impaired on a parallel task, in
which they had to rely on their own, internal cues to
perform the test. The distinction between external
and internal cues may be crucial for understanding
the deficits of PD patients in executive tasks. Patients are impaired in tasks that require the use of internal cues for the control of attention. This
hypothesis explains WCST performance because
subjects must focus their attention and define a
strategy relying only on self-generated internal control. This hypothesis may also explain the inability
of patients to use an internal model in a tracking
procedure (Flowers, 1978).

The second pertinent task-related factor is the
complexity of the task. PD patients performed normally on the three-bead phase of the Tower of
Toronto (Saint-Cyr et al., 1988), indicating preserved problem-solving ability. However, they were impaired in the same task at a higher level of complexity (four beads). In both cases, i.e. non-cued and
complex tasks, performance was impaired because
the demands of the tasks were too great, and exceeded the attentional resources of the patient. For that
reason, PD patients can succeed or fail in tasks according to whether they are more or less resource-
demanding. This interpretation is in line with the
Shiffrin and Schneider model of attention (1977),
which distinguishes between effort-demanding and
automatic tasks, and which explains some cognitive
deficits observed in PD (Weingartner et al., 1984),
especially in learning and memory.

Bradyphrenia

Bradyphrenia is often considered one of the
cognitive symptoms of PD (Agid et al., 1987b;
Rogers, 1986). Yet, the very existence of bradyphrenia in PD is controversial and not formally established, and the exact meaning of the word and of
the concept are still far from precise. Based on its
etymology, bradyphrenia may be defined as slowing

($\beta\rho\alpha\delta\vartheta$-) of the thinking process ($\phi\rho\epsilon\nu o\nu$). The slowing of thoughts has been interpreted in two ways.
According to some authors, it is a purely clinical entity that includes a series of symptoms typically present in PD: apathy, intellectual inertia, slow use of
previously acquired notions (known also as 'psychic
akinesia') and even disorders of attention. In that
sense, bradyphrenia is reminiscent of the concept of
subcortical dementia originally described by
classical neurologists (Von Stockert, 1932) and re-
introduced by Albert et al. (1974), intended to
characterize the intellectual inertia and cognitive
slowing found in subjects with predominantly subcortical lesions. Bradyphrenia is therefore considered by these authors to be an ill-defined *syndrome* to be evaluated in a purely subjective manner. In contrast, some other authors look at
bradyphrenia in a semantically narrower sense,
viewing it as a *symptom* defined as a measurable
lengthening of normal information-processing
time. It is considered a physiological parameter
which can be quantified experimentally.

Bradyphrenia considered as a clinical entity   The
term bradyphrenia was introduced by the French
neurologist Naville (1922) to describe the mental
status of patients afflicted with Von Economo's
lethargic encephalitis. Naville had noticed that when
these patients are confronted with mental operations of increasing complexity, the time required for
thinking of a solution ('réflexion' i.e. analysis) was
considerably increased compared to controls. He
considered bradyphrenia as a syndrome consisting
of a slowing of cognitive processes associated with
attentional difficulties and intellectual inertia. In
this clinical sense, bradyphrenia was later described
in idiopathic PD (De Ajuriaguerra, 1971), and in
PSP (Albert et al., 1974), where it was thought to be,
together with forgetfulness and personality or mood
changes, one of the key cognitive disorders of so-
called subcortical dementia. Subsequently, bradyphrenia and subcortical dementia have sometimes
been equated (Rogers, 1986). The following section
will discuss the concept of subcortical dementia in
greater detail, but it must be stressed that

bradyphrenia and subcortical dementia should not be confused: bradyphrenia refers only to slowing down of the thought processes.

One problem often encountered in the clinical evaluation of cognitive slowing concerns its differentiation from the depressive and motor slowing that are so frequently present in PD. Bradyphrenic patients are often the most akinetic, the most depressed or both. Psychomotor retardation is an important component of depression, which is found in at least 50% of PD patients (Mayeux et al., 1981). The relation between depressive and cognitive slowing has recently been highlighted by Rogers et al. (1987). In their study, the cognitive slowing observed in a group of 30 newly diagnosed PD patients was correlated with affective impairment as assessed by the Hamilton Depression Scale. Cognitive slowing was also observed in a group of 30 patients with primary depressive illness; the cognitive slowing in both groups improved after treatment with dopaminergic agonists, in relation to improvement in the affective symptoms. For these authors, this finding indicates a close relation between cognitive slowing and affective disturbances, which may be based on a common dopaminergic mechanism. In order to appreciate the existence of cognitive slowing in PD, it is necessary to control the depressive component. It is difficult to achieve this goal when the dysphoric mood is missing and when depression is restricted to behavioral slowing. The question then arises of whether it is feasible to separate the two entities.

Similarly, motor slowing may influence the clinical evaluation of intellectual slowing. Most mental operations require a motor response. Akinesia is a basic symptom of PD, directly related to nigrostriatal dopaminergic denervation. Physiological studies have confirmed that both movement time and reaction time are prolonged in PD (Evarts et al., 1981). It may therefore be difficult to evaluate clinically the cognitive component of response time slowing. The frequent association of these two elements justifies the clinical concept of psychomotor slowing. A clearcut dissociation between a sizeable intellectual slowing and the absence of motor slowing is rarely seen in PD patients, in whom this dissociation can usually be studied only by the use of such special techniques as reaction times.

Bradyphrenia considered as a measurable parameter   The reaction time (RT) paradigm allows one to control for movement time, which is known to be increased in PD (Evarts et al., 1981). Moreover, RT procedures allow one to compare the performance of PD patients with that of matched normal control subjects in tasks with different levels of complexity but with the same motor response. The prolongation in response time as a function of task complexity is thought to reflect differences in central processing associated with the identification of different stimulus inputs and selection of response strategies.

Many of the experiments which have used a RT procedure in PD have made low cognitive demands. They are summarized in Table 7. For instance, the difference between choice RT and simple RT performance gives information on central processing time needed for motor programming. In these experiments, no evidence of increased central process-

TABLE 7

Studies assessing central processing time with choice Reaction Times procedures

Study	Test	Results (central processing time)
Evarts et al., 1981	Choice RT vs. simple visual, kinaesthetic RT	Normal
Bloxham et al., 1984	Uncued vs. cued visual RT	Decreased
Girotti et al., 1986	Unpredicted vs. predicted visual RT	Normal
Hietanen et al., 1986	Visual choice RT vs. visual simple RT	Normal
Mayeux et al., 1987	Choice RT vs. simple RT	Normal
Dubois et al., 1988	Unpredicted vs. predicted visual RT	Normal
Pullman et al., 1988	Visual choice RT vs. visual simple RT	Decreased
Rogers and Chan, 1988	Choice RT vs. simple ballistic and tracking RT	Increased

ing time was reported in PD, except by Rogers and Chan (1988) (Table 7). In all other studies, the increase of central processing time in PD patients was either the same (Evarts et al., 1981; Girotti et al., 1986; Hietanen and Teräväinen, 1986; Mayeux et al., 1987; Dubois et al., 1988) or even shorter (Bloxham et al., 1984; Pullman et al., 1988) relative to control subjects. The failure of the choice-RT studies to reveal selective impairment in central processing for more complex tasks was unexpected (Evarts et al., 1981). This finding suggests that additional processing needed for the selection and formulation of central programs is normal in PD, at least for processing involved in motor programming. At least two possible explanations can be offered for the normal performance of PD patients: the central component of the response in choice-RT can be 'distributed between the initiation time and the increased movement time phases of the response' (Brown and Marsden, 1986); alternatively, choice-RT may be too simple to reveal a specific impairment in PD.

For that reason, slowing of thought-processing can be better investigated using more complex tasks with higher cognitive demands than choice-RT (Table 8). Under those conditions, the performance of PD patients is variable (either normal or slowed down), depending on the complexity of the task. For instance, Dubois et al. (1988) found no difference in their multiple-square experiment, an RT procedure with a cognitive component consisting of two different tasks: in the two-square task, subjects were asked to respond only to the red-green combination that appeared in an unpredictable and randomized pattern; in the three-square task, the same rule applied, but the distracting effect of the presence of a third square made the analysis time longer and the task more complex. This additional central processing time, called analysis time, was not greater in a group of 33 PD patients than in control subjects. In contrast, arguments in favor of cognitive slowing derive from other studies. Using a computerized version of the digit symbol substitution test, Rogers et al. (1987) found an increase in matching time of untreated patients when compared to normal con-

trols, but the difference just failed to achieve statistical significance. Similarly, Wilson et al. (1980) have demonstrated that PD patients share a slowing in their ability to scan elements in short-term memory, as shown by their increased reaction time in the Sternberg paradigm, as a function of the size of the memory set. However, the mnemonic slowing was only observed in elderly PD patients.

It should be stressed that cognitive slowing has only been clearly demonstrated on tests that require a high level of processing. A significant increase in response time was reported on a computerized version of the Tower of London Task (Morris et al., 1988), on the Stroop Test (Brown and Marsden, 1988a; Hietanen and Teräväinen, 1988a) and on the 15-Objects Test, a visual discrimination task of 15 superimposed images of objects (Pillon et al.,

TABLE 8

Studies assessing cognitive processing time with complex procedures

Study	Tests	Results (cognitive processing time)
Wilson et al., 1980	Sternberg paradigm	Normal in younger pts (58 yrs) Increased in older pts (69 yrs)
Brown and Marsden, 1986	Spatial choice RT vs. simple RT	Normal
Rogers et al., 1987	Digit symbol substit. test vs. simple RT	Increased
Taylor et al., 1987	Trail-making B vs. Trail-making A	Increased
Brown and Marsden, 1988a	Uncued Stroop RT vs. cued Stroop RT	Increased
Dubois et al., 1988	3 square vs. 2 square visual RT	Normal
Morris et al., 1988	Computerized tower of London	Increased
Hietanen et al., 1988a	Stroop form 3 vs. Stroop form 2	Increased in younger pts (49 yrs) normal in older pts (69 yrs)
Pillon et al., 1989a	Superimposed vs. non-superimposed 15 objects	Increased

1989a). However, in these more complex tasks the greater time required by the patients may indicate a disturbance in cognitive strategy rather than a true slowing of central processing. Analysis of the 15-Objects Test performance favors this hypothesis: in contrast to the constant psychomotor slowing in tasks measuring RT (Brown and Marsden, 1986), the performance slowing on the 15-Objects Test increased from the first to the twelfth object identified, as the task became more difficult. Further, the slowest patients identified objects randomly, extracted details without reference to the global shape, and repeated previous identifications, indicating inappropriate maintenance of a category of activity. Thus, the slowing of cognitive processing demonstrated in this study seems to be partly a by-product of defective strategy, suggesting frontal-lobe dysfunction (Pillon et al., 1989a).

An increase in thinking time was also observed on the Trail Making Test, even when the influence of motor speed was eliminated (difference in time B − A), but only for a subgroup of PD patients characterized by a poor response to L-DOPA therapy (Taylor et al., 1987). It is interesting to discuss some of the physiopathological implications of these results. If one admits that the poor response to L-DOPA may signify the existence of non-dopaminergic lesions of the brain associated with the nigrostriatal lesion, the fact that cognitive slowing was observed in the poor responders but not in the good ones suggests that cognitive slowing is not supported by dopaminergic lesions, contrary to the observations of Rogers et al. (1987). This hypothesis is in agreement with the results of Rafal et al. (1984), who found that overall RT increased when patients were in the untreated state, but without a concomitant slowing of purely cognitive components. Similarly, Pillon et al. (1989a) observed no effect of L-DOPA treatment on the 15-Objects Test score, although the PD motor disability score improved by 54%. Taken together, the results may indicate that cognitive slowing is related to abnormalities of non dopaminergic neuronal systems in the brain.

Conclusion: Does bradyphrenia exist? Bradyphrenia in PD is a valid and useful concept from a clinical standpoint. There are also enough data to suggest that there is a lengthening of response time in some cognitive tasks, even after the motor component has been controlled for. This increase of response time may result from several mechanisms (Table 9). However, cognitive slowing, the most genuine expression of bradyphrenia, is only found on complex tasks which have in common the participation of executive functions supposed to be under the control of the frontal system. This explanation applies in particular to the Trail Making Test (shifting aptitude); to the Tower of London (planning ability); to the 15-Objects Test (self-elaboration of strategy − see above section on 'Executive functions'). The more complex a task from the point of view of requiring the elaboration of a strategy and specific behavioral regulation, the greater is the cognitive slowing. The results described support the conclusion that bradyphrenia, defined as a nonspecific lengthening of information-processing time, is not demonstrated in PD, although a cognitive slowing may result from impaired executive functions.

TABLE 9

Possible reasons for increased response time in cognitive tasks

(A) Nonspecific factors:
Motor slowing
Disorder of concentration
Failure of divided attention
Motivational state
Arousal
Drugs
Psychomotor retardation of depressive illness

(B) Executive dysfunctions:
Concept-formation disorder
Deficit in shifting aptitude
Inability to maintain a mental set
Deficit of programming or of strategy

(C) Bradyphrenia (genuine slowing of central information processing)

Neuronal correlates of cognitive changes in PD

To what extent do specific brain lesions contribute to cognitive disabilities in patients with PD? It is certainly too early to answer this question precisely. Some neuropathological studies have, however, already attempted to shed some light on the problem through estimation of brain atrophy and neuronal loss, and through examination of histopathological and chemical evidence of cell dysfunction.

Estimation of brain atrophy in vivo or post mortem is of little value. In most studies, except that of Hakim and Mathieson (1979), no differences were found either between patients with PD and control subjects or between demented and nondemented PD patients (see review in Jellinger, 1986; Ruberg and Agid, 1988). In fact, the loss of brain weight in PD has been related to the age of the patients and the duration of illness (Jellinger, 1986), thus confirming previous CT-scan studies (Schneider et al., 1979). However, more severe cortical atrophy has been found in demented compared to nondemented PD patients and age-matched control subjects (Steiner et al., 1985). In particular, the frontal lobes (Adam et al., 1983) and the temporoparietal cortex (Portin et al., 1984) have been shown to be more severely affected; correlations have been found between cognitive performance and central but not cortical atrophy (Portin et al., 1984). Altogether these data suggest that the use of brain scans is not a reliable method for detecting neuronal loss or dementia in PD patients. This conclusion is strengthened by recent MRI studies indicating that dementia in patients with PD is not associated with any specific pattern of abnormalities (Huber et al., 1989).

Attempts have been made to associate the cognitive impairment characteristic of PD with lesions of specific neuronal systems, by assigning symptoms to known brain cell losses, interpreting the effect of pharmacological treatment on PD symptoms, and extrapolating from animal experiments. We will examine successively the putative role of dopaminergic and non-dopaminergic subcortical and cortical lesions.

Dopamine-dependent cognitive disorders

Most dopaminergic neuronal systems in the central nervous system are affected by PD (with the possible exception of those of the spinal cord). Dopaminergic neurons, which in humans amount to probably no more than one million cells, are affected to different degrees. The ones most affected are the nigrostriatal neurons, which originate in the substantia nigra and project heavily to the striatum

TABLE 10

Degeneration of the nigrostriatal dopaminergic neurons in Parkinson's disease: main conclusions

1. Within the ventral mesencephalon, not all dopaminergic neurons are damaged. Those containing neuromelanin seem to be more vulnerable than those that do not (Hirsch et al., 1988).

2. The nigrostriatal dopaminergic system is more severely affected (80–90%) than the mesocorticolimbic (50%) system (Price et al., 1978; Javoy-Agid and Agid, 1980).

3. Dopamine depletion is more severe in the putamen than in the caudate nucleus; dopaminergic innervation in the antero-dorsal striatum is preferentially affected (Kish et al., 1988). The loss of dopaminergic innervation follows a gradient, the greatest deficit occurring dorso-laterally, whereas the ventral striatum is relatively spared (Graybriel et al., 1990).

4. The surviving nigrostriatal dopaminergic neurons become overactive as a function of the severity of the lesion (Agid et al., 1973). This mechanism of compensation has not been demonstrated in the mesocorticolimbic dopaminergic system (Agid et al., 1987a).

5. The density of dopaminergic D1 and D2 receptors in the striatum (putamen and caudate nucleus) is not globally different in patients with PD and controls (Pierot et al., 1988; Wagner et al., 1986).

6. It is thought that at least 70% of the nigrostriatal system is already damaged when the first parkinsonian symptoms appear (Bernheimer et al., 1973; Riederer and Wuketich, 1976; Scherman et al., 1989).

7. The 'striatal dopamine deficiency' (Hornyckiewicz, 1975) is a characteristic of parkinsonian syndromes, including post-encephalitic and MPTP-induced parkinsonism (which respond dramatically to L-DOPA) and other degenerative parkinsonian syndromes such as progressive supranuclear palsy (which responds little if at all to L-DOPA).

(caudate nucleus and putamen). The principal characteristics of lesions of the nigrostriatal dopaminergic pathway in PD are listed in Table 10. The neurons least affected are those of the mesocorticolimbic pathway, which originate in the ventrotegmental area and project diffusely to the cerebral cortex (Agid et al., 1987a).

PD was long considered synonymous with dopaminergic denervation in the basal ganglia and cortical regions. In the last 20 years, several studies have attempted to implicate the dopaminergic system in the cognitive deficits found in PD. Some authors have tried to establish correlations between the degree of intellectual deterioration and the severity of the motor deficit because the latter is considered an index of striatal dopaminergic depletion. Other authors have tried to reverse the cognitive impairment in PD by re-establishing normal central dopaminergic transmission through the administration of L-DOPA or other dopaminergic drugs. The main drawback in this kind of in vivo research is that although we can correctly appreciate the nature and severity of the cognitive symptoms, our capacity to discover the exact extent of cerebral dopaminergic damage remains limited. In contrast, clinical-pathological correlations are weakened by the discrepancy between an accurate analysis of the extent of the destruction of the dopaminergic sites and a poor knowledge of the nature and severity of the cognitive changes because, so far, clinical analysis has always been retrospective. For the sake of simplicity, the pharmacological and clinical-pathological approaches will be discussed sequentially in order to best draw conclusions concerning the importance, nature and specificity of the dopaminergic systems implicated in PD.

Relationship between cognitive impairment and estimates of dopaminergic lesions

The approaches used to determine the role played by dopaminergic lesions in the cognitive impairment of PD can be schematically divided into four types: analysis of cognitive disorders in de novo patients and patients with early onset of the disease; correlations between the existence of cognitive impairment

and the severity of motor symptoms; the MPTP model; and relationships between degeneration of brain dopaminergic systems analyzed on autopsy and dementia.

Cognitive disorders in de novo patients and patients with early onset of the disease   It is currently thought that damage of the dopaminergic systems must reach about 70 – 80% before PD motor symptoms appear, and there is a strong probability that only dopaminergic neurons are affected in early stages of the disease (Agid et al., 1987a). These findings suggest that brain dopamine depletion accounts at least partly for the cognitive disturbances in de novo PD patients. Cognitive impairment can be detected in such patients (Levin et al., 1989), but the changes are moderate, and are found only in a minority of patients, particularly when they are older (Canavan et al., 1989). As seen in previous sections, the cognitive changes consist essentially of cognitive slowing (Rogers et al., 1987) and errors on the WCST, where the patients form fewer categories than control subjects (Lees and Smith, 1983). These observations suggest that dopaminergic lesions in their early phase do have cognitive consequences, but that they are relatively minor.

Because long-term response to L-DOPA treatment is found in patients with early-onset PD (i.e. with onset occurring around the age of 40), the latter are considered to have relatively pure brain dopaminergic lesions. Despite the long duration of the disease, the frequency of intellectual impairment in these patients in negligible (Quinn et al., 1987), suggesting that degeneration of brain dopaminergic neurons plays a modest role in the occurrence of dementia.

Correlations between the existence of cognitive impairment and the severity of motor symptoms   The simplest method used to suggest the role of dopaminergic dysfunction in cognitive impairment is to search for a relationship between the severity of PD motor symptoms, particularly akinesia (a symptom known to result from degeneration of the nigrostriatal dopaminergic system) and intellectual mpairment. Such a correlation has been found by ome authors (Marttila et al., 1976; Mortimer et al., 1982; Mayeux and Stern, 1983; Growdon et al., in press). Correlations indicate nothing about causality, however, and the absence of correlation has also been reported (Brown et al., 1984b; Portin et al., 1984; Boller et al., 1984b). Other types of correlation suggest, in fact, that much of the cognitive impairment in PD patients results from the dysfunction of non-dopaminergic neuronal systems because of the lack of correlation between neuropsychological test scores and the L-DOPA-responsive motor score (presumed to reflect the decrease in striatal dopaminergic transmission), contrasting with the strong correlation obtained between cognitive dysfunction and axial symptomatology (including gait disorders and dysarthria), symptoms that respond little, if at all, to L-DOPA treatment (Pillon et al., 1989b).

The MPTP model   The most specific study of the relation between brain dopamine damage and intellectual impairment consists of the investigation of cognitive performance in subjects with MPTP-induced parkinsonian syndrome. In the study by Stern and Langston (1985), most test scores were comparable to those of control subjects; cognitive disorders similar to those of patients with PD (including impairment on tests of general intellectual and frontal-lobe functions) were, however, observed in these patients. Because MPTP-induced parkinsonism probably represents a pure instance of central dopaminergic deficiency, these findings indicate that lesions of ascending dopaminergic systems are sufficient to interfere with mental processes in PD patients. A similar pattern of intellectual change has also been observed in MPTP-exposed but still relatively asymptomatic individuals, thus supporting the idea that a specific set of cognitive deficits is mediated by brain dopamine depletion, even when it is only partial (Stern et al., 1990).

Relationship between degeneration of brain dopaminergic systems analysed on autopsy and dementia   Few neurochemical studies have been performed post mortem on selected populations of demented and nondemented PD patients. Degeneration of nigrostriatal neurons seems independent of mental impairment, as judged from semi-quantitative estimation of striatal concentrations of dopamine (Ruberg and Agid, 1988) and of neuronal loss in the substantia nigra (Gaspar and Gray, 1984), although the latter result has been recently disputed (Rinne et al., 1989). The decrease in dopamine levels in neocortical areas (but not in the hippocampus) is greater in demented than in nondemented PD patients (Ruberg and Agid, 1988). This finding suggests that the degeneration of the mesocortical dopaminergic neurons could contribute to intellectual impairment in PD patients, but these results must be confirmed in a larger series of patients.

All the above studies suggest, but do not prove, that a central dopaminergic deficiency plays a moderate role in the cognitive changes of PD patients. The few in vivo studies performed on cerebrospinal fluid (CSF) have failed to clarify the issue. Levels of HVA, the main metabolite of dopamine, are reduced in the CSF of PD patients, but attempts to detect a correlation between cognitive dysfunction and HVA concentrations have been unsuccessful (Mayeux et al., 1985; Stern et al., 1984b).

Cognitive changes and dopaminergic treatment
If the cognitive functions that deteriorate in PD are dopamine-dependent, they should respond to L-DOPA treatment in a fashion similar to the response of motor symptoms. A number of studies have been performed to assess PD patients versus control subjects before treatment and at various stages during long-term administration of the drug. On average, the initial improvement in mentation (Meier and Martin, 1970; Bearsdley and Puletti, 1971; Loran-

ger et al., 1972b) is followed by a subsequent gradual decline (Botez and Barbeau, 1975; Riklan et al., 1976; Sweet et al., 1976). There have also been reports of impaired mental functions after L-DOPA treatment (Halgin et al., 1977; Agnoli et al., 1984), with psychotic symptoms in some patients (Celesia and Wanamaker, 1972; Barbeau, 1982). This iatrogenic effect may be the consequence of a toxic dose of the drug, especially in demented patients (Sacks et al., 1972). It is difficult to draw firm conclusions concerning the specificity of the action of L-DOPA on cognitive function from these studies because of differences in the clinical pattern of patients and in the techniques of assessment. The first study of a specific effect of L-DOPA was that of Bowen et al. (1975), who found a decreased number of errors, as measured by the WCST. The behavior of PD patients on this test drew attention to the frontal-lobe-like symptoms in PD patients, which could result from brain dopamine depletion. However, the beneficial effect of L-DOPA treatment was attributed to an 'awakening' effect of L-DOPA rather than an effect on specific functions (Marsh et al., 1971).

To avoid nonspecific biases related to sampling of patients and progression of the disease, more recent studies have compared motor and mental performances of PD patients during 'on' (at time of maximal motor improvement, i.e., when dopamine transmission is considered to be restored) and 'off' (when the antiparkinsonian effect is worst, i.e., when striatal dopamine transmission is considered to be reduced or interrupted). These papers (Table 11) are also hard to interpret because it is difficult to match patients in a way that best allows one to extract a signal specifically corresponding to L-DOPA action. Nevertheless, these studies provide information on the importance and specificity of L-DOPA and of central dopaminergic systems in cognitive performance.

The administration of L-DOPA may modify the mental status of PD patients: it has been reported at times to improve memory, 'frontal' signs, depression (Bachman and Albert, 1984) and slowing of cognitive processes (Table 11). However, the im-

provement is moderate at best and is thought b some authors to result from a nonspecific effect o arousal (Marsh et al., 1971; Brown et al., 1986). Fur ther, this improvement is not found in all patients not a surprising finding since the severity o

TABLE 11

Effect of L-DOPA on neuropsychological performances during on and off state

Delis et al., 1982: Worsened memory, disinhibition of language and perseveration during off periods (in a single patient).

Brown et al., 1984b: Mild cognitive dysfunction in only a proportion of patients during off periods, an effect which is essentially related to the levels of mood and alertness.

Rafal et al., 1984: In contrast to the improvement of overall reaction time when patients are on medication, there is no improvement of the slowing of cognitive components assessed during complex reaction time.

Girotti et al., 1986: No variation in cognitive performances but frontal lobe-like symptomatology was not specifically analysed.

Huber et al., 1987: Decreased memory performances when plasma dopamine levels are changed whatever the absolute levels of dopamine.

Mohr et al., 1987: Improvement in delayed verbal memory during on periods.

Gotham et al., 1988: Verbal fluency impaired when patient are off medication; other tests impaired when patients are o levodopa (associative conditional learning and subject-ordered pointing).

Pullman et al., 1988: In patients receiving continuous intravenous levodopa infusion, choice reaction time increases as levodopa levels decrease (i.e. during off periods).

Starkstein et al., 1989a: Significant decrease in the P300 latency of the event-related potentials when patients are off levodopa.

Pillon et al., 1989a: L-DOPA does not improve cognitive slowing, as measured by time needed to identify objects on a visual discrimination task.

Pillon et al., 1989b: No correlation between neuropsychological performances (including 'frontal' tests) and the part of patient's motor score that can be improved by L-DOPA, thought to result from lesions of brain dopaminergic neurons (120 patients).

lopaminergic lesions varies from patient to patient Graybiel et al., 1990). Finally, negative side-effects are also observed at times, perhaps due to hypersensitivity of the dopaminergic receptors in the target structures (secondary to severe dopaminergic neuronal loss), to excessive drug doses (Gotham et al., 1988), or to greater vulnerability due to intellectual deterioration (Hietanen and TerävÄinen, 1988b).

If L-DOPA improves some functions in PD patients, which brain dopaminergic system is involved? Specifically, does the reestablishment of normal dopamine transmission in the striatum improve cognitive functions in patients? Cognitive improvement probably does not take place through the dopaminergic nigroputaminal fibers because the severe damage to these fibers produces a deactivation of the motor loop linking the putamen with the supplementary motor area, which is known to play an important role in motor function. Depletion of dopamine in the caudate nucleus and ventral striatum may be a better candidate through deactivation of the complex neuronal loop originating in the prefrontal and limbic cortex, hippocampus and amygdala, and projecting towards the cingulate and prefrontal cortex via the globus pallidus and substantia nigra (Gotham et al., 1988; Taylor et al., 1986).

Another possibility is that degeneration of the mesocortical dopaminergic system contributes to intellectual impairment in PD patients. This hypothesis is suggested by two observations: the decrease in dopamine concentrations is greater in demented than in nondemented PD patients in the prefrontal and entorhinal cortex (Ruberg and Agid, 1988); in addition, behavioral abnormalities considered to result from dysfunction of prefrontal and limbic regions have been observed in animals after selective destruction of dopaminergic neurons in the ventral-tegmental area (Simon et al., 1980) or of their terminals in the prefrontal cortex (Brozoski et al., 1979). However, these interpretations rest on tenuous ground because in PD, dopaminergic denervation in the caudate nucleus, the ventral striatum and the cortex is generally about $50-60\%$;

yet for this degree of denervation, the compensatory capacities of the remaining neurons are such that dopaminergic transmission is not altered (Agid et al., 1973). Moreover, PET studies with administration of 6-fluoro-DOPA show that depletion of dopamine in the caudate nucleus is found only in about half of PD patients (Nahmias et al., 1985; Martin et al., 1986). How do these results fit with the suggestion that a central dopaminergic deficiency plays a role in cognitive dysfunction and that this deficiency may be partially corrected by L-DOPA? There are two possible explanations: one is that only patients with massive dopaminergic denervation show cognitive disorders, the latter being moderate and variable according to the site of dopaminergic depletion. Another explanation is that partial degeneration of the central dopaminergic systems only produces cognitive deterioration if several groups of neurons are affected simultaneously, whether dopaminergic (nigrostriatal and mesocorticolimbic) or non-dopaminergic (see below).

Non-dopamine-dependent cognitive disorders

Apart from the degeneration of the nigrostriatal and mesocorticolimbic dopaminergic systems, which constitutes the core of the pathology of PD, the other anatomical lesions are mainly confined to deep grey substance nuclei: the locus coeruleus, the raphe nuclei and the substantia innominata, which are sites of origin of the long ascending noradrenergic, serotonergic and cholinergic systems (Fig. 1). Neurons in the basal ganglia and cerebral cortex are, in principle, intact, although cortical neurons are affected in a nonnegligible proportion of patients with dementia.

Role of the degeneration of subcortico-cortical noradrenergic, serotonergic and cholinergic systems in the occurrence of intellectual impairment

The septo-hippocampal and innominato-cortical cholinergic systems In post mortem studies, degeneration of the cholinergic innominato-cortical and septo-hippocampal systems is strongly sug-

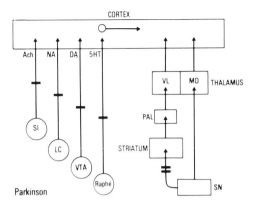

Fig. 1. Principal brain lesions in patients with Parkinson's disease. The black bars indicate lesioned neuronal systems (one bar, moderate lesions; 2 bars, severe lesions). Ach, acetylcholine; NA, noradrenaline; DA, dopamine; 5HT, serotonin; SI, substantia innominata; LC, locus coeruleus; VTA, ventral tegmental area; SN, substantia nigra; PAL, globus pallidus; VL, ventro-lateral thalamic nucleus; MD, medio-dorsal thalamic nucleus.

gested both by the decrease in choline acetyltransferase (CAT) activity in the neocortex and hippocampus, and by the degeneration of neurons in the substantia innominata and septum. Degeneration of these ascending cholinergic systems has been linked to intellectual deterioration as assessed before death: neuronal loss in the substantia innominata (Whitehouse et al., 1983; Jellinger, 1986; Gaspar and Gray, 1984) and the reduced activity of CAT in various cortical areas (Ruberg et al., 1982; Dubois et al., 1985; Perry et al., 1985) are more severe in demented than in nondemented PD patients. CAT activity is also decreased, although to a lesser extent, in the frontal cortex and hippocampus of nondemented patients, indicating that the onset of degeneration of subcortico-cortical cholinergic neurons may precede the deterioration of acetylcholine-dependent cognitive functions (Dubois et al., 1983). Moreover, experimental data in humans and animals and pharmacological observations in PD patients favor the role of a brain cholinergic dysfunction in the genesis of cognitive impairment in PD patients (Table 12).

The noradrenergic coeruleo-cortical system   The noradrenergic pathway from the locus coeruleus (LC) to the cerebral cortex is partially lesioned in PD

TABLE 12

Data suggesting the contribution of brain cholinergic deficiency in cognitive disorders in Parkinson's disease

1. Pharmacological blockade of cholinergic transmission produces memory task impairments in rodents (Squire, 1969), primates (Bartus and Johnson, 1976) and humans (Drachman, 1977; Sitaram et al., 1978).

2. Degeneration of the ascending cholinergic systems, the major source of cortical cholinergic innervation, has repeatedly been demonstrated in senile dementia of the Alzheimer's type, and the resulting cholinergic deficiency is thought to play a role in the associated cognitive disorders (Perry, 1986).

3. Following lesions of the substantia innominata in rats, which result in a cortical cholinergic deficiency, behavioral anomalies indicative of cognitive impairment (disrupted spontaneous behaviours such as exploration, feeding, learned behaviour, spatial memory, inability to suppress previously learned responses) are observed (Dubois et al., 1985; Hepler et al., 1985b).

4. In Parkinson's disease, lesion of cholinergic neurons innervating the neocortex and hippocampus may be implicated in memory disorders, mental confusion and frontal-lobe-like symptomatology.

(a) Administration of anticholinergic drugs in PD patients impairs classical memory paradigms, but not immediate memory (Sadeh et al., 1982).

(b) Confusional episodes which may be considered acute and severe memory disorders are essentially observed in demented rather than nondemented PD patients, especially when they are treated with anticholinergic medications. This suggests that there is a relationship between intellectual deterioration in PD patients and brain cholinergic deficiency (De Smet et al., 1982).

(c) Administration of subthreshold doses of anticholinergics to nondemented PD patients impairs performance on tests of visual memory which require ordered recall of nonfigurative images, whereas the performance of controls is not affected (Dubois et al., 1987). This observation is compatible with a partial decrease in cholinergic transmission which may be masked by compensatory neurochemical mechanisms.

(d) A severe impairment in tests believed to assess frontal-lobe function is observed in PD patients receiving anticholinergics, whereas, at the dose used, intellectual, visuospatial, instrumental and memory functions are not changed (Dubois et al., 1990).

patients, as indicated by cell loss in the LC (Mann et al., 1983) and decreased dopamine β-hydroxylase DBH) activity (Nagatsu et al., 1979) and noradrenaline concentrations (at least 50%) in most cortical areas, particularly in the amygdala, hippocampus and frontal cortex (Scatton et al., 1983). Several types of data support the hypothesis that a cortical noradrenergic deficiency may play a part in the occurrence of mental disorders in PD patients: deficiencies in selective attention, impaired learning and memory, and disorganized complex behavior are observed following lesions of the LC in the rat Iversen, 1984); noradrenaline levels are significantly lower in demented than in non-demented patients, in the LC (Cash et al., 1987) and in the entorhinal cortex (Scatton et al., 1983); RT on continuous performance tasks have been observed to correlate positively with CSF MHPG (3-methoxy-4-hydroxyphenylglycol) concentrations although the levels of the metabolite were normal (Stern et al., 1984b); and tricyclic antidepressants, which are potent synaptic uptake blockers of noradrenaline and are effective in the treatment of depression, prove to be useful in depressed PD patients as well (Strang, 1976).

The serotonergic raphe-cortical neurons The ascending serotonergic neurons are partially lesioned, as suggested by neuronal loss in the raphe nuclei and decreased serotonin concentrations in the striato-pallidal complex (Bernheimer et al., 1961). The decrease is greatest in the hippocampus and frontal cortex, less pronounced in the cingular and enthorinal cortex, but nonsignificant in the amygdala and nucleus accumbens (Scatton et al., 1983). These results are confirmed by the decreased density of imipramine binding sites (some of which are localized on serotonergic nerve terminals and therefore, represent a good index of serotonergic innervation), which are reduced at least in the striatum and frontal cortex of PD patients (Raisman et al., 1986). This central serotonergic deficiency may be responsible for some cognitive disorders in patients because serotonergic systems have been shown to play a role in learning in animals (Green and Heal,

1985). This deficiency may also be implicated in depression: the main metabolite of serotonin (5-HIAA) is found in lower concentrations in the CSF of depressed PD patients compared to those who are not (Mayeux et al., 1984). Mayeux and his colleagues recently found that PD patients who were either depressed or demented had lower CSF concentrations of the metabolite, thereby suggesting that depression and dementia in PD may have common biological mechanisms (Sano et al., 1989). Further, imipramine-like drugs, which are inhibitors of serotonin uptake, have antidepressant activity in these patients as well as in other depressed patients (Mayeux et al., 1984; Green and Heal, 1985).

Role of other cerebral lesions on the occurrence of cognitive deficits

In addition to the massive lesion of the nigrostriatal dopaminergic pathway and the partial degeneration of the long ascending subcortico-cortical systems, dysfunction of other neuronal circuitry may be implicated directly or indirectly in the genesis of cognitive symptomatology in PD patients. Examples include other subcortical neuronal losses, both in the *basal ganglia,* as suggested by the dysfunction of various peptidergic and amino acid-containing neuronal systems (Agid and Javoy-Agid, 1985, p. 130; Agid et al., 1989, p. 468), and in the *brainstem,* where cell loss in the pedunculopontine tegmental nucleus has been found in some patients (Hirsch et al., 1987; Jellinger, 1988). Alterations of neurons in the *cerebral cortex,* which probably occur in a sizeable number of cases (Ruberg and Agid, 1987; Jellinger, 1988), have been proposed to account for cognitive disorders in PD, and especially for dementia.

Table 13 summarizes the histological features commonly found in PD patients and in PD patients with dementia, compared with those of AD patients. Three types of pathology can be found in the post mortem examination of demented PD patients.

The first type consists of large numbers of senile plaques (SP) and/or neurofibrillary tangles (NFT) in the hippocampus and neocortex (Hakim and Mathieson, 1979; Boller et al., 1980). This finding

TABLE 13

Regional neuropathology in Parkinson's disease (PD) and Parkinson's disease with dementia (PD + D) compared to Alzheimer's disease (AD)

Group	Cerebral cortex	Substantia nigra	Locus coeruleus	Nucleus basalis
PD	+	+ + +	+ + +	+
PD + D	Three patterns: (1) SP and/or NFT (2) Diffuse Lewy bodies (3) No SP, NFT	+ + +	+ + +	+ + +
AD	SP and/or NFT	+	+ +	+ + +

The severity of lesion is ranked mild (+), moderate (+ +), or severe (+ + +). SP = senile plaques; NFT = neurofibrillary tangles.

has led some researchers to suggest that in these cases, the neuropathological picture is indistinguishable from AD. However, other authors disagree. To some extent, this is a matter of definition. A recent report exemplifies this issue (Xuereb et al., 1989). Out of a sub-group of 38 autopsied PD patients, only 2 fulfilled the 'criteria for co-existence' of PD and AD. This figure is based on reports from the same group showing that 'a large number of neuritic plaques' could be found in subjects who seemed to have been intellectually normal (Tomlinson and Corsellis, 1984). For that reason, they consider that only the *combined* presence of senile plaques (SP) and neurofibrillary tangles (NFT) warrants the firm diagnosis of AD. This criterion differs from the guidelines recommended by a National Institutes of Health (NIH) panel (Khachaturian, 1985), according to which the diagnosis relies mainly on the number of SP, particularly in elderly subjects. Xuereb et al. point out that, by following the NIH guidelines, the figure for PD patients demonstrating AD-like neuropathological lesions would rise to 20%.

Although the frequency and significance of the cortical changes are still controversial, there is a definite overlap between PD, PD with dementia,

and AD. PD patients without dementia sometimes show cortical AD-like changes in the cerebral cortex (Boller et al., 1980; Gaspar and Gray, 1984; Hakim and Mathieson, 1979). As in AD, a significant decrease in choline acetyltransferase (CAT) activity has been found in the cortex (Ruberg et al., 1982) and in the nucleus basalis of Meynert (Dubois et al., 1983), associated with reduced somatostatin concentrations in the cortex of demented PD patients (Epelbaum et al., 1983). In contrast, Lewy bodies are found in the substantia nigra of a significant number of AD patients (Leverenz and Sumi, 1986; Ditter and Mirra, 1987). This overlap has been confirmed by de la Monte et al. (1989), who compared the histological features of demented PD patients with those showing PD and AD.

The second type of pathology in demented PD patients is known as diffuse Lewy body disease, an entity originally described in a series of single case reports (Okasaki et al., 1961). The prevalence of diffuse Lewy body disease remains to be established, but a recent paper has described 15 cases among 216 brains autopsied consecutively (Byrne et al., 1989). Some features differentiate dementia associated with diffuse Lewy body disease from other dementias in PD: dementia and extrapyramidal symptoms usually develop either at the same time or within a short interval and dementia is 'cortical' in type, with clinical features suggesting temporoparietal damage (Gibb et al., 1989); association with psychiatric disturbances (paranoid delusions, visual and auditory hallucination) is frequent; a marked day-to-day fluctuation of the severity of the dementia, a phenomenon uncommonly seen in other forms of 'cortical dementia', has also been noticed (Byrne et al., 1989). Other alleged distinctive features include prominent gait impairment, and an abnormal EEG with a burst pattern (Dickson et al., 1990). From the point of view of neuropathology, diffuse Lewy body disease may occur with or without AD-like histological changes (Gibb et al., 1989).

Finally, some cases demonstrate no cortical pathology that could explain the dementia and only exhibit the subcortical (mainly mesencephalo-diencephalic) changes typically associated with idiopathic PD (Dubois et al., 1985a; Perry et al., 1985). These cases raise the question of whether the PD lesions of the mesencephalon and other brainstem structures can alone be responsible for the dementia. Alternatively, there may be no neuropathological explanation, as in certain patients diagnosed clinically as having probable AD, who at autopsy are found to have 'dementia lacking distinctive histologic features' (Knopman et al., 1990).

Following Gibb et al. (1989), we conclude that the neuropathology of demented PD patients emphasizes the interaction of three major pathologies responsible for dementia in PD: AD-like changes, subcortical lesions (Lewy bodies and cell loss in the nucleus basalis), and cortical Lewy bodies.

Neurobiochemical correlates hypotheses

Demodulation or destruction of the cognitive programs in PD

A cognitive program is a sequence of neural functions underlying a cognitive performance that is triggered and controlled by a group of topographically organized neuronal systems in the brain. If we assume that cognitive functions depend on the integrity of neuronal circuits programmed for the execution of these functions, cognitive disorders could occur either when neurons in which the program resides are lost, or when the afferent inputs have degenerated or are deficient. In PD, both the subcortical afferents to the cerebral cortex and the cortex itself may be disrupted.

Cognitive disorders can occur when cortical neurons degenerate, as illustrated by the presence of histopathological stigmata (SP and NFT). The identity of the neurons that are lost will not be known until quantitative and qualitative studies of cortical neuronal loss are performed. The hypothesis that cognitive changes in demented patients are related to cortical lesions suggests that the efficacy of classical substitutive treatment to replace effective neurotransmission must be poor because the modulatory systems originate essentially from subcortical areas.

There are reasons to believe that, in most PD cases, cognitive programs are not damaged but rather deactivated. In other words, its normal functions are altered because the program is inappropriately triggered. Most of the selectively damaged afferences are 'modulatory' systems which influence cortical activity. We use the word *demodulation* instead of deafferentation because neuronal loss contributing to the dysfunction of cognitive programs involves systems known to act as neuromodulators (for example dopamine, noradrenaline, acetylcholine and serotonin). In patients whose cognitive programs are partly or entirely intact, it is theoretically possible to provide substitute treatments in order to reestablish subcorticocortical cholinergic or monoaminergic transmission, thereby resulting in reactivation of afferent inputs to the cerebral cortex. Note, however, that while the concept of demodulation may be applied to specific cognitive disorders, it applies less readily to dementia and to the cortical lesions that are thought to be involved.

Threshold of appearance of cognitive disorders

Cognitive disorders may appear beyond a threshold of disruption of a single system of neurons or when more than one neuronal system is damaged (Terry, 1978). Animal work has shown that destruction of one of the ascending subcortico-cortical pathways may cause various behavioral disorders. The example of the degeneration of the cholinergic innominato-cortical pathway (Table 12) is illustrative. It has been shown that degeneration of cholinergic neurons can be severe enough to cause cognitive disorders in some patients, but insufficient in others (Dubois et al., 1983, 1987). This finding suggests that there are two phases in the degeneration of cholinergic input to the cerebral cortex (Agid et al., 1987a): a moderate and asymptomatic neuronal degeneration phase preceding a second period where neuronal loss becomes sufficient for the first cognitive disorders to appear. At the onset of the disease, normal cholinergic transmission may be maintained first by hyperactivity of the remaining cholinergic neurons, and later by postsynaptic supersensitivity of muscarinic receptors. Beyond a certain threshold of cholinergic denervation, intellectual impairment occurs when synaptic adjustments are no longer sufficient to compensate for neuronal loss. At this stage, PD patients become intellectually impaired. At this point, inappropriate administration of anticholinergic drugs can provoke confusional states, as a result of preexistent presynaptic cholinergic denervation, which is abruptly made worse through blockade of cortical cholinergic receptors.

Besides degeneration of the subcortico-cortical cholinergic systems, other ascending neuronal systems are partially affected. Several lines of evidence from experimental studies indicate that cognitive disorders appear when the sum of partial destruction of the afferent modulating systems reaches the necessary threshold. For instance, simultaneous disruption of the nigrostriatal and mesocorticolimbic dopaminergic systems causes marked disruption of the conditioned avoidance response in rats, whereas selective disruption of one or the other of these systems has no effect (Koob et al., 1984). Destruction of one ascending system, such as the cholinergic system, may increase the behavioral consequences of lesions of another system (serotoninergic; Nilsson et al., 1988), but the reverse has also been observed, i.e., that the lesion of one system (noradrenergic) attenuates or suppresses the effects of lesions of another (dopaminergic; Taghzouti et al., 1988). If these results can be transposed to humans, they suggest that disorders of cognition modulated by subcortico-cortical ascending systems may be observed in PD patients, either when there is sufficient partial destruction of several ascending neuronal pathways, or when there is a severe and selective lesion of one of them.

The wide spectrum of mental disorders in PD

Can the symptoms found in the various types of cognitive disorder characteristic of PD be superimposed on the distribution of subcortical and cortical lesions, some of which have been characterized histologically and biochemically? Each of the cognitive syndromes commonly found in PD (name-ly the changes in linguistic, visuospatial, mnestic and 'executive' abilities as well as bradyphrenia and depression) includes a variety of overlapping symptoms. Can each of these symptoms be explained by the different types of lesion known to occur in PD patients? It is likely that degeneration of afferent neuronal systems (cholinergic and monoaminergic modulatory neurons) plays a part in memory disorders and contributes to frontal-lobe-like symptomatology. Degeneration of serotoninergic and noradrenergic ascending neuronal systems is likely to be implicated in the appearance of depression in PD. In summary, there could be some correspondence between the vast spectrum of neuronal lesions in PD and the constellation of cognitive symptoms. The specific features of cognitive impairment in each patient probably depend on the *distribution* of brain lesions, their *severity,* and the *order* in which they develop in the course of the disease.

Neuronal basis of cognitive impairment in the course of the disease

What is the respective role of cortical and subcortical lesions in relation to the cognitive deficits found in PD? This question cannot be answered precisely because no prospective anatomo-clinical study exists so far. In addition, no anatomo-clinical pattern can be generalized to all PD patients. However, some hypotheses can be put forward. Because PD is characterized by striatal and, to a lesser extent, cortical dopaminergic denervation, one can hypothesize that the dopaminergic deficit plays a primary role in the appearance of the moderate frontal-like syndrome found in early-onset PD.

During the evolution of PD, additional subcortical or cortical lesions appear, in addition to the central dopaminergic denervation. These lesions probably contribute to a worsening of the cognitive deficits because of a deactivation of the supposedly intact cortical cognitive programs. This deactivation may explain the accentuation of the frontal-type symptomatology found in PD patients as the disease continues its course years after the onset of the disease.

In a smaller number of patients (see above), dementia according to DSM-III criteria is observed. In these cases, one is tempted to postulate that the neuronal loss and other AD-like cortical histopathological changes play a crucial role in the intellectual deterioration. Thus the dementia would be due to the sum of the subcortical lesions (essentially the ascending modulatory systems) and of the more diffuse cortical lesions. This hypothesis remains speculative since the role of cortical lesions in PD is not clearly established. Moreover, some cases of PD with dementia have been described in patients without apparent cortical lesions (Perry et al., 1985; Dubois et al., 1985), suggesting that subcortical lesions may be sufficiently severe to cause dementia. Conversely, AD-like changes have been observed in the cortex of PD patients without overt evidence of dementia. In those cases, one can hypothesize that intellectual deterioration may appear beyond a certain threshold and that, paradoxically, this threshold is higher in these patients.

In summary, even though these hypotheses are based on clinical, pathological, and experimental observations, they represent oversimplifications. Nevertheless, they may have the merit of stimulating further experiments, particularly longitudinal studies aimed at establishing objective correlates of the clinical observations.

Summary and conclusion

This chapter has shown that in PD, relatively isolated cognitive disorders can be observed in the absence of global intellectual impairment. They include word-finding difficulties in confrontation naming and word fluency tasks; visuospatial disorders which are considered to result mainly in impaired internal representation; defective functional use of memory stores, with impaired performance in delayed response tasks, recency discrimination, temporal ordering, and conditional associative learning; slowing of central processing in complex cognitive tasks; and executive dysfunction, as suggested by behavioral regulation deficits and disorders of programming and strategy.

Each of these disorders results from dysfunction of processes that are commonly considered to be controlled by the frontal lobes. The 'frontal dysfunction' hypothesis, which is offered by several authors to explain the isolated cognitive disorders in PD, is based on this assumption. It should be noticed, however, that the frontal dysfunction of PD patients is somewhat different from the neuropsychological picture observed in patients with lesions of the frontal lobes (Spinnler et al., in preparation). PD patients are less disabled in 'Tower-type' problem-solving tests; they do not perseverate as much as patients with frontal-lobe injuries in sorting and fluency tasks; 'they do not seem to be disinhibited, or to lack insight, or to show unconcern when performing tests' (Cronin-Golomb, 1990, p. 292). Finally, the frontal dysfunction may be amplified by nonspecific factors such as age, depression, attentional disorder or medications.

Age certainly plays some role. Cognitive disorders appear more strikingly in older patients (Lieberman et al., 1979), where they concern mainly frontal-lobe functions, as indicated by the existence of a severe impairment of frontal-lobe-like activity in older patients compared to age-matched control subjects; and by the significant interaction between the effect of age and disease on tests sensitive to frontal-lobe disorders (Dubois et al., 1990). The compounding effect of aging on overall cognition, and on frontal-lobe activities in particular, has been proposed to explain, at least in part, the high frequency of cognitive decline in older PD patients. However, it must be pointed out that defective performance in 'executive' tests has been observed even in younger patients (Hietanen and Teräväinen, 1988), suggesting that age of onset does not entirely explain the frontal dysfunction observed in these patients.

Depression is a common disorder in PD. Its prevalence has been estimated to be about 50% (Mayeux et al., 1981). Depressed mood may affect the reactivity and attentional control of patients in tasks that require a high level of sustained attention and motivation. PD patients with major depression were found to be more severely impaired on tests of cognitive functions than nondepressed patients, particularly on tests believed to assess frontal lobe function (Starkstein et al., 1989). However, depression cannot explain the frontal dysfunction of PD, because many studies have failed to find a significant correlation between depression and cognitive impairment (Santamaria et al., 1986; Taylor et al., 1988; Bieliauskas and Glantz, 1988). Moreover, patients with major depression (those in whom depression is severe enough to alter cognitive performance) are usually excluded in studies of cognitive functions.

Attentional disorders may be particularly important because of their possible effects on cognition in PD and other diseases (see chapter by Spinnler, this volume). In a study in which attentional processes were controlled using the Paced Auditory Serial Addition Test, the number of errors was significantly higher in the PD group than in a group of matched control subjects for fast and slow rate of digit presentation (Brown and Marsden, 1988a). Using the Continuous Performance Task, Mayeux et al. (1987) found more omission errors and fewer correct responses in PD patients than in control subjects or patients with AD. These results suggest the existence of an attentional deficit that has been shown to influence the performance of patients in tests assessing frontal-lobe functions (Wilkins et al., 1987).

Finally, antiparkinson treatment is an important factor to bear in mind because levodopa and anticholinergic therapy may affect the performance of PD patients on tests sensitive to frontal-lobe dysfunction. Gotham et al. (1988) have shown decreased performance in PD patients when ON levodopa but not OFF levodopa compared to control subjects in conditional learning and subject-ordered pointing tests, both tests known to be sensitive to damage of prefrontal cortex (Petrides and Milner, 1982; Petrides, 1985). Comparing two groups of PD patients matched for age, age of onset, motor pattern and L-DOPA treatment, a specific impairment was found only in patients treated with anticholinergic drugs on tests believed to assess frontal-lobe function (Dubois et al., 1990). This

frontal-lobe-test sensitivity to anticholinergic drugs is congruent with the results of Talland's study (1962) on the Necker cube, in which difficulty in controlling the switching of two possible perceptions was observed only in the group receiving mainly anticholinergic drugs and no L-DOPA.

In our opinion, each of the above factors may influence the frontal-lobe-like symptomatology of PD and must be controlled for in further studies by comparing populations matched for age, by excluding patients with major depression and anticholinergic therapy, and by assessing attentional abilities with specific tasks.

The spectrum of specific cognitive disturbances in PD has sometimes been compared to the cognitive deficits reported by Albert et al. (1974) under the name of subcortical dementia. From their initial description and the subsequent restatements (Freedman and Albert, 1985), the core syndrome of subcortical dementia consists of memory loss, frontal-lobe deficits with impaired manipulation of acquired knowledge, concept formation and set-shifting, and usually slowness of thought processes and alterations of personality with apathy or depression. The concept of subcortical dementia has been criticized on clinical and pathological bases mainly because there is significant overlap of both cognitive disorders and neuronal lesions between the so-called cortical and subcortical dementias (Mayeux et al., 1983; Whitehouse, 1986). However, the concept has the advantage of attracting attention to two essential points, which represent the main criteria for subcortical dementia: (1) the absence in most cases of 'cortical' signs such as aphasia and apraxia; (2) the underlying mechanism of cognitive impairment which is supposed to result directly from lesions of subcortical structures via decreased activation of the cerebral cortex. These two conditions are fulfilled in most PD patients. Is it therefore correct to refer to the cognitive disorders of PD as subcortical dementia?

To answer this question, one should probably consider separately the isolated cognitive disorders and the global deterioration of PD. However, this separation is sometimes theoretical because the cognitive disorders often occur along a continuum of deterioration (Pirrozolo et al., 1982), representing a gradient of severity. For this reason, the clear-cut separation of a subgroup of demented patients is difficult, and the choice of a *psychometric score* to define such a subgroup is not obvious. Similarly, a *behavioral criterion* in line with the ones used for other types of dementia may not fit these patients because their autonomy depends in great part on the severity of their motor handicap. The DSM-III criteria, which rely on the existence of a cognitive disorder of sufficient severity to affect social and professional life, cannot always be strictly applied to PD patients.

Many of the studies reviewed in this chapter indicate that even in the absence of a global deterioration of cognitive functions, PD is almost always accompanied by cognitive disorders (Taylor et al., 1986; Pillon et al., in press). These disorders have therefore been considered 'specific', suggesting a lesion of precise neuronal systems (see above). Whatever the mechanism invoked to explain the 'frontal' dysfunction (damage of the nigrostriatal dopaminergic pathway responsible for an interruption of the complex loop; degeneration of long ascending dopaminergic and cholinergic neuronal systems resulting in deafferentation of frontal areas), some data suggest that these disorders are directly related to subcortical pathology. Even if this explanation was always valid, the term subcortical dementia may still be inappropriate because the cognitive disorders are discrete and are observed in the absence of dementia. A preferable term may be 'cognitive disorders of subcortical origin'.

A global deterioration of intellectual functions is observed less frequently than isolated cognitive disorders. As noted in a previous section, the issue of the prevalence of dementia in PD remains under debate, as is the specificity of the pattern of cognitive deficit when compared to other degenerative dementias. Mayeux et al. (1983) found no difference in the cognitive profile, including language, of patients with AD (representative of 'cortical' dementia) and PD. In Mayeux et al.'s study, it may be argued that the matching of the groups on the basis of a modified Mini-Mental state examination may have produced a selection bias, because this test is heavily weighted with items sensitive to language deficits. In fact, further studies were not able to find the same magnitude of impairment in PD patients, even when they were demented, as in patients with AD. This conclusion applies particularly to language (Huber et al., 1986b; Cummings et al., 1988) and memory functions (Helkala et al., 1989; Sagar et al., 1988a), which were shown to be less severely impaired in demented PD patients. We nevertheless agree with the conclusions of Brown and Marsden (1988c), who state that no consistent qualitative features are present to constitute a specific pattern of the dementia of PD.

Other evidence against the use of the term subcortical dementia in PD comes from neuropathology. It is probable, although not conclusively demonstrated, that the numerous cortical lesions observed in patients who die in the end stage of PD play a causative role in the cognitive deficit of earlier stages of PD. If so, PD dementia may be the result of cortical as well as subcortical lesions. The respective role of the two contingents remains to be determined, even if there are good reasons to believe that the subcortical lesions are responsible for the preponderance of frontal dysfunctions observed even in demented PD patients (Pillon et al., 1986). For these two reasons (absence of a specific cognitive profile and presence of associated cortical lesions), it is inaccurate to label the dementia observed in PD a subcortical dementia.

In conclusion, most of the current evidence shows that PD patients exhibit three patterns of cognitive changes. Some patients (probably a small minority) show no cognitive deficits, even when carefully assessed. A large number of patients show relatively isolated cognitive disorders without dementia, probably secondary to subcortical lesions (subcortical cognitive disorders). Finally a sizeable percentage show a dementia without a specific pattern, probably secondary to cortical and subcortical lesions. Neither of the two kinds of cognitive impairment can be accurately called subcortical dementia. On the other hand, the concept of subcortical dementia has some heuristic value because it underscores the importance of the anatomical and functional relationship between the cerebral cortex and subcortical structures, particularly the basal ganglia. We wish to propose that dysfunction of the relationships between these structures constitutes the initial basis of the cognitive impairment of PD.

Acknowledgements

Part of the research presented in this chapter was supported by funds from the Institut National de la Santé et de la Recherche Médicale (INSERM). The authors wish to express their gratitude to Suzanne Corkin Ph.D., Margaret Forbes M.A., Yaakov Stern Ph.D. and Hans Spinnler M.D. for their comments and suggestions.

References

Adam R, Fabre N, Guell A, Bessoles G, Roulleau J, Bes A: Cortical atrophy in Parkinson's disease: correlation between clinical and CT findings with special emphasis on prefrontal atrophy. *Am. J. Neuroradiol.: 4,* 442 – 445, 1983.

Adams RD, Victor M: *Principles of Neurology,* 4th Edition. New York: McGraw Hill, 1989.

Agid Y, Javoy-Agid F: Peptides and Parkinson's disease. *Trends Neurosci.: 8,* 30 – 35, 1985.

Agid Y, Javoy F, Glowinski J: Hyperactivity of remaining dopaminergic neurons after partial destruction of the nigrostriatal dopaminergic system in the rat. *Nature: 245,* 150 – 151, 1973.

Agid Y, Javoy-Agid F, Ruberg M: Biochemistry of neurotransmitters in Parkinson's disease. In Marsden CD, Fahn S (Editors), *Movement Disoders 2. International Medical Reviews, Neurology: Vol. 7.* London: Butterworth, pp. 166 – 230, 1987a.

Agid Y, Ruberg M, Dubois B, Pillon B: Anatomoclinical and biochemical concepts of subcortical dementia. In Stahl SM, Iversen SD, Goodman EC (Editors), *Cognitive Neurochemistry.* Oxford Science Publications, pp. 248 – 271, 1987b.

Agid Y, Cervera P, Hirsch EC, Javoy-Agid F, Lehericy S, Raisman R, Ruberg M: Biochemistry of Parkinson's disease 28 years later: a critical review. *Movement Disorders: 4, Suppl. 1,* 126 – 144, 1989.

Agnoli A, Ruggieri S, Meco G, Casacchia M, Denaro A, Conti L, Bedini L, Stocchi F, Fioravanti M, Franzese A, Lazzari R: An appraisal of the problem of dementia in Parkinson's disease. In Hassler RG, Christ JF (editors). *Advances in*

Neurology, Vol. 40: Parkinson-specific Motor and Mental Disorders. New York: Raven Press, pp. 299 – 306, 1984.

Alberoni M, Della Sala S, Pasetti C, Spinnler H: Problem solving ability of Parkinsonian. *Ital. J. Neurol. Sci.: 9,* 35 – 40, 1988.

Albert ML, Feldman RG, Willis AL: The subcortical dementia of progressive supranuclear palsy. *J. Neurol. Neurosurg. Psychiatry: 37,* 121 – 130, 1974.

Albert MS, Moss M: The assessment of memory disorders in patients with Alzheimer's disease. In Squire LR, Butters N (Editors), *Neuropsychology of Memory.* New York: Guilford Press, pp. 236 – 246, 1984.

Ajuriaguerra (de) J: Etude psychopathologique des parkinsoniens. In de Ajuriaguerra J, Gauthier G (Editors), *Monoamines, Noyaux Gris Centraux et Syndrome de Parkinson.* Paris: Masson, pp. 327 – 351, 1971.

American Psychiatric Association, Committee on Nomenclature and Statistics. *Diagnostic and Statistical Manual of Mental Disorders.* Washington DC: American Psychiatric Association, 1980.

American Psychiatric Association, Committee on Nomenclature and Statistics. *Diagnostic and Statistical Manual of Mental Disorders,* Revised Edition. Washington DC: American Psychiatric Association, 1987.

Asso D: WAIS scores in a group of Parkinson patients. *Br. J. Psychiatry: 115,* 555 – 556, 1969.

Atkinson RL, Shiffrin RM: Human memory: a proposed system and its central processes. In Spence KW, Spence JT (Editors), *The Psychology of Learning and Motivation, Vol. 2.* New York: Academic Press, 1968.

Bachman DL, Albert ML: The dopaminergic syndromes of dementia. In Pilleri G, Tagliavini F (Editors), *Brain Pathology, Vol. 1.* Bern: Brain Anatomy Institute, pp. 91 – 119, 1984.

Baddeley AD: *Working Memory.* Oxford: Oxford University Press, 1986.

Ball B: De l'insanité dans la paralysie agitante. *Encéphale: 2,* 22 – 32, 1882.

Barbeau A: Dopamine and mental function. In Malitz S (Editor), *L-Dopa and Behavior.* New York: Raven Press, pp. 9 – 33, 1982.

Bartus RT, Johnson HR: Short term memory in the rhesus monkey: disruption from the anticholinergic scopolamine. *Pharmacol. Biochem. Behav.: 5,* 39 – 46, 1976.

Bayles KA, Kaszniak AW: *Communication and Cognition in Aging and Dementia.* Boston: College Hill Press, 1987.

Bayles KA, Tomoeda CK: Confrontation naming impairment in dementia. *Brain Lang.: 19,* 98 – 114, 1983.

Beardsley J, Puletti F: Personality (MMPI) and cognitive (WAIS) changes after L-DOPA treatment. *Arch. Neurol.: 25,* 145 – 150, 1971.

Becker J, Nebes R, Boller F: Neuropsychologie du vieillissement. In Botez MI (Editor), *Neuropsychologie Clinique et Neurologie du Comportement.* Masson/Presse Universitaire du Québec, pp. 371 – 379, 1987.

Benton AL: Differential behavioral effects in frontal lobe disease. *Neuropsychologia: 6,* 53 – 60, 1968.

Bernheimer H, Birkmayer W, Hornykiewicz O: Verteilung de-5-hydroxytryptamins (serotinin) im Gehrirn des Menschen und sein Verhalten bei Patienten mit Parkinson Syndrom. *Klin. Wochenschr.: 39,* 1056 – 1059, 1961.

Bernheimer H, Birkmayer W, Hornykiewicz O, Jellinger K, Seitelberger F: Brain dopamine and the syndromes of Parkinson and Huntington. *J. Neurol. Sci.: 20,* 415–455, 1973.

Bieliauskas LA, Glantz TH: Depression type in Parkinson's disease. *J. Clin. Exp. Neuropsychol.: 11,* 597–604, 1988.

Blonder LX, Gur RE, Gur RC: The effects of right and left hemiparkinsonism on prosody. *Brain Lang.: 36,* 193–207, 1989.

Bloxham CA, Mindel TA, Frith CD: Initiation and execution of predictable and impredictable movements in parkinson's disease. *Brain: 107,* 371–384, 1984.

Boller F: Mental status of patients with Parkinson disease. A review. *J. Clin. Neuropsychol.: 2,* 157–172, 1980.

Boller F, Albert ML, Denes F: Palilalia. *Br. J. Disorders Commun.: 10,* 92–97, 1975.

Boller F, Mizutani T, Roessmann U, Gambetti P: Parkinson's disease, dementia and Alzheimer's disease: clinicopathological correlations. *Ann. Neurol.: 7,* 329–335, 1980.

Boller F, Goldstein G, Dorr C, Kim Y, Mossy J, Richey E, Wagener D, Wolfson SK: Alzheimer and related dementias: a review of current knowledge. In Goldstein G (Editor), *Advances in Clinical Neuropsychology, Vol. 1.* New York: Plenum Press, pp. 89–126, 1984a.

Boller F, Passafiume D, Keefe NC, Rogers K, Morrow L, Kim Y: Visuospatial impairment in Parkinson disease: role of perceptual and motor factors. *Arch. Neurol.: 41,* 485–490, 1984b.

Borod JC, Goodglass H, Kaplan E: Normative data on the Boston Diagnostic Aphasia Examination, Parietal Lobe Battery and the Boston Naming Test. *J. Clin. Neuropsychol.: 2,* 209–215, 1980.

Botez MI, Barbeau A: Neuropsychological findings in Parkinson's disease: a comparison between various tests during long-term L-DOPA therapy. *Int. J. Neurol.: 10,* 222–232, 1975.

Bowen FP: Visuomotor deficits produced by cryogenic lesions of the caudate. *Neuropsychologia: 7,* 59–65, 1969.

Bowen FP, Burns M, Yahr MD: Alterations in memory Processes subsequent to short and long term treatment with L-Dopa. In Birkmayer W, Hornykiewicz O (Editors), *Advances in Parkinsonism.* Geneva: Roche, pp. 488–491, 1976.

Bowen FP, Hoehn MM, Yahr MD: Parkinsonism: alterations in spatial orientation as determined by a route-walking test. *Neuropsychologia: 10,* 355–361, 1972.

Bowen FP, Kamieny RS, Burns MM, Yahr MD: Parkinsonism: effects of levodopa on concept formation. *Neurology: 25,* 701–704, 1975.

Bradley VA, Welch JL, Dick DJ: Visuospatial working memory in Parkinson's disease. *J. Neurol. Neurosurg. Psychiatry: 52,* 1228–1235, 1989.

Brown R, McNeill D: The 'tip-of-the-tongue' phenomenon. *J. Verbal Learn. Verbal Behav.: 5,* 325–337, 1966.

Brown RG, Marsden CD: How common is dementia in Parkinson's disease? *Lancet: ii,* 1262–1265, 1984a.

Brown RG, Marsden CD: Visuospatial function in Parkinson's disease. *Brain: 109,* 987–1002, 1986.

Brown RG, Marsden CD: Internal versus external cues and the control of attention in Parkinson's disease. *Brain: 111,* 323–345, 1988a.

Brown RG, Marsden CD: An investigation of the phenomenon of 'set' in Parkinson's disease. *Movement Disorders: 3,* 152–161, 1988b.

Brown RG, Marsden CD: 'Subcortical dementia': the neuropsychological evidence. *Neuroscience: 25,* 363–387, 1988c.

Brown RG, Marsden CD: Cognitive function in Parkinson's disease: from description to theory. *Trends Neurosci.: 13,* 21–28, 1990.

Brown RG, Marsden CD, Quinn N, Wyke MA: Alterations in cognitive performances and affect-arousal state during fluctuations in motor function in Parkinson's disease. *J. Neurol. Neurosurg. Psychiatry: 47,* 454–465, 1984.

Brozoski TJ, Brown RM, Rosvold ME, Goldman PS: Cognitive deficit caused by regional depletion of dopamine in prefrontal cortex of rhesus monkey. *Science: 205,* 929–931, 1979.

Butters N, Salmon DP, Heindel WC: Processes underlying the memory impairment of demented patients. In Goldberg E (Editor), *Contemporary Neuropsychology and the Legacy of Luria.* New York: Laurence Erlbaum, pp. 99–126, 1990.

Byrne EJ, Lennox G, Lowe J, Godwin-Austen RB: Diffuse Lewy body disease: clinical features in 15 cases. *J. Neurol. Neurosurg. Psychiatry: 52,* 709–717, 1989.

Caltagirone C, Carlesimo A, Nocentini U, Vicari S: Defective concept formation in Parkinsonians is independent from mental deterioration. *J. Neurol. Neurosurg. Psychiatry: 52,* 334–337, 1989.

Canavan AG, Passingham RE, Marsden CD, Quinn N, Wyke M, Polkey CE: The performances on learning tasks of patients in early stages of Parkinson's disease. *Neuropsychologia: 27,* 141–156, 1989.

Cash R, Dennis T, L'Heureux R, Raisman R, Javoy-Agid F, Scatton B: Parkinson's disease and dementia. Norepinephrine and dopamine in locus ceruleus. *Neurology: 37,* 42–46, 1987.

Celesia GG, Wanamaker WM: Psychiatric disturbances in Parkinson's disease. *Dis. Nerv. Syst.: 33,* 577–583, 1972.

Charcot JM: Leçons sur les maladies du Système Nerveux. Cinquième Leçon: de la paralysie agitante. Bourneville Ed. Paris: Delahaye: 1872.

Charcot JM, Vulpain A: De la paralysie agitante. *Gaz. Hebdomadaire Méd. Chirurg. 8,* 765–767, 1861: *9,* 54–59, 1862.

Chorover SL, Cole M: Delayed alternative performance in patients with cerebral lesions. *Neuropsychologia: 4,* 1–7, 1966.

Christensen AL, Juul-Jensen P, Malmroe R, Harmsen A: Psychological evaluation of intelligence and personality in Parkinsonism before and after stereotactic surgery. *Acta Neurol. Scand.: 46,* 527–537, 1970.

Cohen J, Squire LR: Preserved learning and retention of pattern analysing skill in amnesia: dissociation in knowing how and knowing that. *Science: 210,* 207–209, 1980.

Como PG, Caine ED: A comparative neuropsychological study of AD and PD (Abstract). *J. Clin. Exp. Neuropsychol.: 9,* 74, 1987.

Connor NP, Ludlow CL, Schulz GM: Stop consonant production in isolated and repeated syllables in Parkinson's disease. *Neuropsychologia: 27,* 829–838, 1989.

Cools AR, Van Der Bercken JH, Horstink MW, Van Spaendonck KP, Berger HJ: Cognitive and motor shifting aptitude disorder in Parkinson's disease. *J. Neurol. Neurosurg. Psychiatry: 47,* 443–453, 1984.

Corkin S: Tactually guided image-learning in man: effects of unilateral cortical excisions and bilateral hippocampal lesions. *Neuropsychologia: 3,* 339–351, 1965.

Critchley EMR: Speech disorders of Parkinsonism: a review. *J. Neurol. Neurosurg. Psychiatry: 44,* 751–758, 1981.

Cronin-Golomb A: Abstract thought in aging and age-related neurological disease. In Boller F, Grafman J (Editors), *Handbook of Neuropsychology, Vol. 4.* Amsterdam: Elsevier pp. 279–309, 1990.

Cummings JL: Intellectual impairment in Parkinson's disease: clinical, pathological and biochemical correlates. *J. Geriatr. Psychiatry Neurol.: 1,* 24–36, 1988.

Cummings JL, Darkins A, Mendez M, Hill MA, Benson DF: Alzheimer's disease and Parkinson's disease: comparison oʹ speech and language alterations. *Neurology: 38,* 680–684, 1988.

Damasio AR: The frontal lobes. In Heilman KM, Valenstein E (Editors), *Clinical Neuropsychology.* New York: Oxford University Press, 1979.

Danta G, Hilton RC: Judgement of the visual vertical and horizontal in patients with parkinsonism. *Neurology: 25,* 43–47, 1975.

Darkins AW, Fromkin VA, Benson DF: A characterization of the prosodic loss in Parkinson's disease. *Brain Lang.: 34,* 315–327, 1988.

Darley FL, Aronson AE, Brown JR: Hypokinetic dysarthria. In Darley FL, Aronson AE, Brown JR (Editors), *Motor Speech Disorders.* Philadelphia: Saunders, pp. 171–197, 1975.

Day BL, Dick JPR, Marsden CD: Patients with Parkinson's disease can employ a predictive motor strategy. *J. Neurol. Neurosurg. Psychiatry: 47,* 1299–1306, 1984.

De la Monte SM, Wells SE, Hedley-White T, Growdon JH: Neuropathological distinction between Parkinson's dementia and Parkinson's plus Alzheimer's disease. *Ann. Neurol.: 26,* 309–320, 1989.

De Lancy Horne DJ: Performance on delayed response tasks in patients with Parkinsonism. *J. Neurol. Neurosurg. Psychiatry: 34,* 192–194, 1971.

Delis D, Direnfeld L, Alexander MP, Kaplan E: Cognitive fluctuations associated with on-off phenomenon in Parkinson's disease. *Neurology: 32,* 1049–1052, 1982.

Della Sala S, Di Lorenzo G, Giordano G, Spinnler H: Is there a specific visuo-spatial impairment in Parkinsonians? *J. Neurol. Neurosurg. Psychiatry: 49,* 1258–1265, 1986.

De Renzi E: *Disorders of Space Exploration and Cognition.* New York: Wiley, 1982.

De Smet Y, Ruberg M, Serdaru M, Dubois B, Lhermitte F, Agid Y: Confusion, dementia and anticholinergics in Parkinson's disease. *J. Neurol. Neurosurg. Psychiatry: 45,* 1161–1164, 1982.

Dickson D, Crystal HA, Lizardi E, Davies P: Antemortem diagnosis of Diffuse Lewy Body Disease. *Neurology: 40, Suppl. 1,* 406, 1990.

Ditter SM, Mirra SS: Neuropathologic and clinical features of Parkinson's disease in Alzheimer's disease patients. *Neurology: 37,* 754–760, 1987.

Drachman DA: Memory and cognitive function in man: does the cholinergic system have a specific role? *Neurology: 27,* 783–790, 1977.

Drewe EA: The effect of type and area of brain lesion of Wisconsin Card Sorting test performance. *Cortex: 10,* 159–170, 1974.

Dubois B, Ruberg M, Javoy Agid F, Ploska A, Agid Y: A subcortico-cortical cholinergic system is affected in Parkinson's disease. *Brain Res.: 288,* 213–218, 1983.

Dubois B, Hauw JJ, Ruberg M, Serdaru M, Javoy-Agid F, Agid Y: Démence et maladie de Parkinson: corrélations biochimiques et anatomocliniques. *Rev. Neurol.: 141,* 184–193, 1985a.

Dubois B, Mayo W, Agid Y, Le Moal M, Simon H: Profound disturbances of spontaneous and learned behaviors following lesions of the nucleus basalis mangocellularis in the rat. *Brain Res.: 338,* 249–258, 1985b.

Dubois B, Danze F, Pillon B, Cusimano G, Agid Y, Lhermitte F: Cholinergic-dependent cognitive deficits in Parkinson's disease. *Ann. Neurol.: 22,* 26–30, 1987.

Dubois B, Pillon B, Legault F, Agid Y, Lhermitte F: Slowing of cognitive processing in progressive supranuclear palsy. *Arch. Neurol.: 45,* 1194–1199, 1988.

Dubois B, Pillon B, Lhermitte F, Agid Y: Cholinergic deficiency and frontal dysfunction in Parkinson's disease. *Ann. Neurol.: 28,* 117–121, 1990.

Dubois B, Pillon B, Sternic N, Lhermitte F, Agid Y: Age-induced cognitive disturbances in Parkinson's disease. *Neurology: 40,* 38–41, 1990.

El Awar M, Becker JT, Hammond KM, Boller F: Learning deficits in Parkinson's disease: comparison with Alzheimer's disease and normal aging. *Arch. Neurol.: 44,* 180–184, 1987.

Elizan TS, Sroka H, Maker H, Smith H, Yahr MD: Dementia in idiopathic Parkinson's disease: variables associated with its occurrence in 203 patients. *J. Neural Transm.: 65,* 285–302, 1986.

Epelbaum J, Ruberg M, Moyse E, Javoy Agid F, Dubois B, Agid Y: Somatosain and dementia in Parkinson's disease. *Brain Res.: 278,* 376–379, 1983.

Evarts EV, Teräväinen H, Calne DB: Reaction time in Parkinson's disease. *Brain: 104,* 167–186, 1981.

Flowers KA: Lack of prediction in the motor behavior of parkinsonism. *Brain: 101,* 35–52, 1978.

Flowers KA, Robertson C: The effects of Parkinson's disease on the ability to maintain a mental set. *J. Neurol. Neurosurg. Psychiatry: 48,* 517–529, 1985.

Flowers KA, Pearce I, Pearce JM: Recognition memory in Parkinson's disease. *J. Neurol. Neurosurg. Psychiatry: 47,* 1174–1181, 1984.

Folstein MF, Folstein SE, McHugh PR: Mini-Mental State: a practical method for grading the cognitive state of patients for the clinician. *J. Psychiatric Res.: 12,* 189–198, 1975.

Freedman M, Albert ML: Subcortical dementia. In Frederiks JAM (Editor), *Handbook of Clinical Neurology. Neurobehavioral Disorders, Vol. 2(46).* Amsterdam: Elsevier. pp. 311–316, 1985.

Freedman M, Oscar-Berman M: Selective delayed response deficits in Parkinson's and Alzheimer's disease. *Arch. Neurol.: 43,* 886–890, 1986.

Freedman M, Rivoira P, Butters N, Sax DS, Feldman RG: Retrograde amnesia in Parkinson's disease. *Canad. J. Neurol. Sci.: 11,* 297–301, 1984.

Frith CD, Bloxham CA, Carpenter KM: Impairments in the learning and performance of a new manual skill in patients with Parkinson's disease. *J. Neurol. Neurosurg. Psychiatry: 49,* 661–668, 1986.

Fuster JM: *The Prefrontal Cortex. Anatomy, Physiology and*

Neuropsychology of the Frontal Lobe. New York: Raven Press, 1989.

Gainotti G, Caltagirone C, Masullo C, Miceli G: Patterns of neuropsychological impairment in various diagnostic subgroups of dementia. In Amaducci L, Davison AN, Antuono P (Editors), *Aging, Vol. 13: Aging of the Brain and Dementia*. New York, Raven Press, pp. 245 – 250, 1980.

Garron DC, Klawans HL, Narin F: Intellectual functioning of persons with idiopathic Parkinsonism. *J. Nerv. Mental Dis.: 154*, 445 – 452, 1972.

Gaspar P, Gray F: Dementia in idiopathic Parkinson's disease. *Acta Neuropathol. (Berl.): 64*, 43 – 52, 1984.

Gibb WRG, Luthert PJ, Janota I, Lantos PL: Cortical Lewy body dementia: clinical features and classification. *J. Neurol. Neurosurg. Psychiatry: 52*, 185 – 192, 1989a.

Gibb WRG, Mountjoy CQ, Mann DM, Lees AJ: A pathological study of the association between Lewy body disease and Alzheimer's disease. *J. Neurol. Neurosurg. Psychiatry: 52*, 701 – 708, 1989b.

Girotti F, Carella F, Grassi MP, Soliveri P, Marano R, Caraceni T: Motor and cognitive performances of Parkinsonian patients in the on and off phases of the disease. *J. Neurol. Neurosurg. Psychiatry: 49*, 657 – 660, 1986.

Girotti F, Soliveri P, Carella F, Piccolo I, Caffarra P, Musicco M, Caraceni T: Dementia and cognitive impairment in Parkinson's disease. *J. Neurol. Neurosurg. Psychiatry: 51*, 1498 – 1502, 1988.

Globus M, Mildworf B, Melamed E: Cerebral blood flow and cognitive impairment in Parkinson's disease. *Neurology: 35*, 1135 – 1139, 1985.

Go RCP, Todorov AB, Elston RC, Constantinidis J: The malignancy of dementias. *Ann. Neurol.: 3*, 559 – 561, 1978.

Goldenberg G, Wimmer A, Auff E, Schnaberth G: Impairment of motor planning in patients with Parkinson's disease: evidence for ideomotor apraxia. *J. Neurol. Neurosurg. Psychiatry: 49*, 1266 – 1272, 1986.

Goldenberg G, Podreka I, Muller C, Deecke L: The relationship between cognitive deficits and frontal lobe function in patients with Parkinson's disease: an emission computerized tomography study. *Behav. Neurol.: 2*, 79 – 87, 1989.

Goodglass H, Kaplan E: *The Assessment of Aphasia and Related Disorders*. Philadelphia: Lea and Fabiger, 1976.

Gotham AM, Brown RG, Marsden CD: 'Frontal' cognitive function in patients with Parkinson's disease 'on' and 'off' levodopa. *Brain: 111*, 299 – 321, 1988.

Gowers WR: Paralysis agitans. In Allbutt, Rolleston (Editors), *A System of Medicine, Vol. VIII*. London: Macmillan, 1899.

Graf P, Schacter D: Implicit and explicit memory for new associations in normal and amnesic subjects. *J. Exp. Psychol. Learn. Mem. Cognition: 11*, 501 – 518, 1985.

Grant DA, Berg EA: A behavioral analysis of damage of reinforcement and ease of shifting to new responses in a Weigl-type card sorting problem. *J. Exp. Psychol.: 38*, 404 – 411, 1948.

Graybiel AM, Agid Y, Hirsch EC: The nigrostriatal system in Parkinson's disease. In Streifler MB, Korczyn AD, Melamed E, Youdin MBH (Editors), *Advances in Neurology, Vol. 53*. New York: Raven Press, 1990.

Green AR, Heal DJ: The effects of drugs on serotonin-mediated behavioural model. In Green AR (Editor), *Neurophar-macology of Serotonin*. Oxford: Oxford University Press, pp. 326 – 365, 1985.

Grossman M, Digby L, Hurtig H, Stern M, Gollomp S: Specific language impairments in Parkinson's Disease (Abstract). *Neurology: 40, Suppl. 1*, 335, 1990.

Growdon JH, Corkin S, Rosen JT: Distinctive aspects of cognitive dysfunction in Parkinson's disease. In Streifler M (Editor), *Parkinson's Disease. Advances in Neurology*. New York: Raven Press, pp. 365 – 376, 1990.

Gurd JM, Ward CD: Retrieval from semantic and letter-initial categories in patients with Parkinson's disease. *Neuropsychologia: 27*, 743 – 746, 1989.

Hakim A, Mathieson G: Dementia in Parkinson's disease. A neuropathologic study. *Neurology: 29*, 1209 – 1214, 1979.

Halgin R, Riklan M, Mishiak H: Levodopa, Parkinsonism and recent memory. *J. Nerv. Ment. Dis.: 164*, 268 – 272, 1977.

Hardyck C, Petrinovich LA: The pattern of intellectual functioning in Parkinson patients. *J. Consult. Psychol.: 27*, 548, 1963.

Heindel WC, Salmon DP, Shults CW, Wallcke PA, Butters N: Neuropsychological evidence for multiple implicit memory systems: a comparison of Alzheimer's and Parkinson's disease patients. *J. Neurosci.: 9*, 582 – 587, 1989.

Helkala EL, Laulumaa U, Soininen H, Riekkinen PJ: Different error pattern of episodic and semantic memory in Alzheimer's disease and Parkinson's disease with dementia. *Neuropsychologia: 27*, 1241 – 1248, 1989.

Hepler DJ, Olton DS, Wenk GL, Coyle JT: Lesions in nucleus basalis magnocellularis and medial septal area of rats produce qualitatively similar memory impairments. *J. Neurosci.: 5*, 866 – 873, 1985.

Hershey LA: Organic mental syndrome in Parkinson's disease. *Arch. Neurol.: 39*, 456 – 457, 1982.

Hietanen M, Teräväinen H: Cognitive performance in early Parkinson's disease. *Acta Neurol. Scand.: 73*, 151 – 159, 1986.

Hietanen M, Teräväinen H: The effect of age of disease onset on neuropsychological performance in Parkinson's disease. *J. Neurol. Neurosurg. Psychiatry: 51*, 244 – 249, 1988a.

Hietanen M, Teräväinen H: Dementia and treatment with L-DOPA in Parkinson's disease. *Movement Disorders: 3*, 263 – 270, 1988b.

Hietanen M, Teräväinen H: Visuospatial rotation in nontreated Parkinsonism (Abstract). *Neurology: 40, Suppl. 1*, 336, 1990.

Hirsch E, Graybiel AM, Duyckaerts C, Javoy-Agid F: Neuronal loss in the pedunculopontine tegmental nucleus in Parkinson's disease and in progressive supranuclear palsy. *Proc. Natl. Acad. Sci. USA: 84*, 5976 – 5980, 1987.

Hirsch EC, Graybiel AM, Agid Y: Melanized dopaminergic neurons are differentially affected in Parkinson's disease. *Nature: 334*, 345 – 348, 1988.

Hoehn MM, Yahr MD: Parkinsonism: Onset, progression and mortality. *Neurology: 17*, 427 – 442, 1967.

Hornykiewicz O: Parkinson's disease and its chemotherapy. *Biochem. Pharmacol.: 24*, 1061 – 1065, 1975.

Hovestadt A, De Jong JG, Meerwaldt JD: Spatial disorientation as an early symptom of Parkinson's disease. *Neurology: 37*, 485 – 487, 1987a.

Hovestadt A, De Jong JG, Meerwaldt JD: Visuo-spatial impairment in Parkinson's disease. Does it exist? Letter to the Editor. *J. Neurol. Neurosurg. Psychiatry: 50*, 1560, 1987b.

Huber SJ, Paulson GW: Relationship between primitive reflexes and severity in Parkinson's disease. *J. Neurol. Neurosurg. Psychiatry: 49,* 1298 – 1300, 1986.

Huber SJ, Shuttleworth EL, Paulson GW: Dementia in Parkinson's disease. *Arch. Neurol.: 43,* 987 – 990, 1986.

Huber SJ, Shulman HG, Paulson GW, Shuttleworth EC: Fluctuations in plasma dopamine level impair memory in Parkinson's disease. *Neurology: 37,* 1371 – 1375, 1987.

Huber SJ, Shulman HG, Paulson GW, Shuttleworth EL: Dose dependent memory impairment in Parkinson's disease. *Neurology: 39,* 438 – 440, 1989a.

Huber SJ, Shuttleworth EC, Christy JA, Chakeres DW, Curtin A, Paulson GW: Magnetic resonance imaging in dementia of Parkinson's disease. *J. Neurol. Neurosurg. Psychiatry: 52,* 1221 – 1227, 1989b.

Huber SJ, Shuttleworth EC, Freidenberg DO: Neuropsychological differences between dementia of Alzheimer's and Parkinson's disease. *Arch. Neurol.: 46,* 1287 – 1291, 1989c.

Huff FJ: Language in normal aging and age-related neurological disease. In Boller F, Grafman J (Editors), *Handbook of Neuropsychology, Vol. 4.* Amsterdam: Elsevier, pp. 251 – 264, 1990.

Illes J, Metter EJ, Hanson WR, Iritani S: Language production in Parkinson's disease. Acoustic and linguistic considerations. *Brain Lang.: 33,* 146 – 160, 1987.

Iversen S: Cortical monoamines and behavior. In Descarries L, Reader TA, Jasper HH (Editors), *Monoamine Innervation of Cerebral Cortex.* New York: Alan R. Liss, pp. 321 – 349, 1984.

Javoy-Agid F, Agid Y: Is the mesocortical dopaminergic system involved in Parkinson's disease. *Neurology: 30,* 1326 – 1330, 1980.

Jellinger K: Pathology of Parkinsonism. In Fahn S, Marsden CD, Jenner P, Teychenne P (Editors), *Recent Developments in Parkinson's Disease.* New York: Raven Press, pp. 33 – 66, 1986.

Jellinger K: The pedunculopontine nucleus in Parkinson's disease, progressive supranuclear palsy and Alzheimer's disease. *J. Neurol. Neurosurg. Psychiatry: 51,* 540 – 543, 1988.

Kertesz A: *Aphasia and Associated Disorders: Taxonomy, Localization and Recovery.* New York: Grune and Stratton, 1979.

Khachaturian Z: Diagnosis of Alzheimer's disease. *Arch. Neurol.: 42,* 1097 – 1105, 1985.

Kish SJ, Shannak K, Hornykiewicz O: Uneven pattern of dopamine loss in the striatum of patients with idiopathic Parkinson's disease – pathophysiologic and clinical implications. *N. Engl. J. Med.: 318,* 14: 876 – 880, 1988.

Knopman DS, Nissen MJ: Implicit learning in patients with probable Alzheimer's disease. *Neurology: 37,* 784 – 788, 1987.

Knopman DS, Mastri AR, Frey DH, Sung JH, Rustan T: Dementia lacking distinctive histologic features: a common non-Alzheimer degenerative dementia. *Neurology: 40,* 251 – 256, 1990.

Koob GF, Simon H, Herman JP, Le Moal M: Neuroleptic-like disruption of the conditioned avoidance response requires destruction of both the mesolimbic and nigrostriatal dopamine systems. *Brain Res.: 303,* 319 – 329, 1984.

Laplane D, Levasseur M, Pillon B, Dubois B, Baulac M, Mazoyer B, Tran Dinh S, Sette G, Danzé F, Baron JC: Obsessive-compulsive and other behavioral changes with bilateral basal ganglia lesions. A neuropsychological, magnetic resonance imaging and positron tomography study. *Brain: 112,* 699 – 725, 1989.

Lavernhe G, Pollak P, Brenier F, Gaio JM, Hommel M, Pellat J, Perret J: Maladie d'Alzheimer et maladie de Parkinson. Différentiation neuropsychologique. *Rev. Neurol.: 145,* 24 – 30, 1989.

Lees AJ: Parkinson's disease and dementia. *Lancet: 1,* 43 – 44, 1985.

Lees AJ, Smith E: Cognitive deficits in the early stages of Parkinson's Disease. *Brain: 106,* 257 – 270, 1983.

Lesser RP, Fahn S, Snider SR, Cote LJ, Isgreen WP, Barret RE: Analysis of the clinical problems in parkinsonism and the complications of long-term levodopa therapy. *Neurology: 29,* 1253 – 1260, 1979.

Leverenz J, Sumi SM: Parkinson's disease in patients with Alzheimer's disease. *Arch. Neurol.: 43,* 662 – 664, 1986.

Levin BE, Llabre MM, Weiner WJ: Cognitive impairments associated with early Parkinson's disease. *Neurology: 39,* 557 – 561, 1989.

Lewy FH: *Die Lehre von Tonus und der Bewegung zugleich systematische Untersuchungen sur Klinik, Physiologie, Pathologie und Pathogenese der Paralysis Agitans.* Berlin: Springer, 1923.

Lezak MD: Executive functions. In Lezak MD (Editor), *Neuropsychological Assessment.* New York: Oxford University Press, 1983.

Lhermitte F, Pillon B, Serdaru M: Human autonomy and the frontal lobes – I: Imitation and utilization behaviors: a neuropsychological study of 75 patients. *Ann. Neurol.: 19,* 326 – 334, 1986.

Lichter DG, Corbett AJ, Fitzgibbon GM, Davidson DR, Hope JK, Goddard GV, Sharples KJ, Pollock M: Cognitive and motor dysfunction in Parkinson's disease. *Arch. Neurol.: 45,* 854 – 860, 1988.

Lieberman A, Dziatolowski M, Kupersmith M, Serby M, Goodgold A, Korein J, Goldstein M: Dementia in Parkinson Disease. *Ann. Neurol.: 6,* 355 – 359, 1979.

Loranger AW, Goodell H, McDowell F, Lee JE, Sweet RD: Intellectual impairment in Parkinson's syndrome. *Brain: 95,* 405 – 412, 1972a.

Loranger AW, Goodell H, Lee JE, McDowell F: Levodopa treatment of Parkinson's syndrome. Improved intellectual functioning. *Arch. Gen. Psychiatry: 26,* 163 – 168, 1972b.

Luchsinger R, Arnold GE: *Voice-Speech-Language.* London: Constable, 1965.

Luria AR: *Higher Cortical Functions in Man.* New York: Basic Books, 1966.

Mann DMA, Yates PO, Hawkes J: The pathology of the human locus coeruleus. *Clin. Neuropathol.: 2,* 1 – 7, 1983.

Marsh GG, Markham CM, Ansel R: Levodopa's awakening effect on patients with Parkinsonism. *J. Neurol. Neurosurg. Psychiatry: 34,* 209 – 218, 1971.

Martin DC, Miller J, Arena V, Kapoor W, Boller F: A controlled study of survival with dementia. Historical prospective study with age/sex matched controls. *Arch. Neurol.: 44,* 1122 – 1126, 1987.

Martin WE, Loewenson RB, Resch JA, Baker AB: Parkinson's disease. Clinical analysis of 100 patients. *Neurology: 23,*

783 – 790, 1973.

Martin WRW, Stoessel AJ, Adam MJ, Ammann W, Bergstrom M, Harrop R, Laihinen A, Rogers JG, Ruth TJ, Sayre CI, Pate BD, Calne DB: Positron emission tomography in Parkinson's disease: glucose and Dopa metabolism. In Yahr MD, Bergmann KJ (Editors), *Parkinson's Disease. Advances in Neurology 45.* New York: Raven Press, pp. 95 – 98, 1986.

Martone M, Butters N, Payne M, Becker JT, Sax DS: Dissociations between skill learning and verbal recognition in amnesia and dementia. *Arch. Neurol.: 41,* 965 – 970, 1984.

Marttila RJ, Rinne UK: Dementia in Parkinson's disease. *Acta Neurol. Scand.: 54,* 431 – 441, 1976.

Matison R, Mayeux R, Rosen J, Fahn S: 'Tip-of-the-tongue' phenomenon in Parkinson disease. *Neurology: 32,* 567 – 570, 1982.

Matthews CG, Haaland KY: The effect of symptom duration on cognitive and motor performance in Parkinsonism. *Neurology: 29,* 251 – 256, 1979.

Mayeux R: Mental State. In Koller WC (Editor), *Handbook of Parkinson's Disease.* New York: Marcel Dekker, pp. 127 – 144, 1987.

Mayeux R, Stern Y: Intellectual dysfunction and dementia in Parkinson's disease. In Mayeux R, Rosen WG (Editors), *The Dementias.* New York: Raven Press, pp. 211 – 227, 1983.

Mayeux R, Stern Y, Rosen J, Leventhal J: Depression, intellectual impairment and Parkinson disease. *Neurology: 31,* 645 – 650, 1981.

Mayeux R, Stern Y, Rosen J, Benso DF: 'Subcortical dementia': a recognizable clinical entity? *Ann. Neurol.: 14,* 278 – 283, 1983.

Mayeux R, Stern Y, Cote L, Williams JBW: Altered serotonin metabolism in depressed patients with Parkinson's disease. *Neurology: 34,* 642 – 646, 1984.

Mayeux R, Stern Y, Williams JBW, Frantz A, Cote L, Dyrenfurth I: Clinical and biochemical features of depression in Parkinson's disease. *Am. J. Psychiatry: 143,* 756 – 759, 1985.

Mayeux R, Stern Y, Sano M, Cote L, Williams JBW: Clinical and biochemical correlates of bradyphrenia in Parkinson's disease. *Neurology: 37,* 1130 – 1134, 1987.

Mayeux R, Stern Y, Rosenstein, Marder K, Hauser A, Cote L, Fahn S: An estimate of the prevalence of dementia in idiopathic Parkinson's disease. *Arch. Neurol.: 45,* 260 – 262, 1988.

McMenemey WH: James Parkinson (1755 – 1824). A biographical essay. In Critchley M (Editor), *James Parkinson (1755 – 1824).* London: MacMillan, 1955.

Meier M, Martin W: Intellectual changes associated with levodopa therapy. *J. Am. Med. Assoc.: 213,* 465 – 466, 1970.

Mildworf B 1978. Cited by Bayles and Kaszniak, 1987.

Milner B: Effects of different brain lesions on card sorting: the role of the frontal lobes. *Arch. Neurol.: 9,* 90 – 11, 1963.

Milner B: Some effects of frontal lobectomy in man. In Warren, Akert K (Editors), *The Frontal Granular Cortex and Behavior.* New York: McGraw-Hill, pp. 313 – 331, 1964.

Milner B, Petrides M: Behavioural effects of frontal-lobe lesions in man. *Trends Neurosci.: 7,* 403 – 407, 1984.

Mindham RHS: Psychiatric symptoms in Parkinsonism. *J. Neurol. Neurosurg. Psychiatry: 33,* 188 – 191, 1970.

Mindham RHS, Ahmed SWA, Clough CG: A controlled study of dementia in Parkinson's disease. *J. Neurol. Neurosurg.*

Psychiatry: 45, 969 – 974, 1982.

Mishkin M, Malamut B, Bachevalier J: Memories and habits: two neural systems. In Lynch G, McGaugh JL, Weinberger NM (Editors), *Neurobiology of Learning and Memory.* New York: Guilford Press, pp. 65 – 77, 1984.

Mjönes H: Paralysis agitans, a clinical and genetic study. *Acta Psychiatr. Neurol. Scand. Suppl.: 54,* 1 – 195, 1949.

Mohr E, Fabbrini G, Ruggieri S, Fedio P, Chase TN: Cognitive concomitans of dopamine system stimulation in Parkinsonians patients. *J. Neurol. Neurosurg. Psychiatry: 50,* 1192 – 1196, 1987.

Mohr E, Fabbrini G, Williams J, Schlegel J, Cox C, Fedio P, Chase TN: Dopamine and memory function in Parkinson's disease. *Movement Disorders, 4:* 113 – 120, 1989.

Morel-Maroger A: Effects of levodopa on 'frontal' signs in parkinsonism. *Br. Med. J.: 2,* 1543 – 1544, 1977.

Morris RG, Downes JJ, Sahakian BJ, Evenden JL, Heald A, Robbins TW: Planning and spatial working memory in Parkinson's disease. *J. Neurol. Neurosurg. Psychiatry: 51,* 757 – 766, 1988.

Mortimer JA, Pirozzolo FJ, Hansch EC, Webster DD: Relationship of motor symptoms to intellectual deficits in Parkinson disease. *Neurology: 32,* 133 – 137, 1982.

Nagatsu T, Kato T, Nagatsu I, Kondo Y, Inagaki S, Iizuka R, Narabayashi H: Catecholamine related enzymes in the brain of patients with parkinsonism and Wilson's disease. In Poirier LJ, Sourkes TL, Bedard PJ (Editors), *The Extrapyramidal System and its Disorders. Advances in Neurology, 24.* New York: Raven Press, pp. 283 – 292, 1979.

Nahmias C, Garnett ES, Firnau G, Lang A: Striatal dopamine distribution in Parkinsonian patients during life. *J. Neurol. Sci.: 69,* 223 – 230, 1985.

Naville F: Les complications et les séquelles mentales de l'encéphalite épidémique. *Encéphale: 17,* 369 – 375, 423 – 436, 1922.

Nelson HE: Modified card sorting test sensitive to frontal lobe defects. *Cortex: 12,* 313 – 324, 1976.

Newcombe F: *Missile Wounds of the Brain: A Study of Psychological Deficits.* London: Oxford University Press, 1969.

Newcombe F, Ratcliff G: Disorders of visuospatial analysis. In Boller F, Grafman J (Editors), *Handbook of Neuropsychology, Vol. 2.* Amsterdam: Elsevier, pp. 333 – 356, 1989.

Newman RP, Weingartner H, Smallberg SA, Calne DB: Effortful and automatic memory: effects of dopamine. *Neurology: 34,* 805 – 807, 1984.

Nilsson OE, Strecker RE, Daszuta A, Bjorklund A: Combined cholinergic and serotonergic denervation of the forebrain produces severe deficits in a special learning task in the rat. *Brain Res.: 453,* 235 – 246, 1988.

Norman DA, Shallice T: Attention to action: willed and automatic control of behaviour. University of California. Report 99, 1980.

Oberg RGE, Divac I: 'Cognitive' functions of the neostriatum. In Divac I, Oberg RGE (Editors), *The Neostriatum.* Oxford: Pergamon Press, pp. 241 – 313, 1979.

Ogden JA: Spatial abilities and deficits in aging and age-related disorders. In Boller F, Grafman J (Editors), *Handbook of Neuropsychology, Vol. 4.* Amsterdam: Elsevier, pp. 265 – 278, 1990.

Ogden JA, Growdon JH, Corkin S: Deficits on visuospatial tests involving forward planning in high-functioning Parkinsonians. *Neuropsychiatry, Neuropsychol. Behav. Neurol.: 3*, 125 – 139, 1990.

Okasaki H, Lipkin LE, Aronson SM: Diffuse intracytoplasmic ganglionic inclusions (Lewy type) associated with progressive dementia and quadriparesis in flexion. *J. Neuropathol. Exp. Neurol.: 20*, 237 – 244, 1961.

Oyebode JR, Barker WA, Blessed G, Dick DJ, Britton PG: Cognitive functioning in Parkinson's disease. *Br. J. Psychiatry: 149*, 720 – 725, 1986.

Parkinson J: *An Essay on the Shaking Palsy*. London: Sherwood, Neely, and Jones, 1817.

Partiot A, Verin M, Dubois B, Pillon B, Agid Y: Delayed response tasks and basal ganglia lesions in man (In preparation).

Patrick HT, Levy DM: Parkinson's disease. A clinical study of 146 cases. *Arch. Neurol. Psychiatry: 7*, 711 – 720, 1922.

Perry EK: The cholinergic hypothesis: 10 years on. *Br. Med. Bull.: 42*, 63 – 69, 1986.

Perry EK, Curtis M, Dick DJ, Candy JM, Atack JR, Bloxham CA, Blessed G, Fairbairn A, Tomlinson B, Perry RH: Cholinergic correlates of cognitive impairment in Parkinson's disease: comparisons with Alzheimer's disease. *J. Neurol. Neurosurg. Psychiatry: 48*, 413 – 421, 1985.

Peterson LR, Peterson MJ: Short-term retention of individual verbal items. *J. Exp. Psychol.: 58*, 193 – 198, 1959.

Petrides M: Deficits in conditional associative-learning tasks after frontal and temporal lobe lesions in man. *Neuropsychologia: 23*, 601 – 614, 1985.

Petrides M: Frontal lobes and memory. In Boller F, Grafman J (Editors), *Handbook of Neuropsychology, Vol. 3*. Amsterdam: Elsevier, pp. 75 – 90, 1989.

Petrides M, Milner B: Deficits on subject ordered tasks after frontal and temporal-lobe lesions in man. *Neuropsychologia: 20*, 249 – 262, 1982.

Piccirilli M, Piccinin GL, Agostini L: Characteristic clinical aspects of Parkinsonian patients. *Eur. Neurol.: 23*, 44 – 50, 1984.

Pierot L, Desnos C, Blin J, Raisman R, Scherman D, Javoy-Agid F, Ruberg M, Agid Y: D1 and D2 type dopamine receptors in patients with Parkinson's disease and progressive supranuclear palsy. *J. Neurol. Sci.: 86*, 291 – 306, 1988.

Pillon B, Dubois B, Lhermitte F, Agid Y: Heterogeneity of cognitive impairment in progressive supranuclear palsy, Parkinson's disease and Alzheimer's disease. *Neurology: 36*, 1179 – 1185, 1986.

Pillon B, Dubois B, Bonnet AM, Esteguy M, Guimaraes J, Vigouret JM, Lhermitte F, Agid Y: Cognitive 'slowing' in Parkinson's disease fails to respond to levodopa treatment: 'The 15 objects test'. *Neurology: 39*, 762 – 768, 1989a.

Pillon B, Dubois B, Cusimano G, Bonnet AM, Lhermitte F, Agid Y: Does cognitive impairment in Parkinson's disease result from non-dopaminergic lesions? *J. Neurol. Neurosurg. Psychiatry: 52*, 201 – 206, 1989b.

Pillon B, Dubois B, Ploska A, Agid Y: Neuropsychological specificity of dementia in Alzheimer's, Huntington's, Parkinson's diseases and progressive supranuclear palsy. *Neurology* (in press), 1991.

Pirozzolo FJ, Hansch EC, Mortimer JA, Webster DD, Kuskowski MA: Dementia in Parkinson disease. A neuro-psychological analysis. *Brain Cognition: 1*, 71 – 83, 1982.

Pollock M, Hornabrook RW: The prevalence, natural history and dementia of Parkinson's disease. *Brain: 89*, 429 – 448, 1966.

Portin R, Rinne UK: Neuropsychological response of parkinsonian patients to long-term levodopa therapy. In Klinger M, Stamm G (Editors), *Parkinsonin's Disease. Current Progress, Problems and Management*. Elsevier: Amsterdam, pp. 271 – 304, 1980.

Portin R, Rinne UK: Predicitve factors for dementia in Parkinson's disease. *Acta Neurol. Scand.: 69 (Supplement 98)*, 57 – 58, 1984.

Portin R, Raininko R, Rinne UK: Neuropsychological disturbances and cerebral atrophy determined by computerized tomography in Parkinsonian patients with long-term levodopa treatment. In Hassler RG, Christ JF (Editors), *Advances in Neurology, Vol. 40: Parkinson-Specific Motor and Mental Disorders*. New York: Raven Press, pp. 219 – 227, 1984.

Price KS, Farley IJ, Hornykiewicz O: Neurochemistry of Parkinson's disease: relation between striatal and limbic dopamine. *Adv. Biochem. Psychopharmacol.: 19*, 293 – 300, 1978.

Proctor F, Riklan M, Cooper ST, Teuber HL: Judgement of visual and postural vertical by Parkinsonism patients. *Neurology: 14*, 287 – 293, 1964.

Pullman SL, Watts RL, Juncos JL, Chase TN, Sanes JN: Dopaminergic effects on simple and choice reaction time performance in Parkinson's disease. *Neurology: 38*, 249 – 254, 1988.

Quinn N, Critchley P, Marsden CD: Young onset parkinson's disease. *Movement Disorders: 2*, 73 – 91, 1987.

Rafal RD, Posner MI, Walker JA, Friedrich FJ: Cognition and the basal ganglia: separating mental and motor components on performance in Parkinson's disease. *Brain: 107*, 1083 – 1094, 1984.

Raisman R, Cash R, Agid Y: Parkinson's disease: decreased density of ³H-imipramine and ³H-paroxetine binding sites in the putamen. *Neurology: 36*, 556 – 560, 1986.

Rajput AH, Rozdilsky B: Parkinsonism and dementia: effects of levodopa. *Lancet: i*, 1084, 1975.

Rajput AH, Offord K, Beard CM, Kurland LT: Epidemiological survey of dementia in parkinsonism and control population. In Hassler RG, Christ JF (Editors), *Advances in Neurology, Vol. 40, Parkinson-Specific Motor and Mental Disorders*. New York: Raven Press, pp. 229 – 234, 1984.

Ransmayr G, Poewe W, Ploerer S, Birbamer G, Gerstenbrand F: Psychometric findings in clinical subtypes of Parkinson's disease. *Adv. Neurol.: 45*, 409 – 411, 1986.

Ransmayr G, Schmidhuber-Eiler B, Karamat E, Engler-Plörer S, Poewe W, Leidlmair K: Visuoperception and visuospatial and visuorotational performance in Parkinson's disease. *J. Neurol.: 235*, 99 – 101, 1987.

Reid WGJ, Broe GA, Hely MA, Morris JGL, Genge SA, Moss NG, O'Sullivan PM, Rail D: The evolution of dementia in idiopathic Parkinson's disease. Neuropsychological and clinical evidence in support of suptypes. Paper presented at the First International Congress of Movement Disorders, Washington DC, April 25, 1990.

Reitan RM, Boll TJ: Intellectual and Cognitive functions in Parkinson's disease. *J. Consult. Clin. Psychol.: 37*, 364 – 369, 1971.

Riederer P, Wuketich S: Time course of nigrostriatal degeneration in Parkinson's disease. *J. Neural. Transm.: 38,* 277 – 301, 1976.

Riklan M, Whelihan W, Cullinan T: Levodopa and psychometric test performance in Parkinsonism – five years later. *Neurology: 26,* 173 – 179, 1976.

Rinne JO, Rummukainen J, Paljärui L, Rinne UK: Dementia in parkinson's disease is related to neuronal loss in the medial substantia nigra. *Ann. Neurol.: 26,* 47 – 50, 1989.

Rogers D. Bradyphrenia in parkinsonism. *Rev. Psychol. Med.: 16,* 257 – 266, 1986.

Rogers D, Lees AJ, Smith E, Trimble M, Stern GM: Bradyphrenia in Parkinson's disease and psychomotor retardation in depressive illness: an experimental study. *Brain: 110,* 761 – 776, 1987.

Rogers MW, Chan CW: Motor planning is impaired in parkinson's disease. *Brain Res.: 438,* 271 – 276, 1988.

Romberg M: *Lehrbuch der Nervenkrankheiten des Menschen.* Berlin: A. Duncker, 1840.

Rosen WG: Verbal fluency in aging and dementia. *J. Clin. Neuropsychol.: 2,* 135 – 146, 1980.

Ruberg M, Agid Y: Dementia in Parkinson's disease. In Iversen L, Iversen SD, Snyder SH (Editors), *Handbook of Psychopharmacology, Vol. 20: Psychopharmacology of the Aging Nervous System.* New York: Plenum Press, pp. 157 – 206, 1988.

Ruberg M, Ploska A, Javoy-Agid F, Agid Y: Muscarinic binding and choline acetyltransferase in Parkinsonian subjects with reference to dementia. *Brain Res.: 232,* 129 – 139, 1982.

Sacks OW, Kohl MS, Messeloff CR, Schwartz WF: Effects of levodopa in Parkinsonian patients with dementia. *Neurology: 22,* 516 – 519, 1972.

Sadeh M, Braham J, Modan M: Effects of anticholinergic drugs on memory in Parkinson's disease. *Arch. Neurol.: 39,* 666 – 667, 1982.

Sagar HJ, Cohen NJ, Sullivan EV, Corkin S, Growdon JH: Remote memory function in Alzheimer's disease and Parkinson's disease. *Brain: 111,* 185 – 206, 1988a.

Sagar HJ, Sullivan EV, Gabrieli JD, Corkin S, Growdon JH: Temporal ordering and short-term memory deficits in Parkinson's disease. *Brain: 111,* 525 – 535, 1988b.

Sahakian BJ, Morris RG, Evenden JL, Heald A, Levy R, Philpot M, Robbins TW: A comparative study of visuospatial memory and learning in Alzheimer's-type dementia and Parkinson's disease. *Brain: 111,* 695 – 718, 1988.

Saint-Cyr JA, Taylor AE, Lang AE: Procedural learning and neostriatal dysfunction in man. *Brain: 111,* 941 – 959, 1988.

Sano M, Stern Y, Williams J, Coté L, Rosenstein R, Mayeux R: Coexisting dementia and depression in Parkinson's disease. *Arch. Neurol.: 46,* 1284 – 1286, 1989.

Santamaria J, Tolosa E, Valles A. Parkinson's disease with depression: a possible subgroup of idiopathic parkinsonism. *Neurology: 36,* 1130 – 1133, 1986.

Saxton J: Correlation of neuropsychological tests with ADL. (In preparation).

Scatton B, Javoy-Agid F, Rouquier L, Dubois B, Agid Y: Reduction of cortical dopamine, noradrenaline, serotonin and their metabolites in Parkinson's disease. *Brain Res.: 275,* 321 – 328, 1983.

Scherman D, Desnos C, Darchen F, Javoy-Agid F, Agid Y:

Striatal dopamine deficiency in Parkinson's disease: role of aging. *Ann. Neurol.: 26,* 551 – 557, 1989.

Schneider E, Becker H, Fischer PA, Grau H, Jacobi P, Brinkmann R: The course of brain atrophy in Parkinson's disease. *Arch. Psychiatr. Nervenhr.: 227,* 89 – 95, 1979.

Schwab RS, Chafetz ME, Walker S: Control of two simultaneous voluntary motor acts in normal and in parkinsonism. *Arch. Neurol. Psychiatr.: 75,* 591 – 598, 1954.

Scott S, Caird FI, Williams BO: Evidence for an apparent sensory speech disorder in Parkinson's disease. *J. Neurol. Neurosurg. Psychiatry: 47,* 840 – 843, 1984.

Shallice T: Specific impairments of planning. *Phil. Trans. R. Soc. Lond. B: 298,* 199 – 209, 1982.

Shiffrin RM, Schneider W: Controlled and automatic human information processing – II: Perceptual learning, automatic attending, and a general theory. *Psychol. Rev.: 84,* 127 – 192, 1977.

Simon H, Scatton B, Le Moal M: Dopaminergic A10 neurones are involved in cognitive functions. *Nature: 286,* 150 – 151, 1980.

Sitaram N, Weingartner H, Gillin JC: Human serial learning: enhancement with arecholine and choline and impairment with scopolamine. *Science: 201,* 274 – 276, 1978.

Spinnler H, Della Sala S: Visuo-spatial impairment in Parkinson's disease. Does it exist? *J. Neurol. Neurosurg. Psychiatry: 50,* 1560 – 1561, 1987.

Spinnler H, Della Sala S, Marchetti C: The riddle of frontal involvement in Parkinson disease. (In preparation).

Squire LR: Effects of pretrial and postrial administration of cholinergic and anticholinergic drugs on spontaneous alternation. *J. Comp. Physiol. Psychol.: 69,* 69 – 75, 1969.

Squire LR: *Memory of Brain.* Oxford: Oxford University Press, 1987.

Squire LR (Topic Editor): Memory and its disorders. In Boller F, Grafman J (Editors). *Handbook of Neuropsychology, Vol. 3.* Amsterdam: Elsevier, 1989.

Sroka H, Elizan TS, Yahr MD, Burger A, Medazu M: Organic mental syndrome and confusional states in Parkinson's disease: relationship to computerized signs of cerebral atrophy. *Arch. Neurol.: 38,* 339 – 342, 1981.

Starkstein SE, Esteguy M, Berthier ML, Garcia H, Leiguarda R: Evoked potentials reaction time and cognitive performance in on and off phases of Parkinson's disease. *J. Neurol. Neurosurg. Psychiatry: 52,* 338 – 340, 1989a.

Starkstein SE, Preziosi TJ, Berthier ML, Bolduc PL, Mayberg HS, Robinson RG: Depression and cognitive impairment in Parkinson's disease. *Brain: 112,* 1141 – 1153, 1989b.

Steiner I, Gomori JM, Melamed E: Features of brain atrophy in parkinson's disease. A CT-scan study. *Neuroradiology: 27,* 158 – 160, 1985.

Stelmach GE, Phillips JG, Chau AW: Visuo-spatial processing in Parkinsonians. *Neuropsychologia: 27,* 485 – 493, 1989.

Stern Y: The basal ganglia and intellectual function. Basal ganglia and behavior. In Schneider J, Lidsky T (Editors), *Sensory Aspects of Motor Functioning.* Hans Huber Publishers, pp. 169 – 174, 1987.

Stern Y, Langston JW: Intellectual changes in patients with MPTP-induced Parkinsonism. *Neurology: 35,* 1506 – 1509, 1985.

Stern Y, Mayeux R, Rosen J, Ilson J: Perceptual motor dysfunction in Parkinson's disease: a deficit in sequential and predictive voluntary movement. *J. Neurol. Neurosurg. Psychiatry: 46*, 145 – 151, 1983.

Stern Y, Mayeux R, Rosen J: Contribution of perceptual motor dysfunction to construction and tracing disturbances in Parkinson's disease. *J. Neurol. Neurosurg. Psychiatry: 47*, 983 – 989, 1984a.

Stern Y, Mayeux R, Cote L: Reaction time and vigilance in Parkinson's disease: possible role of norepinephrine metabolism. *Arch. Neurol.: 41*, 1086 – 1089, 1984b.

Stern Y, Tetrud JW, Martin WR, Kutner SJ, Langston JW: Cognitive changes following MPTP exposure. *Neurology: 40*, 261 – 264, 1990.

Sternberg S: Memory scanning: New finding and current controversies. *Q. J. Exp. Psychol.: 27*, 1 – 32, 1975.

Storandt M: Longitudinal studies of aging and age-associated dementias. In Boller F, Grafman J (Editors), *Handbook of Neuropsychology, Vol. 4.* Amsterdam: Elsevier, pp. 349 – 364, 1990.

Strang RR: Imipramine in treatment of parkinsonism: a double blind placebo study. *Br. Med. J.: 2*, 33 – 34, 1976.

Stroop JR: Studies of interferences in serial verbal reactions. *J. Exp. Neurol.: 18*, 643 – 662, 1935.

Sullivan EV, Sagar HJ: Nonverbal recognition and recency discrimination deficits in Parkinson's disease and Alzheimer's disease. *Brain: 112*, 1503 – 1517, 1989a.

Sullivan EV, Sagar HJ. Gabrieli JD, Corkin S, Growdon JH: Different cognitive profiles on standard behavioral tests in Parkinson's disease and Alzheimer's disease. *J. Clin. Exp. Neuropsychol.: 11*, 799 – 820, 1989b.

Sweet RD, McDowell FH, Feigenson JS, Loranger AW, Goodell H: Mental symptoms in Parkinson's disease during chronic treatment with levodopa. *Neurology: 26*, 305 – 310, 1976.

Taghzouti K, Simon H, Herve D: Behavioural deficits induced by electrolytic lesion of the rat mesencephalic tegmentum are correlated by a superimposed lesion of the dorsal noradrenergic system. *Brain Res.: 440*, 172 – 176, 1988.

Talland GA: Cognitive function in Parkinson's disease. *J. Nerv. Ment. Dis.: 135*, 196 – 205, 1962.

Talland GA, Schwab RS: Performance with multiple sets in Parkinson's disease. *Neuropsychologia: 2*, 45 – 53, 1964.

Taylor A, Saint-Cyr JA, Lang AE: Dementia prevalence in Parkinson's disease. Letter to the Editor. *Lancet: i*, 1037, 1985.

Taylor AE, Saint-Cyr JA, Lang AE: Frontal lobe dysfunction in Parkinson's disease. *Brain: 109*, 845 – 883, 1986.

Taylor AE, Saint-Cyr JA, Lang AE: Parkinson's disease: cognitive changes in relation to treatment response. *Brain: 110*, 35 – 51, 1987.

Taylor AE, Saint-Cyr JA, Lang AE: Idiopathic Parkinson's disease: revised concepts of cognitive and affective status. *Can. J. Neurol. Sci.: 15*, 106 – 113, 1988.

Terry RD: Aging, senile dementia and Alzheimer's disease. In Katzman R, Terry RD, Bick KL (Editors), *Alzheimer's Disease: Senile Dementia and Related Disorders.* New York: Raven Press, 1978.

Teuber HL: The frontal lobes and their functions: further observations in carnivores, subhuman primates and man. *Int. J.*

Neurol.: 5, 282 – 300, 1966.

Teuber HL: Complex functions of basal ganglia. In Yahr MD (Editor), *The Basal Ganglia.* Association for Research in Nervous and Mental Disease. Publ. No. 55. New York: Raven Press, 1976.

Thompson R: Localization of the 'maze memory system' in the white rat. *Physiol. Psychol.: 2*, 1 – 7, 1974.

Todd RB: Paralysis. In Forbes J, Tweedie A, Conolly J (Editors), *The Cyclopedia of Clinical Medicine, Vol. III.* London, 1834.

Tomlison BE, Corsellis JAN: Ageing and the dementias. In Adams JH, Corsellis J, Duchen LW (Editors), *Greenfield's Neuropathology, 4th Edition.* Edward Arnold, pp. 951 – 1025, 1984.

Trousseau A: Tremblement sénile et paralysie agitante. Clinique médicale de l'Hôtel Dieu de Paris. Paris: Baillière, 1861.

Tweedy JR, Langer KG, McDowell FH: The effects of semantic relations on the memory deficit associated with Parkinson's disease. *J. Clin. Neuropsychol.: 4*, 235 – 247, 1982.

Tyler KL: A history of Parkinson's disease. In Koller WC (Editor), *Handbook of Parkinson's Disease.* New York: Marcel Dekker, pp. 1 – 33, 1987.

Villardita C, Smirni P, La Pira F, Zappala G, Nicoletti F: Mental deterioration, visuoperceptive disabilities and constructional apraxia in Parkinson's disease. *Acta Neurol. Scand.: 66*, 112 – 120, 1982.

Von Stockert FF: Subcortical Demenz. *Arch. Psychiatrie: 97*, 77 – 100, 1932.

Wagner HN: Imaging D-2 receptors in Parkinson's disease: a preliminary report. In Fahn S, Marsden CD, Jenner P, Teychenne P (Editors), *Recent Developments in Parkinson's Disease.* Raven Press: New York, pp. 115 – 118, 1986.

Warburton JW: Memory disturbance and the Parkinson syndrome. *Br. J. Med. Psychol.: 40*, 169 – 171, 1967.

Weingartner H, Burns S, Diebel R, Lewitt PA: Cognitive impairment in Parkinson's disease: distinguishing between effort-demanding and autonomic cognitive processes. *Psychiatry Res.: 11*, 223 – 235, 1984.

Whitehouse PJ, Hedreen JC, White CL, Price DL: Basal forebrain neurons in the dementia of Parkinson disease. *Ann. Neurol.: 13*, 243 – 248, 1983.

Whitehouse PJ: The concept of subcortical dementia: another look. *Ann. Neurol.: 10*, 122 – 126, 1986.

Wilkins AJ, Shallice T, McCarthy R: Frontal lesions and sustained attention. *Neuropsychologia: 25*, 359 – 365, 1987.

Wilson RS, Kaszniak AW, Klawans HL, Garron DC: High speed memory scanning in Parkinsonism. *Cortex: 16*, 67 – 72, 1980.

Xuereb J, Perry EK, Irving D, Blessed G, Tomlinson BE, Perry RH: Cortical and subcortical pathology in Parkinson's disease: relationship to parkinsonian dementia. In Boller F, Amaducci LA (Editors), *Clinico-pathological correlations of dementia in Parkinson's disease. Report of the Symposium,* Farmitalia Carlo Erba, Milano, Italy, 9-11-1989.

Yahr MD: a physician for all seasons. James Parkinson 1755 – 1824. *Arch. Neurol.: 35*, 185 – 188, 1978.

Zetuski W, Jankovic J, Pirozzolo P: The heterogeneity of Parkinson's disease. *Neurology: 35*, 522 – 526, 1985.

© 1991 Elsevier Science Publishers B.V.
Handbook of Neuropsychology, Vol. 5
F. Boller and J. Grafman (Eds)

CHAPTER 11

Cognitive impairments in Huntington's disease: insights into the neuropsychology of the striatum

Jason Brandt

The Johns Hopkins University School of Medicine, Baltimore, MD, U.S.A.

Introduction

Huntington's disease (HD) is a progressive neuro-degenerative disease characterized by the insidious onset of uncontrollable choreiform movements, impaired voluntary movement, cognitive deterioration and affective symptoms. Onset of symptoms is typically around age 40, but onset in childhood or late adulthood does occur. Juvenile onset has been associated with a rigid, akinetic form of the illness, severe intellectual impairment, and shorter survival (Merritt et al., 1969; Conneally, 1984; Bryois, 1989). Estimates of the prevalence of HD vary between 5 and 7 per 100,000 population (Conneally, 1984; Folstein, 1989). There is no cure for the illness and, at present, the only treatments are palliative. Symptoms progress relentlessly, with death occurring an average of 15 – 17 years after disease onset.

HD is inherited as an autosomal dominant trait with complete lifetime penetrance. Each son or daughter of an affected person has a 50% chance of inheriting the gene defect and eventually developing the disease. In 1983, a DNA marker very close to the HD gene was discovered distally on the short arm of chromosome 4, but the gene itself remains elusive.

Neuropathologically, HD is characterized by neuronal loss and gliosis in the striatum and, to a somewhat lesser extent, in the globus pallidus (Dom et al., 1976). Cell death typically begins in the dorsomedial region of the caudate nucleus and progresses ventrally and laterally (Vonsattel et al.,

1985). In addition, there appears to be some selectivity in the neuronal populations affected. The small spiny neurons of the caudate are the most severely affected, with relative preservation of somatostatin-containing aspiny neurons (Ferrante et al., 1985). In the later stages of illness, degeneration may also be found in the limbic system, cerebral cortex, and cerebellum (Bruyn et al., 1979).

In many ways, the genetic, epidemiological and clinical features that make HD such a tragic disease also make it extremely valuable for neuropsychological research and the establishment of structure-function relationships. First, unlike illnesses such as Alzheimer's disease (AD) and multi-infarct dementia (MID), HD typically has its onset in middle-age, before age-related cognitive decline typically occurs. Second, diagnosis is usually not too great a problem when the family is well known (cf. Folstein et al., 1986). Adult onset of a progressive movement disorder and cognitive decline or emotional symptoms in a person who has (or had) a parent similarly affected and a pedigree suggestive of autosomal dominant inheritance makes HD the likely diagnosis. Third, the cognitive syndrome is somewhat more selective than that in other dementing illnesses (e.g., AD). Fourth, the neuropathology of HD is relatively circumscribed and consistent. Finally, because HD is inherited as a single-gene dominant trait, half of all offspring of affected persons will develop the disease. This characteristic offers researchers the unique opportunity to study the ontogenesis of dementia, from before the earliest signs to expression of the full clinical syndrome.

Clinical description of dementia in HD

In the century since the early descriptions of HD (Huntington, 1872), there have appeared numerous accounts of its cognitive and psychiatric features. Because of the prominence of lesions in the basal ganglia, HD has been considered (along with Parkinson's disease, progressive supranuclear palsy and Wilson's disease) one of the 'subcortical dementias' (Albert et al., 1974; McHugh and Folstein, 1973, 1975). These disorders have been characterized psychologically by slowed thinking, learning and retrieval inefficiencies, impaired ability to operate on acquired information, and psychopathological symptoms (most notably irritability and apathy). Flagrant aphasia, agnosia and apraxia, the hallmarks of cortical involvement, are typically not seen in these diseases (Cummings and Benson, 1984). The differentiation of subcortical dementias from the cortical dementias (such as those caused by Alz-

heimer's, Creutzfeld-Jakob and Pick's diseases) remains controversial (Whitehouse, 1986). The distinction has been questioned on neuroanatomical grounds (Bruyn et al., 1979; Bondareff et al., 1982; Whitehouse et al., 1982), conceptual grounds (Whitehouse, 1986), and on empirical grounds as well (Mayeux et al., 1983). However, multiple neuropsychological studies have reported qualitative differences between the dementia of HD and dementias of other etiologies (Brouwers et al., 1984; Caine et al., 1986; Fisher et al., 1983; Mayeux et al., 1981; Moss et al., 1986).

In order to determine whether, at a coarse, clinical level, HD patients differ from patients with the paradigmatic cortical dementia, Brandt et al. (1988) studied large samples of HD patients and Alzheimer's disease (AD) patients stratified by overall level of cognitive functioning on the Mini-Mental State Exam (Folstein et al., 1975). Distinct group profiles that were independent of severity of dementia were obtained on the Mini-Mental. At every level of dementia, the HD patients performed worse than the AD patients on the attention item (serial subtraction of 7 from 100). In contrast, the AD patients

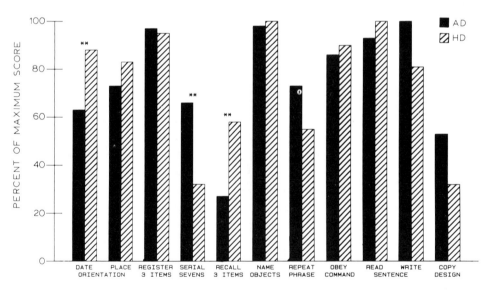

Fig. 1. Mini-Mental State Exam profiles of Alzheimer's disease (AD) patients (*n* = 30) and Huntington's disease (HD) patients (*n* = 31) with total Mini-Mental scores between 20 and 24. Double asterisks indicate that the differences are significant at *p* < 0.001. (From Brandt et al., 1988.)

displayed much more severe memory impairment than the HD patients, again independent of overall level of dementia (Fig. 1). The profile differences were sufficiently robust to classify 229 patients as having AD or HD with 84% accuracy using discriminant function analysis. In a small cross-validation sample of 18 AD and 13 HD patients, correct classification was again 84%. In order to determine whether the discriminant equation would distinguish patients with other cortical and subcortical dementias, it was applied to eight patients with Pick's disease and eight with Parkinson's disease (PD). Seven of the Pick's disease patients (88%) were classified with the ADs, and six of the PD patients (75%) were classified with the HDs. This suggests that the qualitative difference in cognitive functioning seen in AD and HD might also be applicable to other cortical and subcortical dementias. Recently, Salmon et al. (1989) essentially replicated this study, in smaller groups of HD and AD patients, using the Dementia Rating Scale (Mattis, 1976, 1988). Whether the differences found by Brandt et al. and Salmon et al. actually reflect the relative contributions of cortical and subcortical pathology remains unknown. Therefore, the concept of 'subcortical dementia' may be most useful at the clinical-descriptive level and as encouragement to explore the contributions of striatal and dien-cephalic mechanisms to the 'higher' mental functions (Buchwald et al., 1975; Rafal et al., 1984; Stern, 1983).

Cognitive characteristics of Huntington's disease

Intelligence test profiles

Early neuropsychological studies of HD relied extensively on the Wechsler Adult Intelligence Scale (WAIS) for the description of cognitive deficits. Typically, these studies found that HD patients undergo a gradual and generalized loss of cognitive abilities, the course of which roughly parallels that of the movement disorder (Aminoff et al., 1975). Norton (1975) compared six HD patients to a heterogeneous group of six brain-damaged control subjects and found that those with HD were selec-

tively impaired on the Arithmetic, Picture Completion and Object Assembly subtests of the WAIS. Subsequent studies confirmed a specific pattern of impairments on the WAIS, but found that the Arithmetic, Digit Span and Digit Symbol subtests, which have been considered to comprise a concentration and 'freedom from distraction' factor (Cohen, 1957; Matarazzo, 1972), are typically performed most poorly (Caine et al., 1978; Butters et al., 1978; Fedio et al., 1979; Josiassen et al., 1982; Brandt et al., 1984).

Neuropsychological batteries

In an early, comprehensive neuropsychological study of HD, Fedio et al. (1979) administered a large battery of clinical tests, experimental tasks (including perceptual half-field studies) and personality and psychopathology assessment to 10 early-stage patients. Not unexpectedly, the HD patients were impaired on most tests of higher-order cognition. They also had high (abnormal) scores on scales assessing anxiety, depression, peculiarities of thought and interpersonal difficulties. Most noteworthy, however, was the finding that the patients had elevated perceptual thresholds and aberrations in lateral asymmetries on perceptual tasks. The authors speculated that inefficiencies in the encoding of visual, auditory and tactile stimuli may be at the root of the information-processing deficits in HD.

Fisher and associates (1983) compared the neuropsychological performance of 30 HD patients to 9 patients with idiopathic PD and 19 normal control subjects. A large battery of neuropsychological tests was administered, and the data were reduced by principal components analysis. The three factors derived were 'memory' (including the Selective Reminding Test and recall of a categorized list), 'elaborative processing' (including the Stroop Color-Word Test, WAIS Picture Arrangement, and other tasks requiring rapid transformation of stimuli) and 'factual-verbal' (including the Information and Similarities subtests of the WAIS). While the PD patients performed at the 20th percentile on the memory and elaborative tests and approached the control subjects on the factual-verbal tests, the HD patients performed below the first percentile on the memory and elaborative tests and near the 10th percentile on the factual-verbal tests.

Caine et al. (1986) compared the cognitive performance of HD patients to that of patients with multiple sclerosis, another illness having primarily subcortical pathology. While the groups had similar overall profiles, the HD group was more impaired in verbal recognition memory and immediate and delayed recall of geometric designs. Caine and associates also found the HD group to be more impaired in arithmetic computation, a finding consistent with the observations of low WAIS Arithmetic scores (Norton, 1975; Fedio et al., 1979; Butters et al., 1978; Brandt et al., 1984) and impaired serial subtraction on mental status exams (Brandt et al., 1988).

One limitation of some neuropsychological studies of HD is lack of consideration of stage of illness. Early in the progression of the illness, neuropathological changes are relatively focal (restricted to the caudate nucleus and putamen), suggesting that psychological changes may also be focal. Butters and associates (1978) reported that patients tested early in their disease (within a year of diagnosis) had I.Q.s within the normal range, but displayed significant deficits in memory and verbal fluency. Patients tested three or more years after diagnosis displayed an overall lowering of performance on all tests of intellectual and mnestic functioning, with the exception of visual confrontation naming (Boston Naming Test) (Kaplan et al., 1978). Moses and colleagues (1981) studied early, middle-stage and advanced HD patients with the Luria-Nebraska Neuropsychological Test Battery. They confirmed Butters's finding of a prominent memory impairment in the early group and, in addition, found impairments in visuospatial skills in these early patients. The middle-stage and advanced groups had, predictably, more severe and pervasive deficits. Josiassen et al. (1983) also reported that memory and visuospatial deficits appear early in the course of the disease, but, unlike motor impairments, remain relatively stable until the advanced stages of the illness.

Determining the stage of illness in HD patients is often desirable for clinical and research proposes, but is not easily accomplished. Although most researchers group patients according to duration of symptoms, this determination is difficult to make retrospectively. The first signs of the disease are variable, with a sizeable number of patients presenting first with psychiatric syndromes (especially major affective disorder; Folstein et al., 1983a) or emotional symptoms (often increased irritability and/or impulsivity; Folstein et al., 1979). In addition, duration of neurological or psychiatric symptoms is a relatively poor predictor of level of dementia. Brandt et al. (1984) found that severity of impairment of voluntary movement (e.g., diadochokinesis, rapid syllable repetition, gait) at time of assessment is a stronger correlate of I.Q., memory impairment and activities of daily living than is duration of illness.

Shoulson and Fahn (1979) developed an index of total functional capacity (TFC) to be used as a staging variable in HD. The TFC scale rates level of dependence in such daily activities as eating, dressing, engagement in occupation, and managing finances. Shoulson (1981) demonstrated the utility of the scale in tracking the course of the disease and response to symptomatic treatment. Fisher et al. (1983) stratified their HD patients by TFC on the Shoulson-Fahn scale and found that mildly disabled and moderately disabled HD patients differed significantly in their performance on the Stroop Color-Word Test and, to a lesser extent, the Selective Reminding Test. Mayeux et al. (1986) found that cognitive impairment (as assessed by an expanded Mini-Mental State Exam) and depression each contributed significantly to TFC scores, whereas duration of illness, degree of motor disability and age of onset of the illness did not. Recently, Bamford et al. (1989) reported that TFC score was highly correlated with performance in a number of cognitive domains, most notably visuospatial skill (including the Porteus Maze Test and Visual Reproductions from the Wechsler Memory Scale) and 'complex psychomotor' skill (including the Stroop Color-Word Test and the Trail Making Test).

Language in HD

Patients with HD do not have clinically significant language disorders such as would be seen in patients with cortical lesions of the dominant hemisphere or patients with Alzheimer's disease. However, HD patients do have unambiguous impairments in speech and may have subtle linguistic deficits (Gordon and Illes, 1987).

Ludlow et al. (1987) studied speech planning, initiation and production in patients with HD and PD. Among the HD patients, there were impairments in the control of syllable duration, duration of pauses between phrases and duration of sentences, as well as a reduced rate of syllable repetition. The authors suggest that the caudate nucleus may play a major role in controlling the timing of speech movements.

In their description of 18 HD patients, Caine et al. (1978) commented that 'no patient demonstrated specific language impairment suggestive of focal disease. Syntax, word content and usage, comprehension, and repetition were intact. Prosody was abnormal because of involuntary respiratory or vocal movements; articulation was affected by dysarthria' (p. 382). In a later study, however, Caine et al. (1986) reported that early HD patients had defective visual confrontation naming as well as impaired repetition and poor narrative language. Similarly, Butters originally reported that naming was normal in HD, but more recently found impairments in naming and other semantic functions. In the initial study, Butters et al. (1978) found that early-stage HD patients perform poorly on the Controlled Oral Word Association ('FAS') Test, while performing normally on the Boston Naming Test. This was interpreted as indicating impairment in the rapid search of semantic memory in the absence of a general language impairment. A more recent study by Butters and colleagues (Smith et al., 1988) examined semantic processing in patients with mild to moderate HD. Compared to normal control subjects, patients with mild HD were impaired on the WAIS-R Vocabulary subtest and the Boston Naming Test, as well as on measures of verbal fluency (FAS and animal naming). While this finding is in contrast with Butters's previous studies, it should be noted that the naming impairment was relatively mild compared with the language deficits found in cortical dementias (e.g., AD). Nonetheless, the data are consistent with the notion that HD patients are impaired on certain tasks which require efficient access to lexical stores.

A detailed study of language in HD was recently conducted by Podoll et al. (1988). These investigators administered the Aachen Aphasia Test to 45 patients with HD stratified by duration of symptoms and 20 normal control subjects. In conversational language and discourse, the HD patients displayed reduced initiation of speech and short, syntactically simple sentences. Their speech was dysarthric and their writing was dysgraphic, features that are understandable in terms of impairments in motor control. A prominent disorder of visual confrontation naming was found. However, 65% of the misnamings were substitutions of visually similar objects (e.g., calling a *nail* a 'pencil'), leading the authors to conclude that the naming impairment was due primarily to a disorder of visual recognition rather than to problems in lexical retrieval. Performance on tests of language comprehension was normal in the early-stage patients. In more advanced cases, it was highly correlated with the severity of overall dementia.

In a series of semantic priming experiments, Smith and coworkers (1988) found that the more severely impaired an HD patient was, the less likely it was that his performance would reflect a sensitivity to the semantic relatedness of word pairs. While the HD patients showed no impairment in the magnitude of the priming effect per se, they did display a dementia-related decline in the degree to which the associative strength of word pairs affected the priming of semantic relations. Thus, while HD apparently does not involve gross loss of semantic information, as has been suggested of Alzheimer's disease (Martin and Fedio, 1983; Salmon et al., 1988), there is apparently some derangement in the organization of semantic relations, or a disturbance in their activation, which becomes progressively more severe as the disease advances.

Spatial cognition in HD

Impairments in spatial information processing appear to be characteristic of HD, and may distinguish these patients from those with other dementias. Fedio and coworkers (1979) found severe impairments on visuospatial tasks that had prominent motor components, such as copy of the Rey-Osterrieth Complex Figure and stylus maze learning. However, HD patients were also impaired on non-practic tests of spatial perception and judgment, such as the Mosaic Comparisons Test (detecting small differences between two visual patterns) and the Standardized Road-Map Test of Directional Sense (a paper-and-pencil test of right – left orientation).

A later study from the same laboratory (Brouwers et al., 1984) compared the spatial impairments of HD patients to those of AD patients. The AD patients performed more poorly than their control subjects on a large battery of spatial tests, with the exception of the Standardized Road-Map Test. The HD patients were worse than their control subjects on the Mosaic Comparisons Test and Standardized Road-Map Test, but (in contrast to the earlier study) not on copying the Rey-Osterrieth Complex Figure or on stylus maze learning. The results were interpreted as supporting a double dissociation between extrapersonal spatial perception and constructional skill, which are impaired in AD and normal in HD, and egocentric (personal) spatial perception, which is impaired in HD and normal in AD.

In an elegantly simple experiment, Potegal (1971) earlier found evidence for a specific impairment in egocentric spatial localization in HD. His task required subjects to study the location of a black target dot on a table in front of them. After their vision was occluded, their task was to mark the position of the dot with a stylus. The test was administered under several conditions: (1) standard condition, (2) after repeated practice with the stylus with eyes unoccluded, (3) with the head turned to one side, and (4) after taking a single step sideways. Potegal reported deficient localization of the target dot by HD patients only in condition 4, when their body positions vis-à-vis the target had been altered. Based on this finding and his observation of impaired spatial orientation in rats with caudate nucleus lesions (Potegal, 1969), Potegal argued that the caudate plays a role in updating perceived position in space to compensate for self-initiated movements. This notion has obvious similarities to the concept of the corollary discharge. This neural signal, described by Teuber (1976) as originating in the frontal lobes, is purported to be responsible for perceptual constancy in the face of the sensory changes induced by self-initiated movement.

It has been known for over 20 years that damage to the caudate nucleus produces disturbances of spatial learning in animals. For example, monkeys with lesions of the head of the caudate are grossly impaired in the learning of delayed spatial alternations (i.e., respond to the left stimulus on trial 1, the right stimulus on trial 2, the left stimulus on trial 3, and so on) (Battig et al., 1960; Butters and Rosvold, 1968; Divac et al., 1967). Oscar-Berman and associates (1980, 1982) studied cognition in HD and other neurological patients with learning tasks derived from this work with non-human primates. They found HD patients to be markedly impaired on a delayed spatial alternation task, but normal on a delayed response task (Oscar-Berman et al., 1982). This suggests that it is not memory per se, but memory for spatial positions that is mediated by the caudate. Somewhat paradoxically, however, Oscar-Berman and Zola-Morgan (1980) found that HD patients had great difficulty learning a visual pattern reversal task, but not a spatial reversal task (i.e., respond to the left until it is no longer reinforced, then respond to the right until it is no longer reinforced, and so on). The authors were surprised by this finding and raised the possibility that their spatial reversal task may not 'require the egocentric spatial ability supposedly mediated by the caudate' (Oscar-Berman and Zola-Morgan, 1980, p. 509), or may simply have lacked sufficient sensitivity.

Memory in HD
Some form of memory disturbance is a very prominent and early-appearing cognitive feature of HD (Butters et al., 1978; Caine et al., 1977, 1986; Moses et al., 1981). Deficits are displayed in the learning and retention of new information (Caine et al., 1977; Moses et al., 1981; Weingartner et al., 1979), as well as in the retrieval of previously-acquired information (Albert et al., 1981a,b; Beatty et al., 1988; Brandt, 1985).

Anterograde memory Early studies of new learning in HD had suggested impairments in the elaboration of incoming stimuli, resulting in faulty storage of information (Caine et al., 1977; Weingartner et al., 1979). Subsequent studies of patients earlier in the course of their cognitive decline, however, often failed to find significant verbal encoding deficits (Caine et al., 1986; Beatty and Butters, 1986). It has also been demonstrated that the disorder of new learning in HD is qualitatively unlike that found in patients with amnesia due to alcoholic Korsakoff's syndrome and that this might be due to differences in how these patients analyse to-be-remembered information. Korsakoff patients benefit from procedures which increase the opportunity for encoding material (e.g., spaced practice), those which decrease inter-item interference (e.g., varying the similarity of material on consecutive trials), and those which induce 'deep level' encoding (e.g., use of orienting questions). HD patients, on the other hand, do not improve under these conditions (Biber et al., 1981; Butters, 1984). Considered together, these findings suggest that HD patients' encoding deficits are relatively minor and are not central to their memory disorder.

The ability to use verbal mediators as mnemonic aids appears to be relatively intact in HD and differentiates this illness from other dementias. Butters et al. (1983) had patients with HD, AD, Korsakoff's syndrome and right hemisphere strokes recognize visual scenes under two conditions: after free study and after being told a story describing the scene. Only the HD and right hemisphere damaged patients improved significantly in the story condition, suggesting that (1) the verbal material was meaningful only to these patients and (2) it assisted their encoding of the pictures. A similar conclusion was reached by Moss and coworkers (1986). They administered a recognition span memory test to patients with HD, AD or Korsakoff's syndrome, and normal control subjects. Five types of visually-presented stimuli were used: colors, patterns, faces, words and spatial position. The three patient groups performed alike under all the stimulus conditions except the words. Here, the HD patients were superior to the other patients and performed as well (statistically) as normals (Fig. 2). Again, it appears that verbal stimuli are more easily encoded and retrieved by HD patients than are other classes of memoranda (Butters, 1984).

Many studies of new verbal learning in HD have reported relatively normal recognition memory (Butters et al., 1985; Caine et al., 1978; but cf. Caine et al., 1986). Although HD patients are often as severely impaired as Korsakoff amnesics on recall measures of verbal learning, their recognition of verbal material is consistently superior to that of their amnesic counterparts (Moss et al., 1986). Butters et al. (1986), for example, found that HD patients outperformed Korsakoff amnesics on recognition of word-list items (Rey Auditory Verbal Learning Test) and short prose passages. A bit of contradictory evidence is provided by Kramer et al. (1988). Using the California Verbal Learning Test,

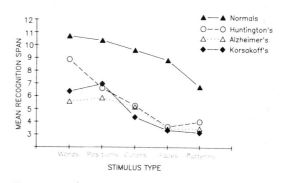

Fig. 2. Performance of patients with Huntington's disease, Alzheimer's disease or alcoholic Korsakoff's syndrome, and normal control subjects on the Delayed Recognition Span Test. The Huntington's disease patients are impaired under all conditions except when the stimuli were words. (From Moss et al., 1986.)

they found that the yes/no recognition of HD patients with Mini-Mental State scores below 24 was as poor as that of AD patients. Only HD patients with Mini-Mental scores of 24 or higher performed better. The three groups (AD, demented HD, mildly impaired HD) did not differ on number of true positive responses ('hits'), but they did differ on false positives. The mildly impaired HD patients made the fewest of these errors, and the AD patients made the most.

The discrepancy between their performance on recall and recognition tests has led to the proposal that the HD patient's verbal memory impairment reflects his inability to initiate systematic search strategies for the retrieval of stored information (Butters, 1984; Butters et al., 1985; Caine et al., 1978). An explicit test of this hypothesis was made by Brandt (1985). Patients with HD and matched normal control subjects attempted to recall items of general factual information. For those items where recall failed, subjects were asked to make 'feelings of knowing' judgments (Hart, 1965, 1967); that is, they were asked to estimate the likelihood that the unrecalled fact would be correctly recognized from among several alternatives. Finally, a multiple-choice recognition test was given for those unrecalled items. The HD patients were as able as the normals in giving accurate feelings of knowing judgments. In both groups, there was a positive correlation between the feeling of knowing estimate given to an item and its likelihood of being recognized. However, the HD patients' response times during the recall test did not reflect their confidence estimates. While the normals took longer to answer (incorrectly) items about which they had a strong feeling of knowing (the typical finding; Nelson and Narens, 1980), no consistent relationship was found for the HD patients. The patients spent no longer in attempting to answer questions about which they had a strong feeling of knowing than they did for those for which they had little confidence of recall (Fig. 3). Thus, there is the strong suggestion that while HD patients' knowledge about their memory stores is relatively intact, their ability to make use of this information in allocating memory search time is

faulty. These results suggest that the dementia of HD includes a defect in the metacognitive control processes that orchestrate retrieval efforts.

Retrograde amnesia   Memory for past events in HD is also qualitatively different from that in other memory-disordered patients. For example, patients with Korsakoff's disease display a marked temporal gradient of retrograde amnesia, with events of the recent past more severely affected than events of the distant past (Albert et al., 1979). Patients with HD, even early in the course of the disease, are equally impaired in remembering public events from all periods of time (Albert et al., 1981a,b) (Fig. 4). Like the verbal recognition data, this finding suggests that retrieval failures, rather than decreasing encoding efficiency as the disease progresses, underlie the memory failure in HD. Recently, Beatty et al. (1988) replicated the finding of a 'flat' retrograde amnesia function in early HD patients. This contrasted to their findings in mildly demented AD patients, who displayed greater recall for events of the 1940s and '50s than for the 1960s, '70s, and '80s.

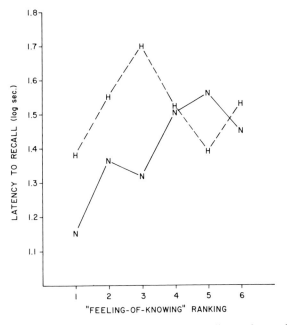

Fig. 3. Latency to incorrect responses on recall test of general knowledge, as a function of feeling-of-knowing. H = Huntington's disease, N = Normal control. (From Brandt, 1985.)

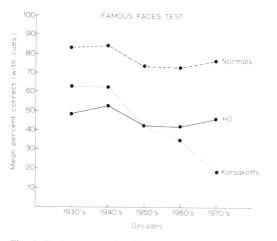

Fig. 4. Performance of patients with Huntington's disease or alcoholic Korsakoff's syndrome, and normal control subjects on the Famous Faces Test of the Boston Retrograde Amnesia Battery. (From Albert et al., 1981a.)

Implicit memory Amnesic patients with lesions of the medial temporal lobes or diencephalon often perform adequately on memory tasks which do not require explicit recollection of prior events (Milner, 1962; Cortin, 1968; and Butters, 1984; Cohen and Squire, 1980; Graf et al., 1984; Shimamura and Squire, 1984). They display normal acquisition of habits and skills, which has come to be called *implicit memory*. In contrast, patients with lesions of the striatum who have mild dementia syndromes and relatively minor impairments in explicit memory (recall and recognition) often show severe defects in implicit memory (Saint-Cyr et al., 1988).

Martone and collaborators (1984) first reported that HD patients are impaired in the acquisition of a perceptual skill. HD and alcoholic Korsakoff patients were administered a task in which mirror-reflected word triads were shown on each of three successive days. The time required to read each triad served as the measure of skill acquisition. Following the third day of word reading, a word recognition test was administered. The results revealed a double dissociation between the two patient groups on the skill learning and recognition memory tests. The amnesic Korsakoff patients evidenced unimpaired skill learning (their rate of improvement in mirror

reading was normal) combined with severely impaired recognition of the verbal stimuli. The HD patients, on the other hand, showed normal recognition performance despite a significant retardation in rate of skill acquisition.

Recently, several research teams have begun to differentiate aspects of implicit memory. Implicit memory encompasses several classes of phenomena, including procedural memory (reflected in tests of motor and rule learning) and activation (reflected in tests of perceptual fluency and semantic priming). Within the domain of motor learning, Bylsma et al. (1990) recently found HD patients to be impaired on some aspects of maze learning, but not others. HD patients and normal control subjects were studied with a computerized stylus maze learning task. The acquisition of the maze skill itself (i.e., improvement across different mazes), the learning of specific routes (i.e., over repeated trials) and the effects of route predictability on performance (i.e., the advantage of patterned over unpatterned routes) were the three aspects of procedural memory examined. The HD group learned individual maze routes at a normal rate but were deficient in generalizing the cognitive skill across mazes. In addition, they failed to demonstrate superior performance on a maze with a predictable route (e.g., right, up, right, up, . . .) relative to mazes with unpredictable routes (Fig. 5). These results support the existence of distinct and separable procedural memory phenomena. They further suggest that the basal ganglia are crucial for generalizing skills across stimulus situations and for making use of the regularity, patterning or organization in to-be-acted-upon stimuli.

The phenomena of implicit memory are differentially affected by different neuropathologies, suggesting their functional independence and reliance on different neural substrates. Heindel et al. (1988) demonstrated that impaired motor learning is not simply a consequence of dementia, regardless of etiology. They studied groups of HD and AD patients, matched for score on the Dementia Rating Scale. The HD group was severely impaired in acquisition of the motor skill underlying the pursuit

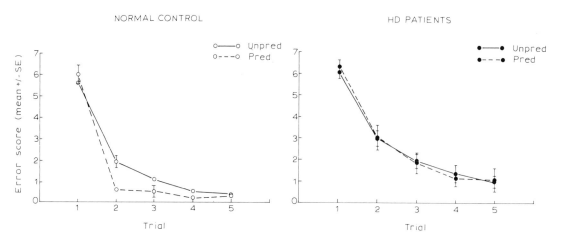

Fig. 5. Errors in learning mazes with predictable routes (Pred) and unpredictable routes (Unpred) in early-stage Huntington's disease patients and normal control subjects. Control subjects learned the maze with the predictable, patterned route in fewer trials than mazes with unpredictable routes. The HD patients performed identically in the two conditions. (From Bylsma et al., 1990.)

rotor task, while the AD group acquired the skill normally, thereby implicating the striatum in this aspect of implicit memory. A more recent study by Heindel and associates (Heindel et al., 1989) demonstrated that HD patients who perform very poorly on the pursuit rotor task are not impaired on a lexical priming task (word-stem completion). This contrasted with the performance of AD patients, who were impaired in lexical priming but not in motor learning (see also Salmon et al., 1988). PD patients with dementia were impaired on both tasks. Taken together, these results suggest that motor skill learning is mediated by a frontal corticostriatal system, whereas verbal priming is neocortically mediated.

'Executive functions' in HD
Since the major subdivisions of the head of the caudate nucleus receive their innervation from the dorsolateral and orbital frontal cortex (Goldman and Nauta, 1977; DeLong and Georgopolous, 1979; Alexander et al., 1986), it is reasonable to expect some features of a 'frontal lobe syndrome' in patients with HD (Mesulam, 1986; Stern, 1983; Stuss and Benson, 1986). In fact, early-stage HD patients often complain of difficulty planning, organizing and scheduling activities (Caine et al., 1978; Fedio

et al., 1979), all well-recognized aspects of frontal-lobe pathology (Stuss and Benson, 1986). Objective testing confirms that many behavioral characteristics of patients with lesions confined to the dorsolateral prefrontal cortex, such as diminished verbal fluency (Butters et al., 1978; Wexler, 1979), poor maze performance (Corkin, 1965; Fedio et al., 1979), inability to compensate for postural adjustments (Potegal, 1971), loss of cognitive flexibility, inability to shift mental sets and perseverative tendencies (Josiassen et al., 1983; Wexler, 1979; Oscar-Berman et al., 1982), are regularly seen in HD.

In the study by Fisher et al. (1983) described earlier, HD patients were compared to equivalently disabled PD patients and normal control subjects on verbal-factual, memory and 'elaborative' tasks. The tests of elaborative functions (Porteus Maze Test, Wisconsin Card Sorting Test, Stroop Color-Word Test), which are known to be highly sensitive to prefrontal pathology, were the most severely impaired in the mildly disabled HD compared to the mildly disabled PD patients. These same tests were also most markedly worse in the moderately disabled HD patients compared to mildly disabled HD patients.

Studies comparing HD, AD and alcoholic Korsakoff patients on perseverative tendencies have suggested that HD patients are *less* prone to these errors of commission than are the other two patient groups (Butters et al., 1983; Butters, 1985). For example, on a verbal fluency task which assesses patients' ability to search their long-term semantic memories, both AD and Korsakoff patients generate more perseverative responses than do patients with HD (Butters et al., 1986). Similarly, Alzheimer and Korsakoff patients produce more intra-test intrusion errors on a picture-context recognition task (Butters et al., 1983) and the immediate recall of short passages (Butters, 1985). AD patients also make many more intrusion errors than HD patients on a multi-trial, word-list learning task (Kramer et al., 1988). Thus, while HD patients may display some cognitive and behavioral abnormalities attributable to prefrontal cortical pathology, such symptoms may be more severe in other dementias and amnesic conditions, especially on non-motor, verbal tasks.

Summary and hypothesis

Several 'core' cognitive defects have been proposed in HD, each of which accounts for a portion of the observed neuropsychological impairments. These include faulty early-stage encoding (Fedio et al., 1979; Weingartner et al., 1979), a defect in egocentric spatial orientation (Potegal, 1971; Oscar-Berman et al., 1980; Brouwers et al., 1984), slow and inefficient access to knowledge stores (Butters et al., 1978; Brandt, 1985; Smith et al., 1988), and impaired implicit memory (Saint-Cyr et al., 1988; Heindel et al., 1988, 1989). To this list, another putative 'core' defect can be added. Much of the evidence reviewed above, including impaired fluency and generativity, faulty allocation of memory search time and the impaired timing of speech, suggest that the tempo of behavior is fundamentally disordered in HD. It may be that intact caudate nuclei are required for the efficient timing of mental and motor acts (Thompson et al., 1962; Schmaltz and Isaacson, 1968), and that a defect in this mechanism may be a major source of the cognitive and motor symptoms of HD. Some very preliminary

support for this hypothesis comes from the observation (Brandt, unpublished) that early- to mid-stage HD patients are as deficient in their perception of the passage of time as much more severely demented AD patients (Fig. 6). While a group of normal subjects underestimated the passage of one minute by an average of 11 seconds, and a group of AD patients (mean Mini-Mental State Exam score = 17.82 ± 4.95) underestimated by an average of 32 seconds, a group of less-demented HD patients (mean Mini-Mental State Exam score = 23.58 ± 3.50) underestimated by an average of 34 seconds. The hypothesis that a fundamental defect in temporal coding underlies many of the cognitive and motor symptoms of this disorder merits further investigation.

Electrophysiological studies

In the past decade, several investigators have turned their attention to event-related brain potentials as markers of information processing in HD. Josiassen et al. (1984) reported that while auditory and visual evoked potentials of HD patients have all the usual early components, the peak amplitudes are greatly reduced. Pattern-shift visual evoked potentials (VEPs) are also clearly reduced in amplitude in HD

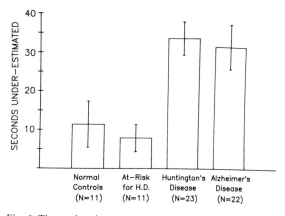

Fig. 6. Time estimation (number of seconds by which one unfilled minute was estimated; mean of three trials) in four groups of subjects. The HD patients had a mean score of 23.58 (± 3.50) on the Mini-Mental State Exam; the AD patients had a mean of 17.82 (± 4.95) (t_{44} = 4.42, $p \leq 0.001$). The difference in mean time estimation score for the AD and HD patients is not significant.

(Lawson et al., 1984). However, it would appear that the prominent disorders of oculomotor control in this population, including impaired ability to maintain visual fixation (Leigh et al., 1983), would make this area of research a problematic one.

The later components of the evoked response are often called 'endogenous' potentials, as they are related to cognitive task demands rather than to stimulus parameters (Hillyard and Kutas, 1983). The P300 component has substantial psychological significance, and is typically generated when a critical stimulus is detected and evaluated. It has been called a 'resolution of uncertainty' wave, and probably plays a role in the updating and modification of cognitive schemata (Pritchard, 1981). Lawson and coworkers (1984) found that the P300 tended to be longer in latency and lower in amplitude in those HD patients where it could be satisfactorily recorded than in normals. Lawson's one HD patient with a clearly abnormal P300 latency was the one who scored lowest on the Mini-Mental State Exam, suggesting a relationship to overall severity of dementia. Rosenberg et al. (1985) found that 12 out of the 13 mild to moderate HD patients they studied had significantly abnormal P300 latencies on either auditory or visual evoked potentials. However, the authors could find no clinical or neuropsychological correlates of P300 latency in these patients. Thus, while evoked potential techniques appear to hold some promise in cognitive studies of HD, their demonstrated utility to date has been limited.

Structural brain imaging in HD

The cardinal neuropathological feature of HD is atrophy of the head of the caudate nucleus and, to a somewhat lesser extent, the putamen (Dom et al., 1976; Vonsattel et al., 1985). However, atrophy of several other brain areas (e.g., neocortex, thalamus, brainstem and cerebellum) is reported in many cases (Dom et al., 1976; Lange, 1981). Several independent studies support the association between atrophy in specific brain areas and cognitive deficits in HD.

Shoulson et al. (1982) studied the CT scans of 42 HD patients. They found that the distance between the caudate nuclei (CC) relative to the outer table of the skull (OT) was highly correlated to total functional capacity ($r = 0.73$). Sax et al. (1983) obtained head CT scans from 26 HD patients. In this study CC/OT was abnormal (> 0.11) in 86% of the patients. Furthermore, many subtests of the WAIS and Wechsler Memory Scale were highly correlated with the CC/OT ratio. In contrast, only a few subtest scores were weakly correlated with frontal horn enlargement (FH/OT as measured on CT scans), a parameter independent of caudate atrophy. Sax and associates also found that severity of chorea was correlated with CC/OT ($r = 0.64$), but not with frontal horn enlargement.

Bamford et al. (1986) performed extensive neuropsychological testing on 60 HD patients who also received CT scans. The test battery was reduced by principal components analysis to four factors: complex psychomotor, verbal memory, visuospatial, and general intelligence. The highest correlation of a CT measure with a neuropsychological measure was between CC/OT and the complex psychomotor factor ($r = -0.46$, $p < 0.001$). The tests loading significantly on the complex psychomotor factor (Stroop Color-Word Test, Digit Symbol subtest from the WAIS-R, and Trail Making Test) are those often found to be most impaired in HD.

Starkstein et al. (1989) obtained head CT scans from 34 patients with HD. For comparison, a group of 24 age-matched normal control subjects was also scanned. The bicaudate ratio (BCR) (i.e., the minimal distance between the indentations of the caudate in the frontal horns divided by the inner table of the skull along the same line, multiplied by 100) was measured by two raters blind to subject group (inter-rater reliability $r = 0.90$). The BCR was much higher in the HD patients than in the normal control subjects, and all HD patients had higher BCR values than their respective age-matched control subjects (see also Barr et al., 1978; Stober et al., 1984). A BCR cut-off point of 14 allowed discrimination of the HD patients from their age-matched ontrol subjects with a sensitivity of 88% and a pecificity of 92%. A significant correlation was observed between several parameters of subcortical atrophy (bicaudate ratio, bifrontal ratio, ventricular ratio) and duration of disease. There was no ignificant correlation between these parameters and age. On the other hand, the frontal fissure and cortical sulci ratios, indices of cortical atrophy, were correlated significantly with age, but not with duration of illness. This study suggests that cortical and ubcortical atrophy are relatively independent processes in HD.

A second study by the same investigators (Starkstein et al., 1988) found significant correlations between the BCR measured on CT scans and three clinical scales used in the evaluation of HD patients: he Mini-Mental State Exam (Folstein et al., 1975), he HD Activities of Daily Living Scale (Brandt et al., 1984), and the Eye Movement Scale from the Quantified Neurological Exam (Folstein et al., 1983b). Unlike the study by Sax et al. (1983), this tudy found no correlations between bicaudate ratio and severity of chorea or impairment of voluntary movement. In a subset of 18 patients who had neuropsychological testing, high correlations were obtained between the bicaudate ratio and performance of the Symbol Digit Modalities Test ($r = 0.65$) and the Trail Making Test ($r = 0.72$ for Part A; $r = 0.80$ for Part B). These data, like those of Bamford et al. (1989), suggest a much larger role for the caudate nucleus in cognitive and oculomotor functions than in motor control, which is probably governed by putamenal and/or subthalamic systems (Alexander et al., 1986).

Recently, Starkstein et al. (unpublished) performed brain magnetic resonance imaging (MRI) scans on 33 HD patients. These same patients were administered a neuropsychological test battery consisting of many tests sensitive to frontostriatal dysfunction. The bicaudate ratio correlated highly with performance on Parts A and B of the Trail Making Test ($rs = 0.57$ and 0.74, respectively), the multiple-choice Benton Visual Retention Test ($r = -0.61$), and all three components of the Stroop Color-Word Test ($rs = -0.55$ to -0.65). There was a significant correlation between size of the left and right heads of the caudate and scores on Part A of the Trail Making Test ($r = -0.51$), and tests of verbal fluency (word list generation) ($rs = 0.41$ to 0.58). However, the area of the *left* caudate and *left* thalamus correlated with score on the interference portion of the Stroop Test (larger areas associated with less interference), while the corresponding areas of the *right* did not. The size of the *left* Sylvian cistern, a marker of left frontotemporo-insular opercular atrophy, correlated with speed and accuracy on Part B of the Trail Making Test, number of losses of set on the Wisconsin Card Sorting Test, Benton Visual Retention Test, a motor go/no-go task, as well as the Stroop Test. The size of the *right* cistern was correlated only with set-losses on the Wisconsin. The stability and significance of these asymmetries in the relationships between cortical and subcortical atrophy and cognitive test performance in HD remain to be determined.

In vitro studies have shown that D_2 dopamine receptors, which normally are in their highest concentration in the striatum, are markedly reduced in HD (Reisine et al., 1977; Whitehouse et al., 1985). Brandt et al. (1990) recently imaged the D_2 receptor in 21 HD patients and eight at-risk individuals using PET scans, and correlated receptor binding with neurological and neuropsychological parameters. A significant reduction in a relative binding of ^{11}C-labelled 3-N-methylspiperone to the D_2 receptor was found in both the caudate and putamen of HD patients. Binding in the caudate was correlated with performance on Part B of the Trail Making Test and on the oral administration of the Symbol Digit Modalities Test, while binding in the putamen was correlated only with duration of illness. The findings indicate that atrophic changes in the striatum seen on CT and MRI are accompanied by receptor alterations. They also support the previous work indicating a larger role for the caudate nucleus in cognition than in motor functions (DeLong and Georgopoulos, 1979; Alexander et al., 1986).

Local cerebral blood flow and metabolism

Regional cerebral blood flow, as measured with the xenon-133 inhalation technique, was found to be reduced in many cortical regions in HD by Tanahashi et al. (1985). The investigators reported that reduced flow in the left frontal and both temporal and parietal lobes was correlated with performance on a Mini-Mental Status Questionnaire. Since flow to subcortical nuclei was not measured in this study, the extent of caudate hypoperfusion is unknown. Weinberger et al. (1988) studied cortical blood flow in HD patients under three conditions. Unlike Tanahashi et al. (1985), they found no reductions in regional blood flow to the cortex, compared to normals, while subjects were at rest. They also found no reductions while patients were performing an automated version of the Wisconsin Card Sorting Test or were engaged in a control task. Although the patients performed more poorly on the Wisconsin Card Sorting Test than the control subjects, blood flow to the prefrontal cortex was equivalent in the two groups. The findings indicate that cognitive deficits usually attributed to pathology of the frontal neocortex may not be due to intrinsic cortical lesions, but rather to the impact of neostriatal pathology on a relatively healthy cortex.

Single photon emission computed tomography (SPECT) scans, which allowed assessment of subcortical blood flow, were obtained from six advanced HD patients by Reid et al. (1988). Reduced blood flow tracer was found in the caudate nucleus in all the patients.

Research teams from the University of California (Kuhl et al., 1982, 1984; Mazziotta et al., 1987), the University of Michigan (Young et al., 1986, 1987; Berent et al., 1988) and the University of British Columbia (Hayden et al., 1986, 1987a; Stoessl et al., 1986) have been especially active in the study of HD patients, and those at-risk, with ^{18}F-2-deoxyglucose (FDG) positron emission tomography (PET) scans. Reductions in striatal glucose metabolism, without significant cortical abnormalities, are typically found in affected patients (Hayden et al., 1986;

Kuhl et al., 1982, 1984; Young et al., 1986, 1987). This hypometabolism correlates highly with clinical severity. Young et al. (1986), for example, reported a correlation (*r*) of 0.91 between glucose metabolic rate in the caudate (relative to the cortex) and total functional capacity on the Shoulson-Fahn scale.

In a recent PET scan study, Berent et al. (1988) found that HD patients have lower cerebral metabolism in both the caudate nucleus and putamen compared to normal control subjects. There was no difference between the groups in cerebral metabolic rate for glucose in the thalamus. Metabolic rate in the caudate correlated highly with digit-symbol substitution, verbal paired-associate learning and Memory Quotient on the Wechsler Memory Scale in HD patients. Much weaker correlations between these memory measures and metabolic rate were observed in the putamen. No significant correlations were found with PET activity in the thalamus. Within the normal control group, there were no significant relationships between cerebral metabolic rate for glucose and cognitive functioning (with the single exception of digit-symbol substitution and activity in the putamen). This study provides further evidence that, of the subcortical nuclei that can be imaged and quantified with PET, the caudate nucleus shows the strongest relationship with memory functioning in HD.

It has been claimed that the striatal PET abnormalities are robust, and are seen even in patients early in the disease who have no caudate atrophy demonstrable by CT scans (Hayden et al., 1986). This has led to the conclusion that defective striatal metabolism precedes brain tissue loss, and may therefore be of use in the pre-clinical diagnosis of HD.

Studies of persons at risk

Each offspring of a person with HD has a 50% chance of having the genetic defect and hence of developing the illness. The possibility that the gene might be expressed before the onset of clear signs and symptoms of the disease has received much attention in the interest of developing a preclinical iagnostic test for use in persons at risk. A number f possible forms of preclinical expression have een proposed and tested (Klawans et al., 1980), anging from response to levodopa administration Klawans et al., 1972) to abnormalities in eyeblink eflexes (Esteban et al., 1981), to peculiarities in humb opposition (Rosenberg et al., 1977).

Several studies have found that individuals at risk or HD, as a group, perform more poorly than non-t-risk individuals on neuropsychological tests on which HD patients perform poorly (Wilson and Garron, 1980). Other studies have found that there re individuals within the at-risk group who per-orm more poorly than expected (Baro, 1973; Wex-er, 1979). Minor deficits are often found on tasks equiring the learning of spatial paths, visuopercep-ual analysis and directional sense (Fedio et al., 979; Josiassen et al., 1983). Wexler (1979) reported hat while the at-risk group she studied was unim-aired in all of the cognitive domains examined, a ubgroup of these subjects (defined by cluster nalysis) had particularly low scores on tests of nemory, digit-symbol coding and response com-etition. Since these are tasks on which HD patients onsistently perform very poorly, Wexler cautiously aised the possibility that his subgroup was compos-d largely of presymptomatic gene-carriers. osiassen and associates (1986) reported that a ubgroup of at-risk individuals with very mild eficits on neuropsychological tests (Tactual Per-ormance Test, Trail Making Test and WAIS Digit ymbol subtest) also produced abnormally low-mplitude somatosensory, auditory and visual voked potentials. They suggested that a combina-ion of electrophysiological and neuropsychological neasure may help identify those at-risk individuals ikely to possess the HD gene.

There have been several explicit attempts to use neuropsychological tests to determine which at-risk ndividuals actually carry the HD gene. Lyle and Quast (1976) performed follow-up psychological ssessments of at-risk individuals 10 to 20 years after hey had initially been assessed. They found that the 2 people who became ill in the interim (out of 156) had lower recall scores on the Bender Gestalt Test on initial assessment. It was later reported that lower scores on the abstraction portion of the Shipley-Hartford Scale and on Wechsler intelligence scales also discriminated at-risks who later developed HD from those who did not (Lyle and Gottesman, 1977). Wexler (1979) suggested that persons who go on to develop the HD phenotype are deficient in the 'capacity to recognize and mentally encode incoming stimuli', and that prediction or very early detection of illness should be possible through examination of the patterning of a number of cognitive performances. An important conceptual and methodological issue in studies of at-risk subjects is defining onset of the disease. If subtle cognitive deficits or emotional symptoms are found in a person at risk, one might reasonably argue that the disease has already begun, even though the diagnosis may not yet have been made.

Two studies have addressed the issue of whether individuals at risk for HD display greater than average *variability* in their performance on the subtests of the WAIS and whether this could be used to predict who carried the disease-causing gene. Josiassen et al. (1982) examined the variance of scores on WAIS subtests and correlations among subtests in a group of 46 at-risk persons. They concluded that the variance was greater than normal and the intercorrelations were smaller than normal. Strauss and Brandt (1985) re-examined Josiassen et al.'s data and raised methodological issues which suggested that their conclusion was premature. A new sample of 38 at-risk individuals was compared on the WAIS to 44 patients with HD and 43 normal control subjects. These new data did not indicate greater variability among the at-risk subjects, either in terms of group variances on each subtest or on the magnitude of intercorrelations among subtests.

The WAIS profiles of patients with HD have been reported to differ from those of normal individuals, independent of overall I.Q. level. Strauss and Brandt (1986) performed discriminant function and hierarchical cluster analyses to explore the utility of WAIS pattern (as opposed to level) information for the pre-clinical identification of HD. A three-variable discriminant function correctly identified

79% of HD patients and normal control subjects. When the discriminant equation was applied to a sample of 38 at-risk subjects, it classified 45% of them with the HD group and 55% with the normal control group. However, there were no clinical differences between the at-risks classified with the HDs and those classified with the normal control subjects. Those classified with affected patients were no more likely to become affected themselves within a three-year period than those classified with normals. Cluster analysis failed to isolate distinct patient, at-risk and control groups. Thus, although performance patterns on the WAIS clearly change in HD, they appear to be of limited value for the preclinical identification of the disease.

Some recent reports suggest that the use of ^{18}F-2-deoxyglucose (FDG) PET scans may also provide a method for presymptomatic detection of the disease state through the demonstration of relative caudate glucose hypometabolism significantly prior to the development of clinical symptoms or structural changes on CT or MRI. UCLA researchers (Kuhl et al., 1982, 1984; Mazziotta et al., 1987) claim that such metabolic findings are present months to years prior to symptomatic onset in some at-risk individuals. Mazziotta et al. (1987) found reductions in caudate metabolism (exceeding the 99% confidence limits of normals) in 18 of the 58 at-risk subjects they studied. In contrast, Young et al. (1987) found that none of the 29 at-risk persons they studied had caudate metabolic rates outside the normal range. The latter authors maintain that caudate hypometabolism in HD occurs only coincident with clinical symptoms, and is not sufficiently sensitive to serve as a presymptomatic marker of the disease. The differences in findings may be due largely to differences between clinical centers in threshold for making the diagnosis of HD and in definition of asymptomatic at-risk status.

Genetic linkage testing for HD

Although the fact that HD is inherited as an autosomal dominant trait has been recognized since its description by George Huntington in 1872, the gene locus for HD remained unknown until 1983. In that year, Gusella and coworkers (1983) reported restriction fragment length polymorphism (RFLP) on chromosome 4 that segregates with the HD phenotype. Subsequent linkage studies of many large, phenotypically different HD kindreds have all confirmed this linkage (Folstein et al., 1985; Haines et al., 1986) and it is now virtually certain that there is only one chromosomal locus for HD. The discovery of this RFLP marker made possible the development of an accurate and reliable presymptomatic test for the illness.

The marker identified by Gusella et al. (1983), called D4S10, is estimated to be approximately 4 to 5 recombination units from the HD gene. This means that in 4 – 5% of meioses, the marker becomes uncoupled from the gene. Thus, any test of a presymptomatic at-risk person using this probe is, at best, 95% accurate. Recently, several new markers have been discovered [D4S43 (Gilliam et al., 1987); D4S62 (Hayden et al., 1988); D4S9. (Wasmuth et al., 1988)]. Some of these new markers are much closer to the HD gene than is D4S10. D4S95, for example, is a highly polymorphic locus that has displayed very few recombinations with the HD gene (Wasmuth et al., 1988). This makes any predictive test with this probe much more informative, with an accuracy of 99% or better.

Meissen et al. (1988) performed the predictive DNA test on 16 individuals at risk. Four people tested positive for the linked marker (high risk of HD), seven tested negative (low risk of HD), and five had uninformative tests (no alteration in risk). Meissen and colleagues reported that two of the four subjects who tested positive had periods of severe depression after testing, but no subjects had required clinical intervention by the time of three-month follow-up.

Hayden et al. (1988b) performed genetic testing on 20 people, including some at 50% risk and some at 25% risk (grandchildren of affected persons whose own parents were clinically well). Twelve subjects tested positive for the marker and therefore were considered at increased risk for HD. Eight tested negative and had a decreased risk. In this latter group, however, were two subjects who had clinical signs consistent with early-stage HD. From this same research group, Jason et al. (1988) reported that there were cognitive neuro-psychological differences between presymptomatic marker-positive and marker-negative individuals. They reported DNA linkage test results on 10 at-risk subjects, all of whom were given an extensive battery of cognitive tests. The seven marker-positive subjects were more impaired than the three marker-negative subjects ($p < 0.05$) on only 4 of 41 variables. While the authors conclude that 'clear neuropsychological impairment may be present in HD even when overt signs and symptoms are not expected for a number of years' (p. 769), the extremely small sample sizes, statistical analyses that capitalize on Type-I error (41 separate independent t-tests, with group sizes of 7 and 4) and very modest statistical effects make the replication of these findings necessary.

Hayden et al. (1987b) combined DNA polymorphism studies with glucose PET studies. In their series, eight at-risk subjects had the HD marker and had a 90% chance of having inherited the HD gene. Three of the eight had abnormally low rates of caudate glucose metabolism (two standard deviations below normal). One individual with a low risk of developing HD from his DNA marker study had abnormally low glucose utilization in the caudate nucleus. Hayden et al. suggested that this indicated a recombination between the linked marker and the HD gene in this individual. They commented that such studies, combining DNA marker analysis and FDG PET, could not only confirm results of the DNA marker in some individuals, but could also detect when DNA results are incorrect due to recombination.

The Johns Hopkins University HD Testing Program

In September 1986, the Baltimore Huntington's Disease Project at the Johns Hopkins University School of Medicine became one of the first two centers in the United States to offer presymptomatic genetic testing for HD to adults at 50% risk for the

illness. Testing has been offered only as part of a research program, designed primarily to determine: (1) the psychiatric, psychological and social consequences of informing people of their HD genetic status, (2) whether pre-test characteristics can discriminate those who adapt well to their genetic status from those who adapt poorly, and (3) whether educational and therapeutic interventions can mitigate morbid psychological and social outcomes. As an increasing number of diseases are being found to have genetic linkages, and as presymptomatic tests are developed for them, it is clearly important to determine whether the application of this new genetic technology carries with it significant psychiatric or social morbidity.

As of September 1989, 127 adult offspring of HD patients voluntarily entered the predictive testing program. (For a full description of the program, see Brandt et al., 1989a,b.) All had Quantified Neurological Examinations (Folstein et al., 1983a), standardized psychiatric interviews (SADS-Lifetime; Endicott and Spitzer, 1978), and extensive psychological and neuropsychological assessments, as well as several counseling sessions prior to DNA analysis. Eighteen subjects were found to be clinically affected with HD during this baseline period and eight opted to serve as untested control subjects. Three people were seriously depressed and their genetic testing was postponed.

DNA analyses using the D4S10, D4S43 and D4S95 locus probes have thus far been performed for 70 participants. There have been 16 positive tests (risk of HD $\geq$ 95%), 43 negative tests (risk of HD $\leq$ 5%) and 11 uninformative tests. The distribution of positive and negative tests is unlikely to be due to chance ($p < 0.001$, binomial test). This is probably due to a combination of factors, including a self-selection bias, the sensitivity of our clinical assessments to very early HD, and our postponing testing of those who were depressed or who had equivocal motor signs of the illness.

The marker-positive and marker-negative groups did not differ in their social or psychiatric histories. Both groups performed in the normal range on the Quantified Neurological Examination and Mini-

Mental State Exam (Table 1). Psychological tests and questionnaires designed to assess personality, coping style, psychological symptoms and life stress (including the Millon Clinical Multiaxial Inventory, Symptom Checklist [SCL-90R], Beck Depression and Hopelessness Scales, Cognitive Failures Questionnaire, Moos Family Environment Scale, Life Events Scale, Social Support Scale, Miller Behavioral Style Scale) failed to discriminate those who would subsequently test positive from those who would test negative. A battery of clinical and experimental neuropsychological tests that are sensitive to early HD was also administered. This included the Symbol Digit Modalities Test, subtests of the WAIS-R, the Hopkins Verbal Learning Test, Standardized Road Map Test of Directional Sense, Wisconsin Card Sorting Test, Stroop Color-Word Test, a visual vigilance task and a choice reaction-time task. On none of these procedures did the marker-positive and marker-negative groups differ (Strauss and Brandt, 1990). These results contrast markedly with those of Jason et al. (1988) and suggest that the gene for HD does not have any measurable manifestations in clinically healthy, at-risk individuals.

At disclosure of DNA test results, initial reactions ranged from extreme joy and relief to disappointment, sadness and demoralization. All participants are re-evaluated at three-month intervals for the first year after disclosure and at six-month intervals thereafter. Preliminary data suggest that there is no increased incidence of psychiatric disorder or social morbidity associated with testing positive for the HD marker (Table 2 and Fig. 7). This sample continues to be followed at regular intervals, and new at-risk persons continue to be entered into the pro-

TABLE 1

Characteristics of at-risk subjects who test positive or negative for the linked DNA marker (data as of September 1989)

	Marker-positive	Marker-negative	
N	16	4[a]	
Age (yrs)	29.44 (SD = 5.09)	35.44 (SD = 7.86)	p < .01
Males: females	6:10	19:22	N.S.
Age of onset of affected parent (yrs)	39.94 (SD = 8.66)	44.20 (SD = 10.28)	N.S.
Married (%)	62	61	N.S.
Children (av. number) (married only)	0.88 (SD = 1.02)	1.73 (SD = 2.00)	p < .05
Education (yrs completed)	14.12 (SD = 2.25)	14.29 (SD = 2.81)	N.S.
Affected parent (father: mother)	9:7	13:28	N.S.
Quantified Neurological Exam	2.12 (SD = 2.99)	1.63 (SD = 2.20)	N.S.
Mini-Mental State Exam	29.07 (SD = 1.10)	29.22 (SD = 1.10)	N.S.

[a] Excludes one suject age 68, and one at 25% risk before testing.

...ocol. Future analyses from this project will allow us ...o address a large number of important neuro- ...sychological issues, including: (1) determining ...ith greater confidence whether the HD gene has ...europsychological manifestations prior to onset of ...iagnosable disease, (2) determining the baseline

cognitive and emotional characteristics of those who cope well and those who cope poorly with news of their genetic status, and (3) determining the very earliest manifestations of striatal cell death as the disease begins its relentless course.

Acknowledgements

The author is grateful to his many colleagues and collaborators, especially Drs. Milton E. Strauss, Marshal F. Folstein, Susan E. Folstein, Frederick W. Bylsma and Kimberly A. Quaid. Mss. Michelle Hall, Laura Krafft and Suzanne Reed provided excellent technical assistance. This work was supported by grants NS16375 and NS24841 from the National Institute of Neurological Disorders and Stroke, grant MH46034 from the National Institute of Mental Health and a grant from the Huntington's Disease Society of America.

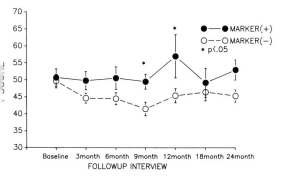

Fig. 7. Psychological symptom severity (SCL-90R Global Severity Index) of marker-positive and marker-negative at-risk subjects at baseline (before disclosure) and at follow-ups. Scores for both groups remain well within the normal range.

TABLE 2

Psychiatric symptomatology in marker-positive and marker-negative subjects at each follow-up, as revealed by the Schedule for Affective Disorders and Schizophrenia – Change Interview (data as of September 1989)

	Proportion with symptoms[a]		Global Assessment Score		
	Marker-positive	Marker-negative	Marker-positive	Marker-negative	
3 months	0/10	1/32	90.20[b] (1.41)	93.14 (0.89)	N.S.
6 months	2/11	4/26	87.55 (3.15)	89.83 (1.64)	N.S.
9 months	1/6	1/15	90.67 (2.11)	92.86 (1.90)	N.S.
12 months	1/5	1/15	85.60 (7.68)	93.20 (1.44)	N.S.
18 months	1/5	1/11	87.40 (4.31)	86.36 (3.16)	N.S.
24 months	0/2	1/4	88.00 (0.00)	89.00 (2.33)	N.S.

[a] Proportion of subjects with clinician ratings of 4 (moderate) or greater on at least one symptom on the SADS-Change Interview.
[b] Mean (S.E.)

References

Albert ML, Feldman RG, Willis AL: The subcortical dementia of progressive supranuclear palsy. *J. Neurol. Neurosurg. Psychiatry: 37,* 121 – 130, 1974.

Albert MS, Butters N, Levin J: Temporal gradients in the retrograde amnesia of patients with alcoholic Korsakoff's disease. *Arch. Neurol.: 36,* 211 – 216, 1979.

Albert MS, Butters N, Brandt J: Patterns of remote memory in amnesic and demented patients. *Arch. Neurol.: 38,* 495 – 500, 1981a.

Albert MS, Butters N, Brandt J: Development of remote memory loss in patients with Huntington's Disease. *J. Clin. Neuropsychol.: 3,* 1 – 12, 1981b.

Alexander GE, DeLong MR, Strick PL: Parallel organization of functionally segregated circuits linking basal ganglia and cortex. *Annu. Rev. Neurosci.: 9,* 357 – 381, 1986.

Aminoff MJ, Marshall J, Smith E, Wyke M: Patterns of intellectual impairment in Huntington's chorea. *Psychol. Med.: 5,* 169 – 172, 1975.

Bamford KA, Caine ED, Kido DK, Plassche WM, Shoulson I: Clinical-pathological correlation in Huntington's disease: a neuropsychological and computed tomography study. *Neurology: 39,* 796 – 801, 1989.

Baro F: A neuropsychological approach to early detection of Huntington's chorea. In *Advances in Neurology, Vol. 1.* New York: Raven Press, pp. 329 – 338, 1973.

Battig K, Rosvold HE, Mishkin M: Comparison of the effects of frontal and caudate lesions on delayed response and alternation in monkeys. *J. Comp. Physiol. Psychol.: 53,* 400 – 404, 1960.

Beatty WW, Butters N: Further analysis of encoding in patients with Huntington's disease. *Brain Cognition: 5,* 387 – 398, 1986.

Beatty WW, Salmon DC, Butters N, Heindel WC, Granholm EL: Retrograde amnesia in patients with Alzheimer's disease of Huntington's disease. *Neurobiol. Aging: 9,* 181 – 186, 1988.

Berent S, Giordani B, Lehtinen S, et al: Positron emission tomography scan investigation of Huntington's disease: cerebral metabolic correlates of cognitive function. *Ann. Neurol.: 23,* 541 – 546, 1988.

Biber C, Butters N, Rosen J, Gerstman L, Mattis S: Encoding strategies and recognition of faces by alcoholic Korsakoff and other brain-damaged patients. *J. Clin. Neuropsychol.: 3,* 315 – 330, 1981.

Bondareff W, Mountjoy CQ, Roth M: Loss of neurons of origin of the senile dementia. *Neurology: 32,* 164 – 168, 1982.

Brandt J: Access to knowledge in the dementia of Huntington's disease. *Dev. Neuropsychol.: 1,* 335 – 348, 1985.

Brandt J, Butters N: The neuropsychology of Huntington's disease. *Trends Neurosci.: 93,* 118 – 120, 1986.

Brandt J, Strauss ME, Larus J, et al: Clinical correlates of dementia and disability in Huntington's disease. *J. Clin. Neuropsychol.: 6,* 401 – 412, 1984.

Brandt J, Folstein SE, Folstein MF: Differential cognitive impairment in Alzheimer's and Huntington's disease. *Ann. Neurol.: 23,* 555 – 561, 1988.

Brandt J, Quaid KA, Folstein SE: Presymptomatic DNA testing for Huntington's disease. *J. Neuropsychiatry Clin. Neurosci.: 1,* 195 – 197, 1989a.

Brandt J, Quaid KA, Folstein SE, et al: Presymptomatic diagnosis of delayed-onset disease with linked DNA markers: the experience in Huntington's disease. *J. Am. Med. Assoc.: 26,* 3108 – 3114, 1989b.

Brandt J, Folstein SE, Wong DF et al: D$_2$ receptors in Huntington's disease: Positron tomographic findings and clinical correlates. *J. Neuropsychiatry Clin. Neurosci.: 2,* 20 – 27, 1990.

Brouwers P, Cox C, Martin A, et al: Differential perceptual-spatial impairment in Huntington's and Alzheimer's dementia. *Arch. Neurol.: 41,* 1073 – 1076, 1984.

Bruyn GW, Bots GTAM, Dom R: Huntington's chorea: current neuropathological status. In Chase TN, Wexler NS, Barbeau A (Editors), *Advances in Neurology, Vol. 23: Huntington's Disease.* New York: Raven Press, pp. 83 – 93, 1979.

Bryois C: [The length of survival and cause of death in Huntington chorea.] *Schweiz. Arch. Neurol. Psychiatr.: 140,* 101 – 115, 1989.

Buchwald NA, Hull CD, Levine MS, Villablanca J: The basal ganglia and the regulation of response and cognitive sets. In Brazier MAB (Editor), *Growth and Development of the Brain.* New York: Raven Press, pp. 171 – 189, 1975.

Butters N: The clinical aspects of memory disorders: contributions from experimental studies of amnesia and dementia. *J. Clin. Neuropsychol.: 6,* 17 – 36, 1984.

Butters N: Alcoholic Korsakoff's Syndrome: some unresolved issues concerning etiology, neuropathology, and cognitive deficits. *J. Clin. Exp. Neuropsychol.: 7,* 179 – 208, 1985.

Butters N, Rosvold HE: The effect of septal and caudate nuclei lesions on resistence to extinction and delayed-alternation performance in monkeys. *J. Comp. Physiol. Psychol.: 65,* 397 – 403, 1968.

Butters N, Sax D, Montgomery K, Tarlow S: Comparison of the neuropsychological deficits associated with early and advanced Huntington's disease. *Arch. Neurol.: 35,* 585 – 589, 1978.

Butters N, Albert MS, Sax D, et al: The effect of verbal elaborators on the pictorial memory of brain-damaged patients. *Neuropsychologia: 21,* 307 – 323, 1983.

Butters N, Wolfe J, Martone M, Granholm E, Cermak LS: Memory disorders associated with Huntington's disease: verbal recall, verbal recognition, and procedural memory. *Neuropsychologia: 23,* 729 – 743, 1985.

Butters N, Wolfe J, Granholm E, Martone M: An assessment of verbal recall, recognition and fluency abilities in patients with Huntington's disease. *Cortex: 22,* 11 – 32, 1986.

Butters N, Salmon DP, Heindel W, Granholm E: Episodic, semantic, and procedural memory: Some comparisons of Alzheimer and Huntington disease. In Terry RD (Editor), *Aging and the Brain.* New York: Raven Press, 1988.

Bylsma FW, Brandt J, Strauss ME: Aspects of procedural memory are differentially impaired in Huntington's disease. *Arch. Clin. Neuropsychol.: 5,* 287 – 297, 1990.

Caine ED, Ebert M, Weingartner H: An outline for the analysis of dementia: the memory disorder of Huntington's disease. *Neurology: 27,* 1087 – 1092, 1977.

Caine ED, Hunt RD, Weingartner H, Ebert MH: Huntington's dementia: clinical and neuropsychological features. *Arch. Gen. Psychiatry: 35,* 378 – 384, 1978.

Caine ED, Bamford KA, Schiffer RB, Shoulson I, Levy S: A controlled neuropsychological comparison of Huntington's disease and multiple sclerosis. *Arch. Neurol.: 43,* 249 – 254, 1986.

Cohen J: The factorial structure of the WAIS between early adulthood and old age. *J. Consult. Psychol.: 21,* 283 – 290, 1957.

Cohen NJ, Squire LR: Preserved learning and retention of pattern-analyzing skill in amnesia: dissociation of knowing how and knowing that. *Science: 210,* 207 – 210, 1980.

Conneally PM: Huntington disease: genetics and epidemiology. *Am. J. Hum. Genet.: 36,* 506 – 526, 1984.

Corkin S: Tactually-guided maze learning in man: effects of unilateral cortical excisions and bilateral hippocampal lesions. *Neuropsychologia: 3,* 339 – 351, 1965.

Corkin S: Acquisition of motor skills after bilateral medial temporal lobe excision. *Neuropsychologia: 6,* 255 – 265, 1968.

Cummings JL, Benson DF: Subcortical dementia: review of an emerging concept. *Arch. Neurol.: 41,* 874 – 879, 1984.

DeLong MR, Georgopoulos AP: Physiology of the basal ganglia-A brief overview. In Chase TN, Wexler NS, Barbeau A (Editors), *Advances in Neurology, Vol. 23: Huntington's Disease.* New York: Raven Press, pp. 137 – 153, 1979.

Divac I, Rosvold HE, Szwarcbart MK: Behavioral effects of selective ablation of the caudate nucleus. *J. Comp. Physiol. Psychol.: 63,* 184 – 190, 1967.

Dom R, Malfroid M, Baro F: Neuropathology of Huntington's chorea: studies of the ventrobasal complex of the thalamus. *Neurology: 26,* 64 – 68, 1976.

Esteban A, Mateo D, Gimenez-Roldan S: Early detection of Huntington's disease: blink reflex and levodopa load in presymptomatic and incipient subjects. *J. Neurol. Neurosurg. Psychiatry: 44,* 43 – 48, 1981.

Fedio P, Cox CS, Neophytides A, et al: Neuropsychological profiles in Huntington's disease: patients and those at risk. In Chase TN, Wexler NS, Barbeau A (Editors), *Advances in Neurology, Vol. 23: Huntington's Disease.* New York: Raven Press, pp. 239 – 255, 1979.

Ferrante RJ, Kowall NW, Beal MF, Richardson EP Jr, Bird ED, Martin JB: Selective sparing of a class of striatal neurons in Huntington's disease. *Science: 230,* 561 – 563, 1985.

Fisher JM, Kennedy JL, Caine ED, Shoulson I: Dementia in Huntington's disease: a cross-sectional analysis of intellectual decline. In Mayeux R, Rosen WG (Editors), *The Dementias.* New York: Raven Press, pp. 229 – 238, 1983.

Folstein MF, Folstein SE, McHugh PR: 'Mini-Mental State': a practical method for grading the cognitive state of patients for the clinician. *J. Psychiatric Res.: 12,* 189 – 198, 1975.

Folstein SE, Folstein MF, McHugh PR: Psychiatric syndromes in Huntington's disease. In Chase TN, Wexler NS, Barbeau A (Editors), *Advances in Neurology, Vol. 23: Huntington's Disease.* New York: Raven Press, pp. 281 – 289, 1979.

Folstein SE, Abbott MH, Chase GA, Jensen BA, Folstein MF: The association of affective disorder with Huntington's disease in a case series and in families. *Psychol. Med.: 13,* 537 – 542, 1983a.

Folstein SE, Jensen B, Leigh RJ, Folstein ML: The measurement of abnormal movement. Methods developed for Huntington's Disease. *J. Neurobehav. Toxicol. Teratol.: 5,* 605 – 609, 1983b.

Folstein SE, Phillips JA, Meyers DA et al: Huntington's disease: two families with differing clinical features show linkage to the G8 probe. *Science: 229,* 776 – 779, 1985.

Folstein SE, Chase GA, Wahl WE et al: Huntington disease in Maryland: clinical aspects of racial variation. *Am. J. Hum. Genet.: 41,* 168 – 179, 1987a.

Folstein SE, Leigh RJ, Parhad IM, Folstein MF: The diagnosis of Huntington's disease. *Neurology: 36,* 1279 – 1283, 1987b.

Folstein SE, Brandt J, Folstein MF: The subcortical dementia of Huntington's disease. In Cummings J (Editor), *Subcortical Dementia.* Oxford University Press, 1990.

Gershon ES, Merrill CR, Goldin LR et al: The role of molucular genetics in psychiatry. *Biol. Psychiatry: 22,* 1388 – 1405, 1987.

Gilliam TC, Bucan M, MacDonald ME et al: A DNA segment encoding two genes very tightly linked to Huntington's disease. *Science: 238,* 950 – 952, 1987.

Goldman PS, Nauta WJH: An intricately pattered prefronto-caudate projection in rhesus monkey. *J. Comp. Neurol.: 171,* 369 – 386, 1977.

Gordon WP, Illes J: Neurolinguistic characteristics of language production in Huntington's disease: a preliminary report. *Brain Lang.: 31,* 1 – 10, 1987.

Graf P, Squire LR, Mandler G: The information that amnesic patients do not forget. *J. Exp. Psychol. Learn. Mem. Cognition: 10,* 164 – 178, 1984.

Gusella JF, Wexler NS, Conneally PM et al: A polymorphic DNA marker linked to Huntington's Disease. *Nature: 306,* 234 – 238, 1983.

Haines JL, Tanzi R, Wexler NS et al: No evidence of linkage heterogeneity between Huntington's disease and G8 (D4S10). *Am. J. Hum. Genet.: 39,* A156, 1986.

Hart JT: Memory and the feeling-of-knowing experience. *J. Educ. Psychol.: 56,* 208 – 216, 1965.

Hart JT: Memory and the memory monitoring process. *J. Verbal Learn. Verbal Behav.: 6,* 685 – 691, 1967.

Hayden MR, Martin WRW, Stoessl AJ, et al: Positron emission tomography in the early diagnosis of Huntington's disease. *Neurology: 36,* 888 – 894, 1986.

Hayden MR, Hewitt J, Martin WRW, Clark C, Ammann W: Studies in persons at risk for Huntington's disease [Letter]. *New Engl. J. Med.: 316,* 382 – 383, 1987a.

Hayden MR, Hewitt J, Stoessl AJ, et al: The combined use of positron emission tomography and DNA polymorphisms for the preclinical detection of Huntington's disease. *Neurology: 37,* 1441 – 1447, 1987b.

Hayden MR, Hewitt J, Wasmuth JJ, et al: A polymorphic DNA marker that represents a conserved expressed sequence in the region of the Huntington disease gene. *Am. J. Hum. Genet.: 42,* 125 – 131, 1988a.

Hayden MR, Robbins C, Allard D, et al: Improved predictive testing for Huntington's disease by using three linked DNA markers. *Am. J. Hum. Genet.: 43,* 689 – 694, 1988b.

Heindel WC, Butters N, Salmon DP: Impaired learning of motor skills in patients with Huntington's disease. *Behav. Neurosci.: 102,* 141 – 147, 1988.

Heindel WC, Salmon DP, Shults CW, Walicke PA, Butters N: Neuropsychological evidence of multiple implicit memory systems: a comparison of Alzheimer's, Huntington's, and Parkinson's disease patients. *J. Neurosci.: 9,* 582 – 587, 1989.

Hillyard SA, Kutas M: Electrophysiology of cognitive processing. *Annu. Rev. Psychol.: 34,* 33 – 61, 1983.

Huntington G: On chorea. *Med. Surg. Rep.: 26,* 317 – 321, 1872.

Jason GW, Pajurkova EM, Suchowersky O, et al: Presymptomatic neuropsychological impairment in Huntington's disease. *Arch. Neurol.: 45,* 769 – 773, 1988.

Josiassen RC, Curry L, Roemer RA, DeBase C, Mancall EL: Patterns of intellectual deficit in Huntington's disease. *J. Clin. Neuropsychol.: 4,* 173 – 183, 1982.

Josiassen RC, Curry LM, Mancall EL: Development of neuropsychological deficits in Huntington's disease. *Arch. Neurol.: 40,* 791 – 796, 1983.

Josiassen RC, et al: Auditory and visual evoked potentials in Huntington's disease. *Electroencephalogr. Clin. Neurophysiol.: 57,* 113 – 118, 1984.

Kaplan E, Goodglass H, Weintraub S: *The Boston Naming Test.* Boston: E Kaplan & H Goodglass, 1978.

Klawans HL, Paulson GW, Ringel SP, Barbeau A: Use of levodopa in detection of presymptomatic Huntington's chorea. *New Engl. J. Med.: 286,* 1332 – 1334, 1972.

Klawans HL, Goetz CG, Perlik S: Presymptomatic and early detection of Huntington's disease. *Ann. Neurol.: 8,* 343 – 347, 1980.

Kramer JH, Delis DC, Blusewicz MJ, Brandt J, Ober BA, Strauss M: Verbal memory errors in Huntington's and Alzheimer's dementias. *Dev. Neuropsychol.: 4,* 1 – 15, 1988.

Kuhl DE, Phelps ME, Markham CH, et al: Cerebral metabolism and atrophy in Huntington's disease as determined by [18]FDG and computed tomographic scans. *Ann. Neurol.: 12,* 425 – 434, 1982.

Kuhl DE, Metter EJ, Riege WH, Markham CH: Patterns of cerebral glucose utilization in Parkinson's disease and Huntington's disease. *Ann. Neurol.: 15 (Suppl.),* S119 – S125, 1984.

Lange H: Quantitative changes of telencephalon, diencephalon, and mesencephalon in Huntington's chorea, postencephalitic, and idiopathic parkinsonism. *Verhandl. Anatom. Gesellsch.: 75,* 923 – 925, 1981.

Lawson EA, Barrett G, Kriss A, Halliday AM: P300 and VEPs in Huntington's chorea. *Ann. N. Y. Acad. Sci.: 425,* 592 – 597, 1984.

Leigh RJ, Newman SA, Folstein SE, et al: Abnormal ocular motor control in Huntington's disease. *Neurology: 33,* 1268 – 1275, 1983.

Ludlow CL, Connor NP, Bassich CJ: Speech timing in Parkinson's and Huntington's disease. *Brain Lang.: 32,* 195 – 214, 1987.

Lyle O, Gottesman I: Premorbid psychometric indicators of the gene for Huntington's disease. *J. Consult. Clin. Psychol.: 45,* 1011 – 1022, 1977.

Lyle O, Quast W: The Bender Gestalt: use of clinical judgment versus recall in the prediction of Huntington's disease. *J. Consult. Clin. Psychol.: 44,* 229 – 232, 1976.

Mattis S: Mental status examination for organic mental syndrome in the elderly patient. In Bellak L, Karasu TB (Editors), *Geriatric Psychiatry.* New York: Grune & Stratton, 1976.

Mattis S: *Dementia Rating Scale.* Odessa, FL: Psychological Assessment Resources, 1988.

Martin A, Fedio P: Word production and comprehension in Alzheimer's disease: the breakdown of semantic knowledge. *Brain Lang.: 19,* 124 – 141, 1983.

Martone M, Butters N, Payne M, Becker JT, Sax DS: Dissociations between skill learning and verbal recognition in amnesia and dementia. *Arch. Neurol.: 41,* 965 – 970, 1984.

Matarazzo JD: Wechsler's Measurement and Appraisal of Adult Intelligence (Fifth Edition). New York: Oxford University Press, 1972.

Mayeux R, Stern Y, Rosen J, Benson DF: Is 'subcortical dementia' a recognizable clinical entity? *Ann. Neurol.: 14,* 278 – 283, 1981.

Mayeux R, Stern Y, Herman A, Greenbaum L, Fahn S: Correlates of early disability in Huntington's disease. *Ann. Neurol.: 20,* 727 – 731, 1986.

Mazziotta JC, Phelps ME, Pahl JJ, et al: Reduced cerebral metabolism in asymptomatic subject at risk for Huntington's disease. *New Engl. J. Med.: 316,* 357 – 362, 1987.

McHugh PR, Folstein MF: Subcortical dementia. Address to the American Academy of Neurology, Boston, MA, April 1973.

McHugh PR, Folstein MF: Psychiatric symptoms of Huntington's chorea: a clinical and phenomenologic study. In Benson DF, Blumer D (Editors), *Psychiatric Aspects of Neurological Disease.* New York: Raven Press, pp. 267 – 285, 1975.

Meissen GJ, Myers RH, Mastromauro CA et al: Predictive testing for Huntington's disease with use of a linked DNA marker. *New Engl. J. Med.: 318,* 535 – 542, 1988.

Merritt AD, Conneally PM, Rahman NF et al: Juvenile Huntington's chorea: In Barbeau A, Brunette TR (Editors), *Progress in Neurogenetics.* Amsterdam: Excerpta Medica Foundation, 1969.

Mesulam M-M: Frontal cortex and behavior. *Ann. Neurol.: 19,* 320 – 325, 1986.

Milner B: Les troubles de la memoire accompagnant des lesions hippocampiques bilaterales. *Physiologie de l'Hippocampe.* Paris: Centre National de la Recherche Scientific, pp. 257 – 272, 1962.

Moses JA Jr, Golden CJ, Berger PA, Wisniewski AM: Neuropsychological deficits in early, middle, and late stages of Huntington's disease as measured by the Luria-Nebraska Neuropsychological Battery. *Int. J. Neurosci.: 14,* 95 – 100, 1981.

Moss MB, Albert MS, Butters N, Payne M: Differential patterns of memory loss among patients with Alzheimer's disease, Huntington's disease, and alcoholic Korsakoff's syndrome. *Arch. Neurol.: 43,* 239 – 246, 1986.

Nelson TO, Narens L: A new technique for investigating the feeling of knowing. *Acta Psychol.: 46,* 69 – 80, 1980.

Norton JC: Patterns of neuropsychological performance in Huntington's disease. *J. Nerv. Ment. Dis.: 161,* 276 – 279, 1975.

Oscar-Berman M, Zola-Morgan SM, Oberg RGE, Bonner RT: Comparative neuropsychology and Korsakoff's syndrome. III – Delayed response, delayed alternation, and DRL performance. *Neuropsychologia: 20,* 187 – 202, 1982.

Phelps ME, Huang SC, Hoffman EJ, et al: Tomographic measurement of local cerebral glucose metabolic rate in humans with ^{18}F-2-deoxy-d-glucose: validation of method. *Ann. Neurol.: 6,* 371 – 388, 1979.

Podoll K, Caspary P, Lange HW, Noth J: Language functions in Huntington's disease. *Brain: 111,* 1475 – 1503, 1988.

Potegal M: The role of the caudate nucleus in the spatial orientation of rats. *J. Comp. Physiol. Psychol.: 69,* 756 – 764, 1969.

Potegal M: A note on spatial-motor deficits in patients with Huntington's disease: test of a hypothesis. *Neuropsychologia: 9,* 233–235, 1971.

Pritchard WS: Psychophysiology of P300. *Psychol. Bull.: 89,* 506–540, 1981.

Reid IC, Besson JAO, Best PV, Sharp PF, Gemmell HG, Smith FW: Imaging of cerebral blood flow markers in Huntington's disease using single photon emission computed tomography. *J. Neurol. Neurosurg. Psychiatry: 51,* 1264–1268, 1988.

Reisine TD, Fields JZ, Stern LZ, Johnson PC, Bird ED, Yamamura HI: Alterations in dopaminergic receptors in Huntington's disease. *Life Sci.: 21,* 1123–1128, 1977.

Rosenberg C, Nudleman K, Starr A: Cognitive evoked potentials (P300) in early Huntington's disease. *Arch. Neurol.: 42,* 984–987, 1985.

Rosenberg S, Metzig E, Snider SR, Ast M, Tobin D: Detection of presymptomatic carriers of Huntington's chorea. *Neuropsychobiology: 3,* 144–152, 1977.

Saint-Cyr JA, Taylor AE, Lang AE: Procedural learning and neostriatal function in man. *Brain: 111,* 941–959, 1988.

Salmon DP, Shimamura AP, Butters N, Smith S: Lexical and semantic priming in patients with Alzheimer's disease. *J. Clin. Exp. Neuropsychol.: 10,* 477–494, 1988.

Salmon DP, Yuen PFK, Heindel WC, et al: Differentiation of Alzheimer's disease and Huntington's disease with the Dementia Rating Scale. *Arch. Neurol.: 46,* 1204–1208, 1989.

Sax DS, O'Donnell B, Butters N, Menzer L, Montgomery K, Kayne HL: Computed tomographic, neurologic, and neuropsychological correlates of Huntington's disease. *Int. J. Neurosci.: 18,* 21–36, 1983.

Schmaltz LW, Isaacson RL: Effects of caudate and frontal lesions on retention and relearning of a DRL schedule. *J. Comp. Physiol. Psychol.: 65,* 343–348, 1968.

Shimamura AP, Squire LR: Paired-associate learning and priming effects in amnesia: a neuropsychological study. *J. Exp. Psychol. Gen.: 113,* 556–570, 1984.

Shoulson I: Huntington disease: functional capacities in patients treated with neuroleptic and antidepressant drugs. *Neurology: 31,* 1333–1335, 1981.

Shoulson I, Fahn S: Huntington disease: clinical care and evaluation. *Neurology: 29,* 1–3, 1979.

Shoulson I, Plassche W, Odoroff C: Huntington disease: caudate atrophy parallels functional impairment. *Neurology: 32,* A143, 1982.

Simmons JT, Pastakia B, Chase TN, Schults CW: Magnetic resonance imaging in Huntington's disease. *Am. J. Neuroradiol.: 7,* 25–28, 1987.

Smith S, Butters N, White R, Lyon L, Granholm E: Priming semantic relations in patients with Huntington's disease. *Brain Lang.: 33,* 27–40, 1988.

Starkstein SE, Brandt J, Folstein S, Strauss M, Wong D, McDonnell A, Pearlson G, Folstein M: Neuropsychologic and neuroradiologic correlates in Huntington's disease. *J. Neurol. Neurosurg. Psychiatry: 51,* 1259–1263, 1988.

Starkstein SE, Folstein SE, Brandt J, Pearlson GD, McDonnell A, Folstein, M: Brain atrophy in Huntington's disease: A CT-scan study. *Neuroradiology: 31,* 156–159, 1989.

Stern Y: Behavior and the basal ganglia. In Mayeux R, Rosen WG (Editors), *The Dementias.* New York: Raven Press, pp. 195–209, 1983.

Stober T, Wussow W, Schimrigk K: Bicaudate diameter — the most specific and simple parameter in the diagnosis of Huntington's disease. *Neuroradiology: 26,* 25–28, 1984.

Stoessl AJ, Hayden MR, Martin WRW, Clark C, Pate BD: Predictive studies in Huntington's disease. *Neurology: 36 (Suppl. 1),* 310, 1986.

Strauss ME, Brandt J: Is there increased WAIS pattern variability in Huntington's disease? *J. Clin. Exp. Neuropsychol.: 7,* 122–126, 1985.

Strauss ME, Brandt J: An attempt at presymptomatic identification of Huntington's disease with the WAIS. *J. Clin. Exp. Neuropsychol.: 8,* 210–218, 1986.

Strauss ME, Brandt J: Are there neuropsychological manifestations of the gene for Huntington's disease in asymptomatic, at-risk individuals? *Arch. Neurol.:* in press.

Stroop JR: Studies of interference in serial verbal reactions. *J. Exp. Psychol.: 18,* 643–662, 1935.

Stuss DT, Benson DF: *The Frontal Lobes.* New York: Raven Press, 1986.

Tanahashi N, Meyer JS, Ishikawa Y, Kandula P, Mortel KF, Rogers RL, Gandhi S, Walker M: Cerebral blood flow and cognitive testing correlates in Huntington's disease. *Arch. Neurol.: 42,* 1169–1175, 1985.

Teuber H-L: Complex functions of basal ganglia. In Yahr MD (Editor), *The Basal Ganglia.* New York: Raven Press: pp. 151–168, 1976.

Thompson RL, Ayers WJ, Mettler FA: Comparison of effects of frontal and caudate lesions on timing and discrimination in monkeys [Abstract]. *Am. Psychol.: 17,* 284, 1962.

Vonsattel JP, Myers RH, Stevens TJ, et al: Neuropathological classification of Huntington's disease. *J. Neuropathol. Exp. Neurol.: 44,* 559–577, 1985.

Wasmuth JJ, Hewitt J, Smith B, et al: A highly polymorphic locus very tightly linked to the Huntington's disease gene. *Nature: 332,* 734–736, 1988.

Weinberger DR, Berman KF, Iadarola M, Driesen N, Zec RF: Prefrontal cortical blood flow and cognitive function in Huntington's disease. *J. Neurol. Neurosurg. Psychiatry: 51,* 94–109, 1988.

Weingartner H, Caine ED, Ebert MH: Encoding processes, learning, and recall in Huntington's disease. In Chase TN, Wexler NS, Barbeau A (Editors), *Advances in Neurology, Vol. 23: Huntington's Disease.* New York: Raven Press, pp. 215–226, 1979.

Wexler NS: Perceptual-motor, cognitive, and emotional characteristics of persons at-risk for Huntington's disease. In Chase TN, Wexler NS, Barbeau A (Editors), *Advances in Neurology, Vol 23: Huntington's Disease.* New York: Raven Press, pp. 257–271, 1979.

Whitehouse PJ: The concept of subcortical and cortical dementia: another look. *Ann. Neurol.: 19,* 1–6, 1986.

Whitehouse PJ, Price DL, Struble RG et al: Alzheimer's disease and senile dementia: loss of neurons in the basal forebrain. *Science: 215,* 1237–1239, 1982.

Whitehouse PJ, Trifiletti RR, Jones BE, Folstein SE, Price DH, Snyder SH, Kuhar MJ: Neurotransmitter receptor alterations in Huntington's disease: autoradiographic and homogenate studies with special reference to benzodiazepine receptor complexes. *Ann. Neurol.: 18,* 202–210, 1985.

Wilson RS, Garron DC: Psychological features of Huntington's disease and the problem of early detection. *Soc. Biol.: 27,* 11 – 19, 1980.

Young AB, Penney JB, Starosta-Rubinstein S, et al: PET scan investigations of Huntington's disease: cerebral metabolic correlates of neurological features and functional decline. *Ann.*

Neurol.: 20, 296 – 303, 1986.

Young AB, Penney JB, Starosta-Rubinstein S, et al: Normal caudate glucose metabolism in persons at risk for Huntington's disease. *Arch. Neurol.: 44,* 254 – 257, 1987.

© 1991 Elsevier Science Publishers B.V.
Handbook of Neuropsychology, Vol. 5
F. Boller and J. Grafman (Eds)

CHAPTER 12

The neurology and neuropsychology of HIV infection

Yaakov Stern and Karen Marder

Departments of Neurology and Psychiatry of the College of Physicians and Surgeons of Columbia University, and The HIV Center for Clinical and Behavioral Studies, New York State Psychiatric Institute and Columbia University, New York, NY, U.S.A.

Introduction

The Acquired Immunodeficiency Syndrome (AIDS) epidemic has sparked a surge of research. Our understanding of infection with the human immunodeficiency virus (HIV) has been modified to incorporate a spectrum of severity, ranging from the seropositive but asymptomatic patient on the one hand, to the patient with AIDS on the other. People with AIDS represent only the tip of the iceberg: as of December 31, 1988, 82,764 cases of AIDS in the US and its territories had been reported to the Centers for Disease Control (CDC). Of these cases, 46,000 have been fatal. In contrast, the CDC's working estimate for total number of people with HIV infection at that same date is $1-1.5$ million, corresponding to a $0.4\% - 0.6\%$ infection rate.

After the description of the medical symptoms of AIDS, cognitive changes and dementia were soon noted as well. Reports of intellectual change in seropositive individuals without AIDS then began to appear, and it became possible to consider the concept of a spectrum of cognitive change paralleling the range of HIV infection.

There are several reasons why the intellectual changes associated with HIV infection should be of interest to the neuropsychologist:

HIV is found centrally, in CSF and brain, even before any medical symptoms are evident, suggesting that there may be a direct effect on the central nervous system.

Reports of cognitive changes in otherwise asymptomatic seropositive individuals raise the possibility that an important early feature of the disease could be impact on intellectual function.

The political and psychosocial ramifications of the possible presence of significant cognitive change in asymptomatic individuals are immense. As an extreme example, some people might unwarrantedly claim that the identification of specific cognitive deficits associated with HIV would mandate consideration of required HIV testing of individuals in 'high risk' occupations.

The pathological changes associated with dementia in AIDS are well described, affording a good opportunity for investigating behavioral concomitants of these changes.

The dementia complex seen in AIDS has been termed a 'subcortical dementia' because it presumably results from disease in subcortical structures. Evaluation of cognitive change in AIDS allows for a re-examination of this issue.

This chapter selectively reviews current findings and opinions regarding cognitive change in the full spectrum of HIV infection. It begins with a brief review of the epidemiology and virology of HIV. Methods for staging the severity of HIV infection are evaluated in order to allow meaningful comparisons between studies, and the systemic and neuropathological aspects of the disease are briefly described. The neurological changes which occur in HIV are reviewed in detail since they provide the necessary background to the evaluation of neuro-psychological changes.

Epidemiology

AIDS was first described in homosexual men in 1981. The following year AIDS was noted in intravenous drug users and Haitians, and by 1983 it was recognized among recipients of infected blood products, infants born to at-risk women, sexual partners of AIDS patients, and Africans (Clumeck et al., 1983). Three main routes of transmission have emerged: (1) sexual – either homosexual, between men, or heterosexual, from men to women or women to men; (2) inoculation of blood via transfusion, needle-sharing among drug users, or needle-stick or open wounds among health workers; or (3) perinatal – either intra-uterine or peripartum (Friedland and Kline, 1987). These three routes of transmission have assumed variable importance since the detection of the epidemic.

As of December 1988, 90% of AIDS cases reported to the CDC were in men over age 13. There has been a decrease in the proportion of men with histories of homosexual activity alone (63%) and an increase in those with only intravenous drug use (IVDU) (20%). There has also been a decrease in the proportion of men who were white (62%) and an increase in those who are black (24%) and Hispanic (13%). Blacks and Hispanics were more likely to have histories of intravenous drug use and less likely to report homosexual activity. The majority of women with AIDS are black (54%) and had a history of intravenous drug use themselves (53%). Among children, 78% are presumed to have acquired HIV infection perinatally from their mothers. Blacks and Hispanics are disproportionately represented among the IVDUs and the women who are sex partners of IVDUs and their children (Update, 1989).

HIV infection

Virology
The virus that causes AIDS, HIV-1, is a human retrovirus discovered in 1983 (Barre-Sinoussi et al., 1983). Although HIV-1 and HIV-2 share 40 – 50% of their genetic makeup, HIV-1 accounts for the overwhelming majority of cases of AIDS (Gallo et al., 1988), while HIV-2 may be less pathogenic and infectious. HIV-1 and HIV-2, along with several other viruses that infect monkeys, sheep, goats and cows, belong to a subfamily of retroviruses called the lentiviruses, and have several features in common. All contain several viral genes, frequently kill infected cells, have long incubation periods, and result in immunological and neurological disorders (Levy, 1989).

Retroviruses are so named because, after entering a cell, a polymerase known as reverse transcriptase makes a DNA copy of the viral RNA. This proviral (double-stranded) DNA then migrates to the cell nucleus, where it is integrated into the cell's genome. Its genetic information can then be duplicated every time the host cell divides, making the infection permanent. After integration, the proviral DNA can exist either in latent form, giving no sign of its presence, or in a productive form leading to creation of new virions that bud from the cell (Haseltine and Wong-Staal, 1988). Why viral latency occurs in some cases is unknown, but probably depends on the levels of one or more of the regulatory proteins that make up the HIV-1 virus (Levy, 1989).

The hallmark of HIV infection is the infection and gradual depletion of the CD4+ helper T lymphocyte (or T4 cell). Preferential replication in this cell line and subsequent destruction of these cells at the time of viral replication seriously impairs an individual's ability to combat certain viral, parasitic and bacterial infections (Redfield and Burke, 1988). Other cells are also infected, notably the monocyte, which may provide the means for infection of the central nervous system by transporting the virus across the blood – brain barrier and then serving as a reservoir for replicating virus (Ho, 1987).

There are probably numerous strains of HIV with different replication properties, pathogenicity, latency and target cells. Viruses recovered from the nervous system can be distinguished from those which cause immune deficiency, but causal implicaions have not been clearly established. Brain-derived virus does not replicate well in CD4 + T cells and does not destroy them. In contrast to virus isolated from blood, brain HIV virus replicates in monocyte-macrophages. Not only is there heterogeneity among strains isolated from different individuals, an individual can have more than one strain, and one viral strain may evolve into a more pathogenic type or emerge as the dominant strain over a period of time (Cheng-Mayer and Levy, 1988).

Staging

HIV infection involves a number of stages of disease, simplistically, an early acute phase, a longer chronic phase and a final phase referred to as AIDS-related complex (ARC) and AIDS. The acute illness is self-limited and may be followed by a latency period during which time the individual is asymptomatic. This will be described in more detail in the section on aseptic meningitis. The length of time that each of these phases comprises has not been delineated. The time from initial inoculation with the HIV-1 virus to the development of AIDS may be as long as 10 years, with a mean of 7.8 years (Lui et al., 1989). A new sensitive technique to detect HIV DNA, the polymerase chain-reaction, has demonstrated the presence of HIV infection at least 35 months prior to the detection of antibodies to HIV-1, the standard means of detecting the virus (Imagawa et al., 1989). However, the presence of HIV infection with the development of an antibody response at such a late stage is extremely unusual.

A number of conventions have been developed to describe patients clinically at various stages of HIV infection. They do not necessarily correspond to the immunological status of the patient and should be considered descriptors of the illness. The term AIDS is reserved for those patients who have had at least one AIDS-defining illness. Pneumocystis pneumonia and Kaposi's sarcoma are the most common AIDS-defining illnesses. The 1987 revision of the CDC surveillance definition for AIDS now includes presumptive diagnosis of some illnesses, without microsocopic or culture confirmation, when sub-jects are known to be HIV+. If HIV status is negative or unknown, AIDS-defining diseases must be definitively diagnosed. All other causes of immunodeficiency must be excluded.

Persistent generalized lymphadenopathy (PGL), also known as lymphadenopathy syndrome (LAS), is a clinical description of patients that may run the gamut from completely asymptomatic and immunologically normal to those with imminent AIDS. It is characterized as lymph nodes 1.0 cm in diameter or greater, present for at least three months in at least two extrainguinal sites. Lymph node enlargement, if not rapidly progressive, is a benign condition, and may be seen in the acute phase of HIV infection or years into the disease course, concurrent with immunosuppression.

Yet another very heterogeneous condition with a variety of definitions is ARC, thought to represent a more advanced stage than LAS. ARC is most often defined as at least two AIDS-related clinical conditions such as lymphadenopathy, persistent fevers, weight loss or oral candidiasis, plus one or more AIDS-related laboratory abnormalities such as decreased T4 lymphocyte count. Like LAS, the clinical manifestations defined as ARC may represent subjects with a wide range of immunological abnormalities. There is clearly overlap in the LAS and ARC categories and, because of the numerous definitions used to define these categories, comparison between studies is very difficult based on these labels alone.

Two staging systems, the CDC (1986) and the Walter Reed (Redfield et al., 1986) classification system, are widely used to characterize the progression of disease (Table 1). The CDC classification is based on clinical parameters and does not relate to the pathobiology of HIV infection in the same way as the Walter Reed system. Patients classified as CDC Group II, asymptomatic infection may be more immunosuppressed than those in CDC Group III, persistent generalized lymphadenopathy. The prognostic significance of the various groups is somewhat doubtful. The Walter Reed system divides the disease into six stages based on a number of indicators of immune impairment, namely

TABLE 1

Staging systems for conditions related to HIV

Walter Reed System

Stage	HIV antibody or culture	Chronic LAD	CD4+ cell count/μl	Cutaneous anergy	Thrush	Opportunistic infection
WRO	−	−	> 400	None	−	−
WR1	+[a]	−	> 400	None	−	−
WR2	+[a]	+[a]	> 400	None	−	−
WR3	+[a]	±	< 400[a]	None	−	−
WR4	+[a]	±	< 400[a]	Partial[a]	−	−
WR5	+[a]	±	< 400	Complete/Partial	+[a]	−
WR6	+[a]	±	< 400	Complete/Partial	±	+[a]

Centers for disease control (CDC) classification system

Group	Description
I	Acute infection
II	Asymptomatic infection
III	Persistent generalized lymphadenopathy
IV	Other disease
Subgroup A	Constitutional disease
Subgroup B	Neurological disease
Subgroup C	Secondary infectious diseases
Category C-1	Specified secondary infectious diseases listed in the CDC surveillance definition for AIDS
Category C-2	Other specified secondary infectious diseases
Subgroup D	Secondary cancers, including those within the CDC surveillance definition for AIDS
Subgroup E	Other conditions

[a] Critical features of each Walter Reed (WR) stage.

CD4+ cell count/μl and cutaneous anergy. The addition of cutaneous anergy testing, with a battery of skin test antigens that must be read 48 hours after application, makes this system cumbersome for outpatient staging. Primary neurological disease and the development of cancer are not included in the Walter Reed staging system since it is not clear how these relate to immune dysfunction (Redfield et al., 1986). It is not clear that either system is better as a staging/prognostic measure than measuring the total number of T4 cells.

Since there are various methods for staging the severity of HIV infection and an optimal system has not been established, it is difficult to compare subject populations utilized in different studies. In par-

ticular, the CDC classifications of ARC and AIDS leave room for a wide range of variation, and even within the seropositive asymptomatic category there is much room for a range of immunological compromise. The most practical solution is for research reports to include information that can be standardly assessed and understood in any research setting. At minimum, this should include T4 counts and complete descriptions of concomitant medical findings.

Systemic manifestations of HIV infection

While this review focuses on the neurological and neuropsychological manifestations of HIV-1 infecion, HIV-1 affects many organ systems, including the pulmonary, gastrointestinal and hematological systems. Most serious systemic illness is caused by opportunistic infections that occur because of the unique form of immunosuppression seen in HIV. Individuals may be more likely to develop certain opportunistic infections depending on their risk group and where they live. Perhaps the most important infection is *Pneumocystis carinii* pneumonia (PCP), which occurs in 80% of patients with AIDS, and will be the first opportunistic infection in 60% (Glatt et al., 1988). Other infections include *Mycobacterium avium* intracellulare, which causes a nonspecific wasting syndrome (Young et al., 1986), oral esophageal candidiasis, and cryptospoidium, which causes a severe diarrheal syndrome in immunocompromised hosts (Soave and Johnson, 1988). These are the most common infections, but by no means an exhaustive list.

Neurological manifestations of HIV infection

HIV infection affects all levels of the nervous system. Diseases of the brain, spinal cord, peripheral nerve and muscle have all been described. Most recently two cases of HIV infection associated with myasthenia gravis have been described (Nath et al., 1990).

Initial estimates of the prevalence of neurological manifestations of HIV infection in homosexual men (Levy et al., 1985) and IVDUs with AIDS ranged from 23% to 39% (Koppel et al., 1985). These were probably underestimates because HIV antibody testing was not yet available and neurological findings may have been attributed to causes other than the direct or indirect effects of the virus. The actual prevalence of neurological changes at various stages of HIV infection remains unestablished. Despite substantial inroads in characterizing the neurological changes in HIV infection, it is unclear how disease of the nervous system relates to other systemic manifestations of HIV, why and how the brain is infected, and what determines the progression of central and peripheral nervous system disease. A major obstacle in the study of this issue

is that in most cases data are confined to prevalence information because the exact time of seroconversion cannot be established.

The neurological manifestations of HIV-1 infection can be divided into three categories: those caused directly by the HIV-1 virus, by opportunistic infections and by CNS neoplasms. The opportunistic infections and the CNS neoplasms are AIDS-defining illnesses. In contrast, the direct infection caused by HIV-1 spans the entire time between acute infection and AIDS.

Opportunistic infections

Numerous bacterial, fungal, viral and parasitic infections have been described in the setting of AIDS (Berger et al., 1987). Some tend to occur only in immunocompromised hosts, while others, such as mycobacterium tuberculosis and syphilis, may occur in the immunocompetent host with HIV-1 infection.

Toxoplasmosis. Toxoplasmosis is the most common nonviral pathogen and the most frequent cause of intracranial masses in the setting of HIV infection (McArthur, 1988). It occurs due to reactivation of previous latent infection. Estimates of prevalence range from 2% to 13%, depending on patient risk group (Levy, 1988b).

Clinically, patients usually present with focal signs such as hemiparesis, aphasia or focal seizures that develop over a period of a few weeks. A diffuse meningoencephalitis, lethargy and even coma may also be the initial presentation of toxoplasmosis.

Diagnosis is usually made by CT scan, which shows multiple ring enhancing lesions in cortical and subcortical regions, notably the basal ganglia. MR is more sensitive than CT, even if double dose contrast is used (Navia et al., 1986a). Lumbar puncture often reveals a CNS pleocytosis and an elevated protein. Serological testing of CSF is often negative, though if intrathecal antibody production is present, it can be very helpful in diagnosis.

Current practice in a patient with a clinical and CT picture compatible with toxoplasmosis is empiric therapy with pyrimethamine and sulfadiazine. Improvement is usually seen both clinically and radiologically in 1 – 2 weeks in up to 90% of cases (McArthur, 1988). Biopsy is reserved for patients who do not respond to therapy, since toxoplasmosis may be confused with lymphoma, tuberculosis, cytomegalovirus, progressive multifocal leuko-encephalopathy and Kaposi's sarcoma. Because relapses are very common, maintenance therapy is required after the usual course of 3 – 6 months.

Cryptococcosis. Cryptococcal meningitis or meningoencephalitis is the most common fungal infection affecting the nervous system in the setting of HIV infection. Prevalence is approximately 5%. IVDUs seem to be at increased risk of developing cryptococcal meningitis (Levy, 1988a).

The presenting features of cryptococcal infection may be fulminant, with involvement at multiple sites including the CNS, blood, skin, lung and liver, or more commonly the presentation can be more subtle, with some but not all signs of meningitis. In a recent series, two-thirds presented with fever, malaise and headache, a quarter with nausea, vomiting or altered mentation, and one-fifth with meningismus (Chuck and Sande, 1989).

Cryptococcal meningitis is probably more accurately detected than other HIV-related CNS diseases because it is easily diagnosed by lumbar puncture. Because the signs and symptoms of cryptococcal meningitis may be subtle, it is important to perform a spinal tap if the diagnosis is even remotely considered. Spinal fluid cell counts, glucose and protein may be only minimally abnormal. India ink capsule staining of the cryptococcal organisms in the CSF is positive in 72 – 100% (Kovacs et al., 1985), but detection of cryptococcal antigen in the CSF is a more reliable diagnostic method. Detection of serum cryptococcal antigen may be even more sensitive than that in CSF (99% compared to 91%) (Chuck and Sande, 1989).

The usual therapy for cryptococcal infection is amphotericin B. The initial response in two studies was 58% (Kovacs, 1985; Zuger et al., 1986). In a study of 89 confirmed cases of cryptococcal meningitis, maintenance therapy with ketoconazole or amphotericin to prevent relapse was associated with improved survival. Extrameningeal cryptococcus

and hyponatremia were associated with shorter survival (Chuck and Sande, 1989).

Viral infections. Progressive multifocal leukoencephalopathy (PML) is a demyelinating disorder that results from the reactivation of a papovavirus, the JC virus. Though in the past this condition was reported most frequently in patients with lymphoma or leukemia or following organ transplantation, HIV is now the leading cause of PML in the immunocompromised patient (McArthur, 1988).

Clinically, the presentation is typically focal, with the onset of hemiparesis, hemisensory loss, aphasia, ataxia or hemianopsia occurring over weeks to months. CT scan reveals non-enhancing hypodense lesions without mass effect. Though usually found solely in the white matter, when multiple lesions occur, some occur in the gray matter. Diagnosis is made by biopsy, which reveals focal myelin loss and enlarged oligodendrocytes with eosinophilic intranuclear inclusions. There is currently no treatment available and survival after diagnosis is usually not longer than 6 months.

Herpes virus group. Cytomegalovirus (CMV) is a common pathogen in patients with AIDS. The majority will develop viremia with CMV when severe HIV infection develops. In addition to causing meningoencephalitis, it is the most common cause of HIV-associated retinitis. It can also cause pulmonary disease, adrenalitis and colitis. Ganciclovir has been largely ineffective in combatting systemic infection with CMV, though CMV retinitis and progressive polyradiculopathy related to CMV may respond to ganciclovir (Miller RG et al., 1990).

Herpes Simplex Virus 1 (HSV I) causes a hemorrhagic necrotizing encephalitis, usually confined to the medial temporal and inferior frontal lobes. The rapidity of disease progression seems to be dependent on the degree of immunocompetence (Levi, 1985).

Though numerous other bacterial, fungal, parasitic and viral infections have been reported to occur with HIV infection, the infectious agents mentioned above are the most common.

CNS lymphoma

HIV infection is now the most common cause of CNS lymphoma, surpassing immunosuppression secondary to organ transplantation or chemotherapy. Prevalence in AIDS is approximately 2%. Clinically, patients present with focal findings such as hemiparesis or hemisensory loss, similar to those with toxoplasmosis or PML, but generally the course is less acute than in those conditions. In addition, patients may present with lethargy or confusion, and one-third eventually develop seizures (Rosenblum et al., 1988). CT scan reveals multicentric contrast-enhancing lesions in 47% (So et al., 1987). Mass lesions tend to occur in the basal ganglia, thalamus, corpus callosum and cerebellum. Lumbar puncture does not usually provide any specific information. Definitive diagnosis is made by brain biopsy, which will often be done in patients with mass lesions which do not respond to antibiotic therapy for toxoplasmosis. Treatment with radiation therapy may lead to some degree of improvement in clinical status and radiological studies, but significant long-term effects on survival have not been seen. The additional benefit of corticosteroids and adjuvant chemotherapy has been controversial.

The direct effects of HIV virus

HIV is both lymphotropic, causing immunodeficiency, and neurotropic, causing disease of the central and peripheral nervous system. Unlike the opportunistic infections seen late in the course of the HIV infection, evidence of HIV viral infection can be detected from the time of inoculation with the virus. The relative timing of the systemic and CNS effects of the virus is a central question in ongoing longitudinal studies. Virus has been repeatedly detected in the CSF of asymptomatic patients, sometimes when it could not be cultured from the serum (Goudsmit et al., 1986; Hollander and Levy, 1987; Marshall, 1988; Goeth, 1989; McArthur et al., 1988).

Other than HIV encephalopathy, also known as the AIDS Dementia Complex (ADC), which will be discussed in detail separately, two major CNS complications are described: aseptic meningitis, acute or chronic, and vacuolar myelopathy. Peripheral nervous system involvement will also be described.

Aseptic meningitis. Abnormalities in CSF, such as pleocytosis or increased protein, have been documented in association with acute meningitis or encephalitis at the time of seroconversion (Carne et al., 1986). An acute mononucleosis-like illness can occur at the time of seroconversion, characterized by fever sweats, myalgias and arthralgias. In seven of 12 subjects who reported such an illness lasting 3 – 14 days, headache and photophobia were prominent, suggesting neurological involvement (Cooper et al., 1985). In another series, two of three homosexual men had pleocytosis at the time of seroconversion and HIV was recovered from the CSF in one (Ho, 1987).

While clinically obvious acute brain infection at the time of seroconversion may be relatively rare, asymptomatic persistent pleocytosis seems to be common. Numerous studies have documented abnormal spinal fluid profiles in HIV+, asymptomatic people (Goudsmit et al., 1986; Hollander and Levy, 1987; Marshall, 1988; McArthur, 1988; McArthur et al., 1989).

After seroconversion, two patterns of symptomatic aseptic meningitis have been described: an acute illness, lasting less than four weeks, characterized by headache, fever and CSF pleocytosis; and a more indolent, chronic illness characterized by either mild or absent complaints and no fever or meningeal signs (Hollander and Stringari, 1987).

Vacuolar myelopathy. A syndrome resembling subacute combined degeneration of the spinal cord, primarily affecting the lateral and posterior columns, occurs in 11 – 22% of patients with AIDS (Petito, 1988; Petito et al., 1986). It does not usually occur until the development of ARC or AIDS. Over a period of weeks to months patients develop a spastic paraparesis characterized by leg weakness, incontinence, ataxia and loss of vibratory and position sense. Pathologically, there is extensive vacuolation and secondary axonal degeneration in the cord (Petito, 1988). The vacuolation is distributed throughout the white matter, especially at the middle to lower thoracic levels. The severity of the myelopathy generally correlates with dementia although it may not be its defining feature; over 90% of the patients with vacuolar myelopathy were demented (Navia et al., 1986c). Myelopathies can also be caused by other viruses such as CMV or herpes simplex type (Britton et al., 1985), or by lymphoma in the epidural space.

Peripheral nervous system. Neuromuscular complications of HIV infection occur in up to 80% of patients. They can be seen at the time of seroconversion in the form of an acute demyelinating inflammatory sensorimotor polyraduculopathy (Guillain-Barre syndrome). The Guillain-Barre syndrome and the chronic inflammatory demyelinating polyneuropathies (CIDP) are the most frequent neuropathies in HIV+ patients who do not have AIDS (Dalakas and Pezeshkpour, 1988). Symptoms include weakness, either acute or subacute, and parasthesias. In the Guillain-Barre cases, there may be a pleocytosis in addition to the elevated protein, which is unusual in the non-immunosuppressed population. These patients and the CIDP patients may respond to plasmapharesis with the development of increased strength, suggesting there is a circulating neurotoxic factor (Dalakas and Pezeshkpour, 1988).

In ARC and AIDS patients, painful, symmetric predominantly sensory neuropathy is the most common neuropathy (Parry, 1988). Patients present with painful dysesthesias and areflexia and sometimes mild weakness. This neuropathy does not remit spontaneously and is often seen accompanying AIDS dementia. The cause of this axonal process may be toxic, metabolic or nutritional. The modest improvement of the sensory neuropathy to AZT suggests that the neuropathy may be due to direct infection with the virus.

The third neuropathy seen is a mononeuritis multiplex which presents as sensory or motor deficits in the distribution of multiple spinal, cranial or peripheral nerves. This neuropathy, usually due to necrotizing vasculitis or an immune complex process, can occur as the first sign of HIV infection or

once AIDS has developed. Prednisone, plasmapharesis and lymphocytopheresis have all proved successful (Lange, 1988a).

Polymyositis, the most common muscle disease seen in patients with HIV infection, can occur at any time during the infection. Patients present with proximal muscle weakness and elevated CPK enzyme. Response to steroids has been improvement in approximately one-half.

Neuropathology

Navia et al. (1986c) explored the neuropathological concomitants of AIDS and AIDS dementia complex in a group of 70 patients with AIDS but without macroscopic focal nervous system diseases (such as toxoplasmosis) or metabolic encephalopathy. Fewer then 10% of all brains were histologically normal, and abnormalities were found predominantly in the white matter and subcortical structures, sparing the cortex. The frequency and severity of abnormalities generally correlated well with the presence of dementia.

Three types of change were noted. In 64 patients, there was diffuse pallor of the white matter of varying severity. This is the least specific change, although it is present in nearly all AIDS patients, often with astrocytic proliferation and scant mononuclear infiltrates. HIV-1 has not been identified in brains where this white matter change is the sole abnormality (Pumarola-Sune et al., 1987).

Vacuolation of the white matter, as described above, was noted in approximately one-half the patients and was generally more frequent and severe in the demented patients.

The conspicuous presence of macrophages, multinucleated cells and reactive astrocytes, along with severe and widespread loss of white matter, was strongly associated with more severe dementia. Scattered multinucleated cells are characteristic of HIV encephalitis and are often present around blood vessels, but can also be noted more diffusely in the parenchyma. The multinucleation is probably a result of virus-induced cell fusion, and productive virus infection occurs principally in these cells and their progenitors (macrophages and microglia) (Brew et al., 1988; Petito, 1988).

The correlation between ADC and the histological features of HIV encephalitis with multinucleated cells is now well established. Diffuse pallor and vacuolar myelopathy are probably not as closely linked to the ADC (Brew et al., 1988).

Methodological issues in the study of cognitive change in HIV

Several issues are repeatedly raised in studies investigating the neuropsychological consequences of HIV. Though in most cases these issues are not unique to the study of HIV, this is a relatively new field and there has been little of the consensus that has often developed in other areas of investigation. In addition, awareness of the public policy ramifications of possible cognitive change in HIV can influence or distort the way that data are analysed and interpreted.

Group means versus case approach

Most papers compare the performance of controls and seropositive groups of varying disease severity on batteries of tests. A standard approach is to compare mean values of individual tests across groups. This approach is particularly appropriate when there is reason to believe that specific aspects of cognition are affected in a particular group. Two disadvantages to this approach are: (1) impairments in individual subjects can be obscured when group means are compared; and (2) some conditions might result in more generalized deficits which may be manifested in poorer performance across a range of tests and might not be obvious in comparisons of individual test scores.

The definition of abnormality for a case

An alternative approach is to establish criteria for impaired or abnormal performance, based on an individual performance across the entire battery of tests. An example is the study by Grant et al. (1987), in which global abnormal performance was defined as defective performance on a single test or borderline performance on two tests. This formulation is probably too restrictive for several reasons: (1) there is an increasing probability of one test yielding a defective score as the number of tests in a battery is increased; (2) from a clinical point of view, most neuropsychologists would not label a patient abnormal on the strength of a poor performance on a single test. In fact, it has been argued that statistical reductions of test scores can be misleading and that it is more productive for a clinician to render an expert opinion based on performance on the entire test protocol. Despite these considerations, most investigators have adopted some criterion for abnormal performance, typically based on a set number of tests falling a specific number of standard deviations below normative values.

The labeling of performance as abnormal based on these types of decision rules can be misinterpreted by the unsophisticated reader. The neuropsychologist readily recognizes that a poor score on one or more tests may have no direct or apparent effect on a person's day-to-day function, and views the tests as tools for uncovering potential relationships between the presence of the HIV and cognitive function. Other readers tend to focus on the label 'abnormal' and begin to wonder whether HIV + individuals should be allowed in the workplace. This observation can be extended to the layperson's understanding of any significant group difference. Since a subtle finding can be misinterpreted as having grave implications for the individual, the clinical implications of any significant finding should be explored. A relationship between a diagnosis of dementia and a person's capacity for social and occupational function is present by definition. However, there is little guidance for determining the functional implications of poor performance on a particular neuropsychological test, or for predicting from tests to 'real world' performance on any task. In fact, this issue presents a particular challenge to neuropsychologists, who are often being asked to move away from exploring brain – behavior relationships and to determine the practical, functional implications of patterns of test performance. Since at this time we are not up to the challenge, special care must be taken in presenting results of studies of HIV and cognition in a fashion that avoids the possibility of misinterpretation by the individual and the public at large.

Still, utilizing criteria for abnormality is one useful technique for evaluating and interpreting the neuropsychological battery as a whole. In most cases the investigator's criteria for 'abnormality' are carefully outlined, and in some cases the ramifications of a series of definitions of abnormality are explored.

Two techniques that have been used less frequently to this point are blind clinical reviews of subjects' performance by a neuropsychologist to elicit judgements of clinical abnormality, and data reduction techniques such as factor and cluster analyses. The latter allow more tests to be considered simultaneously in inter-group and -individual comparisons without introducing a perceived judgement of normality or abnormality.

The definition of abnormality for a test

Another issue that recurs in neuropsychological evaluations of HIV is the definition of abnormal performance for a specific test. Typically, performance that falls 1, 1.5 or 2 standard deviations below the normative mean is chosen to represent defective performance. Clearly this technique is arbitrary, and variation in definitions from study to study makes comparisons difficult. More important, it is not always clear that the normative values employed are relevant for the population being studied. Particularly in studies of drug addict populations, but in studies of homosexual men and other at-risk populations as well, the utilization of an appropriate, well-matched control group allows for more accurate assessment of the possible effects of HIV than comparison with less relevant extant norms.

Screening batteries

In studies of large groups of subjects, one time-efficient technique is to employ a screening battery to identify patients worthy of more in-depth evaluation. While several studies of the effect of HIV on cognition have utilized this approach, it is often counterproductive. Particularly in asymptomatic individuals, the neuropsychological changes, if present, may be quite subtle and are still not well defined. Therefore a screening battery might not provide sufficient sensitivity or breadth of sampled cognitive functions to detect possible changes. When cognitive change is more marked, the screen approach can be more useful both because the salient impairments can be recognized and because a shorter battery is more appropriate for an ill patient.

Cross-sectional versus longitudinal studies

Without longitudinal studies, the significance of neuropsychological changes found early in the course of HIV infection is unclear. It cannot be assumed that any neuropsychological changes uncovered are signs of incipient AIDS dementia complex. Early cognitive changes could conceivably remit, perhaps because they have different causal mechanisms. In addition, only prospective studies provide the opportunity for differentiating neurological or neuropsychological changes associated with HIV itself from other infections, neoplasms and metabolic abnormalities.

AIDS dementia complex

While the initial focus in the characterization of AIDS was on the array of opportunistic infections that could be pathologically and radiologically identified, it soon became clear that a great number of patients suffered from cognitive deficits. Today, CDC criteria for AIDS recognize the presence of dementia as a defining feature.

HIV encephalopathy, or as named by Price and his colleagues, AIDS dementia complex (ADC), was initially attributed to viral encephalitis due to CMV, systemic illnesses, opportunistic infections or tumors affecting the CNS. However, as it eventually became clear that HIV directly affects the CNS, ADC was recognized as a direct, central effect of HIV on the CNS. It affects up to 70% of patients, and can be the presenting symptom of AIDS in up to one-third.

Clinical features

Many studies of ADC are retrospective, and involve chart reviews of patients with AIDS. Prospective studies of this condition are in progress. Navia et al. (1986b) retrospectively reviewed their findings in 70 patients with AIDS but without macroscopic focal nervous system diseases (such as toxoplasmosis) or metabolic encephalopathy. Forty-six of these patients had unexplained cognitive or behavioral changes, which were labelled ADC. AIDS risk factors were similar in those with and without ADC, but those with ADC had a higher median duration of AIDS. In over one-third of those with ADC, it was present either at time of diagnosis of AIDS, prior to the manifestation of AIDS or when they were otherwise medically well. The course of the disease was steadily progressive in most patients although there was rapid acceleration or rapid onset in a substantial proportion.

Early features of the ADC were characterized by impairments in cognitive, motor and behavioral function. Cognitive complaints were noted in 29 patients. Forgetfulness (17) and loss of concentration (11), either alone or in combination, were the most frequent early symptoms. Typical complaints were of losing train of thought in mid-sentence and difficulty reading. Eight patients described mental slowness and 10 had more frank confusion, with spatial or temporal disorientation.

Twenty patients had motor symptoms, including loss of balance (15), leg weakness (9) and deterioration in handwriting (6). Behavioral complaints in 17 patients included apathy and social withdrawal (16), dysphoric mood (5), organic psychosis (2) and regressed behavior (1). In addition 6 patients had headaches and three had seizures.

Bedside mental status in the early stages of the ADC was normal in 12 patients, and in 15 others slowness in verbal or motor responses but preserved cognition was noted. Seventeen others had either mild (9) or moderate (8) cognitive impairment. Eighteen patients at this stage had abnormal neurological examinations, including gait ataxia (15), pyramidal tract signs (14), leg weakness (8) and tremor (8). By the later stages of ADC, 34 patients had severe dementia and 11 had moderate dementia. Psychomotor retardation was prominent (38), with mutism in 18 patients. Neurological signs included ataxia (32), hypertonia (22), moderate to severe motor weakness (15), incontinence (21), tremor (20), frontal release signs (17), myoclonus (9), seizures (9) and organic psychosis (7).

The most salient aspects of clinical characterization of ADC are now considered to be slowing and loss of precision in mentation and motor control. In the early stages of ADC, patients typically complain of difficulty coordinating previously routine tasks. For example, one patient reported that he could no longer pay his bills, because he would lose track of what he was doing. They find they must make lists to remember things and break tasks into their component steps in order to accomplish them. Early motor symptoms can include exaggerated tremor or gait unsteadiness, while neurological examination can reveal slowing of rapid movements of eyes and limbs and abnormal frontal release signs. The intellectual impairment progresses to affect nearly all aspects of cognition (Price and Brew, 1988; Price et al., 1988).

The frequency of ADC in the different stages of HIV infection is not established. Price and Brew (1988) speculate that one-third of patients with ARC have mild ADC, with another one-fourth having 'subclinical' ADC which does not impair functional capacity. However, they suggest that ADC is rare in medically asymptomatic individuals.

While neuropsychological testing is useful in quantifying symptoms of ADC, the presence of functional disability is crucial for establishing its presence. Price and Brew (1988) and Price et al. (1988) require unequivocal evidence of functional intellectual or motor impairment before they classify a patient as having mild ADC.

Relationship of ADC and dementia

The diagnosis of dementia in most other conditions relies on set criteria, typically DSM-III-R for degenerative dementia (APA, 1987). Besides requiring functional impairment, these criteria require impaired memory, as well as impairment in other cognitive functions. In order to retain symmetry with investigations of other dementing illnesses, it would be logical to retain the diagnosis of ADC for patients who meet DSM-III-R criteria. However, ADC was not defined in this manner and many patients labelled with ADC are not really demented according to DSM-III-R criteria, but have a typical array of cognitive, behavioral and motor symptoms. As the disease progresses, there is a point where more standard criteria for dementia are met. Janssen et al. (1989) suggest the term 'HIV-1 associated neurocognitive disorder' to describe cognitive deficits occurring in the context of HIV that do not meet criteria for ADC. Their term might be extended to apply to patients who do not yet meet DSM-III-R criteria for dementia, and ADC reserved for patients who do. At this point, however, these terms are not used in this fashion.

Similar to the process of diagnosing probable Alzheimer disease (McKhann et al., 1984), the diagnosis of dementia in AIDS is a process of exclusion. Systemic effects of HIV that might result in metabolic abnormalities such as hypoxia, and the other central HIV effects that have been described must be considered. While there were preliminary concerns that psychiatric symptoms, particularly depression, might mimic dementia, these have been rare and do not contribute to cognitive change.

Neuropsychological studies
More in-depth studies of the neuropsychological changes associated with AIDS have been conducted. While these studies are prospective, and therefore can offer a clearer picture of the cognitive changes of AIDS, they were often not specifically designed to assess dementia as a clinical entity. The typical study assessed patients with AIDS, often in comparison to other CDC classification groups, and, in a post hoc fashion, categorized patients with sufficient cognitive impairments as having dementia or ADC. A more fruitful approach might be to identify patients with the full range of cognitive and neurological changes associated with ADC or dementia and more carefully characterize their neuropsychological status.

Tross et al. (1988) evaluated 20 HIV −, 16 HIV + asymptomatic, 44 with early (newly diagnosed) AIDS and 40 with late AIDS (referred for neurological evaluation), using a battery of tests including naming, verbal fluency, vocabulary, similarities, block design, immediate and delayed verbal and visual recall digit span, trail making, finger tapping and the grooved pegboard. They found that patients with AIDS could be distinguished from all groups without AIDS by significant impairment in tests assessing motor speed (finger tapping) and fine control (grooved pegboard), visuospatial performance (block design) and sequential problem solving (trails and digit symbol), while groups did not differ on tests of language, memory or attention. The authors set criteria for abnormal performance on each test and evaluated the number of patients in each group with two or three abnormal scores. Using this criterion, the following pattern was seen: HIV −, 0%; asymptomatic HIV +, 12%; early AIDS, 32%; and late AIDS, 71%. The two (out of 16) asymptomatic seropositive patients with abnormalities had 3 and 4 abnormal test scores respectively. While this study does not directly address the issue of which patients are demented, it has been used to characterize the nature of cognitive change in AIDS.

Price et al. (1988) summarized the characteristic neuropsychological abnormalities in ADC as difficulty with complex sequencing, impaired fine and rapid motor movement, and reduced verbal fluency. In contrast, other verbal abilities, including vocabulary and object naming, tend to remain intact longer. It is also their impression that complaints of poor memory can be more severe than the memory deficits documented on formal testing.

Characterization of dementia in AIDS
The pattern of cognitive changes early in ADC, mental slowing, difficulty with visual motor integration and difficulty alternating between mental sets, has been often characterized as being concordant

with subcortical dementia. This term has been used to differentiate the dementias seen in Parkinson's disease, Huntington's disease and progressive supranuclear palsy from Alzheimer's disease. This entity is discussed in more depth in the chapter by Dubois et al. in the present volume. Since the dementias of each of these diseases have their own unique features and the concept of subcortical dementia is still disputed, it is not clear that the application of the term imparts any clarity (Whitehouse, 1986). It is probably more useful in each case to describe the phenomenology of the dementia at each stage of severity. Since the early neuropathological changes of HIV occur primarily in subcortical structures, it would be logical to expect intellectual changes that are associated with these areas. Nondemented patients with Parkinson's disease also manifest mental slowing, visuomotor integration difficulties and set-switching problems, presumably due to the reduced dopaminergic innervation of the basal ganglia (Stern, 1987). However, the severely demented Parkinson's disease patient is difficult to distinguish from a patient with Alzheimer's disease. Similarly, the later stages of ADC are associated with generalized dementia that probably encompasses all of the intellectual impairments seen in Alzheimer's disease. Several studies suggest that other aspects of cognition, including memory, are affected in the HIV spectrum. As discussed above, some of the earlier intellectual changes associated with HIV and labeled as ADC do not meet generally accepted criteria for dementia. The field would benefit more from careful characterization of the progression of the dementia than from the application of labels that are relatively uninformative.

Neuropsychological changes in seropositive individuals without AIDS

Asymptomatic individuals

Positive studies. Grant et al. (1987) compared 11 HIV− with 16 HIV+ asymptomatic, 13 ARC and 5 AIDS homosexual men on a battery of tests including vocabulary, digit span, the Halstead Reitan Category test, trail making, symbol digit associate learning, Wechsler Memory Scale logical and visual memory, and the paced serial addition test (PASAT). Comparisons of test scores across groups revealed a significant difference between AIDS patients and controls on the category test and between AIDS patients and all other groups on the PASAT. They then characterized each subject's overall neuropsychological performance as abnormal if at least one test was 'definitely' impaired or two tests were 'probably' impaired. There was a significant trend towards increased frequencies of impairment across groups, with 9% of the HIV− and 44% HIV+ asymptomatic, 54% ARC and 87% of AIDS patients meeting criteria for abnormality. The authors interpreted these results to suggest that asymptomatic HIV+ people may have incipient central nervous system impairment. While the criteria employed to define abnormality are probably much too liberal, and the subject size was relatively restricted, this study sparked the controversy over the presence of neuropsychological changes in HIV+ asymptomatic individuals.

In the Tross et al. (1988) paper discussed above, in no case did the mean scores in the asymptomatic HIV+ group differ significantly from controls; significant differences were limited to comparisons of the controls to those with early and late AIDS. If overall abnormal performance was defined as abnormal performance on at least one test, then the following distribution of abnormality was seen: HIV−, 20%; HIV+ asymptomatic, 43%; early AIDS, 57%; and late AIDS, 92%. However, they argue that with 17 tests in a battery, each having a nominal impairment criterion of 1 standard deviation below the mean, a single abnormality could occur by chance at the rate of approximately 16%. They consequently preferred the presence of 2 or 3 test abnormalities as a criterion for overall abnormal performance. However, even with this more stringent definition of abnormality, they demonstrated a trend toward increasing frequency of overall abnormal performance across the range of HIV severity. These results, while less provocatively presented than those of Grant et al., also suggest the possibility of increasingly prevalent cognitive deficit as HIV progresses, with even some asymptomatic HIV + patients already affected by marked cognitive impairment.

Stern et al. (in press) assessed neurological signs and symptoms, and administered an extensive neuropsychological battery, including tests of memory, language, executive function, visuospatial ability, attention, motor speed, reaction time, and praxis to 208 homosexual men: 84 HIV −, 49 HIV + asymptomatic, 29 mildly symptomatic and 46 with significant medical symptoms but not AIDS. There was no difference between the HIV − and HIV + men in the frequency of neurological signs or of defective (-2 SD) or borderline (-1 SD) performance on any neuropsychological test. However, HIV + men performed slightly but significantly worse than HIV − men on tests of verbal memory (the selective reminding test), executive function (the Odd Man Out Test) and verbal fluency (controlled oral word association). Similar results were obtained when comparisons were limited to HIV + medically asymptomatic and HIV − men. In order to derive a summary score for the neuropsychological tests, the mean and standard deviation of all subjects' scores on each neuropsychological test was calculated, each subject's score on every test was expressed in terms of z scores and the mean of all z scores for each subject was then calculated. There was a small but significant difference between the mean z scores in the HIV − and HIV + groups (mean z score $= 0.072$ and -0.051 respectively; $p < 0.01$). This difference remained significant when only asymptomatic HIV + men were contrasted with the HIV − group. Ratings of neurological signs and symptoms correlated with neuropsychological summary scores in the HIV + group only. Cognitive complaints were more frequent in the HIV + men; they correlated with actual test performance in the HIV + but not HIV − men. They concluded that the constellation of subjective and objective neuropsychological and neurological findings suggests the possibility of a definable syndrome associated with HIV infection in asymptomatic individuals.

Stern et al. (1990) also assessed the possible presence of cognitive changes in a cohort of seropositive parenteral drug users without AIDS. A similar neuropsychological battery was administered to 198 subjects (64 women, 134 men) at a methadone maintenance clinic and a city hospital ID clinic. Eighty-seven subjects were HIV − and 111 HIV +: 33 asymptomatic, 25 mildly symptomatic and 53 symptomatic but without AIDS. Although HIV − and HIV + groups were comparable in age, education, sex distribution and history of head trauma, all comparisons were controlled for these possible confounders. The HIV + group performed significantly worse than the HIV − group on the trail making test, the Odd Man Out and digit symbol. (The Odd Man Out and similar tests of set switching are discussed in the chapter by Dubois et al. in this volume.) These comparisons remained significant when restricted to the HIV + asymptomatic group only. The frequency of overall abnormal neuropsychological performance, based on blind review of the protocols, was comparable in the two groups. Marder et al. (1990) assessed this cohort neurologically and found increased frequency of extrapyramidal and frontal release signs. Since the HIV + drug abusers performed more poorly on speeded tests and those which tap executive function, functions affected in ADC, they hypothesized that these changes may represent an early manifestation of HIV-related cognitive change.

Wilkie et al. (1990) evaluated 46 HIV + homosexual men relative to 13 HIV − controls. None of the HIV + men met criteria for ARC or AIDS although some had lymphadenopathy. Their neuropsychological battery included tests of language, memory, visuospatial processes, reasoning and attention/reaction time. They also included two tests of information-processing speed: the Posner Letter Matching task to assess long-term memory decoding, and the Sternberg paradigm to assess short-term memory search speeds. The HIV + group was significantly slower on the information-processing tasks and performed significantly below controls on the 45 minute delayed recall portion of the Wechsler Memory Scale Logical Memory subest as well as aspects of the selective reminding test.

Negative studies. Several other investigators have reported no significant differences between seropositive asymptomatic patients and controls. Goethe et al. (1989) compared the performance of 33 HIV+ men to 18 HIV− controls. The HIV+ men were subdivided into Walter Reed Stages 1 (asymptomatic) and 2 (chronic lymphadenopathy). The following tests were administered: controlled oral word association, PASAT, verbal selective reminding, continuous visual memory, finger tapping and trails B. There were no significant differences between the groups on any test. They considered overall neuropsychological performance to be impaired if 3/6 of the test scores fell in the impaired range. Based on this criterion, 7 of the stage 1, and 1 of the stage 2 patients were impaired. Goethe et al. argued that their findings do not support the presence of neuropsychological change in asymptomatic individuals. The major weakness of their study is their choice of controls. While most studies have employed HIV− homosexual men as controls, this study used a convenience sample of men referred for evaluation of possible neuropsychological sequelae secondary to remote head injury. Mean duration of loss of consciousness in these individuals was 1.57 h (SD = 2.15; range 0−7). The authors argue that the controls were experiencing stressors that were similar to the HIV+ groups because their continued enlistment in the USAF was contingent on the outcome of their evaluation. However, the use of a head-injured population as a control group has obvious drawbacks.

The Multicenter AIDS Cohort Study (MACS) groups have consistently found no difference between seropositive asymptomatic patients and controls (McArthur et al., 1989). Their study is notable for their large subject pool and the thoroughness of their accompanying evaluation. They compared 193 seronegative controls to 218 seropositive asymptomatic patients and 52 individuals who had seroconverted during the course of their study. All subjects received a neuropsychological screening battery which included symbol digit modalities, digit span, Rey Auditory Verbal Learning Test, COWAT and the grooved pegboard. A larger neuropsychological battery was reserved for individuals who performed poorly on the neuropsychological battery, had neurological complaints or an objective neurological finding, or who met specific psychiatric criteria. The neuropsychological performance trigger for more extensive testing consisted of scores on two independent tests or more of at least 2 SD, or score on one test of at least 3 SD, below the mean. 15% of the seronegatives, 14% seropositive asymptomatic and 12% of the seroconverters performed abnormally based on this definition. Similarly, there were no differences between the group medians on any individual test. Thirty-nine seronegatives and 68 seropositives met criteria for the second tier of evaluation. Additional neuropsychological testing included the Shipley-Hartford Scale, WAIS-R Block Design, Warrington Recognition Memory Test, Rey Complex Figure and Trail Making. There were no significant differences between groups on the median scores for any individual test. There was also no difference between the two groups in the number of people with abnormal overall neuropsychological performance, defined as 1.5 SD below the mean on two tests or 2.5 SD on one test (HIV−, 23%; HIV+ 22%). The authors attempted to identify factors other than HIV, such as anxiety/depression, alcohol/drug abuse or educational problems, that could potentially contribute to abnormal performance. Interestingly, approximately 78% of the HIV− subjects' abnormal performance had possible explanations, as compared to only 33% of the HIV+ subjects. One drawback to this study is the use of a screen to trigger more extensive testing. As discussed above, in a situation where the nature of a potential HIV-related cognitive deficit is unclear, a screen might not include the sensitive tests, precluding further testing. In addition, 47% of the subjects who met criteria for additional testing by the screen criteria were not assessed, either because of time limitations, scheduling constraints or subject refusal. This adds additional constraints to the generalizability of the results of secondary testing. Still, the neuropsychological tests included in the MACS screen battery are similar to those used by other investigators in the field, and the subject population is one of the largest studied, so the value of this study is incontrovertible.

In a followup to the previous study (Miller EN et al., 1990), the MACS group compared performance on their short battery in 769 seronegative homosexual men to 727 asymptomatic seropositive men and found no significant differences. However, when seronegatives were compared to 84 'symptomatic' (CDC group 4) seropositive patients, significant differences were seen on the symbol digit, Rey Auditory Verbal Learning Test, grooved pegboard and trails B. In addition, no decline in performance on this battery was seen in 132 asymptomatic seropositive men followed for 1.5 years (Selnes et al., 1990).

Janssen et al. (1989) studied the following groups: 157 HIV−, 43 HIV+ asymptomatic, 31 with generalized lymphadenopathy and 26 with ARC. All of these men received a short battery of neuropsychological tests; 85 of them received a larger battery. The short battery consisted of Wechsler Memory Scale Logical Memory (immediate and delayed), Digit Symbol (including immediate and delayed recall), trail making, thumb finger sequential touch and the Boston Naming test. The group with ARC was the only HIV+ group that performed significantly worse than the HIV− group on the test battery. Significant differences were seen on logical memory (immediate and delayed recall) and digit symbol (scaled score, immediate and delayed recall). A summary score was created by averaging each patient's z score on each test, using the seronegative group for reference. Again only the group with ARC differed significantly from the controls (HIV+ asymptomatic mean $z = -0.06$; generalized lymphadenopathy, 0.09; ARC, -0.43). Using cutoffs of 1 or 1.5 SD to define abnormality, a significantly higher percentage of subjects with ARC had neuropsychological impairment than HIV− subjects. The other two groups did not differ from the HIV− group. On the longer battery, abnormal performance as determined by blind clinical rating was more frequent in the ARC group than the other three groups.

This group had previously reported that patients with lymphadenopathy had a specific pattern of neuropsychological abnormalities (Janssen et al., 1988). Upon re-analysis, they determined that those with LAS and cognitive change met criteria for ARC as well. The major drawback of the present paper is in the size of the short neuropsychological battery; it is somewhat less extensive than those in other studies. It is also not clear from the present report whether the longer neuropsychological battery revealed any significant differences between groups on the mean scores of individual tests.

Summary of studies in asymptomatic individuals. This review of studies of seropositive asymptomatic patients is by no means exhaustive, but does capture the issues in this current controversy. (A comprehensive critical review of all papers and abstracts in the area up to 1989 was published by Marotta and Perry (1989).) While there have been many studies with negative findings, the positive findings in a few studies cannot be ignored. It is quite probable that subtle neuropsychological changes can be detected early in the course of HIV infection, prior to advent of medical symptoms. In addition, in a small proportion of patients, more serious cognitive abnormalities may be present. However, without careful longitudinal follow-up the significance of these findings remains unclear. If they are the early manifestation of a later dementia, then they have true prognostic value. However, the presence of subtle cognitive changes may have no relation to a later dementia and may be a function of changes that are unique to the early stages of the disease. In addition, the functional implications of any neuropsychological changes remains to be determined.

Different studies utilized the same or relatively equivalent tests and still had contrasting findings. To some extent, this discrepancy might relate to subtle differences in the severity and manifestations of HIV infection in the populations studied, such as time from seroconversion or degree of immunosuppression. In addition, the influence of potential confounders such as socioeconomic factors, education, history of learning disabilities or head trauma and psychiatric disorders including drug or alcohol abuse cannot be ignored and may differ slightly across studies.

Finally, different tests purporting to assess similar functions might yield divergent results simply because they are not pure measures and are not strictly equivalent. For example, both Stern et al. (in press) and Wilkie et al. (1990) found significant differences between HIV + asymptomatic and HIV − groups utilizing a selective reminding procedure. Other groups used other list-learning tasks, including the Rey Auditory Verbal Memory Test and the California Verbal Learning Test, and found no differences. While these are relatively similar assessments of verbal memory, only in the selective reminding test is the entire word list not read to the subject after each recall attempt. This procedural difference might make additional demands on the patient, tapping attentional or executive functions that the other tests do not. In other cases as well, even when similar tests are utilized, differences in procedures, forms and implementation of tests (e.g. manual vs. computerized) can reduce comparability.

Even in studies with positive findings, their clinical implications are unclear. For example, in Stern et al.'s study of homosexual men (in press), seropositive and negative subjects mean total recall on the selective reminding test differed by 3.3 points. Even if differences such as these have theoretical implications for the central effect of HIV, the presentation of these data must emphasize that they suggest no known relation to abilities to perform daily activities.

ARC

While Janssen et al. (1989) found no cognitive change in seropositive, asymptomatic individuals, they have provided evidence for change in patients with ARC. In their study, patients with ARC performed significantly worse than those HIV − individuals on tests of memory (logical memory and digit symbol recall, immediate and delayed) and motor speed and dexterity (thumb-finger sequential touch). A summary global impairment scale also demonstrated poorer overall performance in the group with ARC. In addition, a significantly higher proportion of patients with ARC had test scores falling 1 or 1.5 standard deviations below normative values. Finally, on a longer battery, 44% of the patients with ARC had batteries judged to be abnormal in clinical review, compared to only 12% of seronegative patients. Similarly, other studies, including those of Grant et al. (1987) and Miller EN et al. (1990) above, have documented more frequent neuropsychological abnormalities in patients with ARC.

Treatment

Many of the neuromuscular complications of HIV infection seem dependent on immune regulation. Strategies such as plasmapheresis and immunosuppression (which is quite dangerous in already immunosuppressed patients) have been somewhat successful in Guillain Barre, inflammatory demyelinating polyneuropathy, mononeuritis multiplex and polymyositis in the setting of HIV infection. At present, zidovudine (AZT), a thymidine analogue which inhibits HIV in vitro, is the only drug licensed for treatment of HIV. Other drugs being studied include 2′,3′-dideoxyinosine (DDI), dideoxycytosine (DDC) and soluble CD4. AZT has been helpful in the chronic symmetric sensory neuropathy believed to be due to the direct effects of the HIV virus and has been reported to decrease mortality as well as the frequency and severity of opportunistic infections associated with HIV.

There is preliminary evidence to suggest that AZT may be beneficial in the treatment of dementia, peripheral neuropathy and myelopathy. In seven patients with a variety of these disorders, there was sustained improvement in six or seven for 5 − 18 months (Yarchoan et al., 1988). In a larger, placebo-controlled, parallel trial of AZT (Schmitt et al., 1988), 281 patients with AIDS or ARC were assessed at baseline and at 16 weeks with tests of attention (two and seven test, memory selective reminding test), visual-motor skills (symbol digit, finger tapping and trails B) and mood and affect (Positive Symptom Distress Index). In the 159 patients with AIDS, significant improvement was seen in all tests administered at week 8 and in all but finger tapping at week 16. In contrast, the patients with ARC showed significant improvement only in consistent long-term retrieval on the selective reminding test and symbol digit, and these changes were seen only at week 16. The more significant improvement in those who had AIDS than in those with advanced ARC is not easily explained; baseline levels of neuro-psychological performance did not differ in the two groups. One interesting feature of this study is that neuropsychological evaluations were conducted at screening and then at the study baseline in an attempt to control for learning effects.

Further studies are needed to demonstrate whether subjects with only mild cognitive changes might benefit from this drug. There are serious side-effects such as bone marrow suppression which must be weighed against possible benefit derived from early treatment.

Conclusions

The result of HIV infection is best viewed as a continuum, along which we should attempt to place each seropositive individual. The presence of cognitive change in the seropositive asymptomatic individual is controversial. There are sufficient positive studies suggesting that some early cognitive changes occur, but the prognostic and functional implications of these changes are unclear. More accepted is the presence of more marked cognitive changes in a subset of patients with ARC and AIDS. The label ADC has been applied to a typical array of cognitive, motor and affective symptoms in ARC and AIDS, which can result directly from the action of HIV on the CNS. Especially in the earlier stages of ADC as described in the literature, many patients might not meet generally accepted criteria for dementia, and to that extent the label is misleading. The HIV spectrum is also associated with a vast array of other neurological conditions that can directly affect the patient's cognitive and functional

capacities. Prospective studies are required to better delineate the relationship between HIV infection and the observed neurological and neuro-psychological manifestations. Many of these are currently under way and promise to clarify many of the issues raised in this review.

Acknowledgement

This work was supported in part by center grant MH43520 from NIMH/NIDA.

Abbreviations

ADC	AIDS dementia complex
AIDS	acquired immunodeficiency syndrome
ARC	AIDS-related complex
AZT	zidovidine
CDC	Centers for Disease Control
CIDP	chronic inflammatory demyelinating polyneuropathy
CMV	cytomegalovirus
CNS	central nervous system
COWAT	controlled oral word association test
CT	computed tomography
DDC	dideoxycytosine
DDI	$2',3'$-dideoxyinosine
DSM-III-R	Diagnostic and Statistical Manual – Third Edition – Revised
HIV	human immunodeficiency virus
HSV	herpes simplex virus
IVDU	intravenous drug use/r
LAS	lymphadenopathy syndrome
MACS	Multicenter AIDS Cohort Study
MRI	magnetic resonance imaging
PASAT	paced serial addition test
PCP	*Pneumocystis carinii* pneumonia
PGL	persistent generalized lymphadenopathy
PML	progressive multifocal leukoencephalopathy

References

American Psychiatric Association. *Diagnostic and Statistical Manual.* Third Edition – Revised. Washington, DC, APA: 1987.

Barre-Sinoussi F, Chermann JC, Rey F, et al: Isolation of a T-lymphotropic retrovirus from a patient at risk for acquired immune deficiency syndrome (AIDS). *Science: 220,* 868 – 871, 1983.

Berger J, Moskowitz L, Fischl M, Kelley RE: Neurologic disease as the presenting manifestation of the acquired immunodeficiency syndrome. *South. Med. J.: 80,* 683 – 686, 1987.

Brew BJ, Rosenblum M, Price RW: AIDS dementia complex and primary HIV brain infection. *J. Neuroimmun.: 10,* 133 – 140, 1988.

Britton C, Mesa-Tejada C, Fenoglio C, Hays A: A new complication of AIDS: thoracic myelitis caused by herpes simplex virus. *Neurology: 35,* 1071 – 1074, 1985.

Carne CA, Tedder RS, Smith A, Sutherland S, Elkington SG, Daly HM, Preston FE, Craske J: Acute encephalopathy coincident with seroconversion for anti-HTLV-III. *Lancet: 2,* 1206 – 1207, 1986.

Centers for disease control: Classification system for human T-lymphotropic virus type III/lymphadenopathy-associated virus infections. *Morbid. Mortal. Weekly Rep.: 35,* 334, 1986.

Cheng-Mayer C, Levy JA: Distinct biologic and serologic properties of HIV isolates from the brain. *Ann. Neurol.: 23,* s58 – s61, 1988.

Chuck S, Sande M: Infections with cryptococcus neoformans in the acquired immunodeficiency syndrome. *N. Engl. J. Med.: 321,* 794 – 799, 1989.

Clumeck N, Mascart-Lemone F, deMaubeuge J, Brenez D, Marcelis L: Acquired immune deficiency syndrome in black Africans. *Lancet: 1,* 642, 1983.

Cooper DA, Gold J, Maclean P, Donovan B, Finlayson R, Barnes TG, Michelmore HM, Brooke P, Penny R: Acute AIDS retrovirus infection: Definition of a clinical illness associated with seroconversion. *Lancet: 1,* 537 – 540, 1985.

Dalakas MC, Pezeshkpour GH: Neuromuscular diseases associated with human immunodeficiency virus infection. *Ann. Neurol.: 23,* s38 – s47, 1988.

Friedland G, Klein R: Transmission of the human immunodeficiency virus. *N. Engl. J. Med.: 317,* 1125 – 1142, 1987.

Gallo R: The cause of AIDS: an overview on its biology, mechanisms of disease induction, and our attempts to control it. *J. Acquired Immune Def. Syn.: 1,* 521 – 535, 1988.

Glatt A, Chirgwin K, Landesman S: Treatment of infections associated with human immunodeficiency virus. *N. Engl. J. Med.: 318,* 1439 – 1447, 1988.

Goethe K, Mitchell J, Marshall W, Brey R, Cahill W, Leger D, Hoy L, Boswell N: Neuroopsychological and neurological function of human immunodeficiency virus seropositive asymptomatic individuals. *Arch. Neurol.: 46,* 129 – 133, 1989.

Goudsmit J, de Wolf F, Paul D, Epstein L, Lange J, Krone W, Speelman H, Wolters E, Van Der Noorda J, Oleske J, Van der Helm K, Coutinho K: Expression of human immunodeficiency virus antigen in serum and cerebrospinal fluid during acute and chronic infection. *Lancet: 2,* 177 – 180, 1986.

Grant I, Atkinson J, Hesselink J, et al: Evidence for early central nervous system involvement in the acquired immunodeficiency syndrome and other HIV infections. *Ann. Int. Med.: 107,* 828 – 836, 1987.

Haseltine W, Wong-Staal F: The molecular biology of the AIDS virus. *Sci. Am.: 259,* 52 – 60, 1988.

Ho D, Pomerantz R, Kaplan J: Pathogenesis of infections with human immunodeficiency virus. *N. Engl. J. Med.: 317,* 278 – 286, 1987.

Hollander H, Levy J: Neurologic abnormalities and recovery of human immunodeficiency virus from cerebrospinal fluid. *Ann. Int. Med.: 106,* 692 – 695, 1987.

Hollander H, Stringari S: Human immunodeficiency virus associated meningitis; Clinical course and correlations. *Am. J. Med.: 83,* 813 – 816, 1987.

Holzman DM, Kaku DA, Yuen T: New-onset seizures associated with human immunodeficiency virus infection: causation and clinical features in 100 cases. *Am. J. Med.: 87,* 174 – 177, 1989.

Imagawa D, Lee MH, Wolinsky S, Sano K, Morales F, Kwok S, Sninsky J, Nishanian P, Giorgi J, Fahey J, Dudley J, Visscer B, Detels R: Human immunodeficiency virus type 1 infection in homosexual men who remain seronegative for prolonged periods. *N. Engl. J. Med.: 320,* 1458 – 1462, 1989.

Janssen R, Saykin A, Kaplan J, et al: Neurological symptoms and neuropsychological abnormalities in lymphadenopathy syndrome. *Ann. Neurol.: 23* (suppl), S17 – 18, 1988.

Janssen RS, Saykin AJ, Cannon L, Campbell J, Pinsky PF, Hessol NA, O'Malley PM, Lifson AR, Doll LS, Rutherford GW, Kaplan JE: Neurological and neuropsychological manifestations of HIV-1 infection: association with AIDS-related complex but not asymptomatic HIV-1 infection. *Ann. Neurol.: 26,* 592 – 600, 1989.

Koppel B, Worsmer, Tuchman A, Maayan S, Hewlett D, Daras M: Central nervous system involvement in patients with acquired immunodeficiency syndrome. *Acta Neurol. Scand.: 71,* 337 – 353, 1985.

Kovacs JA, Kovacs AA, Polis M, et al: Cryptococcosis in the acquired immunodeficiency syndrom. *Ann. Intern. Med.: 103,* 533 – 538, 1985.

Lange D, Britton B, Younger D, Hays H: The neuromuscular manifestations of HIV. *Arch. Neurol.: 45,* 1084 – 1088, 1988.

Levy J: Human immunodeficiency viruses and the pathogenesis of AIDS. *J. Am. Med. Assoc.: 261,* 2997 – 3006, 1989.

Levy R, Bredesen D, Rosenblum M: Neurological manifestations of the acquired immunodeficiency syndrome: experience at UCSF and review of the literature. *J. Neurosurg.: 62,* 475 – 495, 1985.

Levy R, Janssen R, Bush T, Rosenblum M: Neuroepidemiology of acquired immunodeficiency syndrome. In Rosenblum M, Levy R, Bredesen D (Editors), *AIDS and the Nervous System.* New York, Raven: pp. 13 – 27, 1988a.

Levy R, Bredesen D, Rosenblum M: Opportunistic central nervous system pathology in patients with AIDS. *Ann. Neurol.: 23,* s7 – s12, 1988b.

Lui KJ, Darrow WW, Rutherford GW: A model-based estimate of the mean incubation period for AIDS in homosexual men. *Science: 240,* 1333 – 1335, 1989.

Marder K, Malouf R, Doonief G, Bell K, Chenn J, Gorman J, Ehrhardt A, Mayeux R: Neurological signs and symptoms in parenteral drug users. Sixth International Conference on AIDS, 1990.

Marotta R, Perry S: Early neuropsychological dysfunction caused by human immunodeficiency virus. *J. Neuropsychiat.: 1,* 225 – 235, 1989.

Marshall DW, Brey RL, Cahill WT, Houk RW, Zajac RA, Boswell RN: Spectrum of cerebrospinal fluid findings in various stages of human immunodeficiency virus infection. *Arch. Neurol.: 45,* 954 – 958, 1988.

McArthur J: Neurologic manifestations of AIDS. *Medicine: 66,* 407 – 437, 1988.

McArthur J, Cohen B, Farzedgan H, Cornblath D, Selnes O, Ostrow D, Johnson R, Phair J, Polk B: Cerebrospinal fluid abnormalities in homosexual men with and without neuro-psychological findings. *Ann. Neurol.: 23,* s34 – s37, 1988.

McArthur J, Cohen B, Selnes O, Kumar A, Cooper K, McArthur J, Soucy J, Cornblath D, Chmiel J, Wang M-C, Starkey D, Ginzburg H, Ostrow D, Johnson R, Phair J, Polk B: Low prevalence of neurological and neuropsychological abnor-malities in otherwise healthy HIV-1 infected individuals: results from the multicenter AIDS cohort study. *Ann. Neurol.: 26,* 601 – 609, 1989.

McKhann G, Drachman D, Folstein M, et al: Clinical diagnosis of Alzheimer's disease: Report of the NINCDS-ADRDA Work Group under auspices of the Department of Health and Human Services Task force on Alzheimer's disease. *Neurology: 34,* 939 – 44, 1984.

Miller EN, Selnes OA, McArthur JA, Satz P, Becker JT, Cohen BA, Sheridan K, Machado AM, Van Gorp WG, Visscher B: Neuropsychological performance in HIV-1 infected homosex-ual men: The Multicenter AIDS Cohort Study (MACS). *Neurology: 40,* 197 – 203, 1990.

Miller RG, Storey JR, Grecco CM: Ganciclovir in the treatment of progressive AIDS-related polyradiculopathy. *Neurology: 40,* 569 – 574, 1990.

Mills S: Pneumocystis carinii and toxoplasma gondii infections in patients with AIDS. *Rev. Infect. Dis.: 8,* 1001 – 1011, 1986.

Nath A, Kerman RH, Novak IS, Wolinsky JS: Immune studies in human immunodeficiency virus infection with myasthenia gravis: a case report. *Neurology: 40,* 581 – 583, 1990.

Navia BA, Petito CK, Gold JWM, Cho E-S, Jordan BD, Price RW: Cerebral toxoplasmosis complicating the acquired im-munodeficiency syndrome: clinical and neuropathological fin-dings in 27 patients. *Ann. Neurol.: 19,* 224 – 238, 1986a.

Navia BA, Jordan BD, Price RW: The AIDS dementia complex: I. Clinical features. *Ann. Neurol.: 19,* 517 – 524, 1986b.

Navia B, Cho E-S, Petito C, Price RW: The AIDS dementia com-plex: II. Neuropathology. *Ann. Neurol.:19,* 525 – 535, 1986c.

Parry G: Peripheral neuropathies associated with human im-munodeficiency virus infection. *Ann. Neurol.: 23,* s49 – 53, 1988.

Petito CK: Review of central nervous system pathology in human immunodeficiency virus infection. *Ann. Neurol.: 23,* s54 – s57, 1988.

Petito CK, Cho E-S, Lemann W, Navia BA, Price RW: Neuropathology of acquired immunodeficiency syndrome (AIDS): an autopsy review. *J. Neuropath. Exp. Neurol.: 45,* 635 – 646, 1986.

Price RW, Brew BJ: The AIDS dementia complex. *J. Infect. Dis.: 158,* 1079 – 1083, 1988.

Price RW, Brew B, Sidtis J, Rosenblum M, Sheck A, Cleary P: The brain in AIDS: central nervous system HIV-1 infection and AIDS dementia complex. *Science: 239,* 586 – 592, 1988.

Pumarola-Sune T, Navia BA, Cordon-Carlo C, Cho ES, Price BW: HIV antigen in the brains of patients with the AIDS dementia complex. *Ann. Neurol.: 21,* 490 – 496, 1987.

Redfield R, Wright D, Tramont E: The Walter Reed staging classification for HTLV III/LAV infection. *N. Engl. J. Med: 314,* 1986.

Redfield R, Burke D: HIV infections: the clinical picture. *Sci. Am.: 259,* 90 – 99, 1988.

Rosenblum M, Levy R, Bredesen D, So Y, Wara W, Ziegler J: Primary central nervous system lymphomas in patients with AIDS. *Ann. Neurol.: 23,* s13 – s16, 1988.

Schmitt F, Bigley J, McKinnis R, Logue P, Evans R, Drucker J: Neuropsychological outcome of zidovudine treatment of pa-tients with AIDS and AIDS-related complex. *N. Engl. J. Med.: 319,* 1573 – 1578, 1988.

Selnes OA, Miller E, McArthur JA, Gordon B, Munoz A, Sheridan K, Fox R, Saah AJ: HIV-1 infection: no evidence of clinical decline during the asymptomatic stages. *Neurology: 40,* 204 – 208, 1990.

So Y, Choucair A, Davis R, Wara W, Ziegler J, Sheline G, Beckstead J: Neoplasms of the central nervous system in ac-quired immunodeficiency syndrome. In Rosenblum J, Levy R, Bredesen D (Editors), *AIDS and the Nervous System.* New York: Raven, p. 285, 1987.

Soave R, Johnson W: Cryptosporidium and isospora belli infec-tions. *J. Infect. Dis.: 157,* 225 – 229, 1988.

Stern Y: The basal ganglia and intellectual function. In Schneider J (Editor), *Basal Ganglia and Behavior: Sensory Aspects of Motor Functioning.* Toronto: Hans Huber, pp. 169 – 74, 1987.

Stern Y, Sano M, Goldstein S, Richards M, Kloehn J, Mindry D, Chen J, Ehrhardt A, Gorman J: Neuropsychological evalua-tion of seropositive parenteral drug users without AIDS. Sixth International Conference on AIDS, 1990.

Stern Y, Marder K, Bell K, Chen J, Dooneief G, Goldstein S, Mindry D, Richards M, Sano M, Williams J, Gorman J, Ehrhardt A, Mayeux R: Multidisciplinary baseline assessment of gay men with and without HIV infection: III. Neurological and neuropsychological findings. *Arch. Gen. Psychiat.:* in press.

Tross S, Price R, Navia B, Thaler HT, Gold J, Hirsch DA, Sidtis JJ: Neuropsychological characterization of the AIDS Demen-tia Complex: a preliminary report. *AIDS: 2,* 81 – 88, 1988.

Update: Acquired immunodeficiency syndrome-United States, 1981 – 1988. *MMWR: 38,* 229 – 236, 1989.

Whitehouse PJ: The concept of subcortical and cortical demen-tia: another look. *Ann. Neurol.: 19,* 1 – 6, 1986.

Wilkie FL, Eisdorfer CE, Morgan R, Lowenstein DA, Szapocz-nik J: Cognition in early human immunodeficiency virus in-fection. *Arch. Neurol.: 47,* 433 – 440, 1990.

Yarchoan R, Grafman T, Wichman A, Dalakas M, McAtee N, Berg G, Fischl M, Perno C, Klecker R, Buchbinder A, Tay S, Larson S, Myers C, Broder S: Long-term administration of 3'-azido-2',3'-dideoxythymidine to patients with AIDS-related neurological disease. *Ann. Neurol.: 23,* s82 – s87, 1988.

Young L, Inderlied C, Berlin O, Gottlieb M: Mycobacterial in-fections in AIDS patients, with an emphasis on the mycobacterium avium complex. *Rev. Infect. Dis.: 8* 1024 – 1033, 1986.

Zuger A, Louie E, Holzman R, Simberkoff M, Rahal J: Cryp-tococcal disease in patients with the acquired immunodeficien-cy syndrome: diagnostic features and outcome of treatment. *Ann. Intern. Med.: 194,* 234 – 240, 1986.

Section 9

Cognitive, Methodological and Practical Approaches

editors

J. Grafman and F. Boller

© 1991 Elsevier Science Publishers B.V.
Handbook of Neuropsychology, Vol. 5
F. Boller and J. Grafman (Eds)

CHAPTER 13

The role of cognitive theory in neuropsychological research

Andrew Olson and Alfonso Caramazza

Department of Cognitive Science, The Johns Hopkins University, Baltimore, MD 21218, U.S.A.

Introduction

The major aim of cognitive neuropsychology is to understand how the brain enables people to speak and understand, read and write, figure numbers, perceive a melodic line, or do any of many other day-to-day activities that involve the ensemble of human mental capacities. Current (nontrivial) theories of cognition do not refer to the specifics of brain activity. How can such theories map onto the details of brain function given the complexity of the brain's morphology, its interactive circuits, its numerous neurotransmitters, firing patterns, and the like? What kinds of theories must cognitive neuropsychology develop so that our understanding of the cognitive processes involved in, say, spelling a word, can meaningfully relate to our understanding of the brain structures that make spelling a word possible?

Cognitive neuropsychology studies how cognitive functions are altered as a consequence of brain damage. If one accepts the assumption that no new cognitive structures are created as a consequence of brain injury, the patterns of performance shown by brain-damaged subjects reveal an information-processing system that functions with some of its operations impaired. On the assumption that the structure of the normal system limits the transformations that damage can inflict, it is possible to reconstruct the organization of the cognitive system from patterns of impaired performance. (Biologi-

cal/physiological/anatomical organization may limit the possible transformations still further. We will return to this issue in section III.)

In metaphorical terms, data from neurological patients form the shapes of a puzzle and cognitive theory is a frame or board that guides where the shapes can be laid. A theory of the cognitive requirements of a task enables us to put shapes defined by many brain-damaged subjects together to form a coherent picture of how a task is carried out. None of the pieces judged relevant by the theory should be left over, so if some facts cannot be fitted, the framework must either be discarded in favor of some other, or it must be used to show that these facts are not relevant to the issues at hand. Data from sources other than brain-damaged subjects – evidence of linguistic knowledge (e.g. intuitions concerning the grammaticality of sentences) or reaction time studies with normal subjects – may also reveal the processes and representations the brain is using, providing further pieces of the puzzle. Performance consequent to brain damage, however, is a special source of data because it may reveal the workings of brain processes that are not normally evidenced in behavior. It may, therefore, provide some unique or oddly shaped pieces of the puzzle that will set important constraints on theories that describe the structure of cognitive systems.

The metaphor of a mutually dependent board and puzzle pieces should not be taken so literally that one assumes data from brain-damaged subjects reveal well-defined functional components neatly excised by damage. The possible functional effects of brain damage, in fact, are far from clear. We assume that damage cannot create any new cognitive structures, but the range limiting allowable transformations of existing cognitive structures is unknown. Furthermore, isolated deficits that result in circumscribed dysfunction are rare. Instead of neatly removing functional components, damage usually causes several deficits, some of which may interact to transform processing in complex ways. As a result, there is often a complicated relationship between impaired performance and the mechanisms affected by the deficit. Not only are there many pieces to put together to solve the puzzle, it is difficult to identify the pieces of the puzzle themselves. (For a detailed discussion of the metatheoretical and methodological problem associated with the use of impaired performance consequent to brain damage in order to constrain theories of normal cognitive processing see Caramazza (1984, 1986). A related but fundamentally different view is presented by Shallice (1988).) These caveats, however, do not lessen the need for cognitive theory. Quite the contrary, theory will constrain the interpretation of data that have ambiguous significance, and force the consequences of a particular interpretation, even if incorrect, to become apparent.

The argument we will develop in this paper, then, is as follows. In section 1 we will argue that cognitive systems are best understood as information-processing devices and, as such, are describable as a series of independent processing components, each with a specific function. Taking word production in oral reading and spelling (writing) as example domains, we will argue that research in cognitive neuropsychology cannot proceed meaningfully without a computationally oriented theory of the cognitive mechanisms that support normal performance (by 'computational' we mean, after Marr, what is computed and why (Marr, 1982)). In particular, independent processing components and their arrangement (the functional architecture of the cognitive system) must be specified, along with the representations and processes used by each component.

Hypotheses that lay out a functional architecture specify the domains of information that are processed in relatively independent processing systems (e.g. in the case of writing to dictation, phonological information, semantic information, orthographic information), and they specify the possible interactions between systems. When we refer to 'functional architecture' in the text, we are referring to this set of hypotheses. Although details of processing within components may be left unspecified at this level of explanation, the claims made are still substantial. Architectures with different components or with components that are connected differently will account for different patterns of error.

When, on the other hand, we refer to representations and processes within components, we are referring to a more detailed set of hypotheses. Representations specify the information encoded by a component (e.g. phonological features, perhaps in a hierarchical structure), and processes transform one class of representations into another.

A description of the functional architecture and a description of the representations and processes used by each component constitute an account of how information is transformed during a cognitive task. We will call these hypotheses a 'functional' account. The form of a cognitive architecture and the form of its representations and processes will limit each other. A specific functional architecture constrains the representations and processes it can make use of; at the same time, the representations and processes a component uses will determine how it can interact with other components in the architecture. We will argue that a meaningful understanding of cognitive pathology must link a brain-damaged subject's pattern of errors to damaged representations and processes within a functional architecture. The methodological consequences that follow are briefly mentioned.

In section II we will argue that the functional vocabulary we develop, our descriptions of the cognitive operations that the brain performs, will be essential to identifying the brain structures and physiological processes that carry out those operations. Many chemical, electrical and cellular changes occur during brain activity. A mapping of functional descriptions to biology will require that we be able to isolate those changes that are specifically related to information processing (as opposed, for example, to changes that are metabolic but not tied to cognitive operations). The level of detail in our functional description will have to be at least as fine as the level at which information-processing functions are physiologically localized. If the scale is not right, the correlation between measures of neural activity or lesion sites and a functional description of behavior will not be high. Functional descriptions are not a luxury that can be discarded once the biological description advances. Biology may be able to say how functions are carried out by brain tissues, but a functional vocabulary will be required to describe what cognitive operations neural structures are performing.

Finally, in section III we will argue that development of explicit theories of cognition and the mapping of functional theories onto the brain will be aided by the use of biologically oriented and functionally oriented simulation models. The information-processing constraints that are imposed by the physical organization of the brain (if any) and the functional consequences of damage are far from clear. Models based on the physical properties of neurons or more abstract models that explore formal computational properties (e.g. parallel processing) may provide information on these questions where ethical considerations properly limit the range of methodologies that can be used to study human capacities (i.e. forbid lesioning studies or other destructive manipulations). Simulation models of functional architectures will force abstract theories of multi-component systems to be computationally specific. We will stress, however, that not all computational models are equal, and that, to be useful for empirical work, models must have *explanatory perspicuity*. Models, that is, must not only produce a range of outputs that correspond to the behaviors being modelled, they must also make clear what mechanisms are responsible for the outputs they produce. This includes knowing how information in the model is structured, and how the

TABLE 1

Spelling errors made by dysgraphic brain-damaged subjects

Stimulus	Response	Stimulus	Response
fabric	phabrick	cabin	kabbin
journal	jernal	chief	cheef
truck	bus	elbow	leg
leopard	tiger	apple	orange
brush	bpush	count	ount
happy	fappy	faith	faih
soft	ssoft	tiger	tgier
oyster	osyster	church	chucrh
learn	learning	hungry	hunger
powerful	powerfully	bent	bend
picked	pick		

model makes decisions. Computational models that do not reveal how they are structured may be useful as objects of study in themselves, but they cannot function as explanations of phenomena if they are just as opaque as the phenomena they mimic.

I. Cognitive theory: essential for an understanding of cognitive pathology

The issues introduced above will be clearer if they are developed in a specific context. We will initially illustrate them by considering the processing components necessary for spelling, including those components spelling shares with other language functions.

Consider the spelling errors made by various dysgraphic subjects studied in our laboratory (Table 1).

Several aspects of these brain-damaged subjects' performance suggests that the system that produced them has internal structure. First of all, stimuli and the errors made to them can be related to each other along separate dimensions: errors such as *fabric → phabrick* suggest a phonological but not an orthographic relationship between stimulus and response — these errors have traditionally been called phonologically plausible errors (PPE); errors such as *leopard → tiger* indicate a semantic relationship between stimulus and response − these errors have been called semantic paragraphias; errors of the type *brush → bpush* suggest an orthographic but not a phonological relationship between stimulus and response − we will call them orthographically related errors (ORE); and finally, errors of the type *picked → pick* suggest a morphological relationship between stimulus and response − these are termed morphological paragraphias.

Specific relationships between stimulus and response may be noted in error patterns that appear in relative isolation in different brain-damaged subjects. Although all the errors shown in Table 1 have been recorded in patient data, the different types of error shown may be made by single brain-damaged subjects in relative isolation from errors of other types (e.g. the 'phonologically plausible errors' shown between the first set of lines were produced by a dysgraphic subject, JG, whose spelling errors were virtually all of this type (Goodman and Caramazza, 1987)). This non-random patterning of errors, in which relatively homogeneous error patterns may be observed, encourages the hypothesis that there is a spelling system composed of several relatively independent components, each devoted to processing a different aspect of written words, and each vulnerable to damage in isolation.

If different patterns of impairment did not show up in relative isolation, it would be difficult to argue from the data shown that the spelling system had internal structure. If each brain-damaged subject, that is, made errors from the range listed above, the structural implications of their data would be unclear. It could mean that spelling was a functionally homogeneous process, or it could mean that spelling was differentiated functionally, but that the tissue which carried out the various functionally independent operations was intertwined enough that any damage would affect all functions. More on the relation between functional and anatomical issues will follow section II.

Even a common-sense notion of what is involved in writing to dictation, however, would divide the process into several stages. The auditory input must be heard, it must be perceived and identified as a particular word (e.g, /lid/-'lead' vs. /rid/-'read'), the meaning of the word must be accessed (e.g., /rid/: activity with books vs. /rid/: object, plant, part of a musical instrument), the letters that constitute the word have to be retrieved either as part of a whole word (e.g., 'read' vs. 'reed'), or as graphemes corresponding to the word's phonemes, the particular form of the letters to be produced must be decided on (upper or lower case, cursive or printing), and the motor actions to write the word have to be programmed and carried out. This vague, intuitive sense of structure has been given definition and provided with empirical support by neuropsychological data.

Fig. 1 shows a widely accepted version of the major processing components involved in spelling (see Ellis, 1982; Margolin, 1984; Goodman and Caramazza, 1986; Caramazza et al., 1986; Patterson and Shewell, 1987; but see Campbell, 1983, for an alternative view). In the theory represented schematically by the figure, boxes specify the types of informa-

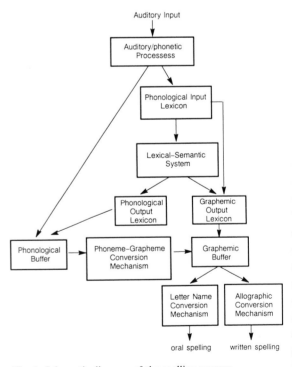

Fig. 1. Schematic diagram of the spelling process.

tion (e.g., phonological) that control processing within autonomous components and also the kinds of processing that occur there (e.g. short-term storage, access of representations etc.). The arrows represent the possible interactions between components. Together, they describe a hypothesis concerning the information processing necessary to spell any word or unfamiliar phonologically legal string. The box marked phonological input lexicon, for example, represents a component that takes abstract phonological information from auditory input and activates stored lexical-phonological representations. If the information (which may also be supplemented by information provided by syntactic and semantic context) matches an entry in the phonological lexicon, the word is 'recognized' and processing begins on its meaning (within the lexical-semantic system). Other boxes represent other relatively independent domains of processing.

The architecture or component structure of cognitive systems has often been elaborated on the basis of evidence from neuropsychological dissociations in performance (that is, evidence of relative impairment in one capacity, while, at the same time, another capacity remains relatively unimpaired), and, in fact, some researchers have argued that dissociation is the *only* pattern on which strong claims about cognitive architecture can be based (Shallice, 1988; Bub and Bub, 1988). Dissociations *have* provided important evidence for some of the basic distinctions made by the theory represented by Fig. 1. The distinction between lexical and nonlexical processing, for example, has been motivated by observation of two opposite patterns of performance. On the one hand, brain-damaged subjects have been described who can spell unfamiliar words (nonwords) and regular words, but who often fail to spell words with inconsistent or irregular spellings (Beauvois and Dèrouesnè, 1981). The opposite pattern has also been described; namely brain-damaged subjects who can spell regular and irregular familiar words, but who have difficulty spelling unfamiliar words — the latter operationally represented by nonwords (Shallice, 1981). The brain-damaged subjects who can spell unfamiliar and regular words are

presumably using a mechanism for converting units smaller than words into letters (termed phoneme-to-grapheme conversion in Fig. 1). In the context of the theory, it is assumed that these brain-damaged subjects cannot access the lexical representations necessary to generate the correct spelling for words which could plausibly be spelled in more than one way, or for words that have irregular spellings. Brain-damaged subjects who spell familiar but not unfamiliar words have a normal ability to access lexical representations for spelling (phonological input lexicon, lexical-semantic system, orthographic output lexicon in Fig. 1), but presumably have damage to the sublexical phonology-to-orthography conversion mechanism needed for spelling novel words. This double dissociation in performance on tasks using familiar and unfamiliar words provides strong evidence that there are independent mechanisms for processing lexical and sublexical orthographic representations.

Dissociations, but also a broader range of neuropsychological evidence (e.g. associations, analysis of error patterns — see discussion below), motivate the other components in the lexical system, including an input orthographic lexicon used for reading; an output phonological lexicon used for naming, reading aloud, repetition, or more generally, any task that requires spoken output; and a lexical-semantic system used by any language task that involves comprehension (see Fig. 2 for a schematized version of the processing components assumed to constitute the lexical system). Data from a series of familiar word and unfamiliar word (nonword) tasks converge to support the existence and arrangement of the components schematized in Fig. 1, and to support a similar set of components for reading (see Ellis (1982) for a review of spelling, and Coltheart (1985) for a review of reading. Caramazza (1988) reviews evidence for the organization of the lexical system).

Dissociations and common-sense applied mechanically, however, can only go so far to reveal the details of a cognitive architecture. Interpretation of dissociations is not always straightforward, and it is not always clear that dissociations are theoretically useful given our present understanding. The informativeness of a dissociation depends on our expectation as to whether abilities *should* dissociate. Dissociations are interesting when there is some question as to whether the structures underlying some ability are, in theory, linked, or, alternatively, whether they are a part of a single domain and yet separate within it. Obviously, for example, a dissociation between spelling and the ability to match color patches does not seem particularly interesting, but this is probably because we imagine that spelling and matching color patches have little to do with each other. Our intuitions reveal a theoretical point. Whether we believe that a dissociation between performance in spelling and performance in some other task will be interesting depends on whether we believe the two tasks have anything in common, and that depends on the theory one proposes to account for performance in each task. Mechanical use of dissociation between color matching and spelling, however, is surely less significant than a dissociation between spelling familiar and unfamiliar words.

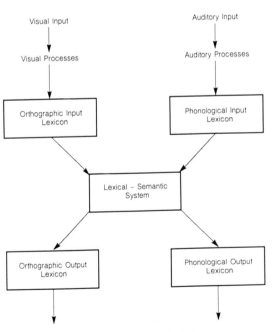

Fig. 2. Schematic representation of the lexical system.

The mechanical use of dissociations does not only fail to make distinctions; it is also too restrictive. Since we are interested in the computational specifics of a cognitive system, a wider range of evidence will be useful when guided by the theory one is pursuing. Associations in which patterns of performance for two tasks closely correspond can and must provide the evidence in those cases where information from two or more different sources converges on a single component (e.g. the graphemic buffer is thought to be shared by both lexical and nonlexical writing systems (Fig. 1). Association evidenced by errors on tasks that require lexical and nonlexical processing was relevant evidence supporting the buffer's location in the spelling process (Caramazza et al., 1987)). No prescription regarding the types of data that will be relevant can be made a priori. Relevance must be judged based on the inferences that connect *patterns* of performance to some cognitive theory. A methodology cannot substitute for theory as a guide for research (see Caramazza (1986) for discussion).

These issues will be clearer in the context of some actual clinical results. In the cases that follow, we will see that inferences from a wide range of data are possible. The interpretations of performance in one task, for example, may depend on performance in some other task, and associated distributions of errors may be informative. Data that shape the functional architecture of a cognitive system will raise questions concerning the internal structure of each component, leading toward further computational detail. Conversely, the representations and processes utilized by particular components will, as they are revealed, constrain the possible architectures that could contain them.

A. Case Study I – Semantic errors. Interpretation of performance depends on performance in other tasks related by theory

Consider two cases drawn from studies in our laboratory concerning the lexical system. These studies examined brain-damaged subjects who made semantic errors in oral reading. The errors were similar to the semantic 'paragraphias' for writing listed above. They involve substitution of a semantically related item for the stimulus to be read.

KE was a well-educated, 52-year-old male who suffered left-hemisphere brain damage as a result of a stroke. In an oral reading task consisting of 144 picturable nouns drawn from several semantic categories he produced 36.1% semantic errors, where these errors accounted for the majority of his incorrect responses (he made 41.7% total errors). Examples of his semantic errors are shown in Table 2 (for a more detailed report on this brain-damaged subject's performance see Hillis et al., 1989).

A second left-hemisphere brain-damaged subject, RGB, also made semantic paralexias in the same reading task as was used with KE. RGB made 36% semantic errors, where again, semantic errors accounted for the majority of the incorrect responses (Table 3). The errors were similar to those made by KE (Table 2) (for a more detailed report of this brain-damaged subject's performance see Caramazza and Hillis, 1989).

Based on their performance on these two tasks, the brain-damaged subjects appear to have identical problems. It would be reasonable to hypothesize damage to processing within the lexical-semantic component (Fig. 2) as a cause for these patterns of performance. Presumably, the semantic entry for a word that causes an error is not accessed normally, and a related word is activated. This is a woefully underspecified account of how semantic access or processing operates, but in the context of the theory we are proposing, the hypothesis of damage to a specific component still allows some predictions. Specifically, brain-damaged subjects with damage to the lexical-semantic component should make semantic errors in any other task that requires lexical semantics, including writing to dictation, written naming of pictures, and spontaneous speech. In addition, these errors should have the same basic distribution as those made in oral reading, provided the brain-damaged subject has no other language-processing deficits.

In KE's case, semantic errors were made in all of the tasks shown in Table 4.

RGB, on the other hand, only made what could loosely be called 'spelling errors' in written naming.

TABLE 2

Semantic errors in oral reading produced by KE

Stimulus	Response
apple	orange
shirt	sock
screw	hammer
nail	pliers
fork	knife
leopard	lion

TABLE 3

Semantic errors in oral reading produce by RGB

Stimulus	Response
pear	apple
cap	hat
kangaroo	giraffe
lemon	lime
celery	lettuce
camel	hump

TABLE 4

KE's semantic errors in different modalities

Stimulus	Writing to dictation
sock	mittens
scissors	paper
mitten	pocket
elbow	tooth
tape	pencil

Stimulus	Written naming of pictures
stapler	paper
spatula	sponge
screw	nail
wrist	leg

Spontaneous speech	Intended production
driving . . . tomorrow	drove . . . yesterday
sore throat	sore tooth
good night	good morning
eat . . . coffee	drink . . . coffee

All of his attempts resembled the stimulus and were recognizable as attempts at such. Semantic errors were absent (Table 5).

Within the theory of the lexical system diagrammed in Fig. 2, there is no way that both RGB's pattern of errors and KE's pattern could result from the same functional deficit. Either different deficits are responsible for the semantic paralexias in the two brain-damaged subjects, or the theory we have proposed is inadequate to accommodate the full range of data and must be discarded or revised.

RGB's pattern *can*, however, be explained by hypothesizing a lesion to the phonological output lexicon and/or its access mechanism from the semantic component. On this account, the proper semantic entry in the lexical-semantic component is available, but it cannot address the proper entry in the phonological output lexicon. As a consequence, a semantically related item is accessed (see Caramazza (1988); Caramazza and Hillis (in press), for discussion). If other evidence supports a locus of damage at the level of the phonological output lexicon, we will not only have evidence to support the component structure diagrammed in Fig. 1; we will also have placed constraints on the possible internal organization of the phonological output lexicon or its access mechanism, as we shall see.

Hypothesizing RGB's locus of damage allows us to predict how he will perform on other tasks. If the deficit affects access to the phonological output lexicon but not the lexical-semantic system, RGB should, after successfully accessing the lexical-semantic component, have a proper understanding of the word, even if his spoken response does not

match this comprehension. When RGB was given words to read and then asked to define them, his definitions did, in fact, match the stimulus, and not the word he spoke aloud (Table 6).

RGB's pattern of performance contrasts with that obtained for KE, whose comprehension of words presented visually or auditorily was no better than his ability to name or write those words.

From the preceding discussion it should be clear that not all semantic errors can be interpreted in the same way. Although KE's and RGB's performance in reading was very similar, their differing performance on other tasks, in the light of the theory we have proposed, implies that damage to different components of the lexical system is responsible for the semantic errors produced by the two subjects.

The point of this section has been to illustrate how the interpretations of performance in a specific task (e.g. reading) may depend on performance in an altogether different task (e.g. spelling to dictation). According to the view presented here, the semantic errors produced by KE and RGB have different bases. This is revealed by the fact that the semantic paralexias produced by the two subjects are *associated* with drastically differing patterns of performance in a set of tasks determined by a theory.

The set of tasks that should be given to a brain-damaged subject cannot be determined a priori;

TABLE 6

RGB's reading responses and definitions

Stimulus	Oral reading response	Definition
records	radio	you play 'em on a phonograph . . . can also mean notes you take and keep
tomato	salad	you get 'em in the summer . . . Jackie used to grow 'em . . . same color as apples
necklace	necktie	you would wear . . . a woman would wear around her neck . . . made out of metal . . . gold or silver
airport	airplane	where they're . . . airplanes are parked . . . where you go to get on the plane at

TABLE 5

RGB's performance in oral reading vs. written naming

Stimulus	Oral reading	Written naming
lime	lemon	lime
fork	eat	fork
leopard	cat	l ap d
shelf	top	shef
finger	ring	figre

they must be selected by considering the alternatives that exist under the theory and deciding which tasks will provide evidence to confirm or deny competing explanations of performance. Selecting tasks according to the theory one is proposing may appear to risk confirming one's biases, but eventually results from tasks that are related in theory will either line up to support an overall account, or else internal contradictions will force the theory to be abandoned. The alternative is to have no criteria for selecting tasks, and to test at random, hoping that a coherent story can be fitted to the data post hoc. Biases are much easier, in fact, to accommodate this way.

The results reported for KE and RGB provide empirical support for a division of the lexical system into components, and for the arrangement of components diagrammed in Fig. 2. In addition to providing evidence concerning the component structure of the lexical system, we must, to fully account for RGB's errors, make certain assumptions about the internal structure of the hypothesized processing components. More specifically, attributing RGB's reading difficulties to a deficit at the level of the phonological lexicon is only the first step in the process of providing an account for the observed pattern of performance. The next step involves articulating specific assumptions about the organization of the phonological output lexicon which would allow a motivated account for RGB's pattern of reading errors.

We have assumed that RGB makes *semantic* errors in reading despite the fact that the component supposedly damaged is the *phonological* output lexicon. This hypothesis follows from the proposed arrangement of the lexical components in which semantic representations access lexical-phonological representations. On this account, however, we are forced to make one other assumption. We must assume that the single most active semantic entry activates all entries in the phonological output lexicon that are *semantically* related to it (because the addresses the semantic system uses to access the phonological output lexicon are organized along semantic dimensions). Each related entry in the phonological output lexicon would be activated, ac-

cording to a logogen principle (Morton, 1969); that is, to a degree determined by its relatedness to the semantic entry. If the correct entry in the phonological output lexicon was not available because of damage, the next most active entry would be a semantically related word. To maintain the hypothesis that RGB's errors result from damage to the phonological output lexicon, it is clear that we must to enrich our theory of the access procedure used by the semantic system, and elaborate the procedure by which a phonological entry is chosen.

In the last example we have seen how it is possible for neuropsychological evidence to motivate a theory concerning the functional architecture of a cognitive system (in this case the lexical system). We also touched briefly on the possibility for data to require theorizing that specifies details *internal* to components that make up the functional architecture. The nature of the evidence connecting data and theory is not fundamentally different whether hypotheses concern the processing domain and arrangement of components making up the functional architecture of a cognitive process or more specific representations and processes internal to components.

We now turn to examples in which detailed analysis of brain-damaged subject performance forces us to make unintuitive claims about the representational structures processed within a component after we initially proposed minimal representational structure. These cases illustrate how the dialogue between cognitive theory and data can lead to an increasingly sophisticated view of the cognitive architecture (allowing us, for example, to explore the interaction between linguistic and non-linguistic mechanisms), and can lead us to enrich our account of the internal workings of components within that architecture.

B. Case Study II – The graphemic buffer. Explication of the representations and processes within cognitive components: theory is crucial to guiding the analysis toward greater detail

Caramazza et al. (1987) described a brain-damaged subject, LB, who made substitutions, insertions, transpositions and deletions of letters in all written spelling tasks (writing words to dictation, writing nonwords to dictation, written naming, and copying after a delay) *and* in oral spelling. They hypothesized that this pattern of performance was the result of damage to the graphemic buffer (see its position in the spelling process in Fig. 1). The graphemic buffer was thought to be a working memory component which keeps active the abstract letter representations computed by the phoneme-to-grapheme conversion component or the orthographic output lexicon (damage would affect both word and nonword tasks). The representations must be held for subsequent processing to compute the specific letter shapes, in writing, or letter names, in oral spelling (damage would affect both oral and written spelling). The orthographic representations in the graphemic buffer were thought to consist, minimally, of an ordered series of abstract letter identities. On this assumption, one would expect damage at this level of the spelling process to affect either of the two dimensions that were hypothesized to characterize the stored representations: order of production and/or grapheme identity. The order of graphemes could change or some positions could be skipped, grapheme identities could be under-specified or deleted, or some combination of the two could occur. By themselves, or in combination, these transformations could lead to the pattern of deletions, substitutions, insertions and transpositions observed for all written and oral spelling tasks this brain-damaged subject performed. Examples of these error types are shown in Table 7.

It should be noted that LB's pattern of spelling performance was *merely consistent* with the

hypothesis that the orthographic representations processed at the level of the graphemic buffer consist of linearly ordered sets of graphemes. Thus, for example, the reported results did not address the hypothesis that orthographic representations might consist of hierarchically organized structures specifying not only the identity of graphemes but also the orthosyllabic organization of the graphemes. To distinguish between alternative accounts, we must articulate and evaluate more detailed issues that concern the organization and processing of orthographic representations. Two issues immediately come to mind: (1) how is order information among graphemes represented? and (2) is there other information besides order and identity of graphemes that must be represented at the level of the graphemic buffer? Exploration of these issues quickly revealed that abstract letter identity and letter order, the minimal structure assumed to be coded by orthographic representations in Caramazza et al. (1987), were inadequate to account for the range of data the theory brought into focus. Data from the following two brain-damaged subjects exemplify patterns which, to be explained, require considerably more specific assumptions concerning both the manner in which order information may be represented and the information given by orthographic structure.

The first case concerns a brain-damaged subject who consistently makes errors on the right side of words in reading and spelling. This pattern suggests that one side of an internally ordered representation is consistently processed inadequately. An unintuitive and significant constraint on representations used for spelling and reading is introduced by the fact that the brain-damaged subject's errors require internal representations, structured in 'spatial' terms (at least the representations must be structured in what are analogous to spatial terms, i.e. ordered so that other mechanisms can affect a section of the representation independent of whether the affected section is produced first or last in tasks such as oral spelling, or oral spelling backwards).

At the time of testing, NG was 76 years old and had an eighth-grade education. She claims to have

TABLE 7

Examples of types of error made by LB

	Stimulus	Response
Substitution error	colore	conore
Insertion error	fritto	frritto
Deletion error	nostro	nos△ro
Transposition error	denaro	derano

been left-handed but was trained to write with her right hand in school. Accordingly, she wrote, pre-morbidly, with her right hand, but used her left hand for other tasks. Four months prior to testing she suffered a stroke that resulted in damage to the left parietal lobe. Her performance was marked by the clinical signs of neglect and so she made gross distortions and omissions on the right side when, for example, reproducing abstract designs or when directly copying drawings of familiar objects. Further details of her clinical profile can be found in Hillis and Caramazza (in press).

NG made similar types and numbers of errors whether she was writing to dictation, spelling orally, spelling from pictures, or copying after a delay. Given the position of the graphemic buffer in the spelling architecture, this pattern implicated damage to the representations stored there (Hillis and Caramazza, 1989). Crucially, NG's spelling errors always involved the right side of words. The dominant error types were letter deletions and substitutions (e.g., *instinct* → *instin*; *facial* → *facer*). The difference between her performance when she was copying words directly, which she did quite well (96.8% correct), and her performance on the same words when she was copying after a delay, which she did quite poorly (33.9% correct), indicates that her difficulty involved using *internally* generated representations.

NG's reading performance was similar to her spelling in both the percentage error and the distribution of different kinds of errors made. In reading tasks she dropped the ends of words (*packed* → *pack*, or *stripe* → *strip*), or completed them inappropriately (*directors* → *direction*, *humid* → *human*). NG made nearly the same percentage and types of errors reading words presented vertically as she made when words were presented horizontally (74.7% vs. 72.3% correct). When she was given orally spelled words and asked to recognize them (e.g. 'What does e-x-c-e-s-s spell?'), her performance was again similar quantitatively and qualitatively.

NG's performance in reading, in reading vertically presented words, in recognizing orally spelled

words and in all spelling tasks was interpreted as support for an argument that NG's deficit involved representations no longer tied to an external arrangement in space. Such an account is consistent with the view that the representations in the graphemic buffer are being neglected when NG spells.

When NG was asked to spell words backwards, her performance suggested that a simple 'first letter produced, second letter produced, third letter, etc.' account of how order is represented in the buffer would not be sufficient. Order in the buffer, for example, could be coded as order of production, so that the last items produced in any sequence would be most degraded. Alternatively, order could be coded as *location* in an abstract left-to-right representation of the items, so that canonical location would determine where errors were made regardless of the order in which they were produced. NG was asked to spell words backwards, borrowing a task from Baxter and Warrington (1983) (e.g. spell 'method' backwards. Correct response: d-o-h-t-e-m). She made errors primarily on the right side of words despite the fact that in backwards spelling the right letters are produced first (as did the brain-damaged subject that Baxter and Warrington tested) (Table 8).

This result is consistent with the view that NG's deficit in processing orthographic representations concerned the location of letters within a canonical left-to-right representation of a word.

The presumably general, non-linguistic, 'attentional mechanism' which operates on spatially organized representations and is responsible for NG's errors remains underspecified. Nonetheless,

TABLE 8

NG's errors when spelling words and nonwords backwards

Stimulus	NG's response
talent	dnelat (talend)
carrer	yeerac (careey)
method	htem (meth)
church	ruhc (chur)

for present purposes it is clear that the analysis of her spelling and reading performance has allowed us to constrain possible hypotheses about the structure of orthographic representations. The 'spatial' quality of the representations in the buffer is not completely unexpected because one of the functions of the buffer is to order letter representations. The apparent 'literalness' of the spatial representation, such that one side can be affected, however, is not intuitive, and requires a significant modification of our original minimal notions concerning ordering of graphemes (see also Ellis, 1988; Hillis and Caramazza, 1989).

When the graphemic buffer was introduced above, simple order and grapheme identity information were said to be represented. We have discussed some evidence which suggests that order is 'spatially' structured in a fairly unintuitive manner. Further analysis of data from the original buffer subject, LB, suggests that the representation of abstract letter identities must also be more highly structured than originally proposed. (A full clinical description and an initial assessment of his performance can be found in Caramazza et al. (1987). A more detailed analysis along the lines presented here can be found in Caramazza and Miceli (1989).)

We now return to LB's case to see how an initial partitioning of the data was necessary to locate his deficit in a particular component of the cognitive architecture, and how this analysis obscured differences that would be important later on when the issues concerned the nature of the representations processed *within* the component initially implicated. The theory under investigation would determine that a different partitioning of the data was relevant to later questions.

LB was an Italian man with university degrees in engineering and mathematics who became dysgraphic as a consequence of a left-hemisphere stroke. He made errors whether he was writing to dictation, writing the names of pictures, or copying upper into lower case after a brief delay. LB's performance was characterized by the substitution, insertion, deletion and transposition of letters regardless of whether the resulting letter strings were

orthographically legal; for example, he made errors such as *scarso → csarso*, where the consonant cluster 'cs' violates orthographic constraints of Italian. Errors were made on both familiar words and unfamiliar words (nonwords), and they were not influenced by frequency, grammatical class or abstractness/concreteness. Stimulus length, on the other hand, had a major influence, with longer words being misspelled more often than shorter words. These aspects of LB's performance help restrict the possible loci of deficit to parts of the spelling system where lexical or phonological factors do not play a role in processing. A plausible candidate is the graphemic buffer.

One piece of evidence that LB's deficit involved the graphemic buffer was the fact that, although the absolute number of errors for words and nonwords differed to some extent, when errors were grouped according to whether the stimulus was a word or a nonword, the distribution of error types for words was closely matched by the distribution of error types for nonwords (see Fig. 3). This evidence helped to establish the locus of deficit by restricting the possible loci of damage to a component of the spelling system involved in processing both familiar and unfamiliar words. This grouping of errors, however, obscured differences which would become important to future analyses.

The hypothesis proposed in Caramazza et al.

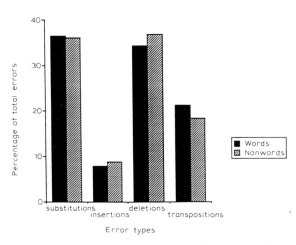

Fig. 3. LB's distribution of errors for words vs. nonwords.

(1987) concerned not only a claim about a mechanism with a specific processing role, that of keeping graphemic information active for subsequent processing, but also a claim about the nature of *representations* being processed by the hypothesized mechanism. The assumptions we are willing to entertain concerning representations and processing role will *determine the analyses* of spelling performance that become necessary to evaluate those assumptions. In this example we will continue to develop this point, showing how the analyses used to describe subject data and the interpretation given to these analyses are dependent on the theory under investigation and on the level of detail at which the theory is stated. We have already seen that order information among the graphemes that comprise the spelling of a word may have to be encoded in a 'spatial' format. Consider now the issue of the nature of orthographic structures themselves.

Caramazza et al. (1987) assumed that orthographic structures consist of linearly ordered sets of grapheme identities. On this assumption, there are no differences between graphemes or combinations of graphemes and, therefore, variation in performance related to these dimensions may be considered random, theoretically unimportant variation. Everything else being equal, the probability of making an error on a particular grapheme or grapheme combination should not differ from that for any other grapheme or grapheme combination. Nor should the probability of producing a particular type of error differ as a function of grapheme or grapheme combination. This reasoning led Caramazza et al. to the *methodological* conclusion that because, by hypothesis, words of the same length are tokens of the same type, performance on these words may be grouped for analysis. If their hypothesis was incorrect, however, and words of the same length were not tokens of the same type, grouping the subject's spelling performance without regard to some other measure of orthographic structure would have the effect of rendering inaccesible (by grouping different structures of the same length together and obscuring the other differences) just the evidence that would have

contradicted the hypothesis. This is precisely what happened in the initial analysis.

A recent, more detailed investigation of LB's spelling performance has brought to light a highly structured and systematic pattern of variation that requires postulating a radically different form of orthographic representation (Caramazza and Miceli, 1989). A few examples from this analysis will serve for present purposes. Consider briefly the case of deletion errors: these errors only occurred for certain types of grapheme and only in certain contexts. Of 141 single-letter deletion errors, 128 (91%) involved a consonant; and of the small number of deletions involving a vowel (13) all but one involved diphthongs (e.g., *compie* → *compe*). The empirical generalization that emerged from the analysis of the distribution of deletion errors *as a function of grapheme type and grapheme combination* is that the deletion of a single letter (virtually) only occurs in the context of a consonant or a vowel *cluster*. When grouped by length, the differing pattern of deletion errors could not be seen because, instead of being analysed by grapheme type, words with different grapheme types and grapheme combinations were lumped together.

Other aspects of LB's performance also seem to depend on units larger than the single grapheme. It was found, for example, that LB made many more errors on stimuli with 'complex' letter clusters (words with consonant clusters or diphthongs – e.g. premio (prize) has the CV structure CCVCVV) than on stimuli with 'simple' letter clusters (words in which consonants and vowels alternate – e.g. tavolo (Table 9) has the CV structure CVCVCV). Important differences in the number of errors and distribution of error types are revealed when the

TABLE 9

Influence of orthographic structure on spelling performance

CV-structure	Example	No. and % correct
CVCVCV	tavolo	1300/1777 (73.2%)
Bisyllabic non-CVCV	fiasco	437/762 (57.3%)
Trisyllabic non-CVCVCV	onesto	244/441 (55.3%)

data are grouped by simple and complex CV structure.

As the discussion of deletion errors indicated, different distributions of errors were observed for simple and complex CV stimuli. Nearly all of the deletion, insertion, and shift errors that LB made were made to complex CV stimuli, and, as a result, substitution errors accounted for a smaller proportion of the total errors for these stimuli. (Transpositions, on this analysis, have been divided into two categories: those cases in which *one* letter moves to a different location in a word, and all other letters remain in their relative positions; and exchange errors, in which two letters are swapped, each moving to the position of the other. This distinction was not drawn arbitrarily. Shift and exchange errors might be expected to occur in response to different kinds of stimuli, and indeed, their distribution across different word types is different. For details see Caramazza and Miceli (1989).) Substitutions, on the other hand, accounted for most of the errors made to simple CV stimuli. A smaller proportion were exchange errors. Fig. 4 shows the distribution of substitution, deletion, insertion, exchange and shift errors as a function of consonant/vowel structure. As may be seen in this figure, LB did not make deletion, insertion or shift errors for stimuli with simple CV structure. LB's spelling performance analysed

from the present perspective allows an important empirical generalization: the probability of making a particular type of spelling error is a function of ortho-syllabic complexity. Thus, to summarize, vowels, the letters that form the nucleus of each syllable, are rarely deleted, but consonants, when they occur with other consonants in syllables larger than the most basic 'single C', 'single V' structure, are particularly vulnerable to errors, and, as a consequence, different kinds of errors are made in response to simple and complex syllable structures. The generalization governing this analysis of the pattern of errors depends on a definition of the theoretical construct *ortho-syllabic unit*, a construct not important to our earlier hypotheses concerning the representations computed during the course of spelling.

LB's data, on a previous analysis, were relevant to locating his deficit within a specific component of the architecture of the spelling system: the graphemic buffer. The same data analysed with the aim of detailing the internal workings of the component now provide evidence relevant to the structure of representations processed by the graphemic buffer. Since the distribution of error types was determined by orthographic factors, including ortho-syllabic structure, the representations that allow this error pattern must include abstract information that specifies, in some form, the difference between consonants and vowels, and the distinction between simple and complex CV structures. They must, in other words, include constraints on the ordering of graphemes with parameters more abstract than letter identity (Caramazza and Miceli, 1989; see also McCloskey et al. (1988) for data and analysis of English-speaking brain-damaged subjects that have similar consequences; for a view of these data from a linguistic perspective, see Badecker (1988)).

The form of this abstract information is the subject of current investigation. Various alternatives are possible. CV information could, for example, be represented directly on a level of slots specified for consonant or vowel identity, or it could be represented more indirectly through structures that identify parts of the syllable that must be filled with

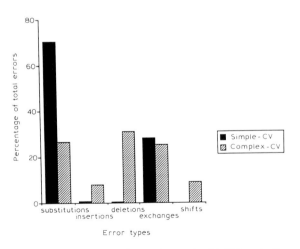

Fig. 4. LB's distribution of errors for words with different orthographic structures.

onsonants or vowels (e.g. onset, nucleus, rhyme, coda) (see for example, Clements and Keyser (1983), Fudge (1969), Halle and Vergnaud (1980) for discussion). Which of these kinds of representation, or some other, accounts for normal and brain-damaged subject data in the most satisfactory manner remains to be seen, but it is at least clear that orthographic representations must specify some form of ortho-syllabic information if we are to give a plausible explanation for LB's highly structured and systematic pattern of errors.

C. Conclusions

The spelling performance of both NG and LB suggests a dysfunction involving the representations at the level of the graphemic buffer. Furthermore, detailed consideration of their error patterns makes it necessary, as we have just seen, to postulate considerably more structure to orthographic representations than the simple order and grapheme identity that was originally thought to be required (i.e. some form of consonant/vowel identity, or syllable onset, rhyme and coda, for example, may need to be represented). The theory required by the new analyses, though not complete by any means, gives us better insight into the internal workings of a component at one level in the spelling process. When examined in detail, the errors produced by LB and NG required an equally detailed theory. The theory, in turn, places specific constraints on the kinds of data that could be accommodated by hypothesizing damage within the graphemic buffer. As a consequence, it not only gives us better insight into the functions of the normal system; it is also easier to falsify.

A number of general theoretical and methodological consequences relevant to work in neuropsychology follow from the examples outlined above. We have seen that the meaning of the data collected from LB was determined by the way they were arranged for analysis, which, in turn, was necessarily determined by the theory the data were meant to address. We have seen how, categorized in one way, these data provided evidence relevant to the position of the deficit within the cognitive architecture, and, analysed differently, they provided

evidence concerning the form of representations processed in the damaged component. These observations are germane to two discussions of neuropsychology in the literature.

If the significance of performance within a single brain-damaged subject must be determined by the way task performance is related to the theory under consideration, even to the point that the same data analysed in different ways will have different consequences for a theory at different levels of detail, it is clear that there can be no a priori or atheoretical classification of errors or subject types. Since there can be no classification of data independent of the theory the data are meant to address, no conclusions about theories of normal cognition can be drawn based on a priori classification schemes. This point holds in the single case, but it is also true of studies that average the performance of groups of brain-damaged subjects based on an a priori classification of errors or on a syndrome category (see Caramazza (1986) for detailed discussion).

Secondly, we have seen that it is possible, from neuropsychological data, to draw conclusions that concern both the functional architecture of a cognitive process *and* the details of components that make up the architecture. It is not the case, then, that neuropsychology can only provide evidence related to general issues that concern the number and arrangement of components in a cognitive system, as some have claimed (Shallice, 1988). Nor is it true that neuropsychological investigations must wander down theoretically irrelevant blind alleys, while cognitive psychology speeds by with data on more direct routes to an understanding of human capacities, as others have claimed (Seidenberg, 1988). The relationship between theory and data in neuropsychology is not significantly different from the relationship between data and theory in cognitive psychology proper or science in general. When guided by theories that try to be as specific as possible, neuropsychological data can address both general and specific issues, alongside cognitive psychology, admittedly subject to all of the missteps and pitfalls that both disciplines may fall prey to.

We have argued that cognitive theory is essential in order to explore the structure of normal cognitive systems as revealed by the patterns of performance displayed by brain-damaged subjects. A theory must specify not only the functional organization of the processing components that are recruited during the performance of a particular task (e.g. spelling), but the details of the processing structure of the hypothesized components (e.g. the structure of lexical-orthographic representations placed in the graphemic buffer). (These two aspects of cognitive theory – the functional architecture and the processing structure of the components that constitute it – are not independent. Given a particular functional architecture, it places severe constraints on the type of processing structure that its component parts may have. For example, the functional architecture of the spelling system shown in Fig. 1 does not allow the phoneme-grapheme conversion component to have access to lexical-orthographic information.) The effort should be, whenever possible, to develop theories that reveal their computational consequences. The number and arrangement of components in the functional architecture and the representations and processes utilized by each component must be specified if we want to use the performance of brain-damaged subjects to contribute significantly to our understanding of the structure of cognitive functions, and both, as we have noted in the case studies cited above, must be specified if we want to be able to explicate significant details and not just gross aspects of brain-damaged subjects' performance. We now argue that cognitive theorizing of this sort will also be necessary if data from brain-damaged subjects are to help reveal the underlying brain mechanisms that support cognitive abilities.

II. Cognitive theory: essential for bridging functional and biological understanding of the brain

Earlier we suggested that cognitive theory would help to join functional and biological understanding of the brain. We now develop more fully the argu-

ment that detail in cognitive theory will be necessary to identify cognitive functions with particular brain regions and circuits.

It is difficult to know precisely how the functional organization of the brain is reflected in its morphology, chemistry and topography. There are many dimensions to the physical system, and the mapping from function to brain organization must specify whether each of these dimensions is important to the information-processing work of the brain, and how. With regard to localization, for example, it could be that cognitive functions are not well isolated in brain regions, so that many functions have important circuitry packed closely in some areas. Alternatively, it could be that there is significant modularization of functional components in brain tissue (see, for example, Mountcastle, 1978). But, even if we could assume that components in some version of a functional theory are discretely localized in the brain, we don't know what the proper scale for matching functional and anatomical descriptions is. If brain functions are highly localized and modular, for example, one would expect the location of brain damage to start to correlate with a functional description of the damage at a fairly gross level of detail. On the other hand, distributed processing would mean that the location of contiguous brain damage would not correlate with functional damage until the functional theory was very specific, and then only for very focal lesions.

Imagine that a component for semantic processing and a phonological output lexicon used for reading exist next to each other in discrete areas of the brain. Lesions in this region might have several kinds of functional consequences. Lesions could be confined to one component, affecting only that component. One lesion could affect the whole of both components, or lesions could lie on the boundary between the two components, affecting both of them to some degree. Clearly, both the size and the location of a lesion will be important, and the different conditions must be distinguishable in the biological description of the lesion site. The detail with which our functional theory describes the components, however, will also be crucial. If our functional theory makes a distinction between 'reading' and 'writing' but does not distinguish different aspects of the reading process, lesions in either or both of the two areas described will impair reading, but so will lesions in other areas, and many of these regions may not overlap. Lesion locations can only be relevant to the localization of cognitive functions when the level of detail achieved by the functional theory is at least as fine as the grain at which the biological distinctions are made. This is also true for other measures of brain function or activity. A successful mapping of function to anatomy, or to some other biological level of analysis, will depend on the scale, in both domains, that is chosen to attempt the mapping. How do we know that we are looking at anatomical lesions on a scale that makes sense for a functional description of the brain?

One would expect to see consistent relations between functional descriptions and localization criteria once the scale of the functional description was sufficiently detailed. At the wrong scale, a brain region associated with some gross functional term would include tissue devoted to several functions so that cognitive and physiological measures will not correlate well. Damage to this area, for example, would produce a variety of symptoms depending on which of the different functions in the area is affected. Alternatively, if there is sufficient variation in brain structures, localizing cognitive functions will always be difficult, and though it might seem that we had not found the proper scale, a consistent relation between a functional description of damage and the location of lesions will always be difficult to find. The former assumption is amenable to investigation; the latter makes an anatomical/functional match very difficult.

In either case, it should be clear that for the project of bringing together cognition and the brain, detailed functional theories are not just superfluous information, engaging in their own way, but a trivial part of the enterprise. Detailed functional theories will be essential. This is particularly obvious if one considers that identifying the function of a brain region has typically involved establishing a consistent relationship between neural activity in an area and behaviors that have some functional element in common. If the account of the functions brains carry out is not sufficiently detailed, one half of this relation has no basis for correspondence with the other, and so there is no way to establish the correlation that signals a successful mapping. When theories of function have been developed in detail we should expect to see correspondences between brain and functional measures. Without a detailed functional theory, however, even what seem to be relatively straightforward correlates between neural activity and environmental stimuli, as in the 'edge detectors' of visual cortex, can have ambigious functional significance (e.g., Lehky and Sejnowski (1988) show that the computation of shape from shading can also rely on receptive units that have some similarity to units that, in the past, have been thought to be devoted to detecting edges).

Biological description and a functional vocabulary will be inseparably intertwined in explanations of brain function because descriptions of events in only (non-functional) neural terms will not make the generalizations needed to meaningfully capture events at the functional level. We are not only emphasizing that some vocabularies will be more efficient than others for building theories in which relevant and irrelevant data can be distinguished (Simon and Newell, 1956), although this is also true. There are at least two other reasons that a functional vocabulary will be indispensable. First, developments in computer science have made us aware of the possibility for virtual machines; machines, that is, in which the physical description of two devices may be different even though they are computing the same function. In this case, the functional identity of the two machines' operations will only be captured at a suitable level of abstraction. So, for example, a digital computer and Charles Babbage's mechanical inference engine can compute the same function, and they can, at a suitably abstract level, even do it in the same *way*. The physical instantiations of the machines, however, with electrical circuits on the one hand, and wheels and cogs on the other, are so different that the sameness of their operations can *only* be captured at a suitably abstract level, but surely this is the most relevant level if one is interested in the task the machines were set up to do (for discussion with further amplification see Pylyshyn, 1986, chapter 4). (Note that these two machines will probably *not* break down in the same way, showing that the transformations due to brain damage are likely to be tied to the *particular* way the brain does a cognitive task. This quality has its attendant promise and peril, i.e. brain damage might provide information about *how* the brain is doing a task, not just what is being done. At the same time, data are always *connected* to *how* a task is being carried out, even if we would prefer to know only what the task is in the abstract.)

Secondly, causal factors at the biological level (neurotransmitters, ion channels, action potentials, neural circuits and the like) will not make connections to function without a complementary functional vocabulary. So, for example, a neuron in visual cortex may be very similar in many respects to a neuron in auditory cortex. It may be physiologically similar, and it may even participate in a very similar neural circuit. To understand the difference between the two neurons, one must know that one is in the *auditory* system and one is in the *visual* system. This requires a functional vocabulary. Although we are not denying that functional descriptions *could* be constructed based on an investigation that proceeds from biology to ever higher levels of abstraction (we *are* saying it would be much more difficult), when such an investigation gets around to theorizing about function it will be forced to use the same theoretical vocabulary and abstractions that would have been necessary if a functional theory had been built independent of biology.

At the same time, neurobiological information, once we begin to get a handle on its functional consequence, may provide significant constraints on how functions can be implemented by the brain, which may, in turn, bear on the forms that brain damage can take and the transformations it can inflict. Such information could be very useful in limiting the

hypotheses one might entertain to explain a pattern of performance resulting from brain damage. Functional inferences drawn from brain-damaged performance, that is to say, are not divorced from implementational issues. Any insight we can gain into the intersection of biological and cognitive theory may allow empirical results in these areas to begin to usefully gain from each other. Computational models are one domain where functional and implementational issues may be explored.

III. Computational models: theoretical tools with the possibility of providing functionally or biologically oriented constraints

Difficulties with the scale and amount of localization in the brain, along with the proper restriction that destructive methods (lesioning and the like) cannot ethically be used to study people, provide the challenge to seek alternative sources of constraint that can be explored to try and converge, from several directions, on an understanding of the link between brain and function. Computer models that are functionally oriented and models that are biologically oriented hold some promise for this enterprise.

For the purpose of what follows we should distinguish between *computational models* and *computer models*. Computational models specify, to use Marr's terminology, *what* is computed and *why* (Marr, 1982), but they do not necessarily go into such detail that the model could then immediately be implemented on a computer. Take, for the sake of simplicity, the initial description of the graphemic buffer mentioned in section 1B above. This description is stated at the *computational* level. It specifies the dimensions represented in the buffer — abstract letter identity and letter order (*what is computed*) — and it says *why* the buffer is needed — to store representations computed over one unit (words or letter combinations) for subsequent processing that requires a different unit (individual letters). To model the buffer on a computer, however, the computational description has to be given specific data structures and algorithms. The order of the letters in the word 'model', for example, could be coded as 'o after m', 'd after o' etc., or as 'm$_1$', 'o$_2$', 'd$_3$', etc., or in one of several other ways. To model the buffer on a computer, one of these ways would have to be chosen. What we are interested in in the following section is how the consequences of a particular *computational* model can be made concrete with the aid of a *computer* model. Obviously, there is some danger that failures arising from the *algorithms* chosen will be attributed to the more abstract description of the model, or that real failures of the abstract description will be attributed to particular algorithms. These caveats must be kept in mind, but the benefits we note in the following sections are substantial.

Models based on the physics of neurons and their receptors or models based on brain anatomy and connectivity (e.g. Reeke and Edelman, 1988) may provide some insight into what the building blocks available to the brain for doing computations are, and what the algorithmic 'style' of the brain is. Models that are more abstract (for a review see Cowan and Sharp, 1988) may, nonetheless, be important for what they can tell us about what learning is (or is not) and for their exploration of parallel processing (to the extent that these areas are their focus, and not limited cognitive demonstrations). They may also provide caveats concerning the interpretation of brain recordings (again, Lehky and Sejnowski (1988) warn about being overly simplistic in the interpretation of single unit response and stimulus correlations. Georgopoulos et al. (1986), from an empirical perspective, argue that *neural populations* and not single neurons are the relevant unit determining behavior). Both biologically oriented models and models of parallel processing may provide some insight into the transformations that can occur as a consequence of brain damage, an area where there are virtually no constraints at present (this information may begin to make contact with functional and anatomical descriptions of brain-damaged subjects, building the first tenuous pieces of a brain/function bridge).

While computer models in neurobiology may help us to understand the medium for computation the brain provides, *functional* computer models will aid in building complex theories of multi-component architectures. Integrating and keeping track of the theoretical details in multicomponent systems will be difficult. Theories will involve complex processing at each stage (of the sort hinted at by the graphemic buffer examples in section I), and, when one considers interactions occurring over the entire system, complexity will be compounded. Following the consequences of changes to some part of such a system will not be easy. In addition, one may be tempted to be vague about the details of some components while focusing on others. Unless there are reasons to be confident that we know the form of the input or the output to these components, however, the details of one component are likely to affect the possible forms we can give to those components it interacts with. If, for example, the representations in the graphemic buffer are found to be more complicated and structured than just ordered abstract letters, this will have implications for components that depend on the graphemic buffer to store information temporarily. It will, that is, have implications for the representations that are either stored in the orthographic output lexicon, or computed from those representations, and it will have implications for the representations computed by the phoneme-to-grapheme conversion component. It is unclear whether additional complexity in buffer representations would also affect the components that follow the graphemic buffer, the allographic conversion system and the letter name conversion mechanism (see Fig. 1).

An additional advantage of computer models is that they force operations to be explicit. In a computer model, descriptions like 'an entry in the phonological input lexicon was activated' or 'phonemes were converted to graphemes' must be fleshed out into specific representations (e.g. phonemes, syllables, letters, etc.) that are operated on by specific processes (e.g. serial search, parallel activation, etc.). The representations and functions chosen to instantiate 'access to the phonological input lexicon' or 'phoneme-to-grapheme conversion' will make predictions that can be compared to empirical results.

Computational models, however, must also have certain characteristics. To function as an explanation, a model must be *perspicuous*. The kind of model we have described in relation to the brain-damaged subject data above has explanatory perspicuity. At the level at which the theory is stated a relationship can be established between the terms of the theory (e.g. 'access to the phonological input lexicon') and the functions and representations the model uses to instantiate those terms. This must also be true of theories implemented by computer models. If it is not, the models cannot be useful as theoretical tools. They would not be part of an explanation, they would be something else that must be explained.

An example may show that the issue of perspicuity is not just a question of whether it is possible to understand how a model works, it relates to whether a model can be useful in guiding experimental work. We have constructed a parallel distributed processing (PDP) model of spelling, using a three layer network and a backpropagation algorithm (Rumelhart et al., 1986). The network contains three layers of interconnected units. Input units are turned on or off to code the sounds of a word. Their signal is transformed once by excitatory or inhibitory lines that connect the input units to 'hidden' (middle layer) units. According to the signal they receive from below, the hidden units turn 'on' to various degrees. Their signal is then transformed again by weighted lines between hidden and output units, and the pattern of 'on' and 'off' units in the output layer is interpreted as a code for a single grapheme. Phonemes are converted one at a time to graphemes, although there is a surrounding phoneme context to aid in the conversion. Other details of the model can be found elsewhere (Olson and Caramazza, in preparation). After training on 1,000 words, 60 times each, the model converted phonemes to graphemes correctly 94% of the time and wrote words correctly 70% of the time. The network did not display the range of error patterns seen in humans with brain damage when it was 'damaged'

by removing weighted lines or adding noise to the weights. (In particular, it made phonologically plausible errors. No damage could make it display the opposite pattern, good performance on words and poor performance on nonwords, as reported by Shallice (1981) for a brain-damaged subject. This suggests it is not an adequate model of the system shown in Fig. 1 (although it may approximate the operation of one of the components, perhaps the phoneme-to-grapheme conversion component).)

This performance failure is not as serious a flaw, however, as the difficulty of judging the model's overall success or failure; a difficulty that results because the method the network has developed to convert phonemes to graphemes is opaque. The algorithm for conversion is contained in the weights of the network, and without interpreting them, we have no idea *how* the network does its job. Did the network fail for fundamental reasons, or because one of the network parameters had a slightly wrong value?

The 'neural plausibility' of the model clearly does not help with this. The neural aspects of the model are not literal enough to be the criteria on which the model is judged, so the model cannot be grounded in physiology. Since we don't know what aspects of neural organization determine the computational structure of the brain, the significance of having *some* resemblance to neurons is not clear. Whether the resemblances are the relevant ones is one difficulty, but, more importantly, the criteria for making this judgement depend on knowing something about the connection between neural organization and cognitive organization, and this is just what the model is supposed to help investigate. Even without these problems, however, the construction of a network is only the beginning. If an in vitro network of cultured neurons could be constructed and monitored, we would still have to discover *what was being done* by the network before we could decide whether something similar was being done by the brain.

As we noted above, graphemic representations used by people while writing apparently refer to representational structure which makes it possible to identify vowel and consonant positions within familiar and unfamiliar words. The network may contain a set of units that are active whenever consonants are processed, and a set of units that are active for vowels so that operations dependent on vowel/consonant identity could refer to these units and perform other operations based on whether the units indicated that a consonant or a vowel was present. It is also possible, however, that the network contains no units with this function. It is suggestive than we know less about the model, in this case, than we do about the kinds of data that would normally be used to build and constrain it.

Part of the problem is that there is no vocabulary that ties the parameters of parallel distributed processing (learning rate, momentum, number of hidden units, etc.) to the functional descriptions we have argued are essential. Some PDP modelers have, in fact, claimed that such symbolic descriptions are epiphenomena arising out of more basic PDP parameters (McClelland et al., 1986). PDP parameters themselves, however, do not give us any guidance when we are faced with a model that does not perform some function in the same way as humans do. Is the learning rate wrong, the number of units, the connectivity, the learning algorithm? When a model fails, there is nothing that ties the level at which success or failure is judged, i.e. the functional level, to the level that changes the network's performance, i.e. the network's parameters. Without a connection between function and parameters, we cannot predict how changes in network parameters will affect performance. All that is possible is to vary parameters at random and hope to hit upon the right model through a search-like procedure.

Another shortcoming of this framework is that it does not allow us to judge the adequacy of the parts of the model imported from the functional domain, notably, the representations that are mapped by the network. The model may not have worked for fundamental representational reasons, or it may not have worked because the number of hidden units was not right (see papers in Pinker and Mehler (1988) for discussions of these issues). This uncertainty makes models that are not perspicuous of dubious value for guiding empirical work (although they may be of great value as objects of study in themselves; that is, to study network dynamics, parallel processing, etc.). Unless we expect to stumble upon the correct theory of how spelling is accomplished in the first effort, the reasons for failures in the models will be as important as the reasons for success. If neither are apparent, it is difficult to see what advance in understanding will have been accomplished by the modelling effort.

If our functional theories are to be as specific as we have argued they need to be to make contact with brain function, the discipline of making computational models out of the theories will be valuable. Computational models, however, must contribute to a sharpening of functional descriptions, so their workings cannot be obscure or opaque. To understand the brain we have to know both *what* is being done, and *how* it is being done. A functional vocabulary will not be a convenient, but disposable, crutch that can be used until we get a chemical or biological understanding of these processes, because although *how* they are carried out may be fundamentally biological or chemical, chemical and biological principles do not have the vocabulary to describe factors important to, for example, lexical access, or writing, or reading, or any of many other cognitive processes: chemical and biological principles do not make the necessary generalizations.

There are no methodologies currently available for mapping descriptions of cognitive processes at a scale that consistently matches measures of the brain. Techniques used on animals cannot ethically be used with people. Animal work may provide information about how brains solve certain kinds of problems, what kinds of circuits are available, and the specifics of neural function. Limitations in areas comparable to human language, however, are a matter of theory, not a technical limitation on the resolving power we can train on the human brain. We don't know enough about what is involved in language processing to go about meaningfully locating it in specific brain structures. Our mission should not be to, for example, locate dysgraphia in the temporal lobe. Rather, the focus should be on those underlying cognitive operations that allow us to write, and then on where and how the operations are carried out in brain tissue.

Many sources of information can help. Computer scientists can tell us about the formal properties of various kinds of parallel machines. Linguistics can provide information about the abstract properties of language. Computer models can help us to be computationally explicit in constructing functional theories, and, when concerned with more or less abstract neural properties, may constrain our view of the kinds of transformations damage can inflict. Even models that are less than perspicuous may, when they are studied further, show us ways of solving computational problems that we hadn't thought of before. Results in these areas will influence the theories required to explain data from studies of normal subjects and brain-damaged subjects. These studies, in turn, are an important source of evidence that concerns how, for example, abstract linguistic properties are instantiated in the brain, and which kinds of computation the brain uses to do so. Under the guidance of detailed theories, the combination of computational models in both functional and biological domains, neurobiology's insight into brain mechanisms, and cognitive studies with normal and brain-damaged subjects should lead to a convergence of results that will expand the intersection of these fields and allow us to proceed in the mapping between brain and function despite all its difficulty.

Acknowledgements

The research reported here was supported in part by NIH Grant NF22201 and by a grant from the Seaver Institute. The authors would like to thank Cristina Romani, Bill Badecker, Brenda Rapp, Argye Hillis, Patrice Drew Dargan, Gabriele Miceli, Rita Capasso, Terry Sejnowski, and Claudia Testa for helpful comments, discussion and/or use of data that went into this paper. We also thank Jordan Grafman for comments on an earlier draft. The fault for any errors or omissions that remain lies with us alone.

References

Badecker W: Representational properties common to phonological and orthographic output systems. Unpublished manuscript, The Johns Hopkins University, 1988.

Baxter DM, Warrington EK: Neglect dysgraphia *J. Neurol. Neurosurg. Psychiatry: 48*, 141 – 144, 1983.

Beauvois MF, Dèrouesnè J: Lexical or orthographic agraphia. *Brain: 104*, 21 – 49, 1981.

Bub J, Bub D: On the methodology of single-case studies in cognitive neuropsychology. *Cognitive Neuropsychology: 5*, 565 – 582, 1988.

Campbell R: Writing nonwords to dictation. *Brain Lang.: 19*, 153 – 178, 1983.

Caramazza A: The logic of neuropsychological research and the problem of patient classification in aphasia. *Brain Lang.: 21*, 9 – 20, 1984.

Caramazza A: On drawing inferences about the structure of normal cognitive systems from the analysis of patterns of impaired performance. The case for single-patient studies. *Brain Cognition: 5*, 41 – 66, 1986.

Caramazza A: Some aspects of language processing revealed through the analysis of acquired aphasia: the lexical system. *Annu. Rev. Neurosci.:11*, 1980.

Caramazza A, Hillis A: Modularity: a perspective from the analysis of acquired dyslexia and dysgraphia. In Malatesha Joshi R. (Editor), *Written Language Disorders*. Dordrecht, Holland: Kluwer Academic Publishers, in press.

Caramazza A, Miceli G: The structure of graphemic representation. *Cognition: 37*, 243 – 297, 1990.

Caramazza A, Miceli G, Villa G: The role of the (output) phonological buffer in reading, writing and repetition. *Cognitive Neuropsychol.: 3*, 37 – 76, 1986.

Caramazza A, Miceli G, Villa G, Romani C: The role of the graphemic buffer in spelling: evidence from a case of acquired dysgraphia. *Cognition: 26*, 59 – 85, 1987.

Clements GN, Keyser SJ: *CV Phonology: A Generative Theory of the Syllable*. Cambridge, MA: MIT Press, 1983.

Coltheart M: Cognitive neuropsychology and the study of reading. In Posner MI, Marin OSM (Editors), *Attention and Performance, (Vol. 11)*. Erlbaum, Hillsdale NJ, 1985.

Cowan JD, Sharp DH: Neural nets and artificial intelligence. *Daedalus: 117*, 85 – 122, 1988.

Ellis AW: Spelling and writing (and reading and speaking). In Ellis AN (Editor), *Normality and Pathology in Cognitive Functions*. London: Academic Press, 1982.

Ellis AW: Normal writing processes and peripheral acquired dysgraphias. *Lang. Cognitive Processes: 3*, 99 – 127, 1988.

Fudge EC: Syllables. *J. Linguistics: 5*, 193 – 320, 1969.

Georgopulos AP, Schwartz AB, Kettner RE: Neuronal population coding of movement direction. *Science: 233*, 1416 – 1419, 1986.

Goodman RA, Caramazza A: Aspects of the spelling process: evidence from a case of acquired dysgraphia. *Lang. Cognitive Processes: 1*, 263 – 296, 1986.

Goodman RA, Caramazza A: Patterns of dysgraphia and the nonlexical spelling process. *Cortex: 23*, 143 – 148, 1987.

Halle M, Vergnaud J: Three dimensional phonology. *J. Linguistic Res.: 1*, 83 – 105, 1980.

Hillis A, Caramazza A: The Graphemic Buffer and mechanisms of unilateral spatial neglect. *Brain Lang.: 36,* 208 – 235, 1989.

Hillis AE, Rapp BC, Romani C, Caramazza A: Selective impairment of semantics in lexical processing. *Cognitive Neuropsychol.: 7,* 191 – 243, 1990.

Lehky SR, Sejnowski TH: Network model of shape from shading: neural function arises from both receptive and projective fields. *Nature: 333,* 452 – 454, 1988.

Margolin DI: The neuropsychology of writing and spelling: semantic, phonological, motor, and perceptual processes. *Q. J. Exp. Psychol.: 6A,* 459 – 489, 1984.

Marr D: *Vision.* New York: W.H. Freeman and Company, 1982.

McClelland JL, Rumelhart DM, Hinton GE: The appeal of parallel distributed processing. In McClelland JL, Rumelhart DE, (Editors), *Parallel Distributed Processing: Explorations in the Microstructure of Cognition, Vol. 1: Foundations.* Cambridge, MA: MIT Press, 1986.

McCloskey M, Goodman-Schulman RA, Aliminosa D: The structure of orthographic representations: evidence from acquired dysgraphia. Paper presented at the meetings of the Psychonomic Society, Chicago, IL, Nov. 1988.

Mountcastle VB: An organizing principle for cerebral functions: The unit module and the distributed system. In Edelman GE, Mountcastle VB (Editors), *The Mindful Brain: Cortical Organization and the Group-Selective Theory of Higher Brain Function.* Cambridge, MA: MIT Press, 1978.

Olson AC, Caramazza A: *Lesioning a connectionist model of spelling.* Paper presented at Venice III: cognitive Neuropsychology and Connectionism, Venice, Italy, October 1988.

Patterson KE, Shewell C: Speak and spell: Dissociations and word-class effects. In Coltheart M, Sartori G, Job R (Editors), *Surface Dyslexia.* London: Erlbaum, 1987.

Pinker S, Mehler J: *Connections and Symbols.* Cambridge, MA: MIT Press, 1988.

Pylyshyn ZW: *Computation and Cognition: Toward a Foundation for Cognitive Science.* Cambridge, MA: MIT Press, 1984.

Reeke GN, Edelman GM: Real brains and artificial intelligence. *Daedalus: 117,* 143 – 174, 1988.

Rumelhart DE, Hinton GE, Williams RJ: Learning internal representations by error propagation. In Rumelhart DE, McClelland J.L. (Editors), *Parallel Distributed Processing: Explorations in the Microstructure of Cognition, Vol. 1: Foundations.* Cambridge, MA: MIT Press, 1986.

Seidenberg MS: Cognitive neuropsychology and language: the state of the art. *Cognitive Neuropsychol.: 5,* 403 – 426, 1988.

Shallice T: Phonological agraphia and the lexical route in writing. *Brain: 104,* 413 – 429, 1981.

Shallice T: *From Neuropsychology to Mental Structure.* Cambridge: Cambridge University Press, 1988.

Simon HA, Newell A: Models: their uses and limitations. In White LD (Editor), *The State of the Social Sciences.* Chicago: University of Chicago Press, 1956.

© 1991 Elsevier Science Publishers B.V.
Handbook of Neuropsychology, Vol. 5
F. Boller and J. Grafman (Eds)

CHAPTER 14

Language processing and language disorders as revealed through studies of syntactic comprehension

David Caplan

Neuropsychology Laboratory, Neurology Department, Massachusetts General Hospital, Boston, MA, U.S.A.

Introduction

This chapter will use results from linguistics, experimental psycholinguistics and aphasiology to build up a picture of the structure of one part of the language-processing system and of its disorders. Its focus will be on 'syntactic comprehension' – the process of assigning syntactic structure to sentences and using that structure to constrain and determine aspects of the meaning of sentences. It will conclude with a brief discussion of the relevance of the results obtained in this domain to other areas of language and cognitive processing.

Basic aspects of language processing

Language and language processing have many characteristics that must be captured by models which attempt to describe and ultimately explain language development, language use and language breakdown. We shall begin this chapter by noting three of these features, which have been explored in contemporary research.

The first is related to the nature of the language code. Intuitions indicate that language consists of multiple different types of structure, each related to different aspects of meaning. Among these linguistic forms are phonemes, words, sentence structures, intonational contours, discourse structures, and others. We have to recognize and inter-

pret many of these forms in the process of language comprehension and to 'get these forms right' when we speak. The number of radically different aspects of form and meaning that make up the language code have led many investigators to a 'modular' view of language processing, in which separate processors are responsible for activating these different aspects of the language code in production and comprehension tasks in each of the normal modalities of language use. This view has penetrated both normative psycholinguistic modelling and aphasiology.

The second set of observations is that the component operations of the language-processing system are extremely efficient. To take one simple example, normal English speakers have a 'production vocabulary' that is estimated to be of the order of twenty thousand words. In normal speech, we search through this large set of items and produce words at the rate of about three per second with an estimated error rate of about one wrong word chosen per million (Levelt, personal communication, 1989). We then integrate the sounds of the words we have activated into supra-lexical prosodic structures with a further error rate of about one mispronounced word per million. This feature of language processing has suggested to researchers that the system operates in a massively parallel fashion.

The third set of observations is that the operations of the language-processing system paradoxically feel effortless and yet demand attention. When we listen to a lecture, converse with an interlocutor or read a novel, we usually have the subjective impression that we are extracting another person's meaning and producing linguistic forms appropriate to our intentions without paying attention to the details of the sounds of words, sentence structure, etc. Moreover, we are unable to inhibit the performance of many language-processing tasks once the system is engaged (e.g., we must perceive a spoken word, not just as a non-linguistic percept). In general, processing that is automatic and unconscious is thought to require relatively little allocation of mental resources (Schneider and Shiffrin, 1977). However, the subjective effortlessness and automaticity of language processing contrasts with our inability to do many other tasks while processing language (e.g., one cannot easily shoot basketball foul shots accurately and quickly while attempting to follow a serious lecture). The difficulties that arise in everyday dual-task situations involving language indicate that language processing requires the allocation of attention and/or processing resources.

These three intuitively appreciable features of language processing are elaborated in proposals regarding three aspects of the language processing system: (1) the components of the system; (2) the organization of these components that supports integrated tasks such as comprehension of spoken language, reading, etc.; and (3) the attentional and working memory resources associated with components of the language-processing system. Studies in formal linguistics, experimental psycholinguistics and aphasiology give rise to specific models of these aspects of language processing. We shall review these aspects of language processing with respect to one part of the system − syntactic comprehension.

Our presentation will consist of the following sections. First, we shall review work in linguistics regarding the nature of syntactic structures. We shall concentrate on theories of syntactic structure developed by Noam Chomsky. However, the goal of this section is not to justify these theories over others, but to illustrate some basic properties of syntactic struc-

tures. Second, we will review studies in psycholinguistics which indicate that one part of the comprehension process involves the computation of syntactic structure (parsing) and begin to describe the processes involved in this task. The remaining sections deal with disorders of syntactic comprehension. The first of these deals with evidence from pathology regarding the existence and nature of a parser. It focusses on the selectivity of deficits in syntactic comprehension. The second of these sections deals with the relationship of the parser to other language-processing and cognitive systems, especially the question of how the short-term memory system might be related to the parser and whether the processes involved in sentence production make use of the same procedures for syntax as do those involved in comprehension. The third of these sections deals with the mental resources required by the parsing process. The final section dealing with pathology describes adaptive stategies used by patients whose syntactic comprehension mechanisms are impaired. The chapter closes with a few general comments on the possible relevance of work on syntactic comprehension to other domains of language processing and on the framework for modelling parsing and its disorders adopted throughout this paper.

Linguistic studies of syntactic representations

Syntactic structures play a particular role in language. They provide the means whereby the meanings of words can be combined to add to the information conveyed by language. Words in isolation convey a limited set of semantic features. Simple (i.e., non-compound) English words generally convey semantic values pertaining to individual items, actions and properties. In addition to these semantic features, language conveys relationships between the items designated by individual words. Information about thematic roles (which person or object is accomplishing an action, which is being acted upon, where actions are taking place, etc.), coreference (which pronouns refer to particular nouns), attribution of modification (which adjectives are associated with which nouns), scope of quantification (which items are qualified by negative and other numerical elements) and other semantic features not inherent in single words depends upon the relationship of words to each other within a sentence.

These relationships are defined by the syntactic structures in which words are located. Syntactic structures are hierarchically organized sets of syntactic categories. Individual lexical items are marked for syntactic category (e.g., *cat* is a noun (N); *of* is a preposition (P)). These categories combine to create non-lexical nodes (or phrasal categories), such as Noun Phrase (NP), Verb Phrase (VP), Sentence (S), etc. The way words are inserted into these higher-order phrasal categories determines a number of different aspects of sentence meaning. Consider, for instance, the very simple sentence, (1):

1. The dog scratched the cat.

In (1), we know that the dog did the scratching and the cat was scratched. This is not because the world is set up so that only dogs can scratch and only cats can be scratched; it is because of the way the words in the sentence are placed in a syntactic structure. The syntactic structure of (1) is shown in Fig. 1. The noun *dog* is part of the NP *the dog* that is attached to the Sentence node, S. We will refer to categories such as P, PP, V, VP, N, NP, etc., as nodes, and say that any node that is connected to another by an upwards-directed line is 'dominated' by that 'higher' node, and that one node is 'immediately dominated' by another if no others intervene along such a line. In this case, the NP *the dog* is immediately dominated by the node S. We shall say that the NP immediately dominated by S is the 'subject' of the sentence. The notion of subject is thus a syntactic

notion, defined by the position of words in syntactic structures. We shall call subject a 'grammatical role', and say that *the dog* plays the grammatical role of subject in (1).

The way this notion is related to the fact that the dog accomplishes the action of scratching (that is, that *the dog* is the 'Agent' of *scratch*) is via the way thematic roles are assigned by the verb. Part of the information associated with a verb is its 'argument structure' – how it assigns actors, recipients of actions, and other thematic roles. The subject of a verb is the 'external argument' of the verb, and the verb *scratch* assigns the thematic role of Agent to its external argument. In a similar way, *the cat* is the 'object' of the verb, the object of the verb is (one of) the 'internal' arguments of the verb, and *scratch* assigns the thematic role of Theme to its internal argument. This is how sentence (1) comes to mean that the dog is doing the scratching and the cat was scratched.

Things can get considerably more complicated than this. Consider sentence (2):

2. The dog that scratched the cat killed the mouse.

In (2) there is a sequence of words – *the cat killed the mouse* – which by itself is a well-formed sentence, but is not understood as a proposition in (2). The reason that this sequence is not understood as a sentence – that is, that sentence (2) does not indicate that the cat actually killed the mouse – is that the structure of (2) does not group together *the cat* with *killed the mouse*. Instead, *the cat* is the object of the verb *scratched*, and the relative clause *that scratched the cat* is predicated of the noun phrase *the dog* which is both the 'head' of the clause and the subject of the main clause. These relationships are expressed in Fig. 2.

The modern study of the nature of syntactic struc-

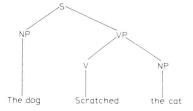

Fig. 1. Syntactic structure of sentence (1).

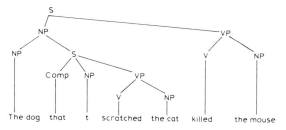

Fig. 2. Syntactic structure of sentence (2).

tures and the way they contribute to sentence meaning began with the pioneering work of Noam Chomsky (1955, 1957, 1965, 1970, 1981, 1985). It was Chomsky who changed the study of syntax from an effort to enumerate the patterns that make for well-formed sentences in a language to the study of the relationship between syntactic structures and aspects of meaning. The relationship between subjects and objects and thematic roles that lies at the basis of the meanings of sentences (1) and (2), though appreciated for many years before Chomsky's work, was integrated into general theories of syntactic representations and their relationship to meaning for the first time in his research.

At the heart of Chomsky's work and subsequent research in modern linguistics lies the effort to represent the syntactic structure of sentences in such a way as to capture regularities in sentence structure. For instance, the fact that subjects of sentences receive the thematic roles assigned to the external arguments of verbs is a regularity of the relationship between sentence structure and sentence meaning. Representing syntactic structure so as to define the notion of subject captures this regularity. In turn, such a representation explains the fact that *the dog* in (1) and *the dog that scratched the cat* in (2) are the Agents of their clauses. Both *the dog* and *the dog that scratched the cat* are NPs in subject position, and this fact determines their thematic role. The fact that they differ in their internal structure (*the dog that scratched the cat* contains a relative clause and *the dog* does not) does not affect the fact that they are both subjects.

Modern linguistics attempts to extend the ability of representations to account for regularites in sentence structure and in the relationship of structure to meaning to cover a wide range of structures. The most complex (and controversial) analyses are those where the structures postulated are more distantly related to the overt form of sentences. For instance, Chomsky has emphasized the fact that thematic roles are the same in sentences of different types such as actives (1) and passives (3):

3. The cat was scratched by the dog.

Chomsky developed models of syntactic structures

that capture this fact. These models postulate so-called 'underlying' syntactic structures in which thematic roles are assigned. These structures are known as 'Deep Structure' in earlier models and as 'D-structure' in more recent work. The D-structure of (1) is shown in Fig. 1 and that of (3) in Fig. 3. In Chomsky's theory, sentences (1) and (3) share aspects of D-structure; namely, the fact that *the cat* is the object of *scratch* in the D-structure of both sentences. This fact guarantees that *the cat* will be the internal argument of *scratch* and play the role of Theme. The role of Agent is assigned to *the dog* because it is the subject of *scratch* in (1), as discussed above, and because it is in a *by*-phrase in (3). This theory thus accounts for the identity of thematic roles in actives and passives on the basis of the fact that these two sentence types share crucial aspects of their D-structure — *the cat* is the object of *scratch*. In this respect, the theory behaves exactly as it did in explaining how *the dog* in (1) and *the dog that scratched the cat* in (2) are the Agents of their clauses — identical grammatical roles lead to identical processes of thematic role assignment.

Chomsky's theory of the passive creates a new question, however: how does *the cat* become the subject of the sentence in (3) and why is it not assigned the role of Agent by virtue of its being the subject of the sentence? Chomsky answers these questions by postulating that *the cat* is moved by a syntactic rule from its position in D-structure to its final position in what is now called 'S-structure', shown in Fig. 4 (S-structure is similar to what was formerly called 'Surface Structure'). In Chomsky's theory, thematic roles are determined by the grammatical roles of NPs in D-structure, not S-structure. Other quite different models of syntactic structure have been suggested by other theoretical syntacticians

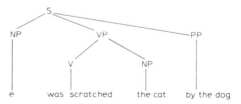

Fig. 3. D-structure of sentence (3).

(e.g., Bresnan, 1982), but all attempt to describe the structures of sentences such as (2) and (3) in such a way that the fact that thematic role assignment remains invariant after passivization in English falls out naturally from the way active and passive sentences are represented (that is, to explain this fact). Chomsky is responsible for the effort to develop theories of syntactic structure that are descriptively detailed and have this sort of explanatory power.

Of course, there must be a motivation for this complication of syntactic structure — the idea that each sentence has several levels of structure, one (or possibly more than one) quite different from that found on the surface. The justification for postulating D-structure and S-structure is complex and cannot be reviewed properly here. However, the rationale behind it can be sketched. In Chomsky's theory, the S-structure of a sentence is due to two different sorts of rules. The first set of rules creates the D-structure; the second set creates the S-structure from the D-structure. Rules of this first sort are known as 'phrase structure rules'. Phrase structure rules (illustrated in Fig. 5) re-write syntactic categories as other syntactic categories. Phrase structure rules are responsible for an important property of sentences — the fact that they are potentially infinite in length. This is because the rules in Fig. 5 are recursive — they can be used over and over again. These rules create structures in which the thematic roles of a sentence are easily related to the position of NPs in the syntax. The second set of rules are so-called 'movement' or 'transformational' rules. These rules move categories in D-structure to their positions in S-structure. These rules (or processes) are responsible for relating underlying structures to overt structures. They move NPs and other elements around in ways that complicate these simple relationships between thematic roles and the surface grammatical positions of lexical items. In the most recent versions of the theory, movement rules are replaced by conditions on which movements are legal, but the basic idea that there are two processes involved in creating syntactic structures has remained an important part of Chomsky's theories over the years. We can see how the effort to describe the syntactic structures of sentences such as (1) – (3) has led to quite an elaborate set of rules and structures, all designed to describe the structure of sentences and to capture (and thus explain) the regularities in the relationship between sentence form and sentence meaning.

The development of theories of syntactic structure that attempted to describe and explain the systematic relationships between syntactic structures and the meanings of sentences naturally led linguists to explore a variety of aspects of meaning that arise at the level of the sentence. One of these which has been extensively studied is co-reference — the relationship of referentially dependent items such as pronouns and reflexives to referring NPs. Consider sentences (4) and (5):

4a. Susan said that a friend$_i$ of Mary's washed herself$_i$.

b. Susan said that a friend$_j$ of Mary's washed her$_j$.

5a. Susan said that Mary's$_i$ portrait of herself$_i$ pleased Helen.

b. Susan said that Mary's$_j$ portrait of her$_i$ pleased Helen.

Herself refers to *friend* in (4a) and *her* cannot refer to *friend* in (4b) (the subscripts indicate identity and distinctness of reference). Similarly, *herself* refers to *Mary* in (5a), and *her* cannot refer to *Mary* in (5b). Pronouns, reflexives and other words that refer to other NPs are said to be 'co-indexed' with those NPs; the NPs with which they are co-indexed are

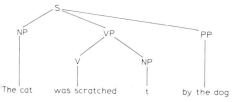

Fig. 4. S-structure of sentence (3).

S --→ NP + VP

NP --→ Determiner + N (+S)

VP --→ V (+NP) (+PP) (+S)

Fig. 5. Sample phrase structure rules.

said to be their 'antecedents'. Sentences (4) and (5) show that there are two constraints on which NP can function as the antecedent of a reflexive and be unable to be the antecedent of a pronoun. First, this NP must be within a particular syntactic domain. In the case of sentences (4a) and (4b), this domain is the clause within which the reflexive or pronoun occurs; in sentences (5a) and (5b), it is the complex NP within which the referentially dependent item occurs. Second, the NP in question must stand in a particular structural relationship to the reflexive or pronoun. In (4a) and (4b), the head of the subject NP stands in that relationship; in (5a) and (5b), the NP that occupies the determiner position in the complex NP stands in that relationship. The relationship – known as 'c-command' – that permits co-indexation of reflexives and rules out co-indexation of pronouns to an NP is defined in terms of the hierarchically organized syntactic structure in which the reflexive or pronoun is found (Chomsky, 1981; Reinhardt, 1981). C-command differs from the structural relationships of 'subject' and 'object' that are relevant to thematic roles.

The assignment of thematic roles and the assignment of co-reference come together in Chomsky's theory in the determination of the meaning of sentences with what are known as 'phonologically null, logically co-referential' elements or 'empty categories' (or 'empty NPs') – referentially dependent items which are not phonologically specified. Passive sentences (such as (3)) have such empty NPs, illustrated by the symbol **t** in Fig. 4, as do sentences with relative clauses, such as (2). So do sentences with question words, such as (6) – (8):

6. John introduced Bill to Mary.

7. Who$_i$ did John introduce **t**$_i$ to Bill?

8. Who$_i$ did John introduce Bill to **t**$_i$?

Who is the Theme of *introduce* in (7) and the Goal of *introduce* in (8). This exactly parallels the role of *Bill* and *Mary* in (6). Furthermore, the grammatical roles occupied by *Bill* and *Mary* in (6) – the direct and indirect object positions – are empty in (7) and (8): an NP is 'missing' after *introduce* in these positions in (7) and (8). In Chomsky's theory, sentence (6) is generated by phrase structure rules, and

sentences (7) and (8) are derived by movement of the pronoun *who* into sentence-initial position when a question is to be created. According to this theory, the application of the movement rule leaves a **trace (t)** in the original position orginally occupied by *who*. The trace is an 'empty NP'. It receives a thematic role (Theme in (7), Goal in (8)), on the basis of its position in a phrase marker, just as the overt NPs *Bill* and *Mary* do in (6). This trace is co-indexed with *who*, and its thematic role is transmitted to its antecedent, *who*. Thus, these sentences begin to illustrate the complex interactions that Chomsky's theory postulates between the assignment of thematic roles and the process of co-indexation – all of which combine to determine aspects of sentence meaning.

According to Chomsky's theory, there are several different types of referentially dependent empty category. The **trace** in (2), (7) and (8) is a **'wh-trace'** because the **trace** is related to 'wh-word' (*who*) acting as a Complementizer. The **trace** in the passive sentence (3) is an **'NP-trace'**, because it is not related to a wh-word, but to a noun appearing in a grammatical position such as Subject. The **NP-trace** in (3), however, functions just like the **wh-trace** in the sense that it receives the thematic role assigned by the verb, is co-indexed with another word in the sentence (the wh-word in Complementizer position), and its thematic role is associated with that word. Chomsky also postulates the existence of an **NP-trace** in sentences such as (9), which the reader can verify also involves the transmission of a thematic role from one syntactic position to another NP (*John* is not the Agent of *seems* but is the Agent of *shaving*).

9. John$_i$ seems to Bill **t**$_i$ to be shaving.

According to Chomsky, sentences (10) – (12) contain a different empty NP, indicated as **PRO**.

10. John $_i$ promised Peter **PRO**$_i$ to shave.

11. John persuaded Peter $_i$ **PRO**$_i$ to shave.

12. It is hard **PRO** to shave.

There are several differences between **PRO** and **trace**. The antecedent of **PRO** can depend upon the verb in the main clause – in (10), **PRO** is co-indexed with *John* and in (11) with *Peter* – or can refer to an entity outsdide the sentence altogether − in (12), **PRO** refers to anyone. The antecedent of **PRO** plays a thematic role around its own verb − *John* is Agent and *Peter* is Theme of *promised* and *persuaded* in (10) and (11). The antecedent of **trace** is always part of the sentence containing the **trace** and can never play a thematic role around its own verb.

The empty NPs **PRO** and **trace** are similar to reflexives and pronouns in that all these NPs share the property of receiving their reference by being related to a noun phrase that directly refers to something in the world − a so called 'referential expression'. In Chomsky's theory, these similarities go deeper. **PRO** and **trace** are similar to pronouns and reflexives, respectively. Like **PRO**, pronouns (e.g., *him*) are allowed to refer to entities outside the sentence they are in. The only restriction on pronouns is that there are certain NPs which they may *not* refer to. Like **trace**, reflexives (e.g., *himself)* must refer to a particular NP in their sentence.

Thus Chomsky's theory establishes several different ways in which referentially dependent NPs can be grouped together. As with the model that relates syntactic structures to thematic roles, the theory that relates syntactic categories and structures to co-reference is complicated. Moreover, as we have seen, the two theories interact, making for yet more interesting complexity. In fact, syntactic structures and their relationship to sentence meaning are considerably more complex than what we have sketched.

Our object in reviewing these aspects of one linguistic theory has been to illustrate some of the goals of modern linguistics, some of the issues that arise in the study of syntactic structures, and the way in which modern syntactic theory has evolved and gained in descriptive and explanatory power. In addition, our sketch of the role of syntactic structures in determining thematic roles and co-indexation illustrates several features of the syntactic structure of language. First, syntactic structures are moderately complex hierarchically organized sets of syntactic nodes coupled with relationships defined over these hierarchical structures (e.g., subject, object, c-command, etc.). Second, different relationships defined over these structures are relevant to different aspects of semantics. Third, linguistic theory groups together language phenomena which are not intuitively related, such as the co-indexation of the subject of *to shave* in (12) and pronouns.

These structures, the relationships between nodes defined over these structures, and the mapping of these structures and relationships to semantic values do not appear to be the same as mental structures used in other aspects of cognition or, indeed, other aspects of language. For instance, we do not know of mental structures that are created during low- or high-level visual processing that have the character of these representations. Other representations in the linguistic domains of phonology, lexical semantics, discourse, etc. − though hierarchically structured − are quite different with respect to both their intrinsic categories and the relationships defined over these structures (such as subject, c-command, etc.). These structural idiosyncrasies suggest that syntactic structures are a special domain of mental representations. These linguistic considerations are thus compatible with a theory which maintains that this aspect of language is processed by a special-purpose mental processing mechanism.

Psycholinguistic evidence regarding the nature of a parser

The syntactic structures we have just briefly described were postulated by linguists in an effort to describe the relationship between the structure of a sentence and certain aspects of its meaning. The data upon which these theories of syntactic structure are based consist of judgements regarding the well-formedness and meaning of different sentences. As we noted above, the structures postulated attempt to explain aspects of meaning (such as the identity of thematic roles in active and passive sentences, or the similar constraints on possible co-indexation of various phonologically overt and phonologically empty referentially dependent categories) by virtue of the similarity of syntactic elements and structures in different sentences.

These linguistic theories are not intended per se to be theories of how sentences are processed. Indeed, judgements of sentence well-formedness and meaning could not provide adequate data upon which to base models of the unconscious processes involved in sentence comprehension or production. What is needed are data from experimental studies in normal subjects that refer to the way these structures are activated in language use. Psycholinguistic research has addressed this topic and has provided data that point to the existence of operations that are narrowly syntactic. Such operations take as input information about the syntactic categories of lexical items (and possible syntactic combinatorial relationships of each word − so called 'subcategorization' facts, such as the fact that the verb *hit* obligatorily requires a direct object) and use them to construct more elaborate syntactic structures. These operations are known as 'parsing' and the mechanism that accomplishes them is called a 'parser'.

The evidence relevant to the existence and nature of parsing operations essentially consists of the demonstration that variation in syntactic structure affects subjects' abilities to understand a sentence, the time it takes to do so, and/or their ability to accomplish a second task while engaged in understanding a sentence. Studies of parsing have used reaction times and error rates to entire sentences in comprehension tasks (Frazier et al., 1983), reaction times in anomaly-detection tasks during sentence comprehension (Stowe et al., 1985; Tanenhaus et al., 1985; Tanenhaus and Carlson, 1989), eye-movement recordings (Raynor et al., 1984), cerebral evoked potential recordings (Garnsey et al., in press), and other techniques. We cannot review all these data here, but shall present one line of argument regarding the nature of the parser, developed by Frazier (1987), that is based upon data from these various sources.

Frazier's case is based on the existence of preferences in interpretation of locally ambiguous syntactic structures. When these preferences lead to an overt misinterpretation of part of a sentence, they go by the name of 'garden path' effects. Perhaps the best-known garden path effect, illustrated in (13), was first brought to psychologists' attention by Bever (1970):

13. The horse raced past the barn fell.

Subjects analyse (13) as containing a main clause, *the horse raced past the barn*, and then do not find a grammatical role for the last word. In fact, the 'correct' (i.e., grammatical) structure of (13) is the same as that of (14):

14. The horse racing past the barn fell.

Sentence (13) is related to (15), with the relative pronoun and auxiliary deleted:

15. The horse that had been raced past the barn fell.

Why is sentence (13) so difficult to structure? Most theorists agree that this is due to the fact that *raced* can be both a main verb and a participle, and that the human sentence comprehension system has a tendency to take it to be a main verb in this sentence context. Pursuing this idea somewhat further, we may ask what it is about this context that leads us to take *raced* as a main verb. Bever (1970) originally suggested that what was crucial about (13) was the sequence of categories NP-V in sentence-initial position. He suggested that listeners match sequences of this form to the grammatical roles of subject-verb, as a sort of template or heuristic. Since these templates or heuristics map syntactic categories onto syntactic structures, they can be viewed as a particular type of domain-specific syntactic operation.

Frazier (1987) agrees with the basic point that the difficulty in structuring (13) is due to the existence of syntactic operations that automatically misanalyse the first words in the sentence. However, she argues that these operations are not template-matching or heuristic in nature. Rather, she argues that there is a parser which incorporates each new word in a sentence into a syntactic structure, using rules that take as input the lexical syntactic category of each new word. The mis-analysis of (13) is due to two principles that guide the operation of these rules: Minimal Attachment and Late Closure. Minimal Attachment specifies that the parser does not postulate any potentially unnecessary nodes. Late Closure specifies that new items are attached to the phrase or clause being processed, if grammatically possible. Minimal attachment leads to the structure (a) in Fig. 6 for (13), rather than the ultimately correct structure (b).

Minimal Attachment and Late Closure are general principles that lead to systematic preferences regarding the higher-order syntactic structures assigned to sequences of words. One or the other, or both, create a whole host of preferences and garden path situations. A partial list, given by Frazier (1987), includes sentences (16) – (19). The syntactic structures associated with the preferred meaning and the garden path interpretation of these sentences are illustrated in Figs. 7 – 10.

16. John hit the girl with a book (preferred reading attaches *with a book* to *hit*, not to *the girl*).

17. Ernie kissed Marcie and her sister laughed (temporary mis-analysis yields the interpretation that Ernie kissed Marcie and her sister).

18. Since Jay always jogs a mile seems like a short distance to him (temporary mis-analysis yields the interpretation that Jay always jogs a mile).

19. Joyce said that Tom left yesterday (preferred reading attaches *yesterday* to *left*, not to *said*. This is the opposite pattern to that seen in (16) because Late Closure operates here while Minimal Attachment operates in (16)).

Minimal Attachment and Late Closure are

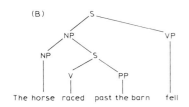

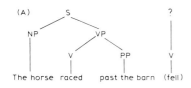

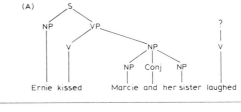

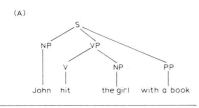

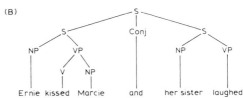

Fig. 6. Garden path (A) and grammatical (B) structural analyses of sentence (13).

Fig. 8. Garden path (A) and grammatical structural analyses of sentence (17).

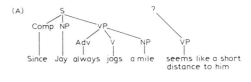

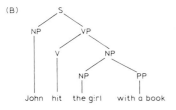

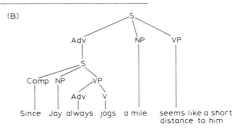

Fig. 7. Preferred (A) and alternative (B) structural analyses of sentence (16).

Fig. 9. Garden path (A) and grammatical (B) structural analyses of sentence (18).

'natural' principles, in the sense that they make first-pass parsing simpler. They preclude the creation of potentially unneeded nodes and keep attachments local, at least initially, thereby presumably reducing both the number of stuctures created by the parser and the number of times the parser must move from place to place in the syntactic tree it is creating. Thus, both principles reduce the workload of the parser. Gorrell (1985) has provided evidence that all the syntactic structures consistent with the subcategorization features of a verb are activated in parallel as a sentence is parsed (see also Shapiro et al., 1987). If this is correct, then the parser apparently rapidly preferentially selects those structures that are created by principles such as Minimal Attachment and Late Closure. This is quite similar to the way lexical ambiguity is handled by on-line comprehension processes (Swinney, 1979; Tanenhaus et al., 1979).)

If the interpretation preferences and garden path phenomena in (13) and (16) – (19) are due to the operation of principles such as Minimal Attachment and Late Closure, it must be the case that these principles guide and constrain the operation of structure-building rules. As stated, Minimal Attachment and Late Closure can only apply to the operation of rules that assign syntactic categories to positions in syntactic trees, and Frazier argues on this basis that such rules exist. In her view, the input

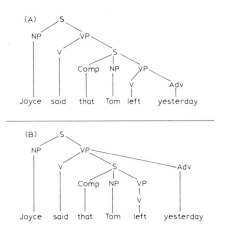

Fig. 10. Preferred (A) and alternative (B) structural analyses of sentence (19).

to these rules is lexical category information and the output is a syntactic structure. There are, however, alternative analyses of the facts just presented as well as other facts regarding sentence processing that have led other researchers to different conclusions.

One alternative to the analyses just presented is to rephrase principles such as Minimal Attachment and Late Closure so as to include semantic notions. For instance, it has been suggested that the garden path phenomenon in (13) does not arise from the application of Minimal Attachment but rather from a principle that sequences of the form NP-V-NP are matched to thematic roles (Agent-Verb-Theme) directly, rather than through the intermediate stage of a hierarchically structured representation (Bates et al., 1982). The Bates et al. analysis denies the existence of a stage of sentence processing that constructs more elaborate syntactic structures. The problem with the Bates et al. approach is that is has only been applied to a very restricted set of syntactic structures. For instance, it has not been applied to the problem created by the structure of sentence (2), in which the sequence of words *the cat killed the mouse* is present but *the cat* is not the Agent of *killed*. In general, the alternatives to a parser have thus far only generated a number of construction-specific heuristics that have no general application and no obvious basis in terms of the requirements of the sentence-processing task. In contrast, Frazier's approach has yielded some very general, principled accounts of preferences and garden path phenomena, and has begun to present serious models of aspects of parsing. The mental processes postulated in both types of model may play a role in sentence comprehension. However, the studies and analyses presented by Frazier and others are convincing (to this author) on at least one point: whether or not more 'direct' mappings from superficial aspects of sentence form to sentential semantic values exist, it is very likely that a parser also exists.

Another rebuttal of the Frazier position is the claim that the phenomena described above are due not to the operation of a parser but to lexical factors. There is a considerable literature regarding the effects of verb structure and meaning on attachment (e.g., Ford et al., 1982; Taraban and McClelland, in press), but the data supporting alternative theories are inconclusive (see for discussion Tyler, 1989; Frazier, 1989; Tanenhaus and Carlson, 1989). Some disagreements reflect different analyses of data. For instance, Holmes (1987) showed that there is a more marked garden path effect in (20) than in (21):

20. The reporter saw her friend was not succeeding.

21. The candidate doubted his sincerity would be appreciated.

The important difference between the sentences is that *saw* is a verb that usually takes a direct NP object, whereas *doubt* is a verb that usually takes a sentential complement. If Minimal Attachment operates independently of the nature of a verb, there should be an identical garden path effect in both (20) and (21). Holmes argues that the reduced garden path effect in (21) indicates that the nature of the verb affects the parser's first-pass attachments. Frazier (1987), however, argues that the existence of a garden path effect at all in (21) is evidence in favour of the operations of Minimal Attachment. Indeed, it appears that Minimal Attachment can, at times, even apply to create structures that are incompatible with the syntactic frames into which a verb can be inserted (i.e., with the subcategorization features of a verb); Mitchell (1987) reported garden path effects in sentences such as (22):

22. After the audience had departed the actors sat down for a well-deserved drink.

Other disagreements reflect different findings based on different experimental techniques. For instance, there is evidence from self-paced reading tasks that the animacy of nouns affects the occurrence of a garden path effect in sentences like (18) (Stowe, 1989), but data from eye-fixation sudies do not find this effect (Ferreira and Clifton, 1986; for discussion, see Tanenhaus and Carlson, 1989). It seems to this author that available data establish a reasonable basis upon which to postulate the existence of a parser that takes as its input the syntactic category of an incoming word and constructs the simplest phrase compatible with that category.

Frazier's work has begun to present serious models of this aspect of parsing. However, this is not to say that other sources of information are not available to the mechanisms that construct syntactic representations. An open question in psycholinguistics is how these other sources of information interact with parsing procedures that are based upon category information.

The third approach that has been contrasted with a parsing explanation of preference and garden path effects is based upon the existence of context effects upon garden path and preference phenomena. Crain and Steedman (1985), Altmann and Steedman (1988) and others have argued that garden paths are artifacts of presenting sentences out of context. They argue that biases such as those seen in (13) and (16) are not due to attachment preferences but rather to referential success. In (16), for instance, attaching *the book* to *the girl* implies that the context has identified more than one girl and that the sentence is referring to the girl with the book (of the girls mentioned in the context). Since presenting the sentence in isolation does not establish a context with more than one girl, the sentence is preferentially interpreted as attaching *the book* to *hit*. Evidence supporting this analysis would come from showing that context reverses preferences such as those seen in sentences like (13) and (16) in isolation. There is evidence that context changes many of these effects, and does so while sentences are being processed (Altmann and Steedman, 1988). However, that evidence is as yet controversial. Ferreira and Clifton (1986), Clifton and Ferreira (1987), Frazier (1987) and others have argued that at least some garden paths remain in effect despite strongly disambiguating context. Moreover, not all preferences can be explained this way; those in (17) – (19) cannot. Since some principles must account for the attachment preferences in (17) – (19), it is reasonable to maintain the claim that these same principles apply to sentences such as (13) and (16).

Thus, despite some lingering uncertainties, there is good evidence from garden path effects and preferred interpretations of locally ambiguous syntactic structures that a parser exists and that it is governed by some basic principles affecting structure-building operations. Indeed, even critics of principles such as Minimal Attachment and Late Closure generally agree that what is at issue is not whether there is a syntactic processor, but how much its initial operations are entirely determined by syntactic information (see the final discussion in Altmann and Steedman, 1988, for instance). The important point is that research in normative psycholinguistics provides quite strong evidence for the existence of a parser – a set of operations that takes as input lexical category information and constructs a syntactic structure.

We have, thus far, been dealing with parsing operations which assign hierarchical structure to lexical category nodes to higher nodes, subject to constraints such as Minimal Attachment and Late Closure. Some researchers have suggested that the parser consists of several different types of process, of which structure-building operations are but one. Frazier (1988) has suggested that structure-building operations are separate from operations that assign thematic roles. On the basis of both theoretical analyses and a reconsideration of work by Freedman and Forster (1985), Weinberg (1987) has argued that structure-building operations are separate from operations that connect referentially dependent items – pronouns, reflexives, reciprocals, various phonologically empty referentially dependent categories (see above) – to their antecedents. Both these analyses separate structure-building operations from other syntactic operations. Together, the two hypotheses suggest that, aside from structure-building operations, there are also several other different types of syntactic operation, such as those related to the assignment of thematic roles and those related to the assignment of reference (co-indexation). We shall briefly review one of these other aspects of parsing – the treatment of referential dependencies (called 'long-distance dependencies' in some of the psycholinguistic literature). This is an area where research in linguistics, psycholinguistics and aphasiology interacts in interesting ways.

Long-distance dependencies involve relationships that exist between discontinuous elements of a sentence. The long-distance dependencies that have been most actively investigated are co-indexation phenomena, called 'filler-gap' constructions in the psycholinguistic literature, in which a word appearing early in a sentence is related to an empty syntactic position occurring later in the sentence. The filler-gap constructions that have been most thoroughly explored involve 'wh-words', as in (23) and (24):

23. What did John buy —?
24. The little girl who the teacher liked — sat on the grass.

In both (23) and (24), the phonologically empty position following the verb is 'filled' by the wh-word that occurs at the beginning of the verb's clause. How is this 'filling' accomplished?

Two aspects of the process of handling these long-distance dependencies must be to identify both potential fillers and gaps, and then to relate the correct ones to each other. For sentences like (23) and (24), the filler-gap relationship can be relatively easily described: the filler is not assigned a thematic role by virtue of its position in a phrase marker, and a single gap exists at a spot where a thematic role must be assigned to complete the argument structure of the verb. It is straightforward to assign this filler to this gap. Moreover, in (23) and (24), there is an overt indication that the sentence contains a filler – the wh-word. Thus, it is possible for the parser to actively search for a gap once the wh-word is encountered in (23) and (24), and some research suggests that such a search in fact occurs (Frazier and Clifton, 1989; Stowe, 1984, 1986). For all these reasons, sentences such as (23) and (24) are ones in which the filler-gap relationships are relatively easy to identify.

Not all constructions with filler-gap relationships are so simple, however. Consider examples (25) – (27):

25. What did John buy (—) the paint with —?
26. What did John buy (—) the paint — $_1$ to decorate — $_2$?
27. What did John buy — $_1$— $_2$ to paint the porch with — $_3$?

In (25), the gap does not occur until after the preposition *with*, but the fact that the verb *buy* is transitive coupled with the fact that the parser has already identified a filler leads to a preliminary assignment of the filler to the role of object of *buy* (Stowe, 1986). That is, sentence (25) creates a local garden path because of the possibility of there being a filler-gap relationship that turns out not to exist in the actual sentence. Sentence (26) contains two gaps — one that functions as the subject of the infinitive *to paint* and that is filled by *John*, and one that functions as the object of *decorate* and that is filled by *what* — and a 'pseudogap' after *buy* as in (25). Sentence (27) is yet more complex. It contains three gaps — the two in (26) plus a real gap after *buy* that is filled with the filler *what*.

In circumstances with more than one filler and/or more than one gap, there seem to be several principles that apply to constrain the parser's first-pass assignment of fillers to gaps. Fodor (1978), Crain and Fodor (1985), Frazier et al. (1983), Engdahl (1983) and Frazier (1987b) have all provided evidence that, in sentences like (27), the parser assigns the more recent of two possible fillers to the first gap, and the more distant to a second. This creates a nested filler-gap structure, illustrated in (29) – (30) (taken from Fodor, 1978):

29. Who$_j$ did you$_i$ want — $_i$ to make a potholder for — $_j$?

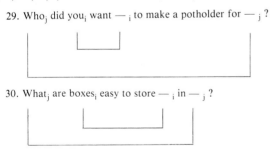

30. What$_j$ are boxes$_i$ easy to store — $_i$ in — $_j$?

Frazier (1987) makes the point that there are several similarities between the handling of these long-distance dependencies and the handling of structure-building discussed above. In both cases, the parser does not wait for all the relevant linguistic input to be available, but makes decisions about structure quite early. In both cases, relatively simple structures are postulated — Minimal Attachment and Late Closure result in the simplest possible at-tachments and the least moving around constructed phrase markers; the most-recent-filler strategy requires a minimum of look-back in cases of long-distance co-indexation.

Finally, we note that there is evidence for a number of distinct processing operations within the related set of procedures that deal with filler-gap relationships. Frazier and Clifton (cited in Frazier, 1987) have argued that the most-recent-filler strategy does not apply in cases where lexical 'control' information determines filler-gap relationships, as in (31). Though research on these topics is too limited to assert any general theory with confidence, it may be that differences among types of fillers and gaps that are expressed in linguistic theory (see above) may map onto different procedures for relating fillers and gaps. One possible generalization is that co-indexation procedures differ for the different empty NPs PRO and WH-trace (Frazier, 1987).

31. John promised Mary — to read the book on vacation.

Thus, studies of sentence comprehension indicate that there is a component of the language-processing system that constructs syntactic phrase markers and uses these phrase markers to constrain and determine aspects of sentence meaning. It is clear that these syntax-building operations are largely unconscious and automatic, and decades-old research has clearly shown that their products are not usually retained in memory for any length of time (Bransford and Franks, 1971; Franks and Bransford, 1972). Nonetheless, psycholinguistic research does seem to show that they exist and has begun to reveal something of their nature.

Disturbances of parsing and syntactic comprehension

The study of sentence-comprehension deficits in aphasic patients supports the idea that there is a parser, and begins to reveal something of its internal structure. In large part, the conclusions drawn from this research on language disorders are consistent with the conclusions drawn from psycholinguistic research on normal subjects.

The first set of observations in aphasiology that bear on the existence of a parser was the finding that some patients had difficulty interpreting some types of semantically reversible sentence despite being able to interpret sentences with similar structures whose meanings could be inferred from lexical meanings and real-world knowledge. Caramazza and Zurif (1976) reported that there were aphasic patients who could not match sentences such as (32) to pictures but who performed well above chance on sentences such as (33):

32. The woman the boy is chasing is tall.

33. The apple the man is eating is red.

These authors argued that the patients in question were unable to assign syntactic structures, but retained knowledge of word meanings and of the real world. They could assign thematic roles 'lexico-pragmatically', but not on the basis of syntactic analyses. It has been widely assumed that these data provide evidence for the existence of a parser (Berndt and Caramazza, 1980; Shallice, 1988).

Other observations appear to indicate that different aspects of sentence interpretation involve different processing components. Linebarger et al. (1983a) have shown that patients who could not understand certain types of semantically reversible sentences, such as the subject-object relative clauses illustrated in (32) and simple passive sentences, were nonetheless able to judge the grammaticality of many sentence types. Linebarger et al. suggested that these patients were able to construct syntactic structures but not interpret them. One version of this interpretation (not necessarily one that the authors would agree with) is that, of the components of the parser described above in connection with the theories of Weinberg and Frazier, the structure-building operations of a parser are intact but the components of a parser that assign thematic roles and co-indexation are affected in these patients. Another interpretation of these and related results (Zurif and Grodzinsky, 1983; Linebarger et al., 1983b; Wolfeck et al., 1989; Cornell et al., 1989) is that these patients retain only certain aspects of grammatical knowledge and apply it to both grammaticality judgements (where it is adequate to accomplish the task successfully) and to sentence interpretation (where it is not). For instance, if a patient knows that a verb can only take two thematic roles, s/he may be able to judge a sentence with three nouns associated with a verb as being ungrammatical, but still not necessarily be able to interpret a passive sentence correctly. In either case, these results would seem to point to selective loss of parsing and/or closely related interpretive operations and thus to the existence of such operations.

However, to base such conclusions on these results is premature. One problem in interpretation involves the possibility of artifactual performances based on how patients cope with the tasks used in this research. For instance, sentence-picture matching requires the use of nonsensical picture foils to depict 'reversed' thematic roles in semantically irreversible sentences. Patients such as those described by Caramazza and Zurif may have performed better on the irreversible sentences than the reversible ones by simply rejecting such foils (Grodzinsky and Marek, 1989). Grammatically judgements in the Linebarger et al. (1983) study may have been based on intonational contours.* The answers to objections of this sort require more careful experimental controls. For instance, an answer to Grodzinsky and Marek's concerns would be the demonstration that the dissociation between interpretation of reversible and irreversible sentences is maintained in tasks, such as object manipulation, which do not require implausible foils (see also Caramazza, 1989). An answer to the concern regarding patients' use of intonation in grammaticality judgements would involve careful controls for this factor. Research has moved in these directions, but

---

* In general, it is difficult to know what a patient bases a grammaticality judgement on. For instance, Linebarger et al. indicate that patients' rejection of sentences such as (i) implies that they are sensitive to constraints on the movement of constituents out of governing categories. (i. How many did John see birds in the park?) However, patients may rule out (i) on the grounds that there are more NPs than argument structure slots in the subcategorization frame of the verb. Thus, the exact analysis of what is retained and lost in patients remains uncertain.

the results are still incomplete. For instance, though many patients have been shown to have difficulty with reversible sentences using tasks such as object manipulation (see, e.g., Caplan et al., 1985), to this author's knowledge, none have also been tested for their ability to do this task with irreversible sentences.* Thus, though many patients have been shown to have syntactic comprehension deficits, there is no firm proof that any of these patients have these deficits in the face of normal ability to comprehend constrained sentences or to make judgements regarding the grammaticality of sentences that are not understood.

Assuming, however, as is likely, that isolated disturbances in syntactic comprehension exist and will be appropriately documented, we must face a second interpretive issue. It is possible that interpreting semantically reversible sentences is simply more difficult than interpreting semantically constrained sentences or judging their grammaticality. This is the 'resource artifact problem' (Shallice, 1988; see also Shallice, 1979, Jones, 1983, and Caplan and Hildebrandt, 1988, for discussion). If task A is harder than task B, a patient may fail on A but do well on B because he has just enough resources available to accomplish B but not A.

In general, the answer to this possibility involves the use of a common methodological technique in neuropsychology – the documentation of a so-called 'double dissociation'. In a double dissociation, one patient does significantly better on one task (A) than a second patient, while the second patient performs significantly better on a second task (B) than the first patient. The inference that is drawn from a double dissociation is that performance on the two tasks does not involve a single processing component; both patterns cannot result from resource reductions.** In the case of syntactic comprehension, there are no descriptions of patients who perform worse on irreversible than reversible sentences or worse on grammaticality judgements than on interpretation of semantically reversible sentences. It is likely that the reason for the absence of a double dissociation involving 'syntactic' and 'non-syntactic' comprehension is that the two processes are not independent: any patient who can apply syntactic operations to reversible sentences could also apply them to irreversible sentences, and any patient who failed to assign thematic roles in irreversible sentences because s/he had lost the concept of thematic relations would also be expected to fail to assign these semantic values in reversible sentences. Thus, we cannot expect double dissociations in this domain, even if syntactic operations are separate from non-syntactic ones in sentence comprehension. Unfortunately, this implies that we cannot clearly conclude on the basis of data of the sort discussed above that parsing is a separate operation from a non-syntactic means of interpreting sentences, or that totally separate structure-building, thematic role assignment and co-indexation components of a parsing mechanism exist.

However, it is possible to look for double dissociations *within* the set of parsing operations. In

---

* Caplan et al. (1985) found no effects of plausibility on object-manipulation performances by aphasic patients but the plausibility effects studied were quite different from those discussed by Grodzinsky and Marek (1988). Bates et al. (1988) documented plausibity effects in a sentence-picture matching task in which many of the stimuli were both implausible and ill-formed. It is hard to evaluate the role of task-specific strategies in patients' approach to this task. Nancy Hildebrandt has brought to my attention one patient she tested who showed a plausibility effect in an object manipulation task under certain conditions.

** Many researchers have defined a double dissociation differently, as a situation in which one patient does well on one task (A) and poorly on a second (B), while a second patient shows the reverse pattern. However, as Shallice (1988, p. 234, Fig. 10.5) has shown, this is not sufficient to rule out resource artifacts as the cause of this performance. Double dissociations, as defined here and in Shallice (1988), do not prove that two deficits underlie performance on the two tasks in question, since one performance may result from a resource reduction and the other from an impairment to a separate processing component. Shallice (1988, pp. 235 – 237) and Jones (1983) have argued that, if a double dissociation is one in which there is a 'strong cross-over interaction' (the 'good' task is performed at normal levels and the affected task is clearly performed at below-normal levels in each of two patients), it is unlikely (or perhaps even impossible) that a resource limitation is the cause of the impaired performance of either patient. Such cases provide the strongest available evidence from pathology that each task includes a functional component not found in the other.

fact, a series of double dissociations has been demonstrated with respect to patients' abilities to interpret aspects of different syntactic structure by myself and Nancy Hildebrandt (Hildebrandt, 1987; Hildebrandt et al., 1987; Caplan and Hildebrandt, 1988a,b, 1989). Our particular concern was patients' abilities to assign referential dependencies. In addition to co-indexation of overt referentially dependent items (pronouns and reflexives), we also studied patients' abilities to co-index empty NPs. We adopted the taxonomy to empty NPs in Chomsky (1981), discussed above, because it specifies the largest number of different types of empty NP at the syntactic level, and thus allows the discovery of the largest number of single and double dissociations of function with respect to empty NPs.

Using an object-manipulation test, we observed isolated disturbances of patients' abilities to assign referents to different referentially dependent items (for details of methodology and interpretation, and for discussion of other cases, see Caplan and Hildebrandt, 1988a). Table 1 summarizes the results of four patients' performances. Two of these patients had difficulties with all empty referentially dependent NPs, but showed a double dissociation between co-indexation of reflexives and pronouns. A.B. showed an impairment in co-indexing pronouns but did well on reflexives; C.V. showed the opposite patterns of performance. Two patients had selective difficulties with co-indexing particular empty NPs. J.V. had difficulty with sentences containing NP-trace, but did well on sentences containing PRO and wh-trace; G.S. did well on sentences with NP-trace but poorly on sentences containing NP-trace and WH-trace.

These double dissociations indicate that patients can have selective difficulties with aspects of syntactic processing. These deficits can be quite restricted. Because of the selectivity of the deficits, especially in cases that show disturbances of particular empty NPs, artifactual causes for these performances seem unlikely: other than the particular co-indexation operation(s) associated with these different referentially dependent NPs, task demands are identical across sentence types. These performances thus

strongly suggest that quite specific parsing operations exist. We have suggested that the dissociations we observed are best accommodated within Chomsky's theory of syntactic structures and an associated parser (Caplan and Hildebrandt, 1988a,b). However, studies of specific parsing impairments are in their infancy, and the range of specific parsing impairments and the ultimate implications of these deficits for the nature of linguistic representations and parsing operations are unknown. The principal conclusion that I believe can be drawn from these studies is that a parser exists and consists of a number of separate operations dealing with different aspects of syntax.

Studies of aphasic patients have also been related to another question regarding syntax-processing mechanisms: is there a special role for certain vocabulary classes in parsing procedures. Several parsing theories (mostly of a slightly older vintage, such as Kimball, 1973) have proposed that the construction of phrase markers is driven by minor lexical categories − determiners, prepositions, complementizers, etc. Data from aphasia have been thought to be relevant to this claim. The argument

TABLE 1

Patient performance on object manipulation test

Sentence type	Patient			
	A.B.	C.V.	J.V.	G.S.
Subject control (John promised Bill to jump)	33%	25%	100%	50%
NP-raising (John seemed to Bill to be jumping)	42%	42%	33%	100%
Object relativization (The man who the woman kissed hugged the child)	17%	0%	93%	25%
Pronouns (The girl said that the woman washed her)	83%	23%	92%	92%
Reflexives (The girl said that the woman washed herself)	42%	100%	100%	92%

from pathology to the normal functional architecture of the system is based on the following logic. If a single processing component is involved in two tasks, damage to that shared component should result in disruption of performance on both tasks. Thus, establishing the role of a single processing component in two tasks requires the documentation of associated processing deficits. Since two deficits can always co-occur in a single case because a neural lesion affects two different functional systems, these co-occurrences must show additional features to provide evidence for a shared processing component. These features include: (1) continued co-occurrence of the deficits in the face of a variability in lesion site and type; and (2) qualitative and quantitative similarity of the two deficits (see Caplan, 1987, 1988 for discussion). In the case of the role of function words in parsing, this logic requires that we identify patients with disturbances affecting function words and examine their parsing abilities.

Some aphasiologists have investigated the co-occurrence of syntactic comprehension disturbances and omission of function words in the speech of a class of patients known as 'agrammatic' aphasic patients. Agrammatism is a disturbance of speech production in which, clinically, patients omit a disproportionate number of affixes and free-standing 'function words'. Agrammatic patients have a variety of other disturbances in processing function words (Rosenberg et al., 1985; Frederici, 1981, 1982). In particular, Bradley et al. (1980) presented evidence that recognition of function words is abnormal in agrammatic aphasics. Caramazza and Zurif (1976), Schwartz et al (1980). Grodzinsky (1986) and others have shown that these patients often have syntactic comprehension disturbances (see below). Some researchers have concluded that both the syntactic comprehension and speech production disturbances seen in these patients are due to specific impairments in activating function words (Zurif, 1982). However, the relationship of these disturbances affecting function words to the syntactic comprehension impairments of agrammatic patients is not clear. Bradley's data have been subjected to both re-analyses and non-

replication (Gordon and Caramazza, 1982), showing that the implications of the original data are not as clear as had been thought at first. No patients have been described in whom a disturbance affecting function words has been related to a comprehension impairment that is restricted to structures containing the affected items. Overall, there is no credible evidence from pathology that function words provide a critical input to the parser.

These studies of aphasic patients are part of a larger set of investigations relevant to the nature of the sentence comprehension system. It appears, from multiple sources, that one part of this system involves a parser, whose operations are specific to the construction of syntactic structures. Brain damage can affect these operations either massively, or in very selective fashion.

The relationsip of a parser to other psycholinguistic processes

The parser does not operate in isolation. It is necessarily dependent upon lexical access processes that provide it with its input (lexical category information, and possibly subcategorization and predicate argument structure information, etc.). In addition to this universally recognized input to the parser, it is clear that multiple sources of information are brought to bear very rapidly on the actions of the parser and on the operations that derive semantic meanings from the structures created by the parser. Some of these may also be part of the input to first-pass parsing. In the oral modality, intonation contours may serve as a guide to major phrasal breaks (Briscoe, 1987), and punctuation may serve a similar function in written language. The role of context in parsing is still controversial (see discussion above).

There are two questions that arise regarding the way different knowledge sources affect parsing: (1) what is the schedule of their interactions, and (2) how do these different knowledge sources actually interact? The first of these questions can be further divided into several separate issues, such as whether different sources of information affect first-pass or second-pass parsing operations, whether different information sources are used to construct different aspects of syntactic form, whether different information sources all interact in a common operation or whether they interact in a complex set of multiple pair-wise operations, etc. The second question requires that we specify a means whereby different information types can influence each other. Frazier (1987) has pointed out that a necessary step in this process is the identification of the primitive elements that are common to that different knowledge source, such as thematic roles being related to both phrase markers and discourse structures.

We cannot answer either of the two basic questions posed above properly on the basis of available data. With respect to the first question, we have presented the controversy surrounding the position advanced by Frazier and others that the initial operations of the parser are uninfluenced by context. It is clear that, at the least, second-pass parsing operations are affected by context. The role of other knowledge sources in parsing is almost unexplored. With respect to the second question, a number of computer simulations have modelled interactions in different ways. For instance, the 'blackboard' of the spoken language comprehension program HEARSAY II used a 'co-operative computational' mechanism that computed most-highly-valued analyses of several levels of language structure and revised earlier structural analyses on the basis of these ratings (Erman and Lesser, 1980). More recently, 'connectionist' (parallel distributed processing — PDP) computational models have provided a general framework for modelling interactions that derives its attractiveness in part from its claims to neural realism (Rumelhart and McClelland, 1986). These computer realizations are frequently cited by researchers whose view of sentence processing holds that a sentence comprehension device is a non-domain-specific system in which individual mental operations combine a variety of information sources (such as Bates et al., 1982). However, none of these different models has been explored to the point

where experiments that would distinguish one from another have been performed.

While we cannot answer these fundamental questions regarding the functional architecture in which the parser is located, we can say that experimental results indicate that the parser usually operates extremely quickly, whatever its input and whatever revisions it must make. First-pass attachments appear to be made on a word-by-word basis (see above). Co-indexation of long-distance dependencies also occurs extremely rapidly: Tanenhaus and his colleagues (Tanenhaus et al., 1985, 1987), for instance, have shown that both word-by-word reading times and features of cerebral evoked potentials are sensitive to anomalies at the point of anomaly (indicated by/) as quickly in (34) as in (35):

34. Which snake did the girl expect **t** to hop / over the log?

35. The girl expected the snake to hop / over the log.

This speed of processing raises questions about another aspect of the functional architecture affecting the parser, one that has been addressed in the literature on aphasia: the role of short-term memory in parsing. Short-term memory is phonologically based (Conrad, 1964), and some researchers have argued that phonological STM is involved in the initial assignment of structure and meaning to a sentence. A characteristic statement of this view is that of Clark and Clark (1977). Their claim, closely related to earlier work by Fodor, Garrett and their colleagues (Garret et al., 1965; Caplan, 1972; Fodor et al., 1974), was that parsing is carried out on a clause-by-clause basis and that material is held in short-term memory until it is structured and interpreted semantically. The Preliminary Phrasal Packager of Frazier and Fodor's 'Sausage Machine' parsing model (Frazier and Fodor, 1978) also suggests a role for short-term memory in parsing. However, the speed of the parsing process suggests that the parser does not make much use of look-ahead. A slightly different model maintains that some lexical items are held in a phonological STM in phrase markers when parsing is difficult and/or when co-indexation operations are required over a large number of intervening NPs (Caramazza and Berndt, 1985; Vallar and Baddeley, 1984; Baddeley et al., 1987). A quite different point of view has been articulated by several other researchers (Warrington and Shallice, 1969; Saffran and Marin 1975; MacCarthy and Warrington, 1987a,b, 1990; Caplan and Waters, 1990). They postulate no role for STM in parsing, but argue that phonological memory systems are involved in processes that arise after sentence meaning is assigned. These processes include mapping propositional content onto motor actions, mapping propositional content onto long-term memory to verify the truth or plausibility of a proposition, checking the meaning derived from the syntactic processing of a sentence against meanings derived lexico-pragmatically, and other reasoning and learning processes (updating semantic and long-term memory) based on propositional content.

Data from brain-damaged patients are relevant to these models. Several patients with STM impairments have been described who have excellent syntactic comprehension abilities (Waters et al., in press; see Caplan and Waters, 1990, for review). For instance, a patient of ours, B.O., has a short-term memory span of 2 – 3 items. If B.O.'s span limited either the look-ahead buffer of her parser or the maintenance of lexical items in phrase markers, she would be expected to show effects of syntactic complexity upon comprehension. If STM was required for long-distance co-indexation, she should show an effect of the number of words intervening between a referentially dependent item and its antecedent. However, neither of these effects was found. B.O. showed excellent comprehension of syntactically complex, semantically reversible sentences, including those containing long-distance dependencies that spanned considerably more than three words. Thus data from B.O. and other STM patients provide strong evidence against any role of STM in parsing itself.*

Studies of aphasic patients have also been related to another question regarding the functional architecture of the sentence-processing system: is there a single mechanism that computes syntactic structure in both input and output tasks (or is there significant overlap between syntactic operations in these tasks)? Again, the discussion focusses on patients with expressive agrammatism (see above). Beginning with the work of Caramazza and Zurif (1976) cited above, many studies have shown that patients with expressive agrammatism often have syntactic comprehension disturbances (Heilman and Scholes, 1976; Schwartz et al., 1980; Grodzinsky, 1986; Caplan and Futter, 1986; etc.). Several authors have argued that the co-occurrence of deficits in sentence production and comprehension seen in these patients indicates that there are 'central' or 'overarching' syntactic operations, used in both comprehension and production tasks (Berndt and Caramazza, 1980; Zurif, 1984; Grodzinsky, 1986).

However, though deficits in syntactic comprehension frequently co-occur with expressive agrammatism, it does not appear that the additional criteria suggesting that a single functional impairment underlies these two deficits are met (see above). When we consider how patients with agram-

---

* On the other hand, the data from STM cases are compatible with the view that phonological memory systems are involved in processes that arise after sentence meaning is determined on the basis of sentence structure. B.O. had particular problems enacting thematic roles in sentences that contained three or more noun phrases, especially if these were proper nouns, independent of their syntactic structure (Waters et al., in press). This suggests that she had trouble mapping three NPs with their thematic roles onto motor actions. She also had more trouble with anomaly judgements in sentences containing two clauses than in sentences with only one clause, again independent of the syntactic complexity of a sentence, suggesting she had trouble mapping propositional meaning onto long-term semantic knowledge (Waters et al., 1987). Other STM patients show comprehension disturbances that seem related to processing that arises after propositional meaning has been extracted. For instance, McCarthy and Warrington (1987a, 1990) reported two STM cases who were unable to map commands onto actions when the task involved a pragmatically unpreferred arrangement of manipulanda. Vallar and Baddeley (1987) reported an STM patient who could not detect the discourse-anomaly of referential dependencies. These data suggest that STM patients show deficits in a variety of situations in which the initial analysis of a sentence must be reviewed (Caplan and Waters, 1990).)

matism perform in syntactic comprehension tasks, we see such a wide degree of variation as to render unlikely the possibility that a single functional disturbance underlies the syntactic comprehension impairments in many individual patients with agrammatism. Several patients with expressive agrammatism have shown no disturbances of syntactic comprehension whatsoever (Miceli et al., 1983; Nespoulous et al., 1988; Kolk and Van Grunsven, 1985). Though some of these patients may be exceptional in certain ways – one of the Miceli et al. patients, for instance, had only a transient aphasic impairment which resolved within a month – many of these patients have classic expressive agrammatism and are not distinguishable from other agrammatic patients who do have disturbances of syntactic comprehension. To the extent that disturbances of syntactic comprehension and expressive agrammatism can be assessed in terms of degree of severity, there seems to be no correlation between the severity of a syntactic comprehension deficit and the severity of expressive agrammatism in an individual patient. These data constitute an argument against the view that there is only one impairment producing expressive agrammatism which necessarily entails a disturbance of syntactic comprehension, and thus are consistent with a model that has separate mechanisms dealing with the construction of syntactic form in the input and output side of processing.

These studies illustrate the first applications of data from pathology to the development of models of the functional architecture of the part of the language-processing system that constructs syntactic representations from verbal input. As more specific models of the interactions between language-processing components are articulated, studies of the patterns of co-occurrence and dissociation of deficits in brain-damaged patients may provide additional information regarding aspects of the functional architecture of the language-processing system.

Resource allocation in the language-processing system

We have indicated at several points that parsing occurs quickly. We have also alluded to the fact that it is automatic (involuntary) and unconscious. Data from experiments with normal subjects confirm these features (Lackner and Garrett, 1973). Since many researchers argue that automatic processing requires little or no deployment of mental resources (Schneider and Shiffrin, 1977; Shiffrin and Dumais, 1981), these observations lead to the question of the resources required by the parser.

Intuitively, sentence comprehension and parsing appear to contradict the view that automaticity and freedom from resource requirements are linked. It is hard to comprehend speech while engaged in other activities. Experimental work suggests that there are different degrees of resource requirements of different parsing operations (Cook, 1975; Wanner and Maratsos, 1978). Thus parsing appears to be both automatic, since it is involuntarily initiated by the presentation of a sentence under ordinary circumstances, and to require processing capacity.

One way to visualize the processing resources required by parsing is to consider the operations involved in assigning the structure of a sentence. Fig. 11a–1 illustrate the development of syntactic representations for a sentence with a relative clause in the 'active node stack' – one part of a computer-based parser developed by Berwick and Weinberg (1984). As the reader can see, the stack becomes quite complex as the parser deals with words in the relative clause. A sentence that did not contain this structure would have a far smaller active node stack. Limitations of mental resources may serve to prevent the parser from processing sentences normally by limiting its ability to construct adequately elaborated structures.

Data from aphasia bear on the resources required by different parsing operations. The logic involves a third methodological approach, analyses of group performance. The differences in the average performance of a group of patients on a single task as a function of certain types of task parameter can be said to reflect the resources required by those parameters on those tasks. In the domain of parsing, we are interested in comparing the performance of groups of aphasic patients on different sentence types.

The results of work in our laboratory (Caplan et al., 1985) provide relevant data. Three groups of patients were examined for their syntactic comprehension abilities using an object-manipulation task. Patients were screened for their ability to understand the vocabulary in auditorily presented sentences. Patients were then presented with nine types of semantically reversible sentence: active, passive, cleft subject, cleft object, dative, dative passive, conjoined, subject object relatives, and object subject relatives. Caplan et al. (1985) report the significant differences in mean correct scores for these different sentences. Though some significant differences may have resulted from differences in the length of sentences, sentences with equivalent number of words, nouns, verbs and function words produced significantly different mean correct scores as a function of their syntactic structure. There are two possible reasons for these differences. Patients might have specific difficulties in accomplishing particular syntactic operations, leading to difficulty on certain sentence types, as described above. Alternatively, or in addition, certain sentence types may require more processing than others and patients may fail on sentences that require more processing.

Additional analyses suggest that these differences in large part reflect the different processing demands associated with different syntactic structures. A clustering analysis based on similarity of performance on individual sentences separated patients into eight groups. Examination of the mean correct scores and standard deviations of each of these groups on each of the nine sentence types showed that, for successive groups of patients, the mean correct score declined on the test as a whole. In addition, in each group, lower scores tended to occur on the sentence types with overall lower scores

for the group as a whole. This relationship between performance on the test as a whole and performance of each subgroup of patients can be attributed to two factors: (1) increased processing demands of certain sentence types and (2) progressive diminution in the resources available for syntactic comprehension in each of the patient groups identified by the clustering analysis. The observed relationship between performance on the test as a whole and performance of each subgroup of patients on specific sentence types would not be expected if patients' performances were determined solely by impairments of specific parsing or interpretive operations. Additional evidence for the importance of resource reduction in determining performance on this task can be found in a principal components analysis, which showed a first factor equally positively weighted for all sentence types that accounted for approximately 60% of the total variance of patient clustering. Given these analyses, the differences in mean correct scores of different sentence types seem to primarily reflect the processing resources associated with the comprehension of each of these sentence types.

Accepting this analysis, the results of the Caplan et al. (1985) study indicate that a number of superficial aspects of sentence structure make demands on processing resources. These include the number of NPs in a sentence, the order of thematic roles, and the number of verbs. These results are unsurprising, except perhaps to a theorist who would maintain that parsing is entirely cost-free. However, this methodology can be more revealing. Butler-Hinz et al. (1990) studied the relationship between sentences containing three thematic roles (e.g., *The monkey pushed the elephant to the tiger*) and sentences containing two thematic roles, one of which is assigned to two noun phrases (e.g., *The monkey pushed the elephant and the tiger*). In a group of 20 brain-damaged subjects, the passive versions of the first of these sentences were significantly harder than the passive versions of the second of these sentences. This finding suggests that the assignment of three different thematic roles to three noun phrases is more demanding of processing requirements than the assignment of two thematic roles to three noun phrases. Hagiwara and Caplan (in press) found that violations of thematic role canonicity (the usual order of thematic roles in a given sentence structure in a given language) were more costly than violations of thematic role markedness (the most common thematic role order for a given sentence structure in the languages of the

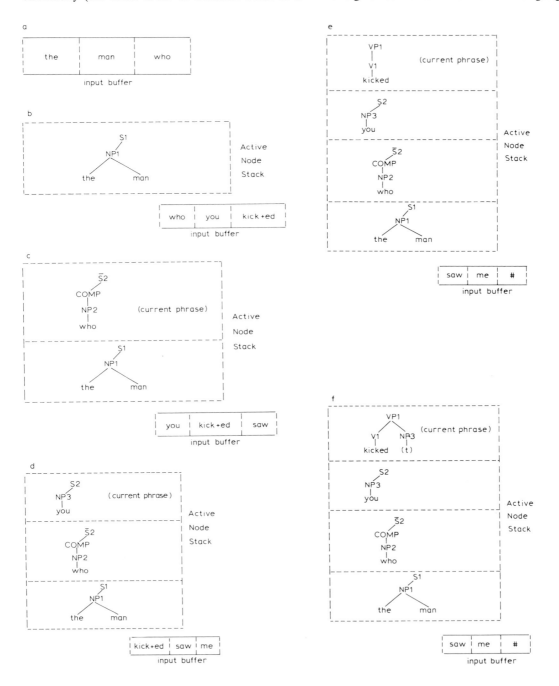

Fig. 11. *a – l.* The structures created in the active node stack, buffer and propositional list during the parsing of the sentence 'The man who you kicked saw me', according to the Berwick and Weinberg parser.

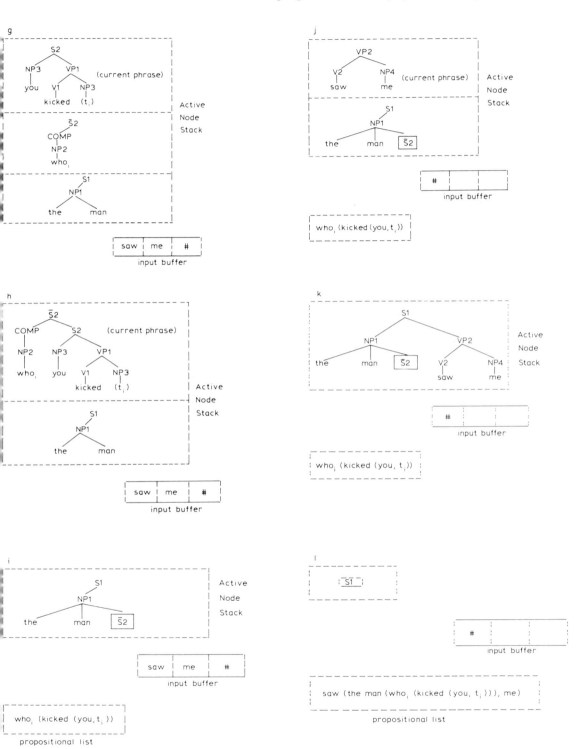

Fig. 11. *g – l.*

world in general), suggesting that the processing of non-canonical thematic role orders demands considerable resources.

Evidence that a decrease in the resources available to a patient is a factor in creating an impairment in syntactic comprehension also comes from the results of individual case studies (Caplan and Hildebrandt, 1988). As noted above, these studies have documented specific syntactic features that contribute to the complexity of processing a sentence. In several cases, a patient could perform specific parsing operations when the overall complexity of the sentence was low but not when other operations also had to be carried out. For example, the patients A.B. and C.V. decribed above, were able to interpret pronouns and reflexives correctly as well as to construct complex NPs in very simple active sentences, but not in sentences that required both the construction of a complex NP and a co-indexation operation. When the combined complexity of concurrent parsing operations exceeded the processing capacity of these patients, the ability to perform individual parsing operations broke down.

We have referred to this aspect of the model of the language-processing system as the Work Space required by a particular operation (Caplan and Hildebrandt, 1988), recognizing that this term is merely an analogy. In the domain of parsing, it would be possible to develop a formal account of this aspect of processing in terms of the number of elementary computational operations that must be accomplished to construct specific syntactic representations, and the space or time requirements of each. This would require a commitment to a model of the specific computations accomplished by a parser. In addition, it is important to establish the relationship of this 'Work Space' to other Working Memory systems, through selected dual-task experiments, and to distinguish allocation of Working Memory resources from allocation of attentional resources as sources of processing limitations. The relationship of resource requirements asssociated with processing particular structures to the frequency of these structures in language usage, and to the

pragmatic and discourse roles of these structures is a topic that largely remains to be explored. Research is slowly providing data that will advance this aspect of psycholinguistic modelling.

Adaptations to parsing impairments

One aspect of aphasic performance that is not immediately relevant to normal language processing, but that is vital to an understanding of language impairments, is the role of compensatory mechanisms in patients' performances. The overt performance of a patient on a language task is the result of his/her deficit and of the compensations s/he makes to that deficit. We can study compensatory mechanisms through yet another methodological technique: qualitative error analysis. Errors patients make reflect failures of normal processing, and systematic errors result from the use of compensatory heuristics for the accomplishment of particular tasks.

In the domain of syntactic comprehension, there are very few reports that contain analyses of errors. Indeed, the most commonly used task − sentence picture matching − does not allow patients to make their own errors. Our studies have reported error types for many sentence types in object-manipulation tasks, where subjects are free to assign any interpretation they wish to the sentence (Caplan and Futter, 1986; Caplan et al., 1985, 1986; Caplan and Hildebrandt, 1988a). Errors made by patients usually respect basic aspects of sentence structure and meaning, such as the number of thematic roles assigned by a verb, the number of propositions expressed in a sentence, and the distinction between referentially dependent noun phrases and referential expressions. We have found that what we have called 'strictly linear interpretations', in which thematic roles are assigned to sequential NPs in canonical order (Agent - Theme - Goal in English), are the most common error type regardless of the syntactic structure of a sentence on the object-manipulation task. In addition, patients appear to be sensitive to the relevance of some minor lexical items for thematic role assignment, such as a *by*-phrase.

We have provided a linguistic analysis of the structures that underlie these errors (Caplan and Hildebrandt, 1988a). The error patterns we have documented can all be accounted for by the application of simple interpretive rules to linear sequences of major lexical categories. The most common erroneous responses in English-speaking aphasics can result from the application of the following rules to the sequence of nouns and verbs in a sentence:

1. In sequences of the form N-V-N or N-N-V, assign either the immediately pre-verbal noun or the first noun in the sentence the role of Agent and assign the remaining noun the role of Theme.

2. In sentences with a verb requiring three arguments, assign the first noun the role of Agent, the second noun the role of Theme, and the third noun the role of Goal.

3. In a sentence with two verbs each of which has two argument places, use Rule 1 iteratively around each verb.

4. Assign the noun in the sequence *by*-N the thematic role of Agent.

Rules (1) – (4) only mention the linear sequences of major lexical categories – nouns and verbs – and one lexically specified preposition (*by*) as the syntactic structures to which interpretive algorithms apply. We have not found it necessary to postulate hierarchically organized phrase markers as the structures to which interpretive rules apply to yield erroneous interpretations. Moreover, the interpretive rules themselves are very simple, they assign thematic roles on the basis of the absolute position of a noun in a sentence, simple precedence relations among items specified in a linear sequence of categories, and a few lexical items (such as *by*). (It is possible that other features of sentence form may also be used to assign thematic roles; for instance, the passive morphology may be important in recognizing a *by*-phrase as relevant to the assignment of the thematic role of Agent as opposed to being interpreted as a locative, and it may also be important in determining the verb whose argument structure is filled by the noun in the *by*-phrase. Even

if these additional features of sentence form slightly complicate these very simple rules, the structures to which interpretive rules apply are still linear sequences of major lexical categories and associated morphological forms.) These structures would result from the operation of lexical identification processes, coupled with a memory system which maintains lexical items and their associated grammatical categories in linear sequences.

The most significant feature of these heuristics is that they are closely related to normal syntactic operations. Linear sequences of major lexical categories (Noun, Verb, Adjective, Preposition) and associated morphological markings are precisely those representations which we indicated were the input to the parser (see above). Adaptive heuristics thus may be derived from aspects of the normal parser. Alternatively, or in addition, both the mechanism for assignment of structure and the interpretive rules that we have suggested to underlie the errors on the Object Manipulation test may make use of what Chomsky calls the primitive conceptual basis for syntax (Chomsky, 1981). In either case, patients' adaptations to parsing impairments make use of a subset of the categories and operations found in normal parsing operations; they do not consist of behaviours based on other cognitive systems, such as spatial arrays, pragmatic factors, etc.* We conclude that patients retain elementary operations within the domain of parsing, and that their first attempts to deal with tasks that normally involve the parser make use of these retained abilities.

General issues

We have indicated how research in linguistics, psycholinguistics and aphasiology comes together to provide the beginnings of a detailed account of

---

* These conclusions are based upon results using the object-manipulation task. Other strategies may arise in different tasks. These may lead to other models of the basis for compensatory heuristics in syntactic comprehension in aphasic patients.

the nature of one aspect of language processing and its disorders. We have argued that research in all three disciplines provides strong evidence for the existence of a set of related operations that create syntactic structures and use them to constrain and determine aspects of sentence meaning (what we have called a parser). We have also illustrated how research in these domains situates this language-processing component with respect to other mental processes. The parser interacts with other linguistic and cognitive systems, but appears to be distinct from them.

Pathological performance can result from disturbances of this part of the language-processing system. Damage to the parser can take two forms: specific parsing operations can be affected (such disturbances can affect a greater or fewer number of operations), and the resources available for parsing can be reduced. Both types of impairment usually co-occur. Overt behaviour on tasks that require the parser reflects both the damage to the parser and the adaptive mechanisms patients use. We have begun to develop a theory of these mechanisms.

Different analyses of data from brain-damaged patients are relevant to different aspects of the model of normal and impaired functioning drawn here. Double dissociations in patients' performances on different tasks and/or with respect to different parameters within a single task provide evidence relevant to the nature of components of the language-processing system. The retention of particular abilities in the face of specific deficits and, under specific circumstances, the co-occurrence of deficits provide evidence regarding the functional architecture of components of the system. In some circumstances, differences in group performance as a function of parameters on a task provide evidence relevant to the processing resources associated with those parameters. Qualitative error analyses provide data regarding compensatory mechanisms.

The domain of syntactic comprehension and its disorders is offered as a possible guide to a general framework within which language disorders may be viewed. Three notions that might be applicable to other language-processing domains emerge from this review. These are: (1) that individual language-processing modules can be selectively impaired; (2) that impairments within a module can affect the operations in the module and/or the availability of processing resources in the module; and (3) that overt behaviour partially reflects adaptations that are tightly linked to the simplest operations of the normal module. Further research will probably demonstrate whether the methods, logic and conclusions presented here are correct and, if so, whether they are of more general usefulness in aphasiology.

The approach to syntactic comprehension disorders adopted here can be placed within a broader context that reflects a certain attitude towards both investigative approaches in neuropsychology and the implications of neuropsychology for the understanding of mental processes. It presents arguments for the existence of specialized mental representations and associated processors. It contrasts with approaches (such as PDP models) that see language processing and other cognitive activities as primarily powerful pattern-recognition and association devices that apply in a similar fashion to many different types of representation. Models that incorporate formal representations and algorithmic processes keyed to these representations are currently far superior with respect to the range of psychological phenomena they describe and explain in the domain of syntactic comprehension than PDP models. Therefore, it is currently necessary to use these models to describe and explain disorders of syntactic comprehension. Future work will almost certainly lead to the development of more empirically adequate PDP-type models of sentence comprehension. It will be interesting to see how well these models fare in describing and explaining disorders of syntactic comprehension.

Acknowledgements

The author wishes to express his appreciation to the Neurology Department of the Massachusetts General Hospital, whose support enabled him to write this chapter. He is also grateful to Jordan

Grafman, Nancy Hildebrandt and Nina Silverberg for helpful comments on earlier drafts. Errors and unclear points are his own responsibility.

Glossary

active node stack: in some computer-based models of parsing, the part of a parser's memory in which the syntactic structure currently being developed resides.

adaptive strategies: mental processes that are used to accomplish a task when the normal processes used in that task are damaged.

affixes: elements that are added to the basic form of a word; prefixes and suffixes.

agent: the initiator of an action.

agrammatism: a language disturbance that occurs after brain damage marked by sparse speech with a disproportionately large number of omissions of minor lexical categories and affixes.

algorithmic processes: operations that active specific representations when presented with other representations.

antecedent: the word to which a referentially dependent item is linked by co-indexation.

argument of a verb: a particular thematic role that is specified by virtue of the lexical representation of a verb; for instance, the verb give specifies two internal arguments (Theme and Goal) and one external argument (Agent).

argument structure: the grammatical roles specified by a verb; for instance, *give* has two argument structures, seen in *John gave the book to Mary* and *John gave Mary the book,* while *introduce* has only one *(John introduced Bill to Mary).*

attribution of modification: the assignment of adjectives to the nouns.

automaticity: cognitive functions that are not under subjects' control; they are initiated by appropriate input and cannot be inhibited; many theorists argue that they are relatively undemanding of processing resources.

c-command: a relationship between nodes in a syntactic structure relevant to the assignment of the antecedent of referentially dependent items.

canonicity: roughly, the most common form of a structure in a given language.

co-indexation: the linking of a referentially dependent item to another item in a sentence or discourse.

co-reference: the fact that two linguistic elements refer to the same entity in the real world.

D-structure: the level of syntactic representation created by phrase structure rules in Chomsky's theory of syntax.

domination: one syntactic category dominates another if the first is higher in a syntactic structure than the second.

double dissociation: a complementary set of performances in which one patient does better on one task than a second patient and the second does better on a second task than the first.

empty categories (empty NPs): items that are not sounded out in a sentence but which exist at an abstract logical and/or syntactic level; in Chomsky's theory, they are referentially dependent items.

external argument: the argument position whose grammatical case is not determined by lexical features of word; in a sentence, the subject is the external argument of the verb.

filler-gap relationships: a relationship between an empty NP and its antecedent.

first-pass parsing: the first set of syntactic structures postulated by a parser.

garden path effects: a (possibly temporary) mis-analyses of the syntactic structure of part of a sentence.

grammatical roles: certain defined relationships between syntactic categories in syntactic structures, such as Subject and Object.

immediate domination: one syntactic category immediately dominates another if the first is directly above the second in a syntactic structure.

internal argument: the argument position whose grammatical case is determined by lexical features of a word; in a sentence, the object is an internal argument of the verb.

intonational contour: the melody of a phrase or sentence, which determines semantic features such as which word is emphasized, etc.

Late Closure: a principle said to guide the parser which ensures that new syntactic categories are first attached to nodes that the parser is currently constructing.

lexical categories: syntactic elements, such as Noun, Verb, etc. that are directly related to words (lexical items): they are contrasted with phrasal categories.

lexical representation: the information about a word in a language user's mental dictionary; this includes information regarding the word's sound, its meaning, and its syntactic features.

long-distance dependencies: a relationship between referentially dependent items and their antecedents that spans a considerable portion of a sentence.

markedness: roughly, the most common form of a structure across the languages of the world.

mental resources: the amount of computational capacity available for a particular cognitive task.

minimal Attachment: a principle said to guide the parser which ensures that new syntactic categories are first attached to existing nodes.

minor lexical categories: all lexical items other than nouns, verbs, adjectives and certain prepositions and adverbs.

modular theories: theories of cognitive function that postulate separate processing components for different sorts of tasks; modular theories can differ with respect to their level of detail and the types of interaction they postulate between modules.

movement rules: rules that move elements from one level of syntactic structure to another, in certain versions of Chomsky's theory of syntax.

object: a noun phrase node immediately dominated by a verb phrase node.

parser: a device that assigns syntactic structure to a sentence.

parsing: the activity of assigning syntactic structure to a sentence.

PDP processing: a mathematical approach to computation inspired by neurophysiology that has been developed to model a number of psychological processes; PDP models make use of massively parallel computational devices.

phoneme: the minimal sound unit in a language that distinguishes one word from another (e.g., /b/ in bat, as contrasted with /p/ in pat).

phrasal categories: syntactic elements, such as Noun Phrase, Verb Phrase, etc., that serve to organize other syntactic categories; they are contrasted with lexical categories.

phrase structure rules: rules that expand phrasal categories as other phrasal and lexical categories.

PRO: an empty category that does not transmit its thematic role to its antecedent.

proposition: the semantic features associated with a sentence.

recursive rules: rules that can generate an infinite number of structures, by rewriting categories in such a way that categories can be re-introduced over and over again.

referential success: the mapping of items in a sentence onto items in the preceding discourse in such a way as to ensure that the specification of the new items is compatible with what is known about previously specified items.

referentially dependent items: words whose reference to items in the real world is determined by the word first being related to another word.

referential expression: an item that achieves its reference by being directly related to an entity in the real world.

relative clause: a clause that modifies a noun phrase, intoduced by a complementizer.

S-structure: the level of representation that occurs after movement of items from D-structure, in Chomsky's theory of syntax.

scope of quantification: the determination of which elements are related to a numerical qualifier (e.g., the third green ball need not be the third ball in an array).

second-pass parsing: revision of the first set of syntactic structures postulated by a parser.

semantically irreversible sentences: sentences in which the nouns can express only one set thematic roles in the real world, such as *The cat drank the milk.*

semantically reversible sentences: sentences in which the nouns can play a variety of thematic roles in the real world, such as *The cat scratched the dog.*

semantics: the meanings of words, sentences, etc.

sentential complement: a clause that is part of the argument structure of a verb, as in *John said* THAT MARY WAS LATE.

short-term memory: a memory system that decays over minutes; verbal short-term memory appears to contain information about word sounds.

structure building operations: operations of a parser that create hierarchical sets of syntactic categories.

subcategorization features: the syntactic structures that are compatible with a verb, specified in the verb's lexical representation.

subject: a noun phrase node immediately dominated by a sentence node.

syntactic ambiguity: sentences in which sequences of words can have more than one meaning because they may be analysed in more than one way syntactically.

syntactic comprehension: the use of syntactic structures to constrain and determine aspects of sentence meaning.

syntactic domain: a portion of a syntactic structure within which a specific syntactic operation, such as co-indexation, is carried out.

syntactic nodes: any syntactic category; the term node has arisen because of linguists' tendency to represent syntactic structures in tree-like diagrams.

syntactic structures: organized sets of syntactic categories that represent the structural relationships between words in a sentence.

thematic roles: information regarding the structure of actions, roughly who is doing what to whom, etc.

trace: an empty category that transmits its thematic role to its antecedent.

working memory: a memory system tied to attentional and cognitive processing in which small amounts of information can be represented and manipulated for short periods.

References

Altmann G, Steedman MJ: Interaction with the context in human syntactic processing. *Cognition: 30,* 191–238, 1988.
Baddeley A, Vallar G, Wilson B: Comprehension and the ar-

ticulatory loop: some neuropsychological evidence. In Colt-heart M. (editor) *Attention and Performance XI.* Hillsdale, NJ: Lawrence Erlbaum, pp. 509 – 530, 1987.

Bates E, McNew S, MacWhinney B, Devescovi A, Smith S: Functional constraints on sentence processing. Cognition: 11, 245 – 299, 1982.

Berndt R, Caramazza A: A redefinition of the syndrome of Broca's aphasia. *Appl. Psycholing.: 1;* 225 – 278, 1980.

Berwick RC, Weinberg A: *The Grammatical Basis of Linguistic Performance: Language Use and Acquisition.* Cambridge: MIT Press, 1984.

Bever TG: The cognitive basis for linguistic structures. In Hayes JR (Editor), *Cognition and the Development of Language:* New York: Wiley, 1970.

Bradley DC, Garrett MF, Zurif EB: Syntactic deficits in Broca's aphasia. In Caplan D (Editor), *Biological Studies of Mental Processes.* Cambridge: MIT Press, 1980.

Bransford JD, Franks JJ: The abstraction of linguistic ideas. *Cognitive Psychol.: 2,* 331 – 350, 1971.

Bresnan J (Editor): *The Mental Representation of Grammatical Relations.* Cambridge, MA: MIT Press, 1982.

Briscoe EJ: *Modelling Human Speech Comprehension, A Computational Approach.* Ellis Horwood Limited, Chicester, 1987.

Butler-Hinz S, Caplan D, Waters GS: Characteristics of syntactic comprehension deficits following closed-head injury vs. left cerebral vascular accident. *J. Speech Hearing Res.: 33,* 269 – 280, 1990.

Caplan D: Clause boundaries and recognition latencies for words and sentences. *Percept. Psychophys.: 12,* 73 – 76, 1972.

Caplan D: *Neurolinguistics and Linguistic Aphasiology: An Introduction.* Cambridge: Cambridge University Press, 1987.

Caplan D: On the role of group studies in neuropsychological and pathopsychological research. *Cognitive Neuropsychol.: 5,* 535 – 548, 1988.

Caplan D, Futter C: Assignment of thematic roles to nouns in sentence comprehension by an agrammatic patient. *Brain Lang.: 27,* 117 – 134, 1986.

Caplan D, Hildebrandt N: *Disorders of Syntactic Comprehension.* Cambridge, MA: MIT Press, 1988a.

Caplan D, Hildebrandt N: Specific deficits in syntactic comprehension. *Aphasiology: 2,* 255 – 258, 1988b.

Caplan D, Hildebrandt N: Disorders affecting comprehension of syntactic form: preliminary results and their implications for theories of syntax and parsing. *Canad. J. Linguistics: 33,* 477 – 505, 1989.

Caplan D, Waters GS: Short-term memory and language comprehension: a critical review of the neuropsychological literature. In Vallar G, Shallice T (Editors), *Neuropsychological Impairments of Short-Term Memory.* Cambridge: Cambridge University Press, in press.

Caplan D, Baker C, Dehaut F: Syntactic determinants of sentence comprehension in aphasia. *Cognition: 21,* 117 – 175, 1985.

Caramazza A: When is enough enough? A Comment on Grodzinsky and Marek. *Brain Lang.: 33,* 390 – 399, 1989.

Caramazza A, Berndt R: A multicomponent view of agrammatic Broca's aphasia. In Kean ML (Editor), *Agrammatism.* New York: Academic Press pp. 27 – 64, 1985.

Caramazza A, Zurif E: Dissociation of algorithmic and heuristic

processes in language comprehension: evidence from aphasia. *Brain Lang.: 3,* 572 – 582, 1976.

Chomsky N: *The Logical Structure of Linguistic Theory.* New York: Plenum, 1955.

Chomsky N: *Syntactic Structures.* The Hague: Mouton, 1957.

Chomsky N: *Aspects of the Theory of Syntax.* Cambridge: MIT Press, 1965.

Chomsky N: *Lectures in Government and Binding.* Dordrecht: Foris, 1981.

Chomsky N: Remarks on nominalizations. In Jacobs RA, Rosenbaum PS (Editors), *Readings in English Transformational Grammar.* Boston, MA: Ginn, 1970.

Chomsky N: *Knowledge of Language: Its Nature, Origin, and Use.* New York: Praeger, 1985.

Clark H, Clark E: *Psychology and Language.* New York: Harcourt, Brace, Jovanovich, 1977.

Clifton C, Ferreira F: Modularity in sentence comprehension. In Garfield JL (Editor), *Modularity in Knowledge Representation and Natural-Language Processing.* Cambridge: Cambridge University Press, pp. 277 – 290, 1987.

Conrad R: Acoustic confusions and immediate memory. *Br. J. Psychol.: 55,* 75 – 84, 1964.

Cook VJ: Strategies in the Comprehension of Relative Clauses. *Lang. Speech: 18,* 204 – 218, 1975.

Cornell T, Fromkin V, Mauner C: A computational model of linguistic processing: evidence from aphasia. Presentation at the Academy of Aphasia Sante Fe, New Mexico, 1989.

Crain S, Fodor JD: How can grammars help parsers? In Dowty D, Kartunnen L, Zwicky A (Editors), *Natural Language Parsing.* Cambridge: Cambridge University Press, 1985.

Crain S, Steedman MJ: On not being led up the garden path: the use of context by the psychological parser. In Dowty D, Karttunen L, Zwicky A (Editors), *Natural Language Parsing.* Cambridge: Cambridge University Press, 1985.

Engdahl E: Parasitic gaps. *Linguistics Phil., 6,* 5 – 34, 1983.

Ermann L, Lesser VR: The HEARSAY-II system: a tutorial. In Lee WA, (Editor). Trends in Speed Regulation, Englewood Cliffs, NJ, Prentice Hall.

Ferreira F, Clifton C: The independence of syntactic processing. *J. Mem. Language: 25,* 348 – 368, 1986.

Fodor JA, Bever TG, Garrett MF: *The Psychology of Language.* New York: McGraw-Hill, 1974.

Fodor JD: Parsing strategies and constraints on transformations. *Linguistic Inquiry: 9,* 427 – 473, 1978.

Franks JJ, Bransford JD: The acquisition of abstract ideas. *J. Verbal Learn. Verval Behav.: 11,* 311 – 315, 1972.

Frazier L: Theories of sentence processing. In Garfield J (Editor), *Modularity in Knowledge Representation and Natural-Language Processing.* Cambridge, MA: MIT Press, 1987.

Frazier L, Clifton C. Thematic relations in parsing. University of Massachusetts Occasional Papers in Linguistics.

Frazier L, Clifton C: Successive cyclicity in the grammar and the parser. *Lang. Cognitive Processes: 4,* 91 – 126, 1989.

Frazier L, Fodor JD: The sausage machine: a new two-stage parsing model. *Cognition: 6,* 291 – 325, 1978.

Frazier L, Clifton C, Randall J: Filling gaps: decision principles and structure in sentence comprehension. *Cognition: 13,* 187 – 222, 1983.

Freedman SA, Forster KI: The psychological status of

overgenerated sentences. *Cognition: 19,* 101 – 132, 1985.

Garnsey SM, Tanenhaus MK, Chapman RM: Evoked potentials and the study of sentence comprehension. *J. Psycholing. Res.:* in press.

Gordon B, Caramazza A: Lexical decision of open- and closed-class words: failure to replicate differential frequency sensitivity. *Brain Lang.: 15,* 143 – 160, 1982.

Gorrell P: Natural language parsing and reanalysis. Proc. NELS: 16, 186 – 196, 1985.

Grodzinsky Y: Language deficits and the theory of syntax. *Brain Lang.: 27,* 135 – 159, 1986.

Grodzinsky Y, Marek A: Algorithmic and heuristic processes revisted. *Brain Lang.: 33,* 316 – 325, 1988.

Hagiwara H, Caplan D: Syntactic comprehension in Japanese aphasics: effects of category and thematic role order. *Brain Lang.: 38,* 159 – 170, 1990.

Heilman KM, Scholes RJ: The nature of comprehension errors in Broca's, Conduction, and Wernicke's aphasics. *Cortex: 12,* 258 – 265, 1976.

Hildebrandt N: A linguistically based parsing analysis of aphasics' comprehension of referential dependencies. Unpublished PhD Dissertation Linguistics, McGill University, 1987.

Hildebrandt N, Caplan D, Evans K: The mani left ti without a trace: a case study of aphasic processing of empty categories. *Cognitive Neuropsychol.: 4,* 257 – 302, 1987.

Hildebrandt N, Waters GS, Caplan D: On the nature and functional role of verbal short-term memory and sentence comprehension: evidence from neuropsychology, *Cognitive Neuropsychology.* in press.

Holmes VM: Syntactic parsing: in search of the garden path. In Coltheart M (Editor), *Attention and Performance XII: The Psychology of Reading.* (London: Erlbaum), pp., 587 – 600, 1987.

Jones GV: On double dissociation of function. *Neuropsychologia: 21,* 397 – 400, 1983.

Kolk HH, van Grunsven JJF: Agrammatism as a variable phenomenon. *Cognitive Neuropsychol.: 2,* 347 – 384, 1985.

Lackner JR, Garrett MF: Resolving ambiguity: effects of biasing context in the unintended ear. *Cognition:* 359 – 372, 1973.

Linebarger MC, Schwartz MF, Saffran EM: Sensitivity to grammatical structure in so-called agrammatic aphasics. *Cognition: 13,* 361 – 392, 1983a.

Linebarger MC, Schwartz MF, Saffran EM: Syntactic processing in agrammatism: A reply to Zurif and Grodzinsky. *Cognition: 15:* 207 – 214, 1983b.

McCarthy R, Warrington EK: Understanding: a function of short-term memory? *Brain: 110,* 1565 – 1578, 1987a.

McCarthy R, Warrington EK: The double disassociation of short-term memory for lists in sentences: evidence from aphasia. *Brain: 110,* 1545 – 1563, 1987b.

McCarthy R, Warrington EK: Neuropsychological studies of short-term memory. In Vallar G, Shallice T. (Editors), *Neuropsychological Impairments of Short-Term Memory.* Cambridge: Cambridge University Press, in press.

Miceli G, Mazzucchi A, Menn L, Goodglass H: Contrasting cases of Italian agrammatic aphasia without comprehension disorder. *Brain Lang.: 19,* 65 – 97, 1983.

Mitchell DC: Lexical gardens in human parsing. In Colheart M (Editor), *Attention and Performance XII.* London: Erlbaum,

pp. 601 – 618, 1987.

Nespoulous J-L, Dordain M, Perron D, Bub D, Caplan D, Mehler J, Lecours A-R: Agrammatism in sentence production without comprehension deficits: reduced availability of syntactic structures and/or of grammatical morphemes. *Brain Lang.: 33,* 273 – 295, 1988.

Reinhart T: *Anaphora and Semantic Interpretation.* London: Croom Helm, 1983.

Rumelhart DE, McClelland JL (Editors): PDP models and general issues in cognitive science. In *Parallel Distributed Processing, Vol. 1.* Cambridge, MA: MIT Press, pp. 110 – 145, 1986.

Saffran EM, Marin OSM: Immediate memory for word lists and sentences in a patient with deficient auditory short-term memory. *Brain Lang.: 2,* 420 – 433, 1975.

Schneider W., Shiffrin RM: Automatic and controlled information processing in vision. In LaBerge D, Samuels SJ (Editors), *Basic Processes in Reading: Perception and Comprehension.* Hillsdale, NJ: Erlbaum, 1977.

Schwartz M, Saffran E, Marin O: The word order problem in agrammatism: I. Comprehension. *Brain Lang.: 10,* 249 – 262, 1980.

Shallice T: Case study appoach in neuropsychological research. *J. Clin. Neuropsychol.: 1,* 183 – 211, 1979.

Shallice T: *From Neuropsychology to Mental Structure.* Cambridge: Cambridge University Press, 1988.

Shapiro LP, Zurig EB, Grimshaw J: Sentence processing in the mental representation of verbs. *Cognition: 27,* 219 – 246, 1987.

Shiffrin RM, Dumais ST: The development of automatism. In Anderson JR (Editor), *Cognitive Skills and Their Acquisition.* Hillsdale, NJ: Erlbaum, 1981.

Stowe L: Parsing wh-constructions: evidence for on-line gap location. *Lang. Cognitive Processes: 1,* 227 – 246, 1986.

Stowe L: Thematic Structures and Sentence Comprehension. In Carlson G, Tanenhaus M (Editors), *Linguistic Structure in Language Processing.* Dordrecht: Reidel, 1989.

Stowe L, Tanenhaus MK, Carlson G: Parsing Filler-Gap Sentences. Paper presented at 26th Annual Meeting of the Psychonomic Society, Amherst, MA, 1985.

Swinney D: Lexical access during sentence comprehension: (re)considerations of context effects. *J. Verbal Learn. Verbal Behav.: 18,* 645 – 659, 1979.

Tanenhaus MK, Carlson GN: Lexical structure and language comprehension. In Marslen-Wilson W (Editor), *Lexical Representation and Process.* Cambridge MA: MIT Press, pp. 529 – 561, 1989.

Tanenhaus MK, Leiman JM., Seidenberg MS: Evidence for multiple stages in the processing of ambiguous words in syntactic context. *J. Verbal Learn. Verbal Behav.: 18,* 427 – 440, 1979.

Tanenhaus M, Stowe L, Carlson G: The interaction of lexical expectation and pragmatics in parsing filler-gap constructions. In Proceedings of the Seventh Annual Cognitive Science Society Meetings, 1985.

Tanenhaus MK, Boland J, Garnsey SM: Lexical structure and language comprehension. Paper presented at Psychonomics Society, Seattle, WA, Nov. 1987, 1987.

Tanenhaus MK, Stowe LA, Carlson G: The interaction of lexical expactation and pragmatics in parsing filler-gap constructions. Proceedings of the Seventh Annual Cognitive. Science Society Conference, Irving, CA, 1985.

Vallar G, Baddeley A: Phonological short-term store, phonological processing and sentence comprehension: a neuropsychological case study. *Cognitive Neuropsychol.: 1,* 121–142, 1984.

Wanner E, Maratsos M: An ATN approach to comprehension. In Halle M, Bresnan J, Miller G (Editors), *Linguistic Theory and Psychological Reality.* Cambridge: MIT Press, 1978.

Warrington EK Shallice T: The selective impairment of auditory verbal short-term memory. *Brain: 92,* 885–896, 1969.

Weinberg A: Modularity in the syntactic parser. In Garfield JL (Editor), *Modularity in Knowledge Representation and Natural-Language Processing.* Cambridge, MA: MIT Press, pp. 259–276, 1987.

Wulfeck BB: Grammatically judgements and sentence comprehension on agrammatic aphasia. *J. Speech Hearing Res.: 31,* 72–81, 1988.

Zurif EB: Psycholinguistic interpretation of the aphasis. In Caplan D, Lecours AR, Smith A (Editors), *Biological Perspectives on Language.* Cambridge, MA: MIT Press, 1984.

Zurif EB, Grodzinsky Y: Sensitivity to grammatical structure in agrammatic aphasics: a reply to Linebarger, Schwartz, and Saffran. *Cognition: 15,* 207–214, 1983.

© 1991 Elsevier Science Publishers B.V.
Handbook of Neuropsychology, Vol. 5
F. Boller and J. Grafman (Eds)

CHAPTER 15

Current methodological issues in human neuropsychology

Giuseppe Vallar

Istituto di Clinica Neurologica, Università di Milano, Milano, Italy

1. Introduction

This chapter aims at discussing a number of basic methodological issues in human neuropsychology. In the last few years the development of neuropsychology has shown as notable features not only the production of a great deal of empirical data, but also an in-depth debate concerning the basic theoretical foundations of this branch of science.

Since its inception neuropsychology has had two basic aims. In a strictly medical perspective, neuropsychology investigates the pathological changes of human behavior produced by brain damage with diagnostic and therapeutic purposes, in patients suffering from a range of diseases including cerebrovascular attacks, tumors, head injury and dementia, such as Alzheimer disease. In clinical practice, neuropsychology also has a therapeutic aim, concerning rehabilitation of cognitive deficits in individuals surviving and recovering from non-progressive diseases such as stroke, trauma, hypoxia, etc. (see a discussion of the past and present role of neuropsychology in clinical practice in the following chapter (Ch. 16)). Neuropsychological research, however, has always had a heuristic scope, taking advantage of the existence of patients in which functions such as language or memory are impaired by brain damage as 'experiments of nature'. Within this second and broader perspective, a distinction can be drawn between two heuristic aims: (1) exploring the neural structures involved in mental functions, where the method of anatomo-clinical correlation, initially developed in the early 1800s, has been used; (2) exploring mental functions per se: patients with selective cognitive deficits produced by brain damage may elucidate the functional architecture of the normal cognitive system.

The chapter includes four sections:

(1) the investigation of the neural correlates of mental function by the method of anatomo-clinical correlation: scope and limits;

(2) two basic approaches to the study of neuropsychological disorders: the traditional clinical method; controlled studies in large series of patients;

(3) cognitive neuropsychology;

(4) three specific contentious issues in human neuropsychology: (a) associations and dissociations among neuropsychological deficits; (b) the concept of neuropsychological syndrome; (c) group vs. single case studies. These three problems will also be discussed, when appropriate, in the first three parts of the chapter.

The ideas and concepts discussed in this chapter will be stated not only as theoretical issues, in the format of general or more specific principles, but I shall give a great deal of illustrative examples providing arguments in favour of and against such principles. The discussion will not be confined to an abstract logical-deductive level of analysis. This approach aims both at making the argument more straightforward and concrete, and at offering the interested reader empirical instances which corroborate or disprove a given theoretical tenet. The choice of the specific illustrative examples, by which some methodological foundations of neuropsychology are discussed, is of course my responsibility and reflects at least in part my specific research expertise, views and perhaps prejudices. I am interested in both the functional architecture of the mind, as investigated by cognitive neuropsychology, and the neural mechanisms of cognitive activity. I hope that this chapter, in addition to providing a critical review of a number of relevant methodological issues, will show that both the cognitive and the neural aspects of human neuropsychology have undergone a remarkable development in recent years and that an increasing degree of interaction may be expected in the near future.

2. The neural correlates of mental processes: the method of anatomo-clinical correlation

Neuropsychology as a science was born in the second half of the 19th century, with an emphasis on the study of aphasia. On the basis of the theoretical approach of Gall, who in the early 19th century suggested a precise cerebral localization of a number of mental faculties, students such as Bouillaud (1825) and Broca (1861, 1865) described an association between damage to specific cerebral regions and specific aphasic disturbances (see references in Hécaen and Dubois, 1969). The apex of this approach was represented by the multi-component models of language of Wernicke (1874) and Lichtheim (1885), where the faculty of language was subdivided into a number of discrete components, which were localized in different regions of the brain.

The main steps of the classical method of anatomo-clinical correlation may be summarized as follows. The behavioural assessment of a given cognitive disorder of the patient (e.g., nonfluent aphasia) is followed by the localization of the cerebral lesion associated with that deficit. The presence of an association between a specific disorder X (i.e., the derangement of a specific function F) and the damage of a specific brain region A allows the inference that F is localized in A. Since the early studies in the 19th century (see Bouillaud, 1825, in Hécaen and Dubois, 1969) this type of inference has made use of the principle of dissociation

of function. Bouillaud's conclusion that the cerebral centre of speech is localized in the frontal regions of the brain rests upon two complementary observations: expressive disturbances are present in patients with frontal lesions, and absent in patients in whom these areas are spared.

The validity of the inference from the pathological association (the abnormal behaviour or symptom X, which reflects the derangement of function F, is associated to a damage of the cerebral region A) to normal brain – behavior relationships (F is localized in A) is not so direct and obvious as it might appear, however.

Jackson (1878, 1915) noted that localizing a lesion and localizing a function cannot be considered as identical. This observation may be read in a number of different ways. Within a totally holistic approach, the view can be taken that the localization of a given mental function in a specific area of the brain is simply nonsense, because its brain correlates are a fully interconnected distributed neural network. The investigation of the anatomical correlates of processes such as language, spatial skills and memory has, however, clearly shown that the holistic positions are not tenable, at least in their more extreme versions (see Phillips et al., 1984; Benton, 1988; the classical holistic approach of Lashley, 1929; see a discussion in Sergent, 1988). A second possibility which should be considered is based on the existence of neural connections between the different cerebral regions: the specific damage of A is associated to the deficit X because the lesions disrupts the circuit C, of which A is one of the components. Accordingly, the appropriate correlation would be between X (and the normal function F) and C, which includes a number of regions A1, A2, A3, . . . An, rather than X and, say, A1.

The hypothesis that a focal cerebral lesion may produce the dysfunction of remote regions is far from being novel (von Monakow, 1914), but only in the last few years has this concept of 'diaschisis' been adequately elucidated at the neurophysiological level, by means of techniques which allow an in vivo mapping of the functional activity of the brain in terms of regional cerebral blood flow and metabolism (see Feeney and Baron, 1986). For over a century anatomo-clinical correlations have used methods such as post-mortem examination, surgical exploration and, only more recently, neuroradiological techniques with a higher and higher resolution power (arteriography, brain scan, computerized tomography (CT), nuclear magnetic resonance (NMR)) which provide neuropathological information concerning the site, size and etiology of a given brain lesion. All such methods suffer a major limitation, however. They cannot reveal functional changes that do not produce neuronal death. Recently developed imaging techniques such as positron emission tomography (PET) have shown that a cortical or subcortical cerebral lesion, in addition to destroying a specific area, may cause a reduction of the neural activity of remote regions which may be revealed by a local hypoperfusion and hypometabolism. Diaschisis is likely to be produced by the interruption of efferent fibers connecting the primarily damaged region to remote areas. These regions, in turn, disconnected by this mechanism, become hypoactive, even though cellular death does not take place. This interpretation of the diaschisis phenomenon is entirely consistent with the view that the neural correlates of mental functions are complex circuits (see, e.g., data from normal subjects in Metter et al., 1984).

Independent of the specific correlation observed (e.g. with a cerebral region or with a complex circuit) the putative mental process cannot, however, be localized. For instance, drawing upon an anatomo-clinical correlation, one cannot conclude that, say, the syntactic parser is 'localized' in a specific brain region. The levels of description of the mental processes and of the brain mechanisms are qualitatively different (see a variety of philosophical approaches to the mind – brain problem in Popper and Eccles, 1977; Bunge, 1980; Churchland, 1986). The 'cerebral localization' of a given mental function is possible if this is reduced at a neurobiological level of description, but this has not so far been the case in human neuropsychological research.

Also, the recent approaches making use of PET technology do not lead to a neurobiological description of mental processes (e.g., in terms of the operation of neural nets or of enzymatic activities), but provide a correlation between the abnormal change of a given mental function and an abnormal pattern of cerebral local blood flow and metabolism (see e.g. Perani et al., 1987). This conclusion also applies to the so-called 'activation studies', which may reveal a correlation between the specific task performed by the subject and the metabolic activity of specific brain regions, but do not reduce the description of the function under investigation to the neurobiological level. A recent illustrative example is offered by a PET study suggesting the existence of a 'colour centre' in the human cerebral cortex (Lueck et al., 1989).

To summarize, the present status of the relationships between brain structures and mental processes is better described by a 'correlation' between these two levels of description, rather than by a 'localization' of a given function in a specific cerebral area or circuit.

With these caveats the correlation methodology may be used with different types of description of neuropsychological deficit and normal mental function, ranging from the traditional Wernicke-Lichtheim taxonomy of the aphasias to the more recent psychological approaches distinguishing different levels of representation and processing (e.g., phonological, syntactic, lexical-semantic; see, e.g., Craik and Lockhart, 1972; Gainotti, 1983), or to the multi-component models of mental function which are a basic feature of the information-processing approach of cognitive psychology and neuropsychology (e.g., Coltheart, 1985, and references therein).

Three anatomo-clinical studies will illustrate these possibilities. In aphasic left brain-damaged patients Mazzocchi and Vignolo (1979) correlated the CT-assessed lesion sites with the traditional aphasic syndromes and confirmed the classical anatomo-clinical views, even though a number of interesting exceptions, such as the so-called 'subcortical aphasias', were noted. Cappa et al. (1981), with a small group of aphasic patients, found a correlation between the error type in a naming task and the lesion site, and suggested that the perisylvian and marginal (farther from the Sylvian fissure) regions of the left hemisphere are the cortical neural correlates of, respectively, the phonological and lexical-semantic levels of speech production. Shallice and Vallar (1990), reviewing the lesion sites of 10 patients with a selective impairment of auditory-verbal immediate memory span, have confirmed an observation of Warrington et al. (1971): the neural counterpart of the selective deficit of phonological short-term memory is a retro-rolandic lesion of the left hemisphere, involving the postero-inferior parietal regions. The anatomo-clinical correlation method has also been applied to nonverbal disorders, such as spatial hemineglect: in humans the damage of the inferior-posterior parietal regions of the right hemisphere is the main cortical correlate of this deficit (see Vallar and Perani, 1987).

The anatomo-clinical correlation method, in principle, can then be applied to the investigation of the neural correlates of various sorts of functional model of mental activities, by studying a succession of comparable single cases or a series of homogeneous patients. The validity of the correlation, in addition to being necessarily related to the value of the functional model (see a discussion in Olson and Caramazza, this volume), also depends on the appropriate control of a number of neurological parameters, such as the temporal interval between the onset of the disease and the correlation time, the available imaging techniques and the etiology of the neurological disease.

The role of the temporal parameters and the technologies used is clearly illustrated by the recent study by Bosley et al. (1987), who investigated the neural correlates of a primary sensory deficit, lateral homonymous hemianopia typically associated with occipital lesions. In three out of five patients with hemianopia a CT assessment revealed occipital lesions, while a PET study showed occipital hypoperfusion in all five cases. A regression of both hemianopia and occipital hypometabolism took place in the two patients in whom the occipital cortex was spared. This was not the case of the three patients with occipital structural lesions, however. This study clearly illustrates the role of two factors in the interpretation of a given anatomo-clinical correlation: the time of correlation and the techniques used. A correlation made in a chronic phase, at least one month after stroke onset, would have indicated that only occipital lesions may produce hemianopia. A study in both the acute and chronic periods, with both CT and PET, indicated instead that extra-occipital lesions involving the afferent projections to the striate cortex may produce temporary hemianopia, which may presumably be traced back to damage to afferent projections (diaschisis).

The role of the factor 'etiology of lesion' is illustrated by the differences between vascular and neoplastic lesions. The latter type of damage has a spontaneous progressive course towards a more and more severe deterioration, while the former lesions typically show a variable degree of spontaneous recovery. The parameter 'duration of disease' then has different implications in the two cases. In addition, when the lesion is neoplastic in nature, factors such as the rate of neoplastic growth should be taken into consideration. Vallar and Perani (1987) have recently noted that spatial hemineglect is frequently associated with rapidly developing tumours, such as glioblastomas, while the association with tumours with a slower rate of growth, such as meningiomas, is comparatively rare. This observation could be traced back to differences in the interaction between development of compensatory mechanisms by undamaged cerebral regions and rate of growth of the tumour: rapidly growing lesions are likely to interfere more substantially with the compensatory processes. Additional examples of the interaction between etiology and clinical syndromes are the association of amnestic aphasia (Hécaen, 1972, pp. 65 – 66) and autotopagnosia (Denes, 1989) with space-occupying tumoral lesions. An anatomo-clinical correlation in a series of patients in whom the factor 'etiology of lesion' has not been controlled might introduce biases as to the frequency of the association between a specific neuropsychological deficit and a given lesion site. This, in turn, would affect the conclusions concerning the role of that brain region in that mental function.

3. The neuropsychological method: the clinical observation of individual positive cases and the experimental study of homogeneous groups of patients

3.1. The traditional method of clinical observation

The anatomo-clinical correlation represents, as noted above, one of the main features of neuropsychology in the 1800s. The traditional correlation studies, however, coupled an often extremely accurate neuropathological analysis with a psychological examination which was non-systematic and non-quantitative, and typically did not exceed the level of clinical observation (see Henschen, 1920 – 1922; Nielsen, 1946; but see also some case reports in Moutier, 1908).

In addition to this dissociation between the accuracies of the neuropathological and psychological assessments, the traditional clinical method was biased towards the selection of positive cases, in whom the neuropsychological deficit was immediately apparent. These clinical observations are therefore a collection of single positive cases who drew the attention of the investigator due to some peculiar feature of their neuropsychological deficits.

The great merits of the traditional clinical method, which paved the way for the development of scientific human neuropsychology, are well known and do not need to be discussed here. This approach, however, ran into difficulties when the discovery of clinically relevant symptoms such as aphasia or apraxia was followed by a phase of systematic research aimed at elucidating their anatomo-functional features, possible relations with other cognitive deficits, and so forth. An index of the weakness of the traditional descriptions is the vagueness of some clinical entities, such as 'constructional apraxia'. This, in turn, determines a great variability in the techniques used for the investigation of a given disorder. In addition, clinical observations may not take into adequate consideration relevant variables such as age, socio-educational level and sex, which may affect the pa-

tient's behavior, in terms both of performance level and of qualitative error patterns.

The final result may be a number of divergent findings, unsuitable for both comparative analyses and attempts to properly replicate (see, e.g., Benton, 1966; Gainotti, 1985, for a critical discussion of the so-called 'clinical' studies on constructional apraxia). Also the long-lasting controversies concerning the existence of specific syndromes (e.g., Gerstmann's syndrome: Hécaen and Albert, 1978; Botez et al., 1985) or the precise nature of some neuropsychological disorders (e.g., visual agnosia: Lissauer, 1890; Bender and Feldman, 1972; Humphreys and Riddoch, 1987) may be taken as an indication of the insufficiencies of the classical clinical method.

3.2. Studies of groups of patients with quantitative and standardized tests

After the Second World War, primarily since the late 1950s, a number of European and North American neuropsychologists (see Benton, 1966; DeRenzi, 1967; Poeck, 1969) attempted to overcome the flaws of the traditional clinical method and suggested that quantitative and standardized techniques of behavioral assessment should be used. This critique was addressed to the methods used in the 1800s, but was relevant neither to the classical anatomo-clinical models nor to the basic underlying psychological concepts. Modification of psychological concepts might be the result of an empirical observation when findings obtained by the new quantitative techniques are not in line with the conclusions based upon the standard clinical method. Benton's critique (1961) of Gerstmann's syndrome is an illustrative example of this approach, which has three main features (see DeRenzi, 1967).

(1) The neuropsychological research is performed in groups of patients. The classical anatomo-clinical approach draws the inference that damage to a specific cerebral region A produces the symptom X, due to the derangement of the function F, on the basis of the observation of single positive cases: patients in whom A is damaged and X is present. This

approach, however, does not take into consideration the 'negative' cases (see, however, Bouillaud, 1825, in Hécaen and Dubois, 1969): patients in whom X is present, but A is spared, or patients in whom X is absent, even though A is damaged. The traditional clinical method, which considers only positive cases, does not rule out the possibility that X is a non-specific effect of brain damage, independent of its specific localization.

A similar line of reasoning may be applied to the analysis of the functional syndromes. Consider a putative syndrome S, comprising four symptoms (A, B, C, and D), produced by the derangement of function F, possibly associated with lesions of the left hemisphere. The study should not be confined to positive cases (i.e., left brain-damaged patients in whom S is present), but, on the contrary, it should include all hemisphere-damaged patients, with both right and left-sided lesions, looking for the presence of the four components of S. The conclusion may be drawn that S does indeed exist if the four symptoms co-occur in the positive cases and are not observed in the negative cases. At the anatomo-clinical level, S should be associated with left hemisphere lesions.

The observation of an individual case may then provide hints for scientific research which, however, relies upon series of patients, where the mere presence of brain damage represents the inclusion criterion. It then becomes possible to investigate whether a putative anatomo-clinical association represents a reliable correlation between a specific symptom and a focal cerebral lesion or reflects some non-specific effects of brain damage. An important corollary of this position is that large samples of patients would be more representative of the general population and would allow firmer conclusions.

(2) The neuropsychological examination is standardized. The traditional clinical examination is not precisely codified. More or less important details of the exam vary across patients and there is no quantitative evaluation of the level of performance. Such clinical reports typically do not mention the precise details of the tests used, making replication difficult, if not impossible. These difficulties may be overcome by the use of tests with fixed procedures, which need to be specified in some detail: e.g., reporting stimuli and response modalities, error classification, quantitative scoring.

(3) The performance of brain-damaged patients should be compared with a matched control group using statistical procedures. The clinical method typically attributes the defective performance of the patient to the cerebral lesion. This may in fact be the case when the deficit is severe or 'clinically' apparent. A suboptimal level of performance may, however, be considered abnormal simply because the patient has a brain lesion. On the other hand, mild deficits might escape the clinical examination. Normal subjects make errors on virtually all psychological tasks, and performance level is influenced by a number of factors, including age, socio-educational level and sex. The performance of the brain-damaged group should then be compared with that of a group of normal subjects, matched for the variables mentioned above.

After the Second World War up to the 1970s there has been a great development of neuropsychological studies based upon this type of methodological approach, both in Europe and in the United States. The research activity of DeRenzi and Vignolo in Italy, of Hécaen in France, of Poeck in Germany, of Bender, Benton, Teuber, and Weinstein in the United States, and their coworkers and pupils, provides illustrative examples (see Mountcastle, 1962; DeRenzi, 1982a,b, Vignolo, 1982).

The typical paradigm of this type of research is the following. The performance of several groups of brain-damaged patients, subdivided according to the side of the lesion (left vs. right) and its intra-hemispheric localization (e.g., pre- vs. post-rolandic) is compared with that of a matched control group of normal subjects. The study aims at assessing whether one side of the brain, and possibly specific cerebral regions, play a specific role in performing a given behavioral task. The reference to modern normal psychology concerns the experimental methodology, but not the architecture of normal mental processes. The main aim of this neuropsychological approach is to establish an anatomo-clinical correlation between the cerebral hemispheres and specific mental abilities, not the investigation of the functional structure of the cognitive processes per se, even though results relevant in this respect may be obtained.

Since this research approach is focused on the anatomo-clinical correlation it is not surprising that: (1) the adopted psychological categories have often been fairly vague (e.g., nonverbal vs. verbal abilities; perceptual and memory processes); (2) views of normal processes developed in the classical period of human neuropsychology are relied upon (e.g., the Wernicke-Lichtheim model of language (1874, 1885); Lissauer's model of visual recognition (1890)); (3) interactions with contemporary normal psychology have been scarce.

Until recently, neuropsychological data have been rarely quoted in normal psychology textbooks. This lack of interest on the part of normal psychology is not surprising, if one considers that the anatomo-clinical approach in neuropsychological research had not aimed at elucidating the functional architecture of mental processes, but at establishing their neural correlates. Seen in this perspective, normal psychology may be useful to neuropsychology, providing models of normal mental activities and behavioral tests suitable for investigating the neural correlates of mental function. The advantage is not reciprocal, however: the results of neuropsychological research concerning anatomo-clinical correlations are of little, if any, interest to students of the functional organization of normal cognitive processes.

4. Cognitive neuropsychology

4.1. Three basic assumptions

In the last twenty years a new neuropsychological approach, now termed 'cognitive neuropsychology', has undergone a remarkable development. The main aim of cognitive neuropsychology is to explore the functional architecture of normal cognitive processes, investigating the patterns of abnormal behavior produced by brain damage. The early and seminal studies in cognitive neuropsychology may

be traced back to the late sixties and early seventies, when in Canada, United States and Britain researchers such as Milner (1966), Drachman and Arbit (1966), Warrington and Shallice (1969), Baddeley and Warrington (1970) and Marshall and Newcombe (1973) investigated individual cases and small and homogeneous series of patients with selective impairments of subcomponents of human memory (short-term memory vs. long-term memory) and of reading (the 'dual-route' model of normal reading).

Since its inception cognitive neuropsychology has taken an information-processing view of mental faculties. Human cognitive activity may be subdivided into a number of inter-related components, with specific functional properties. The functional architecture of modern information-processing models bears clear similarities to the anatomo-clinical models developed in the 1800s (see Fig. 1; a discussion in Morton, 1984). There are, however, two important differences. The classical models are anatomo-functional: each component should be localized in a specific cerebral region. The modern information-processing models do not necessarily imply this point-to-point correspondence, being primarily concerned with the functional architecture of mental processes. Information-processing models tend also to be more explicit as to the functional properties of the different components of the system.

Assuming that the cognitive system comprises a number of discrete subcomponents (see Fig. 1), it is in principle possible that one (some) of them is (are) selectively damaged by brain damage. Patients with brain lesions may then be investigated with a twofold aim: (1) explaining their neuropsychological deficit in terms of the impairment of one or more components of the system; (2) elucidating the functional architecture of the cognitive system. The research methodology used by cognitive neuropsychology, largely derived from normal experimental psychology, is then similar to the quantitative and standardized approach discussed in the previous section and clearly differs from the classical clinical method (see DeRenzi, 1967; Shallice, 1979a; Caramazza, 1984).

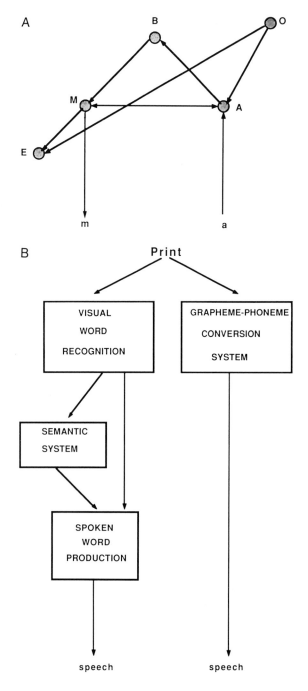

The approach of cognitive neuropsychology has three basic underlying assumptions, which may also be found in the diagrams of classical neuropsychology.

4.1.1. Modularity: the architecture of the human cognitive system is modular (see Marr, 1976, 1982; Fodor 1983, 1985)

In Marr's words (1982, p. 325): 'any large computation should be split up into a collection of small, nearly independent specialized sub-processes'. The modularity assumption may be traced back to Gall, who put forward a primitive version (see Fodor, 1983) and to the classical anatomo-clinical models of the 1800s (see Fig. 1). Modularity is a main feature of the information processing models developed since the 1960s (see, e.g., Norman, 1970) and concerns a variety of mental activities, including vision (Marr, 1982) and language (Chomsky, 1980).

The precise characteristics of modular systems are controversial, however. Fodor's modules (1983) are innate computational mechanisms which deal with specific types of representation and have localized neural correlates. Such modules are fast and automatic, their operation is not affected by the activity of other modules (in Fodor's terminology they are informationally encapsulated), and their content is not accessible to conscious processes. Examples of Fodor's modules, which may be considered analogous to reflexes, are the visuo-perceptual systems and some linguistic processes, such as the syntactic analysis systems. Fodor (1983) in his discussion of modular systems refers only to

from M to the organs of speech. O: centre of visual images. E: writing centre (a centre of motor images from which the organs of writing are innervated). B: centre for the elaboration of concepts. M and A are localized in the inferior frontal convolution and in the temporal convolution, respectively. B is not localized. **B.** A simple dual-route model of adult reading. The component parts of the model are not localized in any specific region of the brain. Source: Coltheart M: Cognitive neuropsychology and the study of reading. In Posner MI, Marin OSM (Editors) *Mechanisms of Attention: Attention and Performance XI.* Lawrence Erlbaum, Hillsdale, NJ, 1985, pp. 3–37, Fig. 4, with permission.

Fig. 1. Two models (a classic and a modern) of aspects of cognitive functions. Both models comprise independent components with specific functions and connections and different levels of representation. **A.** The anatomoclinical model of Lichtheim (1885). A: centre of auditory images. M: centre of motor images. a: afferent branch, which transmits acoustic impressions to A. m: efferent branch which conducts the impulses 'input' perceptual systems. Modularity, however, may be a basic feature of 'output' systems too, such as some motor processes (see Paillard, 1982; Marshall, 1984).

The modular architecture of the cognitive system currently adopted by most cognitive neuropsychologists differs from Fodor's view in a number of important respects. Consider the dual-route model of adult reading (Fig. 1). The components of the system are neither innate nor informationally encapsulated, nor need to have localized neural correlates (Coltheart, 1985). That some modules are innate while others are not may be an important problem in its own right, but such a difference does not prevent the investigation of the functional architecture of the cognitive system and its disorders, at least in adult brain-damaged patients or normal subjects. If cognitive modules are not informationally incapsulated, they might, in principle, have all possible reciprocal connections. Such a fully interconnected architecture might undermine the very concept of modularity, meant as the existence of independent and autonomous components. This extreme possibility, which does not occur in most information-processing models, would not be in line with the vast majority of the neuropsychological empirical data, which suggest instead a modular organization of the cognitive system. Finally, as discussed in the following section, the lack of any correspondence between the functional and the neural architectures would make the occurrence of specific cognitive deficits associated with a cerebral lesions most unlikely.

A modular cognitive system may be organized hierarchically, but this is not necessarily the case. The dual-route model mentioned above represents an illustrative example of a non-hierarchical architecture. A classical example of hierarchical organization is Jackson's distinction (1915; see also the volume edited by Kennard and Swash, 1989, devoted to Jackson's concept of hierarchy) between automatic vs. voluntary/propositional language. A recent illustrative example of a hierarchical model is Tulving's ternary classification (1985) of memory systems: the higher system (episodic memory) depends on and is supported by the immediately lower system (semantic memory), which in turn implies a lower component (procedural memory). A hierarchical model of this sort does not predict double dissociations. In the specific example of Tulving's model (1985), a selective impairment of the episodic system may occur and the suggestion has been made that this might be the case in amnesia (see Kinsbourne and Wood, 1975). According to this hierarchical model, however, the lower semantic and procedural systems cannot be selectively impaired (but see Coughlan and Warrington, 1981; Vallar et al., 1988a).

4.1.2. Correspondence between the functional and neurological organizations

A cerebral lesion is likely to produce a selective damage of a specific subcomponent of the cognitive system only if its neural implementation shares the property of modularity at some neurobiological level. In the classical anatomo-clinical models the level of correspondence is between specific centers and anatomical regions of the cerebral hemispheres. Cognitive neuropsychologists also make this correspondence assumption (neurological specificity or isomorphism: see Shallice, 1981; Ellis and Young, 1988, Ch. 1). Their main interest, however, concerns the functional level: their research, accordingly, is not primarily directed towards a more in-depth specification of the correspondence (see a related discussion in Olson and Caramazza, this volume).

The correspondence between the cognitive modules and the neural architecture might be at the level of anatomical cerebral regions, where the white matter tracts which connect different brain regions represent the neural correlates of the connections between modules, the arrows between boxes of most information-processing systems. This is the classical position (see Fig. 1). These neural correlates may, however, be better conceived in terms of complex circuits, which interconnect different brain structures (see a formal general model in Crick, 1984; a specific model for attentional processes in Mesulam, 1981). This view is in line with both animal (see a review concerning the neural correlates of spatial attention in Rizzolatti and Gallese, 1988) and human (see Metter, 1987; Vallar et al. 1988b). At a finer-grain level of analysis the neural correlates of complex cognitive processes might be described in terms of neural cell assemblies (see Hebb, 1949; Crick 1984; some empirical data concerning neural ensembles involved in coding of movement direction in Georgopulos et al., 1986; a discussion with an explicit reference to 'parallel distributed processing' models in Crick and Asanuma, 1986; Ballard, 1986; also Crick, 1989).

The correspondence might also, it has been argued (see Barlow, 1985), be at the level of the single neuron. Some neurons located in the regions of the superior temporal sulcus in the monkey, which respond to different aspects of facial information (parts of the face, different perspective views, specific faces), provide an illustrative example of this possibility (see Perret et al., 1987). It is finally possible, if not likely, that the level of correspondence is not identical in all systems.

4.1.3. Constancy: the performance of a given brain-damaged patient is produced by the activity of his/her cognitive system minus the component(s) impaired by the cerebral lesion

After a brain lesion and during the recovery phase the cognitive system should not modify its architecture, with the development of new components and/or connections, in order to minimize the effects of the cerebral damage. Were this the case, the cognitive system of a brain-damaged patient would be qualitatively different − would have a different functional architecture − from that of a normal individual. Accordingly, any inference from the patient's behaviour to normal processes would be unwarranted. The investigation of the cognitive impairments of brain-damaged patients would then provide data relevant to our understanding of how the cognitive system reacts to cerebral lesions, by modifying its organization. This type of information, very important in its own right, does not pertain to our knowledge of the normal cognitive system, however.

4.2. Modularity, correspondence and constancy: the plausibility of these assumptions

Neuropsychological research does not aim at a direct verification of these three assumptions: they may be considered a basic core, which, it has been argued (see Caramazza, 1984; Ellis and Young, 1988), cannot be verified directly. Some considerations concerning their plausibility are, however, in order.

4.2.1. Modularity

In a modular structure relatively local modifications do not affect the whole system, while in a non-modular system local changes would have more or less widespread effects. This may represent an evolutionary advantage of the modular system (see Simon, 1969). The positive effects of a local change, which per se would improve the efficiency of the whole system, would run a comparatively minor risk of being reduced or even nullified by unexpected negative modifications in other parts of the system. The modular system has a similar superiority in the case of partial damage. The lesion would destroy a limited number of components, sparing part of the system and producing selective deficits. Were the system non-modular, a global reduction of efficiency would be expected. Finally, the restoration of a partially damaged modular system may be easier. The differences between modular and non-modular systems may be illustrated by a number of analogies. Ellis and Young (1988) suggest the contrast between the highly modular modern hi-fi systems, which include a number of separate components (record decks, cassette decks, amplifiers, etc.), and the less modular radios popular in the 1950s. The human body itself is highly modular, comprising a number of specific organs. In both cases a specific component, such as the hi-fi's amplifier or the human body's heart, may be selectively damaged and may then be repaired or replaced.

A number of empirical observations also suggest a modular architecture. Neurophysiological evidence indicates that the different attributes of a visual scene, such as form, colour and motion, are processed preferentially in anatomically distinct regions of the visual cortex (see e.g., Cowey, 1985; Zeki and Shipp, 1988; see data concerning enzymic correlates in Martin, 1988; see a related discussion in Sergent, 1988). At the psychological level, data from normal subjects argue for a modular organization of some visuo-perceptual (McLeod et al., 1985) and speech production (Shallice et al., 1985) systems.

Some components of the system may be non-modular, however. Lichtheim's anatomo-clinical model (1885) is entirely modular, with one notable exception of the 'B centre' (Fig. 1): 'Though in the diagram B is represented as a sort of a centre for the elaboration of concepts, this has been done for simplicity's sake; with most writers I do not consider the function to be localized in one spot of the brain, but rather to result from the combined action of the whole sensorial sphere. Hence the point B should be distributed over many spots' (op. cit., p. 477). A hundred years later Fodor (1983) takes the view that central cognitive processes, such as problem-solving and decision-making, are non-modular, do not have localized neural correlates and cannot be the object of scientific inquiry.

A clear-cut distinction between central and non-central processes cannot be easily drawn. Evidence from neuropsychology suggests that some relatively central components can be fractionated and are, therefore, modular. This might be the case with the semantic system, which may be selectively impaired (see Shallice, 1987; see a collection of relevant papers in Job and Sartori, 1988). Such central modular systems, however, might have functional characteristics different from those of the more peripheral perceptual or output systems (see Shallice, 1988, Ch. 12). The existence of specific anosognosic disorders is also compatible with the view that some central systems are modular. Some patients may be entirely unaware of a specific neurological deficit, such as hemiplegia or anosognosia, without any associated general mental deterioration or a non-specific denial of illness. For instance, the famous patient M (Anton, 1899),

anosognosic for cortical blindness, was aware of his dysphasia. These observations may be explained by assuming that multiple dedicated control components monitor the activity of perceptual or motor processes (see Bisiach et al., in press). The evidence for modularity of processes which are usually considered central (programming and selection of complex and non-routine actions) is, however, far from certain (see e.g., Shallice, 1982, 1988; Duncan, 1986).

4.2.2. Correspondence
Both the physiological data mentioned above and the existence of patterns of selective neuropsychological impairment are consistent with the view that the neurological and the functional architecture are essentially modular.

4.2.3. Constancy
The assumption that, at least in adult subjects, qualitative changes, such as new components and connections, do not take place in the architecture of the cognitive system is based upon meagre empirical evidence. In most neuropsychological disorders associated with cerebro-vascular attacks or head injury a variable degree of behavioral recovery occurs. This does not necessarily imply a qualitative reorganization and, at a neurophysiological level, may be traced back, at least in part, to the regression of diaschisis in cerebral regions far removed from the structurally damaged area (see Vallar et al., 1988b). Finally, it should be noted that the precise neural mechanisms of recovery of neuropsychological deficits are unclear (see Jeannerod and Hécaen, 1979; Geschwind, 1985). The constancy assumption, which is necessary for any meaningful extrapolation from neuropsychological data to normal function, should be treated with great caution and carefully pondered in any given empirical situation.

The constancy assumption is satisfied if the patient makes a strategic use of his/her residual skills (see two examples concerning agrammatism and disorders of verbal short-term memory in Kolk et al., 1985; Baddeley and Wilson, 1988). Evidence should, however, be provided that the specific behavioural patterns utilized by the patient belong to the normal repertoire, even though they represent infrequent and possibly suboptimal choices. This would require specific experiments. Patient PV (see Vallar and Papagno, 1986), suffering from a selective impairment of phonological short-term memory provides an illustrative example. In the immediate free recall of supra-span lists of words PV adopts a serial recall order, first producing the initial items. Normal subjects typically use an oppposite order, first producing the final items. This choice by PV may be attributed to the abnormally reduced capacity of her phonological short-term memory. Control strategies used to give output priority to items held in this defective system would not secure any advantage to her recall performance; accordingly, the patient shifts to a recall-from-beginning order, which gives priority to the early items of the list, held in the unimpaired long-term memory components. Normal subjects, in contrast, typically recall the final items first, because they are held in an ephemeral memory component (the phonological short-term store), even though the strategy used by PV is a part of their repertoire, as shown by their ability to cope with recall-from-beginning instructions. They then move to the middle and initial items of the list, stored in the more stable long-term components of memory.

The modularity, correspondence and constancy assumptions are plausible and, as noted above, some compatible empirical evidence is available. The cerebral lesions producing neuropsychological deficits, however, are localized according to neural parameters (e.g., the organization of the vascular tree, the preferred sites of thrombotic occlusions and aneurysms, the site and growth pattern of a tumour, etc.), which are not related to specificity of the organization of the neural structures involved in cognitive activities. It then might prove to be the case that the neuropsychological data are contradictory and cannot be meaningfully interpreted in the light of normal cognitive processes (see e.g., Postman, 1975). In addition, even if models of normal cognitive functions may be useful in the interpretation of behavioural disorders produced by brain damage, this does not necessarily imply that

neuropsychological observations may increase our knowledge of normal cognition (see e.g., Crowder, 1982). Seen in this perspective, neuropsychology may be regarded as a parasite of psychology.

This is, however, not the case. Not only have neuropsychological deficits been successfully interpreted on the basis of normal cognitive theory, but data from brain-damaged patients have offered a substantial contribution to the shaping of models of normal function. Consider, as an illustrative example, the selective impairments of human memory. In the 1960s the dominant view in normal psychology distinguished between two serial components, short-term memory and long-term memory. Information enters short-term memory after perceptual processing, and may subsequently gain access to long-term memory (e.g. Waugh and Norman, 1965; Atkinson and Shiffrin, 1968). This architecture predicted the possibility of selective impairments of long-term memory; a short-term memory deficit, however, would produce an associated long-term memory impairment, given the serial organization of the system. The observation that amnesic patients have a selective impairment of the long-term component (e.g., Milner, 1966; Drachman and Arbit, 1966; Baddeley and Warrington, 1970) not only was consistent with the two-component models mentioned above, but was regarded by Atkinson and Shiffrin as 'the single most convincing demonstration of a dichotomy in the memory systems' (op. cit., p. 97), contradicting competing unitary views (see Melton, 1963). The subsequent observation that short-term memory may be selectively impaired, in the absence of any long-term memory deficit (Shallice and Warrington, 1970; Basso et al., 1982; Vallar and Papagno, 1986) is inconsistent with the two-component serial models, suggesting instead a model with parallel access to the two memory components (Shallice and Warrington, 1970). In the same period, normal data inconsistent with the two-component serial model were also published. For instance, Craik and Watkins (1973) found no relation between long-term learning of a given item and the duration of short-term storage (see a discussion in Baddeley, 1990).

A second illustrative example concerns the functional locus of verbal short-term memory along the input-output dimension (see Hitch, 1980; Shallice and Vallar, 1990). In a number of influential multi-component cognitive models developed in the early 1970s (Morton, 1970; Baddeley and Hitch, 1974), the storage system involved in the immediate retention of verbal material was conceived as an articulatory output buffer, also contributing to the programming of fluent speech. In other models the store was acoustic in nature and had an input locus (Sperling, 1967). A number of left brain-damaged patients with a selective impairment of memory span show two features which are not compatible with an output locus of the store. First, the selective deficits of immediate retention may be confined to the auditory input modality, with a substantially better level of performance in the case of visual input (e.g., Luria et al., 1967; Warrington and Shallice, 1969; Basso et al., 1982). Second, speech output may be entirely spared (Shallice and Butterworth, 1977; Basso et al., 1982). Taken together, these data argue for an input locus of the store, which may be conceived of as an auditory-verbal input system (Sperling, 1967; Warrington and Shallice, 1969), where information is coded in a phonological non-articulatory format (Vallar and Baddeley, 1984a). Again, data from normal subjects are consistent with the view that the store has an input locus (Salamé and Baddeley, 1982). The functional architecture of the verbal short-term memory system impaired in the patients discussed above, and its relationships with visual short-term memory and long-term memory systems is illustrated in Fig. 2.

A third example is provided by a recent study by Posner et al. (1984), who applied a model of visuospatial attention developed in normal subjects (see Posner, 1980) to patients with contralateral visual extinction, and suggested that parietal lesions may disrupt the disengagement component of visual attention, when the target is presented in the half-field contralateral to the lesion.

Two lessons can be learned from these examples. First, cognitive impairment in brain-damaged pa-

tients can successfully be interpreted in the light of models of normal function. Second, neuropsychological data may be very useful, if not crucial, in the comparative evaluation of competing models and may shape the architecture of existing models, paving the way to new research developments.

4.3. The neural correlates of cognitive processes

Cognitive neuropsychology is primarily interested in the investigation of normal cognitive processes and their derangement at the functional level. The study of the neural correlates of such processes is a relevant issue in its own right, but, according to

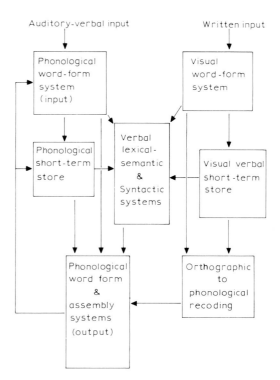

Fig. 2. A functional model of verbal (phonological and visual) short-term memory. The model includes the relationships of the short-term memory systems with the input analysis and speech production components and with the central syntactic and lexical-semantic systems. Redrawn from Shallice T, Vallar G: The impairment of auditory-verbal short-term storage. In Vallar G, Shallice T (Editors) *Neuropsychological Impairments of Short-term Memory*. New York: Cambridge University Press, Fig. 1, 1990).

most cognitive neuropsychologists, this is not an essential component of their investigation (see Shallice, 1979a; Ellis and Young, 1988; cf. Posner et al., 1984; see a related discussion in Caramazza and Olson, this volume).

The existence of a complementarity between the locations of the neural lesions and the differences in the patterns of cognitive impairment may, however, be considered an instance of converging evidence, which corroborates a functional dissociation. This is the case in the distinction between short-term and long-term memory processes (see Shallice, 1979b). Patients with selective impairments of phonological short-term memory and long-term memory typically have left inferior-posterior parietal and bilateral subcortical or medial temporal lesions, respectively (see Shallice and Vallar, 1990; Weiskrantz, 1985). It should be noted, however, that the absence of an anatomical counterpart of a behavioral dissociation does not decrease its value, since the behavioral dissociation does not primarily depend upon neurological data.

According to a widespread opinion among cognitive neuropsychologists (see e.g., *Cognitive Neuropsychology,* Editorial: 1: p. 1, 1984; Mehler et al., 1984) the neurological and psychological levels of descriptions are so different that their correspondence is extremely fragile, even though some neurological specificity is assumed to exist. In addition, attempts to localize specific components of the cognitive systems should be made only when our knowledge of the architecture of the cognitive system is adequate. Seeing the problem of the neural correlates of mental processes in this perspective, psychology should precede neurology (see also Howard, 1985).

This view, though formally correct, may in practice interfere with the development of research concerning the neural correlates of cognitive function. It is not entirely clear what criteria should be used to determine when the functional and neurological descriptions are adequately explicit and precise enough to allow a sensible correlation. Since functional models are frequently revised and modified in a more or less substantial fashion or are replaced by entirely new models, the obvious risk of an endless postponement exists. In addition, relatively poorly specified working hypotheses, based upon incomplete sets of empirical data, might generate new possibly fruitful research fields. For instance, the renowned association between the so-called Broca's area and the faculty of articulated speech was not founded on a precise and detailed functional model of language. Nevertheless this association gave rise to the neuropsychology of language. The aforementioned views concerning the relationship between the neurolological and the psychological level may reflect, at least in part, the prevailing interest of cognitive neuropsychology in linguistic disorders. The attempts to correlate the defective impairment of specific components of the linguistic system to a lesion in specific regions of the left cerebral hemisphere have been far from successful (see, e.g., the case of dyslexia in the anatomic appendices in Coltheart et al., 1980; Patterson et al., 1985). A notable exception is the strong relationship between the selective impairment of phonological short-term memory and left hemisphere lesions involving the infero-posterior parietal regions.

In the neuropsychology of linguistic disorders neural models based upon animal studies are, of course, not available. In the case of non-linguistic deficits, however, some interaction between neuropsychological studies in animals and cognitive research in humans may occur. For example, in the area of spatial attention deficits, Posner et al. (1984) claimed an association between the impairment of a specific sub-component of the attentional system (disengagement from the target) and parietal cortical lesions in humans. They also noted a convergence between neurophysiological data from the study of single neurons in the posterior parietal lobe of the monkey and results from the psychological investigation of the process of orienting of attention in normal subjects.

Finally, the availability of imaging techniques capable of measuring the regional cerebral activity in vivo is likely to provide a valuable contribution to the investigation of the neural correlates of cognitive processes. A recent illustrative example is a PET study of the neural correlates of the different levels of analysis (visual, auditory, lexical-semantic, articulatory codes) which operate in the processing of single words: these different levels are associated with the activation of different cerebral regions and some processes may occur in parallel (Petersen et al., 1988, 1989). In this type of paradigm, the pattern of activation of different cerebral regions when subjects are engaged in different tasks (passive auditory or visual sensory processing; repetition, rhyme judgements, semantic association) is relevant to our knowledge not only of the neural correlates of cognitive processes, but also of the functional architecture of the cognitive system per se. The observation that different cerebral areas may be activated in different tasks, involving putatively different cognitive components, may provide support for specific cognitive models.

Consider as an illustrative example the phonological level. Rhyme judgements performed upon visually presented word pairs activate the left temporo-parietal cortex. This area is also activated when subjects passively listen to words, but not when such words are visually presented. The temporo-parietal cortex is not activated, however, during a repetition task, which involves more anterior regions. This dissociation is considered by Petersen et al. (1989) as an indication that within the phonological code input and output components may be distinguished. Behavioral data from normal subjects (Shallice et al., 1985) and patients (see Shallice and Vallar, 1990) are consistent with this view (see a unitary hypothesis in Allport, 1984a,b).

PET activation data of this sort may complement the lesion localization information in patients with specific cognitive deficits. The association between phonological coding and temporo-parietal cortex found by Petersen et al. (1988, 1989) is in line with data from brain-damaged patients with specific deficits at the phonological level. Cappa et al. (1981) found that the left inferior parietal lobule and the posterior part of the posterior temporal gyrus are frequently involved in fluent aphasics with predominantly phonemic errors in a naming task. In four left brain-damaged patients with phonological agraphia (the disproportionate impairment in writing pronounceable nonwords), the damaged area common to all cases occupies the anterior-inferior supramarginal gyrus (Roeltgen et al., 1983). In ten left brain-damaged patients, a lesion of the left inferior parietal lobule appears to be the neural correlate of the selective deficit of input phonological short-term memory (Shallice and Vallar, 1990).

Both the merits and the limits of activation studies in normal subjects (and of the complementary localization of lesion approach in brain-damaged patients) will be clear from these examples: such studies may provide data relevant for the evaluation of cognitive models, together with information concerning their neural correlates; they are, however, correlational in nature and do not offer a description at the neural level of the operation of the cognitive system.

5. Specific methodological problems

This section concerns three specific methodological issues that have been widely debated in the last few years. The first part deals with the basic tools that allow inferences concerning the modular organization of the cognitive system and its neural correlates: the relative merits and limits of associations and dissociations among symptoms are considered. The basic problem discussed in the second (neuropsychological syndromes) and in the third (single case vs. group studies) parts is whether or not homogeneity across patients is possible. A positive answer to this question has two main implications: neuropsychological syndromes may exist, both group and single case studies can be performed, replication of results across individual patients or groups is possible. A negative answer conjures up a neuropsychology without syndromes, performed on a succession of single cases, where replication does not represent a crucial corroborative criterion.

5.1. Associations and dissociations in neuro-psychology

Since the early studies in the 1800s (see e.g., Bouillaud, in Hécaen and Dubois, 1969) neuropsychology has made use of the method of dissociations between neuropsychological deficits to draw inferences from experimental data. Using this method, two types of dissociation may be distinguished: simple and double (see Teuber, 1955; Weiskrantz, 1968).

5.1.1. The simple dissociation
A group of brain-damaged patients (or a single case) P1 have a defective performance in task A and a normal performance in task B, which probe cognitive function F1 and F2, respectively. Such a finding might indicate that the hemisphere or the cerebral region affected by the brain injury are the neural correlates of F1, and, at a functional level, that these patients have a selective impairment of F1, F2 being spared. This result might, however, be explained in terms of the impairment of a single component F, assuming a greater difficulty of test A, as compared with B. Using cognitive terminology, the appropriate execution of task A requires a greater amount of resource allocation (see Norman and Bobrow, 1975). The brain damage could produce a reduction of available resources so that only B may be performed at the normal level. This difficulty of interpretation may be overcome by a double dissociation.

5.1.2. The double dissociation
This type of dissociation requires the existence of a second group of patient P2, or of a second individual case, who has a defective performance in task B, but not in task A. In this case a single-function interpretation in terms of greater difficulty of one task is not valid and the conclusion may be drawn that F1 and F2 are independent functions. Let us assume that the two tasks represent the activity of a single component and RP1 and RP2, the resource levels available to the two patients or groups. If this is the case, then:

for task A: RP2 > RP1
for task B: RP1 > RP2
where the two inequalities are contradictory.

When a double dissociation between patients exists, the conclusion may be drawn that the two tasks involve two different functions even if performance level is not within the normal range for both tasks. When this is the case the interpretation is less straightforward, since multiple additional deficits or non-specific lesion effects may also be present (see a discussion of this issue in Jones, 1983, who treats double dissociation as a specific instance of 'crossover' interaction).

The history of neuropsychology is rich with double dissociations. Fig. 3 shows an illustrative example from a study of Faglioni et al. (1969) contrasting perceptual-discriminative and semantic-associative disorders in the acoustic modality. Right brain-damaged patients had a defective performance in the perceptual task, which required the *discrimination* of meaningless sounds, but their score was virtually identical to that of normal controls in the semantic-associative task requiring the *identification* of meaningful sounds. Left brain-damaged patients showed an opposite pattern of impairment and their level of performance in the perceptual task was close to the average score of the control group. This example illustrates the double dissociation in

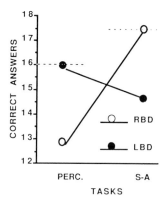

Fig. 3. An example of classical double dissociation (data from Faglioni et al., 1969). PERC.: perceptual task (discrimination of meaningless sounds). S-A: semantic associative task (identification of meaningful sounds). RBD and LBD: right and left brain-damaged patients. Dotted lines: average performance of control subjects.

its classical form. First, the levels of performance in the tasks unaffected by brain damage are within the normal range. Second, the dissociation is between patients: right brain-damaged patients have a better performance level in the semantic task, as compared with left brain-damaged patients, whereas in the perceptual task left brain-damaged patients score better. It will be noted that the performances of the left and right brain-damaged patients, taken in isolation, conjure up a single dissociation, where one group of patients is impaired in one out of two tasks.

A second example of double dissociation is provided by the reading deficits of Anglo-American brain-damaged patients. Phonological dyslexics are severely impaired in reading individual nonwords or novel words, relative to a superior level of performance, which may be virtually errorless, in the case of both regular and irregular words. Surface dyslexics, on the other hand, are able to read nonwords, but their performance with irregular words is defective (see a review in Coltheart, 1985).

This type of inferential procedure may also be used when the comparison is not between tasks but between the effects of two variables on the performances of two patients, or groups of patients (method of the critical variable, see Shallice, 1988). If a crossover interaction is found, this is a specific instance of the classical double dissociation, from which the existence of independent functions can be inferred. This conclusion may also apply to non-crossover interactions (see a discussion of interactions in Kirk, 1982). An illustrative example is the study by Dérouesné and Beauvois (1979), who investigated nonword reading in phonological dyslexic patients: in one case performance was affected by graphemic complexity, but not by a phonemic variable (homophones vs. non-homophones). In a second patient a reversed pattern was found.

The absence of significant differences in the severity of the double-dissociated deficits guarantees that tests with comparable sensitivities to the functions under investigation have been used and that the overall neurological and functional impairment is equivalent in the two groups. Evaluating

whether or not two groups of patients showing a double dissociation have comparable levels of performance may be difficult, however, in particular when both the tasks and the assessed functions are complex. Teuber (1955) illustrates his argument that the levels of impairment of the dissociated deficits should be equivalent by relying on animal research and relatively simple psychophysical studies (visual and tactile discriminative abilities) where comparative evaluations of the levels of severity can be confidently made. This may not be as easily achieved with more complex functions. So, in human neuropsychology a performance well within the normal range and a clear impairment in comparison with a matched control group are usually considered adequate evidence for establishing a double dissociation (see, e.g., the case of selective deficits of long- and short-term memory: Baddeley and Warrington, 1970; Shallice and Vallar, 1990).

The dissociation observed in a given set of experiments is, of course, between tests, and not between functions. The inference from defective performance in a given test to impaired function is not free from problems related to the specific characteristics of the tasks used (see Weiskrantz, 1968). In human neuropsychological research the method of 'converging operations' has been employed to overcome these difficulties: defective performances in a number of different tests which putatively assess the function under investigation concur to suggest a selective impairment. For instance, the observation of an immediate verbal memory deficit confined to the auditory input modality, as revealed by a reduction of memory span and of the recency effect in immediate free recall, and by defective performance in the Peterson task (associated with a preserved performance in a variety of tasks assessing long-term retention), has provided converging evidence for a selective disorder of phonological (auditory-verbal) short-term memory in a number of left brain-damaged patients (see Shallice and Vallar, 1990). The concept of 'converging operations', whereby support for a conclusion comes from more than one source (see Garner et al., 1956), is not confined to sets of data within a given domain, but may include evidence from different research fields, such as human neuropsychology, cognitive psychology and animal data.

5.1.3. The complementary dissociation

The classical double dissociation is between patients (groups or individual cases): as apparent from Fig. 3, right brain-damaged patients have a superior and normal performance in the semantic-associative task and are impaired in the perceptual task, while in left brain-damaged patients a reverse pattern is present. A type of dissociation within patients, confined to tasks, which takes the form of complementary deficits, also exists (complementary dissociations: Shallice, 1979a, 1988; reciprocal disability, Jones, 1983): P1 has a performance level better in task A as compared with task B, P2 vice-versa. In this latter form of dissociation, however, the pattern of performances might be such that P2 has a performance level better than P1 in both tasks A and B, even though, within groups or patients, P1 performs A better than B, and P2 vice versa. If this is the case, the two groups might have performance/resources curves compatible with the existence of a single component involved in both tasks (Fig. 4).

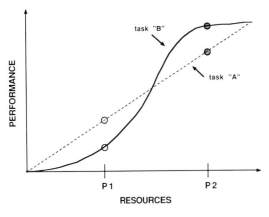

Fig. 4. The complementary double dissociation. A dissociation between tasks but not between patients is compatible with the possibility that a single component is involved in the two tasks, but the patients have different performance/resource curves. Source: Shallice T: *From Neuropsychology to Mental Structure.* Cambridge: Cambridge University Press, 1988, Fig. 10.5, p. 234, with permission.

5.1.4. Associations of deficits and their relationships with dissociations

The interpretation of associations between neuropsychological deficits is more complex. The co-occurrence of a number of different behavioral symptoms (e.g., N1, N2, N3,. . . .Nn) might in principle reflect the damage of a specific single function F, the disorder of which causes all such deficits. Alternatively, the association between, N1, N2, N3, . . . Nn might be attributed to the anatomical contiguity of the neural correlates of functions F1, F2, F3, . . . Fn, the cerebral areas A1, A2, A3, . . . An (see Figs. 5 and 6). In this latter case the association is produced by neurological factors, and anatomical parameters should be taken into consideration, such as the organization of the cerebral vascular tree. For instance, if the vascular territory of a specific artery comprises regions involved in different mental functions, its occlusion would damage such areas, therefore producing an association of symptoms unrelated to functional factors.

An illustrative example of the difficulties in the interpretations of associations is the case of the relationship between defects of phonological short-term memory and disorders of sentence comprehension (see a collection of relevant papers in Vallar and Shallice, 1990). To rule out an interpretation in terms of anatomical contiguity, evidence should be provided in the relevant patients that the comprehension disorder may only be explained in terms of the short-term memory impairment. The ideal candidates for this type of study would be patients with a pure short-term memory deficit, in the absence of other cognitive disorders, such as syntactic or lexical-semantic impairments (see Vallar and Baddeley, 1984b). Secondly, if the memory component is indeed involved in the sentence comprehension process, all patients with a short-term memory deficit should show similar patterns of sentence comprehension impairment (see a review in Vallar et al., 1990a). The existence of dissociated cases (defective immediate verbal memory and normal sentence comprehension: see Howard, 1989), albeit rare, would favour interpretations in terms of close anatomical contiguity of the neural correlates of the relevant functional components, suggesting a less close relationship between processes involved in immediate retention and comprehension.

A second example of association between deficits is the study by Pizzamiglio et al. (1989), who investigated in humans the putative existence of a dissociation between neglect for near and for far extrapersonal space. This dissociation was originally demonstrated in the monkey by Rizzolatti et al. (1983), who made use of tasks requiring motor actions in different parts of the extrapersonal space. Pizzamiglio et al. did not find such a dissociation in a task that required perceptual judgements about stimuli presented in the near and far extrapersonal space without any movement in specific spatial sectors. Pizzamiglio et al. concluded that a single input or sensory component mediates the representation of extra-personal space, while the fractionation between near and far sectors of space is likely to concern output or pre-motor components. This conclusion is based upon a negative finding: the lack of dissociated cases. It remains possible, however, that the crucial dissociated patient simply was not examined, though Pizzamiglio et al. argue that this possibility was unlikely: first, the series of patients was large (28 neglect patients out of 70 right brain-damaged patients); second, the correlation between the severity of near and far extra-personal neglect was high; third, in series of right brain-damaged patients of comparable size other dissociations between components of the so-called neglect syndrome have been repeatedly found (see a review in Bisiach and Vallar, 1988).

The study of associations may provide information relevant to our understanding of the functional architecture of the cognitive system. Consider a model including the component X, involved in the tasks T1, T2 and T3. If a patient has a defective performance in T1, and this impairment can be attributed only to the damage of X, a defective performance in both T2 and T3 will corroborate the conclusion that X is indeed selectively damaged (see a discussion in Caramazza, 1986). An illustrative example is the case study of patient IGR (Caramazza et al., 1986). This patient was severely impaired in

reading aloud, writing to dictation and repeating nonwords, while in the case of words the level of performance was slightly defective or virtually normal. Error analysis showed a phonological relationship between the stimulus and the response given by the patient. Caramazza et al. (1986) interpreted this association in favour of an impaired output phonological buffer component which assembles phonological pre-articulatory segments and feeds more peripheral articulatory (repetition) and graphemic (writing) components. This study, while demonstrating the heuristic value of the association of symptoms, also shows that a set of dissociations is required, to provide evidence that the conjoined failure in the three tasks (repetition, writing, reading) can be attributed only to the deficit of the output buffer. In the study by Caramazza et al. (1986), for instance, the repetition deficit was confined to nonwords and cannot be explained by an associated impairment of phonological analysis.

The efficacy of the conjoined utilization of associations and dissociations is illustrated by a recent study by Grossi et al. (1989), who contrasted two cases: a right brain-damaged patient with a left-sided hemineglect and a left brain-damaged patient unable to generate mental images. The patients' task was to compare the angles between the hands of two clocks in two conditions: in the perceptual test drawings of the two clocks were presented; in the imaginal task the information was given verbally by the examiner ('imagine a clock that says nine o'clock and one that says seven thirty'). The neglect patient showed a dissociation with respect to the spatial positions of the angles to be compared, but not between the tasks, being impaired in both tasks when the angles were on the left-hand side of the clock. In the patient unable to produce mental images a dissociation with respect to the tasks was found: this case was impaired only in the imaginal task, independent of the left- or right-hand side location of the angles.

The association between symptoms may also be used to investigate the precise effects of a rehabilitation treatment. Consider again the functional component X, involved in the tasks T1, T2 and T3. Let us assume a patient in whom X is selectively impaired, that is to say the patient's failure in T1, T2 and T3 may be attributed only to the impairment of X. We might wish to assess whether or not a given treatment TR, which ameliorates the patient's performance in T1, T2 and T3, has specific effects. If this is the case, TR should affect only T1, T2 and T3, but not, say, T4, T5 and T6, which reflect the operation of a different functional component, Y. Seen in this perspective, also the associations between symptoms may be used for investigating the architecture of the cognitive system.

An illustrative example of the investigation of putative associations between symptoms by means of a physiological treatment is offered by the effects of vestibular stimulation upon aspects of the neglect syndrome. In right brain-damaged patients with extrapersonal visual neglect this treatment induces a temporary remission not only of left-sided extrapersonal hemineglect (Rubens, 1985), but also of left personal neglect (Cappa et al., 1987) and of left hemianesthesia (Vallar et al., 1990). These findings suggest a close relationship between these disorders. However, the observation that dissociations between these symptoms also exist (see Bisiach and Vallar, 1988) makes a unitary interpretation unlikely, favouring, instead, explanations in terms of anatomical contiguity of sub-systems all concerned with different aspects of the representation of left contralateral space (extra-personal and personal space, bodily sensation). The close vicinity of these functionally related subcomponents would explain both the frequent co-occurrence of these symptoms, which form the so-called neglect syndrome, and the existence of dissociations. Consistent with this view, the dissociations observed in the monkey are produced by small and precisely localized experimental lesions, which frequently involve adjacent regions (see e.g., Rizzolatti et al., 1983; Rizzolatti and Gallese, 1988). This contiguity might be biologically advantageous in terms of efficiency of the neural system. The sensitivity of all these symptoms to vestibular stimulation might have as a neural correlate the proximity of the vestibular cortical projection area, which, it has been argued (Friberg et al.,

1985), has a posterior-superior temporal location, to the infero-posterior parietal region, which is known to be a major neural correlate of the representation of egocentric space (Vallar and Perani, 1987).

The disorders of the phonological level of processing represent another example of the close anatomical vicinity of related but independent subcomponents. Left perisylvian regions may produce a variety of selective deficits of the phonological level (phonological analysis disorders, impairments of phonological short-term memory, phonemic paraphasias in speech production, phonological agraphia) which frequently, but not necessarily, co-occur (see Shallice and Vallar, 1990).

To summarize, both dissociations and associations are useful tools in neuropsychological research and may provide complementary information. Interpretative problems exist in both cases, but double dissociation in its classical version (see Fig. 3) provides the less ambiguous information and has been, historically, the most effective paradigm for investigating the modularity of the mental processes and their neural correlates.

5.2. Syndromes in neuropsychology

The concept of syndrome has been widely used in clinical medicine. A reliable association of pathological symptoms and signs, related by anatomical, physiological or biochemical factors, might greatly help the diagnostic process, reducing the number of alternative possibilities and suggesting specific lines of investigation (Petersdorf et al., 1983). The associations between symptoms have had a basic role in the development of scientific neuropsychology, defining the taxonomy of the main clinical disorders. The most renowned example is the traditional classification of the aphasias, where entities such as Broca's or Wernicke's aphasia are characterized by the co-occurrence of a number of symptoms, while other deficits are absent. Association of symptoms such as the Gerstmann's and Balint's syndromes represent part of the history of neuropsychology (see Hécaen and Albert, 1978; DeRenzi,

1982a). Deficits such as hemineglect, anosognosia and extinction are frequently associated under the heading of 'neglect syndrome' (see Heilman et al., 1985). In clinical neurology these syndromes have a clear diagnostic value, providing indications concerning the side and location of the lesion. Seen in this perspective, the main neuropsychological syndromes are a basic component of medical knowledge (Adams and Victor, 1983: Mohr and Adams, 1983).

A putative association of n neuropsychological symptoms (N1, N2, N3, N4, . . . Nn) may be produced by three different types of anatomo-clinical pattern, giving rise to three types of syndrome (see Lichtheim, 1885; Brain, 1964; Poeck, 1983; Ellis and Young, 1988).

5.2.1. The anatomical syndrome

The association reflects the anatomical contiguity of the cerebral regions (A1, A2, A3, A4, . . . An), the lesion of which disrupts the functions F1, F2, F3, F4, . . . Fn, therefore producing the symptoms N1, N2, N3, N4, . . . Nn. The value of this type of syndrome concerns the anatomical localization of the lesion. The syndrome is statistical in nature, being related to the probability, which in turn reflects anatomical factors, that the crucial cerebral regions are all damaged by the lesion. The higher the probability, the higher is the localization value of the syndrome. The anatomical syndrome is entirely compatible with dissociations and with incomplete associations of symptoms (e.g., N1, N2, N3, but not . . . N4, Nn) since a lesion might sometimes destroy only A1, A2, A3, but not A4, . . . An (see Fig. 5). The anatomical syndrome, given its probabilistic nature and the possibility of being fractionated into a number of sub-syndromes or partial syndromes, may be considered 'weak' (see a discussion of the classical taxonomy of the aphasias as weak syndromes in Benson, 1979; Poeck, 1983). Finally, it has no theoretical importance from the point of view of the functional organization of the cognitive system.

A well-known example of association of symptoms produced by anatomical contiguity is Gerts-

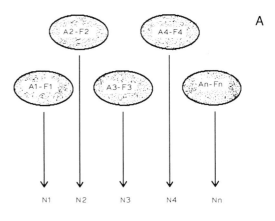

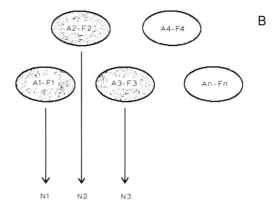

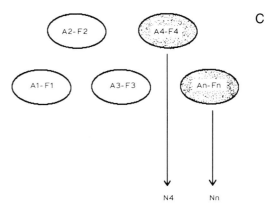

Fig. 5. The anatomical syndrome. The association of symptoms N1, N2, N3, N4,. . . Nn, produced by the impaired activity of the components F1, F2, F3, F4,. . . Fn, localized in the brain regions A1, A2, A3, A4,. . . An, occurs because these cerebral areas are anatomically contiguous. This syndrome may be observed in a complete form (A), when all the relevant cerebral regions are damaged, or in partial forms, when the neurological damage involves only some regions (B and C).

mann's syndrome as interpreted by Strub and Geschwind (1974, 1983). The co-occurrence of the four symptoms (finger agnosia, left-right disorientation, acalculia, agraphia) is valuable in terms of anatomical localization, suggesting a left parietal lesion, but cannot be attributed to the derangement of a single functional component (see Benton, 1961; Heimburger et al., 1964).

5.2.2. *The functional syndrome*
The symptoms N1, N2, N3, N4, . . . Nn co-occur since they are produced by the derangement of a single functional component F (Fig. 6). The neural correlate of F may be a specific circuit or cerebral region. In this case, the term *anatomo-functional syndrome* may be used, where 'anatomo' indicates a localized neural correlate of function F (Fig. 7). This is not a necessary condition, however, since F may well have no localized neural correlates (see, e.g., component B of Fig. 1A). In a functional syndrome, a dysfunction of F should produce all component symptoms. If the syndrome is anatomo-functional, all symptoms should be present and the neural correlate of F should be damaged. Exceptions may be explained only in terms of individual

variability: a number of subjects have a functional architecture of the cognitive system − and, in the case of an anatomo-functional syndrome, of its neural correlates − different from the majority of the population (e.g., left-handers). Similarly, functional and anatomo-functional syndromes, unlike anatomical syndromes, make allowance for partial associations (e.g. N2, N3, but not N1 and N4) only as due to individual variability: they may therefore be considered 'strong' syndromes.

The aphasic disorders of the classical anatomo-clinical models (Wernicke, 1874; Lichtheim, 1885; Luria, 1966) are illustrative examples of strong

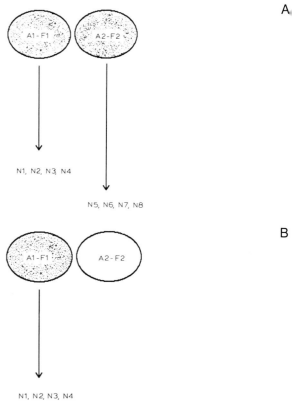

Fig. 7. The anatomo-functional syndrome differs from the functional syndrome in that the involved functional components (e.g., F1 and F2) have specific cerebral correlates (A1 and A2). If the regions A1 and A2 are anatomically contiguous a mixed syndrome, comprising the symptoms N1, N2. . . N8, may occur (A). A mixed syndrome is, however, bound to fractionate into sub-syndromes (e.g., N1, N2, N3, N4), when the cerebral correlate of a single functional component (A1-F1) is selectively damaged (B).

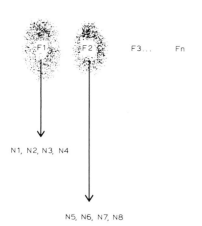

Fig. 6. The functional syndrome. The associations of symptoms N1, N2, N3, N4 and N5, N6, N7, N8 are produced by the dysfunctions of the functional components F1 and F2, respectively. This association is defined in functional terms, with no reference to the neural components involved. This type of syndrome does not make allowance for partial associations (e.g., N1, N2, N3, but not N4).

anatomo-functional syndromes that have both clinical and theoretical significance (see Marshall, 1982): the occurrence of a given association of symptoms reflects the damage of a specific functional component, localized in a region of the brain.

5.2.3. The mixed syndrome

The association between the symptoms N1, N2, N3, N4, . . . N8 reflects both anatomical and functional factors (see Fig. 7). For instance, N1 to N4 might be produced by the dysfunction of F1, localized in cerebral area A1, N5 to N8 by a deficit of F2, localized in A2. The association is produced by the anatomical contiguity of A1 and A2. This might also be conceived in terms of adjacent areas that are members of specific portions of complex circuits which involve various brain structures. A mixed syndrome may fractionate into subsyndromes. In the illustrative example, a lesion confined to A1 would damage F1, bringing about N1 to N4, while a lesion localized in A2 would be associated with symptoms N5 to N8, which reflect the deficit of F2.

Consider now the present status of the classical syndromes. The traditional anatomical correlations of the aphasias have been by and large confirmed (see, e.g., Mazzocchi and Vignolo, 1979; Blunk et al., 1981; Benson, 1988; but see De Bleser, 1988). The availability in clinical practice of CT has, however, shown that in a number of patients aphasic deficits may be associated with 'non-typical' lesion sites. Aphasia may be produced by subcortical lesions (see a review in Cappa and Vignolo, 1983). 'Fluent' and 'nonfluent' aphasic syndromes may sometimes be associated with pre- and retro-rolandic lesions, respectively (Basso et al., 1985). In global aphasia the lesion may be confined to anterior and/or deep structures and, less frequently, to posterior damage (Vignolo et al., 1986). In the case of hemineglect, while the classical postero-inferior parietal correlates have been confirmed, atypical lesion sites, such as frontal and subcortical damage, have also been reported (see a review in Vallar and Perani, 1987).

The use of techniques capable of measuring regional cerebral blood flow and metabolism has shown that the area of functional derangement may extend well beyond the anatomical lesion (see, e.g. Lenzi et al., 1982; Metter, 1987; Perani et al., 1987). These observations have prompted a revision of current views concerning the correlations between patterns of neuropsychological deficits and the damage of specific regions. From the perspective of human anatomo-clinical correlation studies (Perani et al., 1987; Vallar et al., 1988; see related animal data in Rizzolatti and Gallese, 1988), it has been argued that the neural correlates of mental function are better conceived of in terms of complex circuits, rather than, as traditionally maintained, in terms of specific brain centres. On the basis of this sort of data, the theoretical value of the classical syndromes has been denied, since all aphasic patients, both fluent and nonfluent, have temporal hypometabolism (Metter et al., 1989).

In the last few years the theoretical significance of the classical aphasic syndromes has also been attacked with respect to the functional organization of the cognitive system. The argument may be briefly summarized as follows (see for further details, Saffran, 1982; Schwartz, 1984; Caramazza, 1984). The classical aphasic syndromes are based upon a model of cognition developed in the 1800s, which, of course, cannot take into account the subsequent advances of psychological research in normal subjects. When the classical syndromes are analysed in the light of current cognitive models, they may at best be considered anatomical syndromes (but see above), but not functional associations of symptoms. A cognitive investigation or the mere detailed study of the individual patients may reveal a considerable lack of homogeneity among patients classified as belonging to a given traditional aphasic syndrome by a clinical examination or a standard battery (e.g., the Language Examination of the Neuropsychology Centre of the Milano University: Basso et al., 1979; the Boston Diagnostic Aphasia test: Goodglass and Kaplan, 1972). Classic syndromes such as Broca's aphasia (see Mohr et al., 1978; Berndt and Caramazza, 1980) and conduction aphasia (Luria, 1977; Shallice and Warrington, 1977) have been subdivided into new syndromes, in which the symptom-complex has been traced back to a unitary functional deficit. Standard clinical exams, such as the Western Aphasia Battery, may also show, when a numerical taxonomy is used, new associations of symptoms, which may be added to the list of the classic syndromes. Kertesz and Phipps (1977, 1980) subdivide traditional conduction aphasia patients into two subtypes, on the basis of differences in their performance levels in verbal fluency and comprehension tasks.

A further index of the insufficiency of the traditional taxonomy is the high percentage of patients who, under specific circumstances, may be left non-classified as belonging to a specific syndrome. For instance, when the battery is standardized, but, unlike the Western Aphasia Battery, which uses a clustering algorithm, the classification is made by the examiner, over 40% of the patients cannot be classified (Benson, 1979, p. 136; Albert et al., 1981, p. 31).

Thus, the classical anatomo-clinical syndromes have been challenged by cognitive neuropsychologists with new syndromes. In the latter type of association the symptom-complex is analysed with reference to modern information-processing models. This process, which culminated in the late 1970s and the early 1980s, has produced syndromes such as deep, surface and phonological dyslexias (see Coltheart et al., 1983; Patterson et al., 1985).

However, patients classified according to the modern criteria may prove to be nonhomogeneous when their performances are assessed in detail. That the modern syndromes may also suffer from this substantial lack of homogeneity across patients, which characterizes the classical syndromes, is apparent from a review devoted to one noted modern symptom complex, deep dyslexia (Coltheart, 1980). The differences between patients may be attributed to the fact that a given functional component F, the lesion of which was assumed to bring about the symptoms N1, N2, N3, N4, . . . Nn, may fractionate into a number of subcomponents (F1, F2, F3, . . . Fn), giving rise to a variety of new dissociations. One possible response to this state of affairs is the multiplication of syndromes, an occurrence

that might lead to more syndromes than patients. Alternatively, the very concept of syndrome may be abandoned, with every patient investigated as a single case (see Patterson et al., 1985; Caramazza, 1986; Ellis, 1987). In this case the neuropsychological assessment of a specific model of cognitive function is made without the mediation of taxonomical criteria (the syndrome), which allow combining patients into homogeneous groups with respect to the inclusion standards.

An important implication of this neuropsychology without syndromes is that replication across patients is in practice not possible, as each patient is likely to differ from all other patients in more or less important respects. This is a critical difference between this neuropsychological approach and most contemporary science. If replication in a second patient cannot be used as a criterion for corroborating an observation, are there alternative procedures for attempting to classify a neuropsychological result? Replication in the same patient (Ellis, 1987) and the relationships between the novel finding in such patients and both the complete set of the available empirical data and the relevant theoretical models become crucially important (see Caramazza, 1986). The more complete the available data are, the lower is the 'weight' of a single observation. Seen in this perspective, a single finding would be crucially relevant if consistent with the majority of the available data, within a specific theoretical model. A coherent set of results would converge towards a single (the best) available theory.

Were replication across patients impossible, anatomo-clinical correlations in patients would also be impossible. This method is typically based on repeated observations in series of brain-damaged patients and comparisons of the lesion sites and sizes across patients, subdivided into groups according to the presence/absence of a specific symptom or syndrome (see, e.g., Howes and Boller's (1975) method of superimposing the lesion maps; see a review in Damasio and Damasio, 1989). The investigation of the neural correlates of cognitive function would be practicable only in normal subjects, where only the assumption of homogeneity of the neural and functional relevant architectures needs to be made.

When patient replication cannot be obtained, the weight of a single observation is determined both by the complex of the available empirical data and by the theoretical models. This might have dangerous implications, inducing a type of research that aims at producing results consistent with the already published observations and the theoretical models which dominate the scientific area in a given historical period, that is to say, with the status quo. A novel research approach, which breaks with or is outside the dominant paradigms, would be more or less explicitly discouraged.

It may be appropriate to consider this problem in a historical perspective. Empirical observations that have subsequently proven to be very important were frequently not based upon a detailed theoretical model. This is almost always the case in young research areas, where the set of available knowledge is often poor and not well defined. Were replication not considered a corroborative criterion, novel and unexpected findings, peripheral to or inconsistent with the leading theoretical models, would be considered unreliable and irrelevant.

An illustrative example is the discovery that cerebral lesions may bring about a lack of awareness (anosognosia) for specific neurological deficits, such as cortical blindness, hemiplegia and hemianopia, which cannot be explained in terms of a general cognitive impairment or a psychiatric disorder (Anton, 1899; Babinski, 1914; see reviews in McGlynn and Schacter, 1989; Bisiach and Geminiani, in press). This observation has not only become an important symptom in clinical neurology, but has proved to be very relevant to current views concerning conscious mental activity (Bisiach et al., 1990; Bisiach and Geminiani, in press; Shallice, 1988). This happened because the original observations of Anton and Babinski were replicated by subsequent investigators in a number of different patients, namely: replication across patients was obtained. This was crucial, because the current status of neurological knowledge in the late 1800s was not committed to particular views concerning the plausibility of neurological disorders of this

sort. A similar line of reasoning may be applied to the discovery of the role of the right hemisphere in visuo-spatial processes (e.g., Brain, 1941; see a review in DeRenzi, 1982a).

Finally, a position that denies the possible existence of functional syndromes and does not allow replication across patients is directly countered by a specific neuropsychological symptom complex, the selective impairment of phonological short-term memory. A number of patients have been described who have a selective impairment of auditory-verbal span for all verbal stimuli (letters, digits, words, nonwords), which cannot be explained in terms of speech perception or production deficits and has been attributed to the pathologically reduced capacity of the input phonological short-term store. The original observations (see Warrington and Shallice, 1969; similar patients in Luria et al., 1967) have been replicated and localized anatomical correlates have been found (see Shallice and Vallar, 1990).

In different areas of cognitive neuropsychology, such as the reading disorders produced by brain damage acquired in adult age (see Coltheart et al., 1980; Patterson et al., 1985), the situation is likely to be more complex. This could have been an important factor in the development of theoretical views suggesting that the concept of syndrome is devoid of any advantage for research in cognitive neuropsychology, and that replication across patients cannot be confidently used to corroborate empirical observations. In addition to the aforementioned difficulties and problems (excessive reliance on the status quo, impossibility of anatomo-clinical correlations), a concrete case against this position is provided, however, by the disorders of phonological short-term memory.

5.3. Group studies and single case studies in neuropsychology

Neuropsychological research in its development since the 1800s has made use of data from both individual cases and groups of patients selected on the basis of neurological (e.g., side and site of the lesion) and/or functional (e.g., presence/absence of a given deficit) criteria. In different periods, either the group or the single case approach has been the dominant paradigm.

In the 1800s a typical neuropsychological study involved a single patient or a collection of individual cases, in whom the behavioral deficit, described at the clinical level (see section 3.1), was correlated with the anatomical location of the lesion. As noted above, the traditional clinical method has been strongly attacked and, after World War II, group studies and standardized techniques (see section 3.2) have been the leading approach, even though remarkable exceptions, such as case H.M. (see, e.g., Scoville and Milner, 1957), are on record.

The single case approach has been resurrected by cognitive neuropsychologists, with important amendments, however. Briefly, the cognitive study of single patients, as the modern group study approach (see section 3.2), makes use of quantitative and standardized tests, of appropriate control groups, and of statistical methods for assessing the significance of the differences between putatively pathological and normal behaviors (see Shallice, 1979a).

The patient should furthermore be assessed by a wide range of baseline tasks. This would allow both the classification of the patient into a syndrome, if one wishes to do this (see a discussion of this contentious issue in the previous section), and, more importantly, reveal, at least at a coarse-grain level, his/her general pattern of impairment. A wide assessment would indicate whether the patient is likely to be a 'pure' case, with a simple (see Lichtheim, 1885) or single-component (see Shallice, 1988) deficit, and direct the subsequent and more detailed experimental study. For instance, most left brain-damaged patients eventually reported as suffering from a selective impairment of phonological short-term memory have been initially selected because they had a disproportionate impairment of repetition, in a loose sense of the term, as assessed by standard clinical batteries (e.g., WAIS) or language examinations (Milano Aphasia Examination: Basso et al., 1979; Boston Diagnostic Aphasia

Test: Goodglass and Kaplan, 1972). Similarly, experiments aiming at assessing specific hypotheses concerning the nature of hemispatial neglect would identify appropriate patients and their brain-damaged controls on the basis of their behavior in baseline diagnostic tasks (see e.g., DeRenzi et al., 1989). Within a neuropsychology-without-syndromes approach it is less clear how patients suitable for a given study are selected. In principle, all neurological patients should be assessed in full detail from the very beginning of the study.

The main reason for the resurrection of the single case approach has been the increasing awareness that the functional organization of the cognitive system is extremely complex, comprising a number of interconnected components. A cerebral lesion, which has a localization and extension primarily determined by physiological, anatomical and vascular factors, may damage different components in different patients. So, a group study of brain-damaged patients selected on the basis of a coarse-grain functional analysis (e.g., the traditional taxonomy of the aphasias) may include patients who, when assessed in depth, show heterogeneous functional deficits.

In fact, the average behavior of a group may be misleading, concealing heterogeneous deficits. A recent illustrative example is provided by the study by Bisiach et al. (1983), who investigated the line-bisection performance of a group of right brain-damaged patients with neglect using segments of various lengths. An analysis of the performance of the 12 patients as a group revealed a progressive shift to the right of the subjective midline, in direct relation with the length of the lines. When, however, on the basis of a representational model of spatial neglect, the length of the segment 'represented', i.e., taken into consideration by each patient in his/her bisection, was analysed, two qualitatively different patterns were found (see Fig. 8). In one case (RG) the left-sided extremity of the represented segment progressively shifted to the right, as if the right-sided extremity of the actual segment captured the patient's attention. This behavior is compatible with the view that left hemineglect may be traced back to the rightward pathological imbalance of two attentional vectors (see Kinsbourne, 1987). In a second case (CC), the longer the actual segment, the more was the left-sided extremity of the represented segment shifted to the left. This suggests that case CC, in some way, takes into consideration the differences in length between the three segments. Even if the left halves of the segments were entirely neglected, the patient might make such inferences on the basis of the differences in length in their right (non-neglected) halves. This example illustrates both the possibility that averaging across subjects obscures theoretically relevant qualitative differences and the role of the model adopted by the experimenter in guiding all phases of the study (see also Caramazza, 1986). Previous studies (e.g., Schenkenberg et al., 1980) had used the bisection task with segments of various length, a time-honoured clinical test for the diagnosis of hemineglect, but did not apply the concept of represented space.

The detailed investigation of the performance of individual patients may then reveal information missed by a group analysis. In addition, the complexity of the functional architecture of the cognitive system and its relationships with its neural correlates give, in practice, a very important heuristic role to single cases, if the study aims at investigating the modular organization of mental function. Acquired cerebral lesions typically affect more than one component system, and patients with single deficits or impairments confined to a limited number of components are relatively rare. Seen in a historical perspective, a number of relevant advances in neuropsychology have been made possible by the study of single patients with selective impairments. So, Broca's patient suffered from a deficit of 'la faculté du langage articulé', auditory comprehension being relatively preserved (see Hécaen and Dubois, 1969). The patients of Anton (1899) and Babinski (1914) were anosognosic for a specific deficit and this lack of awareness could not be attributed to a general mental impairment. The renowned amnesic patient HM had a selective impairment of long-term episodic memory (see e.g., Milner, 1966). Patients with multiple-component deficits may of course be studied, but the assessment and the interpretation of any given deficit becomes more complex, given the greater number of potentially relevant factors that need to be taken into consideration (see an illustrative and simple example in Baddeley et al.'s analysis (1987) of the double neuropsychological deficit of patient TB).

The single case approach also has practical advantages over group studies: the planning and the execu-

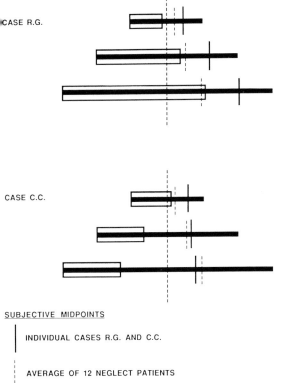

CASE R.G.

CASE C.C.

SUBJECTIVE MIDPOINTS

INDIVIDUAL CASES R.G. AND C.C.

AVERAGE OF 12 NEGLECT PATIENTS

Fig. 8. The average performance (vertical dashed lines) of a group of 12 right brain-damaged neglect patients in a task requiring the bisection of three segments with different lengths (200, 400 and 600 mm). The centre of the segments (long dashed line) was on the midsagittal plane of the patients' trunk. The mean subjective midpoints of the two individual patients (RG and CC, vertical continuous lines) are shown in the upper and lower halves of the figure, respectively. The shaded areas indicate the 'non-represented' portions of the segments (i.e., not taken into consideration by the patients in the bisection task). The non-shaded areas refer to the 'represented' portions of the segments. Source: Bisiach E, Bulgarelli C, Sterzi R, Vallar G: Line bisection and cognitive plasticity of unilateral neglect of space. *Brain Cognition: 2*, 32 – 38, 1983, Fig. 1, with permission.

tion of the experiments are more flexible. In a group study, the experimental procedures cannot be modified during the collection of the data, since this would make the results not comparable across patients. Were a change in the testing procedures or new experiments indeed needed, a new group of patients should be assessed. A group study may be then very long-lasting, unless the group is available for long periods. In a single case study, in contrast, the outcome of an experiment would simply generate new experiments, and the previous data, having been collected in the same patient, may be directly compared with the new observations, assuming of course that the patient's pattern of impairment remains unchanged. Such a single case study, however, may be very long-lasting too, if the appropriate verification of the hypothesis requires long and complex tasks.

This lack of methodological flexibility may delay the collection of the appropriate empirical data in group studies. This, however, does not necessarily diminish their theoretical significance. Major problems may arise from biases in the selection of individual patients. Patients who should be assigned to a group on the basis of the presence of a given behavioral deficit may differ with respect to neurological parameters (aetiology and duration of the disease, patterns of cerebral lateralization: Boller et al., Ch. 16; Vallar and Perani, 1987) which might, in turn, affect the characteristics of the functional impairment. Conversely, if the selection criteria are neurological (e.g., side and site of the lesion), the possible effects of all associated deficits upon the function under investigation should be taken into consideration. Two solutions to these problems have been adopted.

(1) Statistical techniques may be used to correct biases due to factors different from the function under investigation, namely: age, duration of disease, neurological severity, performance in tasks assessing abilities putatively involved in the execution of the task(s) selected to exploring the function that is the object of the study. The statistical treatment may take the form of analyses of co-variance, a method widely used by the Milano group in the

1960s and 1970s. An illustrative example is provided by the study by DeRenzi et al. (1968), who investigated identification and immediate and delayed recognition of faces in right and left brain-damaged patients. In addition to the experimental tasks the patients were also given a simple visual reaction time test, 'to have an indirect measure of the severity of the cerebral lesion not influenced by the hemispheric locus of the damage' (op. cit., p. 22). The performances of brain-damaged patients in the face-perception and memory tasks were then compared by an analysis of covariance, the covariates being age, years of schooling, and reaction time.

(2) Alternatively, the selection criteria may be more cogent. For instance, in Baddeley and Warrington's study (1970), which explored the pattern of deficit of amnesia in the light of the short-term memory/long-term memory dichotomy dominant in the late 1960s, only patients with no detectable evidence of associated deficits, such as subtle semantic disorders, were examined. Similarly, only patients non-aphasic both on a standard language examination and on a sensitive comprehension test, such as the token test (see Boller and Vignolo, 1966), were admitted to the study conducted by Vallar et al. (1988a), who aimed at exploring the long-term memory deficit associated with left brain damage.

Interpretative problems related to the selection of the patients frequently occur in group studies. A major one is the possible confounding role of aphasia. DeRenzi and Faglioni (1965) explained the longer latencies of right brain-damaged patients in simple visuo-motor reaction time, as compared with left brain-damaged patients, in terms of larger lesions in the former group. Assuming that the function involved in simple reaction time has diffuse and non-lateralized neural correlates, the deterioration of performance level would be directly related with lesion size. The factor 'selection of patients' is relevant here as left brain-damaged patients with large lesions are also aphasic and may not enter the study due to the severity of their comprehension disorder. Thus, in a study including left and right brain-damaged patients the former may have a minor neurological deficit and smaller lesions. The bias in the patients' selection might, in turn, affect the results and their interpretation. In a later study, Howes and Boller (1975) confirmed the lengthening of latencies in right brain-damaged patients, but not the hypothesis that their lesions were larger in size. This latter finding does not support an interpretation in terms of selection biases, suggesting instead that the components involved in simple reactions may be localized in some specific regions of the brain, as indeed found by Howes and Boller.

The study of single cases, which aims at elucidating the organization of the cognitive system, does not encounter such problems related to the selection of the patients, provided the three assumptions of modularity, neurological specificity and constancy are fulfilled. It may be useful, however, to record basic neurological information such as cerebral lateralization as inferred by hand preference, aetiology and site of the lesion, etc., not only for anatomo-clinical correlation purposes, but also because such data may sometimes be useful in the interpretation of some behavioral findings. For instance, the associated amnesic deficits found in patient TB (Baddeley et al., 1987), who has a severe impairment of phonological short-term memory, may reflect the diffuse nature of his brain lesion (see Shallice and Vallar, 1990).

The advantages of the single case studies noted above do not necessarily imply that only this approach may provide information relevant to our understanding of the architecture of the cognitive system. In recent years, however, a number of cognitive neuropsychologists (Patterson et al., 1985, pp. 10–11; Ellis, 1987; a detailed discussion in Caramazza, 1986, and Caramazza, 1988) took this view. Briefly, given the complexity of the cognitive system, and the variability of the site and size of the cerebral lesions, which are determined by neurological parameters, it is unlikely that two patients have comparable functional deficits: accordingly, homogeneous groups cannot be made up. Were this possible, however, the homogeneity according to the selection criteria would only concern entering into the group, but would not guarantee homogeneity of the patients with reference to the

results of the experimental study. Accordingly, if the research aims at investigating the organization of the cognitive system, only the study of individual patients, without the mediation of any classical or modern taxonomical syndrome, is appropriate.

This position may be applied to the study of normal behavior, showing that group analyses are also inappropriate in the case of normal subjects, as their performances may also be non-homogeneous (see Shallice, 1988; Caplan, 1988). Group studies in normal subjects are, however, the basic paradigm of cognitive psychology and one of the two basic ingredients of cognitive neuropsychology. McCloskey and Caramazza (1988) reply to this objection by arguing that the assumption of homogeneity can be made in normal subjects, in whom variability may be traced back to background noise. This, however, is not the case with brain-damaged patients, where the pattern of cognitive impairment produced by brain damage may be dissimilar in different patients.

The variability found in normal subjects may, however, not be entirely related to background noise. Let us assume, for example, that ten putatively normal subjects show the standard effect of word length in immediate memory span (i.e., span is superior for short words, as compared with long: see, e.g., Baddeley et al., 1975) while two individuals show no differences (or an opposite effect) at a comparable overall performance level. Such differences might be produced by variations of background noise, even though, were this the case, one might expect a change of overall performance level, without specific effects. If background noise is the relevant factor, these 'aberrant' subjects, when repeatedly tested, should show a behavioral pattern conforming to the average data of the group (see data concerning verbal phonological memory in Logie and Della Sala, 1989). This difference from the normal pattern might, however, be reliable, observed over repeated testing sessions. Such a behavior of the minority might be traced back to various factors: the 'aberrant' subjects might make use of strategies different from those employed by the majority, even though the functional architecture of their cognitive system is identical and such non-typical strategies nevertheless belong to the normal repertoire. Alternatively, the organization of the cognitive system of these divergent subjects might be qualitatively different from the type of functional architecture suggested by the average group data. Were this the case, the assumption of homogeneity could not be applied to normal subjects.

This is more than a remote possibility, as suggested by a number of studies concerning the perceptual behavior of normal subjects in tasks requiring the organization of part of the stimulus pattern in relationship to a specific background field. On the basis of perceptual tasks such as the 'Rod and Frame test' and the 'Embedded Figures Test' normal subjects may be classified, along a continuum, as relatively 'field-dependent' or 'field-independent' (see a review in Pizzamiglio and Zoccolotti, 1982). Such differences are, at least in part, genetic in nature and have been related to functional asymmetries between the cerebral hemispheres. For instance, in a choice reaction time experiment to verbal and nonverbal stimuli Zoccolotti and Oltman (1978) found that the well-known right visual half-field/left hemisphere superiority for letters and the left visual half-field/right hemisphere advantage for faces are present in male 'field-independent' normal subjects, but not in 'field-dependent' individuals. Using a similar paradigm Pizzamiglio and Zoccolotti (1981) have suggested an interpretation in terms of 'field dependency vs. independency', rather than in terms of sex factors, of a number of differences in the hemispheric lateralization of verbal and nonverbal abilities.

The data mentioned above suggest that the assumption of homogeneity also cannot be confidently made in the case of normal subjects. Accordingly, were complete homogeneity a requisite for group studies, the group study method should be used neither in brain-damaged patients nor in normal individuals. This is not the case, however, and group studies are the canonical methodology in normal cognitive psychology. In fact an assumption of complete homogeneity is not needed. The average data are typically taken as indicators of the

behavior, and then of the functional architecture of the majority of the subjects. This position is compatible with the existence of behavioral variations. These, in turn, might reflect individual differences in the organization of the cognitive system, which may be an extremely interesting research field in its own right. The existence of individual differences and the possibility of specific behavioral patterns in a minority of subjects of a given group does not, however, undermine the validity of conclusions based upon the average data that reflect the behavior of most members of the group. Finally, if, as argued above, a complete homogeneity cannot be assumed even in the case of normal individuals, its lack does not represent a strong argument against the validity of the group study approach in brain-damaged patients.

Independent of these potentially dangerous consequences for normal psychology, the aforementioned single case view is based on the very low probability that two patients have identical functional deficits. This does not necessarily imply that group studies cannot be made. At a more pragmatic level of discussion, it may be useful to look for group studies relevant to our understanding of the organization of the cognitive system, even though it should be clear that for the reasons mentioned above the investigation of single patients with selective deficits might be more likely to produce theoretically significant advances.

In the area of memory research, studies in small groups of amnesic patients have shown that the deficit selectively involves long-term memory (Drachman and Arbit, 1966; Baddeley and Warrington, 1970) and, more precisely, its episodic or declarative component (see Cohen and Squire, 1980). In the area of spatial cognition, a group study in neglect right brain-damaged patients provided neuropsychological evidence for the existence of a representation of egocentric space with analogue properties (Bisiach et al., 1979, 1981). Similarly, the neuropsychological fractionation of the processes of orienting of attention, which may be selectively disrupted by parietal damage, has recently been done in a group study comparing parietal and nonparietal left and right brain-damaged patients, even though attention was also paid to the performances of the individual patients (Posner et al., 1984).

Group studies may also be useful for the assessment and development of cognitive models, as the systematic study of a large series of patients may reveal dissociations (or associations) which may be then investigated in more detail. An illustrative example is the group study by DeRenzi and Nichelli (1975), who found dissociations between verbal and spatial short-term memory deficits, which are regarded as relevant to cognitive models of human memory (see Baddeley and Lieberman, 1980; Ellis and Young, 1988, pp. 82 – 84). These authors were also able to find three right brain-damaged patients with dissociated short- vs. long-term spatial deficits: two patients had a selective spatial short-term memory impairment, as assessed by Corsi's block tapping test, which was not associated with spatial disorientation or impairments in the learning of a spatial route; one patient had an opposite pattern of impairment. This set of dissociations suggests that visuo-spatial memory, as its verbal counterpart (see Shallice and Warrington, 1970), has a two-component parallel architecture. Finally, as noted above (see section 5.2), a research program that makes use only of single case studies and does not allow replication across patients prevents any possibility of establishing correlations between the impairment of specific functional components and their neural counterparts.

In conclusion, both single case and group studies may provide data relevant to our knowledge of both the functional organization of mental processes and their neural correlates and there is no sound reason for excluding either method from the arsenal of the neuropsychologist.

6. Summary and conclusions

This chapter has reviewed a number of basic methodological issues in modern neuropsychology.

(1) The foundations of the anatomo-clinical correlation method have been discussed. The suggestion has been made that such a method may be ap-

plied within a variety of neuropsychological approaches, ranging from classical to cognitive neuropsychology, and that the information provided is correlational in nature. Future developments related to the availability of new techniques such as PET are considered.

(2) The main features, scope, underlying assumptions, similarities and differences, and limitations of three popular neuropsychological approaches (the traditional clinical method; the modern standardized group study approach; cognitive neuropsychology) are reviewed.

(3) Three contentious issues in modern neuropsychology are discussed: associations and dissociations; the concepts of anatomical, functional and mixed syndrome; single case vs. group studies. Arguments are put forward to the effect that the concept of syndrome should not be abandoned. Both group and single case studies and associations and dissociations between symptoms may be successfully used in neuropsychological research.

Acknowledgements

I am grateful to Francois Boller, Jordan Grafman and Tim Shallice for their helpful suggestions on an early version of this chapter.

References

Adams RD, Victor M: Syndromes due to focal cerebral lesions. In Petersdorf RG, Adams RD, Braunwald E, et al. (Editors), *Harrison's Principles of Internal Medicine,* 10th edition. New York: McGraw-Hill, pp. 152 – 155, 1983.

Albert ML, Goodglass H, Helm NA, Rubens AB, Alexander MP: *Clinical Aspects of Dysphasia.* Wien: Springer-Verlag, 1981.

Allport DA: Auditory-verbal short-term memory and conduction aphasia. In Bouma H, Bouwhuis DG (Editors), *Attention and Performance X: Control of Language Processes.* Hillsdale, NJ: Lawrence Erlbaum, pp. 313 – 325, 1984a.

Allport DA: Speech production and comprehension: one lexicon or two? In Prinz W, Sanders AF (Editors), *Cognition and Motor Processes.* Berlin: Springer, pp. 209 – 228, 1984b.

Anton G: Ueber die Selbatwahrnehmung der Herderkrankungen der Gehirns durch den Kranken bei Rindenblindheit und Rindentaubheit. *Arch. Psychiatrie Nervenkrankh.: 32,* 86 – 127, 1899.

Atkinson RC, Shiffrin RM: Human memory: a proposed system and its control processes. In Spence KW, Taylor Spence J

(Editors), *The Psychology of Learning and Motivation. Advances in Research and Theory, Vol. 2.* New York: Academic Press, pp. 89 – 195, 1968.

Babinski J: Contribution a l'étude des troubles mentaux dans l'emiplégie organique cérébrale (Anosognosie). *Rev. Neurol.: 27,* 845 – 848, 1914.

Baddeley AD: The development of the concept of short-term memory: implications for neuropsychology. In Vallar G, Shallice T (Editors), *Neuropsychological Impairments of Short-term Memory.* Cambridge University Press, pp. 54 – 73, 1990.

Baddeley AD, Hitch G: Working memory. In Bower GH (Editor), *The Psychology of Learning and Motivation. Advances in Research and Theory, Vol. 8.* New York: Academic Press, pp. 47 – 89, 1974.

Baddeley AD, Lieberman K: Spatial working memory. In Nickerson RS (Editor), *Attention and Performance VIII.* Hillsdale, NJ: Lawrence Erlbaum, pp. 521 – 539, 1980.

Baddeley AD, Warrington EK: Amnesia and the distinction between long- and short-term memory. *J. Verbal Learn. Verbal Behav.: 9,* 176 – 189, 1970.

Baddeley AD, Wilson B: Comprehension and working memory: a single case neuropsychological study. *J. Mem. Lang.: 27,* 479 – 498, 1988.

Baddeley AD, Thomson N, Buchanan M: Word length and the structure of short-term memory. *J. Verbal Learn. Verbal Behav.: 14,* 575 – 589, 1975.

Baddeley AD, Vallar G, Wilson B: Sentence comprehension and phonological memory: some neuropsychological evidence. In Coltheart M (Editor), *Attention and Performance XII. The Psychology of Reading.* Hove and London: Lawrence Erlbaum, pp. 509 – 529, 1987.

Ballard DH: Cortical connections and parallel processing: structure and function. *Behav. Brain Sci.: 9,* 67 – 120, 1986.

Barlow HB: The twelfth Bartlett memorial lecture: the role of single neurons in the psychology of perception. *Q. J. Exp. Psychol.: 37A,* 121 – 145, 1985.

Basso A, Capitani E, Vignolo LA: Influence of rehabilitation on language skills in aphasic patients. *Arch. Neurol.: 36,* 190 – 196, 1979.

Basso A, Spinnler H, Vallar G, Zanobio ME: Left hemisphere damage and selective impairment of auditory-verbal short-term memory. A case study. *Neuropsychologia: 20,* 263 – 274, 1982.

Basso A, Lecours AR, Moraschini S, Vanier M: Anatomoclinical correlations of the aphasias as defined through computerized tomography: exceptions. *Brain Lang.: 26,* 201 – 229, 1985.

Bender MB, Feldman M: The so-called 'visual agnosias'. *Brain: 95,* 173 – 186, 1972.

Benson DF: *Aphasia, Apraxia and Agraphia.* New York: Churchill Livingstone, 1979.

Benson DF: Classical syndromes of aphasia. In Boller F, Grafman J (Editors), *Handbook of Neuropsychology, Vol. 1.* Amsterdam: Elsevier Science Publishers, pp. 267 – 280, 1988.

Benton AL: The fiction of the 'Gerstmann syndrome'. *J. Neurol. Neurosurg. Psychiatry: 24,* 176 – 181, 1961.

Benton AL: *Problemi di Neuropsicologia.* Firenze: G. Barbèra, 1966.

Benton AL: Neuropsychology: past, present and future. In Boller F, Grafman J (Editors), *Handbook of Neuropsychol-*

ogy, Vol. 1. Amsterdam: Elsevier Science Publishers, pp. 3 – 27, 1988.

Berndt RS, Caramazza A: A redefinition of the syndrome of Broca's aphasia: implications for a neuropsychological model of language. *Appl. Psycholing.: 1,* 225 – 278, 1980.

Bisiach E, Geminiani G: Anosognosia related to hemiplegia and hemianopia. In Prigatano GP, Schacter DL (Editors), *Awareness of Deficit after Brain Injury.* New York: Oxford University Press, in press.

Bisiach E, Luzzatti C, Perani D: Unilateral neglect, representational schema and consciousness. *Brain: 102,* 609 – 618, 1979.

Bisiach E, Capitani E, Luzzatti C, Perani D: Brain and conscious representation of outside reality. *Neuropsychologia: 19,* 543 – 551, 1981.

Bisiach E, Bulgarelli C, Sterzi R, Vallar G: Line bisection and cognitive plasticity of unilateral neglect of space. *Brain Cognition: 2,* 32 – 38, 1983.

Bisiach E, Vallar G: Hemineglect in humans. In Boller F, Grafman J (Editors), *Handbook of Neuropsychology, Vol. 1.* Amsterdam: Elsevier Science Publishers, pp. 195 – 222, 1988.

Bisiach E, Meregalli S, Berti A: Mechanisms of production control and belief fixation in human visuospatial processing: clinical evidence from unilateral neglect and misrepresentation. In Commons ML, Herrnstein RJ, Kosslyn SM, Mumford DB (Editors) *Models of Behavior: Computational and Clinical Approaches to Pattern Recognition and Concept Formation, Vol. 9.* Hillsdale, NJ: Lawrence Erlbaum, pp. 3 – 21, 1990.

Blunk R, De Bleser R, Willmes K, Zeumer H: A refined method to relate morphological and functional aspects of aphasia. *Eur. Neurol.: 20,* 69 – 79, 1981.

Boller F, Vignolo LA: Latent sensory aphasia in hemisphere-damaged patients: an experimental study with the token test. *Brain: 89,* 815 – 830, 1966.

Bosley TM, Dann R, Silver FL, Alavi A, Kushner M, Chawluk JB, Savino PJ, Sergott RC, Schatz NJ, Reivich M: Recovery of vision after ischemic lesions: positron emission tomography. *Ann. Neurol.: 21,* 444 – 450, 1987.

Botez MI, Botez T, Olivier M: Parietal lobe syndromes. In Frederiks JAM (Editor), *Handbook of Clinical Neurology, Vol. 1 (45): Clinical Neuropsychology.* Amsterdam: Elsevier Science Publishers, pp. 63 – 85, 1985.

Brain WR: Visual disorientation with special reference to lesions of the right cerebral hemisphere. *Brain: 64,* 244 – 272, 1941.

Brain, Lord: Statement of the problem. In de Reuck AVS, O'Connor M (Editors), *Disorders of Language. CIBA Foundation Symposium.* Gloucester: Churchill, pp. 5 – 20, 1964.

Bunge M: *The Mind-Body Problem.* Oxford: Pergamon Press, 1980.

Caplan D: On the role of group studies in neuropsychological and patopsychological research. *Cognitive Neuropsychol.: 5,* 535 – 548, 1988.

Cappa SF, Vignolo LA: CT scan studies of aphasia. *Human Neurobiol.: 2,* 129 – 134, 1983.

Cappa SF, Cavallotti G, Vignolo LA: Phonemic and lexical errors in fluent aphasia. Correlation with lesion site. *Neuropsychologia: 19,* 171 – 177, 1981.

Cappa SF, Sterzi R, Vallar G, Bisiach E: Remission of hemineglect and anosognosia during vestibular stimulation. *Neuropsychologia: 25,* 775 – 782, 1987.

Caramazza A (Editor): Methodological problems in cognitive

neuropsychology. *Cognitive Neuropsychol.: 5,* 517 – 623. 1988.

Caramazza A: The logic of neuropsychological research and the problem of patient classification in aphasia. *Brain Lang.: 21,* 9 – 20, 1984.

Caramazza A: On drawing inferences about the structure of normal cognitive systems from the analysis of patterns of impaired performance: the case for single-patient studies. *Brain Cognition: 5,* 41 – 66, 1986.

Caramazza A, Miceli G, Villa G: The role of the (output) phonological buffer in reading, writing, and repetition. *Cognitive Neuropsychol.: 3,* 37 – 76, 1986.

Chomsky N: Rules and representations. *Behav. Brain Sci.: 3,* 1 – 61, 1980.

Churchland PS: *Neurophilosophy.* Cambridge, MA: Bradford, The MIT Press, 1986.

Cohen NJ, Squire LR: Preserved learning and retention of pattern analyzing skill in amnesia: dissociation of knowing how and knowing that. *Science: 210,* 207 – 210, 1980.

Coltheart, M: Deep dyslexia: a review of the syndrome. In Coltheart M, Patterson K, Marshall JC (Editors), *Deep Dyslexia.* London: Routledge and Kegan Paul, pp. 22 – 47, 1980.

Coltheart M: Cognitive neuropsychology and the study of reading. In Posner MI, Marin OSM (Eds.) *Mechanisms of attention: Attention and Performance XI.* Lawrence Erlbaum, Hillsdale, NJ: pp. 3 – 37, 1985.

Coltheart M, Patterson K, Marshall JC (Editors): *Deep Dyslexia.* London: Routledge and Kegan Paul, 1980.

Coughlan AK, Warrington EK: The impairment of verbal semantic memory: a single case study. *J. Neurol. Neurosurg. Psychiatry: 44,* 1079 – 1083, 1981.

Cowey A: Aspects of cortical organization related to selective attention and selective impairments of visual perception: a tutorial review. In Posner MI, Marin OSM (Editors), *Mechanisms of Attention: Attention and Performance XI.* Hillsdale, NJ: Lawrence Erlbaum, pp. 41 – 62, 1985.

Craik FIM, Lockhart RS: Levels of processing: a framework for memory research. *J. Verbal Learn. Verbal Behav.: 11,* 671 – 684, 1972.

Craik FIM, Watkins MJ: The role of rehearsal in short-term memory. *J. Verbal Learn. Verbal Behav.: 12,* 599 – 607, 1973.

Crick F: Function of the thalamic reticular complex: the searchlight hypothesis. *Proc. Natl. Acad. Sci. USA: 81,* 4586 – 4590, 1984.

Crick F: The recent excitement about neural networks. *Nature: 337,* 129 – 132, 1989.

Crick F, Asanuma C: Certain aspects of the anatomy and physiology of the cerebral cortex. In McClelland LJ, Rumelhart DE (Editors), *Parallel Distributed Processing. Explorations in the Microstructure of Cognition, Vol. 2.* Cambridge, MA: The MIT Press, pp. 333 – 371, 1986.

Crowder RG: General forgetting theory and the locus of amnesia. In Cermak LS (Editor), *Human Memory and Amnesia.* Hillsdale, NJ: Lawrence Erlbaum, pp. 33 – 59, 1982.

Damasio H, Damasio AR: *Anatomical Correlates of Neuropsychological Disorders.* Oxford: Orford University Press, 1989.

De Bleser R: Localization of aphasia: science or fiction. In Denes

GF, Semenza C, Bisiacchi P (Editors), *Perspectives on Cognitive Neuropsychology.* Hove and London: Lawrence Erlbaum, pp. 161 – 185, 1988.

Denes GF: Disorders of body awareness and body knowledge. In Boller F, Grafman J (Editors), *Handbook of Neuropsychology, Vol. 2.* Amsterdam: Elsevier Science Publishers, pp. 207 – 228, 1989.

DeRenzi E: Caratteristiche e problemi della neuropsicologia. *Arch. Psicol. Neurol. Psichiatria: 28,* 422 – 440, 1967.

DeRenzi E: *Disorders of Space Exploration and Cognition.* Chichester: Wiley, 1982a.

DeRenzi E: Memory disorders following focal neocortical damage. *Phil. Trans. Roy Soc. Lond: B298,* 73 – 83, 1982b.

DeRenzi E, Faglioni P: The comparative efficiency of intelligence and vigilance tests in detecting hemispheric cerebral damage. *Cortex: 1,* 410 – 433, 1965.

DeRenzi E, Nichelli P: Verbal and non-verbal short-term memory impairment following hemispheric damage. *Cortex: 11,* 341 – 354, 1975.

DeRenzi E, Faglioni P, Spinnler H: The performance of patients with unilateral brain damage on face recognition tasks. *Cortex: 4,* 17 – 34, 1968.

DeRenzi E, Gentilini M, Faglioni P, Barbieri C: Attentional shift towards the rightmost stimuli in patients with left visual neglect. *Cortex: 25,* 231 – 237, 1989.

Dérouesné J, Beauvois MF: Phonological processing in reading: data from alexia. *J. Neurol. Neurosurg. Psychiatry: 42,* 1125 – 1132, 1979.

Drachman DA, Arbit J: Memory and the hippocampal complex. *Arch. Neurol.: 15,* 52 – 61, 1966.

Duncan J: Disorganisation of behaviour after frontal lobe damage. *Cognitive Neuropsychol.: 3,* 271 – 290, 1986.

Ellis AW: Intimations of modularity, or, the modelarity of mind: doing cognitive neuropsychology without syndromes. In Coltheart M, Sartori G, Job R (Editors), *The Cognitive Neuropsychology of Language.* London: Lawrence Erlbaum, pp. 397 – 408, 1987.

Ellis AW, Young AW: *Human Cognitive Neuropsychology.* Hove: Lawrence Erlbaum, 1988.

Faglioni P, Spinnler H, Vignolo LA: Contrasting behavior of right and left hemisphere-damaged patients on a discriminative and a semantic task of auditory recognition. *Cortex: 5,* 366 – 389, 1969.

Feeney DM, Baron J-C: Diaschisis. *Stroke: 17,* 817 – 830, 1986.

Fodor JA: *The Modularity of Mind.* Cambridge: MIT Press, 1983.

Fodor JA: Précis of The Modularity of Mind. *Behav. Brain Sci.: 8,* 1 – 42, 1985.

Friberg L, Olsen TS, Roland PE, Paulson OB, Lassen NA: Focal increase of blood flow in the cerebral cortex of man during vestibular stimulation. *Brain: 108,* 609 – 623, 1985.

Gainotti G (Editor): *Struttura e Patologia del Linguaggio.* Bologna: Il Mulino, 1983.

Gainotti G: Constructional apraxia. In Frederiks JAM (Editor), *Handbook of Clinical Neurology, Vol. 1 (45): Clinical Neuropsychology.* Amsterdam: Elsevier Science Publishers, pp. 491 – 506, 1985.

Garner WR, Hake HW, Eriksen CW: Operationalism and the concept of perception. *Psychol. Rev.: 63,* 149 – 159, 1956.

Georgopulos AP, Schwartz AB, Kettner RE: Neuronal population coding of movement direction. *Science: 233,* 1416 – 1420, 1986.

Geschwind N: Mechanisms of change after brain lesions. *Ann. N. Y. Acad. Sci.: 457,* 1 – 11, 1985.

Goodglass H, Kaplan E: *The Assessment of Aphasia and Related Disorders.* Philadelphia: Lea and Febiger, 1972.

Grossi D, Modafferi A, Pelosi L, Trojano L: On the different roles of the cerebral hemispheres in mental imagery: the 'o'clock test' in two clinical cases. *Brain Cognition: 10,* 18 – 27, 1989.

Hebb DO: *The Organization of Behavior.* New York: John Wiley and Sons, 1949.

Hécaen H: *Introduction a la Neuropsychologie.* Paris: Larousse, 1972.

Hécaen H, Albert ML: *Human Neuropsychology.* New York: Wiley, 1978.

Hécaen H, Dubois J: *La Naissance de la Neuropsychologie du Langage.* Paris: Flammarion, 1969.

Heilman KM, Watson RT, Valenstein E: Neglect and related disorders. In Heilman KM, Valenstein E (Editors), *Clinical Neuropsychology.* New York: Oxford University Press, pp. 243 – 293, 1985.

Heimburger RF, Demyer W, Reitan RM: Implications of Gerstmann's syndrome. *J. Neurol. Neurosurg. Psychiatry: 27,* 52 – 57, 1964.

Henschen SE: *Klinische un anatomische Beitrage zur Patologie des Gehirns.* Stockholm: Nordiske Bokandeln, 1920 – 1922.

Hitch G: Developing the concept of working memory. In Claxton G (Editor), *Cognitive Psychology. New Directions.* London: Routledge and Kegan Paul, pp. 154 – 196, 1980.

Howard D: Introduction to 'On agrammatism' by Max Isserlin, 1922. *Cognitive Neuropsychol.: 2,* 303 – 307, 1985.

Howard D: *Does a short-term memory impairment cause impaired sentence comprehension?* Paper presented at the International Conference on Cognitive Neuropsychology. Harrogate (Great Britain) July, 21 – 24, 1989.

Howes D, Boller F: Simple reaction time: evidence for focal impairment from lesions of the right hemisphere. *Brain: 98:* 317 – 322, 1975.

Humphreys GW, Riddoch MJ (Editors): *Visual Object Processing: A Cognitive Neuropsychological Approach.* London: Lawrence Erlbaum, 1987.

Jackson JH: On affections of speech from disease of the brain. *Brain: 1,* 304 – 330. 1878.

Jackson JH: On the nature of the duality of the brain. *Brain: 38,* 80 – 103, 1915.

Jeannerod M, Hécaen H: *Adaptation et Restoration des Fonctions Nerveuses.* Villeurbanne: Simep, 1979.

Job R, Sartori G (Editors): The cognitive neuropsychology of visual and semantic processing of concepts. *Cognitive Neuropsychol.: 5,* 1 – 150, 1988.

Jones GV: On double dissociation of function. *Neuropsychologia: 21,* 397 – 400, 1983.

Kennard C, Swash M (Editors): *Hierarchies in Neurology. A Reappraisal of a Jacksonian Concept.* Berlin: Springer-Verlag, 1989.

Kertesz A, Phipps JB: Numerical taxonomy of aphasia. *Brain Lang.: 4,* 1 – 10, 1977.

Kertesz A, Phipps J: The numerical taxonomy of acute and chronic aphasic syndromes. *Psychol. Res.: 41,* 179 – 188, 1980.

Kinsbourne M: Mechanisms of unilateral neglect. In Jeannerod M (Editor), *Neurophysiological and Neuropsychological Aspects of Spatial Neglect.* Amsterdam: North Holland, pp. 69 – 86, 1987.

Kinsbourne M, Wood F: Short-term memory processes and the amnesic syndrome. In Deutsch D, Deutsch JA (Editors), *Short-term Memory.* New York: Academic Press, pp. 258 – 291, 1975.

Kirk RE: *Experimental Design: Procedures for the Behavioral Sciences.* Monterey, CA: Brooks/Cole, 1982.

Kolk HHJ, Van Grunsven MJF, Keyser A: On parallelism between production and comprehension in agrammatism. In Kean M-L (Editor), *Agrammatism.* Orlando: Academic Press, pp. 165 – 206, 1985.

Lashley KS: *Brain Mechanisms and Intelligence.* Chicago: University of Chicago Press, 1929.

Lenzi GL, Frackoviak RSJ, Jones T: Cerebral oxygen metabolism and blood flow in human cerebral ischemic infarction. *J. Cerebral Blood Flow Metab.: 2,* 321 – 335, 1982.

Lichtheim L: On aphasia. *Brain: 7,* 433 – 484, 1885.

Lissauer H: Ein Fall von Seelenblindheit nebst einem Beitrag zur Theorie derselben. *Arch. Psychiatrie: 21,* 222 – 270, 1890. English translation in: *Cognitive Neuropsychol.: 5,* 153 – 192, 1988.

Logie RH, Della Sala S: *Working memory: a case for neuropsychology.* Paper presented at The International Conference on Cognitive Neuropsychology. Harrogate, Great Britain, July 21 – 24, 1989.

Lueck CJ, Zeki S, Friston KJ, Deiber M-P, Cope P, Cunningham VJ, Lammertsma AA, Kennard C, Frackowiack RSJ: The colour centre in the cerebral cortex of man. *Nature: 340,* 386 – 389, 1989.

Luria AR: *Higher Cortical Functions in Man.* New York: Basic Books, 1966.

Luria AR: *Neuropsychological Studies in Aphasia.* Amsterdam: Swets and Zeitlinger, 1977.

Luria AR, Sokolov EN, Klimkowski M: Towards a neurodynamic analysis of memory disturbances with lesions of the left temporal lobe. *Neuropsychologia: 5,* 1 – 11, 1967.

Marr D: Early processing of visual information. *Phil. Trans. Roy Soc. Lond.: B275,* 483 – 524, 1976.

Marr D: *Vision.* New York: Freman, 1982.

Marshall JC: What is a symptom complex? In Arbib MA, Caplan D, Marshall JC (Editors), *Neural Models of Language Processes.* New York: Academic Press, pp. 389 – 409, 1982.

Marshall JC: Multiple perspectives on modularity. *Cognition: 17,* 209 – 242, 1984.

Marshall JC, Newcombe F: Patterns of paralexia: a psycholinguistic approach. *J. Psycholing. Res.: 2,* 175 – 199, 1973.

Martin KAC: From enzymes to visual perception: a bridge too far? *Trends Neurosci.: 11,* 380 – 387, 1988.

Mazzocchi F, Vignolo LA: Localisation of lesions in aphasia: clinical CT-Scan correlation in stroke patients. *Cortex: 15,* 627 – 654, 1979.

McCloskey M, Caramazza A: Theory and methodology in cognitive neuropsychology: a response to our critics. *Cognitive Neuropsychol.: 5,* 583 – 623, 1988.

McGlynn SM, Schacter DL: Unawareness of deficits in neuropsychological syndromes. *J. Clin. Exp. Neuropsychol.: 11,* 143 – 205, 1989.

McLeod P, McLaughlin C, Nimmo-Smith I: Information encapsulation and automaticity: evidence from the visual control of finely timed actions. In Posner MI, Marin OSM (Editors), *Mechanisms of Attention: Attention and Performance XI.* Hillsdale, NJ: Lawrence Erlbaum, pp. 391 – 406, 1985.

Mehler J, Morton J, Jusczyk PW: On reducing language to biology. *Cognitive Neuropsychol.: 1,* 83 – 116, 1984.

Melton A: Implications of short-term memory for a general theory of memory. *J. Verbal Learn. Verbal Behav.: 2,* 1 – 21, 1963.

Mesulam M-M: A cortical network for directed attention and unilateral neglect. *Ann. Neurol.: 10,* 309 – 325, 1981.

Metter EJ: Neuroanatomy and physiology of aphasia: evidence from positron emission tomography. *Aphasiology: 1,* 3 – 33, 1987.

Metter EJ, Riege WH, Kuhl DE, Phelps ME: Cerebral metabolic relationships for selected brain regions in healthy adults. *J. Cerebral Blood Flow Metab.: 4,* 1 – 7, 1984.

Metter EJ, Kempler D, Jackson C, Hanson WR, Mazziotta JC, Phelps ME: Cerebral glucose metabolism in Wernicke's, Broca's and conduction aphasia. *Arch. Neurol.: 46,* 27 – 34, 1989.

Milner B: Amnesia following operation on the temporal lobes. In Whitty CWM, Zangwill OL (Editors), *Amnesia.* London: Butterworths, pp. 109 – 133, 1966.

Mohr JP, Adams RD: Affections of speech. In Petersdorf RG, Adams RD, Braunwald E, et al. (Editors), *Harrison's Principles of Internal medicine,* 10th Edition. New York: McGraw-Hill, pp. 145 – 152, 1983.

Mohr JP, Pessin MS, Finkelstein S, Funkenstein HH, Duncan GW, Davis KR: Broca aphasia: pathologic and clinic. *Neurology: 28,* 311 – 324, 1978.

Monakow von C: *Die Lokalisation im Grosshirn und der Abbau der Funktion durch Kortikale Herde.* Wiesbaden: Bergmann, 1914.

Morton J: A functional model for memory. In Norman DA (Editor), *Models of Human Memory.* New York: Academic Press, pp. 203 – 254, 1970.

Morton J: Brain-based and non-brain-based models of language. In Caplan D, Lecours AR, Smith A (Editors), *Biological Perspectives on Language.* Cambridge, MA: The MIT Press, pp. 40 – 64, 1984.

Mountcastle VB (Editor): *Interhemispheric Relations and Cerebral Dominance.* Baltimore: The Johns Hopkins Press, 1962.

Moutier F: *L'aphasie de Broca.* Paris: Steinheil, 1908.

Nielsen JM: *Agnosia, Apraxia, Aphasia and their Value in Cerebral Localization,* 2nd Edition. New York: Hafner, 1946.

Norman D (Editor): *Models of Human Memory.* New York: Academic Press, 1970.

Norman DA, Bobrow DG: On data-limited and resource-limited processes. *Cognitive Psychol.: 7,* 44 – 64, 1975.

Paillard J: Apraxia and the neurophysiology of motor control. *Phil. Trans. Roy Soc.: B298,* 111 – 134, 1982.

Patterson K, Marshall JC, Coltheart M (Eds.): *Surface Dyslexia.* London: Lawrence Erlbaum, 1985.

Perani D, Vallar G, Cappa SF, Messa C, Fazio F: Aphasia and neglect after subcortical stroke. *Brain: 110,* 1211 – 1229, 1987.

Perret DI, Mistlin AJ, Chitty AJ: Visual neurones responsive to faces. *Trends Neurosci.: 10,* 358 – 364, 1987.

Petersdorf RG, Adams RD, Braunwald E, et al: The practice of medicine. In Petersdorf RG, Adams RD, Braunwald E, et al. (Editors), *Harrison's Principles of Internal medicine,* 10th Edition. New York: McGraw-Hill, pp. 1 – 5, 1983.

Petersen SE, Fox PT, Posner MI, Mintun M, Raichle ME: Positron emission tomographic studies of the cortical anatomy of single word processing. *Nature: 331,* 585 – 589, 1988.

Petersen SE, Fox PT, Posner MI, Mintun M, Raichle ME: Positron emission tomographic studies of the processing of single word. *J. Cognitive Neurosci.: 1,* 153 – 170, 1989.

Phillips CG, Zeki S, Barlow HB: Localization of function in the cerebral cortex. *Brain: 107,* 327 – 361, 1984.

Pizzamiglio L, Zoccolotti PL: Sex and cognitive influence on visual hemifield superiority for face and letter recognition. *Cortex: 17,* 215 – 226, 1981.

Pizzamiglio L, Zoccolotti PL: Differenze individuali: struttura cerebrale e caratteristiche cognitive. In CA Umiltà (Editor) *Neuropsicologia Sperimentale.* Milano: F. Angeli, pp. 205 – 225, 1982.

Pizzamiglio L, Cappa SF, Vallar G, Zoccolotti PL, Bottini G, Ciurli P, Guariglia C, Antonucci G: Visual neglect for far and near extra-personal space in humans. *Cortex: 25,* 471 – 477, 1989.

Poeck K: Modern trends in neuropsychology. In Benton AL (Editor) *Contributions to Clinical Neuropsychology.* Chicago: Aldine, pp. 1 – 29, 1969.

Poeck K: What do we mean by 'aphasic syndromes'? A neurologist's view. *Brain Lang.: 20,* 79 – 89, 1983.

Popper KR, Eccles JC: *The Self and its Brain.* Berlin: Springer-Verlag, 1977.

Posner MI: Orienting of attention. *Q. J. Exp. Psychol.: 32,* 3 – 25, 1980.

Posner MI, Walker JA, Friedrich FJ, Rafal RD: Effects of parietal injury on covert orienting of attention. *J. Neurosci.: 4,* 1863 – 1874, 1984.

Postman L: Verbal learning and memory. *Annu. Rev. Psychol.: 26,* 291 – 335, 1975.

Rizzolatti G, Gallese V: Mechanisms and theories of spatial neglect. In Boller F, Grafman J (Editors), *Handbook of Neuropsychology, Vol. 1.* Amsterdam: Elsevier Science Publishers, 1988, pp. 223 – 246, 1988.

Rizzolatti G, Matelli M, Pavesi G: Deficits in attention and movement following the removal of postarcuate (area 6) and prearcuate (area 8) cortex in macaque monkeys. *Brain: 106,* 655 – 673, 1983.

Roeltgen DP, Sevush S, Heilman KM: Phonological agraphia: writing by the lexical semantic route. *Neurology: 33,* 755 – 765, 1983.

Rubens AB: Caloric stimulation and unilateral visual neglect. *Neurology: 35,* 1019 – 1024, 1985.

Saffran EM: Neuropsychological approaches to the study of language. *Br. J. Psychol.: 73,* 317 – 337, 1982.

Salamé P, Baddeley AD: Disruption of short-term memory by unattended speech: implications for the structure of working memory. *J. Verbal Learn. Verbal Behav.: 21,* 150 – 164, 1982.

Sergent J: Some theoretical and methodological issues in neuropsychological research. In F Boller and J Grafman (Editors)

Handbook of Neuropsychology, Vol. 1. Amsterdam: Elsevier Science Publishers, pp. 69 – 81, 1988.

Schenkenberg T, Bradford DC, Ajax ET: Line bisection and unilateral visual neglect in patients with neurologic impairment. *Neurology: 30,* 509 – 517, 1980.

Schwartz MF: What the classical aphasia categories can't do for us, and why. *Brain Lang.: 21,* 3 – 8, 1984.

Scoville WB, Milner B: Loss of recent memory after bilateral hippocampal lesions. *J. Neurol. Neurosurg. Psychiatry: 20,* 11 – 21, 1957.

Shallice T: Case study approach in neuropsychological research. *J. Clin. Neuropsychol.: 1,* 183 – 211, 1979a.

Shallice T: Neuropsychological research and the fractionation of memory systems. In Nillson L-G (Editor), *Perspectives on Memory Research*. Hillsdale, NJ: Erlbaum, pp. 257 – 277, 1979b.

Shallice T: Neurological impairment of cognitive processes. *Br. Med. Bull.: 37,* 187 – 192, 1981.

Shallice T: Specific impairments of planning. *Phil. Trans. Roy. Soc.: B298,* 199 – 209, 1982.

Shallice T: Impairments of semantic processing: multiple dissociations. In Coltheart M, Sartori G, Job R (Editors), *The Cognitive Neuropsychology of Language*. London: Lawrence Erlbaum, pp. 111 – 127, 1987.

Shallice T: *From Neuropsychology to Mental Structure*. Cambridge: Cambridge University Press, 1988.

Shallice T, Butterworth B: Short-term memory impairment and spontaneous speech. *Neuropsychologia: 15,* 729 – 735, 1977.

Shallice T, Warrington EK: Independent functioning of verbal memory stores: a neuropsychological study. *Q. J. Exp. Psychol.: 22,* 261 – 273, 1970.

Shallice T, Warrington EK: Auditory-verbal short-term memory impairment and conduction aphasia. *Brain Lang.: 4,* 479 – 491, 1977.

Shallice T, Vallar G: The impairment of auditory-verbal short-term storage. In Vallar G, Shallice T (Editors), *Neuropsychological Impairments of Short-term Memory*. Cambridge: Cambridge University Press, pp. 11 – 53, 1990.

Shallice T, McLeod P, Lewis K: Isolating cognitive modules with the dual task paradigm: are speech perception and production separate processes? *Q. J. Exp. Psychol.: 37A,* 507 – 532, 1985.

Simon HA: *The Sciences of the Artificial*. Cambridge, MA: The MIT Press, 1969.

Sperling G: Successive approximations to a model for short-term memory. *Acta Psychol.: 27,* 285 – 292, 1967.

Strub R, Geschwind N: Gerstmann syndrome without aphasia. *Cortex: 10,* 378 – 387, 1974.

Strub RL, Geschwind N: Localization in Gerstmann syndrome. In Kertesz A (Editor), *Localization in Neuropsychology*. New York: Academic Press, pp. 295 – 321, 1983.

Teuber H-L: Psysiological psychology. *Annu. Rev. Psychol.: 9,* 267 – 276, 1955.

Tulving E: How many memory systems are there? *Am. Psychol.: 40,* 385 – 398, 1985.

Vallar G, Baddeley AD: Fractionation of working memory: neuropsychological evidence for a phonological short-term store. *J. Verbal Learn. Verbal Behav.: 23,* 151 – 161, 1984a.

Vallar G, Baddeley AD: Phonological short-term store, phonological processing and sentence comprehension. *Cognitive Neuropsychol.: 1,* 121 – 141, 1984b.

Vallar G, Papagno C: Phonological short-term store and the nature of the recency effect. Evidence from neuropsychology. *Brain Cognition: 5,* 428 – 442, 1986.

Vallar G, Perani D: The anatomy of spatial neglect in humans. In Jeannerod M (Editor), *Neurophysiological and Neuropsychological Aspects of Spatial Neglect*. Amsterdam: North Holland, pp. 235 – 258, 1987.

Vallar G, Shallice T (Editors): *Neuropsychological Impairments of Short-term Memory*. Cambridge: Cambridge University Press, 1990.

Vallar G, Papagno C, Cappa SF: Latent aphasia after left hemisphere lesions. A lexical-semantic and verbal memory deficit. *Aphasiology: 2,* 463 – 478, 1988a.

Vallar G, Perani D, Cappa SF, Messa C, Lenzi GL, Fazio F: Recovery from aphasia and neglect after subcortical stroke. *J. Neurol. Neurosurg. Psychiatry: 51,* 1269 – 1276, 1988b.

Vallar G, Basso A, Bottini G: Phonological processing and sentence comprehension. A neuropsychological case study. In Vallar G, Shallice T (Editors), *Neuropsychological Impairments of Short-term Memory*. Cambridge: Cambridge University Press, pp. 448 – 476, 1990a.

Vallar G, Sterzi R, Bottini G, Cappa SF, Rusconi ML: Temporary remission of left hemianesthesia after vestibular stimulation. A sensory neglect phenomenon. *Cortex: 123* – 131, 1990b.

Vignolo LA: Auditory agnosia. *Phil. Trans. Roy. Soc. Lond.: B298,* 49 – 57, 1982.

Vignolo LA, Boccardi E, Caverni L: Unexpected CT-scan findings in global aphasia. *Cortex: 22,* 55 – 69, 1986.

Warrington EK, Shallice T: The selective impairment of auditory-verbal short-term memory. *Brain: 92,* 885 – 896, 1969.

Warrington EK, Logue V, Pratt RTC: The anatomical localization of selective impairment of auditory-verbal short-term memory. *Neuropsychologia: 9,* 377 – 387, 1971.

Waugh NC, Norman DA: Primary memory. *Psychol. Rev.: 72,* 89 – 104, 1965.

Weiskrantz L (Editor): Some traps and pontifications. In *Analysis of Behavioral Change*. New York: Harper and Row, pp. 415 – 429, 1968.

Weiskrantz L: On issues and theories of the human amnesic syndrome. In Weinberger NM, McGaugh JL, Lynch G (Editors), *Memory Systems of the Brain*. New York: Guilford Press, pp. 380 – 415, 1985.

Wernicke C: *Der Aphasische Symptomencomplex*. Breslau: Cohn and Weigart. 1874. English translation: *Boston Stud. Phil. Sci.: 4,* 34 – 97, 1966/1968.

Zeki S, Shipp S: The functional logic of cortical connections. *Nature: 335,* 311 – 317, 1988.

Zoccolotti PL, Oltman PK: Field dependence and lateralization of verbal and configurational processing. *Cortex: 14,* 155 – 168, 1978.

© 1991 Elsevier Science Publishers B.V.
Handbook of Neuropsychology, Vol. 5
F. Boller and J. Grafman (Eds)

CHAPTER 16

Neuropsychology in its daily practice: past and present

François Boller[1], Andrew A. Swihart[2], Margaret M. Forbes[3] and Gianfranco Denes[4]

[1]INSERM U 324, Centre Paul Broca, 2ter rue d'Alésia, 75014 Paris, France, [2]Center for Neuropsychological Rehabilitation, Indianapolis, IN, U.S.A., [3]Pittsburgh Alzheimer Disease Research Center, Pittsburgh, PA, U.S.A. and [4]Clinica delle Malattie Nervose e Mentali, Università degli Studi di Padova, Padova, Italy

Introduction

This portion of the *Handbook of Neuropsychology,* dedicated to adult human neuropsychology, began with Professor Benton's discussion of 'Neuropsychology: historical perspectives' (Ch. 1, Vol. 1), and the present volume concludes with this chapter on the daily practice of neuropsychology, both past and present. Our chapter title intentionally echoes Benton's title. Benton adopted a historian's perspective and provided a historical overview emphasizing theoretical and conceptual trends. Our purpose is to discuss the development of the field in terms of its effects on daily practice. We will therefore attempt to capture its changing flavor from the perspective of practicing neuropsychologists, whether they be involved primarily in clinical diagnosis, rehabilitation or research.

Neuropsychology is a rapidly evolving field. It has experienced a spectacular growth in knowledge and a concomitant broadening of the scope of its practice, particularly over the past two decades. We will contrast the character of current practice with that of the past, both in terms of the role of the neuropsychologist and in terms of the content and methods of conducting neuropsychological research and clinical work. As we shall see, differences between past and present roles and content are related to a variety of factors, including advances in the knowledge bases of the disciplines converging to form neuropsychology, theoretical maturation in

both psychology and the neurosciences, technological and methodological improvement in medical knowledge and treatment, and demographic changes in the populations of the industrialized countries. We will review changes in the daily practice of neuropsychology in the areas of assessment and diagnostics, rehabilitation and research. We will conclude our chapter with some brief considerations of the role of neuropsychology in relation to medicine, psychology and the neurosciences. Developmental neuropsychology, a very significant and increasingly important area of neuropsychology, will not be included here since it will be discussed extensively in the next two volumes of the *Handbook.*

Assessment and diagnosis

The neuropsychologist's role
In the past, the clinical practice of neuropsychology consisted almost entirely of diagnostic procedures. Although they were also developed for important research purposes, such as the measurement of 'biological intelligence' (Halstead, 1947), the classical assessment devices such as the Halstead-Reitan Test Battery (Reitan and Wolfson, 1985) were used clinically primarily for identifying and localizing brain dysfunction. Through the 1960s, the role of the practicing neuropsychologist consisted of assessing patients to determine whether they were 'brain damaged' or 'not brain damaged',

and of making differential diagnoses among neurological disorders. This situation changed significantly with the advent of new technologies (e.g., computed tomography), the maturation of psychological constructs (e.g., the development of theoretically more sophisticated, multi-component models of memory processing), and the necessity of improving assessment techniques for neurologically impaired individuals seeking rehabilitation (discussed further below).

Although the precise imaging capabilities of CT, MRI and other associated imaging and diagnostic techniques have reduced the diagnostic role of the neuropsychologist, they have certainly not eliminated it. The neuropsychologist's role in assessment and diagnosis remains crucial in the case of disorders such as Alzheimer's disease, in which neuropsychological assessment is essential for the most definitive diagnosis now possible in the absence of neuropathological findings (McKhann et al., 1984). Furthermore, assessment for the purpose of establishing the presence or absence of neuropsychological dysfunction *per se* documenting current abilities and monitoring potential symptom progression, measuring the effects of treatment on cognitive and neurobehavioral functioning, developing recommendations concerning educational or vocational functioning, and planning specific approaches to rehabilitation are all assessment and diagnostic activities for which the neuropsychologist remains essential.

Additionally, advances in medical technology have created new roles for neuropsychologists in the diagnostic evaluation of the patient. In cases of intractable seizures, for example, when resection or hemispheric ablation is being considered, sodium amytal is administered to inactivate first one hemisphere, then the other, to assess how the patient will function following resection or ablation (the so-called Wada test; Milner, 1975). The neuropsychologist, as part of this assessment team, administers a series of neuropsychological tests to the patient as each hemisphere is inactivated in turn, and from the results develops statements concerning the potential cognitive 'costs' of surgery (Loring et

al., 1989; Milner et al., 1962). Similarly, the neuropsychologist's role during electrocorticographic mapping of functional areas of the brain is crucial and well recognized (see Mateer and Cameron, Ch. 5, Vol. 2).

In summary, the role of the neuropsychologist in assessment and diagnosis has changed dramatically, with a decrease in emphasis on the simple identification and localization of brain damage or dysfunction and an increase in emphasis on assessment of diffuse disorders, quantification of disease progression, evaluation of treatment effects, and, perhaps most significantly, development of rehabilitation goals and methods.

Patients seen in clinical practice

Although some types of cases and kinds of syndromes commonly seen since the beginning of clinical neuropsychology continue to be seen frequently today (e.g., aphasia), others have changed considerably (e.g., dementia). Several factors contribute to both the continuities and the changes. First, advances in medical practice and concomitant demographic shifts have contributed to the vastly increased size of the aged population in the industrialized world and thus to the increased importance of the diseases associated with aging (such as dementia) for the practicing neuropsychologist. Second, shifting historical and political events, as well as advancing industrialization, have resulted in great changes in the type of patient seen in clinical practice. For example, traumatic, penetrating brain injuries incurred by people involved in the world wars created the first major demand for clinical neuropsychologists and, consequently, much of the attention of the profession was focused on relatively young, otherwise healthy men with missile wounds to the brain. However, missile wounds are now relatively rare, and with the advent of almost universal high-speed automobile travel, motor vehicle accidents have resulted in a dramatic increase in the incidence of traumatic non-penetrating brain injuries, which are one of the most common problems referred to the clinical neuropsychologist (see Levin, Ch. 8, Vol. 3). Advances in emergency medicine and immediate medical attention and transportation have further contributed to survival following traumatic brain injury, and thus increased the proportion of head injury patients in the neuropsychologist's practice.

Ever since Broca (1861a,b, 1865) demonstrated the relationship between a vascular lesion in the third frontal convolution of the left hemisphere of the brain and disorders of verbal expression (see Goodglass, Ch. 13, Vol. 1), stroke-induced brain damage has been a major part of clinical practice. For a variety of reasons, however (Forette and Boller, in press), the number of strokes is decreasing, and the development and implementation of increasingly effective programs aimed at prevention and treatment of high blood pressure and atherosclerosis, major risk factors for stroke, foretells an even greater decline in the incidence of strokes and, consequently, of the proportion of stroke patients seen in clinical neuropsychological practice. However, the increased emphasis on neuropsychological rehabilitation for stroke survivors may effectively offset the effects of decreasing incidence on the proportion of stroke victims seen in daily practice.

Other pathological entities have proven more ephemeral. For example, Von Economo's encephalitis and its sequelae of dementia and other behavioral disorders (palilalia, for example) contributed significantly to the pathology seen in the twenties and thirties, but seems to have completely diappeared today. Much more is heard, however, about neuropsychological changes that occur in Parkinson's disease and other diseases of the basal ganglia (Dubois et al., Ch. 10 of this volume). Adverse effects of new drugs have included previously unknown neurological and neuropsychological deficits. Medications used in Parkinson's disease are associated with the on/off phenomenon, for example. Many drugs not usually considered 'psychoactive' may also result in neuropsychological disorders. Digitalis preparations, for example, may produce neuropsychological side-effects in the elderly, even at doses that are quite within the normal range for younger adults.

'Hysterical' syndromes, which constituted such an important part of Charcot's practice and teaching, are rarely seen today. Syphillis, which in either its secondary or tertiary form was frequently responsible for cognitive changes, has not been eradicated, but is certainly now much less common as a cause of neuropsychological deficits. Meanwhile, another group of sexually transmissible diseases, human immunodeficiency virus (HIV) infection and acquired immune deficiency syndrome (AIDS), has become an important etiology of dementia in younger adults (Price et al., 1988), and according to many accounts may become an epidemic of such severity that it may alter the very future of some parts of the world (see Stern and Marder, Ch. 12 of this volume).

Dementia has played a recurring role in the history of neuropsychology. In the early years of the discipline, authors such as Pick and Wernicke wrote about patients with dementing syndromes. Later, several neurologists and neuropsychologists studied and discussed dementia and Alzheimer's disease, even though these entities were not nearly as well known to the general public or even to the scientific and medical community as they are today. As previously stated, the dementias are undoubtedly among the syndromes that have increased the most and have altered to the greatest extent the practice of neuropsychology. This applies to primary (i.e., relatively isolated) dementias such as Alzheimer's and Pick's disease and some vascular dementias, as well as to dementias that appear within the context of other neurological signs, such as Huntington's or Parkinson's disease, or as part of systemic diseases.

There are many reasons for this dramatic increase. As discussed above, significant demographic changes have occurred in North America and in other industrialized countries, and there has been an enormous increase in the number of elderly persons and therefore of age-related neurological disorders, many of which may produce a dementia. Associations of patients and families of patients, such as the Alzheimer Association in the United States as well as similar associations in other countries (for example, France-Alzheimer and the Associazione

Italiana per la Malattia di Alzheimer (AIMA) in France and Italy respectively) have contributed to the increased awareness of Alzheimer's disease and other dementias on the part of physicians, other health professionals and the general public. What is not clear at present is whether there is also an absolute increase in the prevalence of dementia, due, for example, to some exogenous factor (see Amaducci and Lippi, Ch. 1 of this volume).

The marked increase in the number of elderly people and in the number of patients with dementia has been accompanied by a renewed interest on the part of neuropsychologists in the psychology of aging, both normal and abnormal. While age-related problems have influenced the practice of neuropsychology, the converse has also been true, and neuropsychology has changed the way we look at aging and at the aged. For example, aging was long thought to be inexorably accompanied by significant cognitive deterioration, but recent data have indicated that in 'normal' aging this deterioration is often much less important than previously thought (Becker et al., 1987; Swihart and Pirozzolo, 1988). Another example is the introduction of neuropsychological tests designed to be better suited to the capacity of aging or poorly motivated patients, especially those with mild or moderate dementia (Crook, 1985). Such tests are sometimes said to be more ecologically valid than previous tests which failed to take age differences into account in their design, although debate continues about the importance of 'ecological validity' or 'naturalism' in clinical research and practice (Banaji and Crowder, 1989). Irrespective of whether or not these tests are indeed 'better' than traditional ones, one can be almost certain that computerized tests will become more and more common in all areas of neuropsychology (Adams and Brown, 1986).

Rehabilitation

A few years ago, Beauvois and Derouesné (1982) suggested that most neuropsychologists, particularly those engaged in research, had no interest in rehabilitation except perhaps to evaluate its ef-

ficacy. Although historically this may be fairly accurate, it is important to note that there are important exceptions to this statement, particularly in the area of rehabilitation of aphasia. The pioneering work of Weisenburg and McBride (1935) and Aaron Smith and colleagues (1972) are notable in this regard (see also the review by Basso, Ch. 3, Vol. 2). Rehabilitation of nonlanguage neuropsychological deficits also serves as early exceptions to this statement (e.g., Diller, 1971).

Certainly, whatever occurred historically, rehabilitation is rapidly becoming the preeminent component of clinical practice in neuropsychology. Texts on the subject of neuropsychological rehabilitation are numerous (Ellis and Christensen, 1989; Goldstein and Ruthven, 1983; Meier et al., 1987; Miller, 1984; Prigatano, 1986; Rosenthal et al., 1990; Sohlberg and Mateer, 1989; Uzzell and Gross, 1986; Wilson, 1987; Wilson and Moffat, 1984) and, unfortunately, in many ways the practice of neuropsychological rehabilitation has moved ahead in the absence of a solid neurophysiological or neuropsychological understanding of either spontaneous recovery or the effects of various rehabilitation techniques on recovery (see Glisky and Schacter, Ch. 10, Vol. 3, as well as Finger et al., 1988, for a discussion of these issues). However, when confronted with the millions of individuals who have survived traumatic brain injury, stroke and other central nervous system illness and injury producing significant and disabling neuropsychological deficits, the practicing neuropsychologist has little option but to attempt rehabilitation within the constraints provided by current knowledge, while awaiting the development of more effective, theoretically grounded approaches to rehabilitation.

Neuropsychologists have become active in several areas of rehabilitation. Foremost in number are those involved in the treatment of individuals recovering from traumatic brain injuries resulting from motor vehicle accidents, blunt trauma and falls. Others frequently treated include survivors of stroke, hypoxia, infection and tumor. The 'team approach' to rehabilitation is endorsed in most head injury rehabilitation settings (e.g., Christensen and Danielsen, 1987; Laaksonen, 1987; Trexler, 1987), although it is all too often absent from daily practice. When genuinely practiced, the team approach holds a key role for the neuropsychologist in terms of both initial neuropsychological assessment for treatment planning (Goldstein, 1987; Lezak, 1987), and the development and implementation of specific rehabilitation methods and techniques (e.g., Freis et al., 1989 and in preparation; Gordon et al., 1985; Solberg and Mateer, 1987). In contrast to its former focus on deciding whether a patient was or was not brain-damaged, and on localization of damage, neuropsychological assessment and diagnosis in rehabilitation settings focuses on identifying current neuropsychological strengths and weaknesses for purposes of treatment planning and goal setting, and on fine-grained analysis of the nature of the patient's neuropsychological deficits for purposes of specifying remediation approaches.

In addition to the patient populations described above, the problems of the aged and the demented individual have given additional impetus to the development of neuropsychological rehabilitation techniques, particularly in the area of memory. The recent contributions of Wilson and colleagues (e.g., Wilson, 1987, 1989) are notable examples, in that the remediation techniques no longer represent purely rational or empirical efforts, but are based on theoretical models drawn from experimental cognitive neuropsychology. In addition to cognitive and behavioral approaches to remediation of memory deficits (see also, for example, Sheikh et al., 1986), the recent concern with memory disorders of the aged has increased pharmacological research with new drugs to prevent, control or reverse loss of memory and related cognitive disorders (e.g., Amaducci and the SMID Group, 1988; Crook et al., 1986). The preparation and performance of the protocols needed to assess the efficacy of pharmacological therapies for memory disorders and for dementia requires the active participation of the neuropsychologist (see Mohr and Chase, Ch. 5 of this volume).

As efforts at neuropsychological rehabilitation proceed, the need for well-designed efficacy studies becomes increasingly obvious. Research on outcome (variously defined) of both acute and post-acute rehabilitation treatment is beginning to become available (e.g., Ben-Yishay et al., 1987; Burke et al., 1988; Cope and Hall, 1982; Prigatano et al., 1984), although controversy concerning both methodology and findings in such studies continues (for example, Dobkin, 1989; Hachinski, 1989; Reding and McDowell, 1989). Efficacy studies focused on rehabilitation of specific neuropsychological deficits are also becoming more frequent (e.g., Glisky et al., 1986; Ponsford and Kinsella, 1988; Sohlberg and Mateer, 1987), but much more work is needed in this area.

In summary, neuropsychological rehabilitation has become an important aspect of the daily practice of neuropsychology. The unique needs of the brain-injured individual requiring rehabilitation have significantly changed the purposes for which neuropsychologists perform clinical assessment and diagnosis, and are beginning to have a great impact on current neuropsychological research.

Research

In many important ways, the history of research in neuropsychology runs along a relatively continuous thread, with major research issues of the past continuing to be extensively investigated today. Certainly this is true for research concerning disorders of language, memory and visuoperception. Neuropsychological research has also had its trends, sometimes recurrent. To provide just one example, introspection was a popular topic for neuropsychological research at the times of Charcot and Galton but later fell into disrepute. Quite recently, it has been used again to study mental imagery in normal subjects, in patients with focal lesions and in patients with Parkinson's disease (see Bisiach and Vallar, Ch. 11, Vol. 1; Farah, Ch. 21, Vol. 2; Goldenberg, 1989). However, important differences between research past and present are, of course, apparent. Early research on language focused primarily on issues of localization of function and syndrome description (e.g., Broca, 1861a,b, 1865; Head, 1926; Wernicke, 1874). Today these issues continue to be highly relevant and remain the objects of investigation, but a wealth of new questions and concerns is currently of equal interest to the research neuropsychologist. These include such issues as the contribution of subcortical structures to language and its disorders (e.g., Alexander, Ch. 2, Vol. 2; Crosson, 1984), the role of the right hemisphere in language (Gazzaniga, 1983), detailed cognitive models of normal language processing (Coltheart et al., 1986) and linguistic analyses of language deficits (e.g., Caplan and Hildebrandt, 1988; Grodzinsky, in press), among others. Memory has long been an area of great research interest in neuropsychology (e.g., Korsakoff, 1887; Lashley, 1950; Ribot, 1881), with early research addressing primarily the delineation of specific types of memory disorder and the characteristics of each. Contemporary neuropsychology continues to explore these issues (see Section 3, Vol. 3), but a legion of new questions and interests has arisen and gained equal stature with syndrome description. Such issues include the nature of cognitive subsystems of memory (e.g., Baddeley, 1986; Tulving, 1983, 1987), preserved learning abilities in amnesia (Cohen and Squire, 1980; Schacter, 1987), memory in normal aging and dementia (Nebes, 1989; Poon, 1985), rehabilitation of impaired memory (Glisky and Schacter, Ch. 10, Vol. 3; Wilson, 1989; Wilson and Moffat, 1984), and the study of more 'ecologically' valid aspects of human memory performance (e.g., Kopelman et al., 1989). Disorders of visuoperception have been studied for over 100 years (e.g., Jackson, 1876; Kleist, 1934; Lissauer, 1889) and are still of major interest today (see Section 4, Vol. 2). However, new issues include hierarchical organization and functional segregation of visuoperceptual and visuospatial processes (Livingstone and Hubel, 1988; Van Essen and Maunsell, 1983) and the interaction of the visual cognitive systems with other cognitive systems such as attention and memory (Humphreys and Bruce, 1989). Clearly, although much continuity exists between past and present research programs in basic neuro-

psychology, and the traditional core activities of syndrome description and classification have not been supplanted, numerous new areas of research interests have developed from this core, and have greatly broadened the scope of neuropsychological research.

On the other hand, advancing technology has opened important new avenues of research into brain – behavior relationships. Chief among the technological developments that have influenced neuropsychological research are imaging techniques for both structure (CT, MRI) and function (PET), electrophysiological techniques, cerebral blood flow measurement techniques, and refined stimulus presentation techniques, such as tachistoscopic methods and dichotic listening (see Damasio, Ch. 1, Vol. 2; Friedland, Ch. 9, Vol. 2; Hannay, 1986; Pettegrew, Ch. 4 of this volume). In addition to these technological advances and consequent developments in research programs, changes in experimental methods and design have also yielded significant changes in neuropsychological research. Specifically, single case designs are, once again, becoming prevalent in both basic and applied neuropsychological research (Caramazza, 1986; Caramazza and McCloskey, 1988; Shallice, 1979; but see also Zurif et al., 1989). Finally, demographic changes, particularly the shift to a greater proportion of aged individuals in the population than ever before, have produced changes in the focus of neuropsychological research.

Historically important research issues, technological changes and demographic shifts together do not account entirely for the changes that have occurred in the daily practice of neuropsychological research. Numerous complex influences come into play to bring about major changes in a field, and a few of these influences in changing neuropsychological research are briefly described here. Certainly, developments in related disciplines, such as cognitive psychology, have had a dramatic impact on research topics in neuropsychology (see Vallar, Ch. 15 of this volume). Also, cultural influences must certainly be credited with influencing neuropsychological research interests. For example, the exploration of sex differences in brain – behavior relationships and neuropsychological abilities and of the neuropsychology of emotion are relatively new and culturally influenced areas of research. A final factor that should be mentioned is the unexpected consequences of industrialization, which have produced research in such areas as the neurobehavioral effects of various toxic substances in the environment.

Conclusion

This chapter has shown how neuropsychology appears today, compared to the past. Partly as a consequence of these recent changes, there has been an enormous growth in neuropsychological clinical practice and research. This is demonstrated by the rapid growth in membership of specialized disciplinary groups such as the International Neuropsychological Society, the Société de Neuropsychologie de Langue Française, and Division 40 of the American Psychological Association, as well as by the marked increase of neuropsychological research presented at meetings of organizations such as the American Psychological Association and the American Academy of Neurology, and published in reviews such as *Archives of Neurology, Brain* and even *Science* and *Nature.* Correspondingly, following the early steps of *Neuropsychologia* in 1963 and *Cortex* in 1964, the number of reviews specializing in neuropsychology or closely related fields has grown spectacularly and perhaps even excessively. Neurologists known for their work in neuropsychology now occupy several prestigious chairs as department heads in the United States and other countries. Just as significantly, chairs specifically dedicated to teaching and research in neuropsychology have been created within faculties of medicine, psychology and others. Perhaps the apex of the increasing recognition of neuropsychology has been the Nobel Prize awarded in 1981 to Roger Sperry, whose work has inspired research of enormous importance (summarized in part in Section 7, Vol. 4 of this *Handbook*). All of this has resulted in one particularly significant change, the maximum impact of which has yet to be felt: training for physicians (particularly neurologists, psychiatrists and neurosurgeons, but also for geriatricians and others), psychologists and other health-related personnel now almost universally includes an increasing amount of training in the field of neuropsychology and behavioral neurology.

As previously discussed, in the past it was thought (especially by those who were not neuropsychologists) that one of the neuropsychologist's more important functions was to assist physicians in deciding whether or not a given patient had an 'organic' lesion of the CNS and, once it was determined that a lesion was present, to help in its localization. This is clearly no longer the case, for the reasons described above, and the changes in the training of medical practitioners will further solidify this change.

All sciences are the fruit of collaboration and this is particularly true for neuropsychology. In the initial chapter of the *Handbook,* Benton defined neuropsychology as 'a compound discipline in that it represents the confluence of several fields of study'. In his classic manual, Hécaen (1972) had already pointed out that the discipline is at the borderland not only of medicine and psychology, but also of other branches of science such as the neurosciences, linguistics, sociology and anthropology. Currently, in addition, the neuropsychologist has the opportunity to talk with physicists about PET or NMR technologies, with engineers about the design of movement stimulators or recording instruments, and with many others from diverse disciplines. Far from weakening the field, such collaboration is expanding the scope of neuropsychology and can only enhance its attraction and interest for current and prospective professionals in the field.

Acknowledgements

Portions of this work were supported by the Institut National de la Santé et de la Recherche Médicale (INSERM), Paris, France, by the National Institutes of Health (National Institute on Aging) grant N. P50 AG/MH 05133 and by the Center for Neuropsychological Rehabilitation, Indianapolis, IN. This chapter is dedicated to Professor Arthur L. Benton in recognition of his many years of exemplary teaching. We are also indebted to him for his comments on this manuscript.

References

Adams KM, Brown GG: The role of the computer in neuropsychological assessment. In Grant I, Adams KM (Editors), *Neuropsychological Assessment of Neuropsychiatric Disorders*. Oxford: Oxford University Press, pp. 87–99, 1986.

Amaducci L, and the SMID Group: Phosphatidylserine in the treatment of Alzheimer's disease: results of a multicenter study. *Psychopharmacol. Bull.: 24*, 130–134, 1988.

Baddeley A: *Working Memory*. Oxford: Clarendon Press, 1986.

Banaji MR, Crowder RG: The bankruptcy of everyday memory. *Am. Psychol.: 44*, 1185–1193, 1989.

Beauvois MF, Derouesné J: Recherche en neuropsychologie cognitive et rééducation. In Seron X, Laterre C (Editors), *Rééduquer le Cerveau*. Bruxelles: Mardaga, pp. 163–189, 1982.

Becker JT, Nebes RD, Boller F: La neuropsychologie du vieillissement normal. In Botez MI (Editor), *Neuropsychologie Clinique et Neurologie du Comportement*. Montréal & Paris: Les Presses de l'Université de Montréal & Masson, pp. 371–379, 1987.

Ben-Yishay Y, Silver SM, Piasetsky E, Rattok J: Relationship between employability and vocational outcome after intensive holistic cognitive rehabilitation. *J. Head Trauma Rehab.: 2*, 35–48, 1987.

Broca P: Remarques sur le siège de la faculté du langage articulé, suivies d'une observation d'aphémie (perte de la parole). *Bull. Soc. Anatom.: 6*, 330–357, 1861a.

Broca P: Nouvelle observation d'aphémie produite par une lésion de la moitié postérieure des deuxième et troisième circonvolutions frontales. *Bull. Soc. Anatom.: 6*, 398–407, 1861b.

Broca P: Du siège de la faculté du langage articulé, *Bull. Soc. Anthrop.: 6*, 377–393, 1865.

Burke WH, Wesolowski MD, Guth ML: Comprehensive head injury rehabilitation: an outcome evaluation. *Brain Injury: 2*, 313–322, 1988.

Caplan DN, Hildebrandt N: *Disorders of Syntactic Comprehension*. Cambridge, MA: MIT Press, 1988.

Caramazza A: On drawing inferences about the structure of normal cognitive systems from the analysis of patterns of impaired performance: the case for single patient studies. *Brain Cognition: 5*, 41–66, 1986.

Caramazza A, McCloskey M: The case for single patient studies. *Cognitive Neuropsychol.: 5*, 517–528, 1988.

Christensen AL, Danielsen UT: Neuropsychological rehabilitation in Denmark. In Meier M, Benton A, Diller L (Editors), *Neuropsychological Rehabilitation*. New York: Guilford, pp. 381–386, 1987.

Cohen NJ, Squire LR: Preserved learning and retention of pattern-analyzing skill in amnesia: dissociation of knowing how and knowing that. *Science: 210*, 207–209, 1980.

Coltheart M, Job R, Sartori G: *The Cognitive Neuropsychology of Language*. Hillsdale, NJ: Lawrence Erlbaum Associates, 1986.

Cope DN, Hall K: Head injury rehabilitation: benefit of early intervention. *Arch. Phys. Med. Rehab.: 63*, 433–437, 1982.

Crook T: Geriatric psychopathology: an overview of the ailments and current therapies. *Drug Dev. Res.: 5*, 5–23, 1985.

Crook T, Bartus R, Ferris S, Gershon S: *Treatment Development Strategies for Alzheimer's Disease*. Madison, CT: Mark Pawley Associates, 1986.

Crosson B: Role of the dominant thalamus in language: a review. *Psychol. Bull.: 96*, 491–517, 1984.

Diller L: Studies in cognition and rehabilitation in hemiplegia. Final report. Washington, HEW, 1971.

Dobkin BH: Focused stroke rehabilitation programs do not improve outcome. *Arch. Neurol.: 46*, 701–703, 1989.

Ellis DW, Christensen AL: *Neuropsychological Treatment after Brain Injury*. New York: Kluwer Academic Publishers, 1989.

Finger S, LeVere TE, Almli CR, Stein DG: *Brain Injury and Recovery: Theoretical and Controversial Issues*. New York: Plenum, 1988.

Forette F, Boller F: Hypertension and risk of dementia in the elderly. *Am. J. Med.:* in press.

Freis W, Swihart AA, Danek A: Somatosensory substitution of spatial information improves oculomotor performance in visual hemineglect. Paper presented at 'Brain Damage and Rehabilitation: A Neuropsychological Approach.' Ludwig-Maximilians-Universität, Institut fur Medizinische Psychologie: München, October, 1989, and in preparation.

Gazzaniga MS: Right hemisphere language following brain bisection. *Am. Psychol.: 38*, 525–541, 1983.

Glisky EL, Schacter DL, Tulving E: Learning and retention of computer-related vocabulary in memory-impaired patients: method of vanishing cues. *J. Clin. Exp. Neuropsychol.: 8*, 292–312, 1986.

Goldenberg G: The ability of patients with brain damage to generate mental visual images. *Brain: 112*, 305–325, 1989.

Goldstein G: Neuropsychological assessment for rehabilitation: fixed batteries, automated systems and non-psychometric methods. In Meier M, Benton A, Diller L (Editors), *Neuropsychological Rehabilitation*. New York: Guilford, pp. 18–40, 1987.

Goldstein G, Ruthven L: *Rehabilitation of the Brain-damaged Adult*. New York: Plenum, 1983.

Gordon WA, Ruckdeschel-Hibbard M, Egelkos S, Diller L, Shaver MS, Leiberman A, Ragnarsson K: Perceptual remediation in patients with right brain damage: a comprehensive program. *Arch. Phys. Med. Rehab.: 66*, 353–359, 1985.

Grodzinsky Y: *Theoretical Perspectives on Language Deficits*. Cambridge, MA: MIT Press, in press.

Hachinski V: Stroke rehabilitation. *Arch. Neurol.: 46*, 703, 1989.

Hannay HJ: *Experimental Techniques in Human Neuropsychology*. New York: Oxford University Press, 1986.

Halstead WC: *Brain and Intelligence: A Quantitative Study of the Frontal Lobes*. Chicago: University of Chicago Press, 1947.

Head H: *Aphasia and Kindred Disorders of Speech.* Cambridge: Cambridge University Press, 1926.

Hécaen H: *Introduction à la Neuropsychologie.* Paris: Larousse, 1972.

Humphreys G, Bruce V: *Visual Cognition: Computational. Experimental and Neuropsychological Perspectives.* Hillsdale, NJ: Lawrence Erlbaum Associates, 1989.

Jackson JH: Case of a large cerebral tumor without optic neuritis and with left hemiplegia and imperception. *R. Lond. Ophthalmol. Hosp. Rep.: 8,* 434, 1876.

Kleist K: *Gehirnpathologie.* Leipzig: Barth, 1934.

Kopelman MD, Wilson BA, Baddeley AD: The Autobiographical Memory Interview: a new assessment of autobiographical and personal semantic memory in amnesic patients. *J. Clin. Exp. Neuropsychol.: 11,* 724 – 744, 1989.

Korsakoff SS: Disturbance of psychic function in alcoholic paralysis and its relation to the disturbance of the psychic sphere in multiple neuritis of non-alcoholic origin. *Vestnik Psychiatri: 4,* fascicle 2, 1887.

Laaksonen R: Neuropsychological rehabilitation in Finland. In Meier M, Benton A, Diller L (Editors), *Neuropsychological Rehabilitation.* New York: Guilford, pp. 387 – 395, 1987.

Lashley K: In search of the engram. *Symp. Soc. Exp. Biol.: 4,* 454 – 483, 1950.

Lezak M: Assessment for rehabilitation planning. In Meier M, Benton A, Diller L (Editors), *Neuropsychological Rehabilitation.* New York: Guilford, pp. 41 – 58, 1987.

Lissauer H: Ein Fall von Seelenblindheit nebst einiger Beiträge zur Theorie derselben. *Arch. Psychiatrie Nervenkrankh.: 31,* 222 – 270, 1889.

Livingstone M, Hubel D: Segregation of form, color, movement, and depth: anatomy, physiology, and perception. *Science: 240,* 740 – 749, 1988.

Loring DW, Lee G, Meador K: The intracarotid amobarbital sodium procedure: false positive errors during recognition memory assessment. *Arch. Neurol.: 46,* 285 – 287, 1989.

McKhann G, Drachman D, Folstein M, Katzman R, Price D, Stadlen EM: Clinical diagnosis of Alzheimer's disease: Report of the NINCDS-ADRDA Work Group under the auspices of Department of Health and Human Services Task Force on Alzheimer Disease. *Neurology: 34,* 939 – 944, 1984.

Meier M, Benton A, Diller L (Editors): *Neuropsychological Rehabilitation.* New York: Guilford, 1987.

Miller E: *Recovery and Management of Neuropsychological Impairments.* Chichester: John Wiley and Sons, 1984.

Milner B: Psychological aspects of focal epilepsy and its neurosurgical management. *Adv. Neurol.: 18,* 299 – 321, 1975.

Milner B, Branch C, Rasmussen T: Study of short term memory after intracarotid injection of sodium amytal. *Trans. Am. Neurol. Assoc.: 87,* 224 – 226, 1962.

Nebes R: Semantic memory in Alzheimer's disease. *Psychol. Bull.: 106,* 377 – 394, 1989.

Ponsford JL, Kinsella G: Evaluation of a remedial programme for attentional deficits following closed head injury. *J. Clin. Exp. Neuropsychol.: 10,* 693 – 708, 1988.

Poon LW: Differences in human memory with aging: Nature, causes, and clinical implications. In Birren JE, Schaie KW (Editors), *The Handbook of the Psychology of Aging,* 2nd

Edition. New York: Van Nostrand Reinhold, pp. 427 – 462, 1985.

Price RW, Brew B, Sidtis J, Rosenblum M, Scheck AC, Clearly P: The brain in AIDS: central nervous system HIV-1 infection and AIDS dementia complex. *Science: 239,* 586 – 592, 1988.

Prigatano GP: *Neuropsychological Rehabilitation after Brain Injury.* Baltimore: Johns Hopkins University Press, 1986.

Prigatano GP, Fordyce DJ, Zeiner HK, Roueche JR, Pepping M, Wood BC: Neuropsychological rehabilitation after closed head injury in young adults. *J. Neurol. Neurosurg. Psychiatry: 47,* 505 – 513, 1984.

Reding MJ, McDowell FH: Focused stroke rehabilitation programs improve outcome. *Arch. Neurol.: 46,* 700 – 701, 1989.

Reitan RM, Wolfson D: *The Halstead-Reitan Neuropsychological Test Battery: Theory and Clinical Interpretation.* Tucson: Neuropsychology Press, 1985.

Ribot T: *Les Maladies de la Mémoire.* Paris: Alcan, 1881.

Rosenthal M, Griffith ER, Bond MR, Miller JD: *Rehabilitation of the Adult and Child with Traumatic Brain Injury,* 2nd Edition. Philadelphia: F.A. Davis and Company, 1990.

Schacter DC: Implicit memory: history and current status. *J. Exp. Psychol. Learn. Mem. Cognition: 13,* 501 – 518, 1987.

Shallice T: Case study approach in neuropsychological research. *J. Clin. Neuropsychol.: 1,* 183 – 211, 1979.

Sheikh JI, Hill RD, Yesavage JA: Long-term efficacy of cognitive retraining for age-associated memory impairment: a six-month follow-up study. *Dev. Neuropsychol.: 2,* 413 – 421, 1986.

Smith A, Champoux R, Leri J, London R, Muraski A: Diagnosis, intelligence and rehabilitation of chronic aphasics. Monograph: *Social and Rehabilitation Service Grant No. 14-P-55198/5-01,* Department of Health, Education and Welfare, 1972.

Sohlberg MM, Mateer CA: Effectiveness of an attention-training program. *J. Clin. Exp. Neuropsychol.: 9,* 117 – 130, 1987.

Sohlberg MM, Mateer CA: *Introduction to Cognitive Rehabilitation: Theory and Practice.* New York: Guilford, 1989.

Swihart AA, Pirozzolo FJ: The neuropsychology of aging and dementia: clinical issues. In Whitaker HA (Editor), *Neuropsychological Studies of Nonfocal Brain Damage: Dementia and Trauma.* New York: Springer-Verlag, 1988.

Trexler LE: Neuropsychological rehabilitation in the United States. In Meier M, Benton A, Diller L (Editors), *Neuropsychological Rehabilitation.* New York: Guilford, pp. 437 – 460, 1987.

Tulving E: *Elements of Episodic Memory.* Oxford: Clarendon Press, 1983.

Tulving E: Multiple memory systems and consciousness. *Human Neurobiol.: 6,* 67 – 80, 1987.

Uzzell B, Gross Y: *Clinical Neuropsychology of Intervention.* Boston: Kluwer Academic Publishers, 1986.

Van Essen DC, Maunsell JHR: Hierarchical organization and functional streams in the visual cortex. *Trends Neurosci.: 6,* 370 – 375, 1983.

Weisenburg T, McBride KE: *Aphasia. A Clinical and Psychological Study.* New York: The Commonwealth Fund, 1935.

Wernicke C: *Der aphasische Symptomencomplex.* Breslau: Cohn & Weigert, 1874.

Wilson BA: *Rehabilitation of Memory.* New York: Guilford, 1987.

Wilson BA: Remediation and management of disorders of memory. In Van der Linden M, Bruyer R (Editors), *Neuro-* *psychologie de la Mémoire Humaine.* Bruxelles: pp. 160 – 176 Société de Neuropsychologie de langue Française, 1989.

Wilson BA, Moffat N: *Clinical Management of Memory Problems.* London: Croom Helm, 1984.

Zurif EB, Gardner H, Brownell HH: The case against the case against group studies. *Brain Cognition: 10,* 237 – 255, 1989.

Index

1778